The Internal Market Ideal

Professor Stephen Weatherill

The Internal Market Ideal

Essays in Honour of Stephen Weatherill

EDITED BY JEREMIAS ADAMS-PRASSL,
SANJA BOGOJEVIĆ, ARIEL EZRACHI, AND
DOROTA LECZYKIEWICZ

OXFORD
UNIVERSITY PRESS

OXFORD
UNIVERSITY PRESS

Great Clarendon Street, Oxford, OX2 6DP,
United Kingdom

Oxford University Press is a department of the University of Oxford.
It furthers the University's objective of excellence in research, scholarship,
and education by publishing worldwide. Oxford is a registered trade mark of
Oxford University Press in the UK and in certain other countries

First Edition published in 2024

Published in the United States of America by Oxford University Press
198 Madison Avenue, New York, NY 10016, United States of America

British Library Cataloguing in Publication Data

Data available

Library of Congress Control Number: 2023946446

ISBN 978–0–19–286706–3

DOI: 10.1093/oso/9780192867063.001.0001

Printed and bound by
CPI Group (UK) Ltd, Croydon, CR0 4YY

Summary Contents

V. TEACHING EU INTERNAL MARKET LAW

Detailed Contents

V. TEACHING EU INTERNAL MARKET LAW

List of Contributors

Jeremias Adams-Prassl is Professor of Law at Magdalen College in the University of Oxford, with a focus on the future of work and innovation in the European Union and beyond. He read law at Oxford, Paris, and Harvard Law School, and is the author of numerous articles and books, including most recently *Humans as a Service: The Promise and Perils of Work in the Gig Economy* (OUP 2018) and, with Sanja Bogojević, *Great Debates in EU Law* (Bloomsbury 2021). His work has been recognized by prizes and awards including the *Modern Law Review*'s Wedderburn Prize, a British Academy Rising Star Engagement Award, and the 2020 Leverhulme Prize. Since April 2021, he has led a five-year research project on Algorithms at Work, funded by the European Research Council. Jeremias tweets at @JeremiasPrassl.

Albertina Albors-Llorens is a Professor of EU Law at the Faculty of Law in the University of Cambridge and a Fellow of St John's College and was the Deputy Chair of the Cambridge Law Faculty between October 2019 and October 2022. Her research focuses on EU law and competition law, and she has lectured and published widely in these fields. Her recent publications include contributions to *European Union Law* (Catherine Barnard and Steve Peers (eds) (4th edn, OUP 2023), to *Cassis de Dijon: 40 Years On* (Albertina Albors-Llorens, Catherine Barnard and Brigitte Leucht (eds) Hart 2021), and to *The EU Charter of Fundamental Human Rights* (Steve Peers and others (eds) (2nd edn, Hart 2021). She has been one of the editors of the *Cambridge Yearbook of European Legal Studies* (2012–15), a note editor of the *Cambridge Law Journal* (2010–20), and one of the editors for the *Yearbook of European Law* (2015–22). She is a recipient of a Pilkington Prize for Excellence in University Teaching awarded by the University of Cambridge.

Dayana Baleva graduated with an LLM in European Law from the University of Edinburgh in 2021, and a Bachelor of Science in Political Science and International Relations from Leiden University in 2020. Dayana's academic and professional interests are varied and include EU citizenship law, the intersection between economics and social policy in the EU's foreign policy towards developing countries, and social empowerment of vulnerable groups through institutional advocacy. Currently, Dayana is employed in the third sector where she provides policy and project management support for a Scottish government-funded social security project.

Catherine Barnard FBA, FLSW, FRSA is Professor of EU law and Employment Law and fellow and senior tutor of Trinity College. She is the author of *EU Employment Law* (Oxford, OUP, 2012, 5th edn), *The Substantive Law of the EU: The Four Freedoms* (Oxford, OUP, 2022, 7th edn), and (with Peers ed), *European Union Law* (Oxford, OUP, 2020, 3rd edn). She is a member of the European Commission-funded European Labour Law Network (ELLN). She is also a Deputy Director of the UK in a Changing Europe (http://ukandeu.ac.uk/) project. This is an authoritative, non-partisan think tank which does research and provides information about all aspects of Brexit. Part of its remit is to make that information accessible to the general public. So it does a lot of public engagement, especially with the media. She has appeared on the main media channels—BBC, ITV, and Sky—as well as some of the more specialist programmes such as Law in Action, Woman's Hour, Question Time, and the Briefing Room. She has also written for *The Guardian* and *The Telegraph*. She has given evidence to numerous select committees on the legal issues connected with Brexit, immigration, and the European Union (Withdrawal) Act. She has her own podcast, 2903cb, and she blogs on Brexit, mainly for the http://ukandeu.ac.uk/.

Michal Bobek is justice at the Supreme Administrative Court, Czech Republic, and Visiting Professor at the Institute of European, International and Comparative Law, University of Vienna Law Faculty. He has taught in numerous universities in Europe and overseas, including Oxford, College of Europe in Bruges, Prague, or Toronto, as well as (co)authored dozens of books and over one hundred academic articles in areas of EU law, ECHR law, constitutional law, comparative (public) law, and legal theory and history, published in English, Czech, German and French. From 2015 to 2021, he also served as Advocate General at the Court of Justice of the European Union.

Sanja Bogojević is Professor of Law at Oxford University and Fellow at Lady Margaret Hall. Her research interests lie in environmental law and EU law. She is the author of the award-winning *Emissions Trading Scheme: Market, States and Law* (Hart 2013), and her work on EU law includes *Great Debates in EU Law* (with Adams-Prassl, Bloomsbury 2021), as well as *Discretion in EU Public Procurement Law* (co-ed, Hart 2019; paperback 2020), and *Environmental Rights in Europe and Beyond* (co-ed, Hart 2018; paperback 2020). She is the General Editor of *Journal of Environmental Law*.

Nathan Cambien is an associate professor at the University of Antwerp and a Member of the legal service of the European Commission. He previously worked as a legal secretary (*référendaire*) at the Court of Justice of the European Union. Nathan holds a Magister Juris degree from the University of Oxford and a PhD in law from the University of Leuven. He has published widely on various topics of EU law and EU competition law and has been a visiting scholar at several institutions, including Columbia University, the University of Geneva, and the China-EU School of Law.

Fiona Costello is a Research Associate, Faculty of Law, University of Cambridge. Fiona works on the 'EU Migrant Worker Project' examining the experiences of EU nationals living in the UK (post Brexit), particularly in respect of legal status and (employment) rights. The work is part of a programme called 'The UK in a Changing Europe' (http://ukandeu.ac.uk), which is funded by the Economic and Social Research Council. Fiona also works on research connected to administrative justice, access to justice pathways, and everyday law, particularly as experienced by marginalized communities.

Jovan Dimitrijewitsch is a qualified lawyer in Switzerland. He holds a Licentiate and a Doctorate degree in law from the University of Zurich and an LLM in law from the University of Edinburgh. He has worked for several years in public administration and currently practises law with a law firm in Zurich. His main interests cover public law, EU law, Swiss-EU bilateral law, and employment law.

Stefan Enchelmaier studied law, philosophy, and Latin at the Universities of Cologne, Hamburg, and Edinburgh. He obtained his doctorate from the University of Bonn for a thesis on EU competition law, and his habilitation from the University of Munich for a thesis on comparative Anglo-German personal property law. He has worked in Oxford, Munich, York, and again since 2013 in Oxford. His interests are comparative private law, and the law of the European internal market. For several years, he taught a course on European Business Regulation in Oxford together with Stephen Weatherill.

Ariel Ezrachi is the Slaughter and May Professor of Competition Law at the University of Oxford and the Director of the University of Oxford Centre for Competition Law and Policy. He is the co-editor-in-chief of the *Journal of Antitrust Enforcement* (OUP) and the author and co-author of numerous books, including *How Big Tech Barons Smash Innovation* (HarperCollins 2022), *Competition Overdose* (HarperCollins 2020), and *Virtual Competition* (Harvard 2016). His research and commentary have been featured in *The Economist*, *The New Yorker*, *Wall Street Journal*, *Financial Times*, *The Guardian*, Nikkei, *New Scientist*, Politico, WIRED, BBC, and other international outlets.

Michèle Finck is Professor of Law and Artificial Intelligence at the University of Tübingen and Director of the CZS Institute for Artificial Intelligence and Law. Before that, she worked at the University of Oxford, the London School of Economics and the Max Planck Institute for Innovation and Competition. Her work engages with the intersection between law and technology with a particular focus on artificial intelligence.

Laurence W Gormley is Emeritus Professor of European Law, University of Groningen. He is a Professor at the College of Europe, Bruges, and a Bencher of Middle Temple. From 1983 to 1990 he was a European Commission Official, working for most of that time on infringements of the free movement of goods provisions in Community law, and held the Chair of European Law at Groningen from September 1990 until becoming Emeritus in November 2019.

Alicia Hinarejos is Professor of Law at McGill University. Before that, she was a Reader at the Faculty of Law, University of Cambridge, where she was also Director of the Cambridge Centre for European Legal Studies (CELS) and a Fellow of Downing College. Her areas of expertise are EU law and comparative public Law. She is Joint Editor of the *European Law Review*.

Geraint Howells is Executive Dean for Business, Public Policy and Law at the University of Galway. Previously he was Professor of Commercial Law and Associate Dean in Humanities for Internationalisation at Manchester University, where he remains a visiting professor. He has been Dean of Law at the City University of Hong Kong and Head of the Law Schools in Manchester and Lancaster. He has published extensively on consumer law, product liability, and European private law and was a member of the Acquis group developing common principles of European contract law and tort law. A former president of the International Association of Consumer Law, he edited the *Consumer Law Journal* for many years, is on the editorial board of the *Journal of Consumer Policy* and *European Review of Private Law*, and is series editor for Routledge's Markets and Law series.

Rhian Jukes holds an LLB degree from Durham University. Following her undergraduate degree, she graduated from the University of Edinburgh in 2021 with an LLM in European Law where she was awarded the David Edward Prize for her dissertation exploring the relationship between the object and effect dichotomy and Article 101(3) TFEU. She currently works as a Knowledge Management Assistant at Brodies LLP.

Antonín Kotrba completed his LLB at the University of Essex in 2019, soon after continuing his studies at the University of Edinburgh with an LLM in European law (2021). He has also worked as Junior Lawyer for a Prague-based pharmaceutical firm, predominantly dealing with international and EU law. Having recently completed a traineeship at the European Parliament, he is now looking forward to beginning his joint PhD at the University of Edinburgh/KU Leuven in September 2022, researching the EU's constitutional integrity with respect to political disregard for security and human rights in the field of EU external relations.

Dorota Leczykiewicz is Associate Professor of Law, University of Oxford, and a Fellow of St Peter's College. She works in comparative private law, tort law, and EU law. She edited two books with Professor Stephen Weatherill: *The Involvement of EU Law in Private Law Relationships* (Hart Publishing 2013) and *The Images of the Consumer in EU Law*: *Legislation, Free Movement and Competition Law* (Hart Publishing 2016).

Miguel Poiares Maduro is part-time Professor and former Director of the School of Transnational Governance at the European University Institute (EUI). He is also Chair of the Executive Board of the European Digital Media Observatory (EDMO), an STG-led project on online disinformation, funded by the European Commission. His research interests cover EU law, constitutional law, human rights law, and international economic law. From 2013 to 2015, Maduro was Minister Deputy to the Prime Minister and Minister for Regional Development in Portugal. From 2003 to 2009 he served as Advocate General at the European Court of Justice. He has been Member of the European Council of Foreign Relations, Member of the European Council of the World Economic Forum, and Member of the European Commission High Level Group on Media Pluralism and Media Freedom. He was Chairman of the Governance and Review Committee of FIFA from June 2016 to May 2017.

Mislav Mataija is a Member of the Legal Service of the European Commission. He represents the European Commission in litigation before the European Court of Justice in various areas of EU internal market law, advises on EU law matters, and litigates World Trade Organization disputes on behalf of the European Union. He has also been a visiting professor at Columbia Law School; Sciences Po School of Public Affairs, Paris; the Catholic Universities of Lyon and Lille; a lecturer at the University of Zagreb; and a researcher at the European University Institute Centre for Judicial Cooperation. He has published extensively in EU and international law, including a monograph entitled *Private Regulation and the Internal Market: Sports, Legal Services, and Standard Setting in EU Economic Law*, with Oxford University Press in 2016.

Petros C Mavroidis is Professor of Law at Columbia Law School. He has acted as chief reporter for the American Law Institute on the study *Principles of International Trade Law: The WTO*, and his latest manuscript includes *The WTO Dispute Settlement, How, Why, and Where?* (Elgar Publishing 2022).

Hans-Wolfgang Micklitz is Professor of Economic Law at the Robert Schuman Centre for Advanced Studies at the European University Institute, Florence. He held an ERC Grant in years 2011–16 on European Regulatory Private Law, and a grant from the Academy of Finland in years 2015–21 on the External Dimension of European Private Law. His research focuses on European and transnational private and economic law, computer law, and legal theory.

Okeoghene Odudu is Professor of Competition Law and a Director of the Centre for European Legal Studies at the University of Cambridge. He serves on the editorial boards of the *European Competition Journal*, the *Cambridge Yearbook of European Legal Studies*, and *Concurrences*. He was previously a Lecturer in Competition Law at the School of Law, King's College London; a Fellow in Law at Downing College, Cambridge; and attended Harvard Law School at a Scholar of the Kennedy Memorial Trust.

Tamara Perišin, is a Judge at the Court of Justice of the EU—General Court. Previously, Perišin held the Jean Monnet Chair at the University of Zagreb, coordinated the Jean Monnet Centre of Excellence 'EU's Global Leadership in the Rule of Law', was a John Hervey Gregory Visiting Professor of Law and World Organization at Harvard Law School, and participated in Croatia's EU accession negotiations, while she is still teaching at the University of Luxembourg. As regards her academic background, Perišin was a Chevening scholar at the University of Oxford where she earned the degree Magister Juris in European and Comparative Law; she completed her PhD at the University of Zagreb; she was a researcher at the Asser Institute, Georgetown University, the University of Michigan (Fulbright), CEU Budapest, the Max Planck Institute, and Harvard University.

Sacha Prechal studied law (University of Groningen, 1977–83) and Doctor of Laws (University of Amsterdam, 1995). She was Law Lecturer in the Law Faculty of the University of Maastricht (1983–87); Legal Secretary at the Court of Justice of the European Communities (1987–91); Lecturer at the Europa Institute of the Law Faculty of the University of Amsterdam (1991–95); Professor of European Law in the Law Faculty of the University of Tilburg (1995–2003). Prechal is Professor of European Law in the Law Faculty of the University of Utrecht and board member of the Europa Institute of the University of Utrecht (from 2003); member of the editorial board of several national and international legal journals; author of numerous publications; member of the Royal Netherlands Academy of Arts and Sciences; and Judge at the Court of Justice since 10 June 2010.

Thomas Roethe is a former part-time professor at the EUI in the European Regulatory Private Law Project (ERPL) and and Legal sociologist with the methodological focus on the reconstruction of latent structures of meaning in case studies within the framework of 'Objective Hermeneutics'. This is concentrated on the analysis of texts, legal documents of all kinds, such as laws, argumentation of lawyers before national courts, and the ECJ. Transcripts of litigation, written judgments, and open interviews with all parties involved.

Lukas Schaupp is a 2021 LLM graduate in European Law from the University of Edinburgh, with a previous background in political science as part of his undergraduate degree in European Studies from the University of Passau. Since graduating from Edinburgh, he has supported the 'Europe in the World' unit at the Brussels-based Centre for European Policy

Studies (CEPS) as a research intern. Starting in September 2022, he will be conducting PhD research at the European University Institute, focusing on EU-China investment relations. His research examines questions of EU external economic law, with a particular focus on investment and the increasing 'weaponization' of economic measures witnessed in recent years.

Jo Shaw has held the Salvesen Chair of European Institutions at the University of Edinburgh since 2005 and is currently Head of Edinburgh Law School. Her research in the last twenty-five years has focused on questions of citizenship and constitutionalism. She used to regard herself as a generalist EU lawyer, but that no longer holds true.

Niamh Nic Shuibhne is Professor of European Union Law at the University of Edinburgh. She is one of the Joint Editors of the *Common Market Law Review*. She was Joint Editor of the *European Law Review* from 2009 to 2014 and remains a member of its Editorial Board. Her research examines questions of substantive EU law from a constitutional perspective, with a particular focus on principle-based analysis of free movement law and European Union citizenship. She was awarded a Leverhulme Trust Major Research Fellowship (2016–19) to examine how protection of the foundational commitment to equal treatment in EU law has come to represent an ideological challenge to the sustainability of the Union more generally: how it became a 'confounding' rather than founding EU value. Her current research explores the integrity of the EU legal system in a wider sense, with specific focus on the concepts and principles that 'drive' the functioning of that system.

Eleanor Spaventa is Professor of European Law at the Department of Legal Studies, Bocconi University as well as the Director of the Bocconi Lab in European Studies. Her research interests include the internal market, Union Citizenship, EU fundamental rights, Brexit, and the Next Generation EU plan. She has written extensively in these areas and has authored or co-authored reports for the European Parliament and for the European Commission.

Jan Zglinski is Assistant Professor at the London School of Economics and Research Fellow of the Oxford Institute of European and Comparative Law. His research focuses on EU constitutional and internal market law, as well as sports law and policy.

Katja S Ziegler is the Sir Robert Jennings Professor of International Law at the University of Leicester and Co-director of the Centre of European Law and Internationalisation (CELI). Previously, she was Reader in European and Comparative Law, Fellow of St Hilda's College and Deputy Director of the Institute of European and Comparative Law, University of Oxford, of which she is a Visiting Research Fellow. In 2021–22 she held a two-year AHRC-FCDO Knowledge Exchange Fellowship in the Europe Directorate of the Foreign, Commonwealth and Development Office. She has published widely in the areas of international, European, and comparative law, with a particular focus on the interaction of legal orders, human rights and the rule of law, and limits on executive powers in foreign policy. Recent publications include three chapters in the *Research Handbook on General Principles in EU Law: Constructing Legal Orders in Europe* (Katja S Ziegler, Päivi J Neuvonen and Violeta Moreno-Lax (eds), Elgar 2022). She held grants from the European Commission (Jean Monnet actions), the British Academy, and Arts and Humanities Research Council.

Introduction: In Pursuit of the (Internal Market) Ideal

Jeremias Adams-Prassl, Sanja Bogojević, Ariel Ezrachi, and Dorota Leczykiewicz

It is with great joy that we present this collection of essays authored in honour of Professor Stephen Weatherill.

Steve is the Jacques Delors Professor Emeritus of European Law at the University of Oxford, having held the chair from 1998 until 2021. His writing has been central to the development and understanding of European Union law, and his transformative contributions on EU internal market law have enlightened and inspired generations of students, scholars, and policy makers. Steve's engaging and charismatic teaching style has further cemented his standing as a brilliant authority in the field. Everyone fortunate to have worked and studied in his presence delighted in Steve's warm collegiate personality, friendship, and mentorship.

One cannot easily encompass the reach of Steve's contribution to legal scholarship and the legal community, both in Oxford and internationally. And so, on the eve of his retirement, we embarked on a more modest and personal project, a *Festschrift* in which friends and colleagues reflect on key areas of a vast body of work.

Before turning to the substantive contributions ranging from the EU internal market, consumer protection, and the free movement of goods, persons, and citizenship to competition law, sport, and the teaching of EU law, however, it is only fitting to begin with a reflection on Steve's professional journey and pioneering career.

1. In Conversation with Steve

One of the great joys in editing this book has been the personal impressions shared by many of our contributors about Steve—from his early days at Cambridge to his charisma and unique style in the classroom. The lucky recipients of his *Termly Updates* will be familiar with the incisive wit—as well as acerbic sarcasm—with which Steve managed to keep up with developments in EU law. But we still

Jeremias Adams-Prassl, Sanja Bogojević, Ariel Ezrachi, and Dorota Leczykiewicz, *Introduction: In Pursuit of the (Internal Market) Ideal* In: *The Internal Market Ideal*. Edited by: Jeremias Adams-Prassl, Sanja Bogojević, Ariel Ezrachi, and Dorota Leczykiewicz, Oxford University Press.
DOI: 10.1093/oso/9780192867063.003.0001

wondered: what was it that motivated 'a child of the InterRail generation, looking out over the dusty, dirty, wind-blown wasteland of Berlin's Potsdamer Platz in September of 1980',[1] about to begin his second year at University, to devote his life's work to EU law?

In July 2022, we conspired to catch Steve en route to the horses at Ascot. The plan was to explore his career through a reminiscence of key cases from the last four decades—but, as ever, we were treated to so much more: deep reflections not just on how the internal market and the Union at large have evolved, but also on the key role that teaching and scholarship—as well as grubby politics—played in shaping our subject.

Born in Bishop Auckland in 1961, Steve grew up in a family marked by the deep conviction that European cooperation was the only way to avoid the horrors his father and grandfather experienced fighting in the two world wars. The United Kingdom's accession to the EEC brought much joy—but there was little political controversy, even in the lead-up to the referendum of 1975: 'a damp squib, it was always clear where it was going to go'. At Bradford Grammar School, the focus instead was on learning European languages—French and German—and sports: cricket and, above all, football.

In 1979, Steve went up to read law at Queens' College, Cambridge, with contemporaries including Jo Shaw, Richard Hart, and Vivien Rose. Summer travels across the Continent led to an interest in EEC law—then but a fledgling elective. With *Cassis de Dijon*[2] a mere two years old, and heated debates about the intricacies of horizontal direct effect way off the horizon, what little free movement law there was had to be supplemented by a generous dose of the finer points raised by the Common Agricultural Policy. The exam paper survives, as recounted by Jo Shaw's contribution in this volume.

Before the days of Jacques Delors and the Single European Act, there was little specialist interest in the subject, with only two universities—Edinburgh and Exeter—offering a dedicated postgraduate course. Steve went from Cambridge to Scotland, studying at the Centre for European Governmental Studies in 1982–83. The struggle to fill an entire course continued as a theme, with John Usher delighting the four students on the course with fascinating debates surrounding customs classifications and the latest *Hauptzollamt* decision on pyjamas. To while away the time, quizzing their teacher on the most obscure cases and decisions became a favourite game: to no avail, as 'Usher would know them all'. This translated into an early inspiration for Steve's own encyclopaedic knowledge of Union law, nurtured by his daily perusal of *Curia* and the *Official Journal*.

[1] Stephen Weatherill, *Law and Values in the European Union* (Oxford University Press 2016) vi.

[2] Case 120/78 *Rewe-Zentral AG v Bundesmonopolverwaltung für Branntwein* (*Cassis de Dijon*) [1979] ECLI:EU:C:1979:42.

Following a happy period of exploring Europe's football highlights, Steve took up a research job at Brunel University in 1985, working on an EU-funded project on consumer safety. It was during this period that he first began to teach—the joy of which became key in the decision to turn to an academic career.

The first step was a fixed-term post in law at the University of Reading (1986–87), developing a comprehensive course outline which was to become the blueprint for teaching and learning EU law in the decades ahead. This period also saw Steve's first publications, beginning to grapple with many core themes of his work to come: from the relationship between domestic and European consumer protection—the extent to which domestic safety rules are an obstacle to trade, and the ensuing harmonization imperative[3]—to the tension between free trade and effective protection.[4]

In 1987, a permanent lectureship in law brought him to the University of Manchester (1987–90)—and first introduced him to Catherine. EEC law was still an optional subject, but things started to 'feel buzzier', especially following the Single European Act. Litigants, from entrepreneurial managers to staid local authority solicitors, started to encounter free movement law, and set out to challenge long-standing domestic orthodoxy.

In the run-up to *B & Q*,[5] for example, Steve entered into extensive correspondence with county councils to determine their experience with Sunday trading challenges and similar cases. Long before the days of online research, the replies received consistently showed a complete lack of knowledge of EEC law—and indeed surprise that it should apply at all. Whoever first came up with the 'genuinely ingenious' move on part of the UK's largest DIY store, however, 'remains a mystery'.

The 1980s also marked a broader change in direction of the subject, with increasing bulk and coherence in both the work of the Court and the broader scholarship. At the same time, however, it also became clear that EEC norms could be abused by tactical litigants, which heralded a new era altogether. For the first time, there could be a serious discussion as to whether the new legal order might have gone too far.

Closer to home, 1990 saw a joint move with Catherine to the University of Nottingham. The undergraduate course remained fairly consistent, having been successfully developed by Nigel Gravells, a most generous colleague, but for the first time, Steve was able to teach graduates, with an LLM course focused on consumer law, and supervise the first of over 100 research students. The early 1990s also saw the publication of the first edition of *Cases and Materials on EEC Law* (1992), and the Clarendon series' *Law and Integration in the European Union*

[3] Stephen Weatherill, 'Consumer Safety Legislation in the United Kingdom' (1987) 2 European Consumer Law Journal 81.

[4] Stephen Weatherill, '1992 and Consumer Law: Can Free Trade be Reconciled with Effective Protection?' (1988) 6 Trading Law 175.

[5] Case C-145/88 *Torfaen Borough Council v B & Q plc* [1989] ECLI:EU:C:1989:593.

(1995). The latter's cover is famous for its image of a Eurostar train rushing into Waterloo Station—the recently launched highspeed rail service perhaps the perfect metaphor for the next stage of European integration. Indeed, as the preface notes, 'England and Wales are about to follow where Scotland has led. EC law is on the brink of becoming a compulsory part of the undergraduate curriculum in England and Wales.'[6]

The newfound dynamism in the Union was not limited to Treaty revision and the legislator: the Court similarly entered a new stage of assertiveness vis-à-vis the Member States. Whilst there had been some discussion of damages in the run-up to *Francovich*,[7] for example, the Court's bold statements in the case had significant practical impact, despite an apparent lack of follow-up litigation, with lawyers across government departments warning their political masters to 'take EC law seriously'.

It was not just public law aficionados who were starting to pay attention: *Centros*[8] brought the company lawyers to the fray, intrigued by the Court's unusually open recognition of regulatory competition as a central purpose of free movement law. The theme of the Union's overreach continued to rise, as well-entrenched rules were subjected to tough scrutiny: unsurprising to the internal market expert; but also, the stuff of front-page headlines in national tabloids.

Steve's longest academic stint was at Oxford where, in 1998, he became the first Jacques Delors Professor of European Law and Fellow of Somerville College. The subsequent twenty-three years in the post were marked by dynamic and, at times, serendipitous developments of the EU legal order.

Amongst the landmark developments in EU law was the Union's geographic enlargement in the early 2000s, which saw the variety of Oxford graduate students increase to comprise a much wider range of European countries. At the same time, the designation of EU law as a compulsory undergraduate subject meant that an ever-greater pool of colleagues joined arms with EU lawyers in teaching the subject. To help all those new to EU law teaching—at Oxford and beyond—stay on top of the ever-developing jurisprudence and literature in the field, the first *Termly Update* was penned in Michaelmas 2006, quickly becoming an invaluable resource and one of the few genuine highlights to look forward to in Noughth Week. In the St Cross building, the Institute for European and Comparative Law (IECL) was relaunched in 2004, featuring an undergraduate course in Law with Law Studies in Europe (Course II), and spearheaded by Steve as the Director.

Over the years, Steve delivered countless lectures in his uniquely engaging style, as many of the contributors warmly remember. These covered the full range of

[6] Stephen Weatherill, *Law and Integration in the European Union* (Oxford University Press 1995) i.

[7] Joined Cases C–6/90 and 9/90 *Andrea Francovich and Danila Bonifaci v Italian Republic* [1991] ECLI:EU:C:1991:428.

[8] Case C–212/97 *Centros Ltd v Erhvervs- og Selskabsstyrelsen* [1999] ECLI:EU:C:1999:126.

possible topics, from constitutional law and free movement in the internal market for the FHS (undergraduates) to 'European Business Regulation', a BCL/MJur (graduate) course first set up by Derrick Wyatt, and later convened by Steve.

During that period, two cases in particular stood out as 'GTCs' (Good Teaching Cases): *Schmidberger* and *Omega Spielhallen*.[9] Even if these cannot compete with earlier cases such as *Cassis*,[10] *COSTA*,[11] and *Van Gend*[12] in terms of providing the perfect EU law cocktail (take a good splash of free movement provisions, add a few preliminary rulings, and mix in a dash of direct effect incentives to litigate together with Member State concerns over regulatory autonomy), *Schmidberger* and *Omega Spielhallen* 'suddenly provided new questions about justification'.

Any other favourites? *Bosman*, obviously, not least given the fact 'that the older cases are better: crisper and shorter'. But choosing favourites is tough: Steve quickly adds *CIA Security & Lemmens*[13] to the list as an illustration of EU law wielded by ingenious litigants: 'who thought of that?'

But football always comes out top: sharing a birthday with the likes of Ronaldinho, Griezmann, and (in the exact same year) Lothar Matthäus, perhaps it was always Steve's destiny that his academic interests in EU law would eventually spill over into the world of football. He first wrote about discrimination on grounds of nationality in sport in the late 1980s,[14] but these were issues thought interesting 'in theory' with no foreseeable practical impact, not least due to a lack of willing litigants to take on sports' organizing bodies. Along, however, came Mr Jean-Marc Bosman, a Belgian midfielder, who took legal action over football transfer rules—a case which Steve had always been 'waiting for, without ever expecting it to happen'. But happen it did: the judgment in *Bosman*[15] saw a remarkably assertive Court refusing to accept at face value sports bodies' assertions as to their self-regulatory privilege, delivering a clear message to litigants: the European project stops at nothing, not even the murky and powerful world of sports governance.[16]

[9] Case C–112/00 *Eugen Schmidberger, Internationale Transporte und Planzüge v Republik Österreich* [2003] ECLI:EU:C:2003:333 and Case C–36/02 *Omega Spielhallen- und Automatenaufstellungs-GmbH v Oberbürgermeisterin der Bundesstadt Bonn* [2004] ECLI:EU:C:2004:614, respectively.

[10] *Cassis de Dijon* (n 2).

[11] Case 6/64 *Flaminio Costa v ENEL* [1964] ECLI:EU:C:1964:66.

[12] Case C–26/62 *NV Algemene Transport- en Expeditie Onderneming van Gend & Loos v Netherlands Inland Revenue Administration* [1963] ECLI:EU:C:1963:1.

[13] Case C–194/94 *CIA Security International SA v Signalson SA and Securitel SPRL* [1996] ECLI:EU:C:1996:172.

[14] Stephen Weatherill, 'Discrimination on Grounds of Nationality in Sport' (1989) 9 Yearbook of European Law 55.

[15] C–415/93 *Union royale belge des sociétés de football association ASBL v Jean-Marc Bosman, Royal club liégeois SA v Jean-Marc Bosman and Union des associations européennes de football (UEFA) v Jean-Marc Bosman* [1995] ECLI:EU:C:1995:463.

[16] Readers interested in exploring these intricacies will find a great introduction to the (murky) world of sports governance in Miguel Maduro's chapter.

The decision, Steve reflects, 'probably has improved football'—a sense shared by Mr Bosman[17]—even if, as predicted in subsequent publications, fair play may well be better achieved through competition law rather than an exclusive focus on free movement rules.[18]

This leads us to another key theme running through Steve's work: are there any limits to European integration through law? Even though the answer has always appeared to be obvious on the face of the Treaties, it was only in *Tobacco Advertising I*[19] that the Court took a clear stance. The case 'was dynamite' and led to a wholesale change in the Commission's legislative mood: 'every proposal since then has been scrutinised much more carefully', with the Court's jurisprudence becoming a key 'drafting guide'.[20]

That is not to say that Steve saw the sages of Luxembourg as infallible, not least when it comes to careful legal reasoning. *Mangold* and *Kücükdeveci* stand out as examples of a Court failing to show any real respect for countervailing values, such as party autonomy.[21] On occasion, the Court has also proven to be impervious to objections from national courts, sowing the seeds for subsequent domestic revolutions along the lines of *Ajos*.[22] Ever the fair-minded observer, Steve also points to *Dano*[23] as an attempt by the Court to pull back, acting 'remarkably defensively'. The end result 'shook people up'—it may have been that the case was driven by litigants, but it also shows a Court 'ready to listen, conscious about limits of competence'.

What, then, about *Weiss*[24] and the future of negative harmonization—long the most powerful tool in the arsenal of the Court acting as a fearless protector of the internal market? Steve cautions that Luxembourg there was not necessarily 'working with the usual blueprint': EMU issues are 'so obscure', and also, the Court is very cautious in its interactions with Germany's *Bundesverfassungsgericht*. The big picture story thus remains unclear, even if its implications for the rule of law debate in Poland and Hungary, where the 'stakes are much higher than monetary policy', are obvious.

17 James Riach, 'Jean-Marc Bosman: "I think I did something good—I gave players rights"' *The Guardian* (12 December 2015).

18 Stephen Weatherill, '"Fair Play Please!": Recent Developments in the Application of EC Law to Sport' (2003) 40 Common Market Law Review 51.

19 Case C–376/98 *Germany v European Parliament and European Council* (*Tobacco Advertising I*) [2000] ECLI:EU:C:2000:544.

20 Stephen Weatherill, 'The Limits of Legislative Harmonisation Ten Years after *Tobacco Advertising*: How the Court's Case Law Has Become A "Drafting Guide"' (2011) 12 German Law Journal 827.

21 Case C–144/04 *Werner Mangold v Rüdiger Helm* [2005] ECLI:EU:C:2005:709 and Case C–555/07 *Seda Kücükdeveci v Swedex GmbH & Co KG* [2010] ECLI:EU:C:2010:21, respectively.

22 Case C–441/14d *Dansk Industri (DI), acting on behalf of Ajos A/S v Estate of Karsten Eigil Rasmussen* [2016] ECLI:EU:C:2016:278.

23 Case C–333/13 *Elisabeta Dano and Florin Dano v Jobcenter Leipzig* [2014] ECLI:EU:C:2014:2358.

24 Case C–493/17 *Proceedings brought by Heinrich Weiss* [2018] ECLI:EU:C:2018:1000.

Rule of law waters need to be trodden carefully. Whilst *Portuguese Judges*[25] is an 'interesting and elegant judgment', it might itself constitute a violation of the rule of law, by going too far into domestic regulatory autonomy. After all, once the Court enters into the sacred grounds of the rule of law, what could possibly be beyond the limits of its scrutiny? And thus, we return to the central tension found in EU law between conferral and restraint of power. The small, but significant, change in the title of Steve's Clarendon series introduction does not go unnoticed: from *Law and Integration in the European Union* (1995) to *Law and Values in the European Union* (2016).

With the starting gates at Ascot soon to burst open and release their equine occupants, it is time to wrap up with one last question: Steve's greatest sporting memory during his four decades in academia? The answer comes without hesitation: Hull City qualifying for the Europa League in 2014–15. Britain in Europe is, after all, the hallmark of Steve's teaching and scholarship in EU law.

2. Exploring the Internal Market Ideal

The unifying theme of this collection is 'The Internal Market Ideal'. It is an implicit reference to one of Steve's recent books, *The Internal Market as a Legal Concept* (Oxford University Press 2016), but also reflects our hope that a close examination of the legal issues surrounding the semi-integrated market of the European Union could assist in finding, and perhaps delivering, its most desirable version: a Union which benefits from economic growth and pursues non-economic objectives, all whilst carefully balancing respect for Member States' autonomy and the European Union's self-sufficiency.

Chapters in this collection are divided into five parts, addressing many facets of European internal market law. Each chapter offers a different perspective on select aspects of the internal market, its regulatory framework, and legal principles. We hope you will enjoy the intellectual journey through the chapters as much as we have done: it offers a panoramic view of the many elements of the Union's internal market, and, most importantly, an opportunity to appreciate the breadth of Steve's contributions to the field.

3. Part I: The Ever-Developing Nature of Internal Market Law

By its nature, the internal market as a policy objective is an 'ever-unfinished project', experiencing constant evolution. That evolution is guided, and restricted, by

[25] Case C-64/16 *Associação Sindical dos Juízes Portugueses v Tribunal de Contas* [2018] ECLI:EU:C:2018:117.

the European Union's limited competences, the need to project vital interests of the Member States, and the indispensability of their enforcement structures. In his scholarship, Steve has often reflected on economic integration and how it touches upon so much more than trade-related matters. Chapters featured in this part build on the themes explored in Steve's many contributions on point.[26]

In Chapter 1, **Michal Bobek** explores the internal market as an 'incomplete and evolving structure' and picks up the theme of the internal market as a heterogeneous idea. The chapter reflects on the eternal tension between centralization and unification on the one hand and local diversity on the other. Bobek's argument proceeds in three steps. First, it is suggested that the internal market remains a remarkably incomplete structure. Although quite elegant as a model on paper, the default requirement of mutual recognition is an unusually vague principle, the functionality of which at the national level leaves much to be desired. Secondly, the chapter observes that the EU legislature opened up, intentionally or not, a number of other, parallel building sites, ranging from the 'area of freedom, security, and justice' to the 'rule of law crises management', into which the principles and approaches originally developed in the (economic) law of the internal market are being transplanted. Thirdly, the chapter reflects upon what this plethora of the legal construction sites means for the economic law of the internal market. The chapter closes with a broader reflection on whether, while still of course incomplete and evolving, the economic law of the internal market should be approached as any other area of EU law.

In Chapter 2, **Michèle Finck** documents the transformation of EU data law from a legislative ensemble centred primarily around the fundamental right to data protection towards a much broader and more complex area of EU law of which data protection is but one element. The chapter explores the evolution of EU data law through the lens of the internal market and the practical future implications thereof. In doing so, it points to the way new legislative proposals and acts encourage the processing of (personal) data and transform the latter into an object of economic rights, a tradable commodity that can be sold or donated. This paradigm shift, it is argued, will result in tensions that will be keeping practitioners, academics, and judges busy for decades to come.

[26] Steve's vast work in this area includes (but is not limited to) the already mentioned *Law and Economic Integration in the European Union* (OUP 1995). Also noteworthy are his contributions on 'Compulsory Notification of Draft Technical Regulations: The Contribution of Directive 83/189 to the Management of the Internal Market' (1996) 16 Yearbook of European Law 129; 'The Evolution of the Single Market: Harmonisation or Liberalisation' (1990) 53 Modern Law Review 578, with Andrew McGee; 'New Strategies for Managing the EC's Internal Market' (2000) 53 Current Legal Problems 595; 'Why Object to the Harmonization of Private Law by the EC?' (2004) 12 European Review of Private Law 633; 'The Limits of Legislative Harmonisation Ten Years after Tobacco Advertising' (n 20); and the instant classic *The Internal Market as a Legal Concept* (Oxford University Press 2016), followed by 'The Several Internal Markets' (2017) 36 Yearbook of European Law 125 and 'Comparative Internal Market Law: The UK and the EU' (2021) 40 Yearbook of European Law 431.

In Chapter 3, **Alicia Hinarejos** explores the link between the EU's single market and Economic and Monetary Union (EMU). She observes that this link is a longstanding one in that they were conceived of as complementary elements within the European economic constitution and supposed to enhance each other as two sides of the same coin—namely, the project of creating an economic union among the Member States. She discusses how the relationship between the single market and EMU has also changed over time, especially since the euro area crisis. The crisis highlighted the need for changes to make EMU more resilient but reflects that the tools needed to effect change in this area—in the form of EU powers and their corresponding Treaty legal bases—were limited. To address this gap, the single market powers were co-opted. Their use could be perceived as justified due to the complementary nature of the single market and certain aspects of EMU, but the solution has had its drawbacks and, most importantly, limitations. The author concludes by observing that the use of single market legal bases will continue in the future, perhaps changing, to some degree, the nature of the single market itself.

Chapter 4, authored by **Jan Zglinski**, offers reflections on the internal market as a dynamic process. He explores the dynamic nature of the EU internal market and analyses the legal principles and governance structures underlying it. Having traced how these have evolved since the beginning of the European integration project, Zglinski argues that market design choices must be responsive to the political, economic, and institutional context in which they are situated. This context can change over time, rendering old solutions inadequate and structural changes necessary. A look into the future development of the internal market is ventured. Five scenarios are laid out, ranging from more negative integration, to greater positive integration, to the reaching of a stable equilibrium.

4. Part II: The Internal Market, Consumer Protection, and Free Movement of Goods and Persons

In his scholarship, Steve has explored many facets of the internal market. He pioneered the study of EU free movement law, focusing, in particular, on the free movement of goods (who could ever forget his epic lecture series delivered to Oxford undergraduates every Michaelmas term?). Numerous celebrated articles include his scholarship on the subject,[27] as well as a bestselling EU law textbook: *Cases & Materials on EU Law*. Steve has also made a significant contribution to the study

[27] Steve's analysis has found expression in many articles, among them: 'After *Keck*: Some Thoughts on How to Clarify the Clarification' (1996) 33 Common Market Law Review 885; 'Recent Case Law Concerning the Free Movement of Goods: Mapping the Frontiers of Market Deregulation' (1999) 36 Common Market Law Review 51; and repeated 'Free Movement of Goods' articles analysing the implications of the recent case law of the Court of Justice, published in the *International and Comparative Law Quarterly* and the *European Review of Contract Law*.

of EU consumer law. Particularly noteworthy here are two books—*Consumer Protection Law*, with Geraint Howells, and *EU Consumer Law and Policy*—which, together with his many articles, have shaped the field.[28] Of course, Steve's interest reached beyond these themes, and included, in particular, the intersection of both free movement law and consumer law with fundamental rights.[29] The remarkable scope and rigour of his work have inspired many. This part includes five contributions, each exploring related areas of law and policy.

Chapter 5, authored by **Laurence W Gormley**, traces Steve's intellectual journey with the internal market, and in particular the free movement of goods, as portrayed through many of his publications over the years. It uses the images of a shepherd safely grazing sheep and rulers governing well, as portrayed in the Bach/Franck Cantata *Schafe können sicher weiden* (Sheep May Safely Graze). It follows Steve's concerns, critical observations, and level of contentment in the light of judgments of the Court of Justice of the European Union and various actions of the EU legislative actors.

In Chapter 6, **Stefan Enchelmaier** argues that the structure and organization of the Court of Justice of the European Union (CJEU) affect the quality and consistency of the Court's case law on the free movement of goods. The point is illustrated through the analysis of three recent judgments on Article 34 TFEU, and discussion of the way in which cases are allocated to the subdivisions of the Court; judges are attributed to them; and finally, which chambers, judges, and Advocates General participated in the jurisprudence on free movement of goods. The author observes that these judgments have little discursive reasoning, few definitions of key terms, and reference only remotely related earlier judgments that remain without much explanation. From a comparative glance at the Supreme Courts of the United States, United Kingdom, France, and Germany, suggestions are derived

[28] eg 'Consumer Policy in the European Community: Before and After Maastricht' (1993) 16 Journal of Consumer Policy 285, with Hans W Micklitz; 'The Commission's Options for Developing EC Consumer Protection and Contract Law: Assessing the Constitutional Basis' (2002) 13 European Business Law Review 497, 'EU Treaty Revision and Consumer Protection' (2004) 27 Journal of Consumer Policy 367, with Hans W Micklitz and Norbert Reich; 'The Consumer Rights Directive: How and Why a Quest for "Coherence" Has (Largely) Failed' (2012) 49 Common Market Law Review 1279; 'The Links between Competition Policy and Consumer Protection' in Geraint Howells and others (eds), *Yearbook of Consumer Law* (Routledge 2007). One of the editors of the present volume had the pleasure of working with Steve on an edited collection that explored different aspects of EU consumer law and the position of consumer in EU law more broadly: *The Images of the Consumer in EU Law: Legislation, Free Movement, and Competition Law* (Hart 2016), with Dorota Leczykiewicz, to which Steve also contributed a chapter: 'Empowerment is Not the Only Fruit'.

[29] eg note his scholarship in 'From Economic Rights to Fundamental Rights' in *The Protection of Fundamental Rights in the EU After Lisbon* (Hart 2013), also co-edited by Steve (with Sybe Alexander de Vries and Ulf Bernitz), and the broader issues of the EU's intervention into private law, including books jointly edited with other scholars: with Roger Brownsword, Hans-W Micklitz, and Leone Niglia, *The Foundations of European Private Law* (Hart 2011); with Stefan Grundman and Wolfgang Kerber, *Party Autonomy and the Role of Information in the Internal Market* (De Gruyter 2012); and with Dorota Leczykiewicz, *The Involvement of EU Law in Private Law Relationships* (Hart 2013), as well as solo-authored *Contract Law of the Internal Market* (Cambridge University Press 2016).

for a reform of the operation of the CJEU. The chapter calls for specialist chambers of a steady composition that could develop subject-matter expertise, and thus ensure the coherence and quality of the case law.

In Chapter 7, **Sacha Prechal** considers three recent actions brought by the Commission against Hungary, in which the Court of Justice was asked to consider whether an infringement action could be brought on the grounds of an alleged violation of a provision of the Charter of Fundamental Rights (Charter), in addition to an alleged breach of a Treaty freedom. The chapter observes that ever since the *ERT* case[30] (the Greek television monopoly case), it has been standard case law that EU fundamental rights can be relied upon in situations where Member States seek to derogate from provisions of EU law ('derogation situations'), in that any justification of restrictive measures relied upon by a Member State must respect fundamental rights. The author discusses how, in these three recent judgments, the Court built upon this case law and found that the European Commission may start an infringement action based on the Charter in a 'derogation situation' and ask for an independent finding of a breach of the Charter. The chapter reflects that while the Court has yet to address the question of whether a self-standing claim of alleged non-compliance with a Charter provision can also hold where there is only an infringement of a Treaty freedom without a justification being invoked, the case law as it stands is significant for the protection of fundamental rights. The author concludes by pointing out the desirable consequences and value which a separate finding of a breach of fundamental rights in infringement proceedings can entail for EU citizens.

In Chapter 8, **Eleanor Spaventa** explores the intersection between barriers to movement and fundamental rights which leads to the application—or not—of the Charter to acts of the Member States. Here, there are different strands of case law pulling in different directions, and this contribution identifies different approaches in the Court's jurisprudence. In some cases, fundamental rights are more readily applied; for instance, in cases relating to changes of names, extradition cases, *Ruiz Zambrano* cases, and deprivation of citizenship cases. In other instances, including those concerning barriers to movement and access to welfare, fundamental rights are only sometimes relevant—also depending on the way in which the preliminary question has been formulated. Furthermore, there seems to be a link between the fundamental right deemed to be relevant and the rationale of free movement in that particular case. This means that *only* those Charter rights which have the effect of reinforcing or facilitating the right to move may be relied upon, as opposed to *any* Charter right.

[30] Case C-260/89 *Elliniki Radiophonia Tiléorassi AE and Panellinia Omospondia Syllogon Prossopikou v Dimotiki Etairia Pliroforissis and Sotirios Kouvelas and Nicolaos Avdellas* (*ERT*) [1991] ECLI:EU:C:1991:254.

Chapter 9, authored by **Geraint Howells**, reflects on the history of legislative reform relating to consumer product safety at the EU level. He highlights the role of standardization within a co-regulatory approach and the practical dimension of enforcement. Howells also considers the reform proposals recently made at the EU level in response to new technology, as well as potential future UK developments in this field. The chapter concludes by discussing the degree of future alignment between the UK and EU systems in relation to consumer product safety.

5. Part III: The Internal Market, Competition Law, and Sports

This part of the volume ventures into two further domains of EU internal market law prominent in Steve's writing: the interaction between competition law and other goals and values of the EU internal market law,[31] and EU sports law and regulation—an area that has become Steve's unrivalled domain.[32]

In Chapter 10, **Albertina Albors-Llorens** focuses on the interplay between competition law and the single market in the EU. She argues that, in the aftermath of the Modernisation period, the single market imperative remains as alive as ever in the landscape of EU competition law and continues to saturate current challenges, such as those underlying recent legislative initiatives, the fight against cartels, and the digitalization of the economy. The discussion notes how, as the EU and its legal system evolved, criticism was voiced on account of the tensions between that objective and the more traditional goals of competition law. It brings to mind the important question which was asked after market integration had been largely achieved; that is, whether competition law could—and should—begin to live a life independent from that objective. The chapter contends that the single market imperative continues to be an essential aspect of the identity of the EU competition rules and that divesting these rules from it would devalue the impact of one of the most successful areas of EU law and policy.

Chapter 11, by **Miguel Poiares Maduro**, moves our attention to EU sports law. It challenges the current model of sports governance autonomy and argues that only the EU is positioned to bring democratic accountability and rule of law principles into sports governance, and ought to do so. The chapter starts by reviewing the extent to which sports private governance bodies are failing to deliver on the public goods entrusted to them, from sports integrity to the openness and competitive balance of sports competitions. It then proceeds to link those failures to systemic

[31] See eg 'The Links between Competition Policy and Consumer Protection' (n 28).

[32] See eg '"Fair Play Please!": Recent Developments in the Application of EC Law to Sport' (n 18); *European Sports Law: Collected Papers* (TMC Asser Press 2007 and 2014); *Principles and Practice in EU Sports Law* (Oxford University Press 2017); 'The EU as a Sports Regulator' in *Handbook on International Sports Law* (Edward Elgar 2011 and 2022); and 'Saving Football from Itself: Why and How to Re-make EU Sports Law' [2022] Cambridge Yearbook of European Legal Studies 1.

governance failures in those bodies. It identifies and challenges the traditional justifications put forward to validate the almost absolute form of regulatory autonomy and private governance granted to sports governance bodies. It then proceeds to argue not only that autonomy ought to be limited, but that even when and where it does make sense to recognize such autonomy, it needs to be conditioned on subjecting their structures of governance to principles of democracy, rule of law, fundamental rights, accountability, and transparency. The final section argues that only the EU is in a position to do so and puts forward different alternatives on how this can be accomplished. It also argues that, in so doing, the EU presents to its citizens an important democratic added value.

In Chapter 12, **Mislav Mataija** and **Petros C Mavroidis** reflect on the nature of the sports market where rival teams produce and sell competition to the audience. They consider the unique challenges associated with the protection of rivalry in sport markets and the attainment of a 'competitive balance'. The discussion explores the regulatory responses that have been used in American sports markets and uses this to reflect on the EU regime. They note that, broadly speaking, the US-style mechanisms for ensuring competitive balance are absent from European professional sports. Looking at the regulation of football, they note how the EU has been a rather reluctant enforcer. They reflect on the extent to which the organization of sport, which among other things led to the US being a closed league model while the EU is an open league model, may explain the different enforcement approaches used to achieve competitive balance.

Chapter 13, by **Okeoghene Odudu**, considers the role that competition law has played, and continues to play, in the functioning of the market for athletes' services. He asks what role, if any, competition law plays in contributing an environment in which athletes are able to bargain for an increased share of the revenue generated by sport. A question then is whether the ability of athletes to extract an increased share of the revenue generated by the game is somehow harmful. It observes that it has been argued that such salaries have an adverse impact on 'competitive balance' or may otherwise destabilize a sport. The salary distribution hitherto examined is internal to the game, and what has not yet been fully explored is whether a salary disparity between sectors is problematic. The chapter suggests one issue to analyse is whether the disparity of wealth affects accessibility to the sector. It would need to be demonstrated that athletes' salaries harm accessibility and that lower salaries would increase accessibility, rather than be consumed by others in the game.

6. Part IV: EU Values and the Mobilization of EU Law

This part of the volume follows Steve's interest in the interplay between law and politics, a theme rarely addressed directly in academic writings yet frequently highlighted in presentations and conversations with colleagues. There is a sense of a conceptual map here, which includes a demarcation between the fields of law and politics, even if the former can be transformed into the other (and vice versa). Think, for example, about competence sensitivity, managing policy conflicts in free movement law, or safeguarding some scope of Member States' regulatory autonomy: there is a presupposition that law is its own domain and things become 'legal' or need to remain 'legal' to be legitimate.[33] Closely linked is the question of the Union's values, whether constitutionalized or not, and how the institutions contribute to their attainment—and how they can be damaged by imprudent political or adjudicatory choices.[34]

Chapter 14, by **Hans-Wolfgang Micklitz** and **Thomas Roethe**, notes that non-governmental organizations, both self-financed and state-funded, are invoking the CJEU to promote equal treatment, environmental protection, and consumer protection. It observes that, as a result, the CJEU is faced with new challenges. Instead of having to solve a classical case, it needs to decide on policy issues with large implications not only for what might be called the European society, but also, and in particular, for EU law—if not law more generally. The chapter is built around three of the CJEU's landmark decisions, each standing for a particular policy field, and tries to understand whether the proposed solutions remain within the province of law and within legal professionalism. To achieve that, the chapter relies on interviews conducted with the legal actors involved, and on a socio-legal understanding of legal professionalism. Its aim is to highlight the boundaries of law-making through public interest litigation.

In Chapter 15, **Catherine Barnard** and **Fiona Costello** explore the impact of free movement on small, regional locations which previously experienced little to no inward migration. The chapter looks at EU migrant workers working in low-wage, low-skill employment and the problems they experience in and around housing. The authors argue that the requirement of equal treatment, the key right under EU law, means little in practice for the lived experience of migrant workers, yet it creates tensions within the local community.

In Chapter 16, **Katja S Ziegler** reflects on the new relationship between the United Kingdom and EU under the Trade and Cooperation Agreement (TCA). The chapter outlines and contextualizes the paradigm shift of the TCA from supranational EU law to international law in three dimensions and contexts. First, it demonstrates the paradigm shift in economic cooperation, using the rules on trade

[33] See eg one of Steve's most-cited articles: 'Competence Creep and Competence Control' (2004) 23 Yearbook of European Law 1, and also 'Constitutional Issues—How Much is Best Left Unsaid?' in Stefan Vogenauer and Stephen Weatherill, *The Harmonisation of European Contract Law: Implications for European Private Laws, Business and Legal Practice* (Hart 2006).

[34] See, in particular, *Law and Values in the European Union* (n 1), but also many of Steve's articles on competence, free movement, and consumer law. More recently, Steve has also been working on the consequences of Brexit and the Northern Ireland Protocol; see 'Interpreting the Protocol' in Christopher McCrudden (ed), *The Law and Practice of the Ireland—Northern Ireland Protocol* (Cambridge University Press 2022).

in goods as an example. Secondly, it discusses the exclusion of individual rights, and, therefore, enforcement mechanisms accessible to individuals, under the TCA. Thirdly, it analyses the limited role of values, reflected in the basis for cooperation under the TCA in comparison to the role of values in EU law.

In Chapter 17, **Tamara Perišin** and **Nathan Cambien** position the narrative of the building of the single market in the broader framework of the rule of law and the role of individuals in guarding it. The chapter first explores CJEU cases dealing with the rule of law and highlights that such questions arise in different types of judicial proceedings including preliminary reference procedures, infringement actions against Member States, and direct actions against EU institutions or bodies, whereby each of these procedures can be initiated by more than one type of actor. The chapter puts an emphasis on the jurisprudence which arises from actions brought by individual applicants to the General Court. Through this discussion, the chapter illustrates the relevance of individual actions in the possibilities for individuals to have access to the EU courts in light of the most recent jurisprudence on standing in a number of important fields related to the internal market.

7. Part V: Teaching EU Internal Market Law

Steve's devotion to teaching has been acknowledged and celebrated by his students and colleagues alike. Indeed, for Steve, there seemed to be no obvious boundary between teaching and scholarship. He taught the topics on which he had been writing and he wrote about the topics on which he lectured. Anyone who attended Steve's lectures can attest to the fact that they were discursive, inquisitive, and en gaging. They were an invitation into a world of legal concepts, practical questions, policy doubts, and unconstitutional uncertainties. With this in mind, it is only fitting to conclude this collection with two contributions that offer a nod to the art of teaching and the impact it generates.

In Chapter 18, **Niamh Nic Shuibhne**, **Dayana Baleva**, **Jovan Dimitrijewitsch**, **Rhian Jukes**, **Antonín Kotrba**, and **Lukas Schaupp** trace the teaching and learning of the 'Integrity of the EU's Internal Market' LLM course at Edinburgh Law School during the spring semester of the 2020–21 academic year. They illustrate how Steve's research—especially his *Yearbook of European Law* article on 'The Several Internal Markets' (2017) and his subsequent work on Brexit—underpinned the foundations of the course and provoked both teacher and students to interrogate and reflect more deeply on the nature, coherence, and fragility of the internal market. Chiming with Steve's own approach, it considers questions of integrity from a conceptual perspective and then tests and evolves them in the context of complexities within and across the internal market's four freedoms, with respect to how market and non-market objectives intersect, and in terms of how the EU's internal market relates to the markets beyond its borders. The chapter concludes by offering post-course thoughts from the students on what it was like to learn through this thematic approach and from the teacher on the future of education on EU internal market law.

Chapter 19, by **Jo Shaw**, offers a personal reflection inspired by a recently discovered old EEC examination paper, which both she and Steve had to sit as undergraduates in law at the University of Cambridge. Against this backdrop, Shaw explores the intersection of her career with Steve's, fascinatingly placing these careers in the context of the evolution of the EU as legal order and as polity.

***

We hope you will enjoy your journey through the chapters in this collection. We are grateful to the distinguished contributors for their insightful and heartfelt contributions. Particular thanks are due to Lauren Crais, who provided stellar research and editorial assistance in the completion of this volume, and to the Oxford Law Faculty for providing Research Support Funding. We are also thankful to colleagues at Oxford University Press for their support and assistance in publishing the work.

Most importantly, however, our thanks go to Steve: a brilliant scholar, teacher, mentor, and friend—a true mensch, always in the pursuit of the ideal(s) in European Union Law.

PART I

THE EVER-DEVELOPING NATURE OF INTERNAL MARKET LAW

1

The Internal Market as an Incomplete and Evolving Structure: But Evolving Towards Where Exactly?

Michal Bobek

1. An Introductory Flashback

It was one of those still-sunny autumn days. A group of postgrads assembled in one of the smaller lecture theatres of the St Cross Building. I suspect a number of people, myself included, would have preferred to continue admiring the colourful autumn foliage in the University Parks as opposed to the dimness of a stuffy windowless lecture room in an indeed listed—but still brutalist—building. The lecturer who entered the theatre and sat nonchalantly on the front desk certainly brought some brightness to the room. If by nothing else, already by the colour of the jumper under his jacket: canary yellow. Not only did that immediately draw attention to the person in a subliminal way, but it also echoed all the prejudices one might have fostered with regard to the fashion choices of Oxford dons.[1]

Then came the voice. Highs and lows, with sudden changes in melody and cadence. One sentence said slowly, each word weighted and articulated, with the depth and huskiness of James Earl Jones about to announce into the complete silence that *he is* your father. The next sentence started flying into Farinellian heights, with the pronunciation accelerating rapidly, and breath economy akin to somebody trying to finish his last sentence before dropping dead. There is no disguising that that voice would become the object of some parody sessions, over several pints, later on. However, a number of us—who ourselves subsequently went on to lecture, myself included—discovered how efficient that technique is in attracting and keeping the attention of your audience. Our own later imitations were indeed the sincerest form of flattery.

Then came the content. It began with the issue of who should be responsible for regulating the internal market, the principle of attributed competence in regulating business, and the choice of the appropriate legal basis. The (then) recent

[1] Falling into whichever of the categories marvellously set out in Noel Annan, *The Dons: Mentors, Eccentrics and Geniuses* (Harper Collins 2000).

Michal Bobek, *The Internal Market as an Incomplete and Evolving Structure: But Evolving Towards Where Exactly?*
In: *The Internal Market Ideal.* Edited by: Jeremias Adams-Prassl, Sanja Bogojević, Ariel Ezrachi, and Dorota Leczykiewicz, Oxford University Press. DOI: 10.1093/oso/9780192867063.003.0002

judgment of the Court of Justice in the *Tobacco Advertising* case[2] featured prominently during those discussions, together with the notions of competence creep and competence control. What was novel and exciting (certainly for those of us coming from the more dogmatic continental academic tradition) was the independent, critical spirit and sharp analysis, with everything open to discussion.

If you have not guessed by now, you have just joined the first class of the BCL/MJur course on European Business Regulation with Professor Stephen Weatherill.

During the years that have followed, I have had the privilege to continue meeting Steve in various other capacities. They ranged from a fresh fellow at Oxford, coming to see Steve as the EU law teaching group convenor for advice to navigate the rather complex arrangements of a collegiate university, to a sitting member of the Court of Justice (still) avidly awaiting Steve's regular EU law updates for the teaching team, served into one's mailbox at the beginning of each term, and peppered with witty remarks. Especially in later years, it was always refreshing to see that, in the brave new academic world where self-presentation on social media seems to be more important than having anything to say, there remains somebody who (still) first reads, then thinks, and only afterwards passes (a reasoned) judgment.

In one of the regular team updates in the earlier days of my mandate as Advocate General at the Court of Justice, I was referred to as a 'noted poultry expert'. The reason for that honorary title was that poultry featured prominently in my earlier Opinions.[3] My initial reaction, after receiving the invitation to contribute to this *Festschrift*, was therefore to analyse, in Steve's honour, the contribution of poultry to the internal market. My gut feeling (or research hypothesis) would have been that poultry meat, and the flesh of chicken in particular, would have provided a notable contribution to completing the internal market, in particular in the area of the free movement of goods. However, in comparison to, for instance, beer or spirits, I suspect that the contribution of poultry to the evolution of EU law has been overlooked and marginalized. It is therefore crucial to reveal that structural bias in traditional EU law scholarship, thereby encouraging a more global outlook.

However, following a further critical reflection on these peculiar avian inclinations, I decided, for the sake of some residual objectivity, to turn instead to more general reflections on a theme central to Steve's work: the state and the evolution

[2] Case C–376/97 *Germany v Parliament and Council* ECLI:EU:C:2000:544.

[3] For true connoisseurs, who will not chicken out from a little sordid technicality, see (for instance) gems like the Opinion in Case C–134/15 *Lidl* ECLI:EU:C:2016:169 (concerning the scope of labelling obligations on fresh poultry meat, including the issue of whether prices per unit may be affixed only to shelves or must be attached to each individual package, with the somewhat disturbing issue lurking in the background as to how it was technically possible for all individual packages of fresh poultry meat to weigh exactly the same), or the Opinion in Case C–347/17 *A* ECLI:EU:C:2017:720 (which tackled the much more explicit issues of the required sanitary quality of post-mortem inspections of poultry carcasses at the stage after the evisceration but before the chilling of the meat, including the issue of the permissible level of contamination by faeces, bile, or crop).

of the internal market, in particular the eternal tension between centralization and unification on the one hand, and local diversity on the other. The argument presented here proceeds in three steps. First, as Steve has repeatedly argued,[4] the internal market remains a remarkably incomplete structure. Although quite elegant as a model on paper, the default requirement of mutual recognition is an unusually vague principle, the functionality of which at the national level leaves much to be desired—certainly from the point of view of somebody trying to do business, rather than write academic articles. The Mutual Recognition Regulation bears witness to that fact. Secondly, with that one structure far from being complete, the EU legislature (certainly in the past two decades) decided—or was forced—to open up a number of other, parallel building sites, ranging from the 'area of freedom, security, and justice' (a voluntary endeavour) to the 'rule of law crises management' (a less voluntary project). The principles and approaches originally developed in the (economic) law of the internal market are being transplanted and applied in other areas. Thirdly, the plethora of legal construction sites, together with the fact that each of them needs to be serviced with the assistance of a finite amount of resources and manpower, equally mean that ideas and trends developed in these new areas have repercussions on the economic law of the internal market. The argument closes with a broader reflection on whether, while still of course incomplete and evolving, the economic law of the internal market should be approached *as any other area* of EU law.

2. Dogs that do not Bark (but, in the Meantime, Have Acquired New Teeth)

The internal market was supposed to be completed by 1992. At least, that is what had been announced in the Commission's 1985 White Paper, *Completing the Internal Market*.[5] The Annex to that White Paper laid down in detail the individual legislative steps in various fields (in the 'economic' areas of law constituting the internal market, as traditionally understood), that were to be adopted between 1985 and 1992 in order to complete that very structure.

With the passage of time, the Commission's tone in official documents became more circumspect. A fair degree of compulsory institutional optimism was still present. Nonetheless, some more cautious acknowledgments as to the not-so-operational reality crept in.[6] In particular, as the process of sectoral harmonization

[4] See, in particular, Stephen Weatherill, *The Internal Market as a Legal Concept* (Oxford University Press 2017).

[5] Commission to the European Council, *Completing the Internal Market* (White Paper, COM (85) 310 final).

[6] Captured and reproduced in Stephen Weatherill, 'The Principle of Mutual Recognition: It Doesn't Work, Because It Doesn't Exist' (2018) 43 European Law Review 224.

for various types of goods had been gradually halted, the key principle that emerged as the alternative was one of mutual recognition. First coined in the famous *Cassis de Dijon* case,[7] that principle has gradually been elevated to become the cornerstone of the EU level of regulation in the internal market and, later, beyond.

Fans of EU-level harmonization might see that regulatory model as a failure. Indeed, mutual recognition is not one EU-level playing field. It is rather the fall-back option and safety net for the management of the ongoing parallel existence of twenty-seven different regulatory regimes. In a way, mutual recognition does not establish much of an internal market, if the latter is to be understood as an open, internal space in which goods can circulate freely without any regulatory obstacles. Mutual recognition is, rather, a framework for expressing national differences and reservations. That fact is already implied in the very notion of 'mutual recognition': there is a *second point of control*; something needs to be evaluated, recognized, and authorized, once again. One does not normally speak of mutual recognition within one and the same market. The idea that any mutual recognition would be needed for goods travelling from (say) Prague to Brno, with both cities being part of one regulatory space, integrated within the national Czech market, would be seen as absurd.

Certainly, the valid counterargument is that the principle of mutual recognition is as good as it gets at present, where several legal orders must simply coexist within one and the same regulatory space. Vertical shifting of regulatory competence (from the Member States to the EU in matters of regulating the internal market) ended in an incomplete structure. The principle of mutual recognition is thus a good (and the only) tool for managing horizontal diversity and the relationship between the Member States, in the case of the free movement of goods between the Member State of origin (or home Member State, where the goods are produced) and the Member State of destination (the host Member State, where the goods are sold or consumed).

That is certainly correct. However, it requires a critical mind to challenge even that—perhaps more modest—official narrative. In reading some of Steve's more recent writings on the issue, one is strongly reminded of the small child in The Emperor's New Clothes. In particular, to suggest (within the waves of compulsory institutional optimism, which, by that time, were still enchanted with the rise of the new 'principle' of mutual trust and its elevation towards becoming the new meta-principle of EU law) that its older cousin, mutual recognition, is a misnomer, is certainly not mainstream.[8]

[7] Case 120/78 *Rewe-Zentral AG* ECLI:EU:C:18979:42.

[8] Stephen Weatherill, 'Why There is No "Principle of Mutual Recognition" in EU Law (and Why that Matters to Consumer Lawyers)' in Kai Purnhagen and Peter Rott (eds), *Varieties of European Economic Law and Regulation: Liber Amicorum for Hans Micklitz* (Springer 2014). On the other hand, such a strategic choice of a chapter title is bound to secure a great number of references in any academic work dealing with the topic of mutual recognition or the economic freedoms of the Internal Market.

However, matters are put even more sharply in a later piece, entitled, even less euphemistically, 'The Principle of Mutual Recognition: It Doesn't Work, Because It Doesn't Exist'.[9] Here, the gloves come off altogether. It is repeated that the 'principle of mutual recognition' should be expunged from the EU law discourse altogether. But it is, in particular, the practical (non)operation of that principle that caught the author's eye. The model of 'mutual recognition' has an elegance on paper, but it is not matched by success in practice.[10] The fact that a simple case of impeded trade could require the attention of the Court of Justice in 2017 is vivid proof of the deficiencies in the fabric of the internal market:[11] a key piece of legislation that should have formed the backbone of the process of mutual recognition, namely Regulation 764/2008,[12] is irrelevant in practice;[13] the case commented upon provides a glimpse of a malfunctioning system, and Regulation 764/2008 does not even bark, let alone bite.[14] The overall conclusion is that the internal market is not only incomplete in general, but is mundanely incomplete on a daily basis.[15]

What was the case that caused such a damning verdict? The (dis)advantage of a person like Steve who, I suspect, is one of the few people truly reading the entire case law of the Court of Justice relating to the internal market—in particular the four freedoms, and a number of other documents from EU and other institutions—is that he spots cases that do not make headlines, but which are the daily bread and butter of any court.

Noria Distributions SARL[16] was one such seemingly mundane case. Noria was prosecuted for having sold, in France, food supplements containing vitamins and minerals, in particular various types of vitamin B, in quantities exceeding the maximum amount permitted under French law. Noria counterclaimed that it sells the same products lawfully in other Member States. In Noria's view, the marketing of those food supplements should therefore be allowed in France, relying on the principle of mutual recognition. Noria also added that French law was incompatible with EU law because it did not contain any simplified mutual recognition procedure that would allow Noria to import its products into France.

[9] Weatherill, 'The Principle of Mutual Recognition' (n 6), also available as Stephen Weatherill (July 2017) University of Oxford Legal Research Paper Series No 43/2017.

[10] Weatherill, Paper No 43/2017 (n 9) 6.

[11] ibid 9.

[12] Regulation 764/2008 of the European Parliament and of the Council of 9 July 2008 laying down procedures relating to the application of certain national technical rules to products lawfully marketed in another Member State and repealing Decision No 3052/95/EC [2008] OJ L218/21.

[13] Weatherill, Paper No 43/2017 (n 9) 13.

[14] ibid 15, with the reference being made to a famous Sherlock Holmes case, where the key to solving the mystery of the disappearance of a famous racehorse and the murder of the horse's trainer was to find out why the watchdog in the stables did not bark.

[15] ibid 21.

[16] Case C–672/15 *Criminal proceedings against Noria Distribution Sarl* ECLI:EU:C:2017:310.

Steve's indignation at the bleak reality of the application of 'mutual recognition' in the previously quoted article focused on two elements: first, the fact that such a straightforward case would even come before the Court of Justice in 2015; and secondly, the surprising absence in the entire case of any reference to, or use of, a key secondary law instrument that was supposed to govern precisely such types of situations: Regulation 764/2008.[17]

First, the strength—but also potentially the weakness—of the preliminary ruling procedure is that it effectively allows a national court to refer questions to the Court of Justice in cases where there is *subjective* doubt as to the interpretation of EU law. The criterion is not the *objective* importance of the case for the EU legal system.[18] Hence, with the exception of obvious cases that may be disposed of by way of Article 99 of the Rules of Procedure order,[19] any and every case that reaches the Court of Justice under Article 267 of the Treaty on the Functioning of the European Union (TFEU) will be dealt with on the merits. Requests for a preliminary ruling coming from national first instance courts that hear a case and the legal issues put forward for the first time tend to be put differently from those submitted by superior national jurisdictions. The latter jurisdictions often have the benefit of hearing a case where the contentious legal issue concerning the interpretation of EU law has already better crystallized before them.

Moreover, it should be noted that the thrust of the questions raised by the referring court in *Noria* was not concerned with free movement of goods and potential obstacles to it. The referring court was rather explicit in its conclusion that the French rules were an obstacle to trade. The order for reference centred on the scientific assessment and the level of research required from a national administrative authority before deciding the maximum level of permitted daily intake of vitamins, to be carried out in the context of a dedicated secondary law framework in the form of Directive 2002/46.[20] To put it simply, could there be something specific in the French diet that would justify different intake maxima for vitamin B in contrast to, for example, Germany or Ireland? If yes, how are such maxima to be set, following what type of analysis and risk assessment?

Secondly, even with all those allowances made, it is nonetheless legitimate to wonder about the dog that neither barks nor bites: Regulation 764/2008. In that regard, Steve noted that:

[17] Regulation 764/2008 (n 12).

[18] Critically on that point in terms of the purpose of the preliminary rulings procedure, see my Opinions in Case C–561/19 *Consorzio Italian Management* ECLI:EU:C:2021:291 and in Case C–923/19 *Van Ameyde España SA* ECLI:EU:C:2021:125.

[19] Allowing the Court of Justice to dispose of a case by a reasoned order in cases where a question referred to the Court for a preliminary ruling is identical to a question on which the Court has already ruled, where the reply to such a question may be clearly deduced from existing case law, or where the answer to the question referred for a preliminary ruling admits of no reasonable doubt.

[20] Directive 2002/46 of the European Parliament and of the Council of 10 June 2002 on the approximation of the laws of the Member States relating to food supplements [2002] OJ L183/51.

> [T]he Regulation is not mentioned by the referring court in *Noria* and it is absent from the Court's judgment too. A.G. Bobek mentions it, noting in mildly perplexed tones, that neither the national court nor any of the parties had referred to the Regulation, and he contents himself with five brief paragraphs in which he summarises the measure's scheme.[21]

Indeed, the Advocate General in question cannot but confirm having been somewhat perplexed by the fact that what appeared to be a key instrument for managing the process of mutual recognition in another Member State was completely absent from the picture, from the order for reference of the national court, and from the parties' submissions, as well as from the observations of the European Commission and the European Free Trade Association (EFTA) Surveillance Authority submitted in the case. While it cannot but be repeated that the focus of the questions was primarily on the required level of science, in an area which is partially harmonized by Directive 2002/46,[22] that absence is nonetheless striking. That is even more the case given that the national court enquired about the potential for there to be any 'simplified mutual recognition procedure'. While of course that could not be the case with regard to the required level or risk assessment and scientific evaluation,[23] one may view Regulation 764/2008 as having the ambition to do exactly what the referring court asked: to introduce such a simplified recognition track or procedure, putting some flesh on the bare bones of Articles 34 and 36 TFEU.

Such a procedural and factual background, together with the fact that the Court confined the case to a chamber of five judges, deciding without a hearing but with an Opinion, also explains why the Advocate General did not bark either, but contented himself with a modest growl as to the existence of Regulation 764/2008. That course of action was correct not only with regard to the specific issues brought to the attention of the Court by the referring court, but also in view of the potentially far-reaching consequences that could be drawn from non-compliance with Regulation 764/2008, captured and explored very well in the second part of Steve's contribution on the case.

In the past, the Court stated that the failure to notify technical standards under Directive 83/189[24] could deprive those national technical standards of their enforceability, thereby releasing (third-party) private individuals from their obligation to meet such non-notified standards.[25] The Court spent some energy

[21] Weatherill, Paper No 43/2017 (n 9) 10.

[22] However, the specific issue of vitamin maxima was not harmonized by that instrument and, absent any implementing legislation adopted on that matter by the Commission, continued to be governed by national law.

[23] For the reasons that I explained in detail in para 33ff in my Opinion in *Noria* (n 16).

[24] Council Directive 83/189/EEC of 28 March 1983 laying down a procedure for the provision of information in the field of technical standards and regulations [1983] OJ L109/8.

[25] Case C–194/94 *CIA Security International SA* ECLI:EU:C:196:172.

subsequently seeking to limit the impact of that decision so that its reach remains connected to genuine free movement of goods and does not become instrumentalized,[26] as well as to reintroduce at least some balance between the interests of the Union to see its rules enforced in a decentralized and efficient way and the protection of third parties and their legitimate expectations.[27]

Directive 83/189—or its current embodiment in the form of Directive 2015/1535[28]—and Regulation 746/2008 are functional twins. One is concerned with generally applicable technical standards, the other with individual administrative decisions. To wonder, therefore, about the potential analogy to be drawn between the failure to notify a technical standard and the failure to meet the procedural requirements of Regulation 764/2008 is entirely logical.

However, whether it would be sensible to release another non-notification genie out of the lamp is a different question. It is indeed correct that in contrast to the failure to notify technical standards under Directive 83/189, or currently under Directive 2015/1535, a failure to comply with Regulation 746/2008 should normally concern a vertical type of relationship only, involving a public authority refusing to grant authorization, or suspending it, and a trader. No innocent third party should therefore be present.[29]

It is, nonetheless, not entirely obvious what purpose there would be in attaching the non-enforceability sanction to a non-notified administrative decision.[30] Would a negative administrative decision refusing authorization be deprived of any enforceability vis-à-vis the trader? How would that help that trader, who still has no authorization? Rendering a negative administrative decision non-enforceable in respect of a trader simply means that they are reverted to a position as if there had been no decision, which might not be much help if the trader still needs a prior authorization to market. Equally, would the failure to notify the Commission be applicable only to negative decisions, or to any decisions not notified? Could it then lead to a situation in which a trader who received a positive decision still could not import, because that positive decision was not notified to the Commission and is consequently non-enforceable? Perhaps not; this time around, another analogy with the prohibition of reversed vertical direct effect could be relied upon.[31]

[26] Case C-226/97 *Lemmens* ECLI:EU:C:1998:296.

[27] Case C-159/00 *Sapod Audic* ECLI:EU:C:2002:343 and Case C-443/98 *Unilever* ECLI:EU:C:2000:496.

[28] Directive 2015/1535 of the European Parliament and of the Council of 9 September 2015 laying down a procedure for the provision of information in the field of technical regulations and of rules on Information Society services [2015] OJ L241/1.

[29] As contemplated in Weatherill, Paper No 43/2017 (n 9) 20.

[30] With the understanding that the absence of notification would be to the Commission. It is fair to assume that an administrative decision, be it positive or negative, will always be notified to the trader (party in national administrative proceedings) by virtue of national codes of administrative procedure.

[31] eg Joined Cases C-387/02, 391/02, and 403/02 *Berlusconi* ECLI:EU:C:2005:270, paras 73–74, or Case C-321/05 *Hans Markus Kofoed* ECLI:EU:C:2007:408, para 42.

Be that as it may, the point is exactly that there appear to be too many analogies and thorny issues to make the initial analogy as to the procedural consequences that a failure to notify under the two notification regimes should entail. It is, however, probable that such questions are likely to be posed with renewed importance. Regulation 764/2008 has recently been repealed and replaced by Regulation 2019/515.[32] It is intriguing to note that the overall positive tone concerning Regulation 764/2008, previously dominant in the 2012 and 2015 reports on its operation,[33] was somewhat abruptly replaced by a public diagnosis of a malfunctioning regime. It was stated that the regulatory framework has failed in its aim of improving the application of the principle of mutual recognition, equally acknowledging that the requirement to notify administrative decisions restricting or denying market access is rarely complied with.[34]

Whether Steve's analysis contributed to such a change in tack can only be guessed at.[35] What remains clear nonetheless is that the new Regulation 2019/515 takes on board a number of points previously made by him. It seeks to make the notification obligation more visible and robust. The new regulation introduces a system of mutual recognition self-declaration that may be compiled by any trader seeking prior authorization in another Member State. Traders are invited to make such mutual recognition declarations available online.[36] The logic appears to be one of proactive delivery of information by the trader concerned, combined with the obligation incumbent on the administrative authority to continue communicating to the trader concerned in cases of doubt. What is entirely new is the notification obligation being extended under Article 5(9) of Regulation 2019/515 not only to the Commission, but also to other Member States. That is apparently not to be done individually and on paper, but via dedicated notification platforms.[37]

There are further significant novelties. Notification of any administrative decision falling within the scope of Regulation 2019/515 to the economic operator concerned, the Commission, and the other Member States, is to be carried out within twenty days following its adoption (Article 5(9)). A decision shall not take effect before it has been notified to the economic operator (Article 5(13)). Articles

[32] Regulation (EU) 2019/515 of the European Parliament and of the Council of 19 March 2019 on the mutual recognition of goods lawfully marketed in another Member State and repealing Regulation (EC) 764/2008 [2019] OJ L91/1.

[33] Recounted in Weatherill, Paper No 43/2017 (n 9).

[34] See, in particular, recital 7 to the Regulation 2019/515 (n 32).

[35] See also the indications in European Commission, Directorate-General for Internal Market, Industry, Entrepreneurship and SMEs, *Study on the Costs and Benefits of the Revision of the Mutual Recognition Regulation (EC) No 764/2008: Final report* (Publications Office 2018).

[36] Using a standardized form set out in the Annex to that Regulation, available online at <https://ec.europa.eu/docsroom/documents/40922>, last accessed 1 June 2022.

[37] See art 7 and art 11 of Regulation 2019/515 (n 32). See, in particular, Commission Implementing Regulation (EU) 2020/1668 of 10 November 2020 specifying the details and functionalities of the information and communication system to be used for the purposes of Regulation (EU) 2019/515 of the European Parliament and of the Council on the mutual recognition of goods lawfully marketed in another Member State [2020] OJ L377/7.

5(10) and 5(11) of Regulation 2019/515 standardize, in quite some detail, the content of any administrative decision falling within the scope of the Regulation.

Although rather detailed and explicit in some matters, Regulation 2019/515 remains conspicuously silent on the consequences of a failure to comply with its provisions for the case at hand. The already-quoted Article 5(13) goes hardly any further in that direction. It is fair to assume that most national codes of administrative procedure would state that, under normal circumstances,[38] an administrative decision becomes effective/enters into force only after its service on the individual concerned, in cases of authorization requests on the applicant seeking the authorization decision. However, that begs the question: what about the failure to notify an administrative decision to the Commission and to other Member States? What about decisions that fail to meet the requirements as to the content of a decision laid down in Article 5(10) and (11) of Regulation 2019/515?

The fact that the Commission seeks to be more vigilant in enforcing the new regulation may perhaps be deduced equally from another of its novel provisions: Article 8. That article is entitled 'Problem-solving procedure'. On its face, one could assume that it merely serves to incorporate the SOLVIT procedure[39] into the framework of Regulation 2019/515. However, its genuine content is different: Article 8 establishes what can only be described as a 'preliminary rulings procedure' for SOLVIT procedures, with the Commission acting as an arbitrator. An Opinion of the Commission may be issued in any case submitted to the SOLVIT procedure upon the request of either the Home (SOLVIT) Centre or the Lead (SOLVIT) Centre. As the first Opinions issued by the Commission under that procedure illustrate,[40] an Opinion issued under Article 8 of Regulation 2019/515 certainly resembles a judgment on the matter,[41] even leading to a conclusion ('operative part') observing incompatibility of a given administrative decision with Regulation 2019/515.

However, even if a number of failures on the part of the Member States' authorities are observed, those Commission decisions, in line with recital 40 of Regulation 2019/515, remain at the level of stating that a national decision fails to comply with the said regulation. The tenets of that decision should be considered within the given SOLVIT procedure in accordance with Article 8(6) of Regulation

[38] Absent cases of urgency, unknown addresses of an administrative decision, or other special cases.

[39] SOLVIT refers to an informal problem-solving network of the European Commission and the member states of the European Union and the EEA created in 2002. See, in particular, Commission Recommendation 2013/461/EU of 17 September 2013 on the principles governing SOLVIT [2013] OJ L249/10.

[40] See Commission Opinion of 30 September 2021 on the application of the principle of mutual recognition and the requirements of Regulation (EU) 2019/515 regarding food supplements based on Article 8 of Regulation (EU) 2019/515 on the mutual recognition of goods, C(2021) 6950 final, or Commission Opinion of 27 January 2022 on the application of the principle of mutual recognition and the requirements of Regulation (EU) 2019/515 regarding fertilisers, C(2022) 398 final.

[41] Neatly subdivided into sections of 'facts and procedure', 'arguments of the parties', 'applicable legislation and assessment', and 'conclusion'.

2019/515, indeed similarly to a decision on preliminary rulings, which equally formally bind only the referring court within the procedure where the reference was made. While the Commission's right to consider an Article 258 TFEU procedure naturally remains intact, there appears to be (certainly to date) no other procedural sanction with regard to the incompatible national administrative decision or against the defaulting Member State.

In sum, while Regulation 2019/515 contains a number of innovations, it remains to be seen whether and exactly how the new legal framework, and above all the national practice, will differ from the reality prevailing under Regulation 764/2008. Thus, several points raised in Steve's writings and quoted in this section remain very much alive, together with the central issue of enforcement. Moreover, at a more general level, the central principle of mutual recognition leaves a lot to be desired as to its daily operation. The principle is indeed elegant on paper. It appears to be squaring the circle, reconciling EU regulation with local diversity. However, its genuine success in daily practice is much more questionable. Indeed, a trader seeking to import goods to another Member State might be somewhat surprised when encountering that reality, with the only option when faced with the more obstinate national administrations being costly and uncertain litigation. In this regard, the internal market remains a very incomplete structure, and free movement of goods far from fully achieved.

3. A Limited Amount of Butter Stretched too Far and Therefore too Thin?

If one were to believe that the internal market, or the economic regulation of doing business in the Union, is the traditional 'core business' of the Communities and later of the Union, then the last twenty years or so have witnessed a major expansion beyond that core. The Maastricht Treaty, followed by the Amsterdam Treaty and the Lisbon Treaty, have all gradually opened up new areas of EU law and action. If the docket of the Court of Justice were to be an indicator, then consulting an annual report from 1992 and then one from 2022 would reveal just how profoundly the focus of EU law has shifted.

Today, in purely quantitative terms, the area of law most litigated before the Court is the 'area of freedom, security, and justice', followed by taxation, environment, transport, social policy, and intellectual property.[42] However, hidden behind such rather abstract areas are the more infinitely varied and diverse types of cases that are being dealt with, ranging from virtually any and every element of national criminal procedure brought about by a wave of harmonization in that area together

[42] See Court of Justice of the European Union, *Annual Report 2020: Judicial Activity* (Luxembourg 2021) 209–10.

with the advent of the EU Charter of Fundamental Rights, through to the authorization of telecommunication interceptions in order to effectively investigate fraud against the EU budget, as well as to economic sanctions adopted against various states or diverse elements of external Union action around the world, to complex elements of banking supervision, fiscal and monetary transactions, and down to the design of disciplinary proceedings against judges, or the appropriate relationship between a national constitutional and ordinary courts, to name but a few examples by way of illustration. The range and depth of issues is breathtaking. Their only common denominator is that they have very little or nothing to do with the economic regulation of the internal market.

In the past, when the Member States agreed to confer new competences on the Union or the Communities, the most frequently invoked logic was one of 'ancillary necessity' or 'derived legitimacy'. After all, that very structure was embedded in what was formally Article 308 of the Treaty Establishing the European Community (TEC), and before that Article 235 of the Treaty Establishing the European Economic Community (EEC Treaty).[43] For instance, the 'area of freedom, security, and justice' had initially been portrayed as the logical extension and the necessity for having a truly integrated internal market. Indeed, for goods, persons, or capital to move freely, decisions and judgments must move freely with them, without the cumbersome procedures for specific recognition and enforcement.

Over time, in particular following the elevation of the Charter of Fundamental Rights as part of binding primary law, and the more recent and ongoing rule of law backsliding or outright crisis in some Member States, and correlating rediscovery of provisions such as Articles 2 or 19 TEU, made the alternative 'Union based on the rule of law' narrative much more prevalent. There is no doubt that such justification offers a robust reason for the existence of an 'area of freedom, security, and justice', a space of equal protection for all citizens of the Union. Still, as with many other matters concerning European integration in the past, the original narrative was much more down to earth, derived, and instrumental: a truly operational internal market cannot function in a legal vacuum, without the appropriate institutions and procedures. It is, after all, not just about doing business, but rather the proper, decent, and foreseeable *regulation of* doing business.

In any case, EU law has vastly expanded over the course of the past two decades, certainly as far as new areas of regulation are concerned. Nonetheless, some themes and issues have remained the same or very similar. The logic, categories, and vantage points from the field of internal market law have also been relied upon, doubtlessly at least initially, in new areas. The concept of mutual recognition is a

[43] 'If action by the Community should prove necessary to attain, *in the course of the operation of the common market*, one of the objectives of the Community, and this Treaty has not provided the necessary powers, the Council shall, acting unanimously on a proposal from the Commission and after consulting the European Parliament, take the appropriate measures.' My emphasis. It is fair to admit that, in reality, nobody paid that much attention to that condition in practice, since unanimity was required.

prime example. Is the requirement of mutual recognition for goods the same when it comes to judgments in, say, civil matters? How does the requirement of mutual trust, for some time venerated as a 'meta-principle' of EU law before silently ceding its place to more of a 'mutual distrust' in view of non-compliance with basic standards in some Member States,[44] differ from the basic precondition for there being mutual recognition?[45]

A similarly common theme is the issue of maximum or minimal harmonization and the corresponding question of federal pre-emption[46] in any and all areas of regulation. The area of law has changed; the issues remained. *Melloni*[47] offers an example. To what extent has Union action, which harmonized the conditions under which a person could be surrendered to another Member State in cases when such a person did not participate in the trial that led to the conviction for which surrender is now sought, pre-empted any national rules on that matter? The answer of the Court was clear: with regard to the specific issue of surrenders in cases of *in absentia* judgments, the EU rule contained in Article 4a of the re-cast Framework Decision 2002/584/JHA[48] represented in fact the harmonized ceiling. Article 53 of the Charter cannot be used to break it, even if, hypothetically,[49] a Member State would seek to provide a higher level of protection.

The provision in question established a ceiling because, as the Court put it, the Framework Decision provided for an 'exhaustive list of the circumstances' in which the execution of a European Arrest Warrant may be refused.[50] Translated back into the categories of internal market law, with regard to that specific issue, the Framework Decision provided for a maximum level of harmonization. No further Member State legislative intervention *on that specific matter* was allowed.

However, in contrast perhaps to the regulation of the internal market in the narrower, economic sense, 'the subject matter covered'[51] or the 'area covered'[52] by EU action must be understood much more narrowly. It is not an area of law (eg fisheries). It is not even a subject matter understood in the broader sense (eg regulating the activity of fishing trawlers). The analysis of pre-emption focuses on the level of the concrete issue and a specific provision. That is quite logical: whereas in some

44 Critically see my Opinion in Case C–852/19 *Ivan Gavanozov* ECLI:EU:C:2021:346.

45 See further Michal Bobek, 'Epilogue: Of Judges and Trust' in Sara Iglesias Sánchez and Maribel González Pascual (eds), *Fundamental Rights in the EU Area of Freedom, Security and Justice* (Cambridge University Press 2021).

46 In the context of the regulation of the Internal Market, see, in particular, Weatherill, *The Internal Market as a Legal Concept* (n 4) ch 15.

47 Case C–399/11 *Stefano Melloni* ECLI:EU:C:2013:107.

48 Specifically, art 4a(1) of Council Framework Decision 2002/584/JHA of 13 June 2002 on the European arrest warrant and the surrender procedures between Member States [2002] OJ L190/1, as amended by Council Framework Decision 2009/299/JHA of 26 February 2009 [2009] OJ L81/24.

49 Hypothetically, since it would first have to be defined what in fact is a higher level of protection in such a case, and for whom.

50 *Melloni* (n 47) para 44.

51 Weatherill, *The Internal Market as a Legal Concept* (n 4) 209.

52 ibid 218.

areas of market regulation, where the legal landscape tends to be covered by directly applicable regulations, with the consequence being that it may be assumed that the EU legislature, unless it expressly provided otherwise, indeed meant to cover the entire area and all the necessary issues arising, directives (or framework decisions) under Chapter III, Title V TFEU could never have had such a structural, area-driven ambition. They are by their very scope and design 'crafts-on', the proverbial smaller brick to be added here or there to a larger national law structure.

A fortiori, the same must be true in areas where the EU legislature did not even provide for any specific choice as to a concrete rule of behaviour, but instead remained at the level of setting aims and goals. A string of more recent cases in the area of taxation and the protection of Union own resources under Article 325 TFEU might provide an illustration in this regard. The statements that the Member States are to combat fraud and protect the EU's own resources (Article 325 TFEU) or that they are to ensure the correct collection of VAT (Article 273 of Directive 2006/112[53]) cannot be read, absent any further and specific EU secondary law, as harmonizing national laws on prescription periods[54] or, for instance, national rules on the jurisdiction of courts authorizing interceptions of telecommunications when investigating tax fraud.[55]

Two points are of note in lieu of an interim conclusion. First, when entering the new areas of law, the vocabulary, the categories, and the thinking from the established areas are bound to be employed. The Court of Justice, as any other (judicial) body, naturally proceeds by analogy. Gradually, the old categories will be adapted for the new environment. In this way, the conceptualization of the intended level of harmonization by an EU measure has perhaps been adapted in the areas outside the traditional economic law so as to proceed not necessarily by an area of law or even a general subject matter, but by focusing more on a *microanalysis* and a specific provision.[56]

Secondly, with the expansion of the Union competence in several new areas of law beyond the (economic) internal market, together with the constant crisis management plaguing the Union over the last decade, most recently 'enriched' by a full-scale rule of law/constitutional crisis, it is fair to acknowledge that the attention of EU institutions has perhaps been drawn away from the traditional 'core' of the internal market. That is only natural, in a world of infinite complexity but finite resources. However, it also means that the extant resources, persons, and institutions, even if assisted, at the administrative level, by a number of EU agencies and bodies

[53] Council Directive of 28 November 2006 on the common system of value added tax [2006] OJ L347/1.

[54] Case C-42/17 *MAS and MB* ECLI:EU:C:2017:936 or Case C-574/15 *Scialdone* ECLI:EU:C:2018:295. But see Case C-105/14 *Taricco* ECLI:EU:C:2015:555 or indeed Case C-612/15 *Kolev* ECLI:EU:C:2018:392.

[55] Case C-310/16 *Criminal Proceedings against Petar Dzivev* ECLI:EU:C:2019:30.

[56] In detail, see my Opinion, ibid, in particular paras 70–80.

mushrooming like never before, need to cover much more ground and occasionally run the danger of being stretched rather thin over quite a large regulatory area.

4. A Backwards Spillover? Scotch Whisky and Lithuanian Milk

The previous section suggested that older, known areas of law, or any other human activity for that matter, are likely to serve as a springboard for approaching newer areas. What comes next is uncertain. Sometimes, newer areas might take on the principles and approaches of old ones. Sometimes, the new kids on the block might in fact start influencing the old guard. The same is true when it comes to the issue of competence and the degree of harmonization in the internal market. Two recent decisions of the Court deserve to be mentioned in this regard: *Scotch Whisky Association*[57] and *Lietuvos Respublikos Seimo narių grupė*.[58]

Scotch Whisky Association concerned national legislation imposing a minimum price per unit of alcohol with respect to the retail selling of alcoholic drinks in Scotland. The key question referred by the Court of Session (Scotland) was whether such national legislation is allowed in view of the (exhaustive) regulation of the market for agricultural products, including wines, contained in the Single Common Market Organisation Regulation (Single CMO Regulation).[59] In its judgment, the Court stated that the common organization of agricultural markets may include all measures concerning the formation and regulation of prices.[60] The Single CMO Regulation is silent on the specific issue of price fixing by the Member States at the *retail* level. But the Court underlined that the *free formation of selling prices* of agricultural products on the basis of free and open competition *is the foundation* of the entire CMO structure.[61] Moreover, the Court also accepted that price fixing is a measure having equivalent effect to quantitative restriction under Article 34 TFEU, impeding the free movement of goods between the Member States.[62]

However, the Court next held that the national rule at issue pursued *a different objective relating to a general interest* (the protection of public health) other than those covered by the Single CMO Regulation. As such, the national rule would not be precluded if it satisfied the principle of proportionality. The objective of the protection of public health was not specifically part of the equation in the balance

57 Case C-333/14 *Scotch Whisky Association* ECLI:EU:C:2015:845.
58 Case C-2/18 *Lietuvos Respublikos Seimo narių grupė* ECLI:EU:C:2019:962.
59 Regulation (EU) 1308/2013 of the European Parliament and the Council of 17 December 2013 establishing a common organisation of the markets in agricultural products and repealing Council Regulations (EEC) No 922/72, (EEC) No 234/79, (EC) No 1037/2001 and (EC) No 1234/2007 [2013] OJ L347/671 (the Single CMO Regulation).
60 *Scotch Whisky* (n 57) para 14.
61 ibid paras 22–24. My emphasis.
62 ibid paras 31–32.

struck by the EU legislature at EU level when setting the rules for the operation of the common market concerning wine products. That objective was part of a different national regulatory regime, guided by different considerations, which only incidentally overlapped with that of the Union. The national rule at stake was a measure applicable only at the retail stage. Thus, although retail is naturally also a stage (the last stage) of the marketing chain, the overlap and thus ensuing conflict between EU rules and the national rules was said to be marginal.

Lietuvos Respublikos Seimo narių grupė endorsed that approach and pushed it arguably even further. The case concerned Lithuanian legislation adopted to rein in the strong purchasing power of raw milk purchasers and processors. The raw milk market in Lithuania is characterized by atomized supply (with thousands of small raw milk producers) and highly concentrated demand (with only a handful of large purchasing companies). The small producers are not organized. The purchasing companies have thus been able to impose purchase prices upon them, resulting in very low raw milk prices. Reacting to that situation, national legislation established the classification of producers depending on the volume of raw milk sold per day, and obliged purchasers of raw milk to offer the same price to all producers belonging to the same group. It also prohibited purchasers of raw milk from lowering prices without providing justification. A price reduction of 3 per cent or more of the purchase price was only allowed following authorization from the competent administrative authority.

The Single CMO Regulation regulates the raw milk market in a detailed and explicit way. The EU legislature was aware of the unequal bargaining power that might exist between farmers and milk processing companies.[63] Article 148 of the Single CMO Regulation therefore provides for the possibility for a Member State to make the supply of raw milk subject to a number of requirements, including the written form of any such contract, the manner in which the purchase price may be fixed under that contract, and the prohibition to deviate therefrom. At the same time, Article 148(4) of the Single CMO Regulation insists that the price shall remain subject to free negotiation between the parties.

However, even within such a legislative landscape, after having examined whether 'the European Union has exhaustively exercised its competence in the area of contractual relations between the parties to a contract for the delivery of raw milk and, more specifically, in relation to the process of negotiation of that contract',[64] the Court came to the conclusion that there was no 'exhaustive harmonisation in the sector relating to the combatting of unfair commercial practices'.[65] Consequently, Member States have a residual competence to adopt measures to

[63] See, in particular, recital 138 to the Single CMO Regulation (n 59), as well as the legislative history of art 148 of the CMO Regulation recounted at paras 48–49 of my Opinion in that case.

[64] *Lietuvos Respublikos* (n 58) para 42.

[65] ibid para 52.

combat unfair commercial practices which have the effect of restricting the process of free negotiation of prices, even if those measures affect the principle of free negotiation of the price payable for the delivery of raw milk laid down in Article 148 of Regulation No 1308/2013 and, accordingly, on the functioning of the internal market in the sector concerned.[66]

There is no point in re-rehearsing the reason why I was of a different view, believing that, on this particular issue, the Single CMO Regulation *had* exhaustively covered the ground.[67] What is more intriguing is the distinct change of approach in assessing the scope of the Regulation in (previously crucial) areas of market organization. Certainly, the common agricultural policy has recently undergone major reorganization, including the way in which it is regulated.[68] Equally, the common agricultural policy (Title III, Part III TFEU) is now one of the shared competences of the Union under Article 4(2)(d) TFEU. It is not an exclusive competence of the Union under Article 3 TFEU.

However, the entire area was traditionally governed by directly applicable regulations bringing about quite some 'regulatory density' and being rather intolerant towards unilateral Member State action not expressly foreseen by Union measures. To the extent that the directives-driven vocabulary of 'maximum' or 'minimal' harmonization were to be of any use with regard to regulations,[69] the legal unification brought about by a regulation would normally be maximum or exhaustive. That would exclude any Member State action on the same matter not explicitly authorized. The logic was one of establishing and exhaustively regulating the market, with the buzzword indeed being that of one level playing field.

This change of tack appears significant not only in a diachronic comparison (when comparing the two cases to older ones relating to market organization, and more broadly to free movement law in the past), but also in an EU area of law comparison (when contrasting the approach to that in some other areas of EU law action at present). The second point of this contribution already provides some contrasts from the area of judicial cooperation in criminal matters (*Melloni*) or protection of the EU's own resources (*Taricco*). Naturally, to the extent that it is possible to compare those areas of law, would one expect 'federal pre-emption' to play out much more strongly and in a less compromising way in criminal procedure than it does in market regulation?

[66] ibid paras 52 and 53, respectively.

[67] A curious reader might find those in my Opinion, ibid.

[68] Further see ibid paras 19–25.

[69] But why could it not? Indeed, while—at least on paper—in the words of art 288 TFEU, there remains a difference between a regulation and a directive, to tell them apart in practice as to the legislative technique (in particular the level of regulatory detail) used today becomes increasingly difficult. Moreover, more regulations require their own 'transposition', while a number of directives reach such a level of detail that what is left to the Member States is in fact a mere 'transcription' into a source of national law, but hardly transposition and implementation in the traditional sense, ie entailing any real legislative choice.

I wish to stress one point in conclusion to this section: this is not a normative argument on whether more national diversity is a good or a bad thing. That is a value call. The two cases discussed in this section are a (rather empirical) illustration that more diversity has certainly equally arrived in areas previously believed to be firm bastions of the exhaustively governed internal market.[70] That brings me to the closing reflection: should all areas of EU law be treated the same, in so far as the desired or permissible level of diversity to be achieved is concerned?

5. Should There be a 'Core Business' of the Union?

Where does all this leave the regulation of the internal market? Steve's magisterial work on the *Internal Market as a Legal Concept* deftly outlines the permanent tension between regulation and deregulation, on the one hand, and central regulation and local autonomy, on the other, before concluding that 'the internal market as a legal concept is inextricably connected to the internal market as a political, economic and cultural concept [. . .] this is why [. . .] the internal market will never be "completed"; it is evolving, it will never be finalized.'[71]

While such a conclusion may be bad news for variously coloured papers wishing to claim 'mission accomplished' or rather 'market completed', it remains a pertinent summary of the overall predicament of the structure. One might suggest that there is nothing surprising in that statement. *As long as* there is not just one legislative centre, but the EU-level and national ones legislating in parallel, there are bound to be regulatory differences, with new ones created potentially on a daily basis. That is indeed correct. It is equally important nonetheless to occasionally to look beyond that obvious proposition, or the official political or ideological statements of the day, and try to decipher where the reality does in fact stand at present. This calls for three final observations.

First, the law of the internal market, while it was indeed the first one, is not evolving in splendid isolation from other, newer areas of EU law. What it means to be 'federally pre-empted' and when a situation might be 'exhaustively covered' by EU law serve as an example in this regard. The change in approach carried out in other areas, perhaps also caused by the new competence structure of the Treaty of Lisbon, has gradually rendered the traditional internal market categories of 'maximum' or 'minimum' harmonization with regard to certain areas of law somewhat obsolete, certainly if the new approach is to be the one outlined in the previous section. All EU legislation, certainly that within the area of shared competence, will,

[70] For other precursors in neighbouring areas of free movement of goods, see eg Case C–110/05 *Commission v Italy (motorcycle trailers)* ECLI:EU:C:2009:66 or Case C–142/05 *Mickelsson and Roos* ECLI:EU:C:2009:336.

[71] Weatherill, *The Internal Market as a Legal Concept* (n 4) 233. Internal reference omitted.

by default, be the minimal threshold, with the discussion being only whether the concrete measure taken by a Member State was explicitly pre-empted or not, with quite some leeway in the form of 'different objectives pursued' being allowed even in cases of substantive overlaps.

Secondly, ensuring coherence across the board in all areas of EU law might not necessarily mean that all those areas which are lagging behind will be brought up to speed. It might also mean that the vanguard could be brought back. One could perhaps put forward the idea that this is in fact what has been happening to the law of the internal market, certainly in some areas where 'diversity' or 're-nationalization' reappear. That said, even if it were true, this would merely confirm that 'evolving' means potentially changing in whichever direction. European Union integration is not a journey to a known destination of greater harmonization, further integration, and in this sense the inevitable ever-closer Union. It also occasionally means re-nationalization and, thus, from the point of view of the integration orthodoxy, digression or regression.

Thirdly and finally, the outstanding and deeply political question is whether the internal market ought to be treated like any other policy of the Union, or whether it is something special. Connected to this issue is the question of allocation of attention and resources. Should the management of the internal market be viewed as a 'core business' of the Union, with appropriately sufficient attention, energy, and resources being dedicated to it? Or should it become relegated to just an *aim* under Article 3(3) TEU, indeed, in a deeply symbolic way, after the values of Article 2 TEU, and further aims of Article 3(1) and 3(2) TEU?

Certainly, the Union as a value community and the Union as the internal market project are not mutually exclusive.[72] They are complementary and may very well coexist. They simply provide for a different type of justification and narrative. The first is moral, freestanding, and intransitive. The other is more down to earth and instrumental. Even if perhaps only instrumental, in the past, the latter rationale did not serve the Communities and then the Union badly by providing a solid justification for adding yet another EU policy, as well as a justification for the entire structure: it was necessary for *achieving* a (common/internal) market. This is not a call for a return to such instrumental cynicisms, going back to a period where, for instance, third country nationals were to be considered as mere 'service units' for EU citizens.[73] It is, rather, a cautious expression of the worry that someone who desires everything often runs the danger of ending up doing nothing properly. Having a solid and reliable core is crucial for the operation of the outer limbs and peripheries. Moreover, in contrast to the present cacophony of voices arguing over what

[72] After all, the 'internal market' did eventually make it into chapter 6 of Stephen Weatherill, *Law and Values in the European Union* (Oxford University Press 2016).

[73] Epitomized by some older case law that, in the legal and constitutional framework of the day, sought to protect third-country nationals, at least through the rights that they could derive from EU citizens. See eg Case C–60/00 *Mary Carpenter* ECLI:EU:C:2002:434.

exactly the true values of the Union are; who should define them and how; and whether they should be more robust, visible, and enforceable, an operational internal market is the core on which everybody, including the current Article 2 TEU discontents, appear to agree. Thus, my final reflection is quite simple: before one is sure of having built another operational body with a different core, it is unwise not to continue providing special care and attention to the only tried and tested core one has.

2

The Maturation of European Data Law: From Fundamental Rights to Economic Rights

Michèle Finck

1. Introduction

The European Commission has recently put forward various legislative proposals currently being debated as part of the ordinary legislative procedure; namely, the Data Act (DA),[1] the Data Governance Act (DGA),[2] the Artificial Intelligence Act (AIA),[3] the Digital Markets Act (DMA),[4] and the Digital Services Act (DSA).[5] These draft Acts will create new legal rules applicable to data, the lifeblood of the Digital Single Market (DSM).[6] This chapter documents the transformation of European Union (EU) data law from a legislative ensemble centred primarily around the fundamental right to data protection towards a much broader and more complex area of EU law of which data protection is but one element. Whereas data protection law implements data subjects' right to data protection in submitting the processing of personal data to a qualified prohibition, the new legislative proposals encourage the processing of (personal) data and transform the latter into an object of economic rights, a tradable commodity that can be sold or donated. This paradigm shift will undoubtedly result in tensions that will be keeping practitioners, academics, and judges busy for decades to come.

1 Commission, 'Proposal for a Regulation of the European Parliament and of the Council on harmonised rules on fair access to and use of data (Data Act)' COM (2022) 68 final.
2 Commission, 'Proposal for a Regulation of the European Parliament and of the Council on European data governance (Data Governance Act)' COM (2020) 767 final.
3 Commission, 'Proposal for a Regulation of the European Parliament and of the Council laying down harmonised rules on artificial intelligence (Artificial Intelligence Act)' COM (2021) 206 final.
4 Commission, 'Proposal for a Regulation of the European Parliament and of the Council on contestable and fair markets in the digital sector (Digital Markets Act)' COM (2020) 842 final.
5 Commission, 'Proposal for a Regulation of the European Parliament and of the Council on a single market for digital services (Digital Services Act) and amending Directive 2001/31/EC' COM (2020) 825 final.
6 These instruments share the common feature, in that they regulate (personal) data and many factual constellations in which these legal frameworks apply in parallel.

Michèle Finck, *The Maturation of European Data Law: From Fundamental Rights to Economic Rights* In: *The Internal Market Ideal*. Edited by: Jeremias Adams-Prassl, Sanja Bogojević, Ariel Ezrachi, and Dorota Leczykiewicz, Oxford University Press.
 DOI: 10.1093/oso/9780192867063.003.0003

Instead of providing a detailed overview of these tensions, this contribution documents the evolution of EU data law through the lens of the internal market. It surveys the draft Acts to document this paradigm shift, unveils the existence of many incoherencies and incompatibilities between these instruments and data protection law, and ponders the practical future implications thereof. To this end, it is important also to reflect on the function and status of data protection law, which in fact pursues a dual normative objective. On the one hand, data protection law is a fundamental rights framework, giving expression to the fundamental right to data protection as expressed in the EU Charter of Fundamental Rights (the Charter). On the other hand, however, data protection has always also been a mechanism of market integration. While it could be tempting to think that the shared market integration objective facilitates the reconciliation of the tensions between data protection law and the newly proposed Acts, it is argued that the opposite is in fact the case. Indeed, precisely because data protection law already internally balances fundamental rights and market integration objectives, traditional EU law balancing approaches between fundamental rights and economic rights cannot be relied on. As such, the contribution closes with the argument that it is of utmost importance to revise the draft Acts to ensure a stronger degree of legal certainty for those compelled to apply and interpret the legislation once it has entered into force. Otherwise, there is a risk of repeating and exacerbating existing problems in data protection law, which would produce effects opposite to those envisaged by the draft Acts.

2. The Transformation of European Data Law

This section documents the evolution of EU data law from data protection law towards a much richer regime composed of numerous legislative frameworks that exceed a narrow focus on the fundamental right.

2.1 Data Protection Law

European data protection law first emerged as computation technology—and related concerns about its capacities to process personal data—spread. From 1970 onwards, various Member States adopted domestic data protection legislation, each anchored in different national traditions and concepts. This resulted in a fragmented framework of different legal regimes containing different norms rooted in different national legal traditions. These developments eventually led to calls for a harmonized supranational regime and from 1975 onwards, the European Parliament adopted resolutions calling for EU legislation. At first, it failed to gather support from the Commission.[7] Recognizing the need for transnational regulatory cooperation, the Organisation for Economic Co-operation and Development and the Council of Europe moved to adopt transnational data protection guidelines, which put forward some principles that remain foundational in European data protection law today.[8] It was not until 1990, after having been pressured by the Member States' data protection commissioners,[9] that the Commission proposed a directive.[10] The proposal was based on what is now Article 114 of the Treaty on the Functioning of the European Union (TFEU), as fragmented national regimes were considered a threat to the free movement of data across the internal market. The proposal ultimately resulted in the 1995 Data Protection Directive (DPD).[11]

Under the DPD, data protection law was thus initially based on market integration. It was adopted to remedy the fragmentation resulting from the parallel existence of various domestic regimes and was based on TFEU's market harmonization clause. The internal market rationale is also plain when considering the scope of data protection law. In two of its earliest data protection judgments from 2003, *Österreichischer Rundfunk* and *Lindqvist*, the European Court of Justice (ECJ) held that there was no need for an actual cross-border situation. Rather, it interpreted the DPD as intending to generally facilitate the free movement of personal data within the European Union by creating suitable conditions for the internal market overall, rather than giving rise to a right that would only arise where a free movement dimension exists.[12]

A well-functioning market in the digital age does indeed require addressing regulatory hurdles to the movement of the lifeblood of digitalization: data. It is worth stressing that, at the time, there also was no alternative legal basis for the DPD. Indeed, this changed only with the recognition of data protection as a fundamental right of the EU legal order through Article 8 of the Charter[13] and the

[7] European Parliament, 'European Parliament Resolution on the protection of the rights of the individual in the face of developing technical progress in the field of automatic data processing' [1975] OJ C60/48; European Parliament, 'European Parliament Resolution on the protection of the rights of the individual in the face of developing technical progress in the field of automatic data processing' [1976] OJ C100/27; European Parliament, 'European Parliament Resolution on the protection of the rights of the individual in the face of technical developments in data processing' [1982] OJ C87/39.

[8] Organisation for Economic Co-operation and Development, 'OECD Guidelines governing the Protection of Privacy and Transborder Flows of Personal Data' (Privacy Guidelines) (1980); Convention for the Protection of Individuals with regard to Automatic Processing of Personal Data (European Treaty Series 108, Strasbourg 1981). Modernised Convention for the Protection of Individuals with regard to the Processing of Personal Data (European Treaty Series 108+, Strasbourg 2018).

[9] Berlin Resolution of the International Conference of Data Protection Commissioners (1989).

[10] European Parliament, 'Proposal for a Council Directive Concerning the Protection of Individuals in Relation to the Processing of Personal Data' [1990] OJ C277/3.

[11] European Parliament and Council Directive 95/46/EC on the protection of individuals with regard to the processing of personal data and on the free movement of such data [1995] OJ L281.

[12] Case C-101/01 *Lindqvist* [2003] ECLI:EU:C:2003:596 and Joined Cases C-465/00 and 138/01 *Österreichischer Rundfunk* [2003] ECLI:EU:C:2003:294, para 41.

[13] The Charter was solemnly proclaimed in 2000 and became legally binding with the entry into force of the Lisbon Treaty in 2009.

related adoption of Article 16 TFEU, which provides that '[e]veryone has the right to the protection of personal data concerning them' and foresees that the European Parliament and Council lay down data protection rules that ought to be subject to the control of independent authorities.[14]

After the DPD's entry into force, it soon became apparent that, as a directive, it had failed to achieve a sufficient level of harmonization and needed an update to account for ongoing technological change (such as the mainstream adoption of the internet). Consequently, the General Data Protection Regulation (GDPR) was negotiated and became binding in 2018.[15] Alongside the GDPR, the Law Enforcement Directive governs the right to data protection in criminal matters, and Regulation 2018/1725 applies to EU institutions when processing personal data.[16] The e-Privacy Directive protects the fundamental rights to privacy and data protection in electronic communications.[17] Unlike the DPD, Article 16 TFEU forms the legal basis of the GDPR. However, the internal market rationale of data protection law did not disappear with this shift. The GDPR was adopted precisely because the level of harmonization brought about by the DPD was deemed insufficient. Article 1(1) GDPR, which defines its subject matter and objectives, furthermore declares that it 'lays down rules relating to the protection of natural persons with regard to the processing of personal data and rules relating to the free movement of personal data'. Article 1(3) specifies that '[t]he free movement of personal data within the Union shall be neither restricted nor prohibited for reasons connected with the protection of natural persons with regard to the processing of personal data'.

Whereas the legislative text puts the fundamental rights and internal market objectives of the GDPR on par, the GDPR's entry into force and subsequent interpretations have been dominated by the fundamental rights narrative with a much more timid acknowledgement of the GDPR's economic dimension. In recent years, most legal literature as well as judicial interpretations of the GDPR have focused strongly on the fundamental rights dimension of data protection law. For example, the EU judiciary has emphasized that various concepts in the GDPR ought to be

[14] See further, Michèle Finck, 'Data Protection Law' in Sacha Garben and Laurence W Gormley, *Oxford Online Encyclopedia of European Union Law* (Oxford University Press 2022).

[15] European Parliament and Council Regulation (EU) 2016/679 on the protection of natural persons with regard to the processing of personal data and on the free movement of such data and repealing Directive 95/46/EC [2016] OJ L119/1.

[16] European Parliament and Council Regulation (EU) 2018/1725 on the protection of natural persons with regard to the processing of personal data by the Union institutions, bodies, offices and agencies and on the free movement of such data [2018] OJ L295/39; European Parliament and Council Directive (EU) 2016/680 on the protection of natural persons with regard to the processing of personal data by competent authorities for the purposes of the prevention, investigation, detection or prosecution of criminal offences or the execution of criminal penalties, and on the free movement of such data [2016] OJ L119/89.

[17] Directive 2002/58/EC of the European Parliament and of the Council of 12 July 2002 concerning the processing of personal data and the protection of privacy in the electronic communications sector [2002] OJ L201/37–47.

interpreted so as to ensure the 'effective and complete protection of data subjects'.[18] This 'protective rationale' in interpreting data protection law[19] clearly echoes the fundamental rights dimension of data protection law, but the Court has made no similar references to its economic rationale. In contrast, the upcoming additions to the supranational data law regime are explicitly anchored in an internal market rationale.

2.2 The Emergence of Data Law Beyond Data Protection Law

At this stage, EU data law is already more than just data protection law. It comprises, inter alia, the Open Data Directive,[20] which inter alia creates minimum thresholds for Member States to make public sector information available, as well as the Regulation on the Free Flow of Non-Personal Data (RFFNPD), a special legal framework on non-personal data, the goal of which was to stimulate the cross-border exchange of non-personal data in the EU, such as through the elimination of unjustified data localization requirements.[21] Both of these instruments are explicitly about furthering the availability of data in order to stimulate the Digital Single Market. As existing data law instruments have already been studied in detail elsewhere, this section zooms in on the draft Acts. Through this 'actification' of supranational data law, the face of EU data law will irreversibly change.[22] This section introduces the proposals' most relevant characteristics to showcase their objective of strengthening the internal market for the digital age. Of course, any and all provisions of each proposal are subject to change as the legislative process unfolds. It can, however, be expected that their overarching structure and objectives will hold, and that the following analysis will be valid for the specific regulations that will eventually be adopted.

At present, there are no rights or entitlements to data besides intellectual property rights that can guarantee the (exclusive) use thereof by others.[23] Access to data is, hence, by and large controlled by the natural or legal person having physical control

[18] See eg Case C–131/12 *Google Spain* ECLI:EU:C:2014:31, para 38 and Case C–210/16 *Wirtschaftsakademie Schleswig-Holstein* (2017) EU:C:2017:796, Opinion of Advocate General Bot, para 62.

[19] See further, Michèle Finck, 'Cobwebs of Control: The Two Imaginations of the Data Controller in EU Law' (2021) 11 International Data Privacy Law 333–47.

[20] Directive (EU) 2019/1024 of the European Parliament and of the Council of 20 June 2019 on open data and the re-use of public sector information [2019] OJ L172/56.

[21] Regulation (EU) 2018/1807 of the European Parliament and of the Council of 14 November 2018 on a framework for the free flow of non-personal data in the European Union (RFFNPD) [2018] OJ L303/59, 59–68.

[22] 'Act' is a new terminology in EU secondary law that refers to a regulation.

[23] See further, Josef Drexl and others, 'Data Ownership and Access to Data: Position Statement of the Max Planck Institute for Innovation and Competition of 16 August 2016 on the Current European Debate' (2016) Max Planck Institute for Innovation & Competition Research Paper No 16–10 <https://papers.ssrn.com/sol3/papers.cfm?abstract_id=2833165> last accessed on 20 June 2022.

thereover through contractual arrangements. This is inefficient and subject to legal uncertainty as the data protection and consumer law implications of such sharing can be hard to anticipate, which in turn is considered to disincentivize parties from in fact sharing 'their' data. Pursuant to the principle of privity of contract, contractual arrangements also only govern access to data *inter partes*. Moreover, at present, the party having the data in its physical possession has exclusive control over data, even though other parties typically also contribute to the generation thereof. The draft DA would change this by introducing concrete rights designed to facilitate, and hence also increase, the sharing of personal and non-personal data in the internal market.

First, the draft DA introduces sharing obligations for data generated by products and related services (predominantly devices from the Internet of Things). Such products shall be designed and manufactured, and related services provided, so 'that data generated by their use are, by default, easily, securely and, where relevant and appropriate, directly accessible to the user'.[24] Users moreover have a right to make data available to third parties.[25] This empowers consumers by expanding on the limited portability right under Article 20 GDPR, which is full of limitations, such as that portability must be 'technically feasible'.[26] Companies that are defined as gatekeepers under the Digital Markets Act cannot be beneficiaries of the draft DA's access rights given their 'unrivalled ability' to acquire data.[27] While the acquired data shall not be made available for the creation of products that compete with those of the original provider, it remains unclear how this can be enforced in practice.[28] Where a data holder is legally obliged (through the DA or other measures of EU law) to make data available to a recipient, it must do so under fair, reasonable, and non-discriminatory terms and in a transparent manner.[29] Any compensation that is agreed between a data holder and a data recipient must be reasonable.[30] Thus, while the Data Act can be primarily thought of as a legal framework for data-sharing obligations, it at the same time creates contractual and product design requirements for data. Indeed, it provides rules for what contractual terms are acceptable and obliges companies to design their devices and services in a manner that enables the access to related data.

Secondly, the Data Act enshrines an obligation to make data available to public sector bodies and EU institutions, agencies, or bodies based on 'exceptional need'.[31] Such a need is deemed to exist when that data is necessary to prevent or respond to a public emergency or to assist in the recovery thereof,[32] or where the lack of

[24] Draft Data Act (n 1) art 3(1).
[25] ibid art 5(1).
[26] GDPR (n 15) recital 68.
[27] Draft DA (n 1) recital 36.
[28] ibid art 4(4).
[29] ibid art 8(1).
[30] ibid art 9(1).
[31] ibid art 14.
[32] ibid art 15.

available data prevents a public sector body or EU institution from fulfilling a specific public interest task provided for by law.[33] Public emergencies are defined as 'exceptional situations' that negatively affect the population of the EU, a Member State, or part thereof, and which carry a 'risk of serious and lasting repercussions on living conditions or economic stability' or the substantial degradation of economic assets.[34] Climate change comes to mind as a phenomenon that could match these criteria. Seen through this lens, the draft DA is a rare matching point between the EU's Digital Agenda and the European Green Deal. Still, it must be stressed that these access rights are very limited compared to alternatives that were discussed and which would have resulted in generalized access or new data structures.

Thirdly, the draft Data Act enshrines requirements intended to facilitate the switching between different cloud computing providers and the porting of all cloud services to an on-premise solution.[35] Fourthly, it imposes restrictions on international data transfers for non-personal data by cloud providers (general restrictions on international transfers for personal data already exist in the GDPR). However, it does not define what a cloud provider is.[36] Third-country data access requests are only permitted if they are based on international agreements or if the third country's legal system affords protections that are similar to those found in the DA.

The exact contours of the specific rights to be created by the Data Act are yet to be determined, as this Act is still being negotiated. It will undeniably lead to a paradigm shift in data sharing, however, by creating economic rights to data. Indeed, it is necessary to own a connected device in order to enjoy these rights. This is not true for data protection rights, which apply to any data subject. Smart home devices underline the difference: these devices collect data not only about their owners (the homeowners or renters), but also about visitors to the home. While data protection rights apply to any data subjects (owners and visitors alike), only the device's owners benefit from the portability rights created by the Data Act.[37]

The draft DGA sets out a legislative governance framework for data, creating new 'data institutions'. Unlike the draft DA, it does not create new rights to data. Rather, its data governance framework complements the DA's substantive rights to data that can be used to feed various instruments—such as data-sharing services—that are foreseen by the DGA. First, the DGA governs the reuse of certain categories of protected data (such as data subject to commercial or statistical confidentiality arrangements, personal data, and data subject to intellectual property rights) that is held by public sector bodies. As such, it expands current data-sharing obligations

[33] ibid art 16.
[34] ibid recital 10.
[35] ibid art 30ff.
[36] ibid art 27ff.
[37] This also implies that art 20 GDPR is likely to become a fallback option for personal data where the more straightforward access options under the DA are not met.

under the Open Data Directive. While the DGA does not create new obligations on public sector bodies to allow the re-use of data,[38] it enshrines a qualified prohibition of exclusive arrangements granting exclusive access rights to data.[39] The DGA also sets out conditions for the re-use of data[40] and determines that any fees charged for access must meet certain criteria, such as being non-discriminatory, proportionate, and objectively justified, and that they must not restrict competition.[41]

Secondly, the DGA creates a legal regime for data intermediaries. This includes intermediation services between data holders and potential data users that wish to exchange personal and non-personal data[42] as well as data cooperatives (services that data subjects, one-person companies, or small and medium enterprises (SMEs) can rely on to negotiate the terms and conditions for data processing on their behalf).[43] The provisions on data-sharing services are designed to increase legal certainty for the emergent industry of data intermediation services, while also keeping in view the potential to attract or keep existing providers in the internal market. The DGA obliges service providers to register and provide a range of information to competent authorities.[44] This includes information such as the name, address, and legal status of the provider, as well as other details about its activity and identity.[45] The DGA further imposes various conditions that data-sharing services must meet to operate in the EU, including a neutrality obligation according to which the provider may not use the data 'for other purposes than to put them at the disposal of data users'.[46] Similarly, metadata from these operations can only be used for improving the provided service.[47] Access to the service must be fair, transparent, and non-discriminatory.[48]

Thirdly, the draft DGA creates a legal regime for 'data altruism', a notion that refers to data subjects' consent to their personal data being processed, or data holders' permission for the processing of the non-personal data they hold, without seeking a reward, for purposes of general interest, such as scientific research purposes or improving public services.[49] The draft DGA foresees the creation of a register of recognized data altruism organizations[50] and requires that these entities meet a number of transparency requirements.[51]

[38] Draft Data Governance Act (n 2) art 3(3).
[39] ibid art 4(1).
[40] ibid art 5.
[41] ibid art 6.
[42] ibid art 9(1)(a).
[43] ibid art 9(1)(c).
[44] ibid arts 10(1), 10(6).
[45] ibid art 10(6).
[46] ibid art 11(1).
[47] ibid art 11(2).
[48] ibid art 11(3).
[49] ibid art 2(10).
[50] ibid art 15.
[51] ibid art 18.

Finally, the draft DGA creates a legal basis for the creation of the European Data Innovation Board, to be established by the Commission, which will consist of representatives of competent Member State authorities, the European Data Protection Board (EDPB), and the Commission, as well as of representatives from relevant data spaces and competent authorities in specific sectors. They will advise the Commission on numerous aspects of data governance.[52]

The draft DSA is not primarily about data, but does broaden access to data for public authorities in that it requires very large online platforms to provide the European Commission or the Digital Services Coordinator of the member state they are established in with access to data 'necessary to monitor and assess compliance' with the DSA.[53] The draft Digital Services Act would, moreover, prohibit gatekeepers from combining personal data from a core platform service with personal data from other services offered by the gatekeeper or obtained from third parties.[54] It imposes a number of obligations on gatekeeper platforms, including a prohibition on combining certain data without consent and an obligation to ensure the effective implementation of Article 20 GDPR. At first sight, this could be read as strengthening the fundamental right to data protection. Data portability is, however, an atypical provision in data protection law, as it has no equivalent in pre-existing national data protection norms and presents similarities to competition law remedies.[55] Although it can be seen as part of an effort to give data subjects more control over their data[56] through porting their data to other providers, the economic dimension of this right—in contrast to other data subject rights, such as the right to be forgotten—is obvious, as it increases the circulation of data in the internal market and reduces market power of data behemoths.

The draft AIA is dedicated to a specific data processing technique, namely artificial intelligence (AI). The AIA governs AI systems based on their perceived risk.[57] Indeed, it is explicitly not a rights-based framework under which individuals subject to AI-enabled decisions would benefit from novel rights. Rather, it is firmly anchored in EU product liability legislation.[58] This can be taken as a sign that it is predominantly a market-orientated regulation that seeks to strengthen the EU market of 'trustworthy AI' and, with this, the internal market. Under the draft AIA, some practices are subject to a qualified prohibition.[59] 'High-risk' AI systems[60] can

52 ibid arts 26, 27.

53 Draft Digital Services Act (n 5) art 31(1).

54 ibid art 5(a).

55 Orla Lynskey, 'Aligning Data Protection Rights with Competition Law Remedies? The GDPR Right to Data Portability' (2017) 42 European Law Rev 793.

56 ibid.

57 Draft Artificial Intelligence Act (n 3) art 3(1).

58 Michael Veale and Frederik Zuiderveen Borgesius, 'Demystifying the Draft EU Artificial Intelligence Act: Analysing the Good, the Bad, and the Unclear Elements of the Proposed Approach' (2021) 22 Computer Law Rev International 97.

59 See draft AIA (n 3) art 5.

60 ibid art 6.

be used subject to several conditions,[61] some of which are concerned with data and its governance. Where high-risk AI uses trained data, training, validation and testing datasets must meet certain quality criteria[62] for data governance and management practices, such as that the data must be examined for possible biases.[63] The draft AIA also mandates that such datasets shall be 'relevant, representative, free of errors and complete', requirements that can be met at the level of individual datasets or a from combination thereof.[64] It appears doubtful that this provision will eventually be adopted in its current form as, in practice, most datasets will not meet these criteria.

The draft Acts are thus firmly anchored in an economic rationale as they attempt to strengthen the EU internal market for the digital age. Although often forgotten, data protection also pursues economic goals, together with its fundamental rights mandate.

3. European Data Law as Internal Market Law

The above overview has documented the evolution of supranational data law from a legal regime centred primarily around data protection law towards a multifaceted patchwork of different legislative frameworks pursuing economic objectives. Indeed, the legal basis for the draft Data Act, Data Governance Act, Digital Services Act, and Digital Markets Act is Article 114 TFEU, whereas the Artificial Intelligence Act is based on Article 114 TFEU as well as Article 16 of the Treaty on European Union (TEU). This choice of legal basis is unlikely to prove problematic; indeed, as Weatherill has repeatedly illustrated, the Court tends to accept the Commission's stated need for legislative harmonization, so long as a series of formalistic requirements resulting from the Court's own case law are met.[65]

This section first outlines some of the shared features of the proposed legislative regimes that exemplify that objective. Secondly, it will highlight that, although less talked about, data protection legislation also pursues a market integration goal.

[61] ibid arts 8–15.
[62] ibid art 10(1).
[63] ibid art 10(2)(f).
[64] ibid art 10(3).
[65] See further, Stephen Weatherill, 'The Limits of Legislative Harmonisation Ten Years after Tobacco Advertising: How the Court's Case Law has Become a "Drafting Guide"' (2019) 12 German Law Journal 827; Stephen Weatherill, 'The Function and Limits of Legislative Harmonisation in Making the Internal Market' in Robert Schütze and Takis Tridimas, *Oxford Principles of European Union Law*, vol II (Oxford University Press 2018).

3.1 The Draft Acts

The internal market objective of the draft Acts has been stressed time and time again by the European Commission, including—notably—that these initiatives are necessary to avert regulatory fragmentation.[66] The European data strategy was presented as a tool for citizens, employees, and businesses to reap the benefits of digitalization[67] and to strengthen a 'fair and competitive economy' in the EU.[68] While the draft Acts vary in their specific focus, certain common features between them can be identified that illustrate this economic objective, namely (i) data sharing, (ii) the regulation of non-personal data, and (iii) the regulation of data processing techniques. In a way, these Acts can be considered to create an additional internal market in the EU, namely an internal market in data. The resulting 'free movement' of data is of course not formalized in Article 26 TEU, unlike the free movement of goods, persons, services, and capital. Yet, as Weatherill has shown, even these official four freedoms are formalized in different ways and bear different relationships to broader EU policies.[69]

3.1.1 Incentivizing data sharing

The proposed legislative package seeks overall to incentivize the sharing of data. For example, the preamble to the draft DGA announces that it intends to 'improve the conditions for data sharing in the internal market'.[70] While this was already central to the Open Data Directive and the RFFNPD, it contrasts starkly with data protection law, which is in essence a qualified prohibition on the processing of personal data.

Overall, the draft Acts rely on several common techniques conducive to the broader internal market goal. First, they seek to increase the legal certainty inherent in the processing of data. At present, the lack of legal certainty around data sharing is often presented as a reason why data is not shared to a greater extent. Below, numerous hurdles to achieving this goal will be pinpointed. Secondly, the Acts create new rights to data in the expectation that these rights—such as the refinement of the right to data portability under both the draft Data Act and the draft Digital Markets Act—will be relied on to increase the fluidity of data in the internal market. Much like the GDPR, the proposed legislation however remains anchored

[66] European Commission, 'Commission Staff Working Document, Impact Assessment Report accompanying the document Proposal for a Regulation of the European Parliament and of the Council on European Data Governance (Data Governance Act)' COM (2020) 767 final, point 3.1.

[67] European Commission, 'Shaping Europe's Digital Future: Commission presents strategies for data and Artificial Intelligence' (19 February 2020) <https://ec.europa.eu/commission/presscorner/detail/en/ip_20_273> last accessed on 20 June 2022.

[68] European Commission, 'Shaping Europe's Digital Future' (19 February 2020) <https://ec.europa.eu/info/files/communication-shaping-europes-digital-future_en> last accessed on 20 June 2022.

[69] Stephen Weatherill, 'The Several Internal Markets' (2017) 36 Yearbook of European Law 125.

[70] Draft DGA (n 2) recital 3.

in individualism—specifically, the promise of individual initiative in relation to data. Whether this can be successful remains to be seen, but there is a risk of failure considering the limited initiative data subjects have taken with their data protection rights. Thirdly, the Acts will result in new data structures, as envisaged by the draft DGA, which facilitate data sharing between many different parties. The DGA will also create increased legal certainty for existing private sector data-sharing initiatives, as well as public pilot projects that have emerged across the European Union.[71] All in all, these measures are expected to lead to a greater fluidity of data in the internal market.

3.1.2 The regulation of non-personal data

Personal data are subject to the fundamental right to data protection, whereas non-personal data are not. As such, the recent treatment of non-personal data as a regulatory object can only be understood from an economic perspective in the sense that new rules are designed to bring about legal certainty and remove fragmentation along national lines in order to strengthen the Digital Single Market. Interestingly, the proposed regulations take different approaches towards the definition of their regulatory object. The draft DMA embraces the GDPR's definition of personal data, as well as the definition of non-personal data found in the RFFNPD.[72] The draft DGA defines non-personal data in line with the RFFNPD without defining personal data (it should, however, be taken for granted that the GDPR definition applies).[73] The draft DGA, moreover, refers to metadata as a distinct category of data, whereas this can still be personal data under the GDPR.[74]

Furthermore, the draft DA and draft DGA adopt a unitary definition of data as 'any digital representation of acts, facts, or information and any compilation of such acts, facts or information, including in the form of sound, visual or audiovisual recording'.[75] In line with data protection law, data is understood in the semantic sense as information, rather than in the synthetic sense as bits and bytes. Yet the definition of data as any digital representation of 'acts, facts or information' is confusing, as acts and facts are necessarily also information. Further, it can be questioned whether a unitary legislative definition of 'data' makes sense, as personal data will always attract the additional application of the data protection regime and, indeed, both the draft DA and draft DGA create different rules for personal and non-personal data. Hence, there can be no unitary regime applying to a

[71] By way of example, see the Findata project of the Finnish Social and Health Data Permit Authority <https://findata.fi/en/> last accessed on 20 June 2022.
[72] Draft Digital Markets Act (n 4) recitals 20, 21.
[73] Draft DGA (n 2) art 2(3).
[74] ibid art 2(4) ('data collected on any activity of a natural or legal person for the purposes of the provision of a data sharing service, including the date, time and geolocation data, duration of activity, connections to other natural or legal persons established by the person who uses the service').
[75] ibid art 2(1).

unified category of 'data'. These definitional struggles are a prelude to the practical difficulties that will follow at the implementation stage, as outlined further below.

3.1.3 The regulation of data processing techniques

The EU digital agenda does not only focus on data per se but also the processing thereof. This finds the strongest expression in the draft AIA, but provisions related to the techniques used to process data also form part of other instruments. This is to be understood in the context of the EU's goal of developing 'trustworthy technology'[76] or, as the Commission's 2020 digital strategy put it, 'technology that works for people'.[77] These notions imply that technology should be at the service of European citizens, and that they should be able to trust that 'novel' technologies such as AI do not threaten their safety or rights so that they do not avoid adopting them. These are also economic objectives designed to stimulate the creation and adoption of new technologies as well as related goods and services. The positioning of the European Union as the home of trustworthy technologies further constitutes an element of industrial strategy, as it is hoped that expertise in trustworthy technologies will provide a competitive advantage.

The draft AIA pursues this objective in the clearest sense. It creates different regulatory categories of AI based on perceived level of risk. The riskier the AI category, the stronger the legal obligations. Requirements anchored in the desire to produce trustworthy AI can, however, also be found in the other legal frameworks. The draft DA creates 'essential requirements regarding smart contracts for data sharing'.[78] The vendor of an application using smart contracts or a person whose trade, business, or profession involves the deployment of smart contracts for others in the context of an agreement to make data available must meet a number of 'essential requirements', including robustness, the possibility of safe termination and interruption, data archiving, and continuity, as well as access control.[79] Conformity assessments must be carried out to determine compliance with these requirements.[80] The inclusion of such a provision seems somewhat ill-fitting within the broader framework of the draft DA, as smart contracts are not primarily a tool of data sharing. Rather, they are much better understood in the context of the pursuit of trustworthy technology. The draft DSA, moreover, requires the disclosure of 'meaningful information about the main parameters used to determine the recipient' of an advertisement in algorithmic advertising.[81] Additional obligations arise for very large platforms to manage systemic risk. The latter must, inter alia, set out in their terms and conditions the 'main parameters' used in their recommender

[76] European Commission, 'Shaping Europe's Digital Future: Commission presents strategies' (n 67).
[77] European Commission, 'Shaping Europe's Digital Future' (n 68).
[78] Draft DA (n 1) art 30.
[79] ibid art 30(1).
[80] ibid arts 30(2), (3).
[81] Draft DSA (n 5) art 24(c).

systems in a clear, accessible, and easily comprehensible manner, and provide 'options for the recipients of the service to modify or influence those main parameters that they may have made available, including at least one option which is not based on profiling'.[82]

3.2 Data Protection Law as Internal Market Law

Data protection is often primarily thought of as a fundamental right, which of course it is under Article 8 of the Charter, as well as Article 16 TFEU. Data protection is more than a classical fundamental right, however. It is also an instrument of market integration. It was already observed in Section 3.1 that related secondary legislation was adopted to counter regulatory fragmentation in the internal market, and that Article 1 GDPR explicitly states that the Regulation pursues the dual objective of fundamental rights protection and market integration.

Indeed, data protection in many ways diverges from traditional fundamental rights. First, the fundamental right to data protection is implemented through distinct and lengthy legislative frameworks. This creates a much deeper form of harmonization than is known for all other fundamental rights governed by the Charter. Coupled with the Regulation's direct effect, this results in a more firmly harmonized regime. Secondly, the remedies under data protection law are not (only) typical fundamental rights remedies of individual redress. Rather, they are reminiscent of market correction mechanisms, rather than human rights protection measures. This conclusion is confirmed by the fact that the draft Acts adopt very similar remedies, despite not being fundamental rights frameworks. The DSA provides that the Commission may impose on very large online platforms fines up to 6 per cent of their total turnover from the preceding year.[83] Similarly, under the DMA, the Commission can impose upon gatekeepers fines up to 10 per cent of total turnover in the preceding financial year.[84] Thirdly and relatedly, the centrality of regulators in the form of national supervisory authorities highlights the importance of the harmonized application of data protection legislation for the sake of the internal market. Indeed, Article 8 of the Charter is the only Charter provision that refers to a regulator, whose goal is, inter alia, to secure the harmonized interpretation of data protection law. Fourthly, the GDPR has long been accused of being an instrument of industrial policy. The GDPR rules on international transfers have been equated with de facto data localization requirements designed to provide the internal market with a competitive advantage.[85] These are but some features of the

[82] ibid art 29(1).
[83] ibid art 59(1).
[84] Draft DMA (n 4) art 26(1).
[85] Anupam Chander and Uyen P Le, 'Data Nationalism' (2015) 64 Emory Law Journal 677.

GDPR that confirm that it is not just concerned with the fundamental right to data protection but also its implementation in a manner that removes regulatory fragmentation from the internal market. The following section reflects on the related consequences.

4. The Difficult Reconciliation Between the Fundamental Right to Data Protection and Economic Rights Attached to Personal Data

The preceding section has shown that the draft Acts and existing data protection legislation share an internal market objective. This section highlights that, this commonality notwithstanding, many tensions exist between them. While it could be tempting to think that the shared internal market goal facilitates the resolution of these tensions, this section makes the argument that it has the opposite effect. Precisely because secondary law on data protection is already 'internally balanced' between fundamental rights and market goals, the tensions between the GDPR and the proposed Acts will be difficult to resolve in practice.

4.1 Inconsistencies Between Data Law and Data Protection Law

The draft Acts repeatedly stress that the new norms are without prejudice to the GDPR. Unfortunately, this cannot change the fact that, in their current form, there is ample potential for conflict in their future interpretation and application. This tension is obvious even at a broad, conceptual level. While the GDPR creates a qualified prohibition on the processing of personal data, the draft Acts create conditions to stimulate data processing. Inevitably, their implementation will entail an increase in personal data processing (although it remains to be seen to what extent they will achieve that objective). Similarly, legal measures intended to facilitate the further processing of (personal) data seem at odds with the core data protection principles of data minimization and purpose limitation.[86] By way of example, this section introduces two overarching conflicts between the draft Acts and data protection law to highlight troublesome perspectives for future coexistence.

First, it will frequently be difficult to determine which norms apply to which data. The draft Acts blur the boundaries between the processing of personal and non-personal data. This stands in contrast to the GDPR and the RFFNPD and results in numerous conceptual and practical difficulties. Although the draft Acts govern both personal and non-personal data, no unitary regime can apply to both

[86] GDPR (n 15) arts 5(1)(b), (c).

categories given that personal data are always also subject to all GDPR requirements. The practical differentiation between personal and non-personal data is, in many instances, fraught with difficulty,[87] particularly in light of the contextual nature of data (something that is non-personal data to A may be personal data to B in light of additional information to which they have access) and the uncertain threshold of successful anonymization.[88] The quality of data may change with time as more data become available that can be matched to existing data, or as more sophisticated analysis techniques unveil previously invisible correlations. Moreover, a single dataset oftentimes contains both personal and non-personal data. The RFFNPD recognizes this and provides that where a dataset is composed of both categories, the RFFNPD applies to the non-personal data portion of the dataset whereas the GDPR applies to the personal data.[89] However, where personal and non-personal data are 'inextricably linked', the GDPR applies to the entirety.[90] Unfortunately, this leaves open how these distinctions ought to be implemented in practice. The dataset holders and recipients will often not know what specific data are of what quality in a large dataset, and the RFFNPD also leaves open the question of what 'inextricably linked' means. These rules related to mixed datasets are also ominously omitted from the draft DA and draft DGA, which undoubtedly will frequently apply to datasets that contain both personal data and non-personal data.

Secondly, the draft Acts appear to create new legal bases for the processing of personal data. This is antithetical to Article 6(1) GDPR, which requires that one legal basis from an exhaustive list must be met for personal data to be lawfully processed.[91] The draft Acts contradict this. Article 10(5) of the draft AIA appears to create a new legal basis for processing sensitive personal data under Article 9 GDPR, specifically where this is strictly necessary for the purposes of ensuring bias monitoring, detection, and correction in high-risk AI systems. In commenting on the proposal, the EDPB and European Data Protection Supervisor (EDPS) stressed that this provision lacks the necessary precision and additional safeguards to make this a legal basis for processing special category data.[92] Article 11(2) of the draft DGA also appears to create a novel legal basis for the processing of metadata in the operation of a data intermediary—such data can be used for internal development—without mentioning that, under the GDPR, a separate legal basis would be needed in the case of personal data. The same concern also arises in

[87] Nadezhda Purtova, 'The Law of Everything: Broad Concept of Personal Data and Future of EU Data Protection Law' (2018) 10 Law, Innovation and Technology 40.

[88] Michèle Finck and Frank Pallas, 'They Who Must Not Be Identified: Distinguishing Personal from Non-personal Data under the GDPR' (2020) 10 International Data Privacy Law 11.

[89] RFFNPD (n 21) art 2(2).

[90] See ibid art 2(2).

[91] Note the additional application of GDPR (n 15) art 9 for special category data.

[92] EDPB-EDPS, 'Joint Opinion 5/2021 on the proposal for a Regulation of the European Parliament and of the Council laying down harmonised rules on artificial intelligence (Artificial Intelligence Act)' (18 June 2021) <https://edpb.europa.eu/our-work-tools/our-documents/edpbedps-joint-opinion/edpb-edps-joint-opinion-52021-proposal_en> last accessed on 20 June 2022.

relation to Articles 5(6), 7(2)(c), 11(11), and 19(3) of the draft DGA, which all refer to data holders having 'permission' to use data; yet again, the requirements under Article 6(1) GDPR need to be met for personal data. Likewise, the draft DGA's definition of a data holder as 'a legal person or data subject who [...] has the right to grant access to or share certain personal or non-personal data under his control' is problematic.[93] It not only intriguingly excludes natural persons holding non-personal data from its scope but further ignores that the GDPR does not create a right for the data subject to 'share' their data; a legal basis is also needed here (unless this activity falls within the scope of the household exemption and thus is outside the scope of the GDPR).[94]

Beyond these difficulties, many other tensions can be identified. The draft DGA applies to providers of data-sharing services aimed at 'intermediating between an indefinite number of data holders and data users, excluding data sharing services that are meant to be used by a closed group of data holders and users'.[95] Where personal data is concerned, the fact that services are open to an 'indefinite number of data holders and users' would breach the data protection principles of data protection by design and by default, transparency, and purpose limitation.[96] It should also be noted that the draft Acts conflict with other legal frameworks beyond data protection law. It has indeed been stressed that the draft DGA's rules on international transfers of confidential data and data covered by intellectual property rights could conflict with the EU's international trade commitments.[97]

4.2 The Difficult Balancing Between Data Protection Legislation and the Draft Acts

Data protection law can be difficult to conceptualize, given data protection's dual nature as a fundamental right and as an instrument of market integration. The adoption of the draft Acts would force a closer engagement with the nature, and boundaries, of data protection law in their mutual application. The ECJ of course has a long tradition of balancing economic internal market objectives and fundamental rights. As Weatherill has convincingly shown, this has always been a key

[93] Draft DGA (n 2) art 2(5).

[94] 'Sharing' personal data clearly meets the definition of processing in GDPR (n 15) art 4(2).

[95] Draft DGA (n 2) recital 22.

[96] EDPB-EDPS, 'Joint Opinion 03/2021 on the Proposal for a Regulation of the European Parliament and of the European Council on European data governance (Data Governance Act)' (version 1.1, 9 June 2021), 29 <https://edpb.europa.eu/system/files/2021-03/edpb-edps_joint_opinion_dga_en.pdf> last accessed on 20 June 2022.

[97] Julie Baloup, 'The Data Governance Act: New Rules for International Transfers of Non-Personal Data Held by the Public Sector' (*European Law Blog*, 10 June 2021) <https://europeanlawblog.eu/2021/06/10/the-data-governance-act-new-rules-for-international-transfers-of-non-personal-data-held-by-the-public-sector/> last accessed on 20 June 2022.

part of the EU judiciary's docket, before and after the entry into force of the Lisbon Treaty and thus also the Charter.[98]

It can be tempting to think that precisely because data protection law is about not only fundamental but also economic rights, its reconciliation with a framework of economic rights will be straightforward. That is not, however, the case. Rather, the implementation of the right to data protection through secondary legislation already exhaustively determines all permissible limitations to this fundamental right—in this sense it is already 'internally balanced'. Consequently, in data protection law, no further limitations through external norms—including the draft Acts—appear admissible.

This marks a considerable contrast to the ECJ's traditional balancing approach between economic rights and fundamental rights. Here, the ECJ attempts to reconcile fundamental rights and economic interests. By way of example, in the landmark case of *Schmidberger*, Union judges had to reconcile the free movement of goods principle with the right to freedom of expression and assembly. The Court found that, unlike absolute rights such as freedom from torture, the right at issue was not absolute and allowed for balancing—also against economic interests. In such circumstances, 'the interests involved must be weighed having regard to all the circumstances of the case in order to determine whether a fair balance was struck between those interests'.[99] Weatherill noted that *Schmidberger* is of the highest significance in internal market law, as it

> shows that the more sensitive and the more remote from commercial consideration the matters advanced in the context of justification of trade barriers are, the more generous the Court is as regards the available scope for justification and also the breadth of the margin of appreciation enjoyed by the regulator.[100]

Data protection law, however, is not remote from commercial consideration and its additional transposition into secondary law precludes any flexibility in its reconciliation with economic objectives.

Indeed, the GDPR itself already balances fundamental rights and economic concerns and sets the boundaries of possible limitations of the former for the benefit of the latter. This dimension is most obvious regarding data subject rights, such as the right to access in Article 15 GDPR. Although this right is explicitly mentioned as an element of the fundamental right to data protection in Article 8 of

[98] Stephen Weatherill, 'The Internal Market and EU Fundamental Rights' in Sionaidh Douglas-Scott and Nicholas Hatzis (eds), *Research Handbook on EU Law and Human Rights* (Edward Elgar 2017) 364.

[99] Case C–112/00 *Schmidberger* [2003] ECLI:EU:C:2003:333, para 83. See also Case C–341/05 *Laval* [2007] ECLI:EU:C:2007:809; Case C–438/05 *Viking* [2007] ECLI:EU:C:2007:772; and Case C–36/02 *Omega* [2004] ECLI:EU:C:2004:614.

[100] Stephen Weatherill, '*Viking* and *Laval*: The Internal Market Perspective' in Mark Freedland and Jeremias Prassl, *Viking, Laval and Beyond* (Hart Publishing 2014) 32.

the Charter, the GDPR implements it in a manner that does account for economic objectives in making clear that the right is not absolute but rather should not affect 'trade secrets or intellectual property and in particular the copyright protecting the software'.[101] Such limitations are widely considered to be exhaustive. This is also reflected in the EDPB and the EEDPS's Joint Opinion on the Data Governance Act, which concluded that the DGA 'does not duly take into account the need to ensure and guarantee the level of protection of personal data provided under EU law'.[102] The opinion considers the GDPR the 'foundation' upon which the broader data law framework can be built[103] and that new EU legislation 'must not undermine the level of protection and ensure full consistency with all the principles and rules established by the GDPR to effectively guarantee the fundamental rights to the protection of personal data provided under Article 8 of the Charter and Article 16 TFEU'.[104] Thus, in data protection law, the GDPR is a floor and not a ceiling of fundamental rights protection. This is also echoed by the AIA, whose legal basis is both Article 114 TFEU and Article 16 TFEU regarding the data protection-related legal provisions. The AIA explicitly indicates that although an AI system may be compatible with the AIA, that does not imply that its use is lawful, as it may still be unlawful under the GDPR.[105]

4.3 The Importance of Legislative Clarity

It has been argued above that, through its implementation in secondary law, data protection is already internally balanced between fundamental rights and economic interests. Therefore, there is little room for further balancing against external economic objectives, and traditional approaches of balancing between fundamental rights and economic objectives as established in EU free movement law cannot be relied upon. This underlines the importance of working out existing incoherencies between the draft Acts and data protection law at the lawmaking stage. If this is not done, there is a risk of repeating and exacerbating existing shortcomings of the GDPR.

These incoherencies should be remedied to increase legal certainty for those having to apply and interpret these upcoming legal frameworks. This is a practical necessity for the envisaged legal frameworks to have their desired effect. While there is much to be said about specific problems in each proposed Act, this contribution has focused on their prospective interaction with data protection law. From this perspective, it must be stressed that the GDPR, as a technology-neutral,

[101] GDPR (n 15) recital.
[102] EDPB-EDPS, 'Joint Opinion 03/2021' (n 96) 8.
[103] ibid.
[104] ibid 9.
[105] Draft AIA (n 3) recital 41.

principles-based legal framework, has been criticized for failing in many respects to provide the legal certainty needed for the technical translation of legal requirements. The draft Acts risk replicating this lack of legal certainty in two ways. First, internally, with respect to the interpretation of their own provisions. Secondly, they also risk increasing the lack of legal certainty in the GDPR through their mutual interplay. The uncertain definitions of personal and non-personal data are an example of an area that could have both effects. The lack of legal certainty also risks having a range of second-order effects, including burdening the practical implementation as well as public and private enforcement of these norms. Both elements are at the centre of ongoing critiques of the GDPR, confirming that a poorly defined data law regime will suffer from internal weaknesses in addition to exacerbating those already plaguing data protection law.

5. Conclusion

This chapter has outlined the transition of EU data law from a legal framework focused primarily on the fundamental right to data protection to a much more complex legislative patchwork of norms. The various draft Acts that have been put forward by the European Commission will mark a paradigm shift in EU data law as they strive to increase the availability and fluidity of non-personal as well as personal data in the internal market. Although all proposals are said to be without prejudice to the GDPR, there are ample signs that in the practical implementation of these Acts things will not be so straightforward. Rather, we can expect practical uncertainty as to how to reconcile these new norms with established data protection principles.

Ultimately, the Court of Justice of the European Union (CJEU) will be called upon to resolve resulting conflicts. This chapter has illustrated the existence of potential conflicts and predicted that the CJEU will be asked to provide interpretation on how to reconcile tensions between data protection law and the upcoming broader edifice of EU data law. In doing so, its interpretation will need to diverge from the traditional judicial approach to reconciling fundamental rights and fundamental freedoms. Indeed, unlike other fundamental rights protected in EU law, data protection law is already internally balanced in its legislative expression through the GDPR. This leaves less room for additional balancing and hence also increases the risk of serious tensions. To avoid the latter, EU lawmakers should ensure that the new regulations are as unambiguous as possible in order to increase legal certainty. Indeed, the draft Acts need to provide certainty to really achieve their objective of increasing the availability and fluidity of data in the internal market.

3

Economic and Monetary Union and the Single Market: A Coming-of-Age Story?

*Alicia Hinarejos**

1. Introduction

The work of Stephen Weatherill, to whom this volume is dedicated, has fundamentally shaped our understanding of the European Union in general, and the single market in particular, putting the latter in its broader constitutional context in a way nobody else had. Steve's writing and teaching enabled me to see what was at stake—and that it was so much more than bottles of Cassis or German beer. To put it simply: he made me see the constitutional significance of economic integration, and the connections between it and everything else. More generally, he made me see what was special about the European Union experiment and what was not. Just like his writing, this may seem deceptively simple, and yet it got to the heart of how a generation of EU scholars think about their work. For me, it changed everything. In this chapter, I will focus on the connection between the single market and the EU's Economic and Monetary Union (EMU), drawing, in part, on Steve's work on the use and abuse of single market legal bases and, more broadly, on his constitutional approach to economic integration.

The link between the EU's single market and EMU is a long-standing one. The Rome Treaty (1957) set out as the aim of the (then) European Economic Community, 'by establishing a Common Market and progressively approximating the economic policies of Member States, to promote throughout the Community a harmonious development of economic activities'.[1] Many years later, the Werner Report emphasized the link between the single market and a broader economic union.[2] At their summit in Paris in 1972, the Heads of State and Government approved the objective of the progressive realization of an economic and monetary union, which found its way into the wording of the Single European Act 1987. But

* The author is grateful to SSHRC Canada for its support (Insight Grant 2022–26).

[1] Consolidated (2016) Version of the Treaty on European Union (EEC Treaty) [1957] OJ C202/1, art 2.

[2] Report to the Council and the Commission on the realization by stages of economic and monetary union in the Community, 'Werner Report.' Luxembourg, 8 October [1970] OJ Supp C136, 11 November 1970.

Alicia Hinarejos, *Economic and Monetary Union and the Single Market: A Coming-of-Age Story?* In: *The Internal Market Ideal.* Edited by: Jeremias Adams-Prassl, Sanja Bogojević, Ariel Ezrachi, and Dorota Leczykiewicz, Oxford University Press.
 DOI: 10.1093/oso/9780192867063.003.0004

it was the Delors Report, in 1989,[3] that would lay out the blueprint for what was to become today's EMU, explaining its necessity for, and benefits to, the single market in more detail.[4]

The Delors Report recognized that the ongoing process of economic integration within the EU would necessitate 'more intensive and effective policy coordination' in both the economic and monetary fields.[5] The completion of the single market would greatly increase economic interdependence; monetary and economic policy convergence would be necessary to manage this interdependence and to fully realize its benefits.[6] A common currency would ease cross-border trade and eliminate exchange rate instability.[7] Economic coordination of national policies would bring them closer together, avoiding large divergences—which the single market could compound—and asymmetric shocks. And further free movement of the factors of production (notably labour) would be necessary in order to bring a common currency closer to the ideal of an optimal currency area and thus realize its benefits.[8] In this way, the single market and EMU were supposed to enhance each other as two sides of the same coin—namely, the project of creating an economic union among the Member States[9]—essential and complementary elements within the different layers of the European economic constitution.[10]

The relationship between the single market and EMU, however, has also changed over time, especially since the euro area crisis. The crisis highlighted the need for changes to make EMU more resilient; tools to effect change in this area—in the form of EU powers and their corresponding Treaty legal bases—were limited, and the single market ones were co-opted. As we shall see in the following sections, this

[3] Committee for the Study of Economic and Monetary Union, 'Report on Economic and Monetary Union in the European Community' (Delors Report) (1989).

[4] For an overview of the historical evolution and the link between the single market and EMU, see Emmanuel Mourlon-Druol, 'History of an Incomplete EMU' in Fabian Amtenbrink, Christoph Hermann, and René Repasi (eds), *The EU Law of Economic and Monetary Union* (Oxford University Press 2020); Andrew Scott, 'Does Economic Union Require a Fiscal Union?' in Niamh Nic Shuibhne and Laurence W Gormley (eds), *From Single Market to Economic Union: Essays in Memory of John A Usher* (Oxford University Press 2012); Fabian Amtenbrink, 'Denationalizing Monetary Policy: Reflections on 60 Years of European Monetary Integration' in *From Single Market to Economic Union*.

[5] Delors Report (n 3) [11].

[6] ibid [10]–[14].

[7] Thomas Beukers, 'The Eurozone Crisis and the Autonomy of Member States in Economic Union: Changes and Challenges' in Panos Koutrakos and Jukka Snell (eds), *Research Handbook on the Law of the EU's Internal Market* (Edward Elgar 2017).

[8] According to the economic theory of Optimum Currency Areas, a single currency is the efficient choice for areas with a high degree of economic integration; the degree of optimality depends on trade and factor mobility. Robert A Mundell, 'A Theory of Optimum Currency Areas' (1961) 51 The American Economic Review 657. On EMU specifically as a non-optimum currency area, see Paul Krugman, Maurice Obstfeld, and Marc Melitz, *International Economics: Theory and Policy* (9th edn, Pearson 2011) 587–615.

[9] On the link between single market and EMU, see also Jukka Snell, 'The Internal Market and the Philosophies of Market Integration' in Catherine Barnard and Steve Peers (eds), *European Union Law* (3rd edn, Oxford University Press 2020).

[10] Kaarlo Tuori and Klaus Tuori, *The Eurozone Crisis: A Constitutional Analysis* (Cambridge University Press 2014) 13–18.

use is justified due to the complementary nature of the single market and certain aspects of EMU, but it has its drawbacks and, most importantly, limitations. The use of single market legal bases will continue in the future—perhaps changing, to some degree, the nature of the single market itself[11]—and it is an essential condition of solving the problems of EMU, but not a sufficient one. This chapter will provide an overview of the tightening of the relationship between the single market and EMU in the aftermath of the euro area crisis, also showing its limitations. It will then discuss the need for EMU to grow in additional, different ways that do not rely on the legal bases of the single market, in order to 'come of age'.

Section 2 will start by focusing on the measures adopted by the EU and the Member States in the wake of the euro area crisis, highlighting the fact that many of them had to be adopted on the basis of single market provisions. This was the case in the area of financial regulation and banking union, at the intersection between the single market and EMU. The adoption of these measures raised reasonable concerns about the use of Article 114 of the Treaty on the Functioning of the European Union (TFEU) and its boundaries; it also caused broader unease about the co-opting of the single market, which includes all Member States, to pursue an EMU agenda driven by euro countries. This section will finish by considering the likely future use of single market legal bases to continue adopting measures in the financial arena and beyond. Section 3 will argue for the need for EMU to be provided with its own legal bases, given the constraints on the use of single market provisions and the risks associated with overusing them. This need is especially acute when it comes to the next stage of EMU integration, generally considered to require a significant pooling of resources and progress towards a fiscal union. The completion of EMU along these lines cannot happen satisfactorily on the basis of single market provisions and requires a well thought-out, careful Treaty reform—a path that seemed closed for a very long time. Section 4 will explore to what extent the Covid-19 pandemic and the measures adopted to foster economic recovery may have a bearing on this outlook. Section 5 will provide final reflections on the link between EMU and the single market and the future of this relationship.

2. The Euro Crisis and Using the Single Market to Plug Holes: Examples and Limitations

The original design of EMU will not be discussed here in any depth.[12] Suffice it to say that it was created as an asymmetric set of policies involving a highly centralized monetary policy conducted by the European Central Bank (ECB), as well as

[11] ibid 347–51.

[12] For an overview, see Alicia Hinarejos, 'Economic and Monetary Union: Evolution and Conflict' in Paul Craig and Gráinne de Búrca (eds), *The Evolution of EU Law* (Oxford University Press 2021).

the coordination of national economic policies. It also included a series of fiscal rules, embodied in the Stability and Growth Pact (SGP), to foster some degree of budgetary discipline.[13] The theory was that the single currency would help reap the benefits of the single market by easing cross-border trade and taking away the uncertainty of exchange rates. The coordination of national economic policies was necessary to avoid too-great divergences between the (very different) national economies that would now be further bound together. There was a fear that these divergences might be compounded by the dynamics of the single market.

We now know, however, that the original set-up of EMU did not achieve these objectives, and that the lack of effective fiscal discipline and of economic coordination were some of the factors underlying the euro area sovereign debt crisis which started in 2009. The trigger—or immediate cause—was a global financial crisis,[14] itself sparked by a lack of regulation in the financial sector. It was the first time since its creation that the collapse of the euro as a political project seemed like a distinct possibility—and with it, perhaps, untold damage to the single market and to the EU as a whole. The months and years that followed the outbreak of the crisis were hectic ones, as EU institutions and Member States grappled with short- and medium-term fixes to the crisis. Broadly speaking, the fixes fell within the following categories: stabilizing the situation through ECB action and the creation of mechanisms of financial assistance, strengthening budgetary surveillance and economic coordination, and improving regulation of the financial sector to break the toxic link between banks and sovereigns.[15]

2.1 Reacting to the Euro Area Crisis: Limited Tools

If there is one thing that became clear very quickly in the acute phase of the euro area crisis it is that the original EMU tools were inadequate to weather the storm. There was no clear legal basis for the creation of a (permanent) mechanism of financial assistance, for example, and no consensus on how far we could go by using the available Treaty bases to further integrate economic and fiscal policy.[16] In some

[13] The origins of the Stability and Growth Pact lie in a resolution from 1997 (Resolution of the European Council on the Stability and Growth Pact [1997] OJ C236, 17 June 1997). This spawned two regulations (preventive and corrective, respectively): Council Regulation (EC) 1466/97 on the strengthening of the surveillance of budgetary positions and the surveillance and coordination of economic policies [1997] OJ L209/1; and Council Regulation (EC) 1467/97 on speeding up and clarifying the implementation of the excessive deficit procedure [1997] OJ L209/6. The excessive deficit procedure is further detailed in Protocol No 12 attached to the Treaties.

[14] On the financial crisis as immediate cause of the euro area sovereign debt crisis, see eg Scott (n 4) 42ff.

[15] For an overview with further references, see Alicia Hinarejos, *The Euro Area Crisis in Constitutional Perspective* (Oxford University Press 2015) ch 3.

[16] For an overview, see Alicia Hinarejos, 'The Legality of Responses to the Crisis' in Fabian Amtenbrink, Christoph Hermann, and René Repasi (eds), *The EU Law of Economic and Monetary Union* (Oxford University Press 2020).

of these cases, a path outside the Treaties was found: this was the case with the European Stability Mechanism (an intergovernmental and permanent mechanism of financial assistance);[17] the Treaty on Stability, Coordination and Governance, which included the Fiscal Compact (a commitment of the participating states to implement a debt brake); and the Single Resolution Fund, which will be discussed later. In other cases, a single EMU provision acquired star status: a variety of EU measures to strengthen budgetary discipline and surveillance, as well as economic coordination (the Six-Pack and Two-Pack)[18] were adopted on the basis of Article 136 TFEU,[19] which allows for the adoption of measures aimed at strengthening budgetary surveillance within the euro area, and the adoption of economic policy guidelines for the same countries. This legal basis was used to create a new framework for budgetary surveillance (the European Semester) and to introduce new sanctions or strengthen existing ones.[20] For our purposes here, suffice it to say that there was some concern at the time over this very strong reliance on Article 136 TFEU, and its use to seemingly expand or create new powers for the Commission and to introduce a special regime of budgetary surveillance and economic coordination (including through the imposition of new sanctions) for euro countries.[21] While these concerns seem now a thing of the past (the most recent of these rules, the Regulations in the Two-Pack,[22] are almost ten years old and the discussion has moved on), it seems safe to say that the scope of Article 136 TFEU as a tool for the

[17] Treaty on Coordination, Stability and Governance in the Economic and Monetary Union (also known as the fiscal compact) [2012]. Art 136 TFEU was also amended to affirm the power of the Member States to create a mechanism of this kind outside of the EU Treaties.

[18] The Six-Pack consists of five Regulations and one Directive: Regulation (EU) 1173/2011 on the effective enforcement of budgetary surveillance in the euro area [2011] OJ L306/1; Regulation (EU) 1174/2011 on enforcement measures to correct excessive macroeconomic imbalances in the euro area [2011] OJ L306/8; Regulation (EU) 1175/2011 on the strengthening of the surveillance of budgetary positions and the surveillance and coordination of economic policies [2011] OJ L306/12; Regulation (EU) 1176/2011 on the prevention and correction of macroeconomic imbalances [2011] OJ L306/25; Council Regulation (EU) 1177/2011 on speeding up and clarifying the implementation of the excessive deficit procedure [2011] OJ L306/33; and Council Directive 2011/85/EU on requirements for budgetary frameworks of the Member States [2011] OJ L306/41. The Two-Pack, of application only to the euro area, consists of two Regulations: Regulation (EU) 473/2013 on common provisions for monitoring and assessing draft budgetary plans and ensuring the correction of excessive deficit of the Member States in the euro area [2013] OJ L140/11 and Regulation (EU) 472/2013 on the strengthening of economic and budgetary surveillance of Member States in the euro area experiencing or threatened with serious difficulties with respect to their financial stability [2013] OJ L140/1.

[19] In connection with either art 121 or art 126 TFEU, on the preventive arm of the Stability and Growth Pact and the excessive deficit procedure, respectively.

[20] Specifically, new sanctions for euro countries were introduced in the preventive arm of the Stability and Growth Pact, as well as in the macroeconomic imbalance procedure. The sanctions in use in the corrective arm of the Stability and Growth Pact—or excessive deficit procedure—were strengthened.

[21] Tuori and Tuori (n 10) 168–71. The authors argued that art 136 TFEU should have been given a more limited scope, allowing not for the creation of new powers, but simply for the use of the powers set out in arts 121 and 126 TFEU (on the preventive and corrective arms of the SGP) in relation to euro countries.

[22] Treaty on Coordination, Stability and Governance (n 17).

further economic and fiscal integration of euro area countries was exhausted at the time.

2.2 Using Single Market Tools: Better Financial Regulation and Banking Union

Yet in some other cases, the tools of the single market were used: in particular, when it came to strengthening financial regulation and supervision, which was one of the responses adopted by the EU and its Member States in the wake of the euro area crisis. Financial regulation can be said to fall under the single market umbrella, since harmonization of rules relating to financial regulation and supervision have a direct effect on free movement of services and capital. At the same time, it is also an important element of EMU, and failings in this area were one of the underlying causes of the euro area crisis.

The lack of proper financial regulation was considered to be one of the main factors underlying the global financial crisis that started in 2007 and shook the world in 2008 with the fall of Lehman Brothers. The global financial crisis was a precursor to the euro area sovereign debt crisis for various reasons: first, because of the toxic link between weak banks and weak sovereigns, which meant that euro countries that bailed out their banks then struggled to manage the level of debt they had taken on; and secondly, because the global financial crisis worsened the economic problems of certain euro countries and made it more difficult for them to access credit, which in turn increased the pressure on financial institutions. Indeed, the global financial crisis and sovereign debt crisis fed off each other in a toxic loop; in seeking to better regulate financial markets and institutions, the EU sought to break this loop and avoid similar situations in the future. It did so by relying on the tools of the internal market (Article 53 TFEU on the right of establishment, or the general single market clause in Article 114 TFEU), which raised concerns relating to the use of the single market legal bases—and especially Article 114 TFEU—to adopt these reforms at the intersection between the single market and EMU. As we know, Article 114 TFEU is no stranger to this sort of disagreement, and it has not always been easy to draw the boundaries of this potentially broad harmonizing power to pursue the establishment and functioning of the internal market. In its notorious *Tobacco Advertising* decision, the Court of Justice attempted to draw these boundaries by setting out a by-now classic though dull-edged test: essentially, the legislature needs to show that there is an obstacle to free movement (or distortion of competition) within the single market—or that such obstacles are likely to arise—and that the measure in question is suitable to prevent them.[23] Steve

[23] Case C–376/98 *Germany v Parliament and Council (Tobacco Advertising)* [2000] ECR I–08419.

Weatherill's critical assessment of this test and its unavoidable limitations has always been the gold standard in this area.[24]

Subsection 2.2.1 will examine particular reforms in the area of financial supervision and regulation, as well as specific concerns raised by the use of the single market legal bases in this context. This includes whether or not some of these reforms complied with the *Tobacco Advertising* test and were, at heart, 'enough' about the single market and not just about improving EMU, and to what extent Article 114 TFEU can be used to impose significant financial burdens on Member States. Subsection 2.2.2 will then consider broader unease about using the single market provisions to pursue, in effect, an EMU agenda, and discuss the extent to which the single market legal bases will continue to be used in the future to adopt reforms in this area and beyond.

2.2.1 Specific reforms in this area and specific concerns

The reforms adopted at the intersection of the single market and EMU included the adoption of a myriad of new or stricter financial rules for the whole of the EU; the creation of a network of supervision authorities (the European System of Financial Supervision, which includes several supervisory agencies);[25] and the creation of a banking union for the euro area. I will not go into these reforms in detail, but rather only into the matter of their legal basis and some related controversies. First, new or stricter financial rules (a growing 'single rule book') were adopted for all financial institutions operating anywhere within the EU; ie, not only within the euro area.[26] These measures were adopted on the basis of Articles 114 or 53 TFEU, and their object ranges from prudential requirements and supervision of banks and investment firms to harmonization of national deposit guarantee schemes, recovery and resolution of flailing institutions, or the operations of credit rating agencies.[27]

[24] Stephen Weatherill, *Cases and Materials on EU Law* (12th edn, Oxford University Press 2016) 33–41; Stephen Weatherill, *Law and Values in the European Union* (Oxford University Press 2016) 36–45; Stephen Weatherill, 'The Limits of Legislative Harmonisation Ten Years After *Tobacco Advertising*: How the Court's Case Law has Become a Drafting Guide' (2011) 12 German Law Journal 827.

[25] This framework includes the European Banking Authority, the European Insurance and Occupational Pensions Authority, the European Securities and Markets Authority, and the European Systemic Risk Board. See Regulation (EU) 1093/2010 establishing a European Supervisory Authority (European Banking Authority) [2010] OJ L331/12; Regulation (EU) 1094/2010 establishing a European Supervisory Authority (European Insurance and Occupational Pensions Authority) [2010] OJ L331/48; Regulation (EU) 1095/2010 establishing a European Supervisory Authority (European Securities and Markets Authority) [2010] OJ L331/84; and Regulation (EU) 1092/2010 on European Union macro-prudential oversight of the financial system and establishing a European Systemic Risk Board [2010] OJ L331/1.

[26] See generally Kern Alexander and Vivienne Madders, 'Financial Market Regulation in the Internal Market' in Fabian Amtenbrink, Christoph Hermann, and René Repasi (eds), *The EU Law of Economic and Monetary Union* (Oxford University Press 2020).

[27] Directive 2009/111/EC as regards banks affiliated to central institutions, certain own funds items, large exposures, supervisory arrangements, and crisis management [2009] OJ L302/97 (based on art 53 TFEU); Directive 2013/36/EU on access to the activity of credit institutions and the prudential supervision of credit institutions and investment firms (based on art 53 TFEU); Regulation (EU) 575/2013 on prudential requirements for credit institutions and investment firms [2013] OJ L176/1 (based on art 114 TFEU); Directive 2013/36/EU on access to the activity of credit institutions and the prudential

Secondly (and, as it turned out, more controversially), Article 114 TFEU was used to set up a network of financial supervisory authorities:[28] the European System of Financial Supervision, which includes the European Banking Authority, the European Securities and Market Authority (ESMA), the European Insurance and Occupational Pensions Authority, and the European Systemic Risk Board, together with national supervising bodies.[29] The use of Article 114 TFEU in this context did not go unchallenged, particularly its use to harmonize the single market through the creation of, and delegation of powers to, new agencies. The United Kingdom challenged this use of the single market powers in the context of the new ESMA, arguing that the delegation of powers to this agency to prevent or limit short-selling was excessive, and that it went beyond the scope of Article 114 TFEU.[30] The Court of Justice of the EU found that the delegation of powers to agencies such as ESMA—within certain limits—was in compliance with the *Meroni* doctrine,[31] and that harmonization on the basis of Article 114 TFEU can be pursued through delegation of certain powers of implementation to agencies in this area (again, within limits).[32] It had no objection to the use of Article 114 TFEU for the creation of ESMA, or as a legal basis for legally binding decisions taken by ESMA in the context of preventing or limiting short-selling. In both cases, the

supervision of credit institutions and investment firms [2013] OJ L176/338 (based on art 53 TFEU); Directive 2014/49/EU on deposit guarantee schemes (recast) [2014] OJ L173/149 (based on art 53 TFEU); Directive 2014/59/EU establishing a framework for the recovery and resolution of credit institutions and investment firms [2014] OJ L173/190 (based on art 114 TFEU). These rules are applicable to the whole EU single market, while the Single Resolution Mechanism, discussed later, is applicable to Member States participating in the banking union; Regulation (EU) 462/2013 on credit rating agencies [2009] OJ L146/1 (based on art 114); Directive 2013/14/EC [2013] OJ L145/1(based on art 53 TFEU).

[28] See art 114 TFEU generally, in conjunction with art 127(6) TFEU, on the role of the ECB, whenever it was necessary to create a supervisory task for the ECB.

[29] See generally Christoph Ohler, 'Banking Supervision' in Fabian Amtenbrink, Christoph Hermann, and René Repasi (eds), *The EU Law of Economic and Monetary Union* (Oxford University Press 2020).

[30] Case C-270/12 *United Kingdom v Parliament and Council* [2014] ECLI:EU:C:2014:18.

[31] *Meroni* established that only executive powers that did not require the exercise of discretion could be delegated to agencies; *Romano*, for its part, negated that such agencies could adopt acts with the force of law. The Court found that *Meroni* allowed for the delegation of decision-making powers to the new generation of financial supervision agencies (in the case, to ESMA), as long as the powers are precisely delineated in, and reviewable for their accordance with, the delegating act (*UK v Parliament and Council* (n 30) paras 41–55). The Court considered that *Romano* had been superseded by subsequent developments in judicial review (ibid paras 63–68.) See Case 9/56 *Meroni v High Authority of the European Coal and Steel Community* [1958] ECR 133; Case 98/80 *Romano v Institut national d'assurance maladie-invalidité* [1981] ECR 1241.

[32] Extending the Court's late approach to the scope of art 114 TFEU as allowing for the pursuit of harmonization through the delegation of powers to expert bodies (in this case, the Commission working together with the Food Safety Authority), particularly in fields that require technical expertise. (Case C-66/04 *United Kingdom v Parliament and Council (Smoke flavourings)* [2005] ECR I-10553.) In a subsequent case, the Court found that art 114 TFEU could be the legal basis for the creation of a body that would be tasked with contributing to the process of market harmonization (Case C-217/04 *United Kingdom* v *Parliament and Council (European Network and Information Security Agency or ENISA)* [2006] ECR I-3771). Importantly, however, the body in this case was to adopt non-binding supporting or framework measures.

Court found that the result would be genuine market harmonization, and in accordance with the classic *Tobacco Advertising* test.[33]

On this point, the Court's reasoning differed from that of Advocate General Jääskinen, who considered Article 114 TFEU a suitable basis for the creation of ESMA,[34] but not for the downstream measures that ESMA would adopt in relation to short-selling. The Advocate General saw no objection, in principle, to Article 114 TFEU as a legal basis that empowers agencies to adopt legally binding measures with respect to third parties, as long as those decisions amounted to internal market harmonization;[35] he was of the opinion that the specific decision-making powers given to ESMA in the context of short-selling would not lead to harmonization,[36] and thus went beyond the scope of Article 114 TFEU. As we know, the Court disagreed with this assessment; but the fact remains that there is genuine scope for disagreement on the limits to which the scope of Article 114 TFEU is being pushed in this context. While this is not a development that is limited to financial supervision, or to areas with a link to EMU, it is highly relevant in any discussion of how much we can rely on ever-expanding interpretations of Article 114 TFEU to further integration within EMU.

Indeed, similar problems arose in relation to the third set of measures previously mentioned, and adopted in part, too, on the basis of Article 114 TFEU: the creation of a banking union for euro area countries (though open to non-euro countries, should they wish to join). The banking union is one of the most ambitious reforms to come out of the euro area crisis, and it aims to create a much tighter common framework of supervision of financial institutions, as well as a common way of dealing with the risk of their failure.[37] So far, this translates into two pillars: a Single Supervisory Mechanism (SSM),[38] led by the ECB, and a Single Resolution Mechanism (SRM), to contend with ('resolve') failing institutions.[39] It is envisaged that a third pillar will be adopted, namely a European Deposit Insurance Scheme

[33] Case C-270/12 (n 30) paras 97–118. On *Tobacco Advertising*, see nn 23–24 and associated main text.

[34] As the creation of ESMA under art 114 TFEU complied with the same conditions as the creation of ENISA (Case C-217/04 (n 32)), ie its purpose is to improve the conditions for the establishment and functioning of the internal market (Case C-270/12, Opinion of AG Jääskinen delivered on 12 September 2013, paras 27–34.)

[35] ibid para 36.

[36] Instead, he argued that the result would be 'not harmonisation, or the adoption of uniform practice at the level of the Member States, but the replacement of national decision making [. . .] with EU level decision making', ibid para 52.

[37] On banking union generally, see eg Niamh Moloney, 'European Banking Union: Assessing its Risks and Resilience' (2014) 51 Common Market Law Review 1609; Gianni Lo Schiavo (ed), *The European Banking Union and the Role of Law* (Edgar Elgar 2019); and Danny Busch and Guido Ferrarini (eds), *European Banking Union* (2nd edn, Oxford University Press 2020).

[38] See generally Ohler (n 29).

[39] See generally Christo V Gortsos, 'Banking Resolution: The EU Framework Governing the Resolution of Credit Institutions' in Fabian Amtenbrink, Christoph Hermann, and René Repasi (eds), *The EU Law of Economic and Monetary Union* (Oxford University Press 2020).

(EDIS), which has proven extremely controversial and about which discussions continue.[40]

While the banking union failed to make it into the original design of EMU, it is now one of its essential elements.[41] At the same time, it sits at the crossroads between EMU and the single market: its aim is to adopt common rules on financial regulation and supervision of institutions and thus to further the integration of this sector of the single market; at the same time, the adoption of these rules improves the functioning of EMU in that it reduces the risk of shocks and it breaks the toxic link between ailing banks and individual states. What has been called the 'double soul'[42] of the banking union justifies the use of Article 114 TFEU, but this reliance—much as in relation to the measures described earlier in this section—has been 'somewhat strained'.[43]

The SSM is based on Article 127(6) TFEU, which foresees the creation of prudential supervision roles for the European Central Banks.[44] The SRM,[45] on the other hand, is partly based on Article 114 TFEU:[46] a Regulation was adopted on this legal basis to create the SRM itself, and to adopt the common rules that would be applied to failing banks and investment firms. But it was also necessary, as part of the SRM, to create a common fund to be used for the same purpose: a common pool of funds to be used, as a last resort, to guarantee the orderly resolution of

[40] The Commission made a proposal in 2015 that has since stalled: Proposal for a Regulation of the European Parliament and of the Council amending Regulation (EU) 806/2014 in order to establish a European Deposit Insurance Scheme COM (2015) 0586 final. The proposed legal basis is art 114 TFEU.

[41] On how banking union failed to be included in the original design of EMU, to then become one of its most important elements after the crisis, see Gavin Barrett, 'The European Banking Union and the Economic and Monetary Union: A Re-telling of Cinderella with an Uncertain Happy Ever After?' in Gianni Lo Schiavo (ed) (n 37).

[42] A term used by Alberto de Gregorio Merino, 'The Banking Union in EU law: An EU Institutional Law Perspective' in Gianni Lo Schiavo (ed) (n 37).

[43] A term used by Barrett (n 41) 20. For a more detailed overview of the strained relationship between the banking union and the single market, and specific concerns raised by the use of art 114 TFEU as a legal basis, see Tomi Tuominen, 'European Banking Union: A Shift in the Internal Market Paradigm?' (2017) 54 Common Market Law Review 1359.

[44] Council Regulation (EU) 1024/2013 conferring specific tasks on the European Central Bank concerning policies relating to the prudential supervision of credit institutions; Regulation (EU) 1022/2013 amending Regulation (EU) 1093/2010 establishing a European Supervisory Authority (EBA) as regards the conferral of specific tasks on the European Central Bank pursuant to Council Regulation (EU) 1024/2013 (based on art 127(6) TFEU). On the SSM, see Eddy Wymeersch, 'The Single Supervisory Mechanism for Banking Supervision: Institutional Aspects' in Danny Busch and Guido Ferrarini (eds), *European Banking Union* (2nd edn, Oxford University Press 2020).

[45] For a brief overview of both SSM and SRM, see Kern Alexander, 'European Banking Union: A Legal and Institutional Analysis of the Single Supervisory Mechanism and the Single Resolution Mechanism' (2015) 40 European Law Review 154.

[46] Regulation (EU) 806/2014 establishing uniform rules and a uniform procedure for the resolution of credit institutions and certain investment firms in the framework of a Single Resolution Mechanism and a Single Resolution Fund and amending Regulation (EU) 1093/2010 (based on art 114 TFEU). Additionally, all Member States except Sweden and the UK (a Member State at the time) signed an intergovernmental agreement setting out how Member States would levy funds and contribute to the SRM. (Agreement on the transfer and mutualization of contributions to the Single Resolution Fund, signed on 21 May 2014. Final text: Document 8457/14, ECOFIN 342.)

a failing financial institution and limit its negative effects. This fund (the Single Resolution Fund, or SRF) had to be adopted on the basis of an intergovernmental agreement, due to disagreement on the suitability of Article 114 TFEU as a legal basis.[47] Initially, the Commission had proposed to adopt all elements of the SRM (including the SRF) on the basis of Article 114 TFEU, but Germany had misgivings about the use of the single market clause to impose such a financial burden on Member States.[48] The use of a 'supplementary' intergovernmental agreement to deal specifically with the pooling of resources for the Single Resolution Fund was an attempt to minimize legal challenges or, at least, to make it less likely that they would be successful. Indeed, the legality of every element of the banking union was challenged before the German Constitutional Court (surprise!), which found them to be constitutional, though by a rather narrow margin.[49]

Similarly, though the Commission's proposal for a future European Deposit Insurance Scheme (the third and final pillar of banking union) is based on Article 114 TFEU, there are, again, misgivings on the use of the single market clause to impose potentially enormous financial burdens on Member States, and it is likely that certain Member States will continue to insist on the need for Treaty reform instead. Yet again it becomes clear that, while the banking union has been a success (at least those elements that have been adopted so far), the use of Article 114 TFEU or, in general, of the single market legal bases in the Treaty to significantly further integration within EMU is limited, and far from plain sailing.

2.2.2 Broader concerns about using the single market provisions in this area and beyond

Moreover, and apart from the specific concerns discussed so far, there is a broader unease caused by the use of instruments pertaining to the single market (that includes all EU Member States) to ensure the stability of the euro area or, more generally, to the benefit of those Member States that are members of the currency union. This mismatch gives rise to concerns that the euro countries will caucus and drive the single market agenda, and that the measures adopted in this way will interfere with the 'unity' of the single market, disrupting competition and the level playing field.[50] Certain specific arrangements have been put in place to allay these fears in

[47] On the use of art 114 TFEU in the context of the SRM, see Alexander (n 45) 179–81.

[48] Markus K Brunnermeier, Harold James, and Jean-Pierre Landau, *The Euro and the Battle of Ideas* (Princeton University Press 2016) 217–19 and 220–21; Federico Fabbrini, 'On Banks, Courts and International Law: A Critical Analysis of the Draft International Agreement on the Functioning of the Single Resolution Fund' (2014) Centro Studi sul Federalismo Research Paper, 9ff. On the use of art 114 TFEU to mutualize funds, and other specific concerns about the use of art 114 TFEU in this context, see Tuominen (n 43) 1376.

[49] BVerfG, Judgment of the Second Senate of 30 July 2019, 2 BvR 1685/14. For a commentary on the case and its background, see Pietro Faraguna and Donato Messineo, 'Light and Shadows in the Bundesverfassungsgericht's Decision Upholding the European Banking Union' (2020) 57 Common Market Law Review 1629.

[50] de Gregorio Merino (n 42) 36ff.

the context of the SSM and SRM,[51] but the general unease will remain and indeed grow, if this co-opting of the single market continues.[52]

Looking forward, the link between EMU and the single market will continue to be most visible in this area of financial regulation and supervision (what the Five Presidents' Report refers to as the 'financial union' element of EMU).[53] Current proposals aim to make progress within the so-called Capital Markets Union: in other words, to integrate EU capital markets further through the adoption of harmonizing measures that affect companies and investors (including on supervision and taxation).[54] This would increase cross-border capital flows and make it easier to invest across different jurisdictions, thus diversifying and limiting private risk. This, in turn, would diminish public risk and make public risk sharing less necessary.[55] These measures would (rightfully) have single market legal bases; there is no doubt that they would improve the functioning of a sector of the single market (capital markets) that remains fragmented. At the same time, while it is clear that these proposals would also benefit EMU, this complementarity is likely to be less problematic in this area (regulation of private investment) than it is in the framework of the banking union, which involves regulation of public risk and mutualizing Member States' funds, and where the EMU component is, overall, more prominent.

Beyond the realm of financial union—including banking union and the capital markets union project—other attempts to bolster EMU by resorting to the tools of single market integration have also faced difficulties. Notably, the maligned proposal to adopt a Financial Transaction Tax (FTT) on the basis of Article 113 TFEU,[56] for example, had to be abandoned. In this case, while the tax was supposed to contribute to the harmonization of taxation rules among participating Member States (the single market rationale), it would also improve EMU by discouraging risky behaviour, ensuring that financial institutions would contribute to covering the costs of the financial crisis and, more generally, by creating an additional stream

51 ibid 37–39.

52 Snell (n 9) 350. See also Tuominen (n 43).

53 Jean-Claude Juncker, in close cooperation with Donald Tusk, Jeroen Dijsselbloem, Mario Draghi, and Martin Schulz, 'Completing Europe's Economic and Monetary Union' ('Five Presidents' Report'), June 2015. The Five Presidents' Report distinguishes between economic union, financial union, and fiscal union. For a discussion of financial union (which includes banking union and capital markets union), see ibid 10–12.

54 ibid 12.

55 ibid.

56 Once the European Parliament had given its consent in December 2012, the Council adopted a decision in January 2013 authorizing eleven Member States to use enhanced cooperation to adopt a Financial Transaction Tax Directive: Council Decision 2013/52/EU authorizing enhanced cooperation in the area of financial transaction tax [2013] OJ L22/11. The eleven countries were Austria, Belgium, Estonia, France, Germany, Greece, Italy, Portugal, Spain, Slovenia, and Slovakia (Commission Proposal for a Council Directive implementing enhanced cooperation in the area of financial transaction tax, COM (2013) 071 final 2013/0045 (CNS)).

of EU revenue.[57] This was seen as an important step in the (at that time) growing discussion about the need for a significant fiscal capacity for the euro area, and the different ways in which this revenue could be generated. Yet the attempt to use the single market legal bases in this way was once more controversial: this time because of the attempt at using enhanced cooperation and the possibility that the tax (of application only in participating Member States) would give rise to distortions of competition within the single market more broadly, among other concerns.[58] Although ten of the eleven Member States signalled at the time their intention to pursue the adoption of a narrower version of the tax,[59] and Germany put forward a proposal in 2019,[60] there has been no significant progress on the matter so far (though, as will be discussed later, new life may be breathed into this proposal as a result of the Covid-19 pandemic).

3. The Future of EMU Beyond the Tools of the Single Market

As we have seen so far, while there were essential elements of the EU's response to the euro area crisis that were not linked to the single market—the ECB's actions, the creation of mechanisms of financial assistance, the strengthening of budgetary discipline and economic surveillance—reliance on single market bases was an important part of the EU's response to the crisis, and of its longer-term attempt to strengthen EMU. Generally, the post-crisis years have shined a light on, first, the fact that the current Treaties are very limited when it comes to potential legal bases for further integration within EMU and, secondly, that even the use of single market bases in order to pursue integration that has both a single market and an EMU rationale is far from uncontentious. While there have been clear successes such as the partial adoption of the banking union, virtually every use of the single market legal bases in this area has been controversial and limited. And

[57] The revenue was to be shared between the EU (two-thirds) and the participating Member States (one-third).

[58] The UK challenged the legality of the Council Decision authorising the use of enhanced cooperation unsuccessfully (Case C-209/13 *UK v Council* ECLI:EU:C:2014:283). In September 2013, the Council Legal Service concluded in a leaked Opinion that certain aspects of the proposed FTT were illegal (these included the potential for distortions of competition, as well as the broad scope and extra-territorial impact of the tax); another leaked Opinion from the Commission's lawyers came to the opposite conclusion. For an overview of the objections, see Federico Fabbrini, 'Taxing and Spending in the Euro Zone: Legal and Political Challenges Relating to the Adoption of the Financial Transaction Tax' (2013) 39 European Law Review 155.

[59] In a 2014 Joint Statement, ten of the eleven countries admitted that 'complex issues have arisen' and that 'more technical work needs to be conducted', but that their 'commitment to the introduction of a financial transaction tax remains strong'. The tax will 'first focus on the taxation of shares and some derivatives': <www.economie.gouv.fr/files/declaration_des_ministres_des_etats_membres_-_6_mai_2014_version_anglaise.pdf> accessed 1 August 2022.

[60] For an overview of the timeline, see ECOFIN Report to the European Council on tax issues, 14863/19, Brussels 9 December 2019, 29–31.

when it comes to committing to a significant pooling of resources in the future—which is commonly taken to be a natural next step for EMU—the use of Article 114 TFEU seems, so far, out of the question, whether for strictly legal or political reasons. Overall, it is safe to assume that EMU cannot be completed through reliance on the legal bases of the single market. The latter have been invaluable when it comes to putting in place one building block of EMU, the financial union—including banking union and the project of capital markets union—but there is a consensus that EMU needs to add another essential building block: namely, fiscal union.

There have been numerous calls for Member States to share more risk and pool resources to a larger degree since the euro area crisis, in order to make EMU more resilient.[61] This would necessitate the creation of a meaningful fiscal capacity for the euro area, possible in a variety of forms. Yet for a long time this path seemed closed: as we have seen, the single market legal bases are of limited use here and, while there is an ongoing debate as to how much could still be achieved through creative use of current EMU legal bases (albeit that the political will has been lacking), it seems more likely that meaningful action in this area would require a broader debate and Treaty reform, however difficult. National constitutional courts—Germany's in particular—are more likely to be satisfied by the legitimacy of this process than by integration by stealth, to the extent that they may consider significant further integration in the area possible at all. For the longest time, fundamental disagreement on these questions has made further integration within EMU impossible. Does this mean that EMU cannot fully come of age, now that the limits of its own legal bases seem to have been reached (or close to it), and the single market ones cannot be easily co-opted for this part of the journey? As we shall see in the next section, that seemed the likely scenario until recently, but the Covid-19 pandemic and subsequent recovery measures may have lingering effects in this respect.

4. The Effects of Covid-19

The story thus far takes us up to 2020: while it was agreed that further integration within EMU was necessary, the limits of what could be done using EMU's own legal bases and those of the single market had been reached, to a large degree. European Monetary Union needed to make a big leap (towards the pooling of risk and resources) that seemed beyond reach; indeed, EMU could not 'come of age' without a very significant change in political attitudes that would either make Treaty reform possible or open up new ways to proceed.

[61] For a brief overview of the proposals and underlying disagreements, see Hinarejos, 'Economic and Monetary Union' (n 12).

In the midst of this, the Covid-19 pandemic had an unparalleled impact on citizens' lives, national health systems, and economies. It prompted responses such as the suspension of budgetary obligations for Member States—given the enormous spending involved in grappling with the crisis and recovering from it—and ECB measures to help Member States in their efforts.[62] But it also prompted an unprecedented effort to pool resources at the EU level to deal with the crisis collectively.

First, the European Instrument for temporary Support to mitigate Unemployment Risks in an Emergency (SURE) was created.[63] This is a fund from which Member States can obtain loans to deal with shocks to their employment market; it is funded from Member States' voluntary contributions. But far more significant—given its size and nature—was the adoption of Next Generation EU,[64] a recovery package that encompasses the creation of a very sizeable (€750 billion at 2018 prices) pot of money to help Member States rebuild their economy after the pandemic. This is to be funded through EU borrowing; the Commission was authorized to borrow money in the private markets in the EU's name. Slightly more than half of the money will be given to Member States as grants (ie without the need to pay back), the rest as loans. The EU will be responsible for paying back the money disbursed as grants, through its own budget, by 2058. In order to make this possible, it is foreseen that the EU will create new genuine own resources (eg through the creation of new taxes or levies). If this does not prove possible, Member States will have to step in and pay back the borrowed money through their own, much larger contributions to the EU budget. In terms of legal bases, two provisions carry a lot of the weight in the very complex recovery package: Article 122 TFEU, which allows for financial assistance to Member States under certain conditions,

[62] Communication from the Commission to the Council on the activation of the general escape clause of the Stability and Growth Pact, COM (2020) 123 of 20 March 2020. More broadly, the pandemic has lent much currency to the ongoing debate about the permanent reform of fiscal rules; see eg Paul Dermine, 'The EU's Response to the COVID-19 Crisis and the Trajectory of Fiscal Integration in Europe: Between Continuity and Rupture' (2020) 47 Legal Issues of Economic Integration 337. Finally, the ECB has put in place a series of measures that include the adoption of a Pandemic Emergency Purchase Programme (PEPP) to lower borrowing costs and increase lending in the euro area and a series of decisions to increase the funds that banks can borrow from it, as well as making the conditions to do so easier.

[63] Council Regulation (EU) 2020/672 on the establishment of a European instrument for temporary support to mitigate unemployment risks in an emergency (SURE) following the COVID-19 outbreak [2020] OJ L159/1.

[64] Council Regulation 2020/2094 establishing a European Union Recovery Instrument to support the recovery in the aftermath of the COVID-19 crisis [2020] OJ L433I/23; Council Decision (EU) 2020/2053 on the system of own resources of the European Union and repealing Decision 2014/335/EU, Euratom [2020] OJ L424/1; Regulation (EU) 2021/241 establishing the Recovery and Resilience Facility [2021] OJ L57/17. For details on the nature and significance of Next Generation EU, see Bruno de Witte, 'The European Union's COVID-19 Recovery Plan: The Legal Engineering of an Economic Policy Shift' (2021) 58 Common Market Law Review 635. For a rather critical appraisal, see Päivi Leino-Sandberg and Matthias Ruffert, 'Next Generation EU and its Constitutional Ramifications: A Critical Assessment' (2022) 59 Common Market Law Review 433. The legality of the recovery package was challenged unsuccessfully before the German Federal Constitutional Court: BVerfG, 2 BvR 547/21, 2 BvR 798/21, Judgment of 6 December 2022.

and Article 175 TFEU, allowing for specific actions on economic, social, and territorial cohesion, beyond the Funds created for these purposes.[65]

A detailed analysis of Next Generation EU is beyond the scope of this contribution. Suffice it to say that it is extremely significant because of its size and nature: this is a pooling of resources that is unprecedented among Member States in terms of its scale and workings. It is set to be both exceptional and temporary, but it is likely to have an effect in the debate on the creation of a more stable central fiscal capacity. First, because it may shift our perspective on pooling resources, making a central fiscal capacity seem acceptable—part of the status quo. And secondly, because the recovery package does entail an agreement and roadmap to create ways for the EU to raise new own resources. So far, a new national contribution to the budget tied to unrecycled plastic has already been embedded in the Own Resources Decision, but there is a commitment to create a wider variety of resources; the Eurogroup conclusions on Next Generation EU mentioned the potential return of the proposed Financial Transaction Tax, mentioned above. At the time of writing, the Commission has made a proposal for a variety of own resources,[66] with a view to proposing more in 2023 (which may, again, include the Financial Transaction Tax and an own resource linked to the corporate sector).[67] Needless to say, the creation of these avenues for the EU to raise own revenues will be fraught—the more so the more significant these new revenues are—but the Member States do have an incentive to negotiate and find common ground, if they do not want to be responsible for the EU's borrowing when the 2058 deadline rolls around.

What does this mean for our discussion about EMU and the single market? We concluded in the previous section that EMU needed to grow beyond the use of the tools of the single market as its main path towards further economic and fiscal integration. There is a clear link between the single market and EMU, and of course reliance on the single market legal bases will still be necessary to complete certain aspects of EMU. But this reliance is limited and stifling and, in those instances where the limits are pushed too far, it may lead to the discredit of the single market rationale and accusations of competence creep; Steve Weatherill referred to 'real constitutional risks' of the overuse of this powerful market clause.[68] Yet the idea

[65] For discussion of these legal bases, see de Witte (n 64) 652–59.

[66] In December 2021, the Commission proposed to allocate to the EU budget a portion of the revenues raised by a new carbon border control adjustment mechanism, by a reformed and extended Emissions Trading Scheme and, pending future agreement on details, by the adoption of Pillar One of the agreement on a reform of the international tax framework (OECD/G20 Inclusive Framework on Base Erosion and Profit Shifting (BEPS)), which would reallocate a share of the residual profits of the largest and most profitable multinational enterprises to EU Member States (Commission Proposal for a Council Decision amending Decision (EU, Euratom) 2020/2053 on the system of own resources of the European Union, COM (2021) 570 final).

[67] Communication from the Commission to the European Parliament, the Council, the European Economic and Social Council and the Committee of the Regions, 'The next generation of own resources for the EU Budget' COM (2021) 566 final, 5.

[68] Weatherill, *Law and Values in the European Union* (n 24) 41.

that significant integration within EMU would be possible through other means seemed unlikely before the pandemic, because we thought that we had gone as far as possible with the tools granted to EMU within the Treaties, because Treaty reform seemed impossible, or both.

The pandemic may have altered this landscape by giving EMU room to grow in ways that do not rely, at least exclusively or primarily, on the tools of the single market. It is plausible that Next Generation EU, even though it is a one-off, temporary arrangement, will have enduring effects on the nature and future of EMU by shifting our views on the EU as an entity with a significant fiscal capacity. If true, this would be an important legacy. More specific lasting effects may include the creation of a new range of EU own resources (so far not proposed to be adopted on single market legal bases, though this could change in the future)[69] and the revival of Article 175 TFEU, on economic, social, and territorial cohesion, as a viable legal basis for the adoption of macroeconomic tools and maintenance of a significant and stable fiscal capacity for the whole of the EU, beyond Next Generation EU.[70] In this respect, it was significant—though perhaps unsurprising—that a challenge to the legality of the recovery packaged failed before the German Federal Constitutional Court.[71] As always, any further developments will be subject to close judicial scrutiny.

5. Final Reflections

This chapter has provided an overview of the relationship between EMU and the single market legal bases. This relationship has changed over time, especially since the euro area crisis. The latter created a need to act quickly and decisively; at the same time, the Treaty limited what could be done on the basis of EMU provisions alone. The result is that important reforms were adopted on single market legal bases. In all instances, the use of these legal bases has been contentious and limited.

Broadly speaking, this use is justified from the point of view of the *Tobacco Advertising* test: these reforms, though necessary for the purposes of addressing

[69] The proposals for new resources put forward by the Commission at the time of writing (n 66) amount to an amendment of the Own Resources Decision, which would then eventually require implementation through secondary legislation: in the case of a new carbon border adjustment mechanism and the reform of the Emissions Trading Scheme, the natural legal basis would be art 192 TFEU on environmental policy. In the case of the creation of an own resources equivalent to 15 per cent of the share of the residual profits of multinationals that are reallocated to EU Member States under Pillar One of the agreement on a reform of the international tax framework (fn 66), the details remain to be clarified, thought they could include use of art 113 TFEU. The same goes for a potentially revived proposal for a Financial Transaction Tax, should it ever materialize.

[70] De Witte (n 64) 655–59. De Witte concludes that the use of art 175 TFEU to adopt part of the Next Generation EU package means that 'it now serves as the basis for EU macro-economic policy measures, eclipsing the modest legal resources offered by the economic policy chapter of EMU', ibid 680.

[71] BVerfG, 2 BvR 547/21, 2 BvR 798/21, Judgment of 6 December 2022.

the euro area crisis and strengthening EMU, also result in an improvement of the single market. But there has been reasonable disagreement on this question, as well as on others pertaining to the boundaries of Article 114 TFEU: the use of this provision for specific instances of delegation to supervisory agencies, or its potential use to impose substantial financial obligations on the Member States. There are also understandable concerns about the use of the single market legal bases to pursue the aims of a sub-group of Member States only, namely euro area countries, and what that might do to the unity of the single market. More generally, it is possible that this co-opting signals a shift to a different single market paradigm, one that is more centralized and uniform, in order to service economic policy.[72]

Overall, while the single market is inextricably linked to EMU, and the use of its legal bases has been and will continue to be an essential part of certain EMU reforms—especially those concerning banking union and the credit markets union, or the 'financial part' of EMU—this co-opting is necessarily limited and should be undertaken cautiously, lest it damage the legitimacy of both EMU and the single market. The fact is that the chapter of EMU reform that is lagging behind—fiscal union or the creation of a substantial central fiscal capacity for the EU or the euro area—cannot be a result of this co-opting and will eventually need a far more ambitious reform of the EMU provisions. Yet both this sharing of resources and this Treaty reform are extremely difficult political prospects, which for a long time made it unlikely that EMU would ever fully 'come of age'.

It is possible, however, that the Covid-19 pandemic will have an effect on this stalemate. The last section of this chapter has provided a brief overview of the fiscal capacity created to address the effects of the pandemic. This fiscal capacity is exceptional and temporary, but it may open the possibility of a more stable fiscal capacity in the future, whether through Treaty reform or through newly 'discovered' acrobatics akin to the ones that bring us Next Generation EU—albeit there is no question a Treaty reform that is the result of meaningful public debate and which encompasses the necessary reforms to ensure democratic legitimacy and accountability is preferable. Either way, single market legal bases may play a role in this building of a fiscal capacity (depending on what form the latter takes), but a necessarily limited one. Overall, this last stage of reform will unavoidably require that EMU be given its own tools, equal to the task. As this chapter has shown, the relationship between EMU and the single market has been close and fruitful, but also strained—and we cannot continue to rely on single market legal bases to the same degree when it comes to the last stage of EMU: fiscal union. Future reforms aimed at strengthening EMU and making it viable in the long term need to provide it with the necessary tools to 'come of age'.

[72] Snell (n 9) 347–51.

4

The Internal Market as a Dynamic Process: Five Scenarios for the Future

Jan Zglinski

1. Introduction

In hindsight, the biggest miscalculation of the Treaty of Rome may have been the ambition that the 'common market' could 'be progressively established during a transitional period of twelve years'.[1] The Member States of the then newly established European Economic Community agreed on a three-stage plan, which contained a list of specific actions that were to be taken. Once implemented, these actions would—or so it was believed—create an internal market between the participating countries. Yet, when the transitional period passed, that common market was far from being completed. Instead, 'the process of European integration was,' as Karen Alter put it, 'at a virtual standstill, and national barriers to trade were rampant.'[2] The European Commission made a similar 'error' a decade and a half later in its White Paper on 'Completing the Internal Market'.[3] Driven by a vision to revive the economic integration project, it proposed a bold set of policy measures that would remove the remaining physical, technical, and fiscal boundaries to trade in Europe. Again, there was a timetable and a promise to finalize the task of market integration—this time by 1992. And although a large share of the planned legislation was passed, with positive effects on trade and free movement, there could be no talk of having veritably completed the internal market.

Over time, the idea has gained traction that the EU internal market might never be accomplished, or not accomplished in the traditional sense of reaching a final destination. Scholars have argued that it should be viewed as a dynamic process, which can take different forms and shapes, each with their own legal, political, and economic consequences.[4] Steve Weatherill

[1] EC Treaty (Treaty of Rome, as amended) art 7(1).

[2] Karen J Alter, *Establishing the Supremacy of European Law* (Oxford University Press 2001) 212.

[3] Commission to the European Council, *Completing the Internal Market* (White Paper, COM (85) 310 final).

[4] Norbert Reich, 'Der Binnenmarkt als Rechtsbegriff' (1991) 7 Europäische Zeitschrift für Wirtschaftsrecht 203; Damian Chalmers, 'The Single Market: From Prima Donna to Journeyman' in Jo Shaw and Gillian More (eds), *New Legal Dynamics of European Union* (Clarendon Press 1995); Kamiel

Jan Zglinski, *The Internal Market as a Dynamic Process: Five Scenarios for the Future* In: *The Internal Market Ideal*.
Edited by: Jeremias Adams-Prassl, Sanja Bogojević, Ariel Ezrachi, and Dorota Leczykiewicz, Oxford University Press.
 DOI: 10.1093/oso/9780192867063.003.0005

forcefully articulated this position in *The Internal Market as a Legal Concept*:[5]

> The internal market is not 'complete' in any absolute sense. However, it is not just the economics that are incomplete, dynamic and ambiguous. The internal market as a legal concept is incomplete, dynamic and ambiguous too.

The European political process appears, if slowly, to warm up to such an understanding of market integration. A Commission report from 2007 underlines that '[t]he single market is dynamic, constantly evolving and adapting to new realities. As such it will never be "finalised" or "complete".'[6]

This chapter seeks to explore this idea. It proposes a reading of the internal market as a dynamic construct which is subject to periodic changes and developments, and examines the evolution which the internal market has undergone and might still undergo. Three issues will be addressed. The chapter will start with an overview of the internal market's structure, focusing on the institutional actors involved in its creation and maintenance, the governance tools employed for market integration, and the conceptual models underlying them. This will be followed by a short history of how these structural features have developed since the 1950s. The main focus will, then, be on the question of what lies ahead: if the internal market is dynamic indeed, in which direction can we expect it to go in the future? Five possible scenarios will be outlined. They will be used to argue that it may no longer be useful to think about how to 'complete' the internal market, but rather what type of internal market we want for Europe.

2. The Structure of the Internal Market: Actors, Tools, Models

The internal market is firmly anchored in the EU's constitutional materials. Article 26 of the Treaty on the Functioning of the European Union (TFEU) tasks the Union with 'establishing or ensuring the functioning of the internal market', defining it as 'an area without internal frontiers in which the free movement of goods, persons, services and capital is ensured'. In similar terms, Article 3(3) of the Treaty on

Mortelmans, 'The Common Market, the Internal Market and the Single Market, What's in a Market?' (1998) 35 Common Market Law Review 101. More recently, see Inga Govaere, 'Internal Market Dynamics: On Moving Targets, Shifting Contextual Factors and the Untapped Potential of Article 3(3) TEU' in Sacha Garben and Inga Govaere (eds), *The Internal Market 2.0* (Hart 2020).

[5] Stephen Weatherill, *The Internal Market as a Legal Concept* (Oxford University Press 2017) 28.

[6] Commission, 'A Single Market for Citizens' (Communication) COM (2007) 60 final, 3. Similarly, see already in the 2002 *Internal Market Scoreboard*: 'The Internal Market will never be "completed". The effort to maximise its performance is a process, not an event' (Internal Market Scoreboard No 11, November 2022).

European Union (TEU) states that an internal market shall be created and that it ought to contribute to a number of broader policy objectives, ranging from economic growth and price stability, to social progress and full employment, to environmental protection and technological advancement. Despite these stipulations, much of the actual content of the internal market is left open. The Treaties do not specify how exactly the powers between the EU and the Member States are divided, what the relationship between the judicial and political branches should look like, which regulatory standards ought to be adopted, or even what some key concepts—such as free movement—mean. Steve has called the result a 'zone of constitutional and institutional ambiguity'.[7] This ambiguity leaves a wide margin of discretion when it comes to operationalizing the internal market. In the context of how this discretion is used—and what exact shape the internal market ends up taking—three things are important: the actors, tools, and models of market integration.

A variety of actors are involved in the making and administering of the internal market. At the EU level, we have several institutions fulfilling different functions. The Court of Justice adjudicates on disputes concerning (primarily) Member State and (occasionally) EU compliance with the Treaties and secondary legislation. The Commission plays the dual role of legislative engine and main public enforcer of internal market law.[8] The Council and Parliament complement the legislative process, which is supported by various standardization bodies. But market governance is not just done centrally in Europe; Member State institutions play an important role, too. National courts and administrative bodies are required to apply EU rules. National governments and parliaments are expected to remove trade barriers, implement internal market legislation, and even have positive dutics vis-à-vis the Union and other Member States. Finally, we have millions of producers, traders, service providers, and other economic actors who operate across the continent. Although not a formal part of the internal market's governance structure, they play a central role within it as key beneficiaries of the actions taken and private enforcers of the applicable rules.

These actors make use of, or respond to, different tools of market integration. Two main types are typically distinguished in the literature: negative and positive integration.[9] Negative integration denotes the removal of obstacles to trade at the Member State level. The four freedoms are its most important manifestation. These constitute individual rights which can be invoked before EU and national courts against

[7] Weatherill, *The Internal Market* (n 5) 223.

[8] Member States can also enforce internal market rules by means of infringement proceedings, but this option has only rarely been made use of in the past. For a prominent recent example, see Case C-591/17 *Austria v Germany (Infrastructure charge for passenger vehicles)* ECLI:EU:C:2019:504.

[9] This distinction goes back to Jan Tinbergen, *International Economic Integration* (2nd edn, Elsevier 1965). It has gained prominence through the work of Fritz Scharpf: see 'Negative and Positive Integration in the Political Economy of European Welfare States' in Gary Marks and others (eds), *Governance in the European Union* (SAGE 1996) and *Governing in Europe: Effective and Democratic?* (Oxford University Press 1999).

restrictions on the free movement of goods, persons, services, and capital. Positive integration describes the adoption of common European rules through the legislative process. This can be done to harmonize sectors that were previously governed by divergent national rules, and therefore made cross-border trade difficult, or to regulate areas in which Member States had not yet become active. The EU can rely on a number of competence norms for this purpose, including provisions specifically tailored to certain economic sectors (eg agriculture and transport) or policy objectives (eg consumer and environmental protection), as well as to more general legal bases for internal market legislation, the most important being Article 114 TFEU.

Depending on which actors choose to become involved and which tools they decide to employ (and how), the nature of European market integration changes. Maduro has shown that three basic models can be envisaged for the internal market: centralized, competitive, and decentralized.[10] These models do not just embody different approaches to market integration; each comes with distinct constitutional, institutional, and regulatory implications. The centralized model rests on harmonization, which aims at creating uniform rules for all Member States. This puts the emphasis on the EU political process and positive integration. The competitive model protects the autonomy of Member States to adopt their own regulatory standards, while ensuring that each national standard is accepted in other Member States through the principle of (conditional) mutual recognition. This leaves the primary responsibility for economic regulation with the domestic political processes but promotes negative integration through judicial enforcement of the EU free movement and competition rules. Under the decentralized model, Member States also retain the competence to regulate the internal market which is only restricted by the principle of non-discrimination. The result is even greater freedom for national lawmakers and a more confined role for the judiciary.

3. The Evolution of the Internal Market: Law and Policy

None of these features are static: an internal market evolves over time.[11] The US market, which is frequently used as a source of comparison by scholars of

[10] Miguel Poiares Maduro, *We the Court: The European Court of Justice and the European Economic Constitution: A Critical Reading of Article 30 of the EC Treaty* (Hart 1998) 103. Kenneth Armstrong and Jukka Snell draw a similar distinction, but speak of harmonization, home country control, and host country control: see Kenneth Armstrong, 'Mutual Recognition' in Catherine Barnard and Joanne Scott (eds), *The Law of the Single European Market* (Hart 2002); Jukka Snell, 'The Internal Market and the Philosophies of Market Integration' in Catherine Barnard and Steve Peers (eds), *European Union Law* (3rd edn, Oxford University Press 2020) 334. See also Robert Schütze, *From International to Federal Market: The Changing Structure of European Law* (Oxford University Press 2017), who differentiates between a national, federal, and international model, but focuses only on the CJEU and its free movement case law.

[11] For an early articulation of this idea, see Andrew McGee and Stephen Weatherill, 'The Evolution of the Single Market—Harmonisation or Liberalisation' (1990) 53 Modern Law Review 578.

European integration, is an illustrative example. It has experienced periods of decentralization and centralization, regulatory interventionism and economic liberalism, judicial activism and restraint.[12] Similarly, the EU internal market has gone through different phases, or perhaps more precisely, its component parts have.[13] This can be seen in the way in which the law and policies governing it have developed over time.

Let us begin with primary internal market law, as notably embodied in the Court of Justice's case law on free movement. The four freedoms played only a limited role during the first decade and a half of the internal market project. This had partly to do with the transitional period that had been mandated in the Treaty of Rome, which lasted until the end of 1969, and partly with the Court's choice to interpret free movement rights in a traditional, relatively narrow way as prohibitions of discrimination. Things changed in the mid-1970s. In a series of rulings, the Court broadened the scope of the free movement provisions and intensified its scrutiny of Member State regulation. The free movement of goods spearheaded this development. In *Dassonville* (1974), the Court accepted that any national law fell within the scope of Article 34 TFEU if it was 'capable of hindering, directly or indirectly, actually or potentially, intra-[EU] trade'.[14] In *Cassis de Dijon* (1979), it found that the same was true of non-discriminatory product requirements, thus giving birth to what would become known as the principle of mutual recognition.[15] Both the Commission and traders immediately grasped the potential of the two rulings and began to challenge, often successfully, a growing number of domestic regulatory obstacles.[16]

This expansionist logic was transposed to the other free movement rights in the 1990s. One by one, the Court broadened the scope of the free movement of services and workers, and the right to establishment;[17] a little later, free movement of capital followed suit.[18] In line with the spirit of *Dassonville*, it ruled that any Member State measure which was likely to 'impede' free movement, render its exercise 'less attractive', or 'directly affect' market access constituted a prima facie violation of EU law. Around the same time, in an almost contrapuntal movement, the Court

[12] Michelle P Egan, *Single Markets: Economic Integration in European and the United States* (Oxford University Press 2015).

[13] Weatherill speaks of 'The Several Internal Markets' (2017) 36 Yearbook of European Law 125.

[14] Case 8/74 *Procureur du Roi v Benoît and Gustave Dassonville* ECLI:EU:C:1974:82 (*Dassonville*). For an alternative reading of the ruling, see Robert Schütze, 'Re-Reading Dassonville: Meaning and Understanding in the History of European Law' (2018) 24 European Law Journal 376.

[15] Case 120/78 *Rewe-Zentral AG v Bundesmonopolverwaltung für Branntwein* ('*Cassis de Dijon*') ECLI:EU:C:1979:42 (*Cassis de Dijon*).

[16] Karen J Alter and Sophie Meunier-Aitsahalia, 'Judicial Politics in the European Community: European Integration and the Pathbreaking Cassis de Dijon Decision' (1994) 26 Comparative Political Studies 535.

[17] Case C–267/91 *Keck and Mithouard* ECLI:EU:C:1993:905.

[18] Case C–76/90 *Säger v Dennemeyer & Co* ECLI:EU:C:1991:331; Case C–19/92 *Kraus v Land Baden-Württemberg* ECLI:EU:C:1993:125; Case C–55/94 *Gebhard v Consiglio dell'Ordine degli Avvocati e Procurati di Milano* ECLI:EU:C:1995:411.

decided to adjust the scope of the free movement of goods. To counter the excessive use of its jurisprudence as a weapon against any form of economic regulation, including laws with little to no impact on trade, it made one of its more dramatic jurisprudential U-turns in *Keck* and *Mithouard* (1993), ruling that 'selling arrangements' would no longer be caught by the free movement of goods, as long as they did not discriminate against foreign products or traders. This cautious phase did not last, though. Some fifteen years later, the scope of Article 34 TFEU was widened again in *Italian Trailers* (2009) when measures constituting obstacles to 'market access' were introduced as a new, self-standing category of trade barriers.[19]

Just like primary law, secondary law on the internal market has also evolved. The most visible sign of this is its growth into ever-wider economic sectors. In the early days of the European Economic Community, legislative and administrative activity was largely concentrated on a few core areas of the internal market. This notably included measures aimed at implementing the customs union and regulating the agricultural and heavy industries.[20] The situation gradually began to change in the second half of the 1970s, when issues like equal pay, company law, and value added tax began to be covered by harmonization. However, the true impetus for legislative progress came from the 1985 White Paper. Making use of the renewed political enthusiasm for European integration, the Commission decided to fix some outstanding problems (eg concerning national border controls and phytosanitary inspections) but also ventured into new fields such as consumer rights, financial services, and merger control. This was the start of a more high-profile role for the EU legislature with regard to market governance. The story of internal market legislation has, since then, been one of continuous expansion. Notable milestones include the partial liberalization of the network industries in the 1990s, the steps taken towards establishing a banking union in the wake of the euro crisis, and, most recently, the proposed adoption of the Digital Services and Market Acts.

But it is not solely the scope of EU legislation that has changed; the EU's approach to legislating has changed as well. Initially, the European lawmakers sought to harmonize products and sectors by means of adopting detailed regulatory standards. It quickly became evident that this was exceedingly time-consuming and rendered political agreement difficult, especially in times of unanimity requirements and widespread Euroscepticism. In consequence, the traditional approach was replaced by the 'new approach' in the mid-1980s.[21] The EU would henceforth primarily focus on laying down essential safety requirements for products. The nitty-gritty work of setting out technical specifications would be left to European

[19] Case C-110/05 *Commission v Italy* ECLI:EU:C:2009:66 ('*Italian Trailers*').

[20] There were ambitious legislative initiatives outside these core areas, eg regarding the free movement of workers (notably Regulations 1612/68 and 1408/71), but they were few and far between.

[21] Jacques Pelkmans, 'The New Approach to Technical Harmonization and Standardization' (1987) 25 Journal of Common Market Studies 249.

standardization bodies, while free movement in non-harmonized areas would be achieved through the application of the principle of mutual recognition. (In spite of this, legislation based on the traditional approach has not disappeared.) The system, in so far as it applies to goods, underwent another revision in 2008, which resulted in what is called the 'New Legislative Framework'.[22] Among the cornerstones of this framework are rules on accreditation, market surveillance, and conformity assessments. The reforms are driven partly by the need to solve some of the problems that had arisen from the new approach and partly by the desire to promote more efficient market management.

Other, more subtle, developments have also taken place in EU legislative practice. The Union originally relied predominantly on directives, which stipulate a result but leave the decision as to how it is to be achieved to the Member States, as the tool of choice for harmonization. Since the 2000s, it appears to favour regulations, which lay down rules that are binding and directly applicable across Europe, a more centralized form of lawmaking.[23] Similarly, there have been periods in which minimum harmonization (EU rules set mandatory base standards but Member States can adopt more protective requirements) was en vogue and phases in which maximum harmonization (no deviation from EU rules is possible) had the upper hand. The difference between the early measures on consumer rights, such as the Unfair Terms Directive,[24] and more recent ones, such as the Consumer Rights Directive,[25] illustrates this. Finally, traditional 'hard' governance tools like harmonization were complemented with newer 'softer' forms of governance.[26] The EU imposed obligations on Member States to notify the Commission of drafts of legislative projects that might affect trade, created structures enabling administrative cooperation between national authorities, initiated the building of single contact points for foreign economic operators, and established alternative dispute resolution mechanisms for traders and citizens.

These changes—in law and policy—show that evolution has been a constant feature of the life of the internal market. The internal market of the transitional period bears little resemblance to that of the late 1970s which, in turn, significantly differs from that of the early 1990s or today. This is not just in the more practical sense that progress was made in relation to reducing obstacles to free movement and increasing levels of intra-EU trade. There have been significant developments

[22] Council Regulation (EC) 765/2008 setting out the requirements for accreditation and market surveillance relating to the marketing of products [2008] OJ L218/30 and Council Decision 768/2008 on a common framework for the marketing of products [2008] OJ L218/82.

[23] Mario Monti, 'A New Strategy for the Single Market: At the Service of Europe's Economy and Society' (2010) (Monti Report); Jacques Pelkmans, 'What Strategy for a Genuine Single Market?' (2016) CEPS Special Report No 126, 22.

[24] Council Directive 93/13 on unfair terms in consumer contracts [1993] OJ L95/29.

[25] Council Directive 2011/83 on consumer rights [2011] OJ L304/64.

[26] Vassilis Hatzopoulos, 'From Hard to Soft: Governance in the EU Internal Market' (2013) 15 Cambridge Yearbook of European Legal Studies 101.

in the way the internal market has been governed, which have affected its nature and shape.

Institutionally, different actors took the lead at different points in time. The early days were marked by ambitious, if ultimately unsuccessful, efforts of the EU political process to push forward the economic integration agenda, which ended up giving Member States more regulatory autonomy than had been anticipated and desired in the Treaty of Rome. After its first set of activist rulings on the free movement of goods, the Court of Justice became the main driver of market building. The EU political process took up the baton once again in the years leading up to and following 1992, this time with greater success and impact. These shifts have had a bearing on the forms of market governance. Positive integration made way for negative integration, before gradually regaining its role as the predominant method for advancing the internal market (even within these broader movements, smaller but relevant changes occurred, including with regard to legislative techniques, doctrinal principles, and areas of regulatory interest). All of which ended up affecting the type of market integration pursued and achieved. A largely decentralized internal market started leaning towards a competitive and, eventually, a more centralized model.

4. The Road Ahead: Five Scenarios

The foregoing section shows that change has been a constant feature of the internal market's past. It is tempting to contemplate whether the same will be true of its future and, if so, what this future will hold. Where is the internal market headed? Will it continue to evolve? Or have we perhaps reached the 'end of history'? This section gazes into the crystal ball. It discusses the different ways in which the internal market could develop going forward, their respective benefits and drawbacks, as well as the implications they would have for European integration. Five scenarios will be outlined. They constitute simplified ideal types, each revolving around one main theme that would take centre stage in internal market governance. As will become apparent, some of these options are mutually exclusive, while others could potentially co-exist.

There is an inevitable degree of speculation when trying to predict the shape of things to come. If this is true in relation to most things in life, it is even more so in relation to complex phenomena like European integration. Much of what is outlined below depends on a variety of factors, ranging from the political preferences of the Member States, to citizens' attitudes toward Europe, to the behaviour of different EU institutions. What, in hindsight, may look like a strategic choice may, in fact, be the result of the interaction of these manifold, often competing processes. Nonetheless, thinking about some of the options that could materialize, as well as under which conditions they may materialize and what effects they would exert, helps us understand what might lie ahead of us.

4.1 More Negative Integration

The first and—for students of its history—perhaps most obvious path forward for the internal market would be a renewed and strengthened emphasis on negative integration. Given that European economic integration started more seriously only after and, to an important extent, as a result of the CJEU's activist jurisprudence on free movement law, it may appear consequential to envision the internal market's future being best served by a more aggressive application of the four freedoms.

Could free movement rights, which have been given quite an expansive interpretation by the Court already, be applied in an even stricter way? In theory, they could. This might take different forms. One option would be to widen their scope of application. For the free movement of goods, this could entail abolishing the Keck exception and going back to subjecting all national rules that affect cross-border sales to judicial review.[27] For the free movement of persons and services, it could mean renouncing the *de minimis* jurisprudence, which exempts Member State acts that have 'too indirect or uncertain' or otherwise minimal effects on trade from scrutiny.[28] Another option would be to increase the standard of review. The CJEU applies different intensities of review when examining the justification and proportionality of Member State acts, ranging from light touch to strict scrutiny.[29] Intensifying its scrutiny in areas which are currently marked by a deferential approach, such as public health and public policy, would boost the penetrating power of free movement law.

Yet another way of strengthening negative integration would be to limit the possibilities for justifying trade barriers. The UK, no longer part of the EU internal market, has demonstrated how this could be achieved. To regulate trade between its four nations (England, Northern Ireland, Scotland, and Wales) post-Brexit, the UK adopted the Internal Market Act.[30] The Act, in many ways, resembles EU free movement law by drawing on principles like mutual recognition and non-discrimination, and even incorporates some of the finer details from the Court's case law, such as the distinction between discriminatory and non-discriminatory selling arrangements. But there are some crucial differences, the most significant being that the principle of mutual recognition which it establishes is not of

[27] There has been some controversy around whether *Keck*, in fact, has not already been overruled as a result of *Italian Trailers*. Case C-198/14 *Valev Visnapuu v Kihlakunnansyyttäjä (Helsinki)* ECLI:EU:C:2015:751, para 104 and Case C-148/15 *Deutsche Parkinson Vereinigung v Zentrale zur Bekämpfung unlauteren Wettbewerbs* ECLI:EU:C:2016:394, Opinion of AG Szpunar, paras 20ff suggest that the answer is in the negative.

[28] Max S Jansson and Harri Kalimo, '*De Minimis* Meets "Market Access": Transformations in the Substance—and the Syntax—of EU Free Movement Law?' (2014) 51 Common Market Law Review 523.

[29] See, in greater detail, Jan Zglinski, *Europe's Passive Virtues: Deference to National Authorities in EU Free Movement Law* (Oxford University Press 2020).

[30] United Kingdom Internal Market Act 2020.

a conditional but rather a (quasi-)absolute nature.[31] Unlike under European law, there is no possibility of justifying limitations of mutual recognition based on one of the many policy reasons that are listed in Article 36 TFEU or recognized as 'mandatory requirements'. The Act lays down an extremely narrow set of 'exclusions' which are largely limited to measures aimed at preventing the movement of diseases and unsafe food. Consequently, the constituent countries of the UK cannot, in principle, stop goods and services lawfully produced or authorized in other parts of Britain.

Either of the above changes would create the potential for removing a greater number of national trade barriers (and, in addition, general regulatory measures that impede economic freedom).[32] For this potential to be realized, private litigants and/or the Commission would have to take the bait and begin challenging more Member State laws, which would then end up being struck down in proceedings before the CJEU or national courts. The ensuing deregulatory effect would facilitate trade. It could, as in the mid-1970s, deepen market integration through the judicial route.

There are several problems with this scenario, the first of which is practical: how to effect the necessary changes? The jurisprudential *acquis* on (primary) free movement law is notoriously hard to modify.[33] One either needs to push for Treaty amendments or wait for the CJEU to have a change of heart. Both are unlikely. The free movement rules have not, in substance, been touched since the Treaty of Rome and there is no indication that there is or will be a greater appetite for tinkering with them any time soon. The Court of Justice's case law in this area does not seem to go in the direction of greater activism and interventionism, but instead in the direction of deference and self-restraint. Two symptoms of this were already mentioned. The Court has narrowed the scope of the free movement of goods in *Keck*; although it was subsequently re-expanded in *Italian Trailers*, the effects of this line of jurisprudence have, so far, remained largely theoretical. Through remoteness and (in)significance tests, the idea of *de minimis* has entered free movement law. In addition, the Court is granting Member State authorities an ever-wider margin of appreciation in relation to substantive regulatory choices.[34] This trend would have to be reversed for greater negative integration to be achieved.

[31] Stephen Weatherill, 'Comparative Internal Market Law: The UK and the EU' (2021) 40 Yearbook of European Law 431; Kenneth A Armstrong, 'The Governance of Economic Unionism after the United Kingdom Internal Market Act' (2021) 85 Modern Law Review 635.

[32] For a critical analysis of the effects of this strategy in the UK, see Michael Dougan and others, 'Sleeping with an Elephant: Devolution and the United Kingdom Internal Market Act 2020' (2022) 138 Law Quarterly Review 650; Jan Zglinski; 'The UK Internal Market: A Global Outlier?' (2023) 82 Cambridge Law Journal (online first).

[33] Martin Höpner and Susanne K Schmidt, 'Can We Make the European Fundamental Freedoms Less Constraining? A Literature Review' (2020) 22 Cambridge Yearbook of European Legal Studies 182.

[34] Jan Zglinski, 'The Rise of Deference: The Margin of Appreciation and Decentralized Judicial Review in EU Free Movement Law' (2018) 55 Common Market Law Review 1341; cf Catherine Barnard,

More importantly, it is unclear whether an expansion of free movement rights, even if it materialized, would have the desired effect of advancing market integration to a meaningful extent. Although, historically, case law has proven to be a powerful method for kickstarting market integration, it is not an effective tool for market governance in the long term. Disputes are resolved on a case-by-case basis, making it hard to impose a coherent regulatory vision. Also, the idea of achieving further negative integration relies on a steady stream of litigation, which might not come. The evolution of the free movement of goods illustrates this. As explained, the Court of Justice's case law on Article 34 TFEU has gone through different periods, from the expansionist phase following *Dassonville* and *Cassis*, to a more cautious phase after *Keck*, to renewed expansionism post-*Italian Trailers*.[35] The early activist rulings, indeed, provided stimuli for litigants to bring legal action against domestic regulation, a dynamic that led to a swift and significant removal of trade barriers in Europe.[36] By contrast, the more recent broadening of the scope of Article 34 TFEU in *Italian Trailers* had no comparable impact. Not only was there no uptick in case numbers before the Court, but in fact, goods litigation appears to have decreased, and quite considerably so.[37] Part of the reason for this might be that it was not sufficiently clear to traders what they gained from the new 'market access' formula.[38] But other, more structural factors are likely to play a role as well: Member States have improved their compliance with EU law over the past decades; the Commission's priorities have shifted to areas outside free movement; and there has been an increase in internal market legislation, which reduces the number of non-harmonized sectors and prevents disputes by clarifying the rights and duties of economic actors.[39] All of this, combined with the inherent uncertainties connected with bringing legal action, means that free movement litigation is not as appealing as it used to be. And without litigation (further) negative integration is hard to achieve.[40]

'Derogations, Justifications and the Four Freedoms: Is State Interest Really Protected?' in Catherine Barnard and Okeoghene Odudu (eds), *The Outer Limits of European Union Law* (Hart 2009).

[35] Robert Schütze, '"Re-constituting" the Internal Market: Towards a Common Law of International Trade?' (2021) 29 Yearbook of European Law 250.

[36] Alec Stone Sweet, *The Judicial Construction of Europe* (Oxford University Press 2004).

[37] Jan Zglinski, 'The End of Negative Market Integration: 60 Years of Free Movement of Goods Litigation (1961–2020)' (2023) Journal of European Public Policy. There might have been an increase in goods litigation before national courts, although there is so far no evidence—systematic or anecdotal—to support this claim.

[38] Jukka Snell, 'The Notion of Market Access: A Concept or a Slogan?' (2010) 47 Common Market Law Review 437; Gareth Davies, 'Understanding Market Access: Exploring the Economic Rationality of Different Conceptions of Free Movement Law' (2010) 11 German Law Journal 671.

[39] Zglinski, *Europe's Passive Virtues* (n 29).

[40] I say 'hard' instead of 'impossible' as free movement law can also influence Member State action by exerting what has been called a 'shadow effect' (see n 42). This effect is, however, unlikely to materialize without a critical mass of litigation, as the content of any new, more stringent interpretation of the four freedoms would first have to be clarified by the Court and the threat 'from the shadows' would need to be made credible by creating a real risk for national regulation to be overturned judicially.

However, the most serious problem with a revived focus on negative integration would arguably lie elsewhere: it would contribute to a further judicialization of the internal market which is, as many critics argue, already over-judicialized and over-constitutionalized (more on this in a second).[41] This would most visibly affect Member States, whose regulatory autonomy would be constrained to an even greater degree than is currently the case. More national laws would be subjected to judicial review; fewer of them would pass free movement muster. But it would also have a knock-on effect on the EU legislative process. Schmidt has shown that CJEU rulings have a 'shadow effect' on European law-making.[42] They impact on both the content of legislation (by creating rules that influence the substance of secondary measures) and its adoption (by affecting the bargaining conditions in the legislative process).[43] In this way, a more aggressive deployment of free movement rights would be likely to restrict the autonomy of the EU legislature, too.

4.2 Less Negative Integration

Against this backdrop, another way forward for the EU internal market could lie in doing the polar opposite: curbing negative integration. This would entail limiting the role of (primary) free movement law and, relatedly, of the Court of Justice in market regulation. There are several ways in which this objective could be achieved, but two proposals have gained momentum in the literature.[44] The first involves a re-interpretation of the four freedoms. Instead of applying to most, or as some would argue, virtually all restrictions on cross-border trade and economic activity, their scope could be narrowed down to a principle of non-discrimination.[45] The second proposal goes further and involves their de-constitutionalization. The formal status of the four freedoms within the legal hierarchy of European law would be 'downgraded' from primary to secondary law, meaning that they would no longer occupy the elevated position of constitutional

[41] See literature below n 46.

[42] Susanne K Schmidt, *The European Court of Justice and the Policy Process: The Shadow of Case Law* (Oxford University Press 2018). See also Tommaso Pavone and Øyvind Stiansen, 'The Shadow Effect of Courts: Judicial Review and the Politics of Preemptive Reform' (2021) 116 American Political Science Review 322.

[43] See also Fritz Scharpf, 'The Asymmetry of European Integration, or Why the EU Cannot Be a "Social Market Economy"' (2010) 8 Socio-Economic Review 211; Sacha Garben, 'The Constitutional (Im)balance between "the Market" and "the Social" in the European Union' (2017) 13 European Constitutional Law Review 23, 42. More critically, see Sorte Sindbjerg Martinsen, *An Ever More Powerful Court?* (Oxford University Press 2015).

[44] For an overview and discussion of others reform proposals, see Höpner and Schmidt (n 33).

[45] Alexander Somek, 'The Argument from Transnational Effects I: Representing Outsiders Through Freedom of Movement' (2010) 16 European Law Journal 315; Sacha Garben, 'The "Fundamental Freedoms" and (Other) Fundamental Rights: Towards an Integrated Democratic Interpretation Framework' in Garben and Govaere, *The Internal Market 2.0* (n 4).

provisions but be on a par with ordinary legislation and, as such, open to the influence of ordinary politics.[46]

These suggestions might feel counterintuitive at first: how would curtailing free movement rights help advance the internal market? Answering this question requires an understanding of the ideational origins of these proposals. They do not come from a dissatisfaction with insufficient levels of trade between the Member States or a longing for greater economic freedom in Europe. Au contraire, they are rooted in a critique of the status quo which holds that the EU internal market in general, and the Court of Justice's free movement case law specifically, have gone too far, unduly prioritizing deregulation over regulation, and economic interests over democratic and social concerns.[47] In other words, the proposals do not aim at advancing the internal market in the traditional sense of 'more trade, closer economic integration'. They seek to create a more democratic, socially responsive, and, ultimately, legitimate internal market,[48] even if this should come at some economic cost in the form of reducing cross-border exchanges.

Though the details of the two reform proposals vary, the primary consequence of both would be a de-judicialization of the internal market.[49] Limiting the reach of the free movement rights would mean that a smaller share of Member State legislation falls within the scope of EU law and, thus, runs the risk of being overturned by the CJEU or national courts. By the same token, it would send a signal to producers and traders that litigating is less promising as chances of winning have decreased, reducing the number of legal challenges.[50] The main beneficiaries would be domestic political processes. Member States would regain some regulatory autonomy which—so the advocates of this solution hope—would lead to the adoption of higher social standards (which would no longer constitute prima facie breaches of free movement law) and facilitate self-determination through democratic means. There might also be some gains for the EU political process. As noted above, it has been shown that the Court's case law has a significant impact on EU legislation, both by creating a default, fallback option that can be difficult to deviate from and, perhaps more significantly, by influencing the substantive content of European

[46] Dieter Grimm, 'The Democratic Costs of Constitutionalization—The European Case' (2015) 21 European Law Journal 460; Gareth Davies, 'The European Union Legislature as an Agent of the European Court of Justice' (2016) 54 Journal of Common Market Studies 846; Fritz Scharpf, 'De-constitutionalisation of European Law: The Re-empowerment of Democratic Political Choice' in Sacha Garben and Inge Govaere (eds), *The Division of Competences between the EU and the Member States: Reflections on the Past, the Present and the Future* (Hart 2017).

[47] Diamond Ashiagbor, 'Unravelling the Embedded Liberal Bargain: Labour and Social Welfare Law in the Context of EU Market Integration' (2013) 13 European Law Journal 303.

[48] See Jotte Mulder, *Social Legitimacy in the Internal Market* (Hart 2018).

[49] It is widely accepted that the strong judicialization of the EU internal market is an anomaly in comparison with other internal markets across the world. This even goes for the US, which has a notoriously judicialized constitutional and political order; see Egan, *Single Markets* (n 12).

[50] In the US context, see Neil K Komesar, *Imperfect Alternatives* (University of Chicago Press 1997); Andrew Coan, *Rationing the Constitution* (Harvard University Press 2019).

rules.[51] Restricting the case law might free up space for political decision-making and increase the de facto autonomy of the EU legislature.

A de-constitutionalization of the free movement rights would have a similar effect, which would, however, materialize in a slightly different way. The change would not affect the substantive scope of the four freedoms, or at least not necessarily;[52] it would instead simply concern their place in the hierarchy of norms. Currently, free movement rights operate, functionally, as constitutional rights in the EU legal order. As a consequence, the Court's case law in this area is also constitutionally entrenched and, as such, hard to amend and protected from genuine political contestation. If free movement rights were de-constitutionalized, this would change. Contentious CJEU rulings could be modified, or even overturned, through the European political process by means of secondary legislation.[53] This would create room for democratic debate at the EU level. The higher probability of correction could, in turn, have an impact on the case law of the Court, which might render more cautious rulings in order to reduce the potential of conflict.[54] The result would be greater decision-making autonomy for EU and Member States legislatures and, so the hope goes, a shift from deregulation towards (re-) regulation.

There are, hence, weighty arguments in favour of limiting negative integration, yet there are likewise weighty arguments against it. Leaving aside the practical hurdles connected to changing the case law or the Treaties (the resistance to which is likely to be even higher than in the case of expanding the reach of the free movement rights), the main danger would be that the internal market reverts back to the unenviable state in which it found itself in the early 1970s. Especially the re-interpretation of free movement law as a mere prohibition of discrimination would roll back a substantial part of the jurisprudential *acquis*. This would, on the one hand, have the desired effect of preventing contentious, extreme rulings like *Viking* and *Laval*.[55] On the other hand, however, it would equally lead to a scrapping of some landmark cases like *Cassis de Dijon*. Member States would, in all likelihood, use the regulatory space so created to adopt new—or reinstate old—restrictions on trade. This would create significant potential for protectionism. Against this backdrop, less drastic changes to the status quo might be a more promising avenue, such as increasing the level of judicial deference granted to national authorities through

[51] Schmidt (n 42); Scharpf, 'Negative and Positive Integration' (n 9).

[52] Scharpf, 'De-constitutionalisation of European Law' (n 46) has connected his proposal for de-constitutionalizing free movement law with a call for restricting the scope of the four freedoms.

[53] See Martinsen (n 43). It bears noting that this may *de facto* already be possible due to the 'Legislative Priority Rule'; see Eadaoin Ní Chaoimh, *The Legislative Priority Rule and the EU Internal Market for Goods* (Oxford University Press 2022).

[54] Höpner and Schmidt (n 33) 196.

[55] Case C-438/05 *The International Transport Workers' Federation and Finnish Seamen's Union v Viking Line* ECLI:EU:C:2007:772 (*Viking Line*); Case C-341/05 *Laval v Svenska Byggnadsarbetareförbundet* ECLI:EU:C:2007:809 (*Laval*).

doctrines like the margin of appreciation.[56] This would allow keeping the foundational principles on which the internal market rests, while limiting some of the excesses of negative integration and returning agency to the domestic and European political processes.

4.3 More Positive Integration

A third way forward, which could be combined with restricting the role of negative integration, would be a shift towards greater positive integration. This option would involve expanding the reach and force of EU harmonization. The result would be an increase in power for the European legislative process. Further market integration would be brought about through the political route.

There are manifold ways in which this could be done, but the main strategy would inevitably have to revolve around extending EU harmonization to a wider range of economic sectors. Though the number of harmonized areas has significantly risen over time, there is still room for growth. This goes both for fields in which we already see fairly high levels of harmonization, such as the free movement of goods (where over 80 per cent of sectors have reportedly been harmonized[57]), and those in which harmonization is less common or ambitious, such as the free movement of services. New technological phenomena and forms of economic activities open the potential for European legislation, as the General Data Protection Regulation, Digital Service Act, and Digital Markets Act illustrate. In addition, regulatory gaps in existing instruments could be closed. A number of harmonizing measures exempt certain products and activities, or include provisions that make it possible for Member States to derogate from the relevant rules. One example among many is the Services Directive, which explicitly excludes sectors like financial, healthcare, and gambling services from its scope of application. But even in areas that have already been harmonized, further action could be taken. Instruments following the minimum harmonization method could be recast as measures of maximum harmonization, as exemplified by the aforementioned Consumer Rights Directive.

Such reforms would lead to European laws replacing national laws and, thus, creating more regulatory uniformity in the internal market. The core economic benefit of this strategy would be an increase in intra-EU trade. Commission data on domestic consumption in Europe show that the share of goods originating in

[56] Stephen Weatherill, 'The Beauty and the Beast—Is Internal Market Law "Over-Constitutionalised"?' in Tamara Perisin, Tamara Capeta, and Iris Goldner Lang (eds), *The Changing European Union—A Critical View on the Role of Law and the Courts* (Hart Publishing Oxford 2022) ch 6.

[57] Commission, 'Proposal for a Regulation on the mutual recognition of goods lawfully marketed in another Member State—Refit Evaluation' COM (2017) 796 final, 24.

other Member States is over 20 per cent higher in areas that have been harmonized, compared with those that have not or only partially been harmonized.[58] The findings suggest that there is a strong association between harmonization and trade, which makes sense given that the adoption of common European rules renders cross-border sales less burdensome. The same basic dynamic is likely to apply to other areas of free movement.

Positive integration might also bring benefits from a democratic perspective. It would mean that the internal market is regulated to an even greater extent through the legislative process which could, in turn, pave the way for more representation (of voters) and accountability (of regulators). It bears noting that the extent to which the potential of democratization could be realized, of course, depends on the quality of the EU's legislative process in general. There has been a long-standing debate about the Union's 'democratic deficit'.[59] There is wide agreement that, judged by most standard indicators, the EU lags behind traditional representative democracies as can, for instance, be found among the Member States (even if scholars have also highlighted certain advantages, notably when it comes to representing out-of-state interests[60]). Nonetheless, the shift from negative to positive integration would, at the very least, improve the democratic qualities of internal market governance in so far as it would tilt the balance from judicial to political lawmaking at the EU level.[61]

But there would also be costs. The most serious one would be a risk of EU overreach. The positive integration agenda rests on the idea of centralization. Its underlying belief, or focal point, is that regulatory diversity among Member States should be eliminated to the extent possible.[62] Yet there are good reasons for why some diversity should remain in the internal market. From a functional perspective, letting Member States regulate certain areas independently creates the possibility of testing different regulatory strategies and learning from one another; this is the idea of Europe as a 'regulatory laboratory'.[63] Also, it allows for regulation to be tailored to the specific local socio-economic context, where that context

[58] Commission, 'Proposal for a Regulation on the mutual recognition on goods lawfully marketed in another Member State—Impact Assessment' COM (2017) 796 final, 15–16.

[59] Giandomenico Majone, 'Europe's "Democratic Deficit": The Question of Standards' (1998) 4 European Law Journal 5; Andrew Moravcsik, 'In Defence of the "Democratic Deficit": Reassessing Legitimacy in the European Union' (2002) 40 Journal of Common Market Studies 603; Andreas Føllesdal and Simon Hix, 'Why There is a Democratic Deficit in the EU: A Response to Majone and Moravcsik' (2006) 44 Journal of Common Market Studies 533.

[60] Christian Joerges and Jürgen Neyer, 'From Intergovernmental Bargaining to Deliberative Political Processes: The Constitutionalisation of Comitology' (1997) 3 European Law Journal 273.

[61] Similarly, see Martijn den Brink, 'The European Union's Demoicratic Legislature' [2021] International Journal of Constitutional Law 1.

[62] It should be noted that this objective can be pursued to varying degrees; see Stephen Weatherill, 'The Fundamental Question of Minimum or Maximum Harmonisation' in Garben and Govaere, *The Internal Market 2.0* (n 4).

[63] Simon Deakin, 'Legal Diversity and Regulatory Competition: Which Model for Europe?' (2006) 12 European Law Journal 440.

matters. From a constitutional perspective, the EU has committed itself to protecting aspects of national autonomy through the principles of conferral and subsidiarity,[64] the national identity clause,[65] and the various red lines that prevent harmonization in areas in which it, in principle, has a legislative competence.[66] These requirements are intended to ensure that there is sufficient space for national and local self-determination.[67] They also mean that there are boundaries—wherever these might be drawn—to the Union's legitimacy to regulate the internal market.

The difficulties which the EU has experienced with some recent legislative projects illustrate these issues. The attempt to create a common European contract law failed due to pushback at the national level.[68] Member States were not willing to give up their *code civil*, *Bürgerliches Gesetzbuch*, and *Kodeks Cywilny*, which embody their legal traditions, cultural values, and, at times, even historic achievements.[69] The attempt to give trade union rights a firmer footing in EU law by means of the Monti II Regulation did not succeed either. So many national parliaments raised objections against the proposal that the threshold for a 'yellow card' under the Early Warning Mechanism was met, forcing the Commission, politically if not legally, to withdraw its plans.[70] A similar fate befell the original version of the Services Directive, which would have 'only' established the principle of mutual recognition in the field of services, without imposing uniform standards for service providers. The fear of the 'Polish plumber', who became a symbol of social dumping and deregulation, proved too great.[71] These examples should not detract from the fact that, over the same period, the EU has managed to successfully adopt thousands of other legislative acts, including measures of meaningful scope and regulatory impact. However, they do show that the further European legislation tries to reach, the greater the potential for conflict becomes, especially in areas in which Member States feel, rightly or wrongly, that the Union lacks the necessary legitimacy to act.

[64] TFEU, arts 5(1), (3).

[65] TEU, art 4(2).

[66] See eg TFEU, art 79(5) (immigration), art 153(4) (social policy), art 168(7) (public health), art 194(2) (energy).

[67] Floris De Witte, 'Sex, Drugs & EU Law: The Recognition of Moral and Ethical Diversity in EU Law' (2013) 50 Common Market Law Review 1545.

[68] Hans-Wolfgang Micklitz, 'Monistic Ideology versus Pluralistic Reality: Towards a Normative Design for European Private Law' in Leone Niglia (ed), *Pluralism and European Private Law* (Hart 2013).

[69] Bośko Tripković and Jan Zglinski, 'Contestation and Accommodation: Constitutional and Private Law Pluralism(s) in the EU' in Lucila de Almeida and others (eds), *The Transformation of Economic Law: Essays in Honour of Hans-W Micklitz* (Hart 2019) 297.

[70] Federico Fabbrini and Katarzyna Granat, '"Yellow Card, But No Foul": The Role of the National Parliaments under the Subsidiarity Protocol and the Commission Proposal for an EU Regulation on the Right to Strike' (2013) 50 Common Market Law Review 115.

[71] Kalypso Nicolaïdis, 'Trusting the Poles? Constructing Europe through Mutual Recognition' (2007) 14 Journal of European Public Policy 682.

4.4 More Procedural Safeguards

A variation of the positive integration option would be to increase the role of procedural safeguards. As noted in previous sections, the EU has, in addition to hard legislation, adopted various soft law mechanisms and flanking measures that are aimed at improving the functioning of the internal market. This includes, inter alia, obligations of Member States to notify new regulatory standards, the establishing of single contact points for economic operators, and the creation of alternative dispute resolution mechanisms. The commonality of these measures is that they try to make the internal market work more efficiently without imposing common regulatory standards. In other words, they are focused on process, not substance.

What could a further 'proceduralization' of the internal market look like? To begin with, the range of domains in which procedural tools are employed could be expanded. Instruments imposing notification and screening requirements on national authorities before adopting new legislation are a good example. Directive 2015/1535 obliges Member States to communicate to the Commission any draft technical regulation in the field of goods and information society services.[72] Directive 2018/958 requires national authorities to conduct a proportionality assessment before introducing legislation that restricts access to regulated professions.[73] Both could be used as blueprints for other areas of free movement, such as capital and persons. In addition, the control and supervisory powers in existing instruments could be strengthened. The Court has, for instance, already established for Directive 2015/1535 that unnotified national laws cannot be enforced,[74] a sanctioning mechanism that could be transposed to other instruments.[75]

Recently, there seems to be a growing trend in EU law to opt for procedural tools like these, and it is easy to see why. From a Member State perspective, they are attractive as they guarantee that the primary responsibility for regulating stays with the domestic political processes. This not only protects national autonomy but can possibly also yield a democratic dividend. But the benefits from the EU's standpoint are arguably even larger. Procedural safeguards carry the promise of governing the internal market without having to regulate it in minute detail. Member States do the brunt of the regulatory work, while the Union just supervises the outcomes. This may appear particularly appealing, and sensible, as the internal market project has moved from the stage of market creation to that of market maintenance.[76] Moreover, a procedural approach to market governance is,

[72] Directive (EU) 2015/1535 laying down a procedure for the provision of information in the field of technical regulations and of rules on Information Society services [2015] OJ L241/1.

[73] Directive (EU) 2018/958 on a proportionality test before adoption of new regulation of professions [2018] OJ L173/25.

[74] Case C–194/94 *CIA Security International v Signalson and Securitel* ECLI:EU:C:1996:172; Case C–443/98 *Unilever Italia v Central Food* ECLI:EU:C:2000:496.

[75] Stephen Weatherill, 'The Principle of Mutual Recognition: It Doesn't Work Because It Doesn't Exist' (2018) 43 European Law Review 224.

[76] Michelle P Egan, *Constructing a European Market* (Oxford University Press 2001) 272.

in many ways, resource-efficient. It is preventive instead of reactive, requires only relatively limited involvement of EU institutions, and promotes political instead of judicial problem solving.

The reality is more complicated. Some procedural measures have proven to work extraordinarily well; SOLVIT, the informal dispute resolution mechanism for internal market matters, is one of them.[77] The system has demonstrably simplified, sped up, and lowered the costs of dispute resolution and, as a consequence, been very popular with individuals and businesses.[78] In this way, it has contributed to improving the enforcement of internal market law. In other cases, it is harder to assess how efficient an instrument has been. Measures like the Proportionality Directive for regulated professions largely rely on Member States self-correcting and enforcing the obligations imposed on them. To what extent this happens, and to what extent other factors might influence their decision-making, can be difficult to tell.

In yet other cases, it is clear that procedural tools have been ineffective. The Mutual Recognition Regulation is a case in point.[79] It was adopted in 2008 to render the principle of mutual recognition from Article 34 TFEU more tangible and operational. The Regulation applies to situations in which a Member State wants to block the marketing of a product that has been lawfully produced in another Member State. It creates the obligation for the relevant national authority to send the economic operator written notice, in which it explains why the decision is justified based on one of the grounds listed in Article 36 TFEU or other policy objectives in the public interest, and it pursues these objectives in a proportionate manner. The economic operator then has twenty days to draft a response in which they convince the authority that a prohibition is not warranted or necessary, after which the final decision is (supposed to be[80]) taken and notified to them and to the Commission. This is exactly how proceduralization is meant to work: a dialogue that takes place before any real damage is done and resolves disputes through non-judicial means. Despite that, the Regulation turned out to be anything but a success. Four years after its adoption, Commission data showed that only few notifications were made and over 90 per cent of them came from one Member State and one sector, suggesting that the Regulation was 'widely ignored'.[81] The Commission

[77] Commission Recommendation on principles for using 'SOLVIT'—The Internal Market Problem Solving Network [2001] OJ L331/79; now Commission Recommendation on the principles governing SOLVIT [2013] OJ L249/10.

[78] Evgenia Kokolia, 'Strengthening the Single Market through Informal Dispute-Resolution Mechanisms in the EU: The Case of SOLVIT' (2018) 25 Maastricht Journal of European and Comparative Law 108.

[79] Regulation (EC) 764/2008 laying down procedures relating to the application of certain national technical rules to products lawfully marketed in another Member State [2008] OJ L218/21.

[80] Pursuant to art 6(4) of the Regulation, the product was to be deemed to be lawfully marketed if the competent authority did not notify the economic operator of its intention of prohibiting the product.

[81] Weatherill, 'The Principle of Mutual Recognition' (n 75) 229, citing the Commission's First Report on the application of Regulation (EC) 764/2008, COM (2012) 292 final.

has reacted to these problems and amended the Regulation in 2019.[82] It remains to be seen whether the reform will make a difference.

The problems surrounding the Mutual Recognition Regulation raise some broader questions about the potential and limitations of the proceduralization strategy. Procedural measures are a halfway house between negative and positive integration. Despite having their basis in European legislation and giving EU institutions some control powers, they leave many key decisions in the hands of national authorities. There are, as was mentioned, advantages to this approach, but there are also drawbacks. Procedural tools might be able to improve enforcement of EU rules and even prevent conflicts, yet they are unable to eliminate regulatory differences between Member States where such differences exist. Therefore, they are probably best thought of as a useful complementary device that is applied alongside traditional tools of integration (negative or positive), which create substantive regulatory alignment, not as a stand-alone method for market governance.

4.5 Stable Equilibrium

There is one final possibility for what the future of the internal market could look like: everything largely stays the same. This might appear to contradict the analysis provided so far, which emphasized the internal market's dynamic and evolving nature. Yet, it could well be that the largest evolutionary steps occur during the early stages of market creation, whereas later changes are, in comparison, smaller. Once the general course is set and the basic framework is established, development reaches a plateau.

Underlying this vision is the idea of a stable equilibrium. A variety of forces—constitutional, political, and economic—exert influence on the internal market. They pull the internal market in different directions and affect the shape it ends up taking. And it could be that the status quo, the internal market's present form, strikes an acceptable balance between these forces. We have attained a level of intra-EU trade that might not be ideal but is satisfactory. We have achieved a degree of harmonization that does not cover all economic sectors but covers a sufficient range. We have not removed every obstacle to free movement, but most of the serious barriers. We continue to grant Member States a degree of autonomy, but not so much that it jeopardizes the functioning of the internal market. And so on. Accommodating each of these conflicting ambitions to a meaningful extent leaves no one fully content but, likewise, it leaves few actors altogether dissatisfied. It might, thus, create an imperfect but stable internal market.

This need not mean that there is no change at all in the future. It is conceivable that while for the most part the foundations of the internal market remain the

[82] Regulation (EU) 2019/515 on the mutual recognition of goods lawfully marketed in another Member State [2019] OJ L91/1.

same, there will be some developments and reforms at the fringes. These could fall into any of the aforementioned categories. New types of products and activities, emerging as a result of technological progress or social evolution, might be harmonized by the EU, subjecting them to the positive integration logic. Additional procedural tools could be adopted to help with market management. The Court of Justice's case law in certain domains may—in fact, it is likely to—evolve and become more activist or deferential, thus affecting the role of negative integration. These will be limited changes that have an impact on specific areas or features of the internal market, while leaving its general structure intact.

The notion of a stable equilibrium may suggest that maintaining the status quo is an inherently desirable course of action. Yet, as this section has shown, significant criticisms can be and have been voiced against the current framework. It may be argued that the Court of Justice is still playing too important a role in the governance of the internal market, which results in its exceeding judicialization and stifles political debate. Harmonization might be seen as not yet reaching adequate levels (and not doing enough for market integration) or, alternatively, as already interfering with too many economic sectors (and unduly centralizing regulation in Europe, making national self-determination impossible). Some existing market management tools have been shown to be ineffective. Substantive internal market law continues to struggle with accommodating non-economic concerns. The list could go on. Once any of these concerns gains sufficient strength socially, politically, or legally, it might upset the presently existing equilibrium.

5. Concluding Remarks: After *Finalité*

The internal market has traditionally been thought of as a destination, a place to reach, a project that can and eventually will be 'completed'. This chapter has offered a different perspective, one emphasizing its dynamic nature. The internal market has continuously evolved over the past decades. It is a construct that is subject to periodic changes, which are driven by internal and external developments. The extent to which different actors are involved in internal market regulation has varied, the way in which the available governance tools are employed has changed, and the models of market integration which are pursued have shifted. Periods of judicial activism have alternated with periods of judicial self-restraint, phases of legislative inertia with phases of political activity, and movements towards centralization with pushes for decentralization.

Looking at the evolution which the internal market has undergone in the past raises the question about its future: where is the internal market headed? Will it continue to evolve and, if so, how? Five possible paths were sketched. They range from a return to negative integration through a stricter reading and enforcement of the free movement rules, to a strengthening of the role of the domestic or European political processes, to an embracing of the status quo as an embodiment of an imperfect but stable equilibrium. Each has its distinct advantages and disadvantages and will affect the way in which the internal market operates.

Examining the internal market from an evolutionary perspective also brings the question of finalité[83] to the fore: where should it be headed? Is there some kind of endpoint we ought to be aiming towards, even if it can never be fully reached? This appears to be a position that continues to enjoy popularity in many corners. Scholars continue to speak about the need to accomplish the internal market or bemoan that European integration has not yet managed to produce a 'genuine' internal market.[84] Statements like these imply that the current state of affairs is unsatisfactory because the internal market does not yet live up to its own ideal type, which resembles a national market (however defined[85]). This vision may have been helpful at the start of the European project, as an aspirational idea that could be understood relatively easily by politicians and citizens that were, until then, used to thinking in purely domestic terms. It might even have been a useful tool when trying to overcome the Eurosclerosis that had developed by the 1970s, as a reminder of the potential benefits of economic integration. But it is no longer an appropriate way to think about the significantly matured, enlarged, and complex internal market of today.

There are certain choices that we have to make—and periodically remake—in relation to the internal market: how much centralization we want (and how much diversity we want to protect); what importance we seek to accord to free trade (and what place non-economic concerns should occupy); which regulatory standards are appropriate (and which sectors should be regulated at all); and who ought to be entrusted with creating and enforcing the rules that govern economic activity (the political process, the judiciary, or other institutional actors). These, as history demonstrates, are challenging decisions. Every option inevitably involves trade-offs, prioritizing some objectives over others. Yet, when discussing the future of the internal market, thinking in terms of these choices and the consequences they carry is, at this point, more helpful than fantasizing about the promised land of 'completion'. That the internal market 'will never be finalized' need not necessarily be a bad thing.

[83] For a discussion of *finalité* in relation to the EU's constitutional project, see Neil Walker, 'After *Finalité*? The Future of the European Constitutional Idea' in Giuliano Amato, Hervé Bribosia, and Bruno de Witte (eds), *Genesis and Destiny of the European Constitution* (Bruylant 2007).

[84] Pelkmans, 'The New Approach' (n 21) and 'Why the Single Market Remains the EU's Core Business' (2016) 39 West European Politics 1095. Similarly, see Laurence W Gormley, 'Inconsistencies and Misconceptions in the Free Movement of Goods' (2015) 40 European Law Review 925; Vincent Aussilloux and others 'Making the Best of EU's Single Market' (2017) 38 Notes du conseil d'analyse économique 1.

[85] The ways in which particular national markets operate, legally and economically, can differ quite strongly. The Australian and Canadian domestic market structures, for instance, differ considerably from those in the US and the UK, which, in turn, are organized differently from the Swiss and Spanish internal markets.

PART II

THE INTERNAL MARKET, CONSUMER PROTECTION, FREE MOVEMENT OF GOODS AND PERSONS

5

Sheep May Safely Graze

Laurence W Gormley

1. Prelude

At first sight, this title might seem to have little to do with the internal market, an area in which Steve Weatherill has made so many distinguished and thought-provoking contributions over many years. But appearances can be deceptive. Bach's setting of Salomon Franck's words[1] is rightly well-loved, as is indeed the internal market,[2] but in the latter case, whether the shepherd is watchful, and whether those who rule do so with wisdom, is perhaps less certain than it ought to be. Bach and Franck, in the cantata of which *Sheep may safely graze* forms part,[3] laid flattery on with a trowel for the birthday of Christian, Duke of Saxe-Weissenfels; European lawyers are less easily tempted to do the same for the institutions of the Union.

The first requisite for safe grazing is a watchful good shepherd. For European lawyers, this naturally suggests the Commission. Its supervisory and guardian role is of paramount importance in ensuring the establishment and proper functioning of the internal market. Yet it is a role with considerable discretion, or, more cynically, potential for political interference. Less prone to interference, although not acting entirely in a political vacuum, stands the Court of Justice, rather as an *Überhirte*, a superior shepherd. Occasionally it might be compared to the Gods in Brecht's *Der Gute Mensch von Szechuan*, the final scene of which has the Gods disappearing on a pink cloud, leaving the world to sort out its own problems. Fortunately for the development of European law, academic authorities are on hand to cajole, criticize, guide, laud, and persuade. Whether, as a group, they should be seen as varieties of a true shepherd, or more as a series of sheepdogs

[1] '*Schafe können sicher weiden / Wo ein guter Hirte wacht. / Wo Regenten wohl regieren / Kann man Ruh und Friede spüren / Und was Länder glücklich macht.*' (Salomon Franck, '*Schafe können sicher weiden*' libretto for Johann Sebastian Bach, Cantata *Was mir behagt, ist nur die muntre Jagd* ('Hunt Cantata'), BWV 208.)

[2] Despite Jacques Delors' oft-cited observation, 'You cannot fall in love with the single market' (Delors, 'Address to the Members of the European Parliament on the broad lines of Commission policy' (European Parliament, 17 January 1989) <www.cvce.eu/content/publication/2003/8/22/b9c06b95-db97-4774-a700-e8aea5172233/publishable_en.pdf>, last accessed 8 October 2023.

[3] Bach, Cantata *Was mir behagt ist nur die muntre Jagd* (n 1).

Laurence W Gormley, *Sheep May Safely Graze* In: *The Internal Market Ideal*. Edited by: Jeremias Adams-Prassl, Sanja Bogojević, Ariel Ezrachi, and Dorota Leczykiewicz, Oxford University Press.
DOI: 10.1093/oso/9780192867063.003.0006

competing in 'One Man and his Dog',[4] may make for diverting discussions on the Bench at Middle Temple or at High Table at Somerville or even at All Souls. In whatever capacity, Steve Weatherill's writings stimulate debate and point out the wayward reasoning and shortcomings of many a lost sheep (which bleats even more loudly according to the degree to which its acts and reasoning are manifestly misconceived). His writings form a safe haven, *ein feste Burg*: the wolf is kept from the door, and the safety of the flock ensured.

The second requisite is a place where rulers govern well (rule with wisdom). Particularly bearing in mind the Court of Justice's condemnation of *ultra vires* EU measures taken in the name of the internal market,[5] the EU legislature cannot always be said to be endowed with wisdom—although that shortcoming is not unique to the EU; it is true of many legislatures, both in the past and in the present. To the extent that these two requisites are (at least somewhat) satisfied, calm and peace may prevail, and countries may be fortunate as a result. Here too, Weatherill's writings have served as a warning and guiding beacon. This chapter considers various of his writings in the field of the internal market, and their contribution to safe grazing.

2. A Good Shepherd

Particularly in his contributions to the *International and Comparative Law Quarterly*, Weatherill's mastery and understanding of the case law of the Court of Justice on the free movement of goods is evident. Thus, in 1989: 'it is the application of Article 30 [EEC, now Article 34 TFEU] to more subtle, technical barriers to trade that provides the most striking indication of the potency of the prohibition.'[6] Echoing, silently, the Commission's celebrated Communication on the consequences of the *Cassis de Dijon* judgment,[7] Weatherill noted that the result in Case 178/84 *Commission v Germany*[8] meant that the Court was 'not using Article [34] to prevent goods being made in accordance with national tradition'[9] but was ensuring

[4] The venerable sheepdog trial competition broadcast on the BBC between 1976 and 2012. Since 2013, it is broadcast in the context of the BBC's *Countryfile* programme. <www.bbc.co.uk/programmes/m00104fg>; <https://en.wikipedia.org/wiki/One_Man_and_His_Dog> both accessed 8 October 2023.

[5] Celebratedly in Case C-376/98 *Germany v European Parliament and Council* ECLI:EU:C:2000:544 (see the discussion in Section 7).

[6] Stephen Weatherill, 'The Free Movement of Goods' (1989) 38 International and Comparative Law Quarterly 689, 690.

[7] Commission, 'Communication from the Commission concerning the consequences of the judgment given by the Court of Justice on 20 February 1979 in Case 120/78 (*Cassis de Dijon*)' [1980] OJ C256/2. See Laurence Gormley, '*Cassis de Dijon* and the Communication from the Commission' (1981) 6 European Law Review 454, and literature cited there.

[8] Case 178/84 *Commission v Germany* ECLI:EU:C:1987:126. He also referred to Case 407/87 *3 Glocken v USL Centro-Sud* ECLI:EU:C:1988:401 and Case 286/86 *Ministère public v Deserbais* ECLI:EU:C:1988:434.

[9] Weatherill, 'The Free Movement of Goods' (1989) (n 6) 691.

that products made according to different traditions also could be marketed freely outside the Member State where they were produced. He concluded that 'Article [34] is employed as a concerted attack on devious protectionism; the result is in accordance with the fundamental tenets of the plan to complete the internal market.' Weatherill observed that it was 'through the competitive pressures released as a result of these judgments that the huge economic benefits identified in the Cecchini Report[10] will accrue to the citizens of the Community'.[11] In a final floral flourish, he stated that '[t]here can be no more vivid means of creating a popular "People's Europe"[12] than by securing the free movement of the very best of each State's produce throughout the Community'.[13]

If that is the high point of his enthusiasm, a welcome for a somewhat more restrained approach appeared in 1991: Weatherill's observation that the 'European Court is primarily responsible for the development of Article [34] into a vigorous anti-protectionist instrument'[14] was tempered by the view that a common market did not require, in the absence of discrimination or protectionism, the elimination of national diversity in the area of Sunday trading.[15] A year later saw Weatherill observing that while *Cassis de Dijon* had undoubtedly stimulated the process of market integration, the principle in that judgment did 'not automatically sweep aside national law'.[16] He rightly opined that it was 'more accurate to view *Cassis* as a model for testing the interests pursued within national regulatory regimes against the interests of free trade in the Community'.[17] In 1996, Weatherill's discussion of that immaculate misconception, the judgment in *Keck*,[18] noted that the Court's requirement that a legal or factual inequality in the application of measures be shown raised the burden on traders wishing to use Article [34 TFEU] to enhance their freedom of commercial activities. The other side of the coin was that

[10] See Paolo Cecchini, Michael Catinat, and Alex Jacquemin, *The European Challenge 1992: The Benefits of a Single Market* (Gower 1988), summarized in EU Commission, *Europe 1992: The Overall Challenge* (1988) SEC (88) 524 final.

[11] Weatherill, 'The Free Movement of Goods' (1989) (n 6) 691 (internal reference omitted).

[12] See further, Commission, 'A People's Europe: Implementing the conclusions of the Fontainebleau European Council,' COM (84) 446 final, and Committee on a People's Europe, 'Report to the European Council' (the Adonnino Report), Bull EC 1985, supp 7/85.

[13] Weatherill, 'The Free Movement of Goods' (1989) (n 6) 693.

[14] Stephen Weatherill, 'Free Movement of Goods' (1991) 40 International and Comparative Law Quarterly 215, 215.

[15] ibid 218.

[16] Stephen Weatherill, 'Free Movement of Goods' (1992) 41 International and Comparative Law Quarterly 720, 720.

[17] ibid, referring to the judgment in Joined Cases C-1/90 and 176/90 *Aragonesa de Publicidad Exterior and Publivía v Departamento de Sanidad y Seguridad Social de Cataluña* ECLI:EU:C:1991:327. An often-overlooked feature of this judgment is that it confirmed that the protection of public health was a matter that fell within the ambit of art 36 [TFEU] as opposed to being a 'mandatory requirement' under *Cassis de Dijon* (see *Aragonesa*, paras 12–13): in *Cassis*, the Court had erroneously included public health among the list of mandatory requirements; see also Josse Mertens de Wilmars (1984–85) *Rechtskundig Weekblad* No 2, 16, n 2 who admitted, extrajudicially, that this had been due to a drafting error. Mertens was President of the Court at the time of *Cassis*.

[18] Joined Cases C-267/91 and 268/91 *Keck & Mithouard* ECLI:EU:C:1993:905.

stressing market fragmentation as opposed to simply sales suppression shifted the balance in favour of Member States' power to regulate their markets, if they complied with the need for equality in law and in fact.[19] He percipiently observed that this test would be difficult to apply, as indeed it has proved. *Keck* reflected judicial unwillingness to fill lacunae in the Treaty 'in order to acquire a general power of review over local regulatory initiatives that are not shown to imperil the realisation of economies of scale in an integrating market'.[20]

The Court's willingness to fill lacunae or its lack of willingness is scarcely a predictable event, as the Court is perfectly capable of being activist one moment and declining to be so the next; its approach has the whiff of result-oriented case law about it, varying like the proverbial length of the Lord Chancellor's foot.[21] Just a couple of illustrations will suffice to illustrate the point.[22] In Case C–295/90 *European Parliament v Council*,[23] the Court limited the effect of the annulment of a directive, even though the then-Article 174(2) EEC only conferred on the Court the power to do so in respect of regulations.[24] In the circumstances this was uncontroversial, and indeed a very sensible approach,[25] but it was clearly not in accordance with the wording of the Treaty. Sometimes activism is lightly disguised as helping a national court, as in Case 448/98 *Guimont*,[26] Case C–368/95 *Familiapress*,[27] or Case C–142/05 *Mickelsson & Roos*;[28] yet on other occasions the Court is quick to hide behind the skirts of the national judge, and effectively throw the ball back into the latter's court.[29]

Such subtleties did not escape Weatherill's eagle-eyed scrutiny, and in 1996 he perceptively observed that while Community-level measures also had to comply with the requirements of the free movement of goods provisions, the Court implied

[19] Stephen Weatherill, 'Free Movement of Goods' (1996) 45 International and Comparative Law Quarterly 213, 214.

[20] ibid.

[21] See, as to the Lord Chancellor's foot, Edward Fry, 'Life of John Selden' in Frederick Pollock (ed), *Table Talk of John Selden* (Selden Society 1927) 177.

[22] The case law on individual concern is also an area where equitable rabbits are occasionally pulled out of the conjuror's hat (justifiably), while the Court has difficulties in seeing that its traditional interpretation is misconceived: rather mischievously claiming that a Treaty change would be necessary, whereas a simple change in judicial interpretation would solve the problem. See Laurence W Gormley, 'Judicial Review: Advice for the Deaf?' (2006) 29 Fordham International Law Journal 655.

[23] Case C–295/90 *European Parliament v Council* ECLI:EU:C:1992:294, paras 23–27.

[24] Effectively regularizing this approach, the present equivalent provision (art 264 TFEU, 2nd para) confers on the Court the power to state, if it considers this necessary, 'which of the effects of the act which it has declared void shall be considered as definitive'.

[25] The Court noted that simple annulment would be likely to undermine students' right of residence for vocational purposes, which right had been conferred by the Treaty; the essential legislative content of the Directive was not challenged by either the institutions or the Member States, and the date for compliance with the Directive had already passed. *European Parliament v Council* (n 23) paras 23–27.

[26] Case C–448/98 *Guimont* ECLI:EU:C:2000:663, para 22.

[27] Case C–368/95 *Vereinigte Familiapress Zeitungsverlags v Heinrich Bauer Verlag* ECLI:EU:C:1997:325, paras 27–34).

[28] Case C–142/05 *Åklagaren v Mickelsson & Roos* ECLI:EU:C:2009:336, paras 41–44.

[29] eg Case 145/88 *Torfaen Borough Council v B&Q PLC* ECLI:EU:C:1989:593.

'that the standards against which community acts are measured are less exacting than those to which national measures are subjected'.[30] This provided 'an intriguing insight into the legal sensitivity that flows from the effort to develop a multilingual single market'.[31] He noted that in instances of regulation while achieving gradual integration, a less rigorous application of the proportionality principle than was the norm in reviewing national laws, and thus 'perhaps a milder approach to the review of Community rules against the standards of Article [34 TFEU] can be supported in order to allow the Community legislature a discretion in its evolving harmonisation programme that is more flexible than that conceded to national authorities'.[32] While the objective of national obstacles to trade is often more or less blatantly protectionist of the Member State's own purely national interests, that is not the aim of Community-level legislation.

Weatherill's mastery of terse comment combined with an understanding of the subtleties of litigation is well illustrated by his discussion in 1997[33] of the *Semeraro Casa Uno* litigation.[34] The Court rejected the referring court's view that the national measures involved did indeed have discriminatory effects and contented itself with observing that the *Keck* conditions for a measure to fall outside the scope of what is now Article 34 TFEU were fulfilled, adding for good measure that anyway in the *Stoke-on-Trent* judgment[35] it had upheld the legitimacy of non-discriminatory Sunday trading rules as a legitimate choice relating to particular national or regional sociocultural characteristics. Weatherill rightly noted that the Court's approach did not conform to the constitutional division of jurisdiction between the Court and the national court; he also rightly criticized the Court's irrelevant observation that there was no evidence that the aim of the national rules concerned was to regulate trade in goods between Member States. His entirely justified retort was that this should not have been expected, as it was already well established that Article [34 TFEU] was an effects-based provision, rather than an intention-based provision. The Court trotted out the old canard about lack of intention, despite its irrelevance to the legal analysis of the case. Weatherill observed that the Court's ruling in *Semeraro Casa Uno* was 'not entirely satisfactory'. He also perceptively commented that '*Keck* was, at heart, a strategy for extricating the court from judging eccentricities that do not damage integration'. Although the judgment showed that the Court was not minded to relax its determination to leave such

[30] Weatherill, 'Free Movement of Goods' (1996) (n 19) 218, discussing the judgment in Case C-51/93 *Meyhui NV v Schott Zwiesel Glaswerke AG* ECLI:EU:C:1994:312, comparing it with that in Case C-369/89 *Piageme v BVBA Peeters* ECLI:EU:C:1991:256.

[31] Weatherill, 'Free Movement of Goods' (1996) (n 19) 219.

[32] ibid.

[33] Weatherill, 'Free Movement of Goods' (1997) 46 International and Comparative Law Quarterly 704.

[34] Joined Cases C-418/93 and others *Semeraro Casa Uno v Sindaco del Comune di Erbusco* ECLI:EU:C:1996:242.

[35] Case C-169/91 *Council of the City of Stoke-on-Trent v B&Q* ECLI:EU:C:1992:519, paras 11-17.

matters purely to national courts to dispose of, the judgment did 'little to clarify the type of legal or factual inequality of application which litigants must show in order to bring their challenge to national measures within the scope of Article [34]'. In a different context (on the question whether the *Keck* approach would be applied to the free movement of persons, establishment, services, capital, and payments), he felt that the case law was obscure, but regarded it as essential that the Court did not lose sight of the rationale of the free movement provisions, namely 'the elimination of all obstacles to intra-Community trade in order to merge the national markets into a single market bringing about conditions as close as possible to those of a genuine internal market'.[36] With the caveat that the Court stated this in the context of 'the concept of a common market as defined by the Court in a consistent line of decisions'[37] rather than merely in relation to the free movement provisions, that statement by the Court is as relevant today as it was when it was handed down in 1982.

In 1999, Weatherill rightly applauded the Court's judgment in Case C–226/97 *Lemmens*[38] as placing 'the interest in promoting structures for building and maintaining the internal market in its wider context, alongside, not above, other interests in society'.[39] Rules developed for the prevention of the unsupervised proliferation of new obstacles to trade between Member States were not to be misused simply to enable drivers under the influence of drink to escape the consequences of being caught out. Weatherill also rightly welcomed the Court's condemnation in the *Angry Farmers* (*Spanish Strawberries*) case of failure by the French authorities to take steps to ensure the free movement of goods even in the face of public disorder:[40] sins of omission as well as of commission can infringe Article 34 TFEU.

3. Sheep Worrying? Shepherd Worrying!

By 2001, Weatherill's initial welcome for the rather restrained approach in *Torfaen* had worn somewhat thin. He found that the Court had taken a notorious wrong turn in its case law in the 1980s by finding that 'even national rules that inhibited the exercise of commercial freedom which had no direct association with the process of European market-building'[41] would infringe Article [34 TFEU] unless they

[36] Case C–15/81 *Schul* ECLI:EU:C:1982:135, para 33; cited in Weatherill, 'Free Movement of Goods' (1997) (n 33) 706.

[37] *Schul* (n 36) The Court also observed that it was 'important that not only commerce as such but also private persons who happen to be conducting an economic transaction across national frontiers should be able to enjoy the benefits of that market', ibid.

[38] Case C–226/97 *Lemmens* ECLI:EU:C:1998:296.

[39] Stephen Weatherill, 'Free Movement of Goods' (1999) 48 International and Comparative Law Quarterly 217, 219.

[40] Case C–265/95 *Commission v France* ECLI:EU:C:1997:595.

[41] Stephen Weatherill, 'Free Movement of Goods' (2001) 50 International and Comparative Law Quarterly 158, 160.

could be justified. He opined that the risk that Article [34] had been extended beyond its purpose of removing impedimenta to European market integration to become a means of attacking obstacles to freedom to trade in general threatened to destabilize the division of competence between the Member States and the Community.

Another way of looking at this is that the Court was simply requiring that if a measure was experienced as a restriction on trade, it had to be justified if it were to survive. Logically this is in line with the approach evident in Articles 34–36 TFEU themselves—a prohibition unless, as opposed to acceptance unless. The central problem was that the Court had, at least initially, almost encouraged challenges. It quickly realized in the later Sunday trading cases[42] that it had to give clearer guidance itself and take a position on justification, rather than simply leave it to the individual national courts. The trouble was that lawyers and litigants were simply not listening and kept on hammering at the door of the Court. In addition to issues such as Sunday trading, liquor licensing,[43] and sex shop licensing,[44] the Court was confronted with a range of issues relating to how goods were sold (selling practices),[45] as opposed to when or where or even by whom[46] goods were sold. Here too, the results sent mixed signals, but the Court relatively quickly found that there was a measure capable of restricting trade between Member States, and then proceeded to examine whether the alleged justification was acceptable.

Weatherill saw the judgment in *Keck*[47] as 'a step back,' and 'a retreat in [the Court's] reading of [Article 34 TFEU]' which had 'thereby expanded the area of regulatory space left in the hands of national authorities beyond the reach of Article [34 TFEU].'[48] Even though the Court had failed to state what judgments were overruled, he felt that the Sunday trading cases undoubtedly were. With the absurdities of the United Kingdom's Shops Act 1950 in mind, he pithily observed that 'irrational though the rules were, it would be for national constitutional arrangements to correct them.'[49] Inevitably, the result was that the Court got more cases,

[42] Case C-312/89 *Union départementale des syndicats CGT de l'Aisne v SIDEF Conforama* ECLI:EU:C:1991:93; Case C-332/89 *Marchandise* ECLI:EU:C:1991:94; *Council of the City of Stoke-on-Trent* (n 35); Case C-306/88 *Rochdale Borough Council v Stewart John Anders* ECLI:EU:C:1992:510. In *Conforama and Marchandise* and in Case 155/80 *Oebel* ECLI:EU:C:1981:177, worker protection arguments were also advanced.

[43] Case 75/81 *Blesgen* ECLI:EU:C:1982:117.

[44] Case C-23/89 *Quietlynn and Richards v Southend Borough Council* ECLI:EU:C:1990:300; Case C-350/89 *Sheptonhurst Ltd v Newham Borough Council* ECLI:EU:C:1991:194.

[45] Case 286/81 *Oosthoek's Uitgeversmaatschappij BV* ECLI:EU:C:1982:438; Case 382/87 *Buet v Ministère public* ECLI:EU:C:1989:198; Case C-362/88 *GB-INNO-BM v Confédération du commerce luxembourgeois* ECLI:EU:C:1990:102; Case C-126/91 *Schutzverband gegen Unwesen in der Wirtschaft v Rocher* ECLI:EU:C:1993:191.

[46] Case C-369/88 *Delatttre* ECLI:EU:C:1991:137; Case C-60/89 *Monteil* ECLI:EU:C:1991:138; Case C-271/92 *Laboratoire de prothèses oculaires v Union nationale des syndicats d'opticiens de France* ECLI:EU:C:1993:214.

[47] *Keck* (n 18).

[48] Weatherill, 'Free Movement of Goods' (2001) (n 41) 160, 161 (respectively).

[49] ibid 161.

basically asking for clarification of what was meant by the miserable and manifestly unhelpful formulation of the judgment in *Keck*. Weatherill rightly observed that:

> [O]ne might legitimately fear that an unduly narrow, literal reading of *Keck*, showing excessive reverence for the definitional role played by the imprecise notion of a 'selling arrangement', might lead some national courts to reject well-founded submissions based on Article [34 TFEU] without even involving the European Court.[50]

But to be sure, '[t]he theme of inquiry into what type of restriction on trade in the EC is required before a national regulator falls under an obligation to justify choices made against the standards recognised by [EU] law is sure to endure.'[51] Weatherill's advice was that a

> judge should examine each case without preconceptions in order to discover whether the national measure in question exerts a significantly damaging impact on the dynamic process of market-building in Europe to require justification. Legal formulae that direct that attention be paid to selling arrangements, impediments to market access or to the remoteness of the rule from the process of integration should be interpreted as reflecting this underlying economic and social rationale.[52]

4. Red Sky at Night, Shepherd's Delight

By 2003, Weatherill felt that the case law on the free movement of goods was entering calmer waters: 'nothing has lately caused any radical adjustment in the basic framework of the law.'[53] However, he was moved to discuss the distinction between discriminatory and non-discriminatory measures, noting that the 'choice of discrimination as a test presupposes a need to decide what constitute legitimate subjects for comparison.'[54] Moreover, the question of discrimination affects what justifications may be advanced for the measure: discriminatory measures can only be justified on the grounds specified in the TFEU (primarily in Article 36); equally applicable measures, however, may also benefit from the case-law-based justifications[55] originating in *Dassonville*[56] and famously developed in *Cassis de Dijon*[57] and subsequent cases.

[50] ibid.
[51] ibid.
[52] ibid 161–62.
[53] Stephen Weatherill, 'Free Movement of Goods' (2003) 52 International and Comparative Law Quarterly 1021, 1025.
[54] ibid 1026.
[55] eg Case C-2/90 *Commission v Belgium* ECLI:EU:C:1992:310, para 34.
[56] Case 8/74 *Dassonville* ECLI:EU:C:1974:82, para 6.
[57] Case 120/78 *Rewe-Zentral AG v Bundesmonopolverwaltung für Branntwein* ECLI:EU:C:1979:42, para 8.

While arguments have been advanced for assimilation of the Treaty-based and the case-law-based justifications,[58] the Court has maintained the distinction, even though it has then stood logic on its head and claimed that measures that were manifestly discriminatory were not, because of the special nature of the product concerned.[59] If the Court were to simply assimilate the case-law-based justifications with the Treaty-based justifications, it would be very difficult, if not impossible, to maintain the approach that, like all the exceptions to free movement rights, Article 36 TFEU must be strictly interpreted. It is also significant that despite the many opportunities offered by revisions of the Treaties, the Member States have not sought to add environmental protection or any of the other case-law-based grounds of justification to the grounds mentioned in Article 36 TFEU. Weatherill noted that the principal objection to a universally applicable justification test was 'the risk that it would lead to undue loosening of the discipline to which national measures affecting inter-State trade are subjected by [Articles 34–36 TFEU]'.[60] But he felt that 'a growth in inventive excuses for protectionism even in overtly discriminatory guise would not go unchecked by the judiciary and the Court's lack of decisiveness in addressing, let alone accepting, the line proposed by Mr Jacobs is hard for its admirers to defend'.[61] Given the contortions into which the Court twisted itself in relation to environmental protection and free movement of goods, it may be wondered whether the shepherd is, on this point, placing a little too much faith for the safety of his sheep in a somewhat rickety fence.

By 2006, Weatherill sets a slightly more optimistic tone: the case law continued to defy the Commission's view in 1993 that the Court had completed its jurisprudence.[62] While that claim, he argued, was not wholly unfounded, decisions continued to accumulate 'in part to clarify important points of interpretative detail and in part as a reflection of the immense appeal of the Treaty provisions governing free movement to litigants seeking to maximise commercial freedom'.[63] Weatherill observed that the Court was 'gratifyingly resistant to an obstinately formalist reading of *Keck*. It instead envisages a detailed inquiry into the factual impact of the national rule.'[64] The Court's inquiry was, like the structure of [Articles 34–36

[58] eg Case C-379/98 *Preussen Elektra AG v Schleswag AG* ECLI:EU:C:2000:585, Opinion of Advocate General Jacobs, paras 220ff; Stefan Enchelmaier, 'Article 36 TFEU: General' in Peter Oliver (ed), *Oliver on Free Movement of Goods in the European Union* (5th edn, Hart 2010) 216–20. Conversely, Laurence W Gormley, 'Inconsistencies and Misconceptions in the Free Movement of Goods' (2015) 40 European Law Review 925, 938–39, and—as to the purpose of the case-law-based justifications—see Laurence W Gormley, *EU Law of Free Movement of Goods and Customs Union* (Oxford University Press 2009) 505–10.

[59] See *Commission v Belgium* (n 55) para 34.

[60] Weatherill, 'Free Movement of Goods' (2003) (n 53) 1027.

[61] ibid.

[62] Commission, 'Management of the mutual recognition of national rules after 1992' (Communication COM (93) 669 final, [22]).

[63] Stephen Weatherill, 'Free Movement of Goods' (2006) 55 International and Comparative Law Quarterly 457, 458.

[64] ibid.

TFEU] a two-stage rocket: first, was there a trade barrier and secondly, was it justified? Weatherill noted, on the basis of developments in the case law on advertising restrictions,[65] that 'the mere fact that a national rule appears on its face to exert an effect that will be felt equally by all traders and all products is not enough automatically to immunise it from review. A realistic examination of its actual impact in the market is required.'[66] While there was no inconsistency between this approach and *Keck* itself, he observed that these judgments were 'especially helpful in permitting the Court to provide a more nuanced economic context to the application of Article [34] in the service of market integration.'[67]

It is well known that in the vast majority of free movement of goods cases the alleged justification fails—it may be fatuous, disingenuous, wholly artificial, or just downright nannying (as the German arguments on consumer protection have frequently been), or, to put it in more nuanced fashion, even where a measure may be found to be appropriate or suitable for its intended purpose, it can still be found to be disproportionate. Weatherill noted that alleged justifications may be 'no more than an attempt to placate narrow domestic interest groups who would wish to cling to outdated regulatory practices which have no place in an integrated European market.'[68] His surprise that cases where the justifications are, frankly, feeble continue to reach the Court was expressed in no uncertain terms: 'That even today such unmeritorious trade restrictions resist effective suppression short of expensive and lengthy litigation is a blot on the practical achievement of the internal market.'[69]

5. Red Sky at Morning, Shepherd's Warning

By 2009, shepherd Weatherill was rather worried: he acknowledged that 'the Court has laboured to try to fix with precision the necessary extra element pertaining to damage to the internal market with which the challenged national measure must be infected for [Article 34 TFEU] to bite.'[70] However, he felt that we were 'approaching the unhappy position where, just as in the pre-*Keck* era, national courts are understandably baffled as to exactly what is expected of them when faced by speculative claims that national measures infringe [Article 34 TFEU]'.[71] However, perplexity

[65] Case C-71/02 *Herbert Karner Industrie-Auktionen GmbH v Troostwijk GmbH* ECLI:EU:C:2004:181; [2004] ECR I-3025; Case C-239/02 *Douwe Egberts NV v Westrom Pharma NV* ECLI:EU:C:2004:445; [2004] ECR I-7007; Case C-20/03 *Burmanjer* ECLI:EU:C:2005:307; [2005] ECR I-4133.

[66] Weatherill, 'Free Movement of Goods' (2006) (n 63) 459.

[67] ibid.

[68] ibid.

[69] ibid 460.

[70] Stephen Weatherill, 'Free Movement of Goods' (2009) 58 International and Comparative Law Quarterly 985, 986.

[71] ibid, referring to the English case *R (Countryside Alliance) v Attorney General* [2008] 1 AC 719 (HL) (internal references omitted).

and uncertainty were not confined to the House of Lords. Weatherill's discussion of Case C–110/05 *Commission v Italy*[72] concentrates on the relatively short and narrow ruling as a sure sign of disagreement, or at least uncertainty, among the members of the Court. The judgment is remarkable for a number of points. First, the Court attempted to restate what it saw as measures falling within the ambit of Article [34 TFEU], although as examples rather than a limitative list. Secondly, the Court (sitting in Grand Chamber composition) followed the lead of the Third Chamber in Case C–265/06 *Commission v Portugal*[73] in finding that national measures governing the use of products fell within the ambit of [Article 34], and accordingly rejected the invitation by Advocate General Kokott in Case C–142/05 *Mickelsson & Roos*[74] to extend the *Keck* approach to cases involving the use of goods. Thirdly, the Court concluded—in one of the strangest examples of judicial horse-trading in recent years—that the Italian measures were proportionate and, thus, justified. This last point reveals what Weatherill alluded to in his comment about disagreement or uncertainty. The price to be paid for finding that the measures did constitute a hindrance to trade was that the Italian government was allowed to get away with the measures. No less than two Advocates General (Léger[75] and Bot[76]) had convincingly demonstrated that the measures were manifestly disproportionate. However, when a little horse-trading can be done, a lawyer's lot is not a happy one!

Weatherill's fine-tuned antennae were very much in evidence in his discussion of sensitive national interests, noting that in the (to a certain extent inevitable) clash between the economic freedoms guaranteed (now) by the TFEU and national measures protecting social and political rights (such as the right to take collective action[77] or to demonstrate (freedom of expression),[78] or child protection[79]), the Court trod very carefully indeed: a national 'margin of discretion'[80] is

[72] ECLI:EU:C:2009:66. See Laurence W Gormley, 'Free Movement of Goods and Their Use—What is the Use of It?' (2010) 33 Fordham International Law Journal 1589 and Peter Oliver, 'Of Trailers and Jet Skis: Is the Case Law on Article 34 TFEU Hurtling in a New Direction?' (2010) 33 Fordham International Law Journal 1423.

[73] ECLI:EU:C:2008:210.

[74] ECLI:EU:C:2006:782; as to the judgment, see n 28, ECLI:EU:C:2009:336.

[75] ECLI:EU:C:2006:646.

[76] ECLI:EU:C:2008:38.

[77] See Case C–438/05 *International Transport Workers' Federation v Viking Line ABP* ECLI:EU:C:2007:772 and Case C–341/05 *Laval v Svenska Byggnadsarbetareförbundet* ECLI:EU:C:2007:809. See also Weatherill's views on social policy and labour market regulation in Stephen Weatherill, *The Internal Market as a Legal Concept* (Oxford University Press 2016) 187–207 and his views on the internal market aspects of *Viking* and *Laval* in '*Viking* and *Laval*: The EU Internal Market Perspective' in Mark Freedland and Jeremias Prassl (eds), *Viking, Laval and Beyond* (Hart 2014).

[78] See Case C–112/00 *Eugen Schmidberger Internationale Transporte Planzüge v Austria* ECLI:EU:C:2003:333.

[79] See Case C–244/06 *Dynamic Medien Vertriebs GmbH v Avides Media AG* ECLI:EU:C:2008:85.

[80] See *Dynamic Medien*, ibid, para 44 ('margin of discretion'); *Commission v Italy* (n 72) para 65 ('margin of appreciation').

a well-chosen expression. It is not one, however, that implies an unfettered area of reserved powers for the Member States.[81] He observed:

> These decisions involve *such* sensitive balancing of (arguably incommensurable) values that they have (probably inevitably) generated anxieties that ultimately the nature and purpose of [EU] law, and the Court's limited mandate under the Treaty, tends to push economic motivations to the fore, to the detriment of national preferences. Plainly free movement law has become a lot spicier than blackcurrant liqueur.[82]

In 2012, Weatherill reminded readers of the *International and Comparative Law Quarterly* (ICLQ) that the internal market remained a dynamic area of the law, with much detail contested, even though the broad concept of the internal market might be well understood.[83] He returned to the discussion of the 'use cases', examining the judgment in Case C–142/05 *Mickelsson & Roos*.[84] He devoted much attention to the observation that the restriction 'may, depending on its scope, have a considerable influence on the behaviour of consumers, which may, in turn, affect the access of that product to the market of that Member State'.[85] Already in Case C–110/05 *Commission v Italy*, the Court had said: 'a prohibition on the use of a product in the territory of a Member State has a considerable influence on the behaviour of consumers, which, in its turn, affects the access of that product to the market of that Member State.'[86] As a result, consumers had only very limited interest in buying the product.[87]

Weatherill felt that this analysis meant that there was a requirement that the influence on consumer behaviour had to be considerable before an infringement of Article 34 TFEU could be triggered; he argued that using the word 'considerable' was cautious but imprecise and was designed 'to capture the notion that just because national laws vary does not of itself trigger the application of Article 34'.[88] He argued that the threshold at which divergence became a matter of concern for the EU was higher, noting that was also the ambition underpinning the

[81] See Case 35/76 *Simmenthal SpA v Italian Minister for Finance* ECLI:EU:C:1976:180, para 14 and Case 153/78 *Commission v Germany* ECLI:EU:C:1979:194, para 5. See also eg *Dynamic Medien* (n 79) para 45.

[82] Weatherill, 'Free Movement of Goods' (2009) (n 70) 989 (internal references omitted).

[83] Stephen Weatherill, 'Free Movement of Goods' (2012) 61 International and Comparative Law Quarterly 541. This appears to be the last in his series in the ICLQ's 'Current Developments: European Union Law' series.

[84] *Mickelsson & Roos* (n 28).

[85] ibid para 26.

[86] *Commission v Italy* (n 72) para 56.

[87] See *Commission v Portugal* (n 73) para 33; *Commission v Italy* (n 72) para 57; C–142/05 *Mickelsson & Roos* (n 28) para 27.

[88] Weatherill, 'Free Movement of Goods' (2012) (n 83) 542.

judgment in *Keck*. For Weatherill, the problem was pinning down with precision where Article 34 TFEU stopped and where national regulatory autonomy began. He opined that the adjective 'considerable' carried precisely 'that heavy constitutional weight' but it was hard to grasp how one could sensibly measure whether an influence on consumer behaviour was considerable or not; he saw the threshold as crucial but alarmingly elusive, seeming to point to a messy case-by-case application.[89]

The shepherd was concerned. 'The lurking fear is that if the Court delves into a review of national measures which do not affect the construction of an internal market it is intruding into national regulatory autonomy without adequate justification and thereby damaging the legitimacy of EU law.'[90] Yet the shepherd should not be concerned. The sole purpose of using the word 'considerable' was to emphasize that influencing consumer behaviour could indeed result in a barrier to trade between Member States.[91] This was actually already crystal clear in the case law for many years,[92] so in reality the adjective 'considerable' is superfluous, other than to add weight to the conclusion.

The shepherd's fears only increased when in Case C-443/10 *Bonnarde*, the Fifth Chamber of the Court found that 'the requirement that the registration document for demonstration vehicles must state that it was a "demonstration vehicle" in order to be granted the ecological subsidy may influence the behaviour of consumers and, consequently, affect the access of those vehicles to the market of that Member State.'[93] The word 'considerable' (or in this case, 'considerably') had been dropped. Weatherill was scathing:

> And this leap occurs in a decision that does not concern the restriction on use at all but rather a rule of the classic *Cassis de Dijon* type that imposed a 'dual burden' on imports! ... It seems implausible that it really should be taken at face value, so it is probably simply not a reliable decision. In an area where so much has been established—adjusted, adapted—by the case law of the Court over the years, such lack of attention to detail is frankly a source of dismay.'[94]

[89] ibid.
[90] ibid 542–43.
[91] See Gormley, 'Free Movement of Goods and Their Use' (n 72) 1625–26. In particular, there was no intention to seek to imply a revision of the long-standing and consistent 'no *de minimis*' approach in free movement law.
[92] See eg Case 249/81 *Commission v Ireland* ECLI:EU:C:1982:402, para 28; Case 12/74 *Commission v Germany* ECLI:EU:C:1975:23, para 14; Case 193/80 *Commission v Italy* ECLI:EU:C:1981:298, paras 26–27; Case 182/84 *Miro BV* ECLI:EU:C:1985:470, paras 21–22; Case 298/87 *Smanor SA* ECLI:EU:C:1988:415, para 15; Case C-12/00 *Commission v Spain* ECLI:EU:C:2003:21, paras 82–83; and Case 147/04 *De Groot en Slot Allium BV v Ministre de l'Économie, des Finances et de l'Industrie* ECLI:EU:C:2006:7, para 71.
[93] ECLI:EU:C:2011:641, para 30.
[94] Weatherill, 'Free Movement of Goods' (2012) (n 83) 543.

For the reasons outlined above, it is submitted that the shepherd's fear that the doors of Article 34 TFEU were being thrown wide open rather resembles recent newspaper reports of Mark Twain's death.

6. A Question of Faith? For Mutual Recognition, it Takes Two to Tango!

One major aspect of the shepherd's worries, and indeed a good example of the developments in how these worries have been expressed, is the principle of mutual recognition. This has been a mantra for so long in the internal market that it has almost become a dogma. Yet even in the early days of its development, it soon became clear that mutual recognition of goods (and by extension, mutual recognition in the internal market), was neither a panacea nor an absolute rule. A major advantage of mutual recognition was that it enabled the Commission to re-orientate its harmonization programme—no longer was there a need to harmonize everything in sight (as the harmonization activities were often presented); the European institutions could concentrate on removing justified barriers to free movement.[95] Mutual recognition also involved the Member States having confidence in test results from the authorities of other Member States[96] and required Member States to take account of the fact that a trader was authorized to conduct business in its home Member State when evaluating whether the trader was a fit and proper person to be approved to conduct business in the host Member State.[97] In these cases, the Court did not deny the Member States' competence to require testing and compliance, but it set limits on the exercise of that power. The limits of mutual recognition were also exposed in the insurance litigation judgments at the end of 1986.[98] Moreover, despite the obligation on Member States to participate in the removal of obstacles to trade between them, Member States could still,

[95] See the Commission's Communication (n 7).

[96] See eg Case 132/80 *United Foods v Belgian State* ECLI:EU:C:1981:87, para 29 and Case 272/80 *Frans-Nederlandse Maatschappij voor Biologische Producten* ECLI:EU:C:1981:312, para 14. While the Member States were, in the absence of harmonization, free to insist on retesting, the obligation on the authorities of the Member States to assist in bringing about a relaxation of the controls existing in intra-Community trade meant that they were 'not entitled unnecessarily to require technical or chemical analyses or laboratory tests where those analyses and tests have already been carried out in another Member State and their results are available to those authorities, or may at their request be placed at their disposal' (*Biologische Producten*, ibid).

[97] Case 279/80 *Webb* ECLI:EU:C:1981:314.

[98] See Case 205/84 *Commission v Germany* ECLI:EU:C:1986:463; Case 206/84 *Commission v Ireland* ECLI:EU:C:1986:464; Case 220/83 *Commission v France* ECLI:EU:C:1986:461; and Case C–252/83 *Commission v Denmark* ECLI:EU:C:1986:462. The Commission tried to argue that the mutual recognition principle meant that access to the various markets should be granted, but the Court concluded that in the present state of the law, the Member States were entitled to require compliance with their consumer protection legislation; the provision of sufficient consumer protection guarantees at Community level would be necessary.

in the absence of harmonization, in certain circumstances insist on compliance with legitimate health and safety requirements: 'as Community law now stands Member States are not required to allow into their territory dangerous machines which have not been proved to afford users on their territory the same level of protection.'[99] Similarly, the obligation to have confidence in testing did not require an importing Member State—again, absent harmonization—to accept test results carried out by a private testing body, as opposed to a public testing body.[100] More recently, the limits of mutual recognition have been laid out for all to see in relation to gambling supervision,[101] a decision that is hardly surprising in view of the differences in approaches to gambling among the various Member States, the practical unlikelihood of obtaining agreement on harmonization in the field, and the practical difficulties of extraterritorial regulation when not all regulators are well equipped to be ahead of market developments, rather than merely reacting to them. The problems of certificates of conformity issued not by a manufacturer, but by a distributor, were considered by the Court in Case C–354/14 *SC Capoda Import-Export SRL v Registrul Auto Român et al*; here, the Court found that 'it is for the Member States, in the absence of any European Union rules governing the matter, to determine the evidence which may be adduced in that respect, subject to the principles of equivalence and of effectiveness'.[102] It concluded that, subject to that proviso, EU law did

> not preclude a rule that only certificates issued by the manufacturer and not by the distributor are capable, in principle, of establishing that the parts in question have already been approved or homologated or constitute original parts or spare parts of matching quality, for the purpose of national law.[103]

The Court also observed that 'Article 3(26) of Directive 2007/46, which defines the concept of "original parts or equipment" for the purpose of that directive, provides that it is presumed, unless the contrary is proven, that parts constitute original parts if the manufacturer certifies them as being so'.[104]

In 2001, Weatherill rightly observed that:

> *Cassis de Dijon* does not enshrine a principle of absolute mutual recognition or unqualified home country control. Regulatory diversity among the Member

[99] Case 188/84 *Commission v France* ECLI:EU:C:1986:43, para 17.
[100] Case C–293/93 *Houtwipper* ECLI:EU:C:1994:33.
[101] Case C–42/07 *Liga Portuguesa de Futebol Profissional v Departamento de Jogos da Santa Casa da Misericórdia de Lisboa* ECLI:EU:C:2009:519.
[102] ECLI:EU:C:2015:658, para 44.
[103] ibid para 45.
[104] ibid.

> States is in principle respected (pending possible legislative intervention by the EC). However, in practice a regulating authority must persuade the Court that its particular regulatory eccentricities are underpinned by an adequate justification and one may readily suppose this will be difficult where other States show no comparable concern to intervene.[105]

He noted the Commission's complaint that it 'has always found it very difficult to obtain ... a clear and reliable picture of how the principle of mutual recognition is actually applied in practice' and that reliance on the principle by its economic operators remained relatively marginal.[106] But the shepherd was not convinced about the principle:

> [I]n fact, there is no mutual recognition principle in EC trade law: rather, it is a principle of non-absolute mutual recognition, and so litigation against a trade barrier may be deterred by the possibility that justification will be shown and that the case will therefore fail. But, more generally, the problem is that litigation is a costly and time-consuming process, which is frequently simply not worth pursuing.[107]

As will be apparent from the cases briefly noted above, any idea that the mutual recognition principle might be absolute was quickly dismissed by the Court, but it is taking matters rather far to suggest that there is no mutual recognition principle as such. The fundamental principles of the market admit exceptions, in the Treaty and in the case law, but they are still fundamental cornerstones on which the marketplace is founded. At the very least, mutual recognition is a point of departure, a default position—although, like the cedars of Lebanon, it sways with the wind. It is a principle to be applied unless there is good reason not to do so. The shepherd argued further that the statement of the Court in Case C–110/05 *Commission v Italy*[108] that:

> It is also apparent from settled case-law that Article 28 EC reflects the obligation to respect the principles of non-discrimination and of mutual recognition of products lawfully manufactured and marketed in other Member States, as well as the principle of ensuring free access of Community products to national markets

[105] Weatherill, 'Free Movement of Goods' (2001) (n 41) 162.

[106] Commission, *Second Biennial Report on the Application of the Principle of Mutual Recognition in the Single Market*, COM (2002) 419 final [5.1], [5.2].

[107] Weatherill, 'Free Movement of Goods' (2006) (n 63) 460.

[108] See *Commission v Italy* (n 72) para 34.

should go on to say:

> subject to the possibility that the regulating authority may demonstrate general interest which will prevail over that securing free movement of goods.[109]

One may wonder quite how essential this is, given that in that judgment, as normal, the Court proceeded to look first at whether the measure was caught by Article 34 TFEU, and then at whether it was justified. Adding the shepherd's suggestion makes no practical or theoretical difference at all, even though it would have the advantage of stressing once again the availability of justifications which are already known and are not in question. Weatherill's final plea 'Just be a bit more careful please' is, however, a plea which the present author has no difficulty in wholeheartedly supporting.[110]

Weatherill returned to his argument in his discussion[111] of Case C–672/15 *Noria Distribution Sàrl.*[112] Here, the Court declined to look at the case in relation to mutual recognition but was simply able to apply classic procedural conditions.[113] There had to be a procedure in place

> enabling economic operators to obtain the authorisation to market food supplements including nutrients in doses exceeding those authorised. The procedure must be one which is readily accessible and can be completed within a reasonable time, and, if it leads to a refusal, the decision of refusal must be open to challenge before the courts.[114]

Given that the existence of such a procedure was one of the requirements of a justification under Article 36 TFEU, the justification failed. Weatherill criticizes the Court for failing to respond to the question of the national court on mutual recognition, but the short answer to that was that it did not need to get to that stage; once it was clear that the appropriate procedures were not in place, the alleged justification could be dismissed on that ground. On this point, the Court chose economy of effort.

[109] Stephen Weatherill, 'Why There Is No "Principle of Mutual Recognition" in EU Law (and Why That Matters to Consumer Lawyers)' in Kai Purnhagen and Peter Rott (eds), *Varieties of European Economic Law and Regulation Liber Amicorum for Hans Micklitz* (Springer 2014) 410.

[110] See Laurence W Gormley, 'Inconsistencies and Misconceptions in the Free Movement of Goods' (2015) 40 European Law Review 925.

[111] Stephen Weatherill, 'The Principle of Mutual Recognition: It Doesn't Work, Because it Doesn't Exist' (2018) 43 European Law Review 224.

[112] ECLI:EU:C:2017:310.

[113] These are commonly known as the *Vlassopolou/Kraus* conditions; see Case C–340/09 *Vlassopoulou v Ministerium für Justiz, Bundes- und Europaangelegenheiten Baden-Württemberg* ECLI:EU:C:1991:193 and Case C–19/92 *Kraus v Land Baden-Württemberg* ECLI:EU:C:1993:125. The Court cited Case 24/00 *Commission v France* EU:C:2004:70, para 26; Case C–95/01 *Greenham and Abel* EU:C:2004:71, para 35; and Case C–333/08 *Commission v France* EU:C:2010:44, para 81.

[114] *Noria* (n 112) para 22.

More disturbing, though—and certainly correct—is Weatherill's observation that Regulation 764/2008[115] on mutual recognition was simply not working. In view of this, it is scarcely surprising that the Regulation has now been replaced by Regulation 2019/515.[116] This is a considerable improvement, establishing in Article 4(1) a procedure whereby a producer can establish a voluntary mutual recognition declaration. If the importing Member State authorities decide to conduct an assessment procedure under Article 5, they have to take account of test reports or certificates issued by conformity assessment bodies; if the body concerned is accredited in the appropriate field of conformity assessment under Regulation 765/2008,[117] the authorities may not refuse on grounds related to the competence of that body.[118] Unsurprisingly, when an administrative decision is taken as a result of the assessment, full reasons must be given, and the decision must specify the relevant remedies and time limits under national law; it must also refer to the SOLVIT procedure by virtue of Article 8 of Regulation 2019/515.[119] It is a pretty poor state of affairs if regulations are simply not being applied, and it is to be hoped that Regulation 2019/515—including, for the first time, an active element—will fare better than its predecessors.

It would certainly be inappropriate to suggest that the shepherd has had a crisis of faith; it is more of a cry in the wilderness that matters are not what they could be; a plea for clarity *ex abundanti cautela*. In that the shepherd is not alone; there is safety in numbers.

7. Where Rulers Govern Well?

Good government is in short supply or is regarded by many as having been in short supply in recent years, on both sides of the pond, although that should probably not be a surprise, as afficionados of Psalm 146 verse 3 will recall.[120] That makes it all the more important that at the level of the EU, wise decisions are taken, respecting the competence of the Member States and that of the EU itself. Not for nothing is it often said that at least one Member State looks to the EU to solve its problems.

[115] Regulation (EC) 764/2008 of the European Parliament and of the Council of 9 July 2008 laying down procedures relating to the application of certain national technical rules to products lawfully marketed in another Member State and repealing Decision No 3052/95/EC [2008] OJ L218/21.

[116] Regulation (EU) 2019/515 of the European Parliament and of the Council of 19 March 2019 on the mutual recognition of goods lawfully marketed in another Member State and repealing Regulation (EC) No 764/2008 [2019] OJ L91/1.

[117] Regulation (EC) 765/2008 of the European Parliament and of the Council of 9 July 2008 setting out the requirements for accreditation and market surveillance relating to the marketing of products and repealing Regulation (EEC) No 339/93 [2008] OJ L218/30.

[118] ibid art 5(8).

[119] ibid art 5(12). As to SOLVIT, see Preamble recitals 37–39.

[120] 'Put not your trust in princes, nor in the son of man' (King James Version); 'Do not put your trust in men in power, or in any mortal man' (Jerusalem Version).

One of the most important characteristics of Community, now Union, decision-making is the move to, and steady expansion of, qualified majority voting. This was already envisaged in the Spaak Report.[121] This has the great advantage of avoiding decision-making being thwarted by outright blackmail (sometimes in the form of politically linking unrelated dossiers, sometimes in the form of vulgar demands for more money, to name just two examples) and has also inevitably increased the willingness of Member States and others to challenge acts of the EU institutions—sometimes entirely rightly, although often merely to seek to save some local sacred cow or for domestic consumption, to gain favour with voters or vocal interest groups.

The internal market has not been immune from such challenges, and perhaps the most celebrated challenge, on the Tobacco Advertising Directive, was unsurprisingly the subject of considerable comment, not least from Weatherill. The first Tobacco Advertising Directive was an unmitigated disaster, and it was unsurprising that the Court annulled it unceremoniously,[122] reminding the institutions that they too had to act within the limits of their powers. Weatherill observed that 'the Court is scrupulous in expressing its fidelity to the constitutional rule that the limits of the competence conferred on the Community are defined by the Treaty'.[123] There was no general, unfettered competence to regulate the internal market.[124] The Court rightly took the view that prohibiting advertising of tobacco products on ashtrays, parasols, and posters and other hotel, restaurant, and catering articles, and prohibiting cinema advertising slots for tobacco products really had nothing to do with the facilitation of (cross-border) trade.[125] However, the Court confirmed that a prohibition of advertising of tobacco products in periodicals, magazines, and newspapers could be based on the power to adopt harmonizing measures under the then-Article 100a EC (now, after amendment, Article 114 TFEU)[126] in order to ensure the free movement of press products; that provision could also be used to prohibit certain forms of sponsorship.[127] Weatherill commented that:

> [t]he Court has not been lured down a path which envisages the internal market being built by the EC only on the basis of market freedoms unfettered by regulatory prohibition ... The Court has clipped the Community legislature's wings but it has given it a steer towards what may be permissible in future.[128]

[121] Intergovernmental Committee on European Integration, *Rapport des Chefs de Délégations aux Ministres des Affaires Étrangères* (Spaak Report) (Brussels 1956); an English translation is available at <http://aei.pitt.edu/995/1/Spaak_report.pdf> accessed 8 October 2023.
[122] *Germany v European Parliament & Council* (n 5).
[123] Weatherill, 'Free Movement of Goods' (2001) (n 41) 166.
[124] *Germany v European Parliament & Council* (n 5) para 83.
[125] ibid para 99.
[126] ibid para 98.
[127] ibid para 111.
[128] Weatherill, 'Free Movement of Goods' (2001) (n 41) 166.

As ever, his subtle awareness of how the sheep are likely to respond to the sheepdog's actions was also in evidence.

> The very fact that a Member State, having lost the political debate about the desirability of such intervention in the Council, was willing to convert its opposition into a legal challenge to the validity of the measure demonstrates the current sensitivity to the question of demarcating the limits of Community competence.[129]

The extension of qualified majority voting increased the likelihood of dissenting Member States having an incentive to challenge, in the Court, the validity of Community measures the adoption of which they failed to prevent in the Council. Weatherill saw the addressees of this judgment being the political institutions, and—through the Council—the political elites of the Member States. The Court was indicating that it was 'willing to invalidate egregious excesses of legislative ambition'.[130]

However, there was also another message, this time to the national courts, that the Court of Justice was 'serious about patrolling the limits of Community competence'.[131] This, the good shepherd observed, showed that the Court was well aware that (a number of) national courts had become worried that the limits of Community competence might not be observed by the Community legislature and were willing, where they felt that this had occurred, to examine the relevant act against their own constitutional touchstones. Of course, if this were to happen, and various national courts were to deny the validity of Community law, the integrity of the Community legal order would be seriously threatened, or indeed undermined. Weatherill thus argued that it was 'plausible that the Court's rigour in *Tobacco Advertising* is in part an invitation to national courts to trust it, the European Court, with the exclusive function of reviewing the validity of Community laws'.[132] He went on to opine that the rise of qualified majority voting in the Council had created the political conditions in which 'competence sensitivity' has spilled over into the legal arena, and that there was every reason to suppose that such trends would continue, as the Community proceeded further down the path of geographical and functional expansion.

Ten years later, Weatherill viewed the case law on competence as having become no more than a drafting guide for EU legislation in the area of the internal market.[133] The shepherd posed the question whether the first *Tobacco Advertising*

[129] ibid 167.
[130] ibid.
[131] ibid.
[132] ibid.
[133] Stephen Weatherill, 'The Limits of Legislative Harmonization Ten Years after *Tobacco Advertising*: How the Court's Case Law Has Become a "Drafting Guide"' (2011) 12 German Law Journal 827.

case was 'really a constitutionally significant assertion of judicial policing of the limits of EU law or instead simply a glimpse of a moment of legislative laziness'. Legislative compliance with the principles of subsidiarity and proportionality was easily ensured by simple repetition of the formulae which had been approved by the Court. He regarded this as troubling but reflecting 'the intensely political character of the assessments involved which militate against intense judicial review'. However, he found it 'profoundly alarming that determining the limits of the EU's conferred competence pursuant to Article 114 TFEU is also *in practice* subject to a high degree of legislative discretion'. The reality he argued was 'a proliferation of generous judicial approval of wide-ranging regulatory intervention conducted by the EU in the (in practice) unverifiable name of market-making harmonization'.[134]

The shepherd was clearly a rather unhappy bunny! However, this unhappiness was not entirely directed at the sheepdog:

> [One] can easily criticize the Luxembourg Court for lax standards of review and for inventing words—*appreciable*, *likely*—which carry the highest constitutional significance, for they define the limits of EU legislative competence, yet the lowest degree of operational precision ... But the fundamental and inescapable problem here is not primarily the Court but the wording of Article 114 TFEU and of Article 26 TFEU to which Article 114 is explicitly connected. This is a classic instance of the need to confer flexible powers on the EU so that it can effectively perform its broad and ill-defined mission: tightly written controls would militate against effective discharge of tasks. And yet this immediately challenges the principle of conferral in Article 5 TEU. Pure in principle, in practice it is tainted by the functional breadth of the two principal 'problem provisions', Articles 114 and 352.[135]

Echoing Advocate General Fennelly,[136] Weatherill observed that upholding the constitutional division of powers between the Community and the Member States on the basis of objective criteria was indeed a difficult function. He felt the circular pattern by which the Court's analysis of the proper scope of legislative harmonization and the requirements of the principles of proportionality and subsidiarity were simply recycled into the preambles and preparatory documents for legislative harmonization measures revealed how in practice that constitutional division of powers was being unreliably policed.

> Placing a *formal* limit on conferred competence is central to the constitutional strategy for preserving diversity and local autonomy in the EU, but the problem

[134] ibid 849.
[135] ibid 862–63.
[136] Weatherill quoted Fennelly's wise analysis in his Opinion in the first *Tobacco Advertising* case, ECLI:EU:C:2000:32, para 4.

> is the inflation of centralized authority *in practice*. The EU's legitimacy is thereby imperilled. This is why such hope is invested in Lisbon reforms: the fresh—if, in some respect, poorly framed—involvement of national Parliaments in critically reviewing proposals for compliance with subsidiarity (but regrettably not proportionality) and with the scope of Article 352 (regretfully not Article 114). And, more generally, there is pressing need for all actors and institutions to engage with the crucial assessments of how much centralization is worth pursuing where it will damage local autonomy. Centralization versus local autonomy in Europe: the general problems and tensions associated with competence distribution show no inclination to subside.[137]

Constitutional rhetoric often ignores the real rationale behind the supremacy of Union law over national law in the event of a conflict, and the Court's insistence that it, and only it, can annul an EU act. That rationale is essentially socio-economic: if the uniform application, validity, and interpretation of EU law were to be undermined, economic actors would no longer have a level playing field free of artificial distortions of competition, and the very concept of a single market within the EU would be at the least threatened, at the worst destroyed. In fact, behind virtually every challenge to competence, there lurks a socio-economic interest, as is well demonstrated by the plethora of unsuccessful challenges to EU legislation (via references from national courts as well as via direct actions for annulment) on a number of 'sensitive' issues since the first *Tobacco Advertising* judgment.[138]

Weatherill's view of the rulers is essentially that of a shepherd concerned for the safety of his sheep, and of his sheepdog, faced with legislative institutions that often resemble more the proverbial vicar of Bray than wise rulers taking full or at least adequate account of the interests of the people of Europe. The call to respect

[137] Weatherill, 'The Limits of Legislative Harmonization' (n 133) 863–64. See further, Stephen Weatherill, 'Pre-emption, Harmonisation and the Distribution of Competence to Regulate the Internal Market' in Catherine Barnard and Joanne Scott (eds), *The Law of the Single European Market: Unpacking the Premises* (Hart 2002); Stephen Weatherill, 'Supply of and Demand for Internal Market Regulation: Strategies, Preferences and Interpretation' in Niamh Nic Shuibhne (ed), *Regulating the Internal Market* (Edward Elgar 2006), and Stephen Weatherill, 'Competence and Legitimacy' in Catherine Barnard and Okeoghene Odudu (eds), *The Outer Limits of European Union Law'* (Hart 2009). As to his argument that there are, in fact, several internal markets, see Stephen Weatherill, *The Internal Market as a Legal Concept* (Oxford University Press 2016), in which he discusses ambiguities, and Stephen Weatherill, 'The Several Internal Markets' (2017) 36 Yearbook of European Law 125, in which he focuses on aspects of heterogeneity and how the concepts of the internal market are applied in the European Economic Area and further afield.

[138] eg Case C–491/01 *British American Tobacco (Investments) and Imperial Tobacco* ECLI:EU:C:2002:741; Case C–434/02 *Arnold André v Landrat des Kreises Herford* ECLI:EU:C:2004:800; Case C–210/03 *The Queen, on the application of: Swedish Match AB and Swedish Match UK Ltd v Secretary of State for Health* ECLI:EU:C:2004:802; Joined Cases C–154/04 and 155/04 *The Queen, on the application of Alliance for Natural Health and Nutri-Link Ltd v Secretary of State for Health* ECLI:EU:C:2005:449; Case C–380/03 *Germany v European Parliament & Council (Tobacco Advertising II)* ECLI:EU:C:2006:772; Case C–176/09 *Luxembourg v European Parliament and Council* ECLI:EU:C:2011:290; and C–626/18 *Poland v European Parliament and Council* ECLI:EU:C:2020:1000.

subsidiarity and proportionality does not fall on wholly deaf ears, but there is scant consensus about subsidiarity, and the label placed on its definition (now in Article 5(3) TFEU) by Lord Mackenzie Stuart—'a rich and prime example of gobbledygook'[139]—and his question whether the principle more generally was 'a busted flush'[140] are hardly ringing endorsements. Weatherill has opined that:

> [T]he principle of subsidiarity reflects concern about the scope of Community competence and its demarcation from national competence, but that it does little in practical terms to address that concern. It acts as an ill-defined counterweight to the expansion of Community competence agreed at Maastricht and apparent in the intense, multifunctional legislative activity since the entry into force of the Single European Act in 1987.[141]

He felt that the slogan of subsidiarity provided an essentially political framework within which key issues of where power resides could be discussed. Subsidiarity, in his view, intensified the debate about Community competence, rather than resolving it. However, he was relatively mild in his judgement:

> In conclusion, this identification of the subsidiarity principle as essentially fodder for a political talking-shop is not necessarily a point of criticism. It is not feasible that multifunctional activities of the modern Community, characterised by close interdependence with its Member States, could be reduced to a set of rules dictating who does what. Sector by sector, close attention must be devoted to planning the respective contributions of Community and national laws and Community and national implementation and administration of law and policy. If subsidiarity, as a question rather than an answer, has stimulated a more intensive, thoughtful examination of how the evolving European market should be regulated, then it will have fulfilled a valuable function.[142]

The shepherd, at that stage at least, was not really worried. As has been shown, though, his worries have increased considerably over the years.

8. Are Countries Fortunate?

Countries may be fortunate for a variety of reasons: the play of the cards has gone their way; they enjoy economic prosperity and independence; they have freedom

[139] In a letter to *The Independent*, 15 June 1992.
[140] In Dierdre Curtin and David O'Keeffe (eds), *Constitutional Adjudication in European Community and National Law* (*Essays for the Hon Mr Justice Thomas F O'Higgins*) (Butterworths, 1992) 19–24.
[141] Stephen Weatherill, *Law and Integration in the European Union* (Clarendon Press 1995) 172.
[142] ibid 172–73.

(of religion, or from foreign interference, for example); they are at peace with themselves and with others; they experience joy: '*Alle Menschen arden Brüder, Wo dein sanfter Flügel weilt*'.[143] Are they fortunate because of the European Union, and in particular EU law and its internal market? The good shepherd in his wisdom has recently made shrewd observations about thematic questions of the democratic implications of surrendering the right to regulate, to whom, why, and with what implications. With all his subtlety, experience, and understanding, Weatherill has evoked the spirit of European integration inspiringly:

> The answers to the thematic questions vary according to the legal and political context in which they are asked. The EU is neither state nor orthodox international organisation, but rather something in between, and its chosen answers to the key questions are the product of its relatively grand ambitions. Its law reveals a rather broad understanding of a trade barrier and a rather sophisticated approach to justifying such trade barriers. This emerges from its institutionally well-developed design: its powerful Court, and its directly effective and supreme legal order. Part of the EU story ... is its legislative process as well. In the EU, states have surrendered the right to regulate on the basis that they are allowed autonomy where their choices do not interfere with cross-border activity, that they have room to justify such practices even where they do so interfere and, in so far as the decision is taken to replace national rules with common EU rules, states have a voice in the legislative process. Most of all, in the EU, states surrender the right to regulate on these terms because they know that all the other Member States have agreed to the same surrender and because they know the EU puts in place a credible system for holding all participants to keep their bargain. The discipline exerted by the EU over state regulatory choices is a reflection of the EU's ambitions and design more generally.[144]

While those voters in the United Kingdom who allowed themselves to be deluded into voting for Brexit may well repent at leisure, the *communis opinio* is that the Member States of the EU are fortunate indeed. That is not to say that everything in the EU is perfect; a perfect state of affairs has never existed, and most likely never will, but the alternative to the EU—fragmentation, dissonance, unbounded nationalism, disregard for others, and maybe even the continuation of diplomacy by other means—would, just as surely as night follows day, lead to decided

[143] Friedrich Schiller, '*An die Freude*', 1st verse (in this version, posthumously published, 1808); Ludwig van Beethoven, 9th Symphony, 4th movement (tr 'All men will emerge as brothers, Where you rest your gentle wings').

[144] Stephen Weatherill, 'Surrendering the Right to Regulate' in Fabian Amtenbrink and others (eds), *The Internal Market and the Future of European Integration Essays in Honour of Laurence W Gormley* (Cambridge University Press 2019) 132–33.

misfortune. Even relative fortune is something which permits a positive answer to this question.

9. Concluding and Valedictory Observations

This contribution has surveyed Steve Weatherill's intellectual journey, his development as a good shepherd, and his concern for his sheepdog and his flock. Good husbandry and being a good and concerned neighbour have been hallmarks of Steve's professional career. He is a shepherd who understands his sheepdog and his flock in their context—inside and outside the pen, and in the wider (European) world. His concerns have been and are legitimate, but at the end of the day, sheep may indeed safely graze, not least for the reasons which have been quoted above.

Steve has had an outstanding academic career; he is much admired both by those who know him, and by those who only know him through his many works. His tenure of Chairs at Nottingham and at Oxford has been marked by a huge rise in the significance of EU law in academe, in publishing, in legal practice, and, despite Brexit, in the consciousness of the peoples of Europe and beyond. Steve's contribution to the critical understanding and development of EU law has been challenging, thought-provoking, and distinguished. His understanding of the subtleties of the law, its possibilities, and its context is that of a wise guide, philosopher, and friend. A good shepherd indeed, in whose care sheep may safely graze.

6

Chamber Music, Atonal: How the Structure of the CJEU Affects the Jurisprudence on Free Movement of Goods

*Stefan Enchelmaier**

It is not, of course, suggested that all the Court's decisions are poorly reasoned, but simply that this is true of enough of them to be a problem that needs to be addressed.[1]

It is highly regrettable that more time is not given to thinking how the Court should be structured. This is the Cinderella of all intergovernmental conferences.[2]

1. Introduction

Over the last ten years or so, criticism of the substance of the case law of the Court of Justice of the European Union (the Court) has been linked to an investigation into the institutional causes of the shortcomings observed. Woods came to the conclusion that 'the structures in place may not be sufficient to safeguard consistency, coherence and unity of EU law' under Articles 34 and 36.[3] Similarly Favale,

* Patrick Wittum's research assistance with below 5, Alternative Models, is gratefully acknowledged.

[1] Anthony Arnull, 'The Court of Justice Then, Now, and Tomorrow' in Mattias Derlén and Johan Lindholm (eds), *The Court of Justice of the European Union: Multidisciplinary Perspectives* (Hart Publishing 2018) 10.

[2] David Edward, evidence to the House of Lords Select Committee enquiry into the Lisbon Treaty (December 2007), 10th Report of Session 2007–08; HL Paper 62-II, vol II Evidence, Q132–34, cited after Lord Mance, 'The Composition of the European Court of Justice' (talk given to the United Kingdom Association for European Law, 19 October 2011) <www.supremecourt.uk/docs/speech_111019.pdfThis, and all websites subsequently cited, were last accessed on 21 October 2023>.

[3] Loran Woods, 'Consistency in the Chambers of the ECJ: A Case Study on the Free Movement of Goods' (2012) 31 Civil Justice Quarterly 340, 365.

Stefan Enchelmaier, *Chamber Music, Atonal: How the Structure of the CJEU Affects the Jurisprudence on Free Movement of Goods* In: *The Internal Market Ideal.* Edited by: Jeremias Adams-Prassl, Sanja Bogojević, Ariel Ezrachi, and Dorota Leczykiewicz, Oxford University Press. © Stefan Enchelmaier 2024. DOI: 10.1093/oso/9780192867063.003.0007

Kretschmer, and Torremans,[4] as well as Fhima and Denvir,[5] analysed the relationship between the Court's organization and its case law on copyright and trade mark law, respectively. Nic Shuibhne, in her comprehensive study on the (lack of) coherence in the Court's jurisprudence, also attended to the link between incoherence and institutional factors.[6]

This contribution considers some of the shortcomings in the Court's case law on the free movement of goods: namely, a lack of much discursive reasoning and uncertainty as to what constitutes a restriction of free movement. These flaws will be explained as consequences of the peculiar structure and operation of the Court. Those features of the Court are then compared with the organization and operation of the supreme courts of the United Kingdom, France, the United States, and Germany. From this comparison, suggestions will be derived for a reform of the Court.

2. Shortcomings in the Jurisprudence on Free Movement of Goods

Here is not the space for a comprehensive analysis of the case law on the free movement of goods. Rather, a small selection of cases must suffice to illustrate some of the shortcomings in the jurisprudence. They show a plethora of tests that are unclear partly in themselves, partly in their relationship with others. They also show that this is not a mere technicality but can distract from the issues that arise in a case. There is also another strand: namely, the lack of much explanation and the disposal of a case without much concern for the bigger picture of the jurisprudence.

As it happens, all the following judgments come from the Grand Chamber. This chamber, like all other chambers of the Court, frequently changes in its composition. The question will therefore be asked whether the shortcomings in the case law are a consequence of the regular turnover of judges and of the concomitant lack of specialization in the area of free movement of goods.

2.1 *Ålands Vindkraft*

Ålands Vindkraft is an example of a straightforward assessment which the Court (that is, the Grand Chamber) throws into confusion with a seemingly unguarded

[4] Marcella Favale, Martin Kretschmer, and Paul C Torremans, 'Is There an EU Copyright Jurisprudence? An Empirical Analysis of the Workings of the European Court of Justice' (2016) 79 Modern Law Review 31.

[5] Ilanah Fhima and Catrina Denvir, 'An Empirical Analysis of the Likelihood of Confusion Factors in European Trade Mark Law' (2015) 46 International Review of Intellectual Property and Competition Law 310.

[6] Niamh Nic Shuibhne, *The Coherence of EU Free Movement Law: Constitutional Responsibility and the Court of Justice* (Oxford University Press 2013) 54–62; see esp the tables at 57–58.

remark at the end. The eponymous plaintiff in the national proceedings had alleged, and the Court ultimately found, an infringement of Article 34 TFEU. This was said to ensue from Swedish legislation introducing aquota of certificates for green electricity. Suppliers and some consumers in Sweden on a particular date had to hold such certificates, corresponding to a proportion of the electricity they had supplied or consumed. Otherwise, a fee became payable. This scheme in effect reserved just shy of a fifth of the Swedish market for the consumption of electricity to green electricity producers located in Sweden. It worked to the inverse disadvantage of electricity imports from other Member States.[7]

Taking the definition of measures having equivalent effect to quantitative restrictions from *Dassonville* as its starting point,[8] the Court saw at least an indirect and potential hindrance to the importation of green electricity from other Member States. The compulsory quota of certificates could only be satisfied with certificates issued under the national scheme for green energy produced in Sweden. This was capable of impeding electricity imports from other Member States.[9] What is more, domestic producers could offer electricity and certificates together, as a package. This afforded them an advantage when it came to negotiating long-term supply contracts. Therein lay at least a potential disadvantage for imported electricity.[10]

Then the Court added a puzzling codicil. Referring to the advantage that national producers derived from the Swedish scheme, and citing the *Farmers' riots* case among others,[11] the Court explained that:

> [F]ailure by a Member State to adopt adequate measures to prevent barriers to the free movement of goods that have been created, in particular, through the actions of traders but made possible by specific legislation that that State has introduced, is just as likely to obstruct intra-Community trade as is a positive act.[12]

The Swedish rules invited or at least enabled the conduct by national providers that put their competitors from other Member States at a disadvantage. In the *Farmers' riots* case, by contrast, there was mere passivity on the part of the French authorities. No legal framework obliged or even merely encouraged the French farmers to attack lorries carrying produce of Spanish farmers. The more appropriate comparison would be with intellectual property legislation in the Member States. This allows proprietors in certain circumstances to exclude imports from other

[7] Case C-573/12 *Ålands Vindkraft AB v Energimyndigheten* ECLI:EU:C:2014:2037, paras 25 and 38.
[8] ibid para 66.
[9] ibid paras 67–70.
[10] ibid paras 71–73.
[11] The Court's references are to Case C-265/95 *Commission v France* ECLI:EU:C:1997:595 (*Farmers' riots*), para 31, and Case C-112/00 *Schmidberger* ECLI:EU:C:2003:333, para 58. As they are of the same ilk, this text will only deal with *Farmers' riots*.
[12] *Ålands Vindkraft* (n 7) para 74.

Member States into those Member States where the invention, presentation, etc, is protected.

In the case law, however, it was always clear that the point of reference is not the proprietors' availing themselves of the opportunities the legislation affords them. It is instead that legislation itself, and rightly so: commercial operators will seize whatever commercial chances they see, including those that arise from legislation. This is inevitable, and responsibility therefor lies squarely with the Member State that created the legislation. That legislation allows protection beyond the specific subject matter of the intellectual property right in question. It is therefore disproportionate in the sense of the second sentence of Article 36 TFEU. To that extent, it cannot be invoked by proprietors against imports from other Member States.

An analogous treatment of the situation in *Ålands Vindkraft* would, therefore, have required a proportionality assessment of the Swedish policy on green energy. It was rather simple for the Court merely to say the authorities had not done enough to stop Swedish producers playing to their strengths in negotiating long-term supply contracts.

There is another oddity about the Court's referencing the *Farmers' riots* case. The Commission had brought that case before the Court in view of the passivity of the French police over more than ten years of repeated and increasing violence by French farmers against produce imports from other Member States, especially from Spain. The Court's starting point was that Article 34 TFEU did not only catch hindrances to trade that the state itself had created. It also applied 'where a Member State abstains from adopting the measures required in order to deal with obstacles to the free movement of goods which are not caused by the State'.[13] Nevertheless, in deciding how to remove such obstacles caused by private parties, the Member States have a wide margin of discretion, so that only manifestly inadequate countermeasures are in breach of the provisions on free movement.[14]

One should therefore suppose that some similar assessment was called for in the 'omission' case of *Ålands Vindkraft*, too. There is little evidence of it anywhere in the judgment, though. Was the failure of the Swedish government obvious (which would have warranted stating, but was not), or is the *Farmers' riots* test now abandoned? If so, why refer to it first, and then not draw any explicit consequences? Citing *Farmers' riots* might simply be a thought that the Court threw in at the end without much consideration, a confirmation of a result already satisfactorily deduced. It will have to be seen whether this creates any confusion among national courts. They will wonder how much slack they can or must cut a government that argues it had tried its best, but in vain. Undoubtedly, however, it does not reflect well on the technical quality of the Court's judgment.

[13] *Farmers' riots* (n 11) para 30.

[14] ibid paras 33 and 52.

2.2 *TÜV Rheinland*

The Grand Chamber judgment in *TÜV Rheinland*[15] arose from civil litigation in the German courts between a German patient who had in Germany received faulty breast implants made in France. One of the defendants was the German insurance company that had provided cover for the French manufacturer. The insurance contract was governed by French law. Its conclusion had been imposed on the insurer by the competent French authority. Cover was limited to harm that occurred in metropolitan France or in the French overseas territories. The contract also gave injured persons a direct claim against the insurer. In its reference, the German court invited the CJEU to give 'an explicit ruling on whether [Article 18 TFEU] has direct horizontal effect, in the sense that it could be relied upon in a dispute between individuals'.[16]

The Court explained that Article 18 TFEU applied only to situations governed by EU law—that is, those within the scope of EU law—and in the absence of an applicable, more specific prohibition of discrimination.[17] Because no secondary EU law governed the subject matter of the litigation, the Court turned to the four freedoms of the TFEU. Their exercise brings the situation within the scope of the Treaty, provided there is 'a specific connecting factor linking the person, service or goods concerned and the alleged discrimination'. This will be present where the person allegedly discriminated against has moved within the EU, or 'where discrimination is the direct result of the national rules applicable to goods from other Member States'.[18]

No such obstacle had hindered the movement of the breast implants between Member States. It was not the goods' movement that was in issue, but whether the victim could obtain damages from the insurance for the harm the goods had done in one of the Member States. The Court found that the extent of civil liability insurance cover did not impair the marketing in another Member State of the products, or their movement within the EU.[19] The Court contrasted this with its findings in *Phil Collins* that:

> [T]he exclusive rights conferred by literary and artistic property are by their nature such as to affect trade in goods and services and also competitive relationships within the Community. For that reason ... those rights, although governed by national legislation, are subject to the requirements of the Treaty and therefore fall within its scope of application.

[15] Case C-581/18 *RB v TÜV Rheinland LGA Products GmbH, Allianz IARD SA* ECLI:EU:C:2020:453.
[16] ibid para 24.
[17] ibid paras 31–33.
[18] ibid paras 45–46.
[19] ibid paras 55–56.

From this it followed that Article 34 did not come to apply to the litigation in *TÜV Rheinland*.[20]

The judgment is remarkable for the absence of the usual assessment in cases involving the free movement of goods. Granted, the German court had framed its reference pointedly in terms of the application of Article 18 TFEU. This led the CJEU to identify as the salient issue the movement of goods across Member State borders. The answer is, in so many words, 'but they have moved'. Traditionally, however, the fact that goods have moved at all is not decisive,[21] not least because, under the *Dassonville* formula,[22] an indirect and potential hindrance suffices.

In passing, it can be remarked that the obstacle arose, if at all, from the terms of the contract—the conclusion of which was mandated by the French authority. This would bring the case within the ambit of Article 35 rather than Article 34. Never mind, the assessment under both provisions is now the same.[23] Previously, the Court applied Article 35 only to rules that established a separate and more burdensome regime for exports, so-called 'distinctly applicable' measures, as opposed to products made in a Member State, and sold on its domestic market.[24]

The consequent question in *TÜV Rheinland* would, therefore, have been whether the goods found it any more difficult, in law or in fact, to reach customers or users on the German market than products made in Germany. The absence of insurance cover for any damage suffered in Germany might, by the standards of other judgments (not least the one discussed next), at least have been seen as a potential and indirect dissuasion against choosing the French product over a German one.

The Court phrased this as 'discrimination [as] the direct result of the national rules applicable to goods from other Member States'. Nevertheless, all the national court received by way of explanation was a reference to *Phil Collins*. This is a judgment on the question of how intellectual property rights granted by the Member

[20] ibid para 56, referring to Joined Cases C-92/92 and 326/92 *Phil Collins* ECLI:EU:C:1993:847, para 22.

[21] Joined Cases 56 and 58–64 *Consten and Grundig v Commission* ECLI:EU:C:1966:41, para 341:

> [W]hat is particularly important is whether the agreement is capable of constituting a threat, either direct or indirect, actual or potential, to freedom of trade between Member States in a manner which might harm the attainment of the objectives of a single market between States. Thus the fact that an agreement encourages an increase, even a large one, in the volume of trade between States is not sufficient to exclude the possibility that the agreement may 'affect' such trade in the abovementioned manner.

[22] Case 8/74 *Procureur du Roi v Benoît and Gustave Dassonville* ECLI:EU:C:1974:82 (*Dassonville*), para 5. The Court in *Consten and Grundig* derived what undertakings are not allowed to do from the prohibition addressed at the Member States: '[t]he Treaty, whose preamble and content aim at abolishing the barriers between States, and which in several provisions gives evidence of a stern attitude with regard to their reappearance, could not allow undertakings to reconstruct such barriers', (n 21) 340. *Dassonville*, in turn, borrows the formula outlining the duties of Member States under art 34 from the prohibition addressed to undertakings.

[23] Case C-15/15 *New Valmar BVBA v Global Pharmacies Partner Health Srl* ECLI:EU:C:2016:464, paras 36 and 43.

[24] Case 15/79 *PB Groenveld BV v Produktschap voor Vee en Vlees* ECLI:EU:C:1979:253, paras 7 and 9.

States are affected by the rules on the free movement of goods. What this has to do with the facts of *TÜV Rheinland* is not immediately obvious. The referring court may have been somewhat surprised by this reference (if it chose to look it up).

At least the national court knew it need not worry further about either Article 18 or Article 34 TFEU. This is certainly a useful answer for that particular court. The judgment makes no effort, however, to make its findings readily applicable by other courts that might find themselves confronted with similar but not identical questions. The Grand Chamber gives little guidance beyond the case at hand. The Court's responsibility for 'the law' (Article 19(1) TEU) would certainly have allowed for a more principled answer.

2.3 *Austria v Germany (Infrastructure use charge)*

The Grand Chamber judgment in *Austria v Germany*[25] concerned charges that Germany levied on the use of its motorways by all passenger vehicles, whether registered in Germany or in other Member States. Nevertheless, relief by the same amount from motor vehicle tax was granted to vehicles registered in Germany (and hence liable to that tax there). The financial burden of the charge was thus felt only by drivers of passenger vehicles registered in other Member States.[26]

The Court first assessed the German rules under Article 18 TFEU. It held that there was unequal treatment of persons who found themselves in comparable situations, namely as users of German motorways. Moreover, the majority of owners and drivers of vehicles registered in Germany were German nationals, and vice versa for nationals of other Member States regarding vehicles registered in those states.[27] The passage is unremarkable except that it goes against what the Court had convincingly explained in *TÜV Rheinland* about the subsidiary application of Article 18 in relation to the four freedoms: these specific prohibitions take precedence over the general prohibition of discrimination.[28]

Turning to Article 34, the Court opened its assessment with the *Dassonville* formula, as interpreted in the *Moped trailers* judgment:

> [A] measure, even if it has neither the object nor the effect of treating goods coming from other Member States less favourably, also falls within the scope of the concept of a 'measure having equivalent effect to quantitative restrictions', within the meaning of Article 34 TFEU, if it hinders access to the market of a Member State of products originating in other Member States.[29]

[25] C-591/17 *Republic of Austria v Federal Republic of Germany* ECLI:EU:C:2019:504.
[26] ibid paras 1 and 48.
[27] ibid paras 46–51.
[28] See n 17.
[29] *Austria v Germany* (n 25) paras 120 and 121.

The Court found that the German rules restricted the market access of foreign goods delivered in passenger vehicles registered in Member States other than Germany: 'The infrastructure use charge to which, in reality, only the vehicles that carry those goods are subject is liable to increase the costs of transport and, as a consequence, the price of those goods, thereby affecting their competitiveness.'[30]

This again reveals the lack of definition of the Court's 'market access formula'.[31] What is decisive in the end is that the competitiveness of goods from other Member States is reduced more than that of their domestic competitors. The latter have the charges reimbursed; the former remain encumbered. This is, in other words, a discrimination assessment in disguise.

More fundamentally, the Court does not explain why passenger vehicles should be assumed to transport goods in the first place; that is, are involved in commercial transactions somewhere along the supply chain. Some might well be, which would be enough. The next step in the argument would have to be, however, that passenger vehicles registered in Germany are more likely to be used for the transport of goods made in Germany. This is by no means obvious. Passenger vehicles are not likely to be employed for importation. They will more often be the means of local distribution of goods that have earlier been imported or transported on lorries. For this category of vehicles, however, even if registered in Germany, there was no reimbursement of the charges; at least we are not told of any. Once the goods are in the country, however, any inequality (hindrance to market access/reduction in competitiveness) could only be a consequence of German-registered passenger vehicles being predominantly used for the transportation of German-made goods. In other words, the Court's discrimination assessment is sparsely reasoned, whether or not one concurs with the result.

The German government contended that the rules on the charges constituted mere 'rules relating to certain selling arrangements' in the sense of the *Keck* judgment.[32] The Court rejected this argument, holding that 'the concept of "selling arrangements" covers only provisions of national law that regulate the manner in which goods may be marketed, rules concerning the manner in which goods may be transported are not within the scope of that concept'.[33]

This is a condensed version of a passage in Advocate General Wahl's opinion. He had argued that '[t]he concept of selling arrangements covers only national rules that concern the "arrangements under which products may be sold"'. Examples were rules on when, where, how, and by whom products may be marketed. Such rules did not generally hinder market access. In his view, this was different for rules

[30] ibid paras 125–27; the quote is from para 127.

[31] See, in more detail, Stefan Enchelmaier, 'Free Movement of Goods: Evolution and Intelligent Design in the Foundations of the European Union' in Paul Craig and Gráinne de Búrca, *The Evolution of EU Law* (3rd edn, Oxford University Press 2021).

[32] Joined Cases C-267/91 and 268/91 *Keck* ECLI:EU:C:1993:905.

[33] *Austria v Germany* (n 25) para 128.

on the transportation of goods. Transportation rules had a 'more direct effect on the cross-border trade of goods by making imports and exports technically, economically or practically more difficult or even impossible'. They were in that akin to rules on use, which the Court had also not encompassed under *Keck*. The Advocate General saw this confirmed by a number of cases in which the Court dealt with transport restrictions under *Dassonville* and *Cassis de Dijon* rather than *Keck*.[34]

The concept of 'rules relating to certain selling arrangements' continues to vex the case law on free movement of goods. The Advocate General's first formula is circular, merely replacing 'selling' with 'sold'. The Court's is tautological, translating 'selling' into 'marketing', without further elucidating either. Instead, it declares apodictically that transporting does not come under marketing. The Advocate General also gives examples. The trouble with this is that examples presuppose that we already know what they have in common, and that we therefore understand what they are meant to illustrate.

At least the Advocate General provides a reason why rules on transportation are not rules relating to certain selling arrangements: they affect the movement of goods across the borders between Member States more severely than movement within one national market alone. This is part of a discrimination assessment (establishing legal or factual inequality). It does not, however, depend on the slippery concept of rules relating to certain selling arrangements.[35] The same assessment underlies two of the three cases to which the Advocate General refers.[36]

The Court also dismissed the German government's argument that any restrictive effects of the infrastructure use charge were too uncertain and indirect to infringe Article 34 TFEU, reiterating that the charge increased transport costs and thus the price of goods from other Member States.[37] In somewhat more detail, the Advocate General had explained that 'national measures whose restrictive effects were "too uncertain and indirect", "purely speculative" or "too insignificant and uncertain" do not infringe Article 34 TFEU'. That was true, in his opinion, especially with regard to measures that 'make no distinction according to the origin of goods transported' and 'the purpose [of which] is not to regulate trade in goods with other Member States'.[38]

The criteria 'too uncertain and indirect' do not readily lend themselves to judicial application (how long is a piece of string?), nor do the alternative formulations that the Advocate General had quoted from earlier judgments. The Advocate General adds that consequences 'too uncertain and indirect' will follow from indistinctly applicable rules. These rules must not, moreover, be specifically designed to

[34] Case C–591/17 *Republic of Austria v Federal Republic of Germany* ECLI:EU:C:2019:99, Opinion of AG Wahl, para 118.

[35] See, in more detail, Enchelmaier (n 31) 568–72.

[36] The reference to Case C–112/00 *Schmidberger* ECLI:EU:C:2003:333 in fn 62 of the opinion in *Austria v Germany* is puzzling: in paras 51–63 of *Schmidberger*, the Court does not apply the principles from *Cassis*, by contrast with the Advocate General's assertion that it does.

[37] *Austria v Germany* (n 25) para 129.

[38] *Austria v Germany*, Opinion of AG Wahl (n 34) para 123.

regulate trade. There is no explanation for this. It has been established since *Cassis de Dijon* that the uneven factual repercussions of indistinctly applicable measures bring them within the compass of Article 34. What is more, it is irrelevant what a rule is 'designed' to do: it is the rule's effects that count under Article 34's prohibition of measures having equivalent 'effect'. Member States are likely to contend that their legislation was adopted innocently, without so much of a thought about its repercussions on imports. Here, the question is which effects result from the interaction of one provision with others; that is, the rules on the charges and the rules on their reimbursement. What is more, strictly speaking, the Court does not engage with the criteria 'too uncertain and indirect' at all, but merely asserts the inequality created by the charges. This is again part of the discrimination test that permeates the assessment under all freedoms of the internal market.[39]

In all, therefore, much of the judgment is taken up by discussing old questions. The central question, of the link between the levying of the charge on passenger vehicles and its repercussions on goods, is hardly explained, but rather presumed.

2.4 Some Figures on the Case Law on Free Movement of Goods, 2012–2021

The above judgments were all the Grand Chamber's. As it turned out, even between judgments by that same formation of the Court, there were inconsistencies. The Grand Chamber is not the only chamber that hears cases on the free movement of goods, and by far not the busiest in this regard, either. In fact, all chambers are involved. This multiplies the potential for incongruous judgments. Woods[40] analysed the case law of the decade up to 2011 in this regard. Concerning the subsequent ten years' jurisprudence, a search on the Court's website[41] under terms 'quantitative restrictions', 'Article 34 TFEU', 'charges having equivalent effect', 'Article 30 TFEU', and 'Article 110 TFEU' yields sixty-nine judgments. Of those, the following numbers of cases were decided by each chamber:

19: 4th chamber;
11: 2nd chamber; 5th chamber;
8: Grand Chamber;
5: 1st chamber, 3rd chamber;
4: 7th chamber;
2: 6th chamber; 9th chamber;
1: 8th chamber; 10th chamber.

39 See, in more detail, Enchelmaier (n 31) 563–66.
40 Woods (n 3).
41 The search form is available at <https://curia.europa.eu/juris/recherche.jsf?language=en>.

Every chamber thus had at least one case from this area, but the bulk of the jurisprudence came from three chambers, with the Grand Chamber close behind. Even the most prolific chamber, however, had less than two cases per year over the entire period. Still greater intervals come to light when one does not look at the chambers but rather at the judges who produced the first draft of the judgment of the chamber. The following judges were the *juges rapporteurs* in the following numbers of cases:

5: Ilešič, Juhász, Lycourgos, Rodin;
4: Prechal, Vajda, Vilaras, Bonichot;
3: Silva de Lapuerta;
2: da Cruz Vilaça, Jarašiūnas, Jarukaitis, Jürimäe, Levits, Lõhmus, Malenovský, Regan, Schiemann, Šváby, Toader;
1: Arabadjiev, Berger, Fernlund, Jääskinen, Kumin, Lenaerts, Piçarra, Rossi.

In all, twenty-eight judges acted as the *juge rapporteur* in the relevant period. Granted, in this snapshot some were at the end and some at the beginning of their tenure at the Court. Nevertheless, over a period of ten years, both anomalies should roughly cancel each other out. Even the judges most closely involved with the cases on the free movement of goods, therefore, had not quite one case for every year of their six-year tenure. We can ignore reappointments, which would work out at one case every other year in the relevant period. Most judges drafted only one judgment every three (five if reappointed) or even six (ten) years.

Advocates General provided opinions in a total of sixty-four cases (not every one of the above sixty-nine cases was accompanied by an opinion):

9: Bot, Szpunar;
7: Sharpston;
6: Jääskinen, Saugmansgaard Øe;
4: Mengozzi, Wahl;
3: Bobek, Campos Sánchez-Bordona, Hogan, Kokott, Wathelet;
1: Cruz Villalón, Pitruzella, Tanchev, Trstenjak.

This means three cases every two years, at most, for those Advocates General with a single period of tenure of six years at the Court, or three over four years in case of a reappointment. The majority of the sixteen involved, however, have far fewer.

Overall, a picture emerges of a great number of individuals being only sporadically involved in shaping the jurisprudence on free movement of goods. There is no more than a modicum of specialization among the Advocates General, and even less among the judges. A small number of judgments, moreover, are not accompanied by an opinion. On those occasions, the chamber cannot benefit from a prior analysis of the issues at hand, and of the case law in the area. To understand this better requires a look at the organization of the Court into chambers, and at the allocation of cases to the chambers.

3. The Court's Organization

The Court is subdivided into chambers. These have either three or five members (referred to herein as ordinary chambers). Aside from these, there is the Grand Chamber. There are also other formations of the Court, but these have not so far played a role in the development of the case law on the free movement of goods. They will therefore not be discussed here.

3.1 Ordinary Chambers

The Court currently has ten ordinary chambers. Half of the ordinary chambers have five members; the other half, three.[42] The presidents of these chambers are elected for three years (chambers of five judges) or one year (chambers of three judges).[43] The remaining judges are allocated to the chambers, rather than elected. This is done with the help of a list of all judges, on which they appear in order of seniority, calculated from the date they took office.[44]

The allocation for a chamber of five starts with the most senior judge to be allocated to a chamber, then goes to the most junior, back to the second-most senior, and second-most junior; the president will be skipped, should she or he come up in this way.[45] Each chamber of five contains within it a chamber of three, composed of the four judges of the chamber of five, minus that chamber's president. The president of the chamber of three is one of those four judges. For each case heard by a chamber of three, the two judges who are not the president rotate, again in order of seniority.[46] In this way, the sixth chamber is contained within the first, the seventh within the second, and so forth. For the chambers of five and three judges a mix of experience is thus ensured. In the case of both sorts of chambers, their constitution is not determined by subject matter, nor their composition by the substantive legal expertise of the judges allocated.

[42] Assignment of Judges to Chambers [2021] OJ C513/09, 3–4.
[43] Rules of Procedure of the Court of Justice (RoP) arts 12(1) and (2). Consolidated version available at <https://curia.europa.eu/jcms/upload/docs/application/pdf/2012-10/rp_en.pdf>.
[44] ibid art 7(1).
[45] ibid arts 28(1)–(2), 27(4).
[46] ibid arts 28(1) (second sentence) and 28(3).

3.2 Grand Chamber

The Grand Chamber is composed of the President of the Court, its Vice President, three presidents of chambers of five (rotating in order of seniority), a judge who drafts the judgment (*juge rapporteur*), and additional judges to bring the number of members to fifteen (allocated like the judges for the chambers of five).[47] Here again, therefore, the judges are not allocated by expertise, but by seniority. In all, the constitution of the ordinary chambers as well as of the Grand Chamber does not guarantee that any specific subject-matter expertise of the judges involved is enlisted for the legal matter at hand. By the same token, there is no guarantee that the case law will develop in a systematic and coherent manner.

4. The Allocation of Cases

4.1 Ordinary Chambers

After proceedings have been initiated, the President of the Court appoints a *juge-rapporteur* to the case.[48] Similarly, the First Advocate General assigns each case to an Advocate General.[49] The designation of the *juge-rapporteur* will at the same time determine the ordinary chamber to decide the case, namely the chamber of either five or three to which this judge belongs. What size of chamber is chosen depends on the 'difficulty or importance of the case or particular circumstances'.[50] The default choice will therefore, presumably, be the chamber of five, the more difficult cases going 'up' to the Grand Chamber, the easier ones 'down' to the chamber of three judges. The initial choice is made by the Court, acting through the President. The chamber originally chosen can, however, request that the case be assigned to a formation consisting of more judges. In that case, the members of the original chamber will be included among the judges of the larger chamber.[51] The other judges are appointed as described above to hear that case.

Several chambers can thus come to work in the same area, with none having any particular expertise in it. What is more, the possibilities are limited for any coordination on the substance of the judgments, and for the avoidance of incoherence in the case law. After the close of the written procedure in a case, the *juge-rapporteur* presents a preliminary report to the general meeting of the Court pursuant to Article 25 of the Rules of Procedure. This report contains proposals largely of a procedural nature. Substance comes into play only in the *juge-rapporteur's* proposal (if

47 ibid arts 27(1)–(4).
48 ibid art 15(1).
49 ibid art 16(1).
50 ibid art 60(1).
51 ibid arts 60(3) and 29(2).

they so propose) to dispense with a hearing and with an opinion by the Advocate General.[52] The latter would be predicated on the absence of a new point of law.[53] Nevertheless, the general meeting is expressly only called on to take '[d]ecisions concerning administrative issues or the action to be taken upon the proposals contained in the preliminary report'.[54] It is not specifically meant to be a forum for discussing substantive issues in any depth.

Also, there is no realistic chance of correcting case law incoherence or any other flaws once they have arisen. All subsequent formations of the Court suffer from the lack of specialization that brought about the shortcomings in case law in the first place. This can arise because there are no objective, pre-determined criteria for the allocation of cases to the specific and stable formations of the Court.

4.2 Grand Chamber

The allocation of cases to the Grand Chamber follows the same criteria, ie, 'the difficulty or importance of the case or particular circumstances'. A Member State and the institutions of the EU may, however, according to Article 16 of the Protocol on the Statute of the Court of Justice (an annexe to the Treaty) demand that a case to which they are parties be heard by the Grand Chamber.[55]

Regardless of whether a case is originally assigned to the Grand Chamber, or whether it is passed up to it by a chamber of three or five judges, therefore, the selection of judges to the Grand Chamber does not follow their expertise. It merely convenes a larger number of judges and thus, between them, a greater amount of accumulated general experience. This offers the possibility of more contributions to the discussion among the judges, but also creates a greater challenge of making sure everyone is heard equally. There is also the difficulty of ensuring that the discussion among the judges of the Grand Chamber has the same intensity as in the smaller and more static formations. Some of the judges of the Grand Chamber rotate with each case; the members of the smaller formations may or may not be among the judges sitting as the Grand Chamber, depending on where the case was

[52] ibid art 59(2):

> The preliminary report shall contain proposals as to whether particular measures of organisation of procedure, measures of inquiry or, if appropriate, requests to the referring court or tribunal for clarification should be undertaken, and as to the formation to which the case should be assigned. It shall also contain the Judge-Rapporteur's proposals, if any, as to whether to dispense with a hearing and as to whether to dispense with an Opinion of the Advocate General.

[53] Statute of the Court of Justice, art 20(5): 'Where it considers that the case raises no new point of law, the Court may decide, after hearing the Advocate General, that the case shall be determined without a submission from the Advocate General.'

[54] RoP (n 43) art 25.

[55] ibid art 60(1).

originally assigned.[56] In every other respect, the workings of the Grand Chamber are the same as those of the ordinary chambers: following the opinion of the Advocate General, the *juge-rapporteur* drafts a judgment which is then discussed and redacted by all the judges, before it is finalized for publication by the President and the President's staff.

Article 25(1) of the Rules of Procedure of the General Court allows for a principled allocation of cases to chambers,[57] but this provision has no counterpart in the rules for the Court of Justice. More specifically, the Grand Chamber of the CJEU comes into play in accordance with the 'difficulty or importance' of the case, but there are no articulated yardsticks for either. As the judgments analysed above show, the allocation of a case to the Grand Chamber is no guarantee of more profound reflection and clearer articulation of the judgment.

4.3 Nic Shuibhne's Suggestion for a New 'Apex' Court

Nic Shuibhne analysed a number of these problems in her sweeping study on the coherence of the Court's case law on free movement and suggests a solution. She sees the current 'flat' structure of the Court at the root of the problem of incoherence. Once a case is decided by, say, a chamber of three judges, there is no appeal. From then on, incoherent strands coexist in the case law. Corrections can only come from the Court itself (but hardly ever do) or from (even less probable) Treaty amendment by the Member States.

The problem is, in other words, the present combination of first instance and constitutional functions in one court. Nic Shuibhne suggests a number of solutions to this, her preferred option being 'a new apex court … to take direct oversight responsibility of the development of EU law'. By contrast with the current Grand Chamber of fifteen constantly rotating members, Nic Shuibhne argues, such a court needs to be smaller and its composition relatively static. Courts are not meant to be political institutions; she therefore sees no inherent requirement for them to be representative.[58]

[56] Nic Shuibhne (n 6) 57–58 examines the effects of the quicker rotation in the Grand Chamber on recent seminal judgments, three each on the use of goods and on citizenship, respectively. It turns out that no judges or Advocates General (in the goods cases) or only two (citizenship) were involved in more than one judgment from each line, and none in all. The idea of fostering case law coherence through this particular reform was therefore in her judgement 'completely misguided'.

[57] [2015] OJ L105/1, as subsequently amended. Consolidated version available at <https://curia.europa.eu/jcms/upload/docs/application/pdf/2023-03/trib_rp_vers_conso_en.pdf>): 'The General Court shall lay down criteria by which cases are to be allocated among the Chambers. The General Court may make one or more Chambers responsible for hearing and determining cases in specific matters.' This was implemented in the Criteria for the assignment of cases to Chambers [2019] OJ C246/02: Chambers 1–4 are allocated civil service cases; Chambers 5–10, intellectual property cases; all Chambers, competition cases; the cases in each area allocated among chambers in turn.

[58] Nic Shuibhne (n 6) 59–61.

Nic Shuibhne is right in highlighting these concerns. The Member States are likely, however, to require some persuading before they contemplate the creation of a whole new court. Even then, it is anything but certain that the new body would really be smaller or otherwise very different from the existing Court. The Member States' instinct is that 'all must have prizes'.

This was in evidence in the spring of 2015: the General Court had asked for a limited number of new judges, yet the selection of candidates from some Member States but not from others proved politically impossible. As a result, each Member State was given an additional judge, but no new *référendaires* were hired to support them.[59]

This is no surprise: all judges of the Court earn the same salary (as arguably they should). The judges of the Court and General Court, respectively, as well as the Advocate General from a number of Member States each receive the combined salary of several cabinet members in those states. No politician worth his salt would lightly surrender the power of patronage that comes with such a prize (at little or no additional cost to the national budget in a majority of Member States). It can only be hoped that in these circumstances the choice will always be determined purely by the candidates' qualification in matters of EU law. At any rate, the creation of a nimbler new court will be a hard sell to say the least.

Nic Shuibhne asserts that such a new court would not have to be a representative institution. We can only speculate whether this implies that, in her view, the representative nature of the present Court is one of the causes of the lack of coherence in the case law. Nic Shuibhne does not discuss the consequences for her topic of the fact that the first and indispensable qualification of each judge and Advocate General, the *conditio sine qua non* of being called to the Court, is the nationality of the person concerned. This overriding criterion narrows the pool of qualified candidates considerably.

What is more, the vetting committee established under Article 255 TFEU (introduced by the Lisbon Treaty in 2009) contains, among others, former members of the Court. These, as well as the other members of the committee, are appointed by the Council on the initiative of the President of the Court. It is probably too early to say whether, in this way, fresh thinking on a high level can be assured, or whether on the contrary there is an in-built tendency to perpetuate the Court's established modes of judging.

[59] cf Duncan Robinson, 'Judges Multiply as EU States Fail to Agree on Appointments' *Financial Times* (London, 13 April 2015) 6. This resulted in an amendment to art 48 of the Statute of the Court of Justice, which now reads 'The General Court shall consist of:

(a) 40 Judges as from 25 December 2015;
(b) 47 Judges as from 1 September 2016;
(c) two Judges per Member State as from 1 September 2019.'

Consolidated version available at <https://curia.europa.eu/jcms/upload/docs/application/pdf/2016-08/tra-doc-en-div-c-0000-2016-201606984-05_00.pdf>.

5. Alternative Models

All is not lost, however, with the Court as presently organized. On closer inspection, incoherence usually originates in case law that is uncoordinated as between different chambers or different compositions of the Grand Chamber; Nic Shuibhne's tables[60] offer an instructive snapshot of this. Several chambers can come to work in the same area, with none having any particular expertise in it. The Grand Chamber is even more generalist than the smaller chambers. Like the smaller chambers, it has no assigned subject matter, but it draws together even more judges without specific expertise in the subject matter of a given case. These judges, moreover, can come from any chamber, not necessarily from those between whose jurisprudence incoherences have arisen. Not surprisingly, the record of the Grand Chamber is mixed. Not all judgments by that formation have been models of clarity—perhaps the most prominent recent example being the opaque decision at the end of the long-drawn-out *Moped trailers* case.[61] The problem seems to be that with fifteen judges acting in a case of, *ex hypothesi*, heightened importance (howsoever defined), formulaic and vague compromise formulae are hard to avoid, as Nic Shuibhne rightly points out.[62]

5.1 United Kingdom

In a comparative perspective, with its lack of division according to substantive criteria, the Court of Justice resembles the common law courts of last instance. Nevertheless, English judges have virtually all risen from the High Court, whose divisions and specialist lists ensure that each has a defined expertise: the Chancery Division with its specialist lists, viz the Companies Court, Patents Court, and Bankruptcy Court; the Queen's Bench Division with the Admiralty Court, Commercial Court, Technology and Construction Court, and Administrative Court; and the Family Division.

The Court of Appeal still has two divisions, civil and criminal, and in appropriate cases draws on its judges' experience gathered in the High Court. In some specialist matters—intellectual property, say, or tax law—this is always the expertise of individuals, not of a larger number of judges. Permission to appeal may be granted by the High Court or by Court of Appeal itself. This creates at the appeals level the docket control that the High Court does not have when it hears a case at first instance (cases can reach the High Court from courts and tribunals beneath it).

60 Nic Shuibhne (n 6) 57–58.
61 Case C-110/05 *Commission v Italy* ECLI:EU:C:2009:66 (*Moped trailers*).
62 Nic Shuibhne (n 6) 59, fn 109.

In the Supreme Court, there will (also) be a certain deference to individual judges' expertise in specialist subjects so that here, too, there is some meaningful division of labour. In addition, the Supreme Court has control over the number of cases it hears. According to The Supreme Court (Constitutional Reform) Act 2005, s 40(6), it must give permission to appeal. It will only do so if a case raises a 'point of general public importance'. Out of the several hundred petitions in any given year, it accepts only around fifty. When it does so, it will hear a case with an uneven number of at least three judges (s 23(1)). It will allocate more than five judges to a case if, among other things, it is asked to depart from a previous decision or if a conflict between decisions in the (former) House of Lords, the (Judicial Committee of the) Privy Council, and/or the Supreme Court has to be reconciled.[63]

5.2 France

In France, there is even more differentiation. The French *Cour de Cassation* has six chambers, each with defined portfolios of subject areas according to the *Code de l'organisation judiciaire* (COJ):[64] three civil chambers (first, second, third), commercial, economic, and financial chambers; social chamber; criminal chamber; and mixed chamber (*chambre mixte*[65]).[66] The mixed chamber hears a case when a question arises that comes within the jurisdiction of several chambers, when a question has received or is likely to receive divergent solutions before the chambers,[67] or when a case is allocated to the mixed chamber by order of the first president or judgment of a chamber seized.[68] The other chambers are subdivided into sections.[69]

Cases are decided by panels of at least five judges. The chamber president may decide, however, to have the chamber sit *in plenum* instead. This course will be chosen when, for instance, the chamber contemplates departing from its previous case law. The several appeals courts (*cours d'appel*) are similarly subdivided into a *chambre sociale*, *chambre commerciale*, and *chambre civile*. Below it sit the *tribunaux d'instance* for general private law cases of a value of under €10,000, the *tribunaux de grande instance* for those from €10,000, the *tribunaux de commerce*, and the labour courts (*conseil de prud'hommes*).

[63] The complete list is under <www.supremecourt.uk/procedures/panel-numbers-criteria.html>. The judges of the Supreme Court, together with those of the Court of Appeal, also sit on the Privy Council; before long, there will be no more judges who sat in the old House of Lords.
[64] Code de l'organisation judiciaire (COJ) arts L 421-1, R 421-3.
[65] ibid art L 421-4.
[66] See also <https://www.courdecassation.fr/la-cour/lorganisation-de-la-cour-de-cassation/les-six-chambres-de-la-cour-de-cassation>.
[67] COJ (n 64) art L 431-5.
[68] ibid art L 421-7.
[69] ibid art R 421-3.

The *Cour de Cassation* has no control over the number of cases that come before it. The result is a load of around 25,000 cases per year (18,000 civil; 7,000 criminal).[70]

5.3 United States

The competences and procedure of the Supreme Court with its nine justices is determined by 28 USC §1251ff. Of interest here is the Supreme Court's jurisdiction over petitions for writs of *certiorari* (28 USC § 1254ff). The Court can select cases within its discretion (US Supreme Court Rule 10). It will do so only in compelling cases such as conflicts in the interpretation of federal law including the constitution, egregious departures from the accepted and usual course of judicial proceedings, and important questions of federal law. Out of the roughly 7,000–8,000 petitions per year, plenary review is granted to approximately eighty cases. Another 100 or more cases are disposed of without oral argument.[71] The Supreme Court has no internal subdivisions and concomitant division of labour. It usually sits en banc, ie as a plenary court including all justices. Some specialization exists, by contrast, in the federal courts of appeal and in the district courts.

5.4 Germany

The German *Bundesgerichtshof* has thirteen civil panels (senates) with defined specializations (and six criminal senates, with partial specialization among three). The *Bundesgerichtshof* is considered the *primus inter pares* of the five supreme courts, each with its own specialization in administrative (*Bundesverwaltungsgericht*), social (*Bundessozialgericht*), tax (*Bundesfinanzhof*), employment (*Bundesarbeitsgericht*), and general private as well as criminal law (*Bundesgerichtshof*).

Of special interest here is the mechanism for ensuring the coherence of the *Bundesgerichtshof*'s jurisprudence. The jurisdiction of the civil senates is defined by subject matter: the First deals with, inter alia, copyright and select commercial matters; the Second with company law; the Third with state liability; the Fourth with succession; the Fifth with land law; the Sixth with delict; the Seventh with service contracts; the Eighth with sale of goods; the Ninth with credit transactions; the Tenth with patent law; the Eleventh with banking and

[70] <www.courdecassation.fr/institution_1/presentation_2845/>.

[71] <www.supremecourt.gov/about/courtatwork.aspx>.

moveable property; the Twelfth with family law; and the Thirteenth with public procurement.[72]

This ensures specialization, but it cannot prevent overlap. If, for example, a bank seeks to realize security in the insolvency of a company, there may be jurisprudence on the matter by the Second, Ninth, and Eleventh senates. The senate before which the case pends may wish to deviate from a legal principle articulated by one of the other senates (including the Grand Senate mentioned shortly). In that case, the senate that contemplates the deviation explains its reasons and asks other senate(s) that have espoused that principle whether they stand by their view, or whether they agree to the proposed departure. If there is no agreement, the matter is brought before the specially summoned 'Grand Senate' (*Großer Zivilsenat*) consisting of the court's president and one member from each of all the civil senates. The position adopted by the Grand Senate is binding on all senates.[73] In this way, one or several of the positions defined earlier are rejected in favour of the solution adopted by the Grand Senate.

The Law on the Unity of the Jurisprudence (*Rechtsprechungseinheitsgesetz*) provides for a similar mechanism in case a senate of one of the federal courts wants to deviate from the jurisprudence of a senate of another federal court.[74]

5.5 Comparative Conclusions

The common law model of the United Kingdom and of the United States ensures coherence in the case law through a combination of specialization in the lower instances, and docket control at the highest. This cannot easily be transferred to the CJEU. When it comes to the free movement of goods, there is no first instance court whose judgments are reviewed by the CJEU. What is more, under Articles 258 and 267 TFEU, the Court has next to no control over the number of cases that are brought before it. That decision lies instead with the Commission and with the national courts, respectively. The French and German models are more promising

72 For details see <www.bundesgerichtshof.de/DE/DasGericht/Geschaeftsverteilung/SachlicheZustaendigkeit/sachlicheZustaendigkeit_node.html>. Similar specializations are found in the Courts of Appeal (*Oberlandesgerichte*) and High Courts (*Landgerichte*).

73 *Gerichtsverfassungsgesetz* (GVG) [the German equivalent to the UK's Supreme Court Act 1981] ss 132(2), (3), and (5) <www.gesetze-im-internet.de/gvg/index.html>; English version at <www.gesetze-im-internet.de/englisch_gvg/index.html>. For an example, see the decision in [1998] Neue Juristische Wochenschrift 671, in which the Grand Senate decided a controversy between the Ninth (insolvency) and Eleventh (banking) senates on when a secured creditor must release assets whose value exceeds that of the secured debt. In the run-up to this, the Seventh (enforced collection) and Eighth (sale of goods) senates, but not the Eleventh, had been won over by the arguments of the Ninth senate.

74 The full title of the Act is (currently) *Gesetz zur Wahrung der Einheitlichkeit der Rechtsprechung der obersten Gerichtshöfe des Bundes vom 19. Juni 1968 (BGBl. I S. 661), das zuletzt durch Artikel 144 der Verordnung vom 31. August 2015 (BGBl. I S. 1474) geändert worden ist* <www.gesetze-im-internet.de/rspreinhg/index.html>.

because they feature specialization at the level of the highest court itself, rather than below.

6. Suggestions for Reforms to the Structure of the CJEU

At the Court of Justice, the French or German mechanisms for ensuring the coherence of the case law could be replicated, or a similar one created, to give the Grand Chamber a meaningful role in assuring the quality of the case law. According to Article 253 TFEU, final paragraph, the Court itself can, with the approval of the Council, amend its Rules of Procedure. Any amendments must, however, keep within the framework set by the Statute of the Court of Justice.[75] This is because, pursuant to Article 51 TEU, the Statute is laid down in a Protocol which in turn is part of the Treaty. It can, therefore, only be amended in the same way as the Treaty itself. The second, third, and fifth paragraphs of Article 16 of the Statute[76] are the relevant provisions with regard to any reorientation in the role of the Grand Chamber. The second paragraph with its reference to the Rules of Procedure would easily accommodate this reorientation. The third paragraph[77] only stipulates an additional way in which cases can come before the Grand Chamber and hence would be unaffected. The fifth paragraph[78] would also apply in the same way after as before, as it does not say anything about a (potential) conflict between several chambers.[79] Alternatively, 'exceptional importance' can, without any violence to the wording, be read to encompass the prevention or rectification of incoherence in the case law.

Any tinkering with the Grand Chamber aside, specialization among chambers would be the easiest and safest way of ensuring case law coherence. This would, over time, make referrals to the Grand Chamber as rare as they are within the *Bundesgerichtshof* to the Grand Senate.

Again, entirely in keeping with the Statute of the Court, this could be brought about by putting each of the smaller chambers permanently in charge of specific areas of EU law: one chamber for each freedom, one for agriculture and fisheries,

[75] See Treaty on the Functioning of the European Union, art 251.

[76] 'The Grand Chamber shall consist of 15 Judges. It shall be presided over by the President of the Court. The Vice-President of the Court and, in accordance with the conditions laid down in the Rules of Procedure, three of the Presidents of the chambers of five Judges and other Judges shall also form part of the Grand Chamber.'

[77] 'The Court shall sit in a Grand Chamber when a Member State or an institution of the Union that is party to the proceedings so requests.'

[78] 'Moreover, where it considers that a case before it is of exceptional importance, the Court may decide, after hearing the Advocate General, to refer the case to the full Court.'

[79] It is, in that respect, equivalent to §132(4) GVG (n 73), allowing any senate at any time to make a referral to the Grand Senate if a question is of 'fundamental importance' ('*grundlegende Bedeutung*') or if it deems it necessary in order to 'secure the uniformity of the jurisprudence' ('*Sicherung einer einheitlichen Rechtsprechung*').

one for competition (all of these dealing with preliminary references in their respective fields), one for actions between institutions, one for actions brought by individuals, and other subject matters dealt with in the Treaty parcelled out according to their substantive proximity to the portfolio of one chamber or other, the rest so as to balance the workload between chambers. General questions, such as the direct effect of provisions of EU law, would be dealt with by all chambers.

This would, however, only be the first step to creating the 'institutional memory' that is currently lacking; the somewhat haphazard selection of case law references by the Court, and its, at times, idiosyncratic interpretation of previous judgments also does not help to develop a sense of orientation through 'leading cases'.[80] The chamber as such is only an organizational cipher without any awareness of the development of the case law and of the need for coherence. Only the judges have such awareness, and it takes time to form.

It would therefore be necessary to attach each judge, or at least the president of the chamber, to that specific chamber for the whole duration of their tenure at the Court (or at least for one six-year term). One and the same person or group of persons will more easily notice if they are about to contradict what they said on an earlier occasion, or when such a thicket of principles has grown up that even the specialists find it hard to say which applies when.

Advocates General would not be strictly necessary in such a structure, as the newly specialized chambers would need less guidance in their own areas of expertise. The post cannot, however, be abolished without Treaty amendment. Instead, the Advocates General could evolve into custodians of case law coherence, advising chambers when it is not clear whether there is incoherence at all, whether another chamber's opinion should be asked, or whether a specific question should be referred to the Grand Chamber. As hitherto, the Advocates General could also present overviews of the case law and make suggestions regarding the position to be adopted by the chamber in matters where a 'second opinion' appears desirable to the chamber where it is not clear whether a formal passing-on to the Grand Chamber is indicated.

In this way, the Advocates General would be relieved of the duty to deliver opinions in all but the least demanding cases. They would instead be able, in cooperation with the specialist chambers, to concentrate on ensuring that the 'bigger picture' of the case law remains coherent.

Why does the CJEU not follow a more rational model of organizing its business? Why does every judge deal with everything ad hoc, and with nothing on a long-term basis? The reason is probably the fear that judgments would enjoy less acceptance once the chamber dealing with free movement of goods, say, or competition, had been headed for some time (as would be in accordance with the logic of

[80] I am grateful to Dorota Leczykiewicz for this observation.

creating such specializations) by the same judge, and thus came to be viewed as the 'Italian' or the 'Danish' or the 'Greek' chamber.

Also, some chambers might be viewed as more prestigious than others—which judge of any ambition would want to specialize in herring catch quota when another chamber deals with free movement of goods? Such lopsidedness in the distribution of the chambers' portfolios should be avoidable. Nevertheless, chambers of three judges are here to stay, short of Treaty amendment, and so it might be necessary to allocate some 'smaller matters' to these. It is another question whether each five-judge chamber could within it contain a three-judge chamber, to be activated in 'easier' cases or in standard cases, with the five only looking into more complex matters. Neither Statute nor Rules seem to exclude this possibility. Chambers of even size would, at any rate, be preferable, not least in order to avoid the question of what is 'easy' or 'difficult'.

7. Conclusion

The spotlight that was shone above on the case law on the free movement of goods has revealed shortcomings in the judgments that arguably result from a lack of specialization among the formations of the Court. Such specialization is found in other highest courts, of both Member States and non-member states of the EU. The provisions governing the composition and procedures of the CJEU would accommodate a specialization among the Court's chambers. This would also allow the replication of mechanisms that are found in at least two Member States, France and Germany, for ensuring the coherence of the case law as between specialist subdivisions of the highest court. The necessary reforms can be enacted by the Court by virtue of its power of autonomous amendment of its Rules of Procedure. Council approval should not be elusive, as the matter touches few, if any, politically sensitive points.

7
Fundamental Rights and Treaty Freedoms: The 'Derogation Situation' and Infringement Proceedings

*Sacha Prechal**

1. Introduction

The relationship between the fundamental Treaty freedoms and fundamental rights has given—and still gives—rise to various questions, such as how to reconcile the two, whether there is a hierarchical relationship between the two, whether they have the same constitutional standing, whether one should be prioritized over the other and under what circumstances, etc. There is a rich debate going in these matters, to which Stephen Weatherill has actively contributed.[1]

One of the themes of the debate on the interaction between the two concerns the application of fundamental rights in the context of an infringement of a fundamental Treaty freedom. In this respect, as well-established case law of the Court of Justice makes clear, fundamental rights and fundamental Treaty freedoms may indeed interfere with each other.

There are two basic modalities of how fundamental rights function at the level of Treaty freedoms. They may reinforce the Treaty freedoms, or they may function as grounds for restriction of the freedoms. In the latter situation, one of a conflict between free movement on the one hand and fundamental rights on the other,

* All views expressed in this contribution are strictly personal. The contribution was finalized in January 2022.

[1] Roughly speaking, there are two approaches. One of those advocates a harmonious and balanced approach. Here we find, among others, Stephen Weatherill and Sybe de Vries. cf eg Stephen Weatherill, 'From Economic Rights to Fundamental Rights' in Sybe de Vries, Ulf Bernitz, and Stephen Weatherill (eds), *The Protection of Fundamental Rights in the EU After Lisbon* (Hart Publishing 2012) and Sybe de Vries, 'The Protection of Fundamental Rights within Europe's Internal Market after Lisbon: An Endeavour for More Harmony' in Sybe de Vries, Xavier Groussot, and Gunnar Thor Petursson (eds), *Balancing Fundamental Rights with the EU Treaty Freedoms: The European Court of Justice as 'Tightrope' Walker* (Eleven International Publishing 2012). Other scholars argue, however, that there is a built-in bias, which works to the detriment of fundamental rights and that (economic) Treaty freedoms are prioritized over the former. cf eg Stephanie Reynolds, 'Explaining the Constitutional Drivers Behind a Perceived Judicial Preference for Free Movement over Fundamental Rights?' (2016) 53 Common Market Law Rev 643 and Sionaidh Douglas-Scott, 'The European Union and Human Rights After the Treaty of Lisbon' (2011) 11 Human Rights Law Review 645.

Sacha Prechal, *Fundamental Rights and Treaty Freedoms: The 'Derogation Situation' and Infringement Proceedings*
In: *The Internal Market Ideal*. Edited by: Jeremias Adams-Prassl, Sanja Bogojević, Ariel Ezrachi, and Dorota Leczykiewicz, Oxford University Press. © Sacha Prechal 2024. DOI: 10.1093/oso/9780192867063.003.0008

fundamental rights are relied upon in favour of restrictive measures. The classical examples here are the *Schmidberger* case and the *Viking* case.[2] The former situation concerns cases where fundamental rights are relied upon against restrictive measures of the Member States. Ever since the *ERT* case (the Greek television monopoly case),[3] it has been standard case law that *a justification of the restrictive measures relied upon* by the Member State must respect fundamental rights. Yet, this so-called 'derogation situation' was not entirely uncontested.

This came clearly to the fore during the drafting of the EU Charter of Fundamental Rights (CFR). According to some, the application of EU fundamental rights in such situations should be excluded by the final version of Article 51(1) CFR. As is well known, the Article provides that provisions of the Charter are addressed to the Member States 'only when they are implementing Union law'.[4] In this narrow view, 'implement' should refer to the 'agency situation', ie a situation where a Member State adopts measures to implement EU rules.[5]

It has been argued that there was an apparent reluctance to commit the Member States to observing the Charter in other situations than those which are closely linked to the EU and where the Member States have only little or no autonomy.[6] One of the major concerns was that the Charter should not disturb the distribution of powers between the EU and the Member States and, indirectly, also that of jurisdiction between the Court of Justice and national (constitutional) courts.[7]

However, the case law on Article 51(1) CFR has evolved in another direction: the Court, partly assisted by the broader terms of the explanations to the Charter, followed its pre-Charter case law and decided that Article 51(1) also applies when the Member States 'act within the scope of application of Union law'.[8] The derogation situation is a subset of this latter category. While not addressed as such in *Åkerberg Fransson*, two judgments rendered a few years later confirmed explicitly that the *ERT* case law remains good law.[9]

Certain judgments handed down in a preliminary ruling procedure and concerning such a derogation situation do indeed examine the compliance with a Charter provision, next to the restriction/justification analysis under the Treaty

[2] Case C-112/00 *Schmidberger* ECLI:EU:C:2003:333 and Case C-438/05 *Viking* ECLI:EU:C:2007:772.

[3] Case C-260/89 *ERT* ECLI:EU:C:1991:254.

[4] On the drafting history, see Gráinne de Búrca, 'The Drafting of the European Union Charter of Fundamental Rights' (2001) 26 European Law Review 126, in particular at 136–37.

[5] The so-called *Wachauf* line of case law; Case C-5/88 *Wachauf* ECLI:EU:C:1989:321.

[6] de Búrca (n 4) 137.

[7] cf Peter Goldsmith, 'A Charter of Rights, Freedoms and Principles' (2001) 38 Common Market Law Review 1201; Francis G Jacobs, 'Human Rights in the European Union: The Role of the Court of Justice' (2001) 26 European Law Review 331; and Peter M Huber, 'The Unitary Effect of the Community's Fundamental Rights: The *ERT*-Doctrine Needs to Be Reviewed' (2008) 14 European Public Law 323.

[8] Case C-617/10 *Åkerberg Fransson* ECLI:EU:C:2013:105, paras 19–21. For a detailed discussion, see eg Daniel Sarmiento, 'Who's Afraid of the Charter? The Court of Justice, National Courts and the New Framework of Fundamental Right Protection in Europe' (2013) 50 Common Market Law Review 1267.

[9] Case C-390/12 *Pfleger* ECLI:EU:C:2014:281 and Case C-201/15 *AGET Iraklis* ECLI:EU:C:2016:972.

on the Functioning of the European Union (TFEU).[10] In other judgments, while confirming the applicability of the Charter, the examination under the relevant Charter articles is left aside because when it is established that there is a restriction of a fundamental Treaty freedom, the possible limitations of a Charter right are often already covered by this analysis. This is particularly the case where the objective pursued cannot justify the restriction of a Treaty freedom, or where the test of proportionality is not satisfied. A separate examination under the Charter is not deemed necessary in such cases.[11]

A new challenge to the derogation situation line of case law came with three infringement proceedings initiated by the Commission against Hungary. The question was whether an infringement action can be brought on the ground of an alleged violation of a Charter provision, in addition to an alleged breach of a Treaty freedom. The answer to this question was less obvious than one might think. In fact, as was cogently pointed out by Advocate General Saugmandsgaard Øe, this was a new question which required careful consideration.[12]

This chapter will consider under what circumstances the Commission may seek, in an infringement proceeding, a declaration that a Member State has failed to comply with a Charter provision, parallel to an alleged infringement of a Treaty freedom. It will explore the limits and the merits of such an action. In Section 1, I will have a closer look at this new jurisprudential development. Section 2 will briefly address the issue of those situations in which a separate fundamental rights test is allowed and necessary. Section 3 will deal with the question of what added value such an infringement on grounds of a Charter provision violation may have.

2. Infringement Proceedings against Hungary

The first case brought against Hungary concerned national legislation which cancelled, automatically (*ex lege*), rights of usufruct previously created over agricultural land in Hungary between persons who were not close members of the same family.[13] The persons affected by this measure were many nationals of Member States other than Hungary. The Commission argued that by restricting the rights of usufruct, Hungary had infringed Article 49 TFEU (the right of establishment), Article 63 TFEU (free movement of capital), and Article 17 CFR (the right to

[10] *AGET Iraklis* (n 9); Case C–555/19 *Fussl Modestraße Mayr* ECLI:EU:C:2021:89; and Case C–544/19 *ECOTEX BULGARIA* ECLI:EU:C:2021:803.

[11] *Pfleger* (n 9) paras 57–60; Case C–322/16 *Global Starnet* ECLI:EU:C:2017:985, para 50; and Joined Cases C–407/19 and 471/19 *Katoen Natie Bulk Terminals NV* ECLI:EU:C:2021:107, para 56.

[12] Case C–235/17 *Commission v Hungary* (*Rights of usufruct over agricultural land*) ECLI:EU:C:2017:985, Opinion of AG Saugmandsgaard Øe, para 64.

[13] Case C–235/17 *Commission v Hungary (Rights of usufruct over agricultural land)* ECLI:EU:C:2019:432.

property). In this respect, the question was raised whether the Commission could bring a separate complaint based on the infringement of the Charter.

Advocate General Saugmandsgaard Øe found that, in this case, the Court had no jurisdiction to determine the existence of the breach of Article 17 CFR. He recalled the delicate context of the issue, basically repeating the arguments that had been brought up against the *ERT* case law in the past, in particular those concerning the need to respect the division of powers between the EU and the Member States and the distribution of jurisdiction between the Court of Justice on the one hand, and the national constitutional courts and the European Court of Human Rights on the other. Similarly, he observed that the intention of the drafters of the Charter was to limit the circumstances in which the Charter applies to national legislation.[14] Although he noted that, in *Åkerberg Fransson*, the Court had confirmed the 'historical continuity' of its case law, including the proposition that the 'derogation situation' falls within the scope of the Charter,[15] he followed with an insightful analysis of the derogation situation case law itself. In his view, until then the Court had always in principle examined the possible infringement of the Charter of Fundamental Right or of a general principle protecting a fundamental right in connection with a possible justification. Based on this analysis of the *ERT* case law, he concluded that the question of fundamental rights and that of freedom of movement are inextricably linked, a finding which is confirmed by more recent case law.[16]

In the Advocate General's view, this approach is fundamentally different from a separate finding of failure to fulfil obligations under the Charter, independent of the question of a possible justification. This would amount to a review of compliance with fundamental rights without a link to the question of conformity with the freedom of movement.[17] In accepting jurisdiction in the case at hand, the Court would extend or even distort the *ERT* case law, and thus undermine the division of powers between the EU and the Member States where the Charter clearly signals that it was not intended to alter that division.[18] In his view, in cases involving potential violations of free movement principles, the Court should only examine questions of fundamental rights where such an intervention is necessary in order to resolve an issue of freedom of movement.[19]

In the case at hand, such an intervention was, strictly speaking, not necessary to deal with the problem in the context of the free movement of capital as the restriction of this freedom could not be justified anyhow.[20] Nevertheless, in its judgment,

[14] *Commission v Hungary*, Opinion of AG Saugmandsgaard Øe (n 12) paras 68–69.
[15] ibid paras 70–73.
[16] ibid paras 75–94.
[17] ibid paras 75 and 98.
[18] ibid paras 95, 102, and 106.
[19] ibid paras 107 and 110.
[20] cf Joined Cases C-52/16 and 113/16 *SEGRO* ECLI:EU:C:2018:157, para 128.

the Court recalled that the Charter is applicable in all situations governed by EU law and that it must be complied with, inter alia, where national legislation falls within the scope of EU law. In a situation where national legislation restricts one or more of the fundamental Treaty freedoms and the Member State concerned relies on grounds envisaged in Article 65 TFEU, or on overriding reasons in the public interest to justify the restriction, the national legislation has to comply with fundamental rights. In this respect, the use by a Member State of the exceptions provided for by EU law to justify a restriction of a fundamental Treaty freedom must be regarded as an act of 'implementing Union law' within the meaning of Article 51(1) of the Charter.[21] Thus, there was no need to examine independent applicability of the Charter. In the context of examining the justification relied upon by Hungary, the Court examined the question of whether the persons concerned had been deprived of property in the sense of Article 17(1) CFR.[22] Since it concluded that they were, this time the question of possible justification for the fundamental right violation arose. This question was addressed in parallel with the justifications brought forward for the restriction of the free movement of capital, with which it partly overlapped.[23] The final finding of the Court was that Hungary had failed to fulfil its obligations under Article 63 TFEU[24] in conjunction with Article 17 of the Charter.[25]

While this first judgment might seem somewhat ambiguous,[26] further clarification came with the judgment in Case C-78/18 *Commission v Hungary* (*Transparency of associations*).[27] The case concerned obligations of registration, declaration, and publication imposed upon certain categories of civil society organizations which received—directly or indirectly financial support from abroad exceeding a certain threshold. Furthermore, various penalties were provided for, if the organizations failed to comply with the obligations. The Commission sought a declaration that, by these measures, Hungary had breached its obligations under Article 63 TFEU and Articles 7 (respect for private life), 8 (protection of personal data), and 12 (freedom of association) of the Charter. After having dealt with the violation of Article 63 TFEU, which, according to the Court could not be justified by Article 65 TFEU or an overriding reason in the public interest, the Court turned, in a self-standing section of the judgment, to the examination of the alleged breaches of Charter provisions. The difference in structure between this

[21] *Commission v Hungary* (*Rights of usufruct over agricultural land*) (n 13) paras 63–65.
[22] ibid paras 67–89.
[23] ibid paras 123–29.
[24] The restriction of the right to establishment being inextricably linked to the restriction of free movement of capital, it was not necessary to consider the contested legislation in the light of art 49 TFEU.
[25] *Commission v Hungary* (*Rights of usufruct over agricultural land*) (n 13) para 131.
[26] Luca Prete and Ben Smulders, 'The Age of Maturity of Infringement Proceedings' (2021) 58 Common Market Law Review 285, 289–90.
[27] Case C-78/18 *Commission v Hungary* (*Transparency of associations*) ECLI:EU:C:2020:476.

judgment and the 'Usufruct judgment', where the issues of the freedom at stake and the fundamental right were intertwined, is striking. However, for the applicability of the Charter this did not really matter. The Court repeated, with reference to *Aget Iraklis* and *Commission v Hungary* (*Rights of usufruct over agricultural land*),[28] that:

> '[W]here a Member State argues that a measure of which it is the author and which restricts a fundamental freedom guaranteed by the FEU Treaty is justified on the basis of that Treaty or by an overriding reason in the public interest recognised by EU law, such a measure must be regarded as implementing Union law within the meaning of Article 51(1) of the Charter, such that it must comply with the fundamental rights enshrined in the Charter.'[29]

Since Hungary had submitted that the rules at stake were justified by Article 65 TFEU and an overriding reason in the public interest, it was necessary to examine whether they also complied with the Charter. The Court found that the respective Charter rights were limited, but that the Hungarian provisions, which constituted limitations on the relevant Charter rights, could not be justified—and thus Hungary failed to comply with Article 52(1) CFR. In this latter respect, the Court relied on its findings in relation to the alleged justification of the restriction of the free movement of capital. The final outcome was that Hungary failed to fulfil its obligations under Article 63 TFEU and Articles 7, 8, and 12 CFR. However, the link suggested in *Commission v Hungary* (*Rights of usufruct over agricultural land*), namely that a breach of a Charter provision can be examined only in the context of establishing a failure to fulfil the obligations under a Treaty provision such as Article 63 TFEU or other free movement provisions, was not made in the judgment.

The approach of treating the limitation of fundamental Charter rights in such a separate fashion was confirmed in the third judgment, C–66/18 *Commission v Hungary* (*Higher education*).[30] In this case, the Court made an entirely separate statement on the infringement of the Charter rights in the operative part of the judgment. This case concerned two measures introduced by the Hungarian government in relation to teaching activities. The first one required that, in the case of teaching activities leading to a qualification by higher education institutions situated outside the EEA, these institutions were to be subject to the existence of an international treaty between Hungary and the country where that institution has its seat. The second concerned the condition that the foreign higher institutions exercising their activities in Hungary must also offer higher education in the country of their seat.

[28] *AGET Iraklis* (n 9) and *Commission v Hungary* (*Rights of usufruct over agricultural land*) (n 13).
[29] *Commission v Hungary* (*Transparency of associations*) (n 27) para 101.
[30] Case C–66/18 *Commission v Hungary* (*Higher education*) ECLI:EU:C:2020:792.

As far as the application of the Charter is concerned, the Commission argued that these requirements infringed Articles 13 (academic freedom), 14(3) (freedom to found higher education institutions), and 16 (freedom to conduct a business), a position with which the Court agreed. An interesting feature of this case was that, for a part, it concerned a classical 'agency situation'. Hungary was, on the one hand, performing its obligations under the General Agreement on Trade in Services (GATS), in particular Article XVII(1) thereof. These activities are to be considered as implementing EU law within the meaning of Article 51(1) CFR.[31] For another part, in so far as Article 49 TFEU was at stake, the Court recalled that where a Member State is seeking justification of a measure which is restricting a fundamental Treaty freedom on grounds of an overriding reason in the public interest, such a measure must be regarded as implementing EU law within the meaning of Article 51(1) CFR.[32] Interestingly, the Court adds that the same applies with respect to Article 16 of Directive 2006/123. It would seem that the derogation situation (Article 49) and the 'agency situation' (giving effect to Directive 2006/123) are conflated. On reflection, it illustrates that there is no fundamental difference between derogating from a Treaty provision or from secondary law.[33] It also indicates that the distinction between the agency situation and the derogation situation is less important than some may argue.

In any case, it is clear that after these judgments, the Commission may start an infringement action based on the Charter in a derogation situation and may ask for an independent finding of a breach of the Charter.

3. When is a Fundamental Rights Test Appropriate?

In the three cases brought against Hungary, the Commission did not relate an assessment of compliance with fundamental rights to a possible justification of a Treaty infringement. The Commission sought a self-standing finding that a Charter provision had been infringed, without tying the claim to the analysis of a possible justification. However, this does not mean that the justification of a restriction on one of the Treaty freedoms and the issue of a fundamental right violation were entirely disconnected. The application of the Charter was, in all three cases, still triggered by the derogation situation. In this sense, the three cases fit in the logic of the *ERT* case law, as further developed in subsequent preliminary ruling cases. In this respect, another question arises: may the simple restriction or other contravention

[31] ibid para 213.
[32] ibid para 214 with reference to *Commission v Hungary* (*Transparency of associations*) (n 27) para 101 and the case law cited.
[33] cf Koen Lenaerts and José A Gutiérrez-Fons, 'The EU Internal Market and the EU Charter: Exploring the "Derogation Situation"' in Fabian Amtenbrink, Gareth Davies, and Dimitry Kochenov (eds), *The Internal Market and the Future of European Integration: Essays in Honour of Laurence W. Gormley* (Cambridge University Press 2019) 57–59.

of a Treaty freedom, without a justification being brought forward, trigger application of the Charter? The Court has not addressed this question yet. However, according to Advocate General Campos Sánchez-Bordona, it is indeed the operation of the Treaty freedoms as such that draws fundamental Charter rights within the scope of application of EU law. In his view, it would be paradoxical if the Member States had to respect fundamental rights only where they sought to justify a restriction of a Treaty freedom but not where they restricted the freedom without recourse to any justification.[34] Some scholars seem to agree with this position, pointing out that such an interpretation is consistent with the Court's standard case law according to which 'situations cannot exist which are covered ... by European Union law without ... fundamental rights being applicable'.[35] However this may be, such an interpretation of Article 51(1) CFR would, in my view, imply extension of the Charter's application to a situation which is different from the derogation situation, and for this reason would necessitate very careful consideration.

Another—though closely linked—argument against a broad application of the derogation situation raised by Advocate General Saugmandsgaard Øe was the necessity to examine whether a fundamental right was respected in order to resolve the problem of an alleged breach of a Treaty freedom. Only where such a necessity was present should the Charter apply. In my view, in practical terms, this means that whenever it is clear that the justification test cannot be satisfied, there is no need to inquire further into a possible non-compliance with EU fundamental rights. Only where recourse to a justification allowed under the Treaty or the 'imperative reasons' case law seems acceptable would an additional examination under the Charter be necessary.

A comparable approach is reflected in various cases decided upon a preliminary reference from national courts. The Court, often for reasons of judicial economy, may decide that for the solution of a concrete case it is not necessary to look into the matter of a fundamental right violation, since it is clear that the restriction concerned cannot be justified. Similarly, in cases where the Treaty freedoms and the fundamental rights at stake overlap, it may rule that, in any case, the alleged infringement of a fundamental right would not be justified either.[36] Additional analysis of compatibility with fundamental rights is then left aside.

[34] Case C-78/18 *Commission v Hungary (Transparency of associations)* ECLI:EU:C:2020:1, Opinion of AG Campos Sánchez-Bordona, paras 89–91, pointing, in para 87, at the new context, ie that the EU integration process now revolves around the figure of the citizen and its fundamental rights. It would seem that AG Sharpston already held the view that the mere restriction of a Treaty freedom is sufficient to trigger the application of the Charter. See her Opinion in *Pfleger* (n 9) para 45.

[35] Case C-617/10 *Åkerberg Fransson* ECLI:EU:C:2013:105, para 21. cf Matteo Bonelli, '*European Commission v Hungary* (*Transparency of associations*) (C-78/18): The "NGOs case": On How to Use the EU Charter of Fundamental Rights in Infringement Actions' (2021) 46 European Law Review 258, 266. Comparably, see Xavier Groussot, Niels Kirst, and Patrick Leisure, '*SEGRO* and its Aftermath: Between Economic Freedoms, Property Rights and the "Essence of the Rule of Law"' (2019) 2 Nordic Journal of European Law 69, 81.

[36] See cases referred to in n 11 and *SEGRO* (n 20) para 128.

While refraining from an additional analysis of compatibility with fundamental rights may seem acceptable in many preliminary reference cases, in relation to infringement proceedings the question arises as to what purpose would be served by a self-standing finding that, in addition to a breach of a fundamental Treaty freedom, there is an infringement of a fundamental right guaranteed by the Charter. I will discuss this question in the following section of the chapter.

4. Self-standing Infringement of the Charter: What Difference Does it Make?

When answering this question, at least four different points can be made.

In the first place, the purpose of a procedure under Article 258 TFEU is to obtain a declaration that conduct of a Member State infringes EU law. Next, this infringement itself and its consequences have to be eliminated.[37] From this perspective alone, it would seem that a declaration of a breach of a Charter provision in addition to a finding of a breach of a Treaty freedom may be important. This is obviously particularly pertinent in situations where the content of the Treaty freedom at stake and the Charter provision do not overlap. In such a situation it might be possible that the measures that should be put in place by the Member State concerned are different than they would have been if the national rules violated only the Treaty freedom. However, also in situations of overlap of a Treaty freedom and a provision of the Charter the measures to be taken to remedy the infringement are not necessarily the same; certainly not in a situation of a partial overlap. To take the usufruct case as an example, under Article 17 CFR, if a deprivation of property occurs in the public interest, fair compensation must be paid in good time for the loss. It is crystal clear what must be done in terms of a remedy. In the case of a restriction of a free movement right, compensation may indeed also be envisaged,[38] but the matter is less straightforward since the Member States enjoy a degree of discretion in how to remedy an infringement under the Treaty.

In the second place, a separate finding of unjustified interference with a fundamental right seems relevant to me for the imposition of a lump sum or penalty payment under Article 260(2) TFEU.

According to what is by now well-established case law, the principle of imposing a lump sum is essentially based on the assessment of the effects on public and private interests of the failure of the Member State concerned to comply with its obligations, in particular where the breach has persisted for a long period after the judgment initially establishing it was delivered.[39] The imposition of a lump sum

[37] Case C-261/18 *Commission v Ireland* (*Derrybrien Wind Farm*) ECLI:EU:C:2019:955, para 75.

[38] Namely, as a part of the proportionality test. Absence of compensation may render the measures disproportionate.

[39] Case C-270/11 *Commission v Sweden* ECLI:EU:C:2013:339, para 42.

payment and the fixing of that sum depend, in each individual case, on all the relevant factors relating both to the characteristics of the failure to fulfil obligations established and to the conduct of the Member State involved in the procedure initiated under Article 260 TFEU. The lump sum should be an amount appropriate to the circumstances and proportionate to the infringement. The relevant considerations taken into account in this respect include the seriousness of the infringement and the length of time for which the infringement has persisted since the delivery of the judgment establishing it.[40] For the purposes of determining the amount of a penalty payment, the basic criteria are more or less the same.[41]

There is little doubt that non-compliance with the fundamental Treaty freedoms can be qualified, in principle, as a matter of indisputable seriousness.[42] How, then, to assess an infringement of a Charter right? I do not want to enter here into a debate about the relative weight and importance of fundamental Treaty freedoms and fundamental rights.[43] In cases of a parallel breach, infringement of a fundamental right should be seen as a serious aggravating factor, not least because such a breach often creates effects which go beyond purely economic consequences already captured by the infringement of the fundamental Treaty freedom.[44] In other cases, infringement of Charter provisions may be a factor in the assessment and the calculation of a lump sum of the penalty payment itself.

In the third place, the justification mechanisms under the TFEU and Article 52(1) CFR differ. While the grounds for justification and the proportionality test may be identical, Article 52(1) CFR also requires that the limitation for which justification is sought be provided for by law and that it should respect the essence of the right.[45] In many situations, the difference has no important practical consequences. As was already observed above, in cases where the restriction of a Treaty freedom is not justified, there is a good chance that the limitation of a fundamental right will not be justified either.

However, this is not necessarily always the case. For instance, *Fussl Modestraße* concerned national legislation that prohibits television broadcasters from inserting in their programmes broadcast throughout the national territory television advertising whose broadcasting is limited to a regional level.[46] On the one hand, as far as the alleged violation of Article 56 TFEU was concerned, the referring court had to assess whether the legislation was suitable for securing the attainment of the

[40] *Commission v Ireland (Derrybrien Wind Farm)* (n 37) paras 113–14.

[41] ibid para 133.

[42] Case C–842/19 *Commission v Belgique (Revenus immobiliers étrangers)* ECLI:EU:C:2020:915, para 18.

[43] cf the references in n 1.

[44] Case C–66/18 *Commission v Hungary (Higher education)* ECLI:EU:C:2020:172, Opinion of AG Kokott, para 180.

[45] cf also Case C–78/18 *Commission v Hungary (Transparency of associations)*, Opinion of AG Campos Sánchez-Bordona (n 34) paras 95 and 100. The AG points out that the justification test in case of limitation of fundamental rights is more demanding.

[46] *Fussl Modestraße Mayr* (n 10).

objective, namely the protection of media pluralism at regional and local level, and did not go beyond what is necessary. In the case at hand, it was not a foregone conclusion that this justification would succeed.[47] On the other hand, as to the possible infringement of Article 11 CFR, the assessment was different. The Court confirmed that the protection of media pluralism at a regional and local level constitutes an objective of general interest. However, with reference to the European Court of Human Rights case law, the Court found that the proportionality test was satisfied. In fact, in the balancing of the interests involved in this context—namely, the freedom of commercial expression—on the one hand, and the protection of media pluralism at regional and local level, on the other, the German legislature was found not to exceed the broad margin of appreciation to which it is entitled in such a context.[48] Schematically put, the difference in balancing was one between a private interest of commercial speech versus a public interest of contributing to the public debate in the context of examining a Charter violation, and the fundamental Treaty freedom to provide services versus the protection of media pluralism in the context of examining a Treaty violation. The outcome of the review differed accordingly.

In brief, since the analysis and the outcome of the justifications may differ, it would seem important to examine the respective infringements—of Treaty freedoms or of Charter rights—separately.

Finally, an independent finding of a breach of a Charter provision in addition to a breach of a Treaty freedom may assist the individual concerned when he or she considers bringing action for state liability. For example, in addition to seeking compensation for a breach of a Treaty freedom, they may separately claim compensation for the infringement of an EU fundamental right. In any case, the violation of a fundamental right in addition to a breach of a Treaty freedom will also constitute in this context an aggravating factor which may have consequences for the assessment of the damage sustained and the level of compensation to be awarded.

5. Conclusion

The three cases discussed in this contribution concerned the applicability of the Charter in infringement proceedings and the method of assessing a possible infringement of the Charter provisions. They invited a question of how far a self-standing claim about the infringement of the Charter can be brought by the Commission in situations where a fundamental Treaty freedom and the Charter provisions overlap. The Charter was relied upon by the Court in the judgments to assess compatibility of national rules with EU law. The Court treated this matter

[47] ibid paras 52–79.
[48] ibid paras 90–94.

not as controversial, but as a continuation of the derogation case law. An issue that will need clarification in the future is whether such a self-standing claim of an alleged non-compliance with a Charter provision can also hold where there is only an infringement of a Treaty freedom, without a justification being invoked.

Be that as it may, the case law as it stands now is significant for the protection of fundamental rights, and by no means should it be seen in symbolic terms only. The Member States are bound to eliminate the infringement and its consequences. This can be reinforced by financial sanctions. In some cases, an infringement procedure may lead to more concrete and clear outcomes than preliminary ruling proceedings because the practical outcome of the latter may be affected by the vicissitudes of national law, procedural or otherwise. In this sense, the infringement procedure may offer additional—if not better—protection to individuals. The condition is, however, that the Member State concerned faithfully implements the Court's judgment and the Commission performs vigorously its role of the guardian of the Treaty if necessary.

8
The Relationship Between Free Movement of Persons and Fundamental Rights

Eleanor Spaventa

1. Introduction

When I first saw Steve in person, I was a first year DPhil student at Oxford. Being a great admirer of his academic work, but having never actually met him, I decided to attend one of his lectures. In came such a young-looking person that, coming from the Italian system, I immediately thought that the great Professor Weatherill, whom I had imagined as a stern and aged academic, had simply sent one of his academic assistants to lecture on his behalf. My surprise was rather pronounced, then, when the young academic started referring to Professor Weatherill in the first person.

Since then, I have had the chance of benefiting from many academic encounters with Steve—his influence on my professional path has been great, especially since my interest in the internal market was sparkled, unsurprisingly, by some of his writing. His textbook guided me in my first serious encounter with EU law during my LLM studies,[1] and his seminal article on *Keck*[2] contributed greatly to shaping my own thinking on the scope of the free movement of goods and persons provisions. It is not only Steve's writing that provided continuous inspiration for my work, but also his comments at the many academic events where I heard him speak—Steve's relentless analysis of almost any aspect of European integration still stands unrivalled. And so, of course, does his passion for sports law[3] and for football more generally—I remember an occasion in Cambridge when he made clear that his commitment to the Hull City Football Club was non-negotiable. And that, in itself, was a very valuable lesson to a then very junior academic—the fact that one might (in theory) be able to work all the time does not mean we should do so; rather, a personal space must be carved out so that we can cultivate interests and passions outside academia.

[1] Stephen Weatherill and Paul Beaumont, *EC Law* (2nd edn, Penguin 1995).
[2] Stephen Weatherill, 'After *Keck*: Some Thoughts on How to Clarify the Clarification' (1996) 33 Common Market Law Review 887.
[3] See eg Stephen Weatherill, *European Sports Law: Collected Papers* (2nd edn, Springer 2013) and *Principles and Practice in EU Sports Law* (Oxford University Press 2017).

Eleanor Spaventa, *The Relationship Between Free Movement of Persons and Fundamental Rights* In: *The Internal Market Ideal*. Edited by: Jeremias Adams-Prassl, Sanja Bogojević, Ariel Ezrachi, and Dorota Leczykiewicz, Oxford University Press.
 DOI: 10.1093/oso/9780192867063.003.0009

There is no overestimating the effect that Steve's work and interventions had on my academic work and work-life balance, and true to our shared interests I would like in this contribution to return to the boundaries of the free movement provisions, exploring the relationship between barriers to movement to physical persons (hereinafter 'persons') and fundamental rights.[4] Here again Steve's own thinking and suggestions were crucial in shaping my work—first, in relation to the former topic, as Steve was the internal examiner of my doctoral dissertation, which attempted to systematize and explain the notion of barriers to movement across the four freedoms; and secondly in relation to fundamental rights when he invited me to present my work at Oxford, and pushed me to further reflect on my critique of the case law. I cannot think of a better place to try to bring these two topics together than in a book celebrating Steve's contribution to the field of EU legal studies.

In this respect, what I am interested in exploring here is the intersection between barriers to movement and fundamental rights which leads to the application, or otherwise, of the Charter of Fundamental Rights (Charter) to acts of the Member States. This topic is particularly interesting to me because it draws the constitutional boundaries of the EU legal system (or at least one of the constitutional boundaries): since the EU does not have general fundamental rights competence, the application of the Charter to the acts of the Member States affects the repartition of judicial review competences between the European and the national judiciaries.[5] In theory, once the matter falls within the scope of the free movement provisions (or indeed, EU law more generally), then the balancing exercise which is key to judicial review in fundamental rights cases is transferred from the national to the supranational level (regardless of whether the final assessment is done by the Court of Justice or by the national court). Because fundamental rights adjudication almost inevitably requires the juxtaposition of interests and the weighing up of competing aims, the assertion of jurisdiction by the Court of Justice in cases relating to national law affects, and expands, the boundaries of EU law. Furthermore, in the context of European integration, the EU's interest in fostering movement and integration might tilt the balance of the assessment of the conflicting claims towards the result that aids this primary purpose, whereas in the national context that assessment is conducted having regard to the values expressed in the domestic constitution or legal system more generally.

[4] Steve has also published on fundamental rights; see eg Sybe Alexander De Vries, Ulf Bernitz, and Stephen Weatherill (eds), *The EU Charter of Fundamental Rights as a Binding Instrument: Five Years Old and Growing* (Hart Publishing 2016) and his chapter within it; 'The Internal Market and EU Fundamental Rights' in Sionaidh Douglas-Scott and Nicholas Hatzis (eds), *Research Handbook on EU Law and Human Rights* (Edward Elgar 2017); 'Use and Abuse of the EU's Charter of Fundamental Rights: On the Improper Veneration of "Freedom Contract"' (2014) 10 European Review of Contract Law 167.

[5] On these issues see eg Eleanor Spaventa, 'Federalization versus Centralization: Tensions in *Fundamental Rights Discourse in the European Union*' in Michael Dougan and Samantha Currie (eds), *50 Years of the European Treaties* (Hart Publishing 2009), 343.

The fact that national and European interests taken into consideration might well be different is the natural result of the multilevel fundamental rights governance in the European Union. Yet it is not without its problems: take, for instance, cases of clash of rights—*Schmidberger* and *Viking*[6]—where constitutional clashes that could (and perhaps should) have been assessed as clashes between economic and non-economic rights became clashes between free movement rights and non-economic rights. In *Viking*, this led to a paradoxical result where transnational collective action was not seen as a natural counterbalance to the freedom of business to relocate, but rather as a barrier to businesses' free movement rights. This is not necessarily to say that the Court of Justice had or has a pro-business bias,[7] since in the case of the free movement of persons, at least at first, the Court used the same hermeneutic technique to foster the non-economic, and especially the family, rights of the free movers. Once the mover managed to bring themselves within the scope of the Treaty free movement provisions, even rather artificially, then their right to, at least, family life would fall under the umbrella of the European fundamental rights protection, with all the procedural and substantive advantages that this might entail. The most blatant example of this is of course the *Carpenter* ruling, where the Court found that the rules at issue constituted a barrier to movement so as to bring the matter within the scope of EU law and assert the right to family life of the applicant.[8]

This contribution, then, seeks to analyse the grey area of the intersection between the free movement of persons and the application of the Charter.[9] In particular, in the writer's opinion, there are different strands of case law pulling in different directions: in some cases restrictive interpretations, such as in *Dano*, where the Court excluded the relevance of general principles (and thus fundamental rights) to the situation of a Romanian national who was resident in Germany without satisfying the conditions of sufficient resources as provided for in Article 7 of Directive 2004/38;[10] in others, less restrictive interpretations, such as in

[6] Case C-112/00 *Schmidberger* ECLU:EU:C:2003:333; Case C-438/05 *International Transport Workers' Federation and The Finnish Seamen's Union v Viking Line* ECLI:EU:C:2007:772. In the author's opinion, Case C-341/05 *Laval un Partneri* ECLI:EU:C:2007:809 is slightly different, since in that case there was discrimination. Of course, clashes of rights are a common occurrence and also arise in many other areas, and might also entail clashes of rights provided for in secondary legislation and Charter rights; see eg Case C-426/11 *Mark Alemo-Herron v Parkwood Leisure Ltd* ECLI:EU:C:2013:521; C-157/15 *Samira Achbita and Centrum voor gelijkheid van kansen en voor racismebestrijding v G4S Secure Solutions NV* ECLI:EU:C:2017:203; and, for a more nuanced approach, see Case C-414/16 *Egenberger* ECLI:EU:C:2018:257.

[7] But see, for a piercing critique, Sophie Robin-Olivier, 'Fundamental Rights as a New Frame: Displacing the Acquis' (2018) 14 European Constitutional Law Review 96.

[8] Case C-60/00 *Carpenter v Secretary of State for the Home Department* ECLI:EU:C:2002:434.

[9] The scholarship has tended to focus more on the general scope of application of the Charter, especially after cases like Case C-399/11 *Melloni v Ministerio Fiscal* ECLI:EU:C:2013:107 and Case C-617/10 *Åklagaren v Hans Åkerberg Fransson* ECLI:EU:C:2013:280; see also eg Konstanze Von Papp, 'A Federal Question Doctrine for EU Fundamental Rights Law: Making Sense of Articles 51 and 53 of the Charter of Fundamental Rights' (2018) 43 European Law Review 511.

[10] Case C-333/13 *Elisabeta Dano and Florin Dano v Jobcenter Leipzig* ECLI:EU:C:2014:2358 (*Dano*); the ruling in *Dano* provoked considerable academic reaction. See eg Niamh Nic Shuibhne, '"What I Tell

CG,[11] where the Court held that the fundamental rights of an applicant who was resident pursuant to national law, but not meeting the conditions of independency as provided for in Directive 2004/38, were relevant by virtue of Article 21(1) TFEU.

Generally speaking, we can identify different approaches in the Court's jurisprudence: in some categories of cases, fundamental rights are more readily applied (eg in cases relating to changes of name, extradition cases, *Ruiz Zambrano* cases, and deprivation of citizenship cases) whereas in other cases, including those concerning barriers to movement and access to welfare, fundamental rights are only relevant in some instances; this sometimes also depends on the way in which the preliminary question has been formulated. Furthermore, there seems to be a link between the fundamental right deemed to be relevant and the rationale of free movement in that particular case: not just any Charter right may be relied upon in any given case, but only those Charter rights which have the effect of reinforcing or facilitating the right to move.

Before delving into these issues, we will start by providing a short outline of the normative rationale underpinning the application of fundamental rights to free movement cases, then proceed to analyse the more recent case law, trying to understand when fundamental rights are applicable. We will suggest that whether fundamental rights are applied or not depends on a number of variables (which are not always predictable).

2. Free Movement and Fundamental Rights

It is well known that when a Member State is seeking to derogate from a free movement right or limit it pursuant to the mandatory/imperative requirements doctrine, it must justify such rules. In order to be compatible with EU law, derogations and limitations must pursue a public interest and the rule must be necessary and proportionate; ie, the least restrictive means to achieve the stated aims. From an early state of the case law, the Court accepted that when Member States invoked a justification for a barrier to movement, they were acting within the scope

You Three Times is True": Lawful Residence and Equal Treatment after *Dano*' (2016) 23 Maastricht Journal of European and Comparative Law 908; Daniel Thym, 'When Union Citizens Turn into Illegal Migrants: The *Dano* Case' (2015) 40 European Law Review 249; Herwig Verschueren, 'Preventing "Benefit Tourism" in the EU: A Narrow or Broad Interpretation of the Possibilities Offered by the ECJ in *Dano*?' (2015) 52 Common Market Law Review 363.

[11] Case C–709/20 *CG v The Department for Communities in Northern Ireland* ECLI:EU:C:2021:602 (*CG*); from a protection of citizenship perspective, the *CG* ruling is very problematic and might have wide-ranging effects on the rights of EU citizens in the UK caught by Brexit; see also the UK Supreme Court ruling in *Fratila v Secretary of State for Work and Pensions* [2021] UKSC 53, which applies the *CG* ruling. For a critical analysis, see Charlotte O'Brien, 'The Great EU Citizenship Illusion Exposed: Equal Treatment Rights Evaporate for the Vulnerable (*CG v The Department for Communities in Northern Ireland*)' (2021) 46 European Law Review 801.

of EU law. For this reason, Member States had to respect the EU constitutional principles so that the rule not only had to satisfy the proportionality test but also fundamental rights as (then) general principles of EU law.[12] The normative justification for this interpretation is relatively simple, although not uncontested:[13] in the case of Treaty derogations, the state is invoking EU law to justify derogating from its Treaty obligations and, for this reason, it has to respect its constitutional principles, including proportionality and fundamental rights. This reasoning is then also extended to situations in which the Member State is limiting a Treaty right by invoking the mandatory/imperative requirements doctrine. In other words, once the applicant succeeds in bringing herself under the umbrella of the Treaty's free movement provisions, they would benefit from the full protection of EU law. This case law was then incorporated into Article 51(1) of the Charter, which provides that the Member States are bound by its provisions when they are 'implementing' EU law, the explanations to the Charter referring also to the case law relating to situations in which Member States are limiting free movement rights.[14] This said, even accepting the normative justification which is at the root of the applicability of fundamental rights to limitations to free movement rights, it is not entirely clear when and how the Charter applies in those circumstances. Furthermore, the interpretation of Article 51 of the Charter has not been an easy task, since the Court is clearly mindful of the risk that the latter document be applied too readily to situations which in fact have only a very vague and indirect connection with EU law.[15] As mentioned above, the application of the Charter can also have the effect of displacing national constitutional rights (and the interpretation given to those rights), and for this very reason it may become contested both by national judiciaries and by Member States.[16]

Here, the more broadly the Court construes the notion of a barrier to movement, the more it might also impose a fundamental rights scrutiny using as a yardstick its own interpretation of fundamental rights, which might differ from that

[12] The first step towards this doctrine is already apparent in Case 36/75 *Rutili v Ministre de l'intérieur* ECLI: EU:C:1975:137. This doctrine then becomes clearer in Case C–260/89 *ERT* ECLI:EU:C:1991:254 and Case C–368/95 *Vereinigte Familiapress Zeitungsverlags- und vertriebs GmbH v Heinrich Bauer Verlag* ECLI:EU:C:1997:325.

[13] See eg Francis G Jacobs, 'Human Rights in the European Union: The Role of the Court of Justice' (2001) 26 European Law Review 331.

[14] See *Explanations Relating to the Charter of Fundamental Rights* [2017] OJ C303/17. If the situation falls outside the scope of EU law, the Charter does not apply; see eg Case C–40/11 *Lida* ECLI:EU:C:2012:691; Case C–256/11 *Dereci* ECLI:EU:C:2011:734.

[15] See eg Case C–206/13 *Siragusa v Regione Sicilia—Soprintendenza Beni Culturali e Ambientali di Palermo* ECLI:EU:C:2014:126, where the Court tried to provide a test on when the Charter is relevant in relation to acts of the Member States. See also Case C–198/13 *Hernández v Reino de España (Subdelegación del Gobierno de España en Alicante)* ECLI:EU:C:2014:2055.

[16] See eg Italian Constitutional Court Judgment 269/17 (*obiter*) <www.cortecostituzionale.it/action SchedaPronuncia.do?param_ecli=ECLI:IT:COST:2017:269>; and see eg the failure by Romania to give effect to the *Coman* ruling ('Answer given by Ms Dalli on behalf of the European Commission', Parliamentary Question E-005164/2021(ASW) <www.europarl.europa.eu/doceo/document/E-9-2021-005164-ASW_EN.html>), both last accessed on 28 Ocotober 2023.

given by national regulators, and by national courts upon review. The most glaring example of this is the *Carpenter* case. Here, the potential deportation of the wife of Mr Carpenter, a British citizen living in the United Kingdom but also engaged in business transactions with clients based in other European countries, was qualified as a barrier to Mr Carpenter's freedom to provide services in other EU countries, which then had to be assessed in relation to the imperative requirements doctrine. Since the situation fell within the scope of EU law, the refusal by the UK authorities to grant a residence permit to Mrs Carpenter was also assessed vis-à-vis EU fundamental rights—in particular the right to private and family life—and was found to be a disproportionate interference with said right.

Carpenter was really a case about the right to family life of the Carpenter family—yet it was thanks to the intervention of the Court that that right could be effectively protected, since the corresponding right in domestic law (which implemented the European Convention of Human Rights (ECHR)) was not construed as generously, giving more weight to the competing policy aim of controlling immigration. Yet, the normative justification for stretching the scope of the Treaty's free movement of services provisions so broadly was utterly unconvincing,[17] and it left open a more fundamental question: is it sufficient to allege *any* barrier to movement to be able to invoke EU fundamental rights, no matter how artificially connected the situation is to EU law? Furthermore, the expansion of the personal scope of the Treaty as a result of the introduction of Union citizenship rendered the question even more pertinent, not only because of the expansion of the category of those who might invoke the Treaty,[18] but also because of the inextricable connection between *citizenship* and fundamental rights. Already in 1992, Advocate General Jacobs famously argued that a person taking advantage of their free movement rights should be able to 'say "civis europeus sum" and to invoke that status in order to oppose any violation of his fundamental rights'.[19] Such a broad interpretation would, however, considerably blur the line between Member States' qualified autonomy in setting their own fundamental rights standards and the reach of EU

[17] See eg 'Freedoms Unlimited? Reflections on *Mary Carpenter v Secretary of State*' Editorial Comments' (2003) 40 Common Market Law Review 537; Silvia Acierno, 'The *Carpenter* Judgment: Fundamental Rights and the Limits of the Community Legal Order' (2003) 28 European Law Review 398; Gavin Barrett, 'Family Matters: European Community Law and Third-Country Family Members' (2003) 40 Common Market Law Review 369; Eleanor Spaventa, 'From *Gebhard* to *Carpenter*: Towards a (Non-) Economic European Constitution' (2004) 41 Common Market Law Review 743.

[18] In fact, in the author's opinion it is the introduction of Union citizenship, as interpreted by the Court, which puts an end to the artificial notion of barrier; see eg Case C–897/19 PPU *IN v Ruska Federacija* ECLI:EU:C:2020:262, where the Court relied on the free movement of services to bring an Icelandic national within the scope of the EEA agreement in a case relating to extradition since Union citizenship does not extend to EEA citizens, and compare with similar cases (analysed further later in this chapter) in the context of the EU, where the Court can simply rely on Union citizenship to trigger the Treaty.

[19] Case C–168/91 *Christos Konstantinidis v Stadt Altensteig* ECLI:EU:C:1992:504, Opinion of AG Jacobs, para 46. AG Jacobs later adopted a more restrictive approach to this question: see Jacobs (n 13).

fundamental rights, and it has in fact been resisted by the Court. The application of EU fundamental rights in free movement of persons cases is far from being uniform (or even predictable). And yet, we can identify some trends in the case law: in particular, there are some instances which seem to more readily attract the application of EU fundamental rights, whereas in other strands, the application of EU fundamental rights is more variable. We will start our analysis from those cases in which, by and large, once the matter is found to fall within the scope of the Treaty, fundamental rights are always relevant—either as part of the proportionality assessment or independently.

3. Cases that Usually Attract Fundamental Rights Scrutiny

As previously discussed, there are certain categories of cases that seem to attract fundamental rights scrutiny more often: cases concerning names, *Ruiz Zambrano* cases, deprivation of citizenship, and extradition to a third country.

Cases concerning names relate to challenges over the automatic application of rules on names to those who are in a transnational situation, either because they have exercised their right to move or because they possess the nationality of more than one Member State. Here, there is hardly any doubt—at least for those of us who live in heavily bureaucratic states—that having documents drafted using different names because of different rules between countries might lead to very serious administrative difficulties. It was with this fact in mind that the Court, in the first case in which it considered the matter,[20] found that the refusal to recognize and draw up documents using the name acquired by dual-national children from their parents might affect or make more difficult the children's potential future exercise of the right to free movement. Having found that the application of the Belgian rules to dual nationals fell within the scope of the Treaty, the Court could apply the principle of equal treatment in its second limb: the obligation to treat different situations in different ways, which in this case meant not treating dual nationals as if they were Belgian-only nationals. The right to have the documents drafted using the same surname that the children had already registered with the Spanish authorities was therefore safeguarded by a purposive interpretation of the right to free movement, bringing a future potential barrier within the scope of the Treaty provisions, and by requesting the national authorities to take into account the objective difference between the situation of a dual national and a person having only one nationality. The same reasoning is followed in *Grunkin and Paul*,[21]

[20] Case C-148/02 *Garcia Avello* ECLI:EU:C: 2003:539.

[21] Case C-353/06 *Grunkin and Paul* ECLI:EU:C:2008:559; see also Case C-541/15 *Freitag* ECLI:EU:C:2017:432, another case about a discrepancy in a dual national's name in which no reference to fundamental rights was made.

a subsequent case concerning the refusal to recognize the last name of a Member State's own citizen as determined by the rules of the Member State of residence and as stated in the birth certificate.

However, and interestingly, in subsequent cases relating to barriers created by rules relating to determination or transliteration of names, the Court starts from a different premise—it states that names are a constituent element of one's identity and one's own private life, the protection of which is enshrined in Article 7 of the Charter and Article 8 ECHR, only then to proceed to identify a barrier which needs justifying. The Charter is therefore used to reinforce the reasoning of the Court, identifying the right to one's identity as one of the fundamental values protected by the European legal system, but also to clarify that—even taking account EU fundamental rights—the rules could still be justified. In other words, fundamental rights are used here to reinforce the Court's claim of authority both in scrutinizing the national rules and in finding those national rules compatible with the EU legal system. For instance, in both *Sayn-Wittgenstein* and *Bogendorff von Wolffersdorff*,[22] the Court stressed the fact that one's name is a constituent part of one's identity and private life as protected by both the Charter and the ECHR, then found the rules at issue in the main proceedings to be justified by the need to protect competing interests and the principle of equal treatment, itself also protected by the Charter. In *Runevič-Vardyn*,[23] the issue related to a change in the names of the applicants on their marriage certificate. The Court, consistently with prior case law, restated that names are a constituent element of one's identity and are therefore protected by Article 7 of the Charter. In examining the justification for the Lithuanian authorities' refusal to change the marriage certificate, the Court also engaged with the Charter in the assessment of the justification of the relevant rules, balancing the free movement rights of the applicants and their rights under Article 7 of the Charter against Article 22 of the Charter, which provides that the Union must respect cultural, religious, and linguistic diversity, and Article 4(2) TEU, which protects the national constitutional identity, held to include the protection of the state's official language.

Other fields of law where fundamental rights are almost always relevant are those concerning *Ruiz Zambrano* situations and deprivation of citizenship cases. Those cases do not concern barriers to movement, but rather the autonomous application of Article 20 TFEU, which confers EU citizenship on all persons possessing nationality of a Member State. Yet, those cases are equally, if not even more, relevant to our investigation, since EU fundamental rights are applied to the relationship between the citizen and their own state without any need for an existing transnational element.

[22] Case C–208/09 *Sayn-Wittgenstein* ECLI:EU:C:2010:806, para 52; Case C–438/14 *Nabiel Peter Bogendorff von Wolffersdorff* ECLI:EU:C:2016:401, para 35.

[23] Case C–391/09 *Runevič-Vardyn and Wardyn* ECLI:EU:C:2011:291.

A *Ruiz Zambrano* case[24] arises where a Union citizen relies on Article 20 TFEU to prevent the Member State of their own nationality from deporting a third-country national with whom they are in a relationship of dependency.[25] Here, Article 20 TFEU applies to the extent to which deportation of the third-country national would result (or risk resulting) in the EU citizen having to leave the EU territory altogether in order to follow them. In determining the justification of the threatened deportation, the Court considers the protection of the Union citizen's fundamental rights, and in particular their right to private and family life as protected by Article 7 of the Charter and the need to always ensure the best interests of the child as provided for in Article 24(2) of the Charter. Similarly, Article 20 TFEU is triggered in cases of withdrawal of nationality of the Member State, when such a withdrawal would also deprive the citizen of their Union citizenship and therefore of the possibility of enjoying the rights associated with it.[26] In these cases, the Court demands that when assessing the proportionality of the measure, national authorities have full regard to Charter rights and especially to the right to private life and the best interests of the child. For instance, in *Tjebbes*,[27] fundamental rights are used as a way of determining the substance of the rights conferred by Union law by imposing upon national authorities the need to carry out a careful assessment of the personal circumstances of those whose citizenship is withdrawn.

Finally, another area where the Charter is always relevant concerns the extradition of Union citizens to a country outside the EU. These cases focus on the extent to which Member States might give effect to an extradition treaty with a third country in relation to a Union citizen resident in their territory who, by virtue of moving, has engaged Article 21 TFEU.[28] Here, the Court consistently requires

[24] See eg Case C-836/18 *Subdelegación del Gobierno en Ciudad Real v RH* ECLI:EU:C:2020:119; Joined Cases C-451/19 and 532/19 *Subdelegación del Gobierno en Toledo v XU and QP* ECLI:EU:C:2022:354; Case C-32/16 *KA* ECLI:EU:C:2018:308; Case C-133/15 *HC Chavez-Vilchez* ECLI:EU:C:2017:354, para 70; Case C-304/14 *CS* ECLI:EU:C:2016:674, para 36; Case C-165/14 *Rendón Marín* ECLI:EU:C:2016:675, para 66. In the earlier case of *Dereci* (C-256/11, ECLI:EU:C:2011:734), before the Court developed the notion of dependency, it indicated to the national court both the relevance of art 7 of the Charter, if the matter fell within art 20 TFEU, *and*, failing the applicability of the Charter, the duty to respect art 8 ECHR; and in Joined Cases C-356 and 357/11 *O and S* ECLI:EU:C-2012:776, when the notion of dependency was still rather restrictive, the Court fails to take into account fundamental rights in relation to art 20 TFEU, but it takes them in full account in relation to the family reunification Directive.

[25] For a comprehensive definition of dependency, see eg Case C-82/16 *KA* (n 24) and Case C-133/15 *HC Chavez-Vilchez* (n 24). See also pending Case C-459/20 *X v Staatssecretaris van Justitie en Veiligheid* ECLI:EU:C:2022:475.

[26] Case C-221/17 *Tjebbes* ECLI:EU:2019:189; Case C-118/20 *JY v Wiener Landesregierung* ECLI:EU:C:2022:34. The Charter naturally also applies to national rules determining the franchise for the European Parliament; see Case C-650/13 *Delvigne* ECLI:EU:C:2015:648.

[27] See also Hanneke van Eijken, '*Tjebbes* in Wonderland: On European Citizenship, Nationality and Fundamental Rights' (2019) 15 European Constitutional Law Review 714.

[28] Case C-398/19 *BY Generalstaatsanwaltschaft Berlin* ECLI:EU:C:2020:1032, where the Court again subjected the extradition to a third country of an EU citizen non-national to the requirement that extradition would not prejudice the rights provided for in art 19 of the Charter; Case C-247/17 *Raugevicus* ECLI:EU:C:2018:898; in Case C-897/19 PPU *IN v Ruska Federacija* (n 18), the Court also extended this protection to a European Economic Area (EEA) citizen who fell within the scope of the EEA by virtue

national courts to apply the Charter in examining whether extradition can take place. However, this review of extradition measures has so far been limited to assessing compliance with Articles 19(2) and 4 of the Charter. Article 19(2) protects individuals from removal or extradition to a country where there is a serious risk that they would be subjected to the death penalty, torture, or other inhuman or degrading treatment or punishment, and Article 4 of the Charter protects against torture and inhuman and degrading treatment more generally.[29] As previously mentioned, other rights, including procedural rights and the right to private and family life, have so far not been relevant in the Court's assessment.[30]

Overall, in all the cases examined above, there is a close connection between the fundamental right invoked and the scope of the free movement right, and it is this proximity that explains the more ready application of the Charter, both in justifying a claim of authority and in internalizing fundamental rights in the proportionality test. We shall now analyse other strands of cases where the application of fundamental rights is less consistent.

4. Cases Where the Applicability of the Charter is Variable

We have seen above that in certain instances, Charter rights are more commonly applied by the Court, either within the proportionality assessment or as free-standing rights because the Member State is implementing EU law. However, in other situations, particularly in relation to migrant Union citizens' residence rights and access to welfare, as well as in cases of circular migration, the applicability of the Charter is more variable. We shall look at these different strands of case law in turn. However, before we start, we should recall briefly the *Dano* case, possibly now overruled at least in part by the ruling in *CG*, which will be examined later in this chapter.[31]

of receiving services in Croatia; even though the Charter does not bind the EEA states, it was applicable *ratione loci*.

[29] See Case C–182/15 *Petruhhin* ECLI:EU:C:2016:630.

[30] Fundamental rights are also relevant in relation to penalties imposed on Union citizens for administrative breaches relating to free movement rights; see eg Case C–35/20 *A* ECLI:EU:C:2021:13, where fundamental rights form part of the proportionality assessment.

[31] Fundamental rights were absent from the Court's reasoning in the first wave of Union citizenship cases; see eg Case C–85/96 *María Martínez Sala* ECLI:EU:C:1998:217; Case C–224/98 *D'Hoop* ECLI:EU:C:2002:432; Case C–184/99 *Rudy Grzelczyk* ECLI:EU:C:2001:458. In Case C–413/99 *R v Baumbast* ECLI:EU:C:2002:493, fundamental rights were relevant in relation to the first of the two cases, concerning the derived right to reside of a divorced parent of children in education, but not in relation to the direct effect of art 21 TFEU (then art 18 TEC) where the Court limited its assessment to the proportionality of the measure. Some of us, rightly or wrongly, assumed that if proportionality as a general principle of EU law was applicable in the case of barriers to the free movement of citizens, so too would be fundamental rights as general principles. See eg Michael Dougan and Eleanor Spaventa, 'Educating Rudy and the English Patient: A Double-Bill on Residency Rights under Article 18 EC' (2003) 28 European Law Review 699.

It is well known that *Dano* related to a claim to welfare provision by a Romanian citizen living in Germany. Here, the Court held that Article 18 TFEU, providing for the general right to non-discrimination on grounds of nationality within the scope of the Treaty, was given 'more specific expression' in Article 24(1) of Directive 2004/38, which provides a general right to equal treatment in relation to situations falling within the scope of that Directive. Since Ms Dano did not meet the requirement of economic self-sufficiency necessary to claim a right to reside in Germany by virtue of Article 7 of Directive 2004/38, she did not fall within the scope of the Directive and hence could not claim equal treatment. Moreover, there was no residual role for Article 21 TFEU: the fact that Ms Dano had exercised her free movement rights did not mean that the general principles of EU law (equal treatment, proportionality and fundamental rights) were applicable: rather, the failure to fulfil the conditions provided for in the Directive placed her outside the reach of EU law. The national court had also enquired specifically about the applicability of the Charter of Fundamental Rights and in response to this question the Court of Justice excluded the relevance of the Charter, finding that in this case Germany was not implementing EU law. Whereas this part of the ruling referred to the notion of 'non-contributory' benefits pursuant to Regulation 883/2004, the exclusion of the Charter is consistent with the first part of the ruling where the Court denied any residual relevance to Article 21 TFEU when the claimant did not meet the conditions provided for in Directive 2004/38. The ruling in *Dano* is of relevance to our analysis because the Court does not call into discussion the case law on the constitutional principles of EU law (proportionality and fundamental rights); rather, it restricts the personal scope of the Treaty provisions precisely to avoid applying those constitutional principles. In other words, while *Dano* changed the relationship between primary and secondary law as developed in *Baumbast*, it did not change the constitutional landscape in relation to fundamental rights. The subsequent case law does not clarify in a consistent way the extent to which EU fundamental rights apply once the situation falls within the scope of the Treaty because the national rule imposes a barrier to movement.

The first line of cases to be examined are those where the Member State is seeking to restrict or deny the right of residence to Union citizens or their family members, including cases concerning circular migration.[32] Here, and as mentioned earlier, the legal landscape is very fragmented and the applicability of fundamental rights haphazard. Take, for instance, the cases of *Alokpa* and *Bajratari*.[33]

[32] We are not considering, unless particularly relevant, cases of straightforward implementation of Directive 2004/38, since in those cases the Charter is applicable through the medium of secondary legislation rather than the free movement provisions; see eg Joined Cases C–331 and 366/16 *K v Staatssecretaris van Veiligheid en Justitie and HF v Belgische Staat* ECLI:EU:C:2018:296; Case C–129/18 *SM (Child placed under Algerian kafala)* ECLI:EU:2019:248.

[33] Case C–86/12 *Alokpa and Moudoulou* ECLI:EU:C:2013:645; Case C–93/18 *Bajratari v Secretary of State for the Home Department* ECLI:EU:C:2019:209.

Both cases concerned the derived residence rights in a host state of third-country national parents of minor Union citizens resident in a host state. The children/family had no particular link with the Member State of nationality in either case, and both cases centred on the availability of sufficient resources, which would allow the children to claim a right of residence pursuant to Article 7(1)(b) of Directive 2004/38, and through which a derivative right to reside would be conferred on their carers.[34] In the first case, Ms Alokpa had a job offer which she could not take up for lack of a residence permit. In the second case, Mr Bajratari was working without a work permit. In *Alokpa,* the Court held that since the children did not possess sufficient resources (given that their mother could not legally take up employment despite a job offer) they did not have a right to reside, and they should, if anything, go back to their state of nationality and claim a *Ruiz Zambrano* right to reside for their mother there, regardless of the fact that neither the mother nor the children had any connection with the children's state of nationality. In *Bajratari,* on the other hand, the Court found that income from irregular work could be taken into account in relation to establishing the sufficient resources necessary for the applicability of Directive 2004/38. In neither case, however, did the Court take into consideration the Charter. This is particularly striking in *Alokpa,* given that the national court had explicitly enquired about the applicability of the Charter, and given that minors were involved whose forced return to a state of nationality with which they had no connection might well be a disproportionate interference with their rights under Articles 7 and 24 of the Charter and Article 8 ECHR.

Even more striking is the case of *NA*,[35] which concerned a third-country national victim of domestic violence whose ex-husband, a German national, fled and subsequently divorced her. One of the issues for determination was whether Mrs NA could claim a derived right to reside as the former spouse of a Union migrant citizen. Despite the fact that she had been the victim of domestic violence, the Court found that she had no such right because at the time of the divorce the main right-holder had already left the host state. Instead, her right to reside was derived from her children's right to education. The Court did not mention fundamental rights, even though the referring court had made it clear to the Court that the national tribunal competent for the assessment of facts had found that the

[34] The fact that Union citizens' children need to have a carer/parent/relative to ensure that their right to free movement and residence is effective even beyond the right to remain in education is consistent case law; see eg Case C–200/02 *Chen and Zhou* ECLI:EU:C:2004:639.

[35] Case C–115/15 *NA* ECLI:EU:C:2016:487, para 30 question 2; see also *Ahmed v Secretary of State for Home Department* [2013] UKUT 89 (IAC) where the UK Upper Tribunal applied the *Ruiz Zambrano* test in relation to German minors resident in the UK, since the prospect of them going to Germany was negligible. On divorce, see also Case C–218/14 *Singh (II)* ECLI:EU:C:2015:476 (again no mention of fundamental rights). The ruling in *NA* was partially overruled in Case C–930/19 *X v Belgium* ECLI:EU:C:2021:657, para 40ff. Again, in relation to this issue the Court does not mention fundamental rights.

forced return of Mrs NA's children to their state of nationality would be a breach of Article 8 ECHR and Article 7 of the Charter.

On the other hand, in both *Coman* and *VMA* fundamental rights formed a significant part of the Court's assessment. *Coman* was a case of circular migration in that Mr Coman was coming back to his Member State of nationality after having exercised his free movement rights.[36] Pursuant to the case law,[37] circular migrants have a right to family reunification analogous to that conferred upon migrant Union citizens by Directive 2004/38. In *Coman*, however, the authorities had denied Mr Coman's spouse a residence permit on the grounds that they were in a same-sex marriage, which is not recognized in Romania. The Court of Justice found that the situation fell within the scope of Article 21 TFEU and that the refusal to grant a residence permit to Mr Coman's spouse was an interference with such a right. Accordingly, such refusal had to be justified, and any justification would have to comply with the Charter and, in particular, Article 7 thereof. Since the ECtHR had already declared that Article 8 ECHR encompassed the situation of a homosexual couple in the same way as that of a heterosexual couple, the failure to recognize the right to reside of Mr Coman's spouse was incompatible with Article 21 TFEU.

Similarly, in *VMA*,[38] the issue related to the Bulgarian authorities' refusal to issue a birth certificate to a child whose birth had been registered in Spain, on the grounds that according to Bulgarian law the birth certificate should identify the mother (and the father). As the parents of the child were two women, and since they had refused to acquiesce to the request of disclosing who between them (if any) was the biological mother, the certificate was refused, with also the (possible) consequence that the Bulgarian authorities would not issue a Bulgarian ID or passport to the child. The Court found that the refusal constituted a barrier to movement and therefore it had to be justified. Any justification invoked would have to respect the right to private life as enshrined in Article 7 of the Charter, as well as the rights of the child provided for in Article 24 of the Charter, including the child's right to have their best interest treated as the primary consideration and their right to maintain a personal relationship with both parents. Noting that Article 24 of the

[36] Case C-673/16 *Coman* ECLI:EU:C:2018:385.

[37] See Case C-456/12 *O v Minister voor Immigratie, Integratie en Asiel and Minister voor Immigratie, Integratie en Asiel v B* ECLI:EU:C:2014:135, where fundamental rights were not mentioned; in Case C-89/17 *Banger* ECLI:EU:C:2018:570, rather than the right to private and family life, it was the right to an effective judicial remedy. In this case, however, the Charter was applicable by virtue of the applicability of Directive 2004/38. In Case C-230/17 *Deha Altiner and Ravn* ECLI:EU:C:2018:497, in relation to a circular situation having to decide if family life between a Union (own citizen) and the son of her third-country national husband had been created or strengthened in the host Member State before they returned, since the son only joined them at a later stage, the Court did not carry out any fundamental rights assessment, albeit it naturally referred to family life. No reference was made, however, to the Charter or to the best interests of the child, perhaps because the Court did not consider this to be a barrier to movement.

[38] Case C-490/20 *VMA* ECLI:EU:C:2021:1008.

Charter had given effect at Union level to the rights of the child as contained in the Convention on the Rights of the Child,[39] the Court drew on this latter document, and especially on the child's right not to be discriminated against (also in relation to the parents' sexual orientation); their right to be registered immediately at birth; their right to a name; and their right to a nationality, to find that it would be inconsistent with the Charter to deprive or render excessively difficult the child's ability to travel with the parent not mentioned in the birth certificate.

Coman and *VMA* are particularly interesting because in both cases the Member States invoked the constitutional identity clause found in Article 4(2) TEU. Yet, in both cases, the Court resisted the temptation of allowing Article 4(2) TEU to become a sort of 'relativist' bridge, permitting a different standard of rights depending on the country of destination. And, given the cultural 'sensitivity' of the issue, the Court's decision is perhaps best understood as having regard to its reliance upon the ECHR and the Convention on the Rights of the Child, where both instruments are binding upon all Member States as a matter of international law. Any accusation of judicial activism can then more easily be fended off as the obligations relied on by the Court against the Member State had arisen first and foremost from international law, and only in the second place from EU law.

Finally, there is another strand of cases where the application of fundamental rights is anything but consistent. Those cases relate to the right to access welfare provision in a host state by economically inactive (or semi-active) EU citizens. At first, the Court held that a person lawfully resident in the host state had the right to equal treatment, including in relation to welfare benefits, regardless of whether their residence had been conferred by national or EU law (*Sala*).[40] This interpretation was qualified in *Grzelczyk* by acknowledging that, when the right to reside was derived from EU law, exercising the right to equal treatment might result in the EU citizen becoming an unreasonable burden with the effect that the Member State might legitimately terminate residency.[41] In *Baumbast*,[42] the Court stated that the right to reside was a Treaty-derived right so that any limitation to it, even in pursuance of the conditions provided for in the then-residency directives, had to comply with the proportionality principle (and presumably with fundamental rights). While in *Vatsouras*[43] the Court also gave a broad interpretation of the principle of equal treatment and a narrow interpretation of the derogation contained in Article 24(2) of Directive 2004/38, with time it accepted that the provisions of Directive 2004/38 (that is, the political compromise contained therein) should be

[39] UN Convention on the Rights of the Child (adopted 20 November 1989 UNGA Res no 44/25, entered into force 2 September 1990) <www.ohchr.org/en/instruments-mechanisms/instruments/convention-rights-child>.

[40] Case C-85/96 *María Martínez Sala* (n 31).

[41] Case C-184/99 *Rudy Grzelczyk* (n 31).

[42] Case C-413/99 *R v Baumbast* (n 31).

[43] Joined Cases 22 and 23/08 *Vatsouras and Koupatantze* ECLI:EU:C:2009:344.

given greater, if not predominant, value.[44] This approach culminated in the restrictive interpretation of the personal scope of EU law in *Dano*, with the effect that a Union citizen who does/did not meet the conditions of the right to reside pursuant to Directive 2004/38 would not qualify for equal treatment, nor would they fall within the scope of the Treaty. Thus, neither general principles nor fundamental rights would be relevant in their case. Similarly, in *Alimanovic*, the Court gave a more restrictive interpretation of the rights of migrant jobseekers and made no mention of Charter rights.[45]

In *Job Centre Krefeld* and *GMA*,[46] the Court changed gear again in relation to the rights of Union citizens, this time leaning towards a more generous interpretation of jobseekers' rights. In *Job Centre Krefeld*,[47] the issue related to whether the claimant (JD) had a right to a jobseekers' allowance. The Court found that since JD had previously been a worker, his children, who were in education, derived their right to reside from Article 10 of Regulation 492/2011, and their father in turn derived his right to reside from his children's Article 10 rights. For this reason, Article 7(2) of the same regulation, guaranteeing a right to equal treatment in relation to social and tax advantages, was applicable, and JD was entitled to the benefit. In *GMA*, on the other hand, the national court enquired about jobseekers' right to stay beyond the first three months (Article 14(4)(b) of Directive 2004/38).[48] The Court of Justice clarified that after the first three months of unqualified residence, the Member State must afford the jobseeker a reasonable time to acquaint themselves with the job market. It is only after that period has expired that the Member State can request that the Union citizen provide evidence that they were still looking for a job and had genuine chances of being engaged. In both cases, the expansive reading of the rights of jobseekers was grounded firmly in the free movement provisions and secondary legislation, with no mention of the Charter. Of course, this might also be because of the way the preliminary questions had been phrased. Yet, in *GMA*, the Court decided not to answer the national court's question as to whether the Charter was relevant in determining

[44] See also Case C-158/07 *Förster* ECLI:EU:C:2008:630.

[45] Case C-67/14 *Jobcenter Berlin Neukölln v Nazifa Alimanovic* ECLI:EU:C:2015:597, and see Anastasia Iliopoulou-Penot, 'Deconstructing the Former Edifice of Union Citizenship? The *Alimanovic* Judgment' (2016) 53 Common Market Law Review 1007.

[46] Case C-181/19 *Jobcenter Krefeld—Widerspruchsstelle v JD* ECLI:EU:C:2020:794; Case C-710/19 *GMA v Belgium* ECLI:EU:C:2020:1037.

[47] For an analysis, see Fulvia Ristuccia, 'The Right to Social Assistance of Children in Education and Their Primary Carers: *Jobcenter Krefeld*' (2021) 58 Common Market Law Review 877; see also Maxime Tecmenne, 'Migrant Jobseekers, Right of Residence and Access to Welfare Benefits: One Step Forward, Two Steps Backwards?' (2021) 46 European Law Review 765.

[48] For analysis, see Rufat Babayev, 'Setting Out the Boundaries of Jobseekers' Residence Status and Beyond: Case C-710/19 *GMA v État Belge*' (2022) 29 Maastricht Journal of European and Comparative Law 286; Tecmenne (n 47); Alice Welsh, 'A Genuine Chance of Free Movement? Clarifying the "Reasonable Period of Time" and Residence Conditions for Jobseekers in *GMA*' (2021) 58 Common Market Law Review 1591.

a jobseeker's right to reside. In other words, until the recent ruling in *CG*,[49] the Court did not take into account the special connection between welfare entitlement and fundamental rights, focusing rather on access to welfare as a tool to enhance free movement.

In *CG*, the issue related to a Union citizen who had arrived in the United Kingdom before the end of the transition period and was resident in the United Kingdom pursuant to domestic law which, in the light of the withdrawal of the United Kingdom from the EU, granted an unconditional right to reside to EU citizens present in its territory (the pre-settled status). Ms GC had arrived with her partner, with whom she had two children. Being a victim of domestic violence, she later escaped and was living in a women's shelter. When she applied for universal credit, she was denied the benefit on the grounds that she did not meet the conditions provided for by domestic law. The Court, consistently with the *Dano* approach, ruled that the right to equal treatment did not apply to a Union citizen who did not meet the requirements of the right to reside provided for in Article 7 of Directive 2004/38, that is, economic activity or economic independence. However, differently from *Dano*, the Court also held that Ms CG fell within the scope of the Treaty by virtue of her having exercised the right to move and reside conferred by Article 21(1) TFEU. Although the requirements of Directive 2004/38 had not been met, the United Kingdom—by granting her a right to reside—was still implementing Union law for the purpose of Article 51(1) of the Charter, so that the latter applied.[50] The Court held that the state, in accordance with Article 1 of the Charter, had an obligation to ensure that a Union citizen lawfully resident pursuant to national law and who is in a vulnerable situation could live in dignified conditions. Furthermore, pursuant to Articles 7 and 24(2) of the Charter, the Member State was also required to ensure that the children could live with the parent(s) responsible for them in dignified conditions.

5. Conclusions

The analysis of the application of the Charter to national rules limiting free movement rights shows that there is no 'principled' approach to the application of fundamental rights in those cases. In this respect, the fear expressed in the wake of the *Carpenter* ruling of an overreach of EU fundamental rights through the medium

[49] Case C–709/20 *CG* (n 11).

[50] We shall not enter into that other thorny area which is the extent to which fundamental rights apply in relation to national rules which go beyond the requirements imposed by EU law. On this, see the seminal article by Francesco de Cecco, 'Room to Move? Minimum Harmonization and Fundamental Rights' (2006) 43 Common Market Law Review 8; see also Francesco de Cecco, 'Minimum Harmonization and the Limits of Union Fundamental Rights Review: *TSN* and *AKT*' (2021) 58 Common Market Law Review 187.

of the free movement provisions seems to have been unjustified. Rather, the application of fundamental rights to cases involving barriers to movement is far from consistent, and, in the writer's opinion, depends on many variables.

Thus, as is the case in relation to Article 51 Charter more generally, the level of proximity between the EU right invoked as a trigger and the fundamental right itself seems very relevant to the applicability of the Charter. When there is close proximity, as in the context of the right to family reunification, which is a specific expression at Union level of the right to family life, the Court readily applies Articles 7 and 24 of the Charter. The same is true in relation to the *Ruiz Zambrano* type of cases, one of the premises of which is that the child, who is a Union citizen, would have to abandon the territory of the EU in order to maintain their family life. Furthermore, if a given interpretation of a fundamental right is also guaranteed by international law, such as was the case in *Coman* and *VMA*, but also in relation to the extradition cases, then the Court is more ready to give effect to those rights in EU law, even when the application of the Charter touches upon culturally sensitive issues. And, if the right is relatively 'cost free', such as in relation to names, then it will also be more readily enforced through fundamental rights reasoning. Conversely, more caution is exercised in using fundamental rights to assert citizens' rights to welfare provision. Where the Court wants to guarantee the latter, it tends to derive it directly from the free movement provisions and secondary legislation rather than by enforcing Charter rights. Finally, *CG* might signal a move towards a more rights-based approach, at least to protect a minimum core of rights for vulnerable migrants. In this way, the decision of the Member State to confer residency rights beyond what is required by EU law comes with the obligation to guarantee the enjoyment of at least some of the Charter rights, and primarily that of living in dignified conditions. Welfare entitlement, or at least some welfare entitlement, is therefore seen not only as a tool to enhance and guarantee free movement, but as a fundamental right of Union citizens when lawfully present in the host territory.

9

The Evolving Regulation of Consumer Safety in the Internal Market

*Geraint Howells**

1. Introduction

I met Stephen Weatherill four decades ago when he was a talented researcher in the Consumer Law Research Centre at Brunel University. This work would eventually lead to the significant edited volume, *Federalism and Responsibility: A Study on Product Safety Law and Practice.*[1] He has set out his views on consumer safety both in our joint book on UK consumer law[2] and in his authoritative work on EU consumer law.[3] He has been an important commentator on product safety at key times, pointing out the need to incorporate standards into the regulatory framework[4] and to ensure effective enforcement.[5] Both these themes appear in this contribution. This product safety scholarship aligns with two of Stephens's twin passions in the legal realm—ensuring an effective internal market and, at the same time, ensuring European citizens benefit from effective consumer protection. Consumer safety must have been a pleasurable field for him to plough, for in my opinion it has been a success story with many interesting regulatory innovations and, with one hiccup, a history of reflective regulatory reform.

This brief comment—it is not intended to be a full-blown scholarly exposition—has five objectives. First, some general comments will be made about the legislative process with regard to consumer product safety at the EU level. Secondly, the co-regulatory approach will be praised, for it has been a trailblazer in ensuring soft law is made effective by placing it within a regulatory framework. Thirdly, the practical dimension of enforcement and particular cross-border cooperation will be

* The author would like to thank Jonathon Watson for his research assistance.

[1] Hans-W Micklitz, Thomas Roethe, and Stephen Weatherill (eds), *Federalism and Responsibility: A Study on Product Safety Law and Practice in the European Community* (Gralsam & Trotman 1994).

[2] Geraint Howells and Stephen Weatherill, *Consumer Protection Law* (2nd edn, Routledge 2017).

[3] *EU Consumer Law and Policy* (2nd edn, Edward Elgar 2014).

[4] 'A General Duty to Supply Only Safe Goods in the Community: Some Remarks from a British Perspective' (1990) 13 Journal of Consumer Policy 79.

[5] 'Reinvigorating the Development of Community Product Safety Policy' (1991) 14 Journal of Consumer Policy 171.

Geraint Howells, *The Evolving Regulation of Consumer Safety in the Internal Market* In: *The Internal Market Ideal.*
Edited by: Jeremias Adams-Prassl, Sanja Bogojević, Ariel Ezrachi, and Dorota Leczykiewicz, Oxford University Press.
 DOI: 10.1093/oso/9780192867063.003.0010

highlighted. The discussion then moves from these broad themes to consider the most recent reform proposals at the EU level as well as future UK developments.

2. EU Legislative History and Reform

When the EU first adopted a General Product Safety Directive in 1992,[6] it was seen as completing a regulatory framework for product safety that had witnessed the development of broad-based sectoral directives adopted under the new approach.[7] These had set out essential safety requirements and encouraged producers to comply with standards that fleshed out how they could be complied with. The General Product Safety Directive ensures that all consumer products are covered—even if not addressed by any new approach directives—and that all consumer risks are covered, even if not mentioned in the new approach directives. Other obligations such as reporting mechanisms apply where the new approach directives do not address them. It was a pretty good start. Although some Member States, like the United Kingdom, had already introduced a general safety requirement,[8] an overarching obligation to provide safe products across Europe was a major step forward. As important on a practical level was the requirement that every Member State have a body responsible for product safety, with powers to enforce the rules.

In 2001, the Directive was reformed.[9] Some of the most significant reforms were intended to oblige businesses to lift the veil of secrecy surrounding their safety problems and cooperate more openly with agencies. Businesses had to inform the authorities when products posed risks incompatible with the general safety requirement. It was also made clear that unsafe goods should be recalled from consumers who had purchased them, and whilst the preference was for the business to organize this, the enforcement agency could mandate it.

At this time, the contrast between product safety and product liability reform was stark. Product safety was being proactively reviewed whereas product liability was the subject of a few short reports, with little sign the Commission was interested in reform beyond relatively minor reform regarding the inclusion of primary agricultural produce. What were the reasons for this? Product safety was being operationalized by officials who were seeing problems and wanting to make enforcement more effective. They had an incentive to demand reforms and, as part of government, had the means to influence law reform agendas. By

[6] Council Directive 92/59/EEC of 29 June 1992 on general product safety [1992] OJ L228/24.

[7] Council Resolution of 7 May 1985 on a new approach to technical harmonization and standards [1985] OJ C136/1.

[8] Consumer Protection Act 1987, s 10.

[9] Directive 2001/95/EC of the European Parliament and of the Council of 3 December 2001 on general product safety [2002] OJ L11/4. See Duncan Fairgrieve and Geraint Howells, 'General Product Safety—A Revolution through Reform' (2006) 69 Modern Law Review 59. Subsequent to writing the article, Regulation (EU) 2023/988 on general product safety [2022] OJ L35/1 was adopted.

contrast, product liability was being used by private practice lawyers, who would seek what advantage they could from the new civil liability rules but were not organized in the same way to lobby for reform. Indeed, the number of serious product liability cases in many countries remained low and so the evidence base for reform was slow in accruing. Perhaps most important was the feeling that the EU had dipped its toes in dangerous waters when legislating for strict product liability and yet, so far, the results had not been too problematic. The consumer lobby had gained the political goal of strict liability, albeit subject to some important caveats such as the development risks defence, and industry seemed to be managing the liability risk. There had been no US-style liability crisis and no un-insurability problems.

The contrast between the Commission's enthusiasm for reform in the two areas heightened when, in 2013, the Commission issued proposals to turn the General Product Safety Directive into a regulation.[10] It would also have imposed greater obligations on manufacturers to demonstrate compliance, required greater traceability, ensured that all links in the supply chain more actively promoted safety, enhanced market surveillance, promoted wider disclosure of dangerous products, and linked penalties to the size of the economic operator. This reform stumbled, seemingly over a requirement that the country of origin would need to be disclosed. It was perplexing that these reforms should have been held up over a provision that was only at best tangentially related to product safety. Clearly there were some politics or other factors at play of which I was unaware.

Momentum for reform has now been given to these areas due to technological developments related to digitalization and artificial intelligence (AI). These will be explored later. These same drivers are also finally forcing the Commission to undertake a fundamental review of product liability.[11]

Alongside the explicit consumer safety rules, the EU has developed rules on accreditation of conformity assessment bodies.[12] These bodies are vital to the *ex-ante* control of products, and their approval can be a requirement for the award of the CE mark. Also, within the field of harmonized products, the Commission has developed rules on market surveillance,[13] some of which are informing the reform proposals for a General Product Safety Regulation.[14]

[10] Commission, 'Proposal for a regulation of the European Parliament and of the Council on consumer product safety' COM (2021) 346 final.

[11] Commission, 'Proposal for a directive of the European Parliament and of the Council on liability for defective products' COM (2022) 495 final; Commission, 'Proposal for a directive of the European Parliament and of the Council on adapting non-contractual civil liability rules to artificial intelligence' COM (2022) 496 final.

[12] Regulation (EC) 765/2008 of the European Parliament and of the Council of 9 July 2008 setting out the requirements for accreditation and market surveillance relating to the marketing of products [2008] OJ L218/30.

[13] Regulation (EU) 2019/1020 of the European Parliament and of the Council of 20 June 2019 on market surveillance and compliance of products [2019] OJ L169/1.

[14] COM (2021) 346 final (n 10).

3. Co-regulation

Soft law is a theme of our times as governments seek ways to regulate economic activity in a manner that does not place undue burdens on either the state apparatus or the businesses being regulated. When done well, it can produce efficient means to target the real problems that are well known to those in the sector. However, there are always fears that rogue traders will operate outside the self-regulatory structures and a risk that those within them will be policed in a relaxed manner. Therefore, integrating self-regulation into a regulatory framework provides the opportunity to have the best of all worlds. This has been attempted in many sectors, but product safety was an early adopter of this co-regulatory approach. It has been pretty successful in integrating standards into the process.

Standards are a key element of harmonization under the new approach. Producers remain free to meet the essential safety requirements set out in annexes to the new approach directives in any way they see fit, but the easiest route to a safer harbour for compliance is provided by adhering to standards developed by the European standardization body (CEN) and adopted by national standards bodies. Where third-party certification is required, this is also achieved by notified bodies that meet set criteria. Standards also play a role within the context of proving compliance with the general safety requirement. A product is presumed to be safe—as far as the risks and risk categories covered by relevant national standards are concerned—when it conforms to voluntary national standards transposing European standards, the references of which have been published by the Commission in the *Official Journal of the European Communities*.[15] Otherwise, assessment of the safety of the product should take into account the voluntary national standards transposing relevant European standards that have not, however, followed the specific procedure leading to publication and the standards drawn up in the Member State in which the product is marketed.[16]

Criticisms can be made of the reliance on voluntary standards. The standardization process has been criticized for being too lengthy.[17] Consumers have limited input to the process of standards creation and the process can even be dominated by a few key industry players, raising potential competition concerns. There have also been suggestions that some producers might shop around for conformity assessment bodies that apply more flexible interpretations when assessing products. Indeed, for many consumer products, the CE mark can be added by the producer

[15] General Product Safety Directive, art 3(2).

[16] ibid art 3(3).

[17] Commission, 'Report from the Commission to the European Parliament and the Council on the implementation of Directive 2001/95/EC of the European Parliament and of the Council of 3 December 2001 on general product safety' COM (2021) 342 final, 10.

themselves, without the involvement of the third party. There are certainly plenty of examples of dangerous products that still infiltrate the EU market (eg toasters[18]). Yet the EU standards do provide a measure of reassurance, and this is placed within a regulatory framework that still allows action to be taken when unsafe products are detected. This system probably works reasonably well, as most mainstream players want to produce safer products and not risk the publicity attached to product recalls or the liability risks posed by strict product liability. However, this co-regulatory system probably only works because there is an effective enforcement structure to support it.

4. Enforcement

Enforcement structures vary from one state to another. In the UK, as Weatherill has noted,[19] local enforcement dominates. This is pragmatic and effective as local officers tend to know the businesses and local issues. There is some degree of consistency introduced for business through the home authority principle whereby a lead authority will liaise with particular businesses to ensure consistency. Also, national and regional issues can be coordinated by the National Trading Standards Board. However, in a European context there is a need for a national focal point, whatever the underlying local arrangements are underneath. In the UK, this is now the Office for Products and Standards. There has been a long tradition of consumer safety authorities cooperating and sharing information. This preceded the EU structures and was formerly coordinated within the framework of the Organisation for Economic Co-operation and Development (OECD).[20] The focus of attention has shifted to EU mechanisms with Rapid Exchange of Information System (RAPEX) and other systems for exchanging information. The value and importance of such cooperation is underpinned by the EU-UK Trade and Cooperation Agreement, expressly providing for continued exchanges of information on product safety between the EU and the UK. Thus, at least in this sensitive area, it is to be hoped that the links between enforcement authorities will be retained. The natural incentives to promote the common good of protecting consumers' safety should provide the glue to make sure the EU and UK authorities remain in contact. However, this will be easier if the underlying regulations remain aligned, and it is to this future that our attention now turns.

[18] See European Parliament, 'Briefing Paper on General Product Safety Regulation' (September 2022) 2.

[19] See 'Reinvigorating the Development of Community Product Safety Policy' (1991) 14 Journal of Consumer Policy 171 and Geraint Howells and Stephen Weatherill, *Consumer Protection Law* (2nd edn, Routledge 2017) 483.

[20] See eg OECD, 'Report on enhancing information sharing on consumer product safety' (June 2010).

5. EU Reform

The 2013 reform proposals and the latest proposal both favour replacing the Directive with a Regulation. This seems appropriate, given that the aim is to insert the European regime into the national systems and to provide common means for communication and coordination. There is also limited interaction with other national law. In this respect, regulatory law is different from private law, where any EU rules need to fit into the matrix of national laws.

The latest proposals are, however, clearly influenced by the desire to ensure safety law is fit for the digital age. Thus, AI and cybersecurity risks are both made relevant to the assessment of safety. Article 7(1) of the proposed General Product Safety Regulation[21] would require that the following factors should be taken into account when assessing safety:

(c) the effect that other products might have on the product to be assessed, including the effect of non-embedded items that are meant to determine, change or complete the way another product falling under the scope of this Regulation works, which have to be taken into consideration in assessing the safety of that other product; ...
(h) the appropriate cybersecurity features necessary to protect the product against external influences, including malicious third parties, when such an influence might have an impact on the safety of the product;
(i) the evolving, learning and predictive functionalities of a product.

Specific attention is paid to the online marketplace, for which a definition is provided.[22] The EU already has a voluntary EU Safety Pledge that a number of organizations have signed up to.[23] The Regulation would move away from the hands-off approach of the E-Commerce Directive,[24] which only required action to be taken when a site was informed of illegal activity, such as the sale of dangerous products. It goes beyond the proposal in the Digital Services Act that would make sites liable under consumer law where they appeared to be providing the product or service or acting under the authority or control of someone who was.[25] It provides specific rules in the safety context, requiring online marketplaces to establish a single point

[21] COM (2021) 346 final (n 10).
[22] ibid art 3(14).
[23] For details and reports, see <https://ec.europa.eu/info/business-economy-euro/product-safety-and-requirements/product-safety/product-safety-pledge_en> accessed 12 October 2022.
[24] Directive 2000/31/EC of the European Parliament and of the Council of 8 June 2000 on certain legal aspects of information society services, in particular electronic commerce, in the Internal Market [2000] OJ L178/1.
[25] Commission, 'Proposal for a Regulation of the European Parliament and of the Council on a Single Market For Digital Services (Digital Services Act)' COM (2020) 825 final, art 5(3). Subsequent to writing the article, Regulation (EU) 2922/2965 (Digital Services Act) [2022] OJ L277/1 was adopted.

of contact, register with the Safety Gate portal, provide specific information, and promote voluntary compliance and cooperation with authorities. It also includes powers for enforcement authorities to require the removal of illegal content referring to dangerous products from their online interface. The control of the internet sale of unsafe goods is also enhanced by including within the definition of 'economic operator' not only the manufacturer, the authorized representative, the importer, and the distributor, but also the fulfilment service provider. Fulfilment service providers are vital to the delivery of online goods from outside the EU, but their legal status was unclear.[26] The goal is to ensure that someone within the EU is responsible for the product's safety.

Fulfilment service providers were introduced as a legal category in Regulation 2019/1020 on market surveillance and compliance of products.[27] This had put a modern regime in place for products covered by harmonized EU rules. In comparison, the regime for non-harmonized consumer products looked ragged, and this problem was resolved by importing the rules from Regulation 2019/1020 wholesale into this proposal. Enhanced powers to impose traceability requirements are also included.[28] Specific rules will identify what can be required when a product is recalled.[29] Interestingly, in another example of regulatory law and compensation being blended,[30] a remedy also has to be provided on recall. This must include one of the following: repair, replacement, or refund.[31]

The Regulation would also rename RAPEX as the Safety Gate[32] and include a Safety Business Gateway portal.[33] The relationship with the more general Information and Communication System would be clarified to prevent the need for duplicate entries. Cooperation between Member States' enforcement authorities is ensured by the Consumer Safety Network.

The Community maintains the ability to intervene when Member States' reactions to product safety issues differ significantly.[34] An arbitration mechanism is introduced.[35]

There are many other small nuggets included within the Proposal. The overall assessment is of a very welcome package that modernizes the law to reflect changing

[26] See Commission, 'Commission Notice on the market surveillance of products sold online' [2017] OJ C250/1, 3.2.

[27] See recital 13 and art 3 no 11.

[28] COM (2021) 346 final (n 10) art 17.

[29] ibid art 34.

[30] See also the requirement to provide redress for unfair commercial practices, according to art 11a of Directive 2005/29/EC of the European Parliament and of the Council of 11 May 2005 concerning unfair business-to-consumer commercial practices in the internal market [2005] OJ L149/22 as amended by the Directive 2019/2161 [2019] OJ L328/7.

[31] COM (2021) 346 final (n 10) art 35(1).

[32] ibid art 23.

[33] ibid art 25.

[34] ibid art 26.

[35] ibid art 27.

supply practices following the growth of online sales, many of which involve products coming from outside the EU. It allows the concerns around AI and the integration of software into products to be addressed. It modernizes enforcement procedures and aligns the rules for harmonized and non-harmonized products. However, this framework may be easier to set up than to apply. It is well known that compliance with regulatory rules by online sites can be low.[36] That is why the sanctions are important, and it is useful that, in line with other consumer protection laws, the requirement has been introduced that the maximum penalty should be at least 4 per cent of the turnover of the economic operator or online marketplace.[37] It is also unclear how the rules relating to AI and cybersecurity should be applied. Saying they should be taken into account is one thing; applying them in practice raises many difficult questions. There is also the relationship to be considered with the proposed EU Artificial Intelligence Act[38]—which sets standards but reserves the most stringent controls only for high risk products, and it is not clear that all consumer products will be classified as high risk[39]—and the rules for AI liability, which have just been published.[40]

6. United Kingdom

The United Kingdom has issued its own Product Safety Review and released its response to the evidence from the consultation.[41] This makes interesting reading. It is broader than merely dealing with the general consumer safety requirement and also encompasses, inter alia, standardization and conformity assessments as well as, tangentially, some issues relating to product liability. It also links into the debate about the circular economy. However, it touches on some of the same issues as those that are raised by the EU recent proposal.

There is clearly the same concern as there is within the EU about the need to regulate the online marketplace, with unfair competition being cited by businesses as a concern—with a gentle side swipe by the UK at the EU Safety Pledge, which, it is suggested, is not very effective. There is some general discussion about new technology and product safety, but few specifics, though there was acknowledgment of a shared view across stakeholder groups that clarity was needed in some areas.

[36] See eg OECD, 'Online Product Safety: Trends and Challenges' [2016] OECD Digital Economy Papers No 261 at 5–6.

[37] COM (2021) 346 final (n 10) art 40.

[38] Commission, 'Proposal for a regulation of the European Parliament and of the Council laying down harmonised rules on artificial intelligence (Artificial Intelligence Act)' COM (2021) 206 final.

[39] See eg Christiane Wendehorst, 'The Proposal for an Artificial Intelligence Act COM (2021) 206 from a Consumer Policy Perspective', study commissioned by the Austrian Federal Ministry of Social Affairs, Health, Care and Consumer Protection (2021) 112. <https://ssrn.com/abstract=4087402>.

[40] COM (2022) 496 final (n 11).

[41] Office for Product Safety & Standards, 'UK Product Safety Review: Call for Evidence Response' (November 2021).

Examples of such points are whether the definition of 'product' includes software, what the requirements for software updates are, and where liability lies.[42] There was also an interesting point made about the problems of 'drop-shipping' when goods are sent from overseas, so it is difficult to hold someone responsible locally.[43] There was also clearly some pride in the fact that the UK had taken steps to improve recalls through the standardization process.[44]

There is also much discussion of simplification and clarification of laws, with an attempt clearly to seek to lay the blame for much of the complexity with the EU.[45] It is indeed understandable in the current climate that this government review would seek to emphasize any benefits that might potentially stem from Brexit. This opportunity is duly noted: 'Following the UK's departure from the EU, we have a genuine opportunity to think boldly about how we regulate product safety and take an approach that puts UK consumers and businesses first.'[46] It is also seen as important that '[e]nsuring that the future framework takes full advantage of having left the EU, is adaptable and responsive to the challenges of the future and is better calibrated to the best evidence of risk will likely require legislative change'.[47] The one example of necessary legislative change cited is e-labelling.[48] Is it to be implied from that one example being listed that other issues can be addressed by interpretation of existing rules and soft law measures such as standardization? The Report itself notes that that a significant majority of respondents were sceptical of the EU voluntary approach to online marketplaces.[49]

It would be strange if product safety were an area of significant divergence between the UK and the EU, given that coordination in this area was considered sufficicntly important to include it in the EU UK Trade and Cooperation Agreement. It is most likely that the UK will fall into line with the broad thrust of EU policy as similar issues are clearly affecting both systems. The EU has a clear proposal, whereas the UK still seems to be in the formative stage and will have to choose how close a regulatory alignment it will have with the EU. But the wider the divergences, the more problematic this will be, not only at the political level but also in practical terms for businesses. Even leaving aside substantive policy, it is clear that there are a range of regulatory tools that can be chosen. The extent to which the UK and EU systems could drift apart due to different views on the role of soft law and how technology is used in enforcement (another theme from the UK review) is something

42 ibid 16.
43 ibid 19.
44 See PAS 7100:2018 Code of practice on consumer product safety related recalls and other corrective actions <www.bsigroup.com/en-GB/pas7100-supporting-better-product-recalls/>.
45 Office for Product Safety & Standards (n 41) 6: 'the current map of product safety legislation is large and, like much of the EU law on our statute book, complex.'
46 ibid 25.
47 ibid 26.
48 ibid.
49 ibid 14.

that should be watched. On a positive note, both systems may learn from one another. But there needs to be a willingness to be open to such learnings. Left to the consumer safety professionals, there should be confidence that these issues will be worked out and coordination will continue. In these strange political times, one can never be quite sure where politics will take us. It is to be hoped the final solution provides for free circulation of goods and consumer protection both within the EU and between it and the UK. That is what Stephen Weatherill has striven to support through his scholarship, and it is for the rest of us to be vigilant to ensure we maintain a safe consumer products market in the face of new challenges currently being driven by technology and internationalization of the consumer market. These developments should be viewed positively, and the Regulation should aim to give us confidence in the emerging products and markets. Consumer safety regulation should be a win-win-win for business, consumers, and states wanting to support innovation.

PART III

THE INTERNAL MARKET, COMPETITION LAW, AND SPORTS

10

The Ties that Will Always Bind: EU Competition Law and the Single Market

Albertina Albors-Llorens

1. Introduction

Speaking in 2015, Commissioner Margrethe Vestager alluded to the unbreakable and enduring bond between the EU competition rules and the single market. She famously averred:

> Competition Policy is very much at the core of the process of European integration. Our work is based on Treaty articles that have not changed since 1958. The founding fathers of Europe understood that there would be no genuine integration without a Single Market—and no functioning Single Market without a strong competition policy enforced by a central competition authority. Six decades later, here we are. The Single Market has been—and still is—a powerful engine of European integration in the economic sphere and beyond. And this will continue into the future.[1]

Commissioner Vestager's iconic words[2] encapsulate with remarkable clarity and simplicity a truth that, while occasionally challenged, remains constant in EU law. This is that, amongst the manifold objectives that competition law and policy serve in the EU, the promotion of the single market imperative has always been intended to play a very significant role. There is general agreement that this objective was inextricably woven into the original fabric of the EU competition law provisions. The reason for this is simple. The achievement of market integration was dependent not only on ensuring the free movement of all the factors of production (goods, persons, services, and capital), but also on making sure that a system of competition

[1] Commissioner Margrethe Vestager, 'Keynote Speech: The Values of Competition Policy' (CEPS Corporate Breakfast: 'One Year in Office', Brussels, 13 October 2015) <https://wayback.archive-it.org/12090/20191129202939/https://ec.europa.eu/commission/commissioners/2014-2019/vestager/announcements/values-competition-policy_en>.[last accessed on 12 October 2023]

[2] Leading commentators in the field have often referred to them. See Alison Jones, Brenda Sufrin, and Niamh Dunne, *EU Competition Law* (7th edn, Oxford University Press 2019) 43 and Richard Whish and David Bailey, *Competition Law* (10th edn, Oxford University Press 2021) 51.

Albertina Albors-Llorens, *The Ties that Will Always Bind: EU Competition Law and the Single Market* In: *The Internal Market Ideal*. Edited by: Jeremias Adams-Prassl, Sanja Bogojević, Ariel Ezrachi, and Dorota Leczykiewicz, Oxford University Press.
 DOI: 10.1093/oso/9780192867063.003.0011

law existed so that undertakings could not replicate barriers to trade by means of anti-competitive practices, and that public authorities could not provide unfair competitive advantages—to national sectors or undertakings—that could distort the operation of the internal market.[3] The very reason for the inclusion of a set of competition provisions in the founding Treaties was their indispensability to the internal market project.[4] It therefore followed that these rules had to be, in turn, interpreted in pursuit not only of the objectives traditionally ingrained in the genetic code of any system of competition law but also of market integration. It is in this sense that scholars described the EU competition law system as 'special' from its inception.[5]

Ascertaining the meaning of the single market objective is not straightforward, because a unique definition of the internal market remains elusive. As Stephen Weatherill has pointed out, the internal market as a legal concept is 'broad and ambiguous'[6] and 'inextricably connected to the internal market as a political, economic and cultural concept'.[7] Moreover, he has convincingly argued that the vagueness of the Treaty parameters has led to the existence of several internal markets in the EU,[8] which of course also complicates the identification of their objectives. In this chapter, we will explore the continuing commitment of the competition rules to the achievement and development of the 'single' or 'internal' market,[9]

[3] See European Commission, 'First Report on Competition Policy' (April 1972) 13 <https://op.europa.eu/en/publication-detail/-/publication/418817dc-c69b-42b1-a787-013fd545017d> [last accessed on 12 October 2023]. This reasoning was endorsed by the Court of Justice in some of its seminal decisions interpreting what are today arts 101 and 102 TFEU, such as in Joined Cases 56 and 58/64 *Consten and Grundig v Commission* ECLI:EU:C:1966:41, para 340.

[4] See Intergovernmental Committee on European Integration, *Rapport des chefs de délégation aux Ministres des Affaires Étrangères* (Spaak Report) (Brussels, 21 April 1956) 16–17 <https://archives.eui.eu/en/fonds/94975?item=CM3%2FNEGO-91> [last accessed on 12 October 2023]. An (unofficial) English translation is available at <http://aei.pitt.edu/995/1/Spaak_report.pdf> [last accessed on 12 October 2023].

[5] See David J Gerber, 'The Transformation of European Community Competition Law?' (1995) 35 Harvard International Law Journal 97, 98.

[6] Stephen Weatherill, *The Internal Market as a Legal Concept* (Oxford University Press 2017) 76.

[7] ibid 233.

[8] Stephen Weatherill, 'The Several Internal Markets' (2017) 36 Yearbook of European Law 125, 178.

[9] The Court of Justice has tended to use all three terms ('common', 'single', and 'internal' market) as interchangeable (Case 15/81 *Gaston Schul Douane Expediteur v Inspecteur der Invoerrechten en Accijnzen* ECLI:EU:C:1982:135, para 33). However, while academic commentators have generally agreed that the terms 'internal' and 'single' market are synonymous (see Kamiel JM Mortelmans, 'The Common Market, the Internal Market and the Single Market. What is in a Market?' (1998) 35 Common Market Law Review 101, 107), some have pointed out that the concept of 'common market' encompassed a wider and more complex reality than the 'internal market', arguing that the latter does not include essential elements of the common market such as the rules on competition (see Pierre Pescatore, 'Some Critical Remarks on the Single European Act' (1987) 24 Common Market Law Review 9, 11). Today, both the TEU (ie art 3(3)) and TFEU (ie art 4(2)(a), art 26) consistently refer to the internal market. For the purposes of this chapter these potential differences are not significant, since what we are exploring here is the commitment of the competition provisions to serve the single market *objective* rather than whether these rules are formally *included* in the set of provisions that constitute the single market.

understanding this objective in the narrow economic sense of an overarching quest for market integration.

As the European Union and its legal system evolved, criticism was voiced on account of the tensions arising between the single market imperative—itself a dynamic construct—and the more traditional goals of competition law, which, as we will see later, also continued to evolve. An important question was whether, after market integration was largely achieved, EU competition law could—and should—begin to live a life independent from that crucial objective, as it is the case for other systems of competition law. This chapter will argue that, in the aftermath of the modernization process, the single market imperative remains alive in the landscape of EU competition law and pervades current challenges such as the fight against cartels and the digitalization of the economy. In relation to the former, the Commission has made it a priority to investigate behaviour that attacks the foundations of market integration, such as price fixing and market sharing. In relation to the latter, the new Digital Markets Act strikingly shows the complementarity between competition law and internal market law values. Furthermore, this chapter will contend that this objective continues to be an important aspect of the identity of the EU competition rules and that divesting these rules from it would devalue the impact of one of the most successful areas of EU law and policy.

2. The Early Evolution of EU Competition Law and the Development of the Single Market Project

The primary system of substantive competition rules provided in the Treaty on the Functioning of the European Union (TFEU) has, in structure and content, remained essentially unchanged since the founding European Economic Community (EEC) Treaty. It adopts the form of a set of broadly framed prohibitions on anti-competitive behaviour. Thus, it covers prohibitions on anti-competitive agreements and abuses of dominant position (Articles 101 and 102 TFEU), adapts the principles in these rules to the behaviour of public undertakings (Article 106 TFEU), and includes a general prohibition on state aid subject to certain exceptions (Article 107 TFEU). Following a long and controversial process, an EU system of merger control was added as a final normative pillar and is today contained in the current EU Merger Regulation (EUMR).[10]

[10] A first proposal for a Merger Regulation had been put forward by the Commission in 1973 (Proposal for a Regulation (EEC) of the Council on the control of concentrations between undertakings [1973] OJ C92/1). This was amended several times and it was not until 1989 that the Council finally adopted the first EEC Merger Regulation (Regulation 4064/89 [1989] OJ L395/1). See further, HG Sevenster, 'At Last: An EEC-Regulation on the Control of Concentrations' (1990) 3 Leiden Journal of International Law 63. Following a process of review that began in 2001, the current EU Merger Regulation was adopted in 2004. This is Council Regulation 139/2004 on the control of concentrations between undertakings ([2004] OJ L24/22). The Regulation operates a 'one stop shop' model, according

The Treaties have never provided guidance as to the objectives that should shape the application of these rules. The open-ended nature of these provisions became both their weakness and their strength. Their weakness because, following the entry into force of the founding Treaties, there would be endless debates as to what should be the goals of EU competition law and controversy as to the interpretation given to these rules by the EU Commission and the Court of Justice.[11] Their strength, because it granted great freedom to the Commission and to the Court of Justice—at a time where national systems of competition policy were underdeveloped and less able to exert an influence on the emerging EU regime[12]—to fashion a largely new legal framework[13] that would later show its adaptability to the political and economic evolution of the European Union. However, it is significant that all the forms of anti-competitive behaviour—and anti-competitive mergers under the EUMR—set out in the Treaty were, and continue to be, prohibited 'as incompatible with the internal market'. In other words, the rationale for their illegality ostensibly seems to reside in their incompatibility with the single market imperative, even if we can also discern from their wording that they are also concerned with the protection of other values, such as the competitive process itself[14] or consumer interests,[15] and the fairness and non-discriminatory nature of market behaviour and transactions.[16] It is therefore possible to argue that, on the relatively blank

to which the Commission has exclusive jurisdiction to investigate mergers that transcend national borders and to prohibit those that significantly impede effective competition in the EU (see art 2(3) of Regulation 139/2004).

[11] Valentine Korah, writing in 1986, explained: 'in the EEC there is no agreement as to what objectives should be pursued by competition policy. Probably the most important in the view of the Commission and the Court is the integration of the common market' ('EEC Competition Policy: Legal Form or Economic Efficiency' (1986) 39 Current Legal Problems 85, 85). See also the excellent work by Laura Parret, 'Shouldn't We Know What We Are Protecting? Yes, We Should! A Plea for a Solid and Comprehensive Debate about the Objectives of EU Competition Law and Policy' (2010) 6 European Competition Law Journal 339.

[12] In this respect, competition law differed from other areas such as, for example, the protection of fundamental human rights, where the national constitutional traditions of the Member States were recognized as providing a source of inspiration for the developing standards at EU level. See Case 11/70 *Internationale Handelsgesellschaft mbH v Einfuhr- und Vorratsstelle für Getreide und Futtermittel* ECLI:EU:C:1970:114, para 4.

[13] On the innovative nature of the competition provisions set out in the Founding Treaties, see Desmond Dinan, *Europe Recast: A History of European Union* (2nd edn, Palgrave MacMillan 2014) 59–60.

[14] One of the elements to engage the prohibition in art 101(1) TFEU is that a form of cooperation should have as its 'object or effect the prevention, restriction or distortion of competition within the internal market'. This element also appears in the prohibition in art 107(1) TFEU. In the case of art 102 TFEU, the notion of abuse has been interpreted to include the element of distortion of competition (Case 85/76 *Hoffmann-La Roche v Commission* ECLI:EU:C:1979:36, para 91).

[15] See art 101(3) TFEU, referring to consumer benefit as one of the conditions for the application of the legal exception contained in that provision to the art 101(1) TFEU prohibition, or art 102 TFEU, which cites as a form of abuse limiting 'production, markets, or technical development to the prejudice of consumers'.

[16] See art 101(1)(d) TFEU, which gives as an example of anti-competitive agreements the application of 'dissimilar conditions to equivalent transactions,' or art 102 TFEU, which lists as forms of abuse the

canvas provided by the Treaties, the service to the internal market was one of the few elements that was made explicit, even if, as we have seen, the legal construct of the 'single' or 'internal' market is also a relatively vague one.

While the preamble to the Treaty of Rome revealed in 1957 the real scale of the ambition of the European integration project, the content of that Treaty provided a more realistic reflection of the degree of integration to which the European Union could aspire in the shorter term. At the core of this was the achievement of economic integration through the creation of a 'common' market. Alongside the removal of barriers to the free movement of goods, persons, services, and capital, the provision of the first harmonization mechanisms to eliminate distortions to trade and competition arising from divergences between national legislations and a set of common policies, a system of rules to ensure that competition was not distorted in the common market appeared as the remaining piece of the foundational jigsaw. After some years of stagnation and slow progress, accentuated by the constraints imposed by the legislative processes operating at the time, crucial impetus was given to what would be increasingly referred to as the 'single' or 'internal' market. This came about through the broad interpretation given by the Court to the free movement provisions[17] and the adoption of the Single European Act (SEA) in 1986. The SEA not only set out a deadline for the completion of the internal market for the end of 1992 and espoused a broader and more effective approach to harmonization but also began to loosen the institutional hurdles that stood in the way of the adoption of legislation, mainly by setting out the system of qualified majority voting and beginning to increase the role of the European Parliament in the legislative process. All these changes meant that a workable single market was broadly accomplished—albeit inherently never 'completed'[18]—and that further economic, political, and social integration was soon on the agenda, with successive Treaty amendments increasing the array of competences of the Union well beyond the economic sphere.

In the meantime, the competition rules set out in primary legislation had begun to yield their true potential, buoyed by the exclusive competence granted to the Union in this field and the flexibility offered by the Treaties. The EU Commission soon emerged as the 'central competition authority' to which Commissioner Vestager referred in 2015[19] as necessary to enforce a strong system of competition

imposition of 'unfair purchase or selling prices or other unfair trading conditions' and the application of 'dissimilar conditions to equivalent transactions with other trading parties'.

[17] In particular, the delivery of the seminal decision of the Court in *Cassis de Dijon* (Case 120/78 *Rewe-Zentral AG v Bundesmonopolverwaltung für Branntwein* ECLI:EU:C:1979:42) and the recognition of the principle of mutual recognition had a decisive effect in unfolding the true potential of negative integration as a de-regulatory technique for the achievement of the internal market.

[18] As Weatherill lucidly argues, drawing from Commission sources, the ambiguity of the internal market concept means that the single market will never be 'completed'. Weatherill, *The Internal Market as a Legal Concept* (n 6) 233.

[19] See n 1.

policy in the single market. This was reflected in Regulation 17/62,[20] the first enforcement Regulation, which gave the Commission the exclusive power to apply Article 101(3) TFEU—devising a centralized authorization system[21] as well as very strong powers to gather evidence in the course of its investigations into suspected infringements of antitrust prohibitions in the Treaties.[22] These parameters contributed for a long time to the prominence of the system of public enforcement of the EU antitrust prohibitions by the Commission over the system of private enforcement[23] and the public enforcement at the national level by National Competition Authorities (NCAs).[24] Tellingly, the reason why the Commission was initially given the monopoly in the application of Article 101(3) TFEU was to secure a uniform interpretation of that provision 'at a time the Community's primary objective was the integration of national markets'.[25] So, again, the service of competition law to the single market was the driving force in the crucial choice made by the legislator at the time to single out the importance of Article 101(3) TFEU and to decide in favour of an authorization system instead of a directly applicable exception system. At the substantive level, the Council adopted parent measures in the field of competition law but extensively delegated the power to legislate to the Commission in many areas,[26] and this corpus of legislation was supplemented by Commission decisions, notices, and guidelines. As a result of all these factors, the powerful position of the Commission at the apex of competition law and policy in the EU was firmly entrenched.[27]

[20] Regulation No 17: First Regulation implementing Articles 85 and 86 of the Treaty [1962] OJ 13/87 (English Special Edition Series I vol. 1959–1962).

[21] ibid arts 9(1) and 4(1).

[22] ibid arts 11 and 14.

[23] Arts 101(1), 101(2), and 102 TFEU were held to be directly effective early in the case law and hence capable of being invoked by private parties before the national courts (Case 121/73 *Belgische Radio en Televisie and Société belge des auteurs, compositeurs et éditeurs v SABAM (BRT I)* ECLI:EU:C:1974:6, para 16). However, both the fact that national courts were not able to apply the conditions in what is today art101(3) TFEU and, at the time, the underdevelopment and existence of profound disparities across the national legal systems in terms of the remedial rules applicable to these claims resulted in a dearth of private litigation (see eg in relation to actions for damages, Commission, *Green Paper on Damages for Breach of the EC Antitrust Rules* COM (2005) 672 final).

[24] Again, the fact that only the Commission could apply art 101(3) TFEU, and that NCAs would, under art 9(3) of Regulation 17, only remain competent to apply the core antitrust prohibitions so long as the Commission had not initiated an investigation, considerably weakened the role of public enforcement in the hands of the NCAs.

[25] See Commission, *White Paper on Modernisation of the Rules Implementing Articles 85 and 86 EEC Treaty* [1999] OJ C132/1, Executive Summary [4].

[26] See, for the early body of Commission block exemption regulations on vertical agreements that emanated from the enabling Council Regulation 19/65/EEC (OJ ***English special edition: Series I Volume (1965-1966) p. 35 - 37***)Regulation 1983/83 on the application of Article 85(3) to categories of exclusive distribution agreements [1983] OJ L173/1) or Regulation 1984/83 on the application of Article 85(3) to categories of exclusive purchasing agreements [1983] OJ L173/5.

[27] The decisional practice of the Commission as public enforcer of the competition rules showed a clear commitment to the goal of market integration (see Claus-Dieter Ehlermann, 'The Contribution of EC Competition Policy to the Single Market' (1992) 29 Common Market Law Review 257, 261.

In those early days, the other institution that played a vital role in what effectively was the development of a new legal system was the Court. As the Commission put it:

> The Court of Justice played its part to the full: sometimes upholding, sometimes annulling, but always contributing to a better understanding of the competition rules as they affected the everyday life of consumers and undertakings in the nascent common market.[28]

There is no doubt that the Court was well placed not only to give meaning to the broadly framed elements in Articles 101 and 102 TFEU,[29] but also to develop the competition rules in tandem with the free movement provisions with a view to achieving the common goal of market integration.[30] As the years passed, seminal decisions of the Court delivered on the eve of the past century and the dawn of the new one, such as those in *Eco Swiss*[31] and *Courage v Crehan*,[32] emphasized in very explicit terms the indispensability of the EU competition rules for the good functioning of the internal market. Together, therefore, the Commission and the Court added a great deal of colour to the canvas provided by the Treaties and, in time, the legal framework that emerged would have a decisive influence on the alignment of the national systems of competition law with the EU system.

Reflecting on the early development of the single market project and of the system of EU competition law, it is difficult not to compare the ease and success in the evolution of EU competition law with the rockier path and political compromises that led to the achievement of the single market. Of course, the application of the competition rules by the Commission and the Court was the subject of criticism on several fronts—as we shall see, the commitment to the single market ideal was one of them—but, ultimately, the challenge of creating both a 'culture of competition'[33] and a new body of legal rules to deploy it was met with efficiency and speed.[34] In the next section we will explore two themes. First, whether, once a

[28] See Commission, *White Paper on Modernisation* (n 25) [2].

[29] Thus, the Court began to give meaning to the elements in art 101(1)—see egthe notion of concerted practice (Case 48/69 *Imperial Chemical Industries v Commission* ECLI:EU:C:1972:70, para 64); the notion of effect on trade (Case 56/65 *Société Technique Minière (LTM) v Maschinenbau Ulm (MBU)* ECLI:EU:C:1966:38, para 249)—in very similar terms to those found later in the *Dassonville* formula (Case 8/74 *Procureur du Roi v Dassonville* ECLI:EU:C:1974:82, para 5); the meaning of the expression anti-competitive 'object or effect' (*Société Technique Minière*, para 249); or the notion of abuse in art 102 TFEU (see *Hoffmann-La Roche* (n 14)).

[30] Apart from the fact that, at the time, the Court was unaided by a court of first instance and hence decided on all the cases stemming from the application of both sets of rules, the Court was often asked to consider the combined application of the free movement and competition rules. See eg*Dassonville* (n 29) and Case 229/83 *Leclerc v 'Au blé vert'* ECLI:EU:C:1985:1.

[31] Case C-126/97 *Eco Swiss v Benetton* ECLI:EU:C:1999:269, para 36.

[32] Case C-453/99 *Courage v Crehan* ECLI:EU:C: 2001:465, para 20.

[33] See Commission, *White Paper on Modernisation* (n 25) *Executive Summary* [4].

[34] Speaking in 1998, forty years after the entry into force of the EEC Treaty, Commissioner Karel van Miert observed: 'European competition policy is certainly a success story. From humble and highly

workable single market was largely realized in the EU and competition law began to face new pressures, the commitment to the single market became diluted as other values and objectives sought to claim priority in the application of the rules.[35] Secondly, whether the tensions that continued to come to light between the single market objective and other goals of competition law meant that there was a case for the former to be compromised in favour of the latter.

3. The Coming of Age of EU Competition Law and the Controversies Surrounding the Single Market Imperative

Towards the end of the twentieth century, some years after a workable single market seemed to have been established, the Commission led a process destined to 'modernize' EU competition law. Such a process was deemed to be necessary to face important changes in the evolution of the EU such as the progress towards economic and monetary union, the rapid enlargement of the Union, and the increasing globalization of the economy, as well as the specific resource constraints that the Commission experienced in the light of the burdensome system of notifications and individual exemptions. Generally, this process is used to refer to the changes enabled by Regulation 1/2003,[36] which brought about the end of the monopoly of the Commission in the application of Article 101(3) TFEU and the move from a centralized authorization system to a system of 'directly applicable exception'. In the new decentralized system, national courts and NCAs acquired the power to fully apply Articles 101 and 102 TFEU. However, as Gerber argued, the modernization of EU competition law had two equally important facets. He referred to Regulation 1/2003 as ushering in an 'institutional' or 'procedural' modernization but also used the term 'substantive' modernization to allude to the 'reorientation of much of the thinking about substantive competition law'.[37] Thus, in parallel with the decentralization reforms, the Commission began to espouse a 'more economic approach',[38] a goal that was soon to infuse the extensive reform of the substantive

controversial beginnings it has become a cornerstone of the Commission's activities' (van Miert, 'The Future of European Competition Policy' (Presentation of the Ludwig Erhard Prize, Bonn, 17 September 1998) <https://ec.europa.eu/competition/speeches/text/sp1998_042_en.html>[last accessed on 12 October 2023]).

[35] In this respect, see Gerber, who pointed out in 1994 that once economic integration had been largely achieved, the system of EU competition law should 'redefine its mission'. David J. Gerber, 'The Transformation of European Community Competition Law?' (n 5) 143.

[36] Council Regulation 1/2003 on the implementation of the rules on competition laid down in Articles 81 and 82 of the Treaty [2003] OJ L1/1.

[37] David J Gerber, 'Two Forms of Modernization in European Competition Law' (2007) 31 Fordham International Law Journal 1235, 1245–55.

[38] See Mario Monti, 'A European Competition Policy for Today and Tomorrow' (2000) 23 Journal of World Competition 1, 2. See also, for a detailed account, Anne C Witt, *The More Economic Approach to EU Anti-Trust Law* (Hart 2017) chs 1–3.

rules concerning the application of not only Articles 101 and 102 TFEU but also those on merger control and on state aid.[39]

What was the effect of these seismic changes on the commitment of the EU competition rules to the single market objective? We will look first at the articulation of the key principles and body of legislation and notices that were to guide, to use Gerber's terminology, the 'institutional' and 'substantive' dimensions of the modernization process. Then, we will consider the case law to examine the tensions arising between the single market objective and other goals of EU competition law, and the criticism levelled at the Court in those instances where primacy seemed to have been accorded to the single market objective over other values.

3.1 The Modernization Principles and the Commitment to the Single Market

We saw previously how the key reason for granting to the Commission the exclusive power to apply Article 101(3) TFEU had been the need to ensure a uniform application of that particular provision at a time when economic integration was under construction in the EU.[40] In that sense, one of the concerns anticipated in relation to the transition to a system where national courts and NCAs would be able to apply that provision was whether this change would act to the detriment of such steadfastly guarded uniformity and, for our purposes, indirectly, of the commitment to the internal market rationale embedded in forty years of decisional practice of the Commission and case law of the Court. However, it was clear both from the preparatory documents[41] and from Regulation 1/2003 itself[42] that the need to ensure legal certainty and uniformity in the interpretation of the competition rules was a crucial concern underlying the reforms. Correspondingly, mechanisms of cooperation between the Commission and national courts and NCAs were incorporated in Regulation 1/2003[43] to ensure a degree of centralized guidance from the

[39] The 'substantive' dimension of modernization was developed through a mixture of 'soft law' documents and legislative reforms, while the primary provisions in the Treaties remained untouched. See, for instance, in the context of Article 101 TFEU, the *Green Paper on Vertical Restraints* (COM (1996) 721) that then paved the way for the reform of the system of block exemption regulations on vertical agreements (see Regulation 2790/99 [1999] OJ L336/21) and was followed by the review of the system of block exemptions on horizontal cooperation agreements (see Regulation 2658/2000 [2000] OJ L304/3 and Regulation 2659/2000 [2000] OJ L304/7). Next came the overhaul of the system of merger control through *Green Paper on the review of Council Regulation (EEC) 4064/89* (COM (2001) 745) that led to the adoption of a new EUMR (Council Regulation 139/2004 (n 10)) and of state aid policy (see Commission, 'State aid action plan: Less and better targeted state aid: a roadmap for state aid reform 2005–2009' COM (2005) 107). Finally, this approach extended to the application of art 102 TFEU (Commission, 'Guidance on the Commission's enforcement priorities in applying Article 82 of the EC Treaty to abusive exclusionary conduct by dominant undertakings' [2009] OJ C45/7).

[40] See n 25 and accompanying text.

[41] Commission, *White Paper on Modernisation* (n 25) [101]–[107].

[42] See Council Regulation 1/2003 (n 36) preamble recitals [15]–[22].

[43] ibid arts 11, 15, and 16.

Commission. These were developed further in the accompanying modernization package.[44] It is suggested, therefore, that the determination of the legislator to guarantee a uniform and consistent interpretation of the rules in the new decentralized system of enforcement simultaneously contributed to a continuing commitment to the single market objective.

Turning to the process of 'substantive' modernization or the infusion of a 'more economic' approach to the application of the EU competition rules, this broad-ranging expression was understood to embrace, inter alia, a redefinition of the goals of competition law and the use of rigorous economic tools and analysis to investigate and approach the existence of anti-competitive behaviour.[45] Both of these aspects are significant when considering the potentially changing role of the single market imperative in the interpretation of EU competition law. The first, because its principal manifestation was the apparently sudden elevation of consumer welfare to the rank of primary objective of EU competition law by the Commission.[46] Apart from the difficulties in defining what was really meant by consumer welfare,[47] the shift from a position where the competition rules had been acknowledged to serve a variety of objectives[48] to give prominence to a particular one over the others could have raised concerns as to whether the single market imperative was no longer as important as it once was. Therefore, it could have been argued that perhaps it was no longer necessary for the competition rules to pursue market integration with the same intensity as before. The second, because it might be posited that the emphasis placed on the use of economic standards could exacerbate the clashes between the solutions derived from these methods and those emanating

[44] See Commission, 'Notice on cooperation within the Network of Competition Authorities' [2004] OJ C101/03 [3.1] and [3.2] and Commission, 'Notice on the cooperation between the Commission and the courts of EU Member States in the application of Articles 81 and 82 EC' [2004] OJ C101/4.

[45] Heike Schweitzer and Kiran Klaus Patel, 'EU Competition Law in Historical Context: Continuity and Change' in Jiran Klaus Patel and Heike Schweitzer (eds), *The Historical Foundations of EU Competition Law* (Oxford University Press 2013) 220 and Anne C Witt, 'The European Court of Justice and the More Economic Approach to EU Competition Law: Is the Tide Turning?' (2019) 64 The Antitrust Bulletin 172, 173.

[46] See eg the famous speech by Commissioner Joaquín Almunia, who declared: 'Consumer welfare is not just a catchy phrase. It is the cornerstone, the guiding principle of EU competition policy.' Joaquín Almunia, 'Competition: What's in it for Consumers?' (European Competition and Consumer Day, Poznan, 24 November 2011) <https://ec.europa.eu/commission/presscorner/detail/en/SPEECH_11_803>[last accessed on 12 October 2023] . Before that, see Commissioner Monti, 'The Future for Competition Policy in the European Union' (London, 9 July 2001) <https://ec.europa.eu/commission/presscorner/detail/en/SPEECH_01_340> [last accessed on 12 October 2023].

[47] In this respect, see the seminal work by Joseph F Brodley, 'The Economic Goals of Antitrust Efficiency, Consumer Welfare and Technological Progress' (1987) 62 New York University Law Review 1020, 1032–41.

[48] Before the Modernisation, the Commission often referred to a panoply of objectives that included the promotion of the single market imperative, the protection of the competitive process, ensuring fairness and economic freedom, the protection of small and medium-sized undertakings, and even taking account of the interests of workers, users, and consumers. For an example, see Commission, 'Ninth Report on Competition Policy' (Publications Office 1980) 9–10 <https://op.europa.eu/en/publication-detail/-/publication/26e12860-4710-46be-bcfc-60582d4e51b2/language-en> [last accessed on 12 October 2023].

from the need to preserve the single market ideal. This chapter will explore later some of the tensions that have traditionally arisen between the need to pursue the ideal of market integration and economic efficiency criteria such as those affecting the competition law case law on territorial vertical restraints or parallel importation.

It is argued here, focusing now on the general principles and the body of 'soft law' and legislation yielded by the 'substantive' modernization process, that neither the Commission's emphasis on the goal of consumer welfare nor the use of economic methods to investigate the existence and effects of anti-competitive behaviour appear to have displaced or even weakened the single market imperative.

First, while it is true that the goal of consumer welfare may have occupied a prominent place in the Commission's rhetoric at the time,[49] the objective of market integration continued nonetheless to be consistently and robustly acknowledged in the Commission guidelines issued during the modernization period. For instance, the 2000 Guidelines on Vertical Restraints mentioned the protection of competition as a means to secure consumer welfare as a 'primary' goal and market integration a an 'additional' goal of EU competition law.[50] The 2010 Guidelines on Vertical Restraints adopted a more nuanced wording and referred to the prevention of restrictions of competition to the detriment of consumers and to the 'wider objective 'of achieving an integrated internal market'.[51] Further, the 2004 Commission Guidelines on the Application of Article 101(3) TFEU talked about the objective of protecting competition as 'a means of enhancing consumer welfare and ensuring an efficient allocation of resources' but immediately referred to market integration as jointly serving the same goals.[52] Finally, the 2009 Guidance on the Commission's enforcement priorities in applying Article 102 TFEU alluded to the 'wider objective of achieving an integrated internal market' alongside helping 'markets to work better for the benefit of businesses and consumers'.[53] Simultaneously, while some decisions of the General Court initially might have been read as supporting a shift towards singling out consumer welfare as the main objective of EU competition law,[54] decisions from the Court of Justice reined in any such suggestions by

[49] See n 46. However, it is noteworthy that, even in the same 2011 speech by Commissioner Almunia where he singled out consumer welfare as a central goal of EU competition law, he also referred to the ruling in *Pierre Fabre* as one that supported cross-border sales in the EU and underlined 'the need for a strict application of Single Market imperatives' (Case C–439/09 *Pierre Fabre Dermo-Cosmétique v Président de l'Autorité de la concurrence and Ministre de l'Économie, de l'Industrie et de l'Emploi* ECLI:EU:C:2011:649).

[50] Commission, 'Guidelines on Vertical Restraints' [2000] OJ C291/1 [7].

[51] Commission, 'Guidelines on Vertical Restraints' [2010] OJ C130/01 [7].

[52] Commission, 'Guidelines on the application of Article 101(3) TFEU (formerly Article 81(3) TEC)' [2004] OJ C101/08) [13].

[53] See Commission, 'Guidance on the Commission's enforcement priorities' (n 39) [1].

[54] See eg Case T–168/01 *GlaxoSmithKline v Commission* ECLI:EU:T:2006:265, para 118. However, even in that case, where the General Court stated that the objective of art 101(1) was 'to prevent undertakings, by restricting competition between themselves or with third parties, from reducing the welfare of the final consumer', the Court immediately prefaced this by also reiterating that that provision constituted

continuing to favour a pluralist view[55] and to reinforce the need to interpret the EU competition rules also in light of the single market goal.[56]

Secondly, the transition to the use of more economics-based methods of analysis of market behaviour did not appear to diminish the significance of market integration considerations. One area that epitomizes this is the reform of the legal system applicable to vertical agreements, generally acknowledged as the starting point of the 'substantive' modernization process. Traditionally, this had been one of the most controversial areas of EU competition law. This was on account of a very formalistic approach (which had generated an over-inclusive application of the prohibition in Article 101(1) TFEU), the rigidity of the framework of exemption and of the excessive importance accorded to the protection of economic freedom, and the single market objective to the detriment of rigorous economic analysis.[57] The new regime that was to emerge from the reforms carried out by the Commission—first by the 1996 Green Paper on Vertical Restraints,[58] leading to the adoption of the first 'umbrella' Block exemption Regulation on Vertical Restraints (Regulation 2790/99) and the accompanying Guidelines[59]—ushered in a major shift towards a more flexible system based on a more thorough economic analysis that evaluated market power and the effects—not only the form and content—of the agreements in question. However, it is very significant that all those documents and legislative documents continued to reflect a deep commitment to the single market objective.

The 1996 Green Paper on Vertical Restraints, while clearly endorsing a more economics-based approach, devoted very considerable attention to analysing the aspects of vertical restraints that were beneficial and those that were harmful to market integration, reiterating that 'competition is vital to obtain the economic gains from the single market'.[60] Likewise, an examination of Regulation 2790/

'a fundamental provision indispensable for the achievement of the missions entrusted to the Community, in particular for the functioning of the internal market' (ibid). For a more direct endorsement by the General Court of consumer welfare as the 'ultimate purpose' of the competition rules, see Joined Cases T–213/01 and 214/01 *Österreichische Postsparkasse v Commission* ECLI:EU:T:2006:151, para 115.

[55] Case C–501/06P *GlaxoSmithKline v Commission* ECLI:EU:C:2009:610, para 63; Case C–8/08 *T-Mobile Netherlands v Raad van bestuur van de Nederlandse Mededingingsautoriteit* ECLI:EU:C:2009:343, para 38, and Case C–52/09 *Konkurrensverket v TeliaSonera Sverige* ECLI:EU:C:2011:83, paras 22, 20.

[56] For a practical application in the context of the restriction of parallel imports, see Joined Cases C–468/06–478/06 *Sot Lélos kai Sia EE v GlaxoSmithKline* ECLI:EU:C:2008:504, para 65. As explained earlier in this chapter, the single market objective as used in this piece is confined to the pursuit of market integration, and the arguments made are about the service of the competition rules to that narrow goal. A richer conception of the internal market that would also consider consumer welfare—another notably difficult concept to define from a legal perspective—as an objective of the single market would introduce other interesting issues such as the potential overlap between the goals of competition law and free movement law, or at least the interaction between their shared values.

[57] See the seminal article by Barry E Hawk, 'System Failure: Vertical Restraints and EC Competition Law' (1995) 32 Common Market Law Review 973, 985.

[58] See n 39.

[59] See nn 39 and 51, respectively.

[60] See, Commission, *Green Paper on Vertical Restraints*, n 39, [71] and, more generally, [70]–[84].

99 and the accompanying Guidelines and, later, of the 2010 Block exemption Regulation on Vertical Restraints (Regulation 330/2010) and Guidelines[61] reveals signs of the continuing attachment to the pursuit and protection of market integration. Examples of this are some of the hardcore territorial and customer restrictions listed in those regulations that removed the benefit of the block exemption. These include, for example, restrictions on passive sales imposed on a distributor into the exclusive territory reserved to the supplier or to another distributor[62] or restrictions on cross supplies between distributors in a selective distribution system.[63] For their part, the 2004 Guidelines on the Application of Article 101(3) TFEU list vertical agreements that are considered to be restrictive of competition 'by object'—thus making unnecessary an analysis of the effects of these agreements to justify intervention—as 'those providing absolutely territorial protection (ATP), including restrictions on passive sales'.[64] Again, this is consistent with a long line of case law[65] and shows the clear influence of the market integration rationale. The importance of safeguarding the single market imperative has remained an important concern in the latest process of revision of the policy concerning vertical restraints.[66]

Another example, this time drawn in the context of Article 102 TFEU, is the 2009 Commission Guidance Paper on Enforcement Priorities. This represents, overall, one of the clearest examples yielded by the 'substantive' modernization process of a shift towards an effects-based approach in the application of the Treaty competition provisions. Although the Guidance itself focuses on exclusionary abuses, it crucially also reveals that the Commission might act in the future 'against certain behaviour that undermines the efforts to achieve an integrated internal market'.[67]

[61] Commission Regulation (EU) No 330/2010 of 20 April 2010 on the application of Article 101(3) of the Treaty on the Functioning of the European Union to categories of vertical agreements and concerted practices [2010] OJ L102/1 and Commission, 'Guidelines on Vertical Restraints' [2010] OJ C130/01 (n 51).

[62] See Regulation 330/2010 (n 61) art 4(b)(i); Commission, 'Guidelines on Vertical Restraints' [2010] OJ C130/01 (n 51) [51]; and, previously, Regulation 2790/99 (n 39) art 4(b)(i). On this point, see further, Patrick F Todd, who argues that 'if the Single Market Imperative were not a goal of EU Competition Law, there would be no need to treat restrictions on passive sales more harshly than restrictions on active sales' (Todd, 'Vertical Restraints, the Single Market Imperative and UK Competition Policy after Brexit' (2019) 18 Competition Law Journal 122, 124). Other commentators had already pointed out that making a distinction between restrictions on active sales (covered by the Block exemption) and passive sales (that constitute a hardcore restriction) appeared to be 'somewhat at odds with economics.' See Patrick Rey and Thibaud Vergé, 'Vertical Restraints in European Competition Policy' (2014) 4 Concurrences 44, 51.

[63] Regulation 330/2010 (n 61) art 4(d) and, previously, Regulation 2790/99 (n 39) art 4(d).

[64] See 'Guidelines on the application of Article 101(3)' (n 52) [23].

[65] See eg *Consten and Grundig* (n 3).

[66] See the Communication from the Commission approving the new 'Guidelines on Vertical Restraints' (10 May 2022, C(2022) 3006 final), where the pursuit of the single market continues to be a crucial theme—eg at [18](d), where the creation of obstacles to market integration is listed as a negative effect of vertical restraints, or at [222] alluding to the fact that, in general, passive sales cannot be prohibited in territories exclusively allocated to a buyer so as to prevent market partitioning.

[67] See Commission, 'Guidance on the Commission's enforcement priorities' (n 39) [7].

This seems to be an implicit recognition that, even within a more economics-based framework of analysis, the service of the competition rules to the internal market remains a driving force.

It follows from what we have considered so far that, although the modernization period brought about a change in focus and approach in the application of the competition rules, the legislation and notices that embodied these changes maintained both the commitment to the single market objective as one of the goals of EU competition law and policy and its importance as a factor in determining the thresholds for intervention. This was further supported by the decisional practice of the Commission in its role as public enforcer of Articles 101 and 102 TFEU.[68]

3.2 The Case Law of the CJEU: The Single Market Imperative at Play in the Application of the EU Competition Rules

The case law of the CJEU has, from the early years of the EU integration process, reflected not only the importance of the single market imperative in the application of the EU competition rules but also the occasional tensions between it and other values subscribed to by competition law, notably those upholding economic and consumer welfare. This chapter will use only a range of examples from a very extensive body of case law as a narrative to support the main argument. This is that despite those frictions and the criticism that followed, and that the modernization period reorientated the priorities and methodology used by EU competition law, the Court has continued to view the goal of market integration as playing an important role in the application of the antitrust rules.

The commitment of the Court to the single market ideal was shown in the trailblazing decision in *Consten and Grundig*.[69] There, the Court remarked that agreements that might lead to the partitioning of national markets were at variance with the creation of an internal market, a fundamental objective of the (then) Community and one that Article 101 TFEU was designed to serve.[70] This assertion by the Court became central to several strands of the case law. In *Consten and Grundig*, an exclusive distribution agreement that shielded the exclusive distributor from intra-brand competition by providing absolute territorial protection (ATP) against imports was held to constitute a restriction of competition

[68] See eg, among others, the Commission Decision of 5 October 2005 relating to a proceeding pursuant to Article 81 of the EC Treaty against Automobiles Peugeot SA and Peugeot Nederland NV (Cases COMP/E2/36623, 36820 and 37275 *SEP/Automobiles Peugeot SA*) [2005] OJ L173/20 and Commission Decision of 30 October 2002 relating to a proceeding pursuant to Article 81 of the EC Treaty and Article 53 of the EEA Agreement (COMP/35.587 *PO Video Games*, COMP/35.706 *PO Nintendo Distribution*, and COMP/36.321 *Omega–Nintendo*) [2003] OJ L255/33.

[69] *Consten and Grundig* (n 3).

[70] This is particularly clear in the French language version of the judgment (Affaires Jointes 56 et 58–64 *Établissements Consten S et Grundig* contre *Commission* ECLI:EU:C: 1966:41, 494).

by object, contrary to Article 101(1) TFEU. There is general agreement that the ruling of the Court in that case responded not only to an evaluation of the negative effects that such an agreement might yield on competition but also to the demands arising from the single market rationale—the latter given that the purpose of that agreement was to insulate a national market.[71] The fact that the Court chose to treat such an agreement as anti-competitive by object supported this conclusion. This is because an economics-based argument might be made that such vertical restraints on intra-brand competition should not be treated as automatically in breach of the Article 101(1) TFEU prohibition—and potentially only saved through the (unlikely) satisfaction of the Article 101(3) TFEU conditions—but, rather, that a full inquiry should be deployed as to their effects on the market.[72] As Monti suggested, the case illustrated well the difficulties that might arise in balancing the market integration rationale with efficiency considerations.[73] In subsequent years, the Court continued to appraise severely vertical agreements, including clauses that might facilitate the division of national markets, and hence be inimical to the project of market integration. This was the case, for instance, of agreements containing export bans,[74] discouraging exports,[75] or generally restricting parallel trade.[76]

During and following the process of modernization, the attachment to the single market goal continued to emerge in the analysis of agreements granting territorial exclusivity and which could therefore contribute to the isolation of national markets.[77] Further, similar tensions between that goal and other objectives of competition law persisted in some areas of the case law. The body of decisions concerning agreements aiming to limit parallel imports in the pharmaceutical markets is a case in point. As has already been pointed out by leading scholars, restrictions on parallel trade raise competition concerns, but there is also evidence that parallel trade may not always be beneficial for consumers or yield efficiency gains,

[71] See Giuliano Amato, *Antitrust and the Bounds of Power: The Dilemma of Liberal Democracy in the History of the Market* (Hart 1997) 49; Barry E Hawk, 'Antitrust in the EEC: The First Decade' (1972) 41 Fordham Law Review 229, 231.

[72] The ruling was in contrast with the Opinion of AG Roemer, who had argued for an analysis of the *effects* of the agreement on competition rather than categorizing it, as the Commission and the Court each did, as restrictive of competition by object (*Consten and Grundig* (n 3) paras 358–60). In this respect, it is noteworthy that other systems of competition law, such as the US system, have moved from treating some territorial restrictions as per se illegal to subjecting them to a full competition enquiry.

[73] See Giorgio Monti, 'Article 81 EC and Public Policy' (2002) 39 Common Market Law Review 1057, 1065–66.

[74] Case 19/77 *Miller International v Commission* ECLI:EU:C: 1978:19, para 7.

[75] Case T-77/92 *Parker Pen v Commission* ECLI:EU: T:1994:85, para 37.

[76] Case 96/82 *IAZ International Belgium v Commission* ECLI:EU:C:1983:310, paras 23–29 and the emergence of the same single market rationale in the section of the judgment concerning the non-application of the art 101(3) TFEU conditions at para 35. See also Case C-32/78 *BMW v Commission* ECLI:EU:C: 1979:191, para 32.

[77] See Joined Cases C-403/08 and 429/08 *Football Association Premier League v QC Leisure* ECLI:EU:C: 2011:631, paras 139–44], which involved a licensing agreement that granted absolute territorial exclusivity to a broadcaster in the area covered by the licence.

particularly within the special structural features that converge in those markets.[78] Yet, in *GlaxoSmithKline*, the Court reiterated that such agreements were aimed at partitioning national markets[79] and continued to treat them as restrictive of competition by object, without thinking it necessary to demonstrate that consumers would be deprived of competitive advantages as a result of these agreements.[80] In the context of Article 102 TFEU, the *Syfait II*[81] decision seemed again to be heavily influenced by the single market imperative,[82] and held that a refusal to supply by a dominant company aimed at avoiding parallel exports would be prima facie abusive.[83] However, this decision also provided evidence of the Court's willingness to attach weight to economic considerations, like the need of an undertaking to protect its own commercial interests, which could objectively justify such ostensibly abusive behaviour—presumably even in the face of a potential threat to market integration.[84] In other words, while the ruling of the Court could be seen as formalistic because it did not lean towards a fully-fledged consideration of the effects of the practice[85] (most likely as a result of the intervention of the single market rationale), it also reflected an attempt to strike a compromise between a powerful integration rationale and other considerations through the deployment of the notion of objective justification.

Cases dealing with discriminatory practices have also illustrated frictions between the single market principles and efficiency considerations. It could be argued, for instance, that the charging of discriminatory prices for the same goods or services depending on geographical location is misaligned with the objectives of market integration.[86] It ostensibly offends the basic principle of non-discrimination—in the absence of objective justification—that lies at the foundation of the internal market.[87] However, from an economic perspective, it is not clear that price discrimination is always inefficient or detrimental to consumer

[78] See Ioannis Lianos, Valentine Korah, and Paolo Siciliani, *Competition Law* (Oxford University Press 2019) 146–50 and the literature cited therein.

[79] See *GlaxoSmithKline v Commission* (n 55) paras 59–61 and *Sot Lélos kai Sia EE v GlaxoSmithKline* (n 56) para 65.

[80] See *GlaxoSmithKline v Commission* (n 55) para 63.

[81] *Sot Lélos kai Sia EE v GlaxoSmithKline* (n 56).

[82] ibid para 66.

[83] ibid.

[84] ibid para 69.

[85] In this sense, it is worth comparing the Court's approach with the suggestions made by AG Ruiz-Jarabo Colomer in his Opinion, where he advocated for an effects-based analysis of art 102 TFEU (ECLI:EU:C:2008:180, paras 62–75).

[86] Although some commentators have argued that a common market does not require the existence of identical prices in each region, but rather the absence of barriers to import and export. See W Bishop, 'Price Discrimination under Article 86: Political Economy in the European Court' (1981) 44 Modern Law Review 282, 289.

[87] For an example where the Commission applied art 102 TFEU to a situation where the practice in question discriminated based on nationality and constituted 'a breach of fundamental Community principles', see Commission Decision Case IV/36.888 *1998 Football World Cup* [2000] OJ L5/55, particularly at para 122.

welfare and that it should be automatically presumed to come within the scope of the antitrust prohibitions.[88] It is therefore revealing that cases involving geographical price discrimination where the practices have been aimed at the partitioning of the EU markets appear to have been treated more strictly by the Court, using a reasoning that has alluded to the single market imperative,[89] than other forms of price discrimination.[90]

Finally, some of the cases concerning restrictions on online sales have also evinced additional dimensions of a pervading single market rationale. Thus, in *Pierre Fabre*,[91] the Court considered a selective distribution agreement that included a clause whereby the products could only be sold by retailers and distributors in a physical space and with a pharmacist present. Effectively, this amounted to a ban on internet selling. The consistent view of the Court in relation to selective distribution agreements has been that while they may affect competition, they can be objectively justified when they pursue legitimate aims,[92] and are capable of improving competition in relation to factors other than price—eg maintenance of a specialist trade—subject to the fulfilment of certain conditions.[93] Despite the categorization of the ban on online sales as restrictive of competition by object, the Court remained open to the possibility of objective justification, even if those arguments were ultimately unsuccessful. For our purposes, this is the most interesting part of the judgment. One of the arguments advanced was that the clause in the agreement was necessary to protect consumers from an incorrect use of the products. In dismissing the suggestion that this could be a legitimate aim to justify the de facto ban on online sales, the Court borrowed strands of reasoning from the case law on free movement of goods, where similar arguments had been rejected in cases concerning bans on internet sales.[94] We

[88] See, among others, Bishop (n 86) 286–88; Rey and Vergé (n 62) 49–50. See also the Opinion of AG Wahl in Case C–525/16 *MEO v Autoridade da Concorrência* ECLI:EU:C: 2017:1020, paras 61–69.

[89] See Case 27/76 *United Brands v Commission* ECLI:EU:C:1978:22, paras 227–34, particularly paras 232–33. The ruling of the Court was criticized for a lack of engagement with a rigorous analysis of the effects of the practice and the single market rationale pointed out as the key motivation in the decision. See Bishop (n 86) 289. See also Case T–83/91 *Tetra Pak International v Commission* ECLI:EU:T:1994:246, para 170.

[90] See Robert O'Donoghue, 'The Quiet Death of Secondary-Line Discrimination as an Abuse of Dominance: Case C-525/16 MEO' (2018) 9 Journal of European Competition Law & Practice 443. See also Case C–209/10 *Post Danmark v Konkurrencerådet* ECLI:EU:C:2012:172, para 30.

[91] Case C–439/09 *Pierre Fabre Dermo-Cosmétique v Président de l'Autorité de la concurrence and Ministre de l'Économie, de l'Industrie et de l'Emploi* ECLI:EU:C:2011:649.

[92] Case 107/82 *AEG-Telefunken v Commission* ECLI:EU:C:1983:293, para 33.

[93] In a long line of case law (see Case 26/76 *Metro v Commission* ECLI:EU:C:1977:167, para 20) and, very clearly, in *Fabre* (n 91) the Court explained that these conditions are that:

> [Re]sellers are chosen on the basis of objective criteria of a qualitative nature, laid down uniformly for all potential resellers and not applied in a discriminatory fashion, that the characteristics of the product in question necessitate such a network in order to preserve its quality and ensure its proper use and, finally, that the criteria laid down do not go beyond what is necessary. (para 41)

[94] *Pierre Fabre* (n 91) para 44.

know for certain that the Commission viewed that judgment as one supporting the single market project.[95] By contrast, unlike other cases considered above, the Court did not make a direct allusion to the fact that such a clause could offend the internal market principles and seemed to conduct a pure competition law analysis. However, it is suggested that the reliance on the case law on free movement revealed at least a degree of influence of those principles in the application of Article 101(1) TFEU.

The conclusion that emerges from this microcosm of the case law is neither that the Court accords primacy to the market integration rationale over other objectives of competition law nor that the single market principles and traditional objectives of competition law always pull in opposite directions, but rather that they may work to complement one another. That complementarity between the rules would be all the more evident if we were to adopt a broader concept of the single market that would encompass not only the aim of market integration but other values including fairness and consumer welfare.[96] However, even in the narrow sense explored in this chapter that uses market integration as the main objective of the single market, the case law has always shown that the market integration rationale is relevant in the application of the competition rules and that it has an impact on the threshold for intervention. It suggests that this rationale may have an influence in tipping agreements within Article 101(1) into the 'object' category and unilateral practices under Article 102 into the ostensibly abusive category, thus creating presumptions of illegality that either need to be saved through the application of the Article 101(3) conditions or objectively justified. Inherently, therefore, some of the cases we have discussed can be seen as reflecting a compromise between the plurality of goals of competition law.[97] The acknowledgment of a variety of objectives and of the need to devise mechanisms to balance them reflects a constructive rather than an antagonistic approach and is commonplace in legal analysis.

[95] In this respect, see the 2011 speech by Commissioner Almunia, where he declared, in relation to that judgment: 'Limiting a distributor's freedom to sell to a consumer that visited its website is a hardcore restriction of competition law. It denies the very existence of Europe's Single Market', Almunia (n 46).

[96] See Joined Cases T-213/01 and 214/01 *Österreichische Postsparkasse* (n 54), where the General Court explained: '[T]he ultimate purpose of the rules that seek to ensure that competition is not distorted in the internal market is to increase the well-being of consumers... Competition law and competition policy ... have an undeniable impact on the specific economic interests of final customers who purchase goods or services' (para 115). See Section 1 for the existence of different dimensions to the notion of the 'single' or 'internal market'.

[97] For an excellent account that highlights the pluralism of goals served by competition law today and which approaches these as being both independent and complementary, see Ariel Ezrachi, 'EU Competition Law Goals and the Digital Economy' (6 June 2018) Oxford Legal Studies Research Paper 17/2018, 4. A broader conception of the single market to which we have alluded in this piece would make the argument that the internal market also serves a plurality of objectives.

4. Concluding Observations

This chapter set out to argue that the link between the EU competition rules and the commitment to market integration is an enduring one and not only applicable to the formative years of development of the single market project. As we have seen, the very reason for the inclusion of a set of rules to address certain types of anti-competitive behaviour in the original version of the EU Treaties was that such a system was regarded as essential to achieve the internal market. However, after this project was broadly achieved, we continue to see how the seminal value of market integration continues to play a role, both in the approach of the EU Commission and in the case law of the Court of Justice. Further, even after the process of modernization of EU competition law, which reorientated EU competition law by adopting a more economics-based approach and a fully decentralized system of enforcement, the market integration rationale was not abandoned. Rather, this thread continues to run through the application of the competition rules as a prominent part of their identity.

That the service of the EU competition rules to market integration is not redundant but abiding continues to be demonstrated in developments arising from the challenges faced by EU competition law today. For instance, the fight against cartels has become one of the main enforcement priorities of the EU Commission, which has used its newly freed resources following the decentralization reforms to focus on the detection of cartels.[98] There is, of course, agreement that cartels are one of the most harmful violations of competition law and one of the greatest threats to an open market economy.[99] However, the Commission's fight against cartel activity also continues to directly serve the single market ideal as evinced, in particular, by the treatment of market-sharing agreements, which have always been considered as inimical to market integration.[100]

Further, the inexorable digitalization of the economy over the last three decades has yielded a host of new questions about the suitability of the existing competition rules and of theories of harm to control new forms of anti-competitive behaviour

[98] See Mario Monti, 'Fighting Cartels, Why and How? Why Should we be Concerned with Cartels and Collusive Behaviour?' (3rd Nordic Competition Policy Conference, Stockholm, 11–12 September 2000) <https://ec.europa.eu/commission/presscorner/detail/en/SPEECH_00_295>;.[last accessed on 12 October 2023]

Margrethe Vestager, 'A New Era of Cartel Enforcement' (Italian Antitrust Association Annual Conference, Rome, 22 October 2021) https://ec.europa.eu/newsroom/comp/items/724530[last accessed on 12 October 2023]

[99] See the famous words of Judge Scalia, who referred to cartels as the 'supreme evil of antitrust' in *Verizon Communications Inc. v Law Office of Curtis V Trinko,* (2004) 540 US 398, 408, or (former) Competition Commissioner Mario Monti, who referred to them as 'cancers on the open market economy.' (Monti, 'Fighting Cartels, Why and How?' (n 98)).

[100] See eg Commission Decision of 18 July 2001 relating to proceedings pursuant to Article 81 of the EC Treaty (now Article 101 TFEU) and Article 53 of the Agreement on the European Economic Area against *SAS Maersk Air* (Case COMP.D.2 37.444 *SAS Maersk Air* and Case COMP.D.2 37.386 *Sun-Air versus SAS and Maersk Air*) (2001) OJ L265/15, paras 69–72.

derived from the accumulation of market power, where the traditional parameters of dominance and abuse are difficult to apply. An intense academic debate as to the appropriate policy options to address new harms and as to the respective roles of competition and regulation in this new economic landscape has followed and is still ongoing.[101] Yet, among the discussion of these fundamental concerns, the inextricable link between the EU competition rules and the single market remains. This is reflected both in the decisional practice of the EU Commission and in emerging legislative initiatives to ensure a form of regulation of core platform services to achieve fair and open markets in the digital sector.

In relation to the former, the Commission has continued to take the view that behaviour that tends to restore the divisions between national markets frustrates the integration objective of the Treaty and is restrictive of competition by object.[102] In relation to the latter, the Digital Markets Act (DMA)[103] is highly relevant. This legal instrument uses, as a legal base, Article 114 TFEU—the provision most frequently used to harmonize national measures in order to eliminate obstacles to the establishment and functioning of the single market.[104] The Regulation asserts that the competition rules have as their objective the protection of undistorted competition in the common market and that these remain of application to certain aspects of the behaviour of providers of core platform services—or 'gatekeepers'—such as those involving the acquisition of a dominant position or multilateral anticompetitive conduct.[105] It acknowledges that the DMA aims to protect a different legal interest, which is to ensure that markets where these providers are present 'are and remain contestable and fair'.[106] Putting aside the issue that such a neat separation may be, in practice, difficult to achieve, the Regulation crucially highlights that these objectives, while presented as independent, are also 'complementary'.[107]

[101] See, among others, Ariel Ezrachi and Maurice E Stucke, *Virtual Competition: The Promise and Perils of the Algorithm-Driven Economy* (Harvard University Press 2019); Nicholas Petit, *Big Tech and the Digital Economy: The Moligopoly Scenario* (Oxford University Press 2020); Pablo Ibañez-Colomo, 'Self-Preferencing: Yet Another Epithet in Need of Limiting Principles' (2020) 43 World Competition 417.

[102] See *Holiday Pricing*, where the Commission took the view that a clause in the standard term contracts between a hotel company and tour operators that restricted the ability of the latter to sell freely the hotel accommodation in all EEA countries by differentiating between consumers on the basis of their country of residence was restrictive of competition by object, contrary to art 101 TFEU and art 53 EEA Agreement. Commission Decision of 21 February 2020 relating to a proceeding under Article 101 of the Treaty on the Functioning of the European Union and Article 53 of the EEA Agreement Case AT.40528 *Meliá* (*Holiday Pricing*) [2020] OJ C182/07, paras 39–49.

[103] See Regulation (EU) 2022/1925 of the European Parliament and Council of 14 September 2022 on contestable and fair markets in the digital sector (Digital Markets Act), OJ [2022] L 265/1.

[104] See Commission, 'Explanatory Memorandum to the Commission Proposal for a Digital Markets Act' (Brussels, 15 December 2020) s 2, where the rationale for the use of art 114 TFEU is provided, namely the need to address the regulatory fragmentation created by diverse national rules dealing with the problems arising from the unfair conduct of gatekeepers vis-à-vis business users which is exacerbated by the cross-border nature of core platform services.

[105] See Commission Proposal for the *Digital Markets Act* (n 103), preamble [5], [10] and Regulation 2022/1925 (n 103), preamble [5], [10].

[106] See Regulation 2022/1925 (n 103), preamble [11].

[107] ibid.

This complementarity is evident in the examination of the specific obligations imposed on gatekeepers by Articles 5 and 6 of the DMA, which reveals practices that have already been relevant in a competition enforcement context.[108] This would indicate that there might be situations where it could be challenging to delimit the separate or concurrent application of the two sets of rules. More importantly for our purposes, however, it also chimes with the idea that the single market objective and the competition rules are still called to work in tandem to address any threats that emerge in the path of the achievement of a full and lasting picture of European integration.[109]

Finally, the indelible link between competition law and the single market objective has transcended the application of the substantive rules. Thus, Directive 2014/104 on antitrust damages,[110] one of the most significant developments of recent times in the field of private enforcement of Articles 101 and 102 TFEU, has a dual legal base: it is based both on Article 114 TFEU and on Article 103 TFEU.[111] This key harmonizing instrument thus brings together the objectives of securing full compensation for victims of anti-competitive behaviour, securing a better co-ordination of the systems of public and private enforcement of the competition rules and seeking to foster the internal market principles by aiming to secure equivalent judicial protection across the Union.[112] This indicates that not only the interpretation of the substantive rules but also the remedies that are used to give force to these continue to entrench the bond between EU competition law and the internal market project.

As Weatherill put it, writing in 2017, competition law is 'explicitly tied to the service of the internal market by both Articles 101 and 102 TFEU'.[113] It is argued here that this service remains today as strong as it ever was.

[108] For another example of the complementarity between the two sets of rules, see Article 14 of Regulation 2022/1925 (n 103). The Commission Proposal for the *Digital Markets Act* (n 105), preamble, [33] when considering the obligations laid down by the proposed Regulation in relation to gatekeepers, had provided that these 'obligations should correspond to those practices that are considered unfair by considering the features of the digital sector and *where experience gained, for example in the enforcement of the EU Competition rules,* shows that they have a particular negative impact on the business users and end users'. (emphasis added)

[109] Furthermore, if we adopt a richer conception of the single market that goes beyond the quest for market integration to which we have alluded in this chapter, this complementarity indicates that internal market law and competition law both tend to be attracted by goals of fairness and consumer welfare.

[110] Directive 2014/104/EU of the European Parliament and of the Council on certain rules governing actions for damages under national law for infringements of the competition law provisions of the Member States and of the European Union [2014] OJ L349/1.

[111] ibid, preamble [8].

[112] ibid art 1.

[113] Weatherill, 'The Several Internal Markets' (n 8) 129.

11

EU Law and Sports: A Match Made in Hell or in Heaven?

Miguel Poiares Maduro

1. Introduction

I share with Steve a passion for EU law and for sport (and football in particular), and so it seems only appropriate for this piece to focus on the relationship between the two. Perhaps to the surprise of many, EU law has become the most relevant legal order in shaping the law and governance of sports. The autonomy of a sport's private governance regimes escapes the control of almost any legal order in almost all aspects—with the notable exception of EU law. The reason has little to do with the substantive scope of EU law. Most sports issues that have fallen under the scope of EU law could, as well, fall under the scope of national laws. For example, much of what the European Court of Justice (ECJ) decided in *Bosman*[1] under the scope of the free movement of workers could be decided under the right to work or the freedom of contract in most national constitutions. Indeed, many of the questions involving the application of EU competition law to sports and their governance bodies could also have been raised and addressed in the competition law regimes of other legal orders. They are not, for a simple but crucial reason: individual state legal orders do not have effective jurisdiction over a sport's transnational governing bodies. In fact, when state legal orders have tried to exercise such jurisdiction, they have faced threats of exclusion of their national and club teams and athletes from international sports by those sports' transnational governing bodies. The reason why the Union of European Football Associations (UEFA), Fédération Internationale de Football Association (FIFA), or the International Olympic Committee (IOC) federations appear before the ECJ and respect its decisions on EU law is because they cannot afford to exclude the teams and athletes from twenty-seven European states. European Union law is, at the moment, one of the few—if not the only—legal orders that can exercise effective jurisdiction over the private transnational regimes and governing bodies of sports.

[1] Case C–415/93 *Bosman* ECLI:EU:C:1995:463.

Miguel Poiares Maduro, *EU Law and Sports: A Match Made in Hell or in Heaven?* In: *The Internal Market Ideal*.
Edited by: Jeremias Adams-Prassl, Sanja Bogojević, Ariel Ezrachi, and Dorota Leczykiewicz, Oxford University Press.
 DOI: 10.1093/oso/9780192867063.003.0012

This is of great consequence: not for sport alone, but for the EU itself. Sports provide a unique example of the democratic added value that EU law can bring in terms of public accountability and legal and democratic oversight of transnational power and private governance that impact our collective life, but which national governments are no longer capable of regulating.[2] As I teach my students: the role of EU law in sports is a counter-intuitive example that challenges the idea that the benefits of European integration come at the expense of state sovereignty. It is unfortunate that the EU political institutions do not seem to fully grasp this. Were it not for the ECJ, and the role of legal scholars such as Steve Weatherill, the EU would seemingly be content to abdicate an important part of market and social regulation to transnational private entities that are not truly accountable to anyone.

The position taken by EU institutions and national governments in the recent *Superleague* case is revealing in this regard.[3] The case (pending before the Court as I write this chapter) examines the extent to which, in the light of competition rules, governing bodies in sports can be entrusted with the role of authorizing competing events to those they organize and, if so, under what conditions. National governments and EU institutions have largely bought into UEFA's framing of the case as regarding not UEFA's and FIFA's monopolist power, but rather the Superleague itself. In fact, the Court is not going to decide if the Superleague should be authorized, nor will the decision of the Court in any way prejudge any assessment to be made of the Superleague and its own compatibility with EU rules. It is likely that around the time this book will see the light of day , we will know whether the Court resisted the narrative spun by powerful sport organizations such as UEFA and FIFA. Let us hope it will. As Steve has convincingly argued, EU law should strengthen, instead of weakening, its role in sports. This chapter is an attempt at supporting such an argument. It is, therefore, as a particular tribute to Steve's visionary work on the relation between EU law and sports that I decided to focus on EU sports law. As such, my argument is not a simple product of a coincidence between leisure and work. Rather, it is based on the idea that sport is an entry point to discuss what ought to be the soul of European integration.

[2] I have been making this point for a long time. See eg 'Passion and Reason in European Integration' (2010) Forum Constitutionis Europae 03/10 <http://ssrn.com/abstract=1709950> (accessed 1 October 2023) and 'Europe and the Constitution: What If This Is As Good As It Gets?' in Marlene Wind and Joseph Weiler (eds), *Constitutionalism Beyond the State* (Cambridge University Press 2003) 74.

[3] Case C-333/21, *Request for a preliminary ruling from the Juzgado de lo Mercantil no 17 de Madrid (Spain) lodged on 27 May 2021—European Super League Company, SL v Union of European Football Associations (UEFA) and Fédération Internationale de Football Association (FIFA)*, pending (*European Super League v UEFA and FIFA*) [2021] OJ C382/10.

2. Failing to Deliver the Public Goods of Sports

2.1 Integrity in Sports: Rules Without the Rule of Law

Over the past years, sport has increasingly been engulfed in scandals. Many of these scandals are of a criminal nature. Corruption seems to be widespread, from cases involving key FIFA figures uncovered by US criminal authorities in 2015 to the more recent example of systemic and generalized corruption revealed in Belgian football. But aside from these well-known public cases, journalistic investigations and several institutional reports assume that such scandals are only the tip of the iceberg, the product of systemic governance problems.[4] Sport (football, in particular) is also considered by the European Commission to be among the economic activities more at risk of being used for money laundering.[5]

The greater financial importance of online gambling has also further increased cases of match fixing, involving players, referees, and even team owners.[6] Revelations of tax evasion have also multiplied, leading to the conviction of some of sport's greatest names. The European Parliament Report on the inquiry into money laundering, tax avoidance, and tax evasion identifies football as an area susceptible to tax evasion, due to 'loopholes and mismatches' in the legislation.[7] The problems with criminal activities in sport have reached such levels that a Director General of the World Anti-Doping Agency (WADA) has claimed that organized crime controls over 25 per cent of world sport.[8]

But sport's integrity problems do not stop there. There are multiple tensions with human rights, for example, that gain particular visibility in the context of the organization of sports events by regimes with a poor human rights record (FIFA World Cup Qatar 2022 being only one example). It is certainly not unanimously agreed, and hard to enforce in practice, to argue that sports events ought to be limited to democracies. On the other hand, it is far from certain that sports events will always

[4] See eg European Parliament, European Parliament resolution of 2 February 2017 on an integrated approach to Sport Policy: good governance, accessibility and integrity [2017] OJ C252/2; Council of Europe, Parliamentary Assembly 2200 (2018) on Good Football Governance <https://pace.coe.int/en/files/24284>; and Parliamentary Assembly of the Council of Europe, Motion for a resolution, 'The Legitimacy Crisis in International Sports Governance' <https://pace.coe.int/en/files/22442>.

[5] In 2019, the European Commission added football to the list of activities more at risk of being used for money laundering, mentioning that 'questionable sums of money with no apparent or explicable financial return or gain are being invested in sport'. See European Commission, 'Towards better implementation of the EU's anti-money laundering and countering the financing of terrorism framework' (Communication) COM (2019) 360 final.

[6] Declan Hill, *The Fix: Soccer and Organized Crime* (McClelland & Stewart 2010).

[7] European Parliament, 'Report on the inquiry into money laundering, tax avoidance and tax evasion' (2017/2013(INI)), notably paras 21 and 171 <www.europarl.europa.eu/cmsdata/131460/2017-11-08%20PANA%20Final%20Report.pdf>.

[8] Kathryn Henne, 'Reforming Global Sport: Hybridity and the Challenges of Pursuing Transparency' (2015) 37 Law and Policy 325.

be a force for good, no matter which states and political regimes host them. The extent to which they can promote human rights and positive changes or, instead, reinforce autocratic regimes depends, to a large extent, on the conditions and human rights frameworks to which sports organizations link the arrangement of such events. Another human rights issue relates to compliance with human rights in the context of the organization of the events themselves: from the labour rights of the workers involved, to the freedom of association, the right of non-discrimination, or the freedom of expression of fans and athletes during the events. This requires a clear commitment to such rights but also independent monitoring and enforcement.[9] Furthermore, human rights issues in sports go well beyond the tensions of particular political regimes organizing certain sporting events; they also relate more specifically to the ways in which sports governing bodies regulate sports activities. This includes—on and off the field—limits on freedom of expression for athletes and other participants; the right to due process for athletes and officials; and non-discrimination rules regarding gender, race, religion, sexual orientation, etc. In all these areas, examples of human rights violations unfortunately abound, often with the complicity—if not direct involvement—of sports governing bodies.

Unfortunately, much more could be included in this parade of horrors. For instance, I have left out issues relating to how sports organizations have dealt with doping and, in particular, with state-sponsored doping.

This is all to say that sports governance has increasingly been exposed in its failure to deliver on what is, perhaps, its primary function: protecting the integrity of sport. As I hope to demonstrate, this is also a consequence of its own failure to act under the rule of law and undermines its claim to self-governance.

2.2 Competitive Balance, Openness, and Solidarity

In addition to multiple integrity problems, sports governance is also failing to deliver on what may be, after integrity, the second most important public good entrusted to it: balanced and open competitions. While competitive balance may be achieved within closed leagues (as is the case in the United States), that is not the European model. As enshrined in Article 165(2) of the Treaty on the Functioning of the European Union (TFEU), competitive balance requires 'promoting fairness and openness in sporting competitions'. This refers to open leagues, based on the

[9] When I briefly chaired the FIFA Governance Committee, we promoted the adoption of a FIFA Human Rights Policy (our Committee made the proposal, but the final adoption belonged to the FIFA Council). The cause of more tension was our insistence on guaranteeing independent monitoring and enforcement. The final version does mention independence in monitoring and enforcing, but in an ambiguous and not fully satisfying way. Such a policy was, unfortunately, applicable in full only to future events, which meant that the World Cups in Russia and Qatar were not bound by all its aspects. See FIFA, 'FIFA's Human Rights Policy' (May 2017) <https://digitalhub.fifa.com/m/1a876c66a3f0498d/original/kr05dqyhwr1uhqy2lh6r-pdf.pdf>.

model of promotion and relegation. While competitive balance does not require openness, openness requires competitive balance. A league with formal promotion and relegation rules, but where those that remain and those that are relegated are always the same, is not really an open league. Competitive balance is, therefore, even more important in such a context to guarantee openness. Additionally, the concept of fairness requires both integrity of the competition (that everybody plays under the same rules) and competitive balance (as a competition can only be said to be fair where there is some competitive balance among those competing). However, competitive balance and openness appear to be decreasing, at least in European sports. An important example is European football, where we are witnessing increased competitive asymmetry and reduced openness.[10]

Solidarity is a key principle that ought to drive the actions of sports governance bodies considering their responsibility for sports development and competitive balance. Financial advantage is the biggest competitive advantage in sport.[11] It is well known that achieving and protecting competitive balance requires, both in closed and open leagues, some degree of solidarity. Increased wealth concentration and the lack of effective equity and solidarity mechanisms explain the increase in competitive asymmetry in European football. In addition, the emergence of teams de facto funded by state aid increasingly distorts competition and financial fairness.

Securing both efficient and transparent mechanisms of financial fairness and solidarity is crucial to the protection of the so-called European sports model. As mentioned, this is reflected in Article 165(2) TFEU, which talks of 'developing the European dimension in sport, by promoting fairness and openness in sporting competitions'. Openness of sport competitions at the European level involves, in my view, two dimensions: first, as already mentioned, open leagues, organized under the principle of promotion and relegation; and secondly, the protection of multi-level leagues; in other words, the development of pan-European league or leagues should not undermine open and competitive *national* leagues. In such a context, solidarity at both national and European levels becomes even more important for the purpose of safeguarding competitive balance and openness in all these different leagues.

That is not, however, how European football (and, I suspect, other sports) have progressed. Various reports and studies identify a decrease in competitiveness and openness of football at the European and national levels.[12] Not only do football

[10] See the analysis and references below.

[11] The best predictor of a team's placement in a league is how much it spends on players: Ahmed Murad, 'Liverpool Wins Champions League Battle of the Budgets' *Financial Times* (2 June 2019) <www.ft.com/content/9ede30d0-84c1-11e9-a028-86cea8523dc2>. For a broader analysis of the economics of football, see Simon Kuper and Stefan Szymanski, *Soccernomics* (Nation Books 2014).

[12] See eg Raffaele Poli, Loïc Ravenel, and Roger Besson, 'Competitive Balance: A Spatio-temporal Comparison' (CIES Football Observatory Monthly Report 40, November 2018) <https://football-observatory.com/IMG/sites/mr/mr40/en/phone/index.html>; Steve Menary, 'The Same Clubs Dominate Champions League Despite the Corona Pandemic: Champions League Diversity Index' (*PlaytheGame.org*,

governance bodies seem incapable of protecting and promoting competitive balance and openness, but the instruments they have set up appear to have aggravated wealth concentration and reduced competitive balance and the genuine openness of national and European leagues.

The Champions League has become, de facto, a Superleague.[13] In the last two decades, only around 5 per cent of the semifinal teams in the Champions League came from outside the five big leagues (England, Spain, Germany, Italy, and France), when previously, the figure was ten times more. The rules regarding the redistribution of revenue actually favour (instead of mitigating) teams who have had more success in the past—therefore reinforcing, instead of mitigating, their dominant role in the competition. Furthermore, the groups are designed to favour those same teams. A recent reform has even introduced a factor taking into account historical performance, allowing certain teams access to the Champions League even if they have not gained sufficient promotion under their national league. These 'historical rights' are clearly opposed to the European open model of promotion and relegation. There may be reasons in favour of the current rules and developments in the European Champions League. What is clear is that they do not contribute to more competitive balance and greater openness, but, instead, undermine them.[14]

Perhaps even more dramatic, however, has been the impact of the Champions League on national leagues. For many teams, particularly those of small and medium size, the impact of Champions League revenue on their total budgets is substantial and can easily more than double their usual revenue. This means that the teams that get to the Champions League acquire a substantial advantage as compared to the teams with which they compete at the national level. This is, moreover, an advantage that tends to reinforce itself. Once a team has that first advantage, it will benefit from it at the national level, which increases the likelihood of repeating its presence in the Champions League and further entrenching itself as the dominant financial force and sports team at the national level. It becomes the incumbent of national football. This decrease in competitive balance is taking place in a significant way across Europe, albeit to varying degrees.[15]

24 August 2020) <www.playthegame.org/news/the-same-clubs-dominate-champions-league-despite-the-corona-pandemic-cl-diversity-index-202021/>; 'Champions League Round of 16—The Richer Take it All' (*FootballBenchmark.com*, 19 February 2019) <www.footballbenchmark.com/library/champions_league_round_of_16_the_richer_take_it_all>.

[13] Jonathan Wilson, 'By Stealth Rather than in One Swoop, the European Super League Has Arrived' *The Guardian* (23 April 2022) <www.theguardian.com/football/blog/2022/apr/23/by-stealth-rather-than-in-one-swoop-the-european-super-league-has-arrived>.

[14] The emergence of a European Superleague as a consequence of the Champions League was anticipated (and argued for) by John Vrooman, 'Theory of the Beautiful Game: The Unification of European Football' (2007) 54 Scottish Journal of Political Economy 314.

[15] See Poli, Ravenel, and Besson (n 12).

The impact of the Champions League on the reduction of competitive balance in national leagues seems clear: competition has strongly decreased in national leagues, measured in terms of both diversity of champions and the concentration of points in the top teams.[16] It is true that other factors may have contributed to this (correlation is not necessarily causality), but the link seems obvious, given the reasons mentioned previously—and if for no other reason than that the Champions League and football governance bodies regulations have not chosen to reverse this trend of decreased competitive balance at the national and European levels.[17]

This increased competitive asymmetry impacts the uncertainty of sports, which has both moral and economic effects. It also undermines the open character of competitions that is supposed to be enshrined in the European model of sports. As stated, one can only talk about genuinely open leagues when, aside from relegation and promotion, they include mobility within the league and between the national and European Champions leagues. In other words, when those being promoted and relegated and those participating in the Champions League (at its different stages) are not always the same teams. As we have seen, however, that is no longer the case, and the closing of European and national leagues is happening both in fact and in law.

The reduction of competitive balance has an additional negative effect: it aggravates integrity risks. For example, where competition is severely unbalanced and sport outcomes are not uncertain, many matches not only lose public interest but, deprived of the sports competition incentive, become more susceptible to match fixing. Similarly, competitive imbalance makes make many teams more easily dependent on other teams (through the loans of players, for example) or other economic interests (such as sports agents and sports investors), which multiplies the risk of conflicts of interest. One cannot ignore, for example, the tendency for multi-ownership of clubs at the European level, which generates risks of conflict of interest and in terms of integrity of competitions.

The previous two sections have highlighted the extent to which sports governance is failing to deliver on the goals 'entrusted' to it. First, sport has become an economic area more susceptible to illegal activities. Not only is the integrity of sport increasingly questioned, but sport is seen as particularly susceptible to being captured by criminal activities unrelated to sport itself. Secondly, sports governance is also failing to deliver on some of the most important public goods entrusted to it, such as competitive balance, solidarity, and, in Europe, the open model of sports. This undermines the claim to self-government put forward by sports governance

[16] See studies cited in Wilson (n 13).

[17] Kuper and Szymanski argued that, as designed, even the Financial Fair Play System rules would simply serve to protect the already dominant clubs ((n 11) 85ff).

bodies that, in turn, supports what someone has described as 'the extraordinary autonomy of sports bodies'.[18]

3. Challenging the Alleged Institutional Comparative Advantage of Sports Governance Bodies

3.1 A Critical Assessment of Justifications for Sports Self-governance

The 'extraordinary autonomy' of sports governance and regulation may be justified by different arguments which are frequently proposed.

3.1.1 Private autonomy

A first justification is to be found in the connection made between the well-established principle of private autonomy and the idealized and romantic traditional presentation of sport as a grassroots activity. As highlighted in a recent article, it is paradoxical how, in spite of the hyper-commercialization of sport, its primary cultural and cognitive regulatory framework is so deeply dominated by an idyllical vision that is far from corresponding to that reality.[19] In fact, a lot of the regulatory deference from which sports private governance bodies benefit seems to be based on this assumption of sport as a voluntary grassroots association movement, that would fall under a purely private domain of free association. In fact, this idealized representation of sport is far from its current reality. Sport is, nowadays, a multi-million-euro business activity comprising companies, workers, and consumers. Many of these are heteronomously subject to the regulation of sports governance bodies. They are not voluntarily adhering to such regulations but are de facto subject to them, by virtue of both the economically dominant position of sports governance bodies and, in some cases, the legal rules reinforcing that power. The fact that we are not in the realm of voluntary association but of collective regulation is increasingly being recognized by courts. As the ECJ mentioned in *Bosman*, these rules 'cannot be seen as necessary to ensure enjoyment of that freedom [of association] by those associations, by the clubs or by their players, nor can they be seen as an inevitable result thereof'.[20]

That we are in the realm of the collective regulation of a market by sports governance bodies is a consequence of the economic nature of much of sports activity,

[18] Margareta Baddeley, 'The Extraordinary Autonomy of Sports Bodies under Swiss Law: Lessons to be Drawn' (2020) 20 The International Sports Law Journal 3.

[19] Henk Erik Meier and others, 'The Capture of EU Football Regulation by Football Governing Bodies' [2022] Journal of Common Market Studies 1, 13–14, making a point about football that is, however, equally applicable to other sports.

[20] *Bosman* (n 1) para 80.

together with the power held over that economic activity by those sports governance bodies. Sport is likely the most important leisure activity in society. It seems to be an area of societal life that we spend a great deal of time on (as players, spectators, or in any other form) and, arguably, most of us give attention to. The cumulative audience of a football World Cup is said to be in the realm of 40 billion people. Two-thirds of the world's population is also said to watch at least part of the Olympic Games. This societal interest has a corresponding economic impact through sports events themselves, but also through the growing relevance of related industries such as broadcasting, merchandise and gear, other goods and services, gambling and video games, etc. It is revealing that some of the companies that have moved furthest up the ranking of the FT 500 top global companies are from the sports domain. It is not easy to measure the direct global economic impact of sport, but some existing studies measure the global sports market somewhere between 500 and 750 billion euros.[21] In the European Union (EU), sports' GDP value is estimated at 2.12 per cent of the EU GDP,[22] and it is one of the fastest-growing areas as we move into a more leisured-oriented economy. As such, sport is a dynamic and significant market.

Sports governance bodies regulate these markets, and they do so through heteronomous rules linked to deeply hierarchical relationships of power. The ECJ has, in multiple cases, been the most important institution in understanding and challenging the idealized presentation of sport as a domain of private autonomy and calling it what it is: a regulatory power based on a vertical relation of power. There is no reason why this power ought not to be scrutinized as other similar governance and regulatory powers are.

3.1.2 The representation claim

It could also be argued that sports governance bodies' institutional advantage comes from their representation of all the relevant stakeholders. According to this line of thinking, they would be in a better position to represent all the interests impacted by sports regulation. This is, to some extent, a follow-up to the idyllic associative vision of sports governance. Private governance bodies often present themselves as driven by a bottom-up culture of representation of different stakeholders; however, the reality of sports governance could not be further away from this presentation.

[21] The Business Research Company 2022, *Sports Global Market Report 2022* and Amir Somoggi, 'Coronavirus' Economic Impact on the Sports Industry' (*Sports Venue Business*, 19 March 2020) <https://sportsvenuebusiness.com/2020/03/19/coronavirus-economic-impact-on-the-sports-industry/>.

[22] European Commission, 'Study on the economic impact of sport through sport satellite accounts' (Research Report, April 2018) 10 <https://op.europa.eu/en/publication-detail/-/publication/865ef44c-5ca1-11e8-ab41-01aa75ed71a1/language-en>.

There is no evidence that sports organizations are actually representative of all the different interests involved in and impacted by sports; indeed, the reality appears quite the contrary. A first clear indicator is the lack of diversity of representation (in both leadership positions and also the electoral constituencies themselves). For a start, there are almost no women: a recent study identified that eleven women (versus 195 men) are presidents of national Olympic committees, and that only 5 per cent of presidents of national sports associations in Europe are women; their presence in governing bodies is less than 10 per cent.[23] Another report paints an even darker picture beyond the European borders.[24] It is therefore not surprising that Richard Lapchick identified as the overwhelming conclusion of the 2016 International Sports Report Card on Women in Leadership Roles that '[t]he leadership in international sport is an exclusive club of men'.

A report on FIFA, preceding the 2015 reforms, identified a similar scenario, with women comprising only 8 per cent of FIFA's governing body.[25] The judicial scandals of 2015 were, however, an opportunity to change this status quo. Moya Dodd and Catherine Ordway describe how a group of women (mobilized by Moya Dodd) were able to use the crisis to push for reforms in the area of gender equality.[26] The main reform imposed a minimum for female representation on the FIFA Council: each confederation was required to elect at least one woman among its representatives to the FIFA Council.

Some confederations implemented this by creating a female position, for which all female candidates were to compete. As such, they would elect one woman but not more than one woman, transforming the minimum requirement into a ceiling. A rule aimed at promoting female representation was thereby converted into a rule limiting female representation.[27]

[23] Council of Europe, 'Balance in Sport: Training about Gender Equality in Sport' <https://rm.coe.int/ppt-balance-in-sport-training-paris-18nov-m-forest/16808c347c>.

[24] Centre for Olympic Studies & Research, Gender Equality and Leadership in Olympic Bodies: *Women, Leadership and the Olympic Movement* (April 2010). This was a report commissioned by the IOC Women and Sport Commission; also revealing was the fact that only around half of the sports associations replied to the questionnaire.

[25] See Aidan Ormond, 'FIFA, Football and Women: Dodd's Reform Push' (*MyFootball.com.au*, 21 November 2015) <www.myfootball.com.au/news/fifa-football-and-women-dodds-reform-push>. The original report of that FIFA task force does not seem to be available any longer, but Moya Dodd (the author of the report) described the status quo and attempts at changing it in Moya Dodd and Catherine Ordway, 'FIFA Governance: How Crisis Opened the Door for Gender Equality Reforms' (2020) Jean Monnet Working Paper 14/20, 1 <https://jeanmonnetprogram.org/wp-content/uploads/JMWP-14-Moya-Dodd-Catherine-Ordway.pdf>.

[26] ibid 15ff.

[27] I followed this case closely, as I was then the chair of the FIFA Governance Committee, in charge of monitoring such reforms and the elections for the FIFA Council. The Committee actually adopted at that time a set of guidelines aimed at helping confederations to implement such rules and promote female representation in the FIFA Council: FIFA Governance Committee, 'Guidelines for Promoting the Involvement of Women in the FIFA Council' (2016) <https://digitalhub.fifa.com/m/1e432c645600e569/original/oxkmv00wclfngjsgs6ob-pdf.pdf>.

This led to an actual conflict between the (then-)newly set up Governance Committee (which I briefly presided over at the time) and one of the confederations (which refused to correct this discrimination against women and postponed its elections). Later, when the elections took place (and I was no longer on the Committee), a case was brought against the confederation by a female candidate, before the Court of Arbitration for Sport (CAS).[28] The Court confirmed the existence of discrimination, as well as third-party interference in the elections, but declared it could not, in this instance, annul the elections and order them to be re-held. The exact reason why no effective remedy could be provided is unknown, since CAS's decision was not published.[29] Moreover, FIFA, including its Ethics Committee, appears to have taken no action against those involved in both the discriminatory actions and third-party interference in the elections that have been established by CAS. This case illustrates the extent to which the governance culture of sports is opposed to effective female non-discrimination and representation.

The limited scope of representation of all affected interests by sports governance bodies is also visible in the absence of forms of representation and participation afforded to athletes, supporters, and other stakeholders. In fact, the political cartels dominating sports associations start with a closed and highly controlled electoral universe of voters. For example, it is no surprise that women continue to be underrepresented at the level of FIFA and its confederations, when only 2 per cent of voting association presidents are female.[30]

Evidence of the capture of sports governance bodies by a limited group of people and interests is also to be found in the absence of power renewal. This is immediately visible in the long periods that sports leaders stay in power and the fact that they are almost always unchallenged. João Havelange was president of FIFA for thirty-five years. He was followed by his de facto number two, Joseph Blatter, who remained in power for seventeen years and would have stayed longer, were it not for the judicial investigation initiated by American authorities over FIFA (he was even overwhelmingly re-elected after the first scandals came to light). Juan Antonio Samaranch was president of the IOC for twenty-one years. His son is the current vice-president and is considered to be the frontrunner for the next presidency.

This highlights the extent to which the selection pool for political offices in sports is small and cartelized. There is no genuine power renewal. Not only is it extremely

[28] Miguel Poiares Maduro and Benedita Menezes Queiro, 'You Can't Sit with Us. Discrimination against Women in Football: A Commentary of the *Mariyam Mohamed vs. Asian Football Confederation (AFC)* case' (2022) Catolica Global School of Law Working Paper No 1/2022 <https://catolicalaw.fd.lisboa.ucp.pt/asset/2066/file> and also published in (2021) 9 Revista do Direito do Desporto.

[29] CAS, 'Media Release: The Court of Arbitration for Sport (CAS) Partially Upholds the Appeals of Mariyam Mohamed Related to the 2019 Asian Football Confederation (AFC) Elections' (25 January 2021) <www.tas-cas.org/fileadmin/user_upload/CAS_Media_Release_6310_6496.pdf>. The lack of transparency inherent in the publication policy of CAS is one of the criticisms most often levied against the 'sports court'.

[30] Dodd and Ordway (n 25) 31.

rare for an incumbent to lose an election, but it is also rare for incumbents to even be challenged. The normal state of affairs is for presidents of sports associations and governance bodies to be in power for long periods, never being challenged, and playing vital roles in the choice of their successors from a limited pool of insiders. A recent survey of elections across all the Olympic sports federations concluded that two-thirds of their presidents had run unopposed.[31] Genuine electoral competition is so rare that it has even become usual to dispense with the vote and elect the next president by acclamation. For example, FIFA changed its rules at the Congress of 2019 to allow President Gianni Infantino to be re-elected simply by acclamation during the same Congress.[32]

For those who may think that, without opponents, a secret ballot would only be a formality, remember that the rule required the candidate to have at least a majority of votes in favour. As a consequence, it would actually be possible in a secret ballot for a candidate running unchallenged not to be elected. The use of voting by acclamation is, therefore, the final brick in an effective strategy preventing any form of dissent. Without secret ballots, there is no risk that any form of hidden dissent could express itself (assuming that those who might use the secret ballot to express dissent wouldn't dare to express it publicly). This reveals the extent of the democratic problems facing sports as well as how rules are manipulated to prevent effective democracy and to protect the existing political cartels.

Similar factors explain why votes are so often unanimous (or almost unanimous) in congresses. They impress even by comparison with the most effective autocratic regimes. Dissent is a rarity. All this hints—to say the least—at an extremely high level of voting control in sports organizations.

3.1.3 Governance and rule of law

While claiming a bottom-up representative legitimacy, sports organizations actually operate from the top down. It starts with a very high concentration of power in the president, without any effective separation of powers or checks and balances. This means that, among many other things, presidents control the administrations in charge of organizing the elections. Such concentration of power is not limited to relationships with the administration and other 'political' bodies. There is also no effective separation of powers with regard to the (supposedly) independent bodies.[33]

[31] Liam Morgan, 'Lack of Contested Elections Paints a Dictatorial Picture of Olympic Movement' (*Inside the Games*, 10 June 2019) <www.insidethegames.biz/articles/1080421/liam-morgan-lack-of-contested-elections-paints-a-dictatorial-picture-of-olympic-movement>.

[32] ibid.

[33] I explain and discuss this point in more detail in Miguel Poiares Maduro and Joseph HH Weiler, '"Integrity", "Independence" and the Internal Reform of FIFA: A View from the Trenches' in Arnout Geeraert and Frank van Eekeren (eds), *Good Governance in Sport: Critical Reflections* (Routledge 2021) and, with Ioannis Galariotis and Benedita Menezes Queiroz, 'The Transnational Governance of Sports: Key Issues and Proposals' (2019) Policy Paper, European University Institute.

The latter are often dependent on the political bodies, subject to both renewal and dismissal by the latter. It is also not uncommon (albeit not necessarily frequent) for members of independent bodies to come from previous positions in other political structures within sport. In fact, this culture is so widespread that it permeates what is supposed to be the highest judicial structure of sport. The past two presidents of the International Council of Arbitration for Sport (ICAS, the board that oversees CAS, including selecting the arbitrators) were previously leading officials of the IOC. This is a bit like having ministers or heads of government transition into Chief Justices. The overwhelming majority of ICAS members are appointed by sports governing bodies, and the rest are then chosen by those initial members. Arbitrators themselves often have links with sports associations, are subject to renewable terms, and are not subject to any effective mechanism monitoring, preventing, or sanctioning conflicts of interest. In addition, the criteria used to appoint the presidents of the panels or to determine the publication of CAS decisions are, to a large extent, unclear. These are only a few of the numerous problems that lead many to question the extent to which CAS is independent and complies with due process.[34]

The absence of genuine checks and balances undermines the compliance of sports governance with the rule of law. This represents an additional challenge to the recognition of its autonomy and self-government. It is a well-known fact that democracy cannot survive without the rule of law and checks and balances, in the same way that no genuine competition exists without independent umpires guaranteeing an equal application of the rules. The concentration of power, political cartelization, absence of renewal of power, and the 'autocratic-like' voting records that dominate sports governance bodies are not the product of a mysterious and unique consensus in this area of life. Nor should they be treated as fun facts to be ignored. They are evidence of profound systemic problems in the governance of sports organizations that undermine any good governance, democratic, and representative claim on their part.[35]

[34] Antoine Duval, 'Lost in Translation? The European Convention on Human Rights and the Court of Arbitration for Sport' (2022) 22 The International Sports Law Journal 132; Helen Lenskyj, 'Sport Exceptionalism and the Court of Arbitration for Sport' (2018) 4 Journal of Criminological Research 5; Grit Hartmann, 'Tipping the Scales of Justice: The Sports and Its "Supreme Court"' *Play the Game* (November 2021) <www.playthegame.org/publications/tipping-the-scales-of-justice-the-sport-and-its-supreme-court/>. Some of these issues were addressed in a controversial judgment of the European Court of Human Rights (*Mutu and Pechstein v Switzerland* App nos 40575/10 and 67474/10 (ECHR, 2 October 2018). This decision would deserve its own article.

[35] It is therefore not surprising that several of the cases uncovered in 2015 by the US Department of Justice involved instances of buying votes. The absence of a transnational entity empowered to systematically monitor and investigate sports elections makes it hard, however, for many other cases to come to life. The power system described also deters anyone interested in preserving their position in sports from bringing any such cases to light. As stated by Richard Pound, whistleblowers and those who talk about the problems 'are now treated far more harshly than the perpetrators, so there is a distinct lack of encouragement to have the facts known'. (Interview with *Transparency International* <https://blog.transparency.org/2016/01/15/richard-pound-the-corruption-risks-in-sport/index.html>). An exception is the case of *Mariyam Mohamed vs Asian Football Confederation (AFC)* (<www.tas-cas.org/en/gene

3.1.3.1 The expertise claim

An additional argument, often invoked in support of sports autonomy, relies on the greater expertise of their governance bodies in matters pertaining to their respective sports. This argument fails on two grounds. First, the claim to greater expertise can only extend as far as that which is unique to sport. That has, in fact, been the basis of the application of EU law to sports by the ECJ. It applies to sports in its economic dimension. In other words, it applies to rules adopted by sports governing bodies that regulate the economic activity inherent in sports. It does not apply to rules specific to sport itself (such as what is a penalty or an offside). What sports governance bodies cannot do is to claim a sports exception to insulate their regulation of economic activities (and their own economic activities) from EU law. The ECJ has recognized the difficulty of severing the economic from the sports dimension (when, for example, sports disciplinary sanctions prevent a club or an athlete from exercising their economic activity). It is in this light that it recognizes that non-economic grounds, unique to sport, may justify restrictions to EU economic rules—but these need to be necessary and proportional, as with any other exception to those rules.[36]

With respect to the economic dimension of the business of sports there is no *a priori* greater claim from sports governing bodies than that of other business associations with respect to their own markets. In order for sports governing bodies to claim some sort of institutional advantage in regulating these markets, they should comply with at least two conditions: (i) they should not be engaged in business activities in the market they want to regulate, and (ii) they should secure the representation of all the interests involved in such market (from the providers of services and goods to their consumers). Neither of these, however, is the case. First, the most profitable sports businesses are those undertaken by the sports federations themselves (such as the Olympics, the World Cup, the European Championship, or the Champions League). This puts their regulatory activity of the sports markets in a permanent conflict of interest with their business interests in those markets. They claim to be acting on behalf, and for the greater good, of the broader interests linked to sports and all its stakeholders. Yet their institutional set-up does not

ral-information/news-detail/article/cas-partially-upholds-the-appeals-of-mariyam-mohamed-related-to-the-2019-asian-football-confederatio.html>), where the CAS panel, aside from recognizing that she was a victim of discrimination on the basis of gender, also established that there had been third-party influence in the elections. The follow-up to the case, however, confirms Richard Pound's diagnosis. Nothing happened to those elected or involved in such electoral corruption, while Ms Mohamed has been ostracized from sport. In addition, it is important to note that voting control does not always involve criminal activity. It may be easily done under the current system of sport governance by exchanging political favours through appointments to well-paid positions or by favouring transfer of funds to federations with 'loyal' presidents. Many other problems could be raised, including the absence of campaign rules.

[36] For an example of this reasoning in the ECJ, see *Bosman* (n 1) paras 73–78. The Court replicated this reasoning in many other judgments.

appear to reflect that, and, as illustrated above, there is no evidence of success in their regulation of the public goods associated with sport. The current outcomes of their regulatory action demonstrate the opposite: corruption and integrity problems are widespread, and the competitive balance and open character of competitions is decreasing. Secondly, as also described above, there is a lack of genuine democracy and a limited scope of representation of all stakeholders' interests. In addition, their proximity to particular interests creates capture risks and additional conflicts of interest.

A concrete example highlights these problems and the risks of the inherent systemic conflict of interest in which they often operate. In 2018, the Adjudicatory Chamber of UEFA's Financial Fair Play Body—the independent body set up within UEFA to monitor clubs' compliance with financial fair play rules—took a decision requiring Paris St-Germain (PSG) to be investigated and (later) sanctioned for violation of financial fair play rules. The club appealed on procedural grounds (arguing, contrary to the view of the Adjudicatory Chamber, that the investigation was time-barred). The case ended favourably for PSG at CAS, but, since the reasoning of the decision was not made public (by agreement of both UEFA and PSG), it was only when the *New York Times* gained access to the case proceedings and made them public that it was possible to find out why: UEFA's lawyers actually argued in favour of PSG's position, against the decision taken by UEFA's own independent body.[37] In other words, the administration and political leadership of UEFA sided with PSG and undermined, in the proceedings before CAS, the decision of its own independent body, de facto reverting the decision of its independent Financial Fair Play Body.[38] Another more recent piece by the *New York Times* casts further suspicions on the relationship between UEFA and PSG.[39] The article describes how UEFA disciplinary bodies ignored a flagrant violation of the rules of conduct by the president of PSG, Nasser al-Khelaifi, reported by the referee of a crucial Champions League match. It happens that the president of PSG is also a member of UEFA's most important governance body, its Executive Committee (he is there as a 'representative' of football clubs). This is the case notwithstanding that he is also the owner of a company (beIN Media Group) that is one of UEFA's most important business partners.

[37] Tariq Panja, 'In P.S.G. Case, Documents Show UEFA Surrendered Without a Fight' *The New York Times* (24 July 2019) <www.nytimes.com/2019/07/24/sports/psg-uefa-ffp.html>.

[38] UEFA has stated that it was actually agreeing with the position of the president of the lower chamber within the Financial Fair Play Body. This would be the equivalent of a government not complying with a decision of its supreme or constitutional court because it preferred the decision of a lower court in the same proceeding. Not surprisingly, most independent members of the Financial Fair Play Body have by now resigned or been replaced (arguably by more 'friendly' figures: see Wilson (n 13)).

[39] Tariq Panja, 'At Top of European Soccer, Fears That Rules Don't Apply to All' *The New York Times* (24 August 2022) <www.nytimes.com/2022/08/24/sports/soccer/champions-league-psg-nasser.html> (accessed 7 February 2023).

It is impossible to know for sure the extent to which this conflict of interest was relevant in UEFA's actions favourable to PSG. Still, the conflict of interest is clear and casts an immediate shadow of suspicion over such decisions. In fact, independent of al-Khelaifi's personal business dealings with UEFA, it is clear that UEFA has little interest in having PSG (and other important clubs) out of its most important competition, as this would likely decrease its revenues. Consequently, this casts serious doubts on its capacity to exercise its regulatory function in a genuinely independent and fair manner with respect to all clubs. In other words, the systemic conflict of interest at the heart of many sports governing bodies' regulatory functions undermines the independence with which they can be trusted to exercise such functions.

3.2 A New Approach to Sports Autonomy

The previous analysis highlights that, not only there is no *a priori* claim of institutional superiority for sports governance bodies with respect to market regulation of sports, but, on the contrary, their selective representation of the relevant stakeholders and proximity to some of the regulated interests may generate increased risks of capture. This is even more true if the governance of these sports bodies, in charge of regulation, does not limit such risks of capture and is permeated by other institutional malfunctions, such as those described previously, linked to the absence of separation of powers and the rule of law.

In the words of a great figure of sport himself, Richard Pound (former vice-president of the IOC and of WADA), the truth is that, in the current context, sport's 'mantra' of autonomy 'is an outdated relic from an earlier era'.[40]

This is not to deny that there may be aspects where sports governance bodies may indeed present an institutional advantage. An important argument, often advanced in support of sport's autonomy, including the autonomy of its legal and judicial systems, is the need for sports issues to be decided expediently and at the transnational level.

The organization of sports competitions requires decisions to be taken in time frames that may be incompatible with the regular procedures of ordinary courts or of the usual legislative and regulatory state procedures. This is an argument that does not extend to all issues, however. More importantly, even with respect to matters where such advantage is indeed relevant, it is an argument in favour of granting *some* autonomy and regulatory powers to such organizations. It says nothing, however, of the conditions that ought to be required for such autonomy to be recognized. It seems crucial for such recognition to be conditional upon compliance

[40] Richard Pound, 'Global Sport: A SWOT Assessment' (*Play the Game Conference Remarks*, October 2015) <www.playthegame.org/media/gpvlkqhj/25-10-sunday-1400-richard-pound.pdf>.

with certain principles of governance that would correct, or at least mitigate, the institutional malfunctions that I have highlighted.

The same could be said with respect to the claim arising from the transnational nature of sports. This is not compatible with the fragmentation that could result from being subject to a web of different national regulations. It is therefore argued that granting such regulatory authority is the only way to protect the transnational dimension of sports and prevent them from being fragmented and nationalized. This is, however, an argument in favour of transnational regulation of sports, and not necessarily one in favour of private transnational self-regulation. In addition, sports bodies have often used this argument to shield themselves from matters that could be nationally regulated without creating obstacles to transnational sports. The transnational private governance of sports has served to protect the absolute autonomy of sports organizations from any form of regulation (or even national judicial decisions) that they oppose, instead of serving only to protect the transnational dimension of sports. There is no reason for that, if not for the fact that national governments are either unwilling to or incapable of (and perhaps both) imposing such regulation, for reasons I will describe next.

Furthermore, there are other transnational areas of activity where governments have not hesitated to act to protect public interests without fear of fragmentation. A good example is the digital domain, where there has been an increase in public regulation, particularly in the EU. What often happens is that effective regulation of these areas requires transnational cooperation or supranational action (such as the EU provides). In other words, the transnational dimension of sports makes it harder to develop a constitutional and rule of law architecture for sports and enforce it but does not dispense it. On the contrary, it makes it more important for us to develop it.

Both expediency and the transnational dimension of sports are therefore relevant arguments to a discussion on the extent of the autonomy to be granted to sports federations and on the form and locus of the regulation and oversight they ought to be subject to. They do not, however, justify granting to sports federations the unconditional 'extraordinary degree of autonomy' they have been given so far.

If they exercise regulatory power over an important area of social and economic life, they ought to comply with the same principles with which we expect all regulatory authorities to comply. To the extent that their regulatory power is anchored in an independent structure of governance, this structure of governance ought to be subject to principles of democracy, rule of law, fundamental rights, accountability, and transparency. This should cover their political, administrative, and judicial bodies. But who can and ought to do that? The final section argues that only the EU is in a position to do this (or to promote it) and puts forward different alternatives on how this can be done.

4. EU Law is the Answer

As outlined above, there are good arguments for sports governance to be different from public governance, and even to continue to be dominated by private governance. Transition costs into a totally new model and political choice arguments may concur with that. What it does not have to be (and ought not to continue to be) is subject to this form of private governance: a de facto political cartel, neither representative nor accountable. It is necessary, therefore, to set a mechanism guaranteeing that the regulatory powers exercised by such private governance regimes are subject to similar constitutional values and constraints as those of public governance: that they adequately represent all affected interests; that they operate subject to internal democracy and forms of checks and balances; and that they adopt and enforce their rules, in compliance with the rule of law and fundamental rights.

This could assume the form of an international independent agency with competences to review and supervise the different sports governance bodies in matters such as the integrity and fairness of elections, the effectiveness of the mechanisms of checks and balances and separation of powers, as well as ethical and integrity issues. This agency would, therefore, not replace the regulation of sports by sports governance bodies, but rather guarantee the conformity of their governance with principles of democracy, transparency, accountability, checks and balances, and the rule of law.

The problem with this alternative is its feasibility. In theory, this independent agency could be set up through an intergovernmental agreement between like-minded states. These states would then require any sports international association to accept the jurisdiction of the agency. Without that requirement, the states would not recognize their competitions and regulations. This could be done even in the form of soft law by an informal agreement between states and sports associations, whereby the latter would commit to set up such an independent agency under the terms agreed with the states, with the implicit threat that if they did not do so, then public authorities would start asserting their powers.

The likelihood of this happening is extremely low, however. First, there are several states that do not object to the current state of affairs, as it gives them much more influence than the alternative would. Sports organizations also cultivate that proximity, particularly with states that do not bring with them accountability. A former president of a sports federation and IOC member (in)famously stated that '[d]ictators can organize events such as [the Olympics] without asking the people's permission . . . For us, everything is easier in dictatorships.'[41]

[41] See Sam Borden, 'Olympics 2022: How We Ended up with a Winter Games amid China's Human Rights Crisis' (*ESPN.com*, 2 February 2022) <www.espn.com/olympics/story/_/id/33192322/olympics-2022-how-ended-winter-games-amid-china-human-rights-crisis>.

Despite sports associations' usual claim to political neutrality, the reality is often the opposite. It is common for sports associations to include in their governing bodies political officials, thereby simultaneously co-opting politics and being captured by part of it. State funding of sports associations has also increased in an indirect way via the number of state-owned or controlled companies that are now major business partners of sports associations. The proximity between sports and politics, and the problems this proximity generates, became very visible during the most recent Olympics, when the IOC often took the position of supporting Chinese authorities in the midst of multiple human rights controversies. It is revealing of the promiscuity of interests involving politics, sports, and its officials that the IOC appointed Juan Samaranch Jr to head the Coordination Committee for the Beijing Olympics. As mentioned earlier, he is the son of a previous Olympic president but, of more significance here, he has significant business interests in China and with the Chinese government.[42] The Qatar World Cup is a further illustration of this problem.

All this, together with the usual capture of domestic politics by sports bodies,[43] makes it unlikely for the project of an international agency to gather the support of a sufficient number of states to become a genuine international endeavour.

Something akin to this can only be set up under the leadership of the EU. If, on the one hand, it is unlikely for there to be the collective will at the international level to do it, on the other hand, national governments cannot do so even if they do have the will. Indeed, if a state assumes such a position on its own, such state's national and club teams and athletes risk being excluded from sports competitions organized by the international federations. It is well known that the principle of political neutrality is mostly invoked to oppose any form of public regulation, arguing that any state regulation capable of questioning the power and rules of sports governing bodies constitutes a political interference in the autonomy of sport. Consequently, teams and athletes from states attempting such regulation have been faced with the threat of being, in practice, excluded from the sport. This is a rather effective tool to preserve their absolute self-governance and private regulatory power and extends as far as judicial decisions.[44]

Yet, international sports federations have not acted in the same way when required, by either the Commission or the ECJ itself, to amend their rules and procedures. The reason is simple: they do not have the same bargaining power with respect to the EU as they have with respect to individual Member States. They cannot credibly threaten to exclude the teams and athletes from the twenty-seven

[42] See Li Yuan, 'Its Human Rights Record in Question, China Turns to an Old Friend' *The New York Times* (14 December 2021) <www.nytimes.com/2021/12/14/business/china-olympics-peng-shuai-samaranch.html>.

[43] That, according to a recent article, extends as far as the EU itself: see Meier and others (n 19).

[44] The most recent example that comes to mind is FIFA's threat to exclude the Spanish national team from the World Cup in light of a judicial review of Spanish FA elections.

EU Member States. The EU is the only public regulatory authority that they are forced to take seriously. Even Switzerland, under whose law most international sports federations are established, does not have effective regulatory power. It is unclear, because of the financial advantages Switzerland enjoys from hosting such organizations, whether the Swiss authorities would ever seriously consider regulating and scrutinizing such organizations. If they did (as some in Switzerland itself think they should), the most likely outcome would be for such organizations to move to a more 'friendly' jurisdiction. They would search for an even 'more favourable' regulatory haven. In fact, the Swiss laws were made to grant international sports federations the largest possible autonomy with the purpose of getting them to establish themselves in Switzerland.[45] The problem is that such autonomy gives them an effective regulatory power over markets that are not in Switzerland.

It is because these federations act and exercise power in our market and society that the EU is entitled to regulate them. It is because their power exerts itself in an economic market, and not simply within a game, that the EU has a clear legal basis to act under its internal market powers. And it is because of the particular nature of such power that the EU is likely the only political entity with the effective authority to scrutinize and make such power accountable. This is an interesting case of what I have defined, in previous writings, as the EU democratic added value. It is at the EU level that EU citizens can reinstate democratic control over a form of private regulatory power that Member States cannot effectively regulate and scrutinize on their own. This is an example of an EU policy that does not erode state sovereignty, but instead reinstates it.

In its case law, the ECJ seems to be well aware of the EU's legal authority to do so, and also of the need to do it. As argued by Antoine Duval and Ben Van Rompuy, the 'CJEU tried to impose a democratic check on the exercise of transnational authority by SGBs [Sports Governing Bodies] in football and beyond'.[46] As they also argue, the deregulatory approach sometimes attributed to the ECJ in this area is false and 'a blessing for some SGBs willing to find a scapegoat to blame for their failure to regulate their own sport'.[47]

Instead, what the ECJ does can better be represented as the reverse: requiring the power of collective regulation held by sports governance bodies to be exercised in a way that respects minimum regulatory and governance democratic standards. That it has fallen almost exclusively on the ECJ to do so is a testament to the degree of influence that sports governance bodies have on the alternative institutions that

[45] See Baddeley (n 18) and Suren Gomtsian and others, 'Between the Green Pitch and the Red Tape: The Private Legal Order of FIFA' (2018) 43 Yale Journal of International Law 85 and TILEC Discussion Paper No 2017-03.

[46] Antoine Duval and Ben Van Rompuy (eds), *The Legacy of* Bosman: *Revisiting the Relationship between EU Law and Sport* (TMC Asser Press 2016) 6.

[47] ibid 5.

could accomplish it, including the political process. This much has been stated by former Advocate General Carl Otto Lenz (the AG in *Bosman*) who, in an unusually candid way, noted after the *Bosman* case: '[i]n no other case in my career of almost 14 years at the Court have I been exposed to such efforts to take influence on a case. The political influence and power of football cannot be overestimated.'[48] Interestingly, the same disproportionate support from political authorities (and the Commission itself) for the power of sports governance bodies that surprised then-AG Lenz in *Bosman*[49] was again on display in the (misleadingly labelled) *Superleague* case, mentioned above.[50] That UEFA and FIFA have, apparently, managed to co-opt Member States and EU institutions into their framing of the case is a replay of how former AG Lenz described the *Bosman* proceedings before the ECJ. By the time this chapter has been published, we will see whether, as in *Bosman*, the Court will ignore such framing and the political context and focus on the actual issues of EU law at stake.

In my view, the case law of the ECJ provides the foundations on which to build a coherent EU approach to the democratic accountability and regulation of sports governance bodies. First, the ECJ has (re-)established legal control over the transnational private governance of sports economic activities. It did so by explaining why sports autonomy ought not to be confused with immunity from legal and judicial scrutiny and did not entail an unsupervised power to regulate without democratic accountability. The ECJ attributes to sports governance bodies a power of collective regulation similar to that of states.[51] Subsequently, it notes that many of the rules adopted by these bodies do not regulate the sport activity itself, but rather the economic activity inherent in or linked to sport.[52] In addition, it has recognized that even rules regarding the sports activity itself may actually limit the economic activity linked to that sport and are, for that reason, also subject to its judicial scrutiny. Finally, it has even expressly questioned the regulatory role played by such sports governance bodies 'which constitutes policing of an economic activity and touches on fundamental freedoms [falling] within the competence of the public authorities'.[53]

[48] Carl Otto Lenz, 'Foreword' in Duval and Van Rompuy (n 47) viii.

[49] ibid.

[50] Case C-333/21 *Request for a preliminary ruling* (n 3).

[51] See *Bosman* (n 1); Case 36/74 *BNO Walrave and LJN Koch v Association Union cycliste internationale* ECLI:EU:C:1974:140; and, particularly, Case T-193/02 *Laurent Piau v Commission of the European Communities* ECLI:EU:T:2005:22, paras 76–78.

[52] ibid.

[53] *Piau* (n 51) para 78. It is surprising to me that the litigants against UEFA in the *Superleague* case have not, in light of what the Court of Justice argues in *Piau*, directly challenged FIFA's regulatory power with respect to the fundamental freedoms of the Treaty. In *Piau*, the Court makes clear in paras 76–79 that it believes that there would be a stronger challenge against the holding of the regulatory power itself if done under the free movement provisions as opposed to under competition rules. The case being a reference from a national court will allow the Court, however, to introduce such free movement analysis—but in the hearing, no party or Court member appears to have raised the issue.

The second pillar of the ECJ's case law regards the nature of that judicial scrutiny. In a first line of cases, what it does is assess the proportionality of the rules adopted by sports governance bodies that are under-challenged. It balances the legitimacy and adequacy of the goals pursued by those roles with the restriction they impose on the economic activity.[54] In a second line of cases, the ECJ focuses, instead, on the legitimacy of that regulatory role itself and/or the institutional (or governance) requirements that have to be guaranteed by sports governance bodies in order for EU law to respect their regulatory authority in a certain domain.[55] In *Motoe* in particular, the ECJ made clear that, even when that regulatory power is granted by the state, when the sports governing body is in a conflict of interest with respect to its own economic activity in the sport, it needs to be subject to restrictions, obligations, and review.[56] It is unclear if the ECJ will admit at all, in the absence of a power granted by the state, the exercise of regulatory power in case such systemic conflict of interest exists (such as when it is involved in the authorization of competing sports). But in *Piau*, as mentioned, the Court seems to admit that the exercise of certain regulatory powers by private entities may be unlawful outside a public framework regulating such exercise.

5. Conclusion

The ECJ is increasingly confronted with (and appears increasingly aware of) the systemic problems and conflicts of interest that arise in the transnational private governance of sports. As a consequence, its case law has paid growing attention to the institutional requirements necessary for such governance to be legitimate and acceptable under EU law. At the same time, one cannot ignore that the ECJ is limited in the scope of powers at its disposal to remedy such situations. First, it does not decide which cases are brought to it. It has no power to set its own agenda.[57] This means that many of sports' regulatory and governance problems may never reach the Court. This is particularly so because of the litigation costs imposed on any athlete or official challenging a decision from a sports federation. Athletes are often suspended for having sought recourse to an ordinary court instead of using the 'mandatory arbitration' of the CAS.[58] Officials are ostracized

[54] See eg *Bosman* (n 1); *Walrave* (n 51); and Case C–519/04 P *David Meca-Medica and Igor Majcen v Commission* ECLI:EU:C:2006:492, among many others.

[55] See Case C–49/07 *Motosykletistiki Omospondia Ellados NPID (MOTOE) v Elliniko Dimosio* ECLI:EU:C:2008:376 (*Motoe*).

[56] ibid para 52.

[57] It is true that both admissibility criteria and the different degrees of judicial scrutiny employed in different areas are used by courts both to filter and promote (by encouraging or discouraging litigation) the issues they may be more or less keen to address. But this is a rather limited form of regulating their judicial agenda (unless, of course, they have *a certiori* power as in the US Supreme Court, though even this is always dependent on what is 'brought' to them).

[58] Case C–415/93 *Bosman* (1995) ECLI:EU:C:1995:293, Opinion of Advocate General Lenz and *Mutu and Pechstein* (n 35).

and treated as pariahs by the political cartel described above. Secondly, judicial decisions are, by definition, piecemeal. In addition, when reviewing the exercise of regulatory powers, courts define what cannot be done and, while on occasion pointing at what ought to be done, they cannot do it themselves. Even when, as has often been the case in sports, the Court points to the institutional or procedural requirements necessary for the exercise of a certain power to be lawful, it is in no position to monitor and guarantee that such will actually be done, or even how those requirements would be interpreted and implemented.

It is for these reasons that an EU answer to the severe problems in sports regulation and its private governance requires the other EU institutions to step up their game.[59] The systemic approach developed by the ECJ provides the best starting point from which to build a more general EU approach to private transnational sports governance. It requires, however, other EU institutions to assume their own responsibilities. What the Court can do is to increase the incentives for that to happen if, for example, it will no longer accept the regulatory role of sports governance bodies in certain domains, absent a certain public framework and/or until they comply with the systemic governance requirements it defines as necessary to guarantee compliance with EU law.

The description of sports regulatory and governance failures helps us to identify what should be part of the constitutional architecture imposed upon sports governance bodies:

- Guarantees of representation for all sports stakeholders and of the democratic organization of the governance bodies;
- Separation of powers and effective checks and balances, including for investigating corruption and integrity issues (as well as by performing fit and proper tests and reviewing possible conflicts of interest);
- Clear separation of regulatory and business functions;
- Principles and obligations regarding transparency and accountability; and
- Independent judicial review; in other words, even if the specificities of sport may authorize a distinct judicial system (such as CAS), this needs to be set up so as to guarantee effective independence and adherence to principles of due process.

The EU could promote this directly by setting up an EU agency established under the internal market legal basis. It can also act so as to require sports governance bodies to set up an international independent agency (a model of which might be the recently proposed WACA: World Anti-Corruption Agency).[60] The

[59] I have argued this much in an editorial opinion piece with Steve, Joseph Weiler and Petros C Mavroidis: 'Only the EU Can Save Football from Itself: View' (*Euronews.com*, 21 November 2021) <www.euronews.com/2021/11/12/only-the-eu-can-save-football-from-itself-view>.

[60] Hartmann (n 34).

EU has at its disposal a variety of tools and levers that it can use to require this from sports federations and to make sure such an international agency would be genuinely independent and have the necessary scope of powers. In its softer form, political leverage might be enough, but it needs to be effectively used.[61] A stronger instrument would be for the Commission to adopt a communication under competition rules, whereby it would condition its deference towards the competitive restrictions inherent in the current forms of sports governance and regulation on the establishment of such an agency and compliance with its rules and decisions. An even stronger instrument would be to adopt legislation establishing certain licensing requirements for international sports federations operating in the EU internal market.

There is no lack of instruments for the EU to do what is necessary. It is, moreover, an area where the EU has a clear democratic added value with respect to its Member States.[62] It is the EU that can bring back under democratic control this process of transnational private governance. I believe the importance that sports has had in Steve's treatment of EU law is a recognition of that as much as it is of his personal passion for the topic. The ECJ too has recognized such importance. It is time for the political institutions to do so too.

[61] Meier and others (n 19).
[62] See various articles by Maduro (n 2).

12
The Crusade for the Holy Grail of Competitive Balance

*Mislav Mataija and Petros C Mavroidis**

1. Competitive Balance in Sports Markets

Unlike 'typical' markets, a sports market is not a zero-sum game, as competitors jointly produce the marketed good. In sports markets, rival teams produce and sell competition to the audience. Neale was probably the first who, because of this feature, inquired seriously into what he termed 'the peculiar economics of sports'.[1]

The regulatory challenge for the sports authorities is the same as that of antitrust authorities in 'typical' markets: how to maintain rivalry in the market? The means employed, nevertheless, are not the same. Whereas antitrust is used to this end in, say, the soft drinks market, by constraining dominant firms and preventing cartels, sports regulation (especially in the United States) generally aims at levelling the playing field across competitors. In some cases, this translates into regulatory interventions that would be suspect, or even flat out illegal, under 'normal' antitrust. Such interventions are done in the name of competitive balance, a concept that is intuitively easy to understand—ensuring some sort of long-term comparability in strength among competing teams—yet hard to define precisely.

Assuming that some regulatory intervention is necessary, how should we understand 'competitive balance'? Antitrust analysis knows similar difficulties. Even if we could define the optimal level of rivalry, there is nothing like a 'rivalry-meter' at our disposal. Antitrust authorities, aided by the HHI-Index (the Herfindahl-Hirschman Index, measuring the degree of concentration in a given market),[2] will use the incidence of a given practice on consumer welfare as proxy to decide how rivalry has been affected. What is the corresponding proxy for levelling the playing field, for preserving competitive balance (the term preferred in sports law)

* European Commission (all views are personal and do not necessarily reflect the views of the European Commission), and Columbia Law School respectively.

[1] Walter C Neale, 'The Peculiar Economics of Professional Sports: A Contribution to the Theory of the Firm in Sporting Competition and in Market Competition' (1964) 78 The Quarterly Journal of Economics 1.

[2] See, in this context, P Dorian Owen, Michael Ryan, and Clayton R Weatherston, 'Measuring Competitive Balance in Professional Team Sports Using the Herfindahl-Hirschman Index' (2007) 31 Review of Industrial Organization 289.

Mislav Mataija and Petros C Mavroidis, *The Crusade for the Holy Grail of Competitive Balance* In: *The Internal Market Ideal*. Edited by: Jeremias Adams-Prassl, Sanja Bogojević, Ariel Ezrachi, and Dorota Leczykiewicz, Oxford University Press.
 DOI: 10.1093/oso/9780192867063.003.0013

in sports markets? There are some regulatory responses in this context, originating in the US sports markets, and we will be discussing them in what follows. But the question in which we are most interested in this essay is: why have similar initiatives appeared in the United States only, and much less in the EU?

Section 2 focuses on semantics and aims to lay out the conceptual parameters for a generic understanding of 'competitive balance', irrespective of a given sports market with defined characteristics. In Section 3, we shift gears, and discuss competitive balance in a contextual manner. Competitive balance has been addressed in different ways in different markets, and the risk for sample bias looms large when discussions focus on a subset of the whole. We have picked the US sports market, admittedly the most sophisticated regulatory paradigm of competitive balance there is. The various US sports (baseball, basketball, football, ice hockey, soccer) are asymmetrically regulated in this respect and do not share the same legal relationship with US antitrust either. We privileged a discussion of the common elements across the various sports so that the reader can leave this section with a good understanding of the quintessential elements of competitive balance across US sports. In Section 4, we discuss regulation of the most popular sport in Europe, football. We will insist on the differences with the US, while highlighting some of the potential explanatory variables for the relative legislative inertia reigning over Europe in this respect. Section 5 provides concluding reflections on what seems to be a key question; namely, whether the ability to regulate with a view to achieving competitive balance is constrained (and, if yes, to what extent) by the 'open' (promotion/relegation) or 'closed' character of the sports market at hand. This is a question that has also occupied the attention of Professor Stephen Weatherill and, hence, a very fitting tribute to his scholarship.

2. Understanding Competitive Balance

Zimbalist quipped:

> Competitive balance is like wealth. Everyone agrees it is a good thing to have, but no one knows how much one needs.[3]

While competitive balance is the centrepiece in sports regulations—in the US model anyway—it has not managed to win overwhelming support worldwide. Intuitively, it seems rational and even appealing to aim for competitive balance. Crucially, however, the typical criterion used for regulatory intervention in the name of competition is the maximization of interest in a sports market. Understood

[3] Andrew Zimbalist, 'Competitive Balance in Sports Leagues: An Introduction' (2002) 3 Journal of Sports Economics 111, 111.

in this way, its policy attraction beyond the US coasts is still very much in doubt. And there is more. Some of its intellectual premises have been questioned as well, thus eviscerating even more its potential appeal.

Theoretically, perfect competitive balance in a team sport implies that each team enjoys the same probability of winning in respect of each game in the competition. How do we measure the probability of winning in a precise manner, however? Comprehensive surveys on this score, like that put together by Humphreys and Watanabe,[4] and earlier by Fort and Maxcy,[5] point to the need to employ proxies. But we are getting ahead of ourselves, as the obvious starting point is: why does competitive balance matter?

2.1 Why Does Competitive Balance Matter?

The central argument in favour of competitive balance is that it contributes to uncertainty of outcome, and thus increases sports attendance (whether understood as attendance in stadiums or, say, TV ratings). Competitive imbalance, implicitly, will reduce interest in sport and, thus, the rate of return on the investment in clubs, even the ones that are the most successful on the sporting front. Low attendance will lead to reduced sales of merchandise, sponsoring, TV income, and so on and so forth. Uncertainty as to the sporting outcome, conversely, influences the marginal utility for consumers, and thus operates as an attendance booster. The rest follows: increasing attendance leads to additional investment, value and volume of TV rights, sales of merchandising, sponsoring, etc.

And there are other benefits as well. Increasing the size of the pie means that top talents will be attracted to the sport, and the quality in the market will increase as a result (which, in turn, will help attract more money into the business, etc).[6]

A rather unexplored question is whether competitive balance could serve objectives other than increasing the pie. Are there legitimate reasons why, to put it in simpler terms, a smaller but more equally distributed pie might be preferable, and what might those reasons be? We are not speaking here of very specific regulatory interventions that may incidentally have such an effect. For example, regulating doping may reduce the overall pie and provide a leg up to smaller teams whose players are (one could hypothesize at least) less likely to partake. This is not relevant

4 Brad R Humphreys and Nicolas M Watanabe, 'Competitive Balance' in Leo H Kahane and Stephen Schmanske (eds), *Oxford Handbook of Sports Economics: The Economics of Sports*, vol 1 (Oxford University Press 2012).

5 Rodney Fort and Joel Maxcy, 'Competitive Balance in Sports Leagues: An Introduction' (2003) 4 Journal of Sports Economics 154.

6 There is a plethora of writings on this score. For a recent paper referencing previous work on this score, see Daniel Read, Aaron CT Smith, and James Skinner, 'A Comparative Analysis of Competitive Balance Between a Closed and an Open League in Rugby League' (2021) 22 Journal of Sports Economics 871.

to our topic. The question is, rather: could a measure taken directly in order to improve competitive balance or increase uncertainty be justified on grounds such as fairness, or integrity of sporting competitions, regardless of the impact on attendance and revenues? Even if this might be possible legally speaking, there is a clear measurement problem, and such an approach may appear as rather deferential to sporting bodies.

Uncertainty of outcomes can be further subdivided into:

- Short-term uncertainty: uncertainty about the outcome in a specific game (eg it is unclear whether Arsenal FC will beat Hull FC next time they meet);[7]
- Mid-term uncertainty: uncertainty about the outcome of a competition (will Arsenal FC win the Premiership in 2024?)
- Long-term uncertainty: uncertainty about domination over a more extended time period (will Arsenal FC, for example, win the Premiership eight to ten times in the next ten seasons?)

Despite definitional problems, competitive balance is regarded as desirable. Regulators tend to strive for medium- to long-term uncertainty, as the marginal utility of consumers increases correspondingly. We stated above that there are theoretical underpinnings for regulators' pursuit of competitive balance in sports. But is there empirical support showing that it matters in terms of affecting the interest to attend? It is of course difficult to construct the counterfactual, as there is no appropriate treatment-control group. Comparing, say, the NFL (National Football League) in the United States, where there is regulation of competitive balance with the British Premiership where there is (almost) none cannot lead to any robust conclusions. Still, within this caveat, there have been some attempts to look for empirical support.

Szymanski looks into attendance data for the US NBA (National Basketball Association) and finds no clear empirical evidence that uncertainty is correlated to attendance increase.[8] He cites the example of Chicago Bulls—a dominant team by any reasonable benchmark during the late eighties and early nineties—and finds that its period of dominance correlates with record attendances.

Pawlowski and Anders asked roughly the same question in the realm of the Bundesliga, the top German professional football league. Their results highlight a positive effect on attendance, when either the home or the away team (or both) still have a theoretical chance to win the championship. Paradoxically, perhaps, they find no comparable supportive evidence when the same teams still compete to

[7] Even though there is nothing uncertain about this contest. Not even the most ardent fan of Hull FC would harbour a tinge of hope that his team could ever prevail over mighty Arsenal FC.

[8] Stefan Szymanski, 'Incentives and Competitive Balance' (2003) 3 European Sport Management Quarterly 11.

qualify for the UEFA Champions League. While they find no evidence that spectators prefer the home team to play an inferior team, their results suggest that visiting superstars' teams (the equivalent to the Chicago Bulls) boost attendance figures in the German Bundesliga.[9] The latter suggests that the correlation between uncertainty of outcome and attendance is not so straightforward.

Of course, various other factors might have influenced this outcome. It should also be kept in mind that an additional difficulty in measuring competitive balance is that changes occur over a relatively long time period, and that any increase or drop in attendance may not follow immediately. The Chicago Bulls' dominance, for example, did not lead to a sudden drop in attendance, even though the outcome of sports encounters was largely a foregone conclusion for a considerable amount of time, Szymanski has claimed.[10] He goes on to argue that being a sports fan is often a lifetime allegiance, and fans could expect a similar dominance by their team in the medium to long run. If the purpose of regulation is long-run uncertainty, not even the Bulls managed to defy the realization of this objective. Of course, the strength of this argument depends on whether a period of six to eight years is representative, whether dominance should be measured with respect to the performance of one club, or rather of all clubs that make it to playoffs, etc.

The next question is how express competitive balance in regulatory language.

2.2 Approximating Competitive Balance

A few imaginative proposals have been offered in the literature as to how competitive balance, or lack thereof, could be measured. Among these proposals, Noll-Scully[11] measurements have attracted a lot of attention. This method compares the standard deviations of winning percentages in the league with the standard deviations one would expect in a perfectly competitive league. A perfectly competitive league is one where every team has a 50 per cent chance of winning a game. On the other hand, the Spearman rank correlation coefficient (named after Charles Spearman, who developed it for a different field)[12] looks at correlation between finishing positions of clubs in, say, two consecutive seasons. In a perfectly competitive league, there should be no correlation between the position where clubs had finished in the previous and the following season. This exercise can be repeated. If the league becomes less competitive, the Spearman value will move away from

[9] Tim Pawlowski and Christoph Anders, 'Stadium Attendance in German Professional Football: The (Un)importance of Uncertainty of Outcome Reconsidered' (2012) 19 Applied Economics Letters 1553.

[10] Szymanski, 'Incentives and Competitive Balance' (n 8).

[11] See Roger Noll, 'The Organization of Sports Leagues' (2004) 19 Oxford Review of Economic Policy 530.

[12] Charles Spearman, 'The Proof and Measurement of Association Between Two Things' (1904) 15 American Journal of Psychology 72.

zero. Teams who do better will obtain positive values, whereas teams who do worse will have negative ones.

The US MLB (Major League Baseball) commissioned a blue-ribbon report, which suggested a different measurement of competitive balance: namely, the RRRPP, the acronym for 'regularly recurring hope of reaching postseason play'.[13] Why the focus on postseason? In US sports, the postseason (playoffs) is key to winning overall. Clubs that do not make it to postseason are eliminated from pursuing the championship. RRRPP is, of course, a proxy for competitive balance, and an 'idiosyncratic' proxy one might add, as postseason does not exist in the British Premiership, for example. RRRPP is also tough to measure, but the key is this: it allows leeway, as it does not strive for absolute parity. *Ex post facto*, one can always assess the precision of RRRPP measurements by comparing predictions with the position of clubs. And, of course, alternance of clubs in playoffs would be the best indicator of competitive balance in line with this benchmark.

2.3 Takeaways for Regulating Competitive Balance

The key points of our discussion so far are:

First, the case for competitive balance is contested. The argument in favour of pursuing it certainly relies on strong theoretical underpinnings, but the empirical proof that it matters is not fully supportive of the theoretical case for regulation. If at all, the takeaway for regulators is that addressing competitive balance is probably warranted, but the importance of such initiatives should not be unduly exaggerated either.

Secondly, to promote competitive balance, regulation should impose disciplines on the conduct of participants and not require particular outcomes. Indeed, it would make little sense to regulate to ensure an (alternating) *ex-ante* identified champion, when the intellectual foundation for regulating competitive balance is the promotion of uncertainty.

Thirdly, absolute parity across competitors is an illusion, and it is perhaps unwarranted as well. Absolute parity would be akin to knowledge *ex ante* of the outcome, and of course this would have eliminated uncertainty in the first place. Some room is left for uncertainty, and there are good reasons for it: with the same (symmetric) means, if some room is left for ingenuity to produce results, there will be gains from innovation as some agents will produce winning formulas that others might find it plausible to imitate, and so on and so forth. We thus use here the term 'uncertainty' as Knight[14] and Keynes[15] understood the term; that is, when precise

[13] Paul C Weiler and others, *Sports and the Law: Texts, Cases, and Problems* (6th edn, West Publishing 2018), discuss it in sufficient detail.

[14] Frank H Knight, *Risk, Uncertainty, and Profit* (The Riverside Press 1921).

[15] John Maynard Keynes, *A Treatise on Probability* (Macmillan 1921).

probabilistic estimations are hard to obtain ('radical uncertainty' is the term that Kay and King,[16] who have recently revisited the definitions used by Knight and Keynes, have chosen to express that concept).

3. Competitive Balance in US Sports

The United States was the first country to seriously reflect upon the regulation of competitive balance in sports. There is no unitary model that has been followed across sports, and variations do exist. Some overlapping elements, which we will be discussing shortly, show a decisive turn away from 'leaving it to the market'.

3.1 The Context: Closed Leagues

In 1876, William A Hulbert of the Chicago White Sox laid down the foundational arguments and design for a closed professional league. Closed referred to the *numerus clausus* (limited number) of teams that would be invited to participate in the competition. The competition had to be organized professionally: businesspeople would be called in to invest and run teams, and players would concentrate on playing. The rate of return on investment would be buoyed by the *ex ante* assurance that teams would stay in the market ('closed' leagues), as well as by the geographic exclusivity that the teams enjoyed. From each defined geographic area, only one team would participate in the league. Assuming the league was the relevant product market, this would bestow a monopoly position and lock in the resulting profits. New teams could be admitted (expansion), but under stringent rules.[17] Rules would develop in this context over time. Nowadays the vast majority of the baseball clubs (three-quarters of the clubs) must approve an expansion, and if the location of a new club (or the location to which an existing club is moving) is less than 100 miles from where an incumbent is located, the latter must agree. Of course, none of this prevents the emergence of a new competing league. However, in practice, such challengers in US baseball have not proved successful. Nor have the competing leagues (including leagues abroad) been a significant competitor in the recruitment of top players.

The idea of a closed league offered a few advantages to the owners: with no external competitors realistically able to bid for the best players (precisely because the leagues have been closed), the available players could only be hired by one

[16] John Kay and Mervyn King, *Radical Uncertainty: Decision-Making Beyond Numbers* (WW Norton & Company 2020).

[17] Weiler and others (n 13) offer a very detailed account of the historical evolution. Compare Gerald W Scully, *The Market Structure for Sports* (University of Chicago Press 1995) 8ff.

league. Thus, the payroll burden would be lower and the supply of talent larger than it would otherwise have been. Owners of clubs became a self-regulated cartel, and some even requested and obtained exemption from antitrust (eg in baseball). Antitrust prosecution did not undo these basic characteristics. In *Mid-South Grizzlies v NFL*,[18] the federal court rejected the complaint by the team that had been denied access to the football league. In the court's view, there was no violation of either section 1 or section 2 of the Sherman Act. The argument was that cities without a team might have found it profitable to organize a rival league. The NFL, in other words, was not an essential facility in this court's view.

Szymanski and Ross criticized this outcome, arguing that the viable antitrust claim was not that a team had been unfairly excluded from the NFL, but that the NFL provided no means to allow new teams to enter the competition. In their view, the maintenance of a closed monopoly league like the NFL constituted a violation of federal antitrust laws.[19]

3.2 The Key Features of Competitive Balance *à l'americaine*

United States sports exhibit three key characteristics that reflect the spirit of 'competitive balance' as understood on the North American continent:

Revenue sharing: while different sports have introduced different modalities, the idea is that some of the total income made will be shared across clubs, to compensate teams with lower revenues (since they also participate in the production of the output sold to the general public).

Draft system for recruitment: the quintessential idea is that teams that performed worse in the previous year are allowed first pick of the new players entering the professional league. The contribution of the best players in the draft to weaker clubs is a boost to competitive balance. Top talents will of course command the highest salaries; this is where the next element, a salary cap, kicks in to ensure equitable distribution of talent across teams. And, of course, top talents do not necessarily make top players over time. There is uncertainty as to how talents will develop, even though the increasing professionalization of sports (through the very

[18] *Mid-South Grizzlies v NFL*, 720 F2d 772 (3d Cir 1983).

[19] Stephen F Ross and Stefan Szymanski, 'Open Competition in League Sports' (2000), available at SSRN <https://ssrn.com/abstract=350960 (last accessed on 18 October 2023)>. In a twin paper (Stephen F Ross and Stefan Szymanski, 'Antitrust, Promotion and Relegation' (2002) 3 Wisconsin Law Review 625), the authors discuss the antitrust issues against the background of both a closed and an open league. No one has ever mounted an antitrust challenge along these lines so far against US closed leagues, and it seems unlikely for various reasons that it would succeed, if submitted. There is the legal issue, and there is of course a wider policy issue. Szymanski discusses the pros and cons of closed leagues leaning on contest theory (meaning a situation in which agents invest irreversibly toward winning a prize) (Szymanski, 'Economics of League Design: Open Versus Closed Systems' in Kahane and Schmanske, *Oxford Handbook of Sports Economics* (n 4)).

sophisticated treatment of data) has been reducing the size of the problem to some extent.

Salary caps: US sports utilize both hard and soft caps (per team, as well as per individual player).[20] Baseball allows overspending by a fixed amount, but those practising it are taxed more. A luxury tax has been introduced, whereby offenders will pay 20 per cent of the overspent amount, 30 per cent if they repeat the offence, and 50 per cent of all overages for any additional offence.

The above does not exhaust the regulatory means aimed at establishing a competitive balance. There are other instruments which in our view are of lesser importance. There are, for example, statutory debt limits (teams cannot spend beyond an agreed percentage of their turnover on players), roster and waiver limits (the least competitive team chooses first from the pool of players about to enter the league; the new drafts, that is), etc.

Some of the means used to bring about a competitive balance have been criticized in literature.[21] Fort and Quirk[22] offer a comprehensive discussion in this realm. It is not the purpose of this contribution to delve in depth into the adequacy of the regulatory means used to ensure competitive balance. Suffice it to state that practice has been receptive to criticism. Rottenberg, for example, in a classic study, criticized the reserve clause in baseball, under which part of a player's contract with a team would be retained upon the contract's expiry—with the result that the players under these contracts were not free to enter into a contract with another team.[23] The reserve clause has been abolished, enabling players to sign with other clubs as free agents. A similar development has taken place in European football since the *Bosman* judgment (discussed in Section 4).

3.3 Empirical Assessment

Fort and Quirk,[24] writing twenty-five years ago, stated that the empirical assessment of the means purporting to ensure competitive balance is a job that still

[20] The difference between the two is largely confined to the consequences of breaking the rule, as both a soft and a hard cap do impose a maximum amount that teams dispose of. But a team can overspend above a soft cap, as long as it is prepared to pay a fee, which is usually known as a 'luxury tax'. Conversely, when a hard cap has been introduced, no team is allowed to spend over the amount fixed, regardless of the circumstances.

[21] Palomino and Rigotti (2000), for example, have argued that revenue sharing increases competitive balance on the one hand, but decreases incentives to win on the other. In their view, under demand maximization, a performance-based reward scheme (used by European sports leagues) may be optimal. Nevertheless, under joint profit maximization, full revenue sharing (used by many US leagues) emerges as the optimal solution. Frederic Palomino and Luca Rigotti, 'The Sport League's Dilemma: Competitive Balance Versus Incentives to Win' (2000) CentER Discussion Paper 2000-109.

[22] Rodney Fort and James Quirk, 'Cross-subsidization, Incentives, and Outcomes in Professional Team Sports Leagues' (1995) 33 Journal of Economic Literature 1265.

[23] Simon Rottenberg, 'The Baseball Players' Labor Market' (1956) 64 Journal of Political Economy 242.

[24] Fort and Quirk (n 22).

needed to be done. This is still nowadays largely the case. If we pick participation in playoffs, then the emerging picture with respect to the MLB (a league with luxury taxes but no salary caps) and the NBA (a league with hard salary caps), as per the RRRPP benchmark, is not that different. In the MLB, only one out of thirty teams did not make it to playoffs in the last ten years (2011–20). Up to sixteen teams in total participated in playoffs during these ten years. In the NBA as well, only one out of thirty teams did not make it to playoffs in the last ten years, whereas up to twenty-two teams in total participated in the playoffs in the given years.

Eight different teams were crowned champions during the same decade in the MLB, and only two (the San Francisco Giants and the Boston Red Sox) won twice. The New York Yankees, the team that is arguably the league's biggest spender, have not won since 2009. In the NBA, seven teams won the championship, with the Golden State Warriors prevailing three times and the Miami Heat twice. But each of these two reached the finals five times, and the Cleveland Cavaliers four times, whereas the San Antonio Spurs were very respectably represented twice in the finals. Based on this information only, it looks as though there are more dominant teams in the NBA than in the MLB. But such conclusions would fail to account for various factors: the importance of network externalities across differently talented players, for one, which are more important in basketball than in baseball. Individual talent and performance count for substantially less in basketball than they do in baseball, which, by any reasonable account, is a very individualistic sport.

For the sake of argument, a look into various European football championships reveals that the distribution of champions across states is practically the same today as it was in the 1950s, and, if at all, even fewer clubs vie for the national title in today's world. Indeed, the dominant teams come out as champions today even more than in the past (see Table 12.1). This may suggest that the absence of strong competitive balance measures leads to greater dominance by fewer clubs. However, as already explained, such direct comparisons across leagues and sports are difficult to draw and could be influenced by a number of factors.

Budzinski and Pawlowski[25] have advanced an interesting defence of regulating competitive balance. Irrespective of the conclusive empirical evidence supporting competitive balance measures, they have argued that what matters is perceived (as opposed to de facto) competitive balance. It matters even more if we accept that what affects market participants' behaviour is how they perceive sports market regulation. Fans, athletes, and/or investors will be attracted to a regulated sport (where competitive balance is the centrepiece of the regulatory scaffolding),

[25] Oliver Budzinski and Tim Pawlowski, 'The Behavioural Economics of Competitive Balance: Implications for League Policy and Championship Management' (2014) Ilmenau Economics Discussion Paper No 89.

Table 12.1 Distribution of European football championships across states, 1951–1960 and 2011–2020*

	Championships 1951–1960	Championships 2011–2020
Germany	5	2 (Bayern 8/10)
Spain	4	3 (Barcelona 6/10)
England	6	6 (Man City 4/10)
France	4	4 (PSG 7/10)
Italy	4	2 (Juventus 9/10)
Portugal	3	2 (Benfica 5/10)

*Table by authors.

because they will believe that, in light of the equality of means available to different competitors, the chances to win are even across the participants. What matters, thus, is not so much what the regulation of competitive balance has produced de facto. What matters is the expectations created by the regulation.

4. Competitive Balance (or the Lack Thereof) in the EU Context

Broadly speaking, the US style mechanisms for ensuring competitive balance are absent from European professional sports.

There is only indirect influence on the competitive balance, as we will see in what follows. There is no draft system, there are no European salary caps, and revenue sharing is more limited. So, the question, when moving into a discussion of the EU legal framework, is more why the issue of competitive balance has not been addressed, rather than how Europe regulates competitive balance.

Football governing bodies have, however, frequently invoked competitive balance in order to justify a number of regulations, with varying success. Famously, in *Bosman*, the Union of European Football Associations (UEFA) claimed that transfer rules preventing players from freely changing clubs upon contract expiry were justified 'by the need to maintain a financial and competitive balance between clubs', an argument which the Court rejected.[26]

[26] Case C-415/93 *Bosman* ECLI:EU:C:1995:463. In ss 105–07, the Court held that transfer rules 'neither preclude the richest clubs from securing the services of the best players nor prevent the availability of financial resources from being a decisive factor in competitive sport, thus considerably altering the balance between clubs'.

In this section, we will concentrate on the regulation of European football ('soccer' in US parlance), which follows the 'European sport model' or the 'pyramid' system: an open hierarchy of leagues with promotion and relegation, where professional and amateur sport are under the remit of the same national governing bodies and even take part in the same pyramid. There is no *numerus clausus* and clubs do not have geographical monopoly (unless one considers de facto monopolies due to market power).

Under the circumstances, any comparison with the US model is limited, not just due to the different organization of the leagues, but also conceptually. The term 'competitive balance' is used in European legal and policy debates in a deeply ambiguous way. The same measure is sometimes described as a tool for achieving competitive balance, and sometimes as indicating a distortion to competitive balance.

4.1 Who Does What? National Federations, UEFA, and the EU

Before discussing competitive balance in the European context, it is useful to say a few more words about the regulatory set-up. Unlike the US model, where closed professional leagues essentially regulate themselves, the European model is based on a single governing federation for the sport as a whole on both the national and European levels. Clubs are, in turn, members of those federations. National football federations are bound to follow the rules of the European federation (UEFA), and, in turn, UEFA is subordinate to the global federation, the Federation International of Football Associations (FIFA). Thus, football is regulated by national football federations at the national level, by UEFA at the European level, and by FIFA at the global level. In this context, and for the purposes of this study, UEFA is particularly important as, historically, it has been the author of important measures linked to competitive balance considerations, such as the rules on transfers, training compensation, and financial fair play. The authority of UEFA to enact these rules is, of course, not God-given, but stems from a conferral of powers by its members (one that is, however, not so easy to reverse).

In practice, in other words, UEFA emerges as the main 'football legislator' in Europe. While originally confined to organizing European competitions, its role shifted towards legislating the conditions for participating in its club and national team competitions, specifically the Champions League, the Europa and Conference Leagues, and the Euros. Given the enormous economic significance of these events, UEFA was able to impose licensing conditions that clubs needed to observe, which go far beyond what are usually considered purely sporting rules (eg the permissible number of substitutes used in a match) and introduce, among other things, nationality rules, rules on transfers, and, most recently, financial discipline (Financial Fair Play, or 'FFP'), etc.

While football, like sport in general, is to a large extent privately regulated, public regulators at the national and EU level still have a role to play. In this respect, the EU has historically taken an outsized role, due in large part to the transnational nature of the sports business. In particular, the EU has 're-regulated' sports by applying the rules on free movement of workers and services and competition to discipline measures taken by sports federations. This has been achieved both through Court decisions and decisions of the Commission as an antitrust authority. The *Bosman* case, outlawing nationality caps and restrictive transfer rules, is usually held up as an important example. More recently, the *ISU* case has confirmed that the European Commission as an antitrust regulator can also take decisions that have an impact on the organization of sports competitions.[27]

The so-called 'sporting exception', which used to be a prominent element of EU sports law debates, has by now effectively vanished, and has been replaced by softer arguments invoking the 'specificity' of sport. Instead of autonomy from EU law, the sporting world can, at best, hope that the specific nature of sport will be given some weight at the stage of justifying certain restrictive measures.[28] Thus, whenever UEFA or others seek to regulate sports, at least outside of 'pure' sporting rules such as the number of players on the pitch or the tasks of referees, it has to take account of the limits imposed by EU law.

Therefore, EU law is certainly capable of having some impact on competitive balance, even though it does not regulate competitive balance head on. The question is, however, in which direction regulatory intervention through EU law is taking sport competitions. For example, striking down a measure taken by a sports federation under the free movement rules has typically meant facilitating the movement of players from one club to another, making it more difficult for clubs to retain the players they trained or contracted with. The effect of such rulings on competitive balance is ambiguous. *Bosman*, for example, is typically portrayed as having *reduced* the competitive balance by helping the small group of rich leagues and teams more easily sign the best players from across the EU. Binder and Findlay show that, while *Bosman* has not had significant negative effects on competitive balance within leagues 'importing' the greatest number of players, it has reduced the competitive balance across national leagues, ie in the Champions League.[29] What is implicit in this argument is that greater player mobility between leagues and clubs *reduces* competitive balance. Pearson has argued, on the other hand, that the

[27] Case T–93/18 *International Skating Union v European Commission*, ECLI:EU:T:2020:610, Judgment of 16 December 2020.

[28] See eg Stephen Weatherill, 'Anti-Doping Revisited-the Demise of the Rule of "Purely Sporting Interest"?' (2006) 27 European Competition Law Review 645 and Borja Garcia and Stephen Weatherill, 'Engaging with the EU in Order to Minimize Its Impact: Sport and the Negotiation of the Treaty of Lisbon' (2012) 19 Journal of European Public Policy 238.

[29] John J Binder and Murray Findlay. 'The Effects of the *Bosman* Ruling on National and Club Teams in Europe' (2012) 13 Journal of Sports Economics 107.

post-*Bosman* UEFA transfer rules reduce competitive balance by still making the free movement of players too difficult due to ever-increasing transfer fees.[30] This assumes, conversely, that greater player mobility *increases* competitive balance.

Similar uncertainty arises with respect to competition law. At first sight, competition law would seem to improve competitive balance. After all, it is meant to facilitate competition by increasing rivalry between competitors (in this case, clubs). However, the measures that sports federations take to (ostensibly) improve competitive balance typically involve an agreement among competitors to jointly engage in or refrain from some activities, which may be prohibited by Article 101 of the Treaty on the Functioning of the European Union (TFEU). For example, agreements to share revenue, jointly allocate players to clubs (such as a draft), or cap salaries, would in all likelihood be at least prima facie considered anti-competitive. Alternatively, the rules adopted by sporting bodies could be challenged as unilateral abuses of a dominant position under Article 102 TFEU; indeed, sporting bodies have in the past been found to hold a position of dominance.[31]

To the extent they have pro-competitive aspects by effectively addressing a real competitive balance concern, they may escape the competition law scrutiny, whether under Article 101 or under Article 102 TFEU. And, of course, competition authorities may be reluctant to challenge such measures in the first place. The fact remains, however, that competition law is, at best, neutral, and, at worst, an obstacle to the adoption of competitive balance measures. A different picture may emerge when it comes to rules that are, at the same time and perhaps for the same reasons, anti-competitive and *reduce* competitive balance. In that scenario, competition law would incidentally prevent harm to competitive balance. But the fact remains that, when it comes to genuine proactive attempts to tackle it, competition law is more likely to get in the way than help.

All of this does not, however, mean that EU bodies are actively on the lookout for competitive balance measures to strike down. Recent history shows that the EU has been a rather reluctant enforcer, at least in the area of football. European Union institutions, including the European Commission, have preferred a negotiated approach. While constantly pointing out that EU law can be applied to scrutinize the sporting world, the focus has rather been on its autonomy, conditioned upon somewhat vaguely described 'good governance' principles. This is at least partly related to Article 165 TFEU, the first Treaty provision expressly dealing with sports, introduced by the Treaty of Lisbon in 2009.[32] While Article

[30] Geoff Pearson, 'Sporting Justifications under EU Free Movement and Competition Law: The Case of the Football "Transfer System"' (2015) 21 European Law Journal 220.

[31] Some examples can be found in the judgments in *Piau* (Case T–193/02, *Laurent Piau v Commission* [2005] ECLI:EU:T:2005:22); *Meca-Medina* (Case C–519/04 P, *David Meca-Medina and Igor Majcen v Commission* [2006] ECLI:EU:C:2006:492); and *MOTOE* (Case C–49/07, *Motosykletistiki Omospondia Ellados NPID (MOTOE) v Elliniko Dimosio* [2008] ECLI: EU:C:2008:376).

[32] Stephen Weatherill, *Principles and Practice in EU Sports Law* (Oxford University Press 2017) ch 6 offers an excellent discussion of this provision.

165 lays the groundwork for an active EU sports policy, it also enjoins EU institutions to 'take account of the specific nature of sport' and does not provide a basis for harmonization of Member State laws. On the face of it, this provision does not prevent the Commission or the Court from scrutinizing the measures of sporting bodies as they have done in the past and may even in some respects be read as reinforcing future scrutiny (eg the emphasis on 'openness in sporting competitions' and 'moral integrity of sportsmen and sportswomen'). Nevertheless, it seems to have shifted the emphasis from enforcement onto coordination and supporting action.[33]

4.2 Little or Nothing on Competitive Balance

While UEFA justifies many of its measures by invoking competitive balance, there are no 'classic' US-style competitive balance instruments in European football. Rhetoric aside, there is currently no instrument that directly serves the competitive balance objective in European football competitions. At best, some UEFA instruments pursue that objective partly, indirectly, or inconclusively.

As explained above, UEFA has in the past unsuccessfully defended restrictions on player transfers by invoking competitive balance. Several aspects of UEFA's current transfer rules, based on a 2001 arrangement with the European Commission, also invoke that objective.

This is true, for example, of UEFA's training compensation and solidarity mechanism, entitling clubs that initially trained young players to payments on the occasion of their subsequent transfers. It is questionable to what extent the 'trickle-down' logic of the training compensation and solidarity payments is a genuine competitive balance tool. For one thing, the clubs making the payments will frequently not even be competing with the beneficiary clubs, because they play in different countries or different leagues. Moreover, while undoubtedly redistributive in nature, the financial effects of the mechanism are too small to have a meaningful impact on competitive balance. Indeed, as Laskowski shows,[34] the solidarity mechanism has an almost negligible effect on competitive balance, and most of its beneficiaries are concentrated among the largest leagues and clubs. Thus, a 2018 study for the European Commission points out that, 'overall, solidarity compensations directly linked to transfers (i.e. training compensation and solidarity mechanism), account for less than 2% of the total international transfer fees … As a result, the

[33] For different takes on this see Mislav Mataija, *Private Regulation and the Internal Market* (Oxford University Press 2016); Tom Serby, 'The State of EU Sports Law: Lessons from UEFA's "Financial Fair Play" Regulations' (2016) 16 The International Sports Law Journal 37; Stephen Weatherill, Stephen, *Principles and Practice in EU Sports Law* (Oxford University Press 2017).

[34] Jakub Laskowski, 'Solidarity Compensation Framework in Football Revisited' (2019) 18 The International Sports Law Journal 150.

redistribution linked to transfers has no significant positive impact on addressing the issue of competitive balance.'[35]

As the solidarity and training compensation mechanism illustrates, a system of resource redistribution is not necessarily a competitive balance system. This is a solidarity scheme that generally tackles, albeit to a minimal extent, the distribution of economic resources among football clubs. It simply does not target the uncertainty of outcomes in any particular competition. In other words, even if it were much larger in scope, it would be a rather poor mechanism for broadening the pool of competitive clubs in the Champions League, to take one of these metrics as an example. The clubs that the solidarity scheme is benefiting may not even be competing in the Champions League in a particular season, or they may very well already be among the top teams in the league.

The so-called 'home-grown player rule', requiring clubs to have on their roster a minimum number of locally trained players, is also sometimes portrayed as a competitive balance measure. Of course, vertical integration is costly. Young players who make their reputation in feeder clubs can leave at the end of their contract, the feeder clubs receiving, at best, a compensation fee which could be a far cry from the market value of their trainees. The uncertainty surrounding the future evolution of young trainees can only act as a disincentive for feeder clubs that cannot pass on the training costs to the families of the trainees. The actual effects of the home-grown players rule are, however, also ambiguous from a competitive balance point of view,[36] as this regime walks on a tightrope with respect to compatibility with EU free movement rules, since favouring locally trained players amounts de facto to favouring the nationals of the club's state.[37]

Finally, probably the biggest tool capable of addressing competitive balance available to UEFA is the revenues from European competitions, which it distributes. From one point of view, revenues from European competitions offer a boost to smaller clubs, because they are quite significant relative to their other revenues. Nevertheless, the distribution is obviously regressive, as the larger and more successful clubs are entitled to significantly larger shares, not just due to their success in any given year, but also depending on 'coefficients' reflecting results in previous years and the size of their TV markets.[38] Thus, it seems quite clear that UEFA's

[35] Commission, 'An Update on Change Drivers and Economic and Legal Implications of Transfers of Players, Final Report to the DG Education, Youth, Culture and Sport of the European Commission' (March 2018) 59 <https://sport.ec.europa.eu/sites/default/files/report-transfer-of-players-2018-en.pdf>.

[36] Laskowski (n 35).

[37] Paul Downward and others, 'An Assessment of the Compatibility of UEFA's Home Grown Player Rule with Article 45 TFEU' (2014) 39 European Law Review 493. Case C–325/08, *Olympique Lyonnais SASP v Olivier Bernard and Newcastle UFC* [2010] ECLI:EU:C:2010:143, shows that such schemes could, generally speaking, be justified. However, UEFA's Home Grown rules have not yet been tested.

[38] Distribution to clubs from the 2021/22 UEFA Champions League, UEFA Europa League and UEFA Europa Conference League, and the 2021 UEFA Super Cup, 'Payments for the Qualifying Phases,

distribution of revenues does not help the competitive balance among the clubs participating in European competitions. It may also have a negative effect on the competitive balance in national leagues as it reinforces the economic strength of the most successful teams qualifying for European competitions. This effect may be particularly strong in the smaller leagues because of the relative size of UEFA payments (even if those payments are very small slices of UEFA's pie) compared to the other revenues of domestic clubs. It is true that UEFA attempts to offset this through 'solidarity payments' (not to be confused with solidarity payments based on transfer fees, discussed earlier in this chapter) to non-participating clubs. However, these payments are, relatively speaking, small, and as they are distributed to a large number of clubs, unlikely to have a real impact on the competitive balance.[39] This effect is compounded by the fact that access to UEFA competitions is skewed. Bigger clubs in lucrative national championships have a higher chance to access UEFA competitions. As future participation is to a large extent a function of past performance, for some clubs, participation in UEFA competitions comes close to a self-fulfilling prophecy.

4.3 Indirectly: The FFP?

The FFP rules of UEFA were designed to ensure the financial stability of clubs after the magnitude of debt of some European behemoths was revealed. The debt, to be sure, was sometimes towards third parties and on one occasion to the owner of the club, who had acted as a 'sugar daddy' (wealthy benefactor). Since medium- to long-term viability cannot be conditioned on similar behaviour, UEFA moved in and, through the FFP, aimed to provide a framework to guarantee the financial sustainability of clubs. Some have claimed that FFP is a competitive balance instrument.[40] Others have deplored it, as smaller clubs were deprived of potential 'sugar daddies' and had to live within the confines of a meagre income.

The core of the FFP rules[41] is a break-even requirement, under which the licence of a club to participate in UEFA competitions depends on expenses not significantly exceeding income (no more than 5 million euros) over a period of three years. There is a limited possibility for clubs to maintain a deficit of up to 30 million

Solidarity Payments for Non-participating Clubs' (20 May 2021) <https://editorial.uefa.com/resources/0269-125fde34ba54-30a4c9aeea13-1000/20210520_circular_2021_35_en.pdf>.

[39] 4 per cent in 2021/2022, ibid.

[40] Vsevolod Grabar and Konstantin Sonin, 'Financial Restrictions and Competitive Balance in Sports Leagues' (2018), available at SSRN <https://ssrn.com/abstract=3242351>; Daniel Plumley, Girish Ramchandani, and Rob Wilson, 'Mind the Gap: An Analysis of Competitive Balance in the English Football League System' (2018) 18 International Journal of Sport Management and Marketing 357.

[41] UEFA Club Licensing and Financial Fair Play Regulations; UEFA Club Licensing and Financial Sustainability Regulations, accessible through <www.uefa.com/insideuefa/news/0246-0e796c23daa9-41f78afb0c7a-1000--financial-sustainability/>.

euros if such deficit is covered by its shareholders or related parties. All this is, at the moment of writing, effectively suspended through flexibilities introduced due to the Covid-19 pandemic. This has helped trigger a reconsideration of the entire FFP regulation, which has led to a concrete proposal endorsed by the UEFA competent authorities in April 2022. While the basic disciplines are still those embedded in the 2018 edition of the statute,[42] the sanctions for violating rules have changed, and luxury taxes have been introduced (emulating thus the logic of some US sports, and possibly approximating more closely a classic competitive balance instrument): a European club overspending its football-related income defined in the statutes (and the ensuing break-even rules) will pay additional luxury taxes to a pot that UEFA will administer. Furthermore, clubs cannot spend more than 70 per cent of their football-related income on salaries for their professional players. Together, the introduction of luxury taxes and salary caps constitute the main innovations of the new regulation.[43]

The rules define income as including gate receipts, broadcasting rights, income from merchandising and sponsoring, and the transfer fees received. Expenses cannot overshoot the income thus defined. This is, for all practical purposes, what UEFA calls the 'break-even rule', which all clubs participating in its competitions must observe. Importantly, section E of Annex X of the above-cited regulation imposes a cap on acceptable deviations from the break-even rule, meaning that a subsidy from the club's owners cannot, in principle, compensate a deficit. Expenses include wages and various operating expenses, but also the transfer fees. Certain categories of expenses are excluded from consideration, such as expenditures on stadiums and youth facilities.

Consequently, the current version of the FFP on paper does not address revenue sharing, salary caps, and the like. Its effects on competitive balance are secondary at best, as we explain below. Before we do that, a few words on the institutional dimension of FFP seem warranted.

The FFP rules are applied by a body specifically set up for this purpose by UEFA, the Club Financial Control Body (CFCB). The CFCB's decisions can be appealed to an Appeals Board, a UEFA body comprising jurists and former judges (in its original composition at least). Appeals against the final decision are subject to a review by the Court of Arbitration for Sports (CAS). The UEFA bodies and the CAS have, over the years, dealt with a number of cases. In a notable recent decision, for example, Manchester City successfully appealed a UEFA decision imposing a two-year suspension for violations of the FFP rules, with the CAS significantly reducing the sanction and thwarting the ban altogether.[44]

[42] 2018 UEFA Club Licensing and Financial Fair Play Regulations <https://documents.uefa.com/v/u/MFxeqLNKelkYyh5JSafuhg>.

[43] See arts 65ff of UEFA Club Licensing and Financial Sustainability Regulations <https://documents.uefa.com/r/LjQqEb3_Iy8CFzkDqPkK2Q/I5SB6jzim0MofZDhT4g6gw>.

[44] *Manchester City FC v UEFA* CAS 2020/A/6785.

We have argued that it is important to understand what the FFP rules do, and what they do not do. Recall that, while sometimes held up as a competitive balance instrument, the rules themselves never even mention that concept. In fact, Article 2 of the UEFA Club Licensing and Financial Fair Play Regulations provides a rather detailed list of objectives of the FFP in which competitive balance simply does not figure: 'economic and financial capability' of clubs, their 'transparency and credibility', protection of creditors, 'discipline and rationality in club football finances', encouraging clubs to 'operate on the basis of their own revenues' and spend responsibly, and, more vaguely, 'the long-term viability and sustainability of European club football'. This makes clear what is already evident from the substance of the rules: the objective is to improve the clubs' financial stability and prevent excessive spending.

Thus, the FFP may improve competitive balance only indirectly, if at all. For example, if we assume that the more successful clubs are the ones that are more likely to violate FFP (because they overspend on transfers and wages, making them more successful), implementing FFP rules will provide a leg up for the other competitors. Generally, however, there is no reason to think that this assumption holds.

On the other hand, even if all clubs were equally likely to violate FFP, more successful clubs stand to lose more through the application of FFP, in absolute terms, as they tend to attract wealthier investors. Similarly, wealthier clubs may be more likely than others to seek to draw on the income of their owners or shareholders, which the FFP impedes them from doing.

Furthermore, one could argue that spotty enforcement or a lack of agreement over what the FFP rules entail will increase the risk of clubs seeking to game the system by violating the rules to obtain an advantage over their competitors. In other words, the competitive balance problem could arise because some clubs 'defect' from the FFP rules while others do not. In those circumstances, strictly applying the FFP rules may be necessary in order to restore competitive balance. But this does not mean that the FFP rules are a competitive balance instrument, when compared to the baseline scenario.

All in all, the FFP is a highly imprecise instrument. It is club-specific, and not competition-wide. In other words, the FFP rules do not take into account the clubs' position relative to their competitors in the national league. Vast disparities in terms of income as well as sporting success within a single league are not a concern for the FFP, as long as both the more successful and less successful clubs respect the FFP rules. Moreover, the FFP binds only clubs participating in UEFA competitions. A club that usually does not qualify (eg a mid-level club in a league from which only few teams qualify to European competitions) is not disciplined by the UEFA's FFP rules. While some national leagues have their own versions of FFP rules, this is by no means universal.

As for the European competitions themselves, the effects of FFP on competitive balance are also likely to be indirect or ambiguous, because the application of the rules does not depend on any club's competitive position within, say, the Champions League. Nevertheless, the impact (if any) may be more pronounced here to the extent that some clubs are more likely to be repeat players, and the UEFA's FFP rules only apply to clubs participating in European competitions.

One may go even further and argue that true competitive balance instruments can only work in the context of a closed league, as in the US examples. This is because the effect of a competitive balance measure, like a salary cap, can be directly measured from one season to the next, with more or less the same set of clubs subject to the mechanisms. Any instrument that is applied in an open league (such as a national league with promotion and relegation, which partly changes the set of participants every year) or in a competition which draws participants from different leagues every year (like European club competitions, whose set of participants depends on the final standings in national leagues as well as yearly qualifications) is by definition less direct, and its effect is more difficult to measure. As an example, Gayant and Le Pape propose an adjusted model for measuring competitive balance in open leagues.[45] But it is by no means excluded that a 'classic' competitive balance instrument like a salary cap can be used in the context of an open league; one example is English rugby, which we will discuss later.

Empirical studies disagree on whether FFP rules have (so far) helped the competitive balance in European football. Even those that do find a positive effect tend to suggest that it has not been large. A few authors portray FFP as a long-term risk for competitive balance. Sass has suggested that FFP prevents smaller clubs from overspending, ie investing for the future. As a result, incumbents will become even more entrenched because of the 'glory hunter phenomenon': 'If a club becomes more successful, it is able to attract more and more spectators, which increases the club's market size and future success, which in turn increases market size even further.'[46] Peeters and Syzmanski come to a similar conclusion.[47] Birkhäuser, Kaserer, and Urban similarly argue that the FFP 'freezes existent hierarchies and reduces competition'.[48] Based on a study of the five top leagues in Europe, Plumley, Ramchandani, and Wilson conclude that there has been a statistically significant decline in overall competitive balance in Spain, Germany, and France, but not in England and Italy, where there is no significant difference. Like Sass, they suggest that this decline in competitive balance may be an 'unintended consequence' of

[45] Jean-Pascal Gayant and Nicolas Le Pape, 'Mesure de la "Competitive Balance" dans les ligues de sports professionnels. Faut-il distinguer les ligues fermées des ligues avec promotion et relégation?' (2015) 66 Revue économique 427.

[46] Markus Sass, 'Glory Hunters, Sugar Daddies, and Long-Term Competitive Balance under UEFA Financial Fair Play' (2016) 17 Journal of Sports Economics 148.

[47] Thomas Peeters and Stefan Szymanski, 'Financial Fair Play in European Football' (2014) 29 Economic Policy 343.

[48] Stephan Birkhäuser, Christoph Kaserer, and Daniel Urban, 'Did UEFA's Financial Fair Play Harm Competition in European Football Leagues?' (2019) 13 Review of Managerial Science 113.

FFP.[49] Freestone and Manoli, by contrast, argue that FFP has not reduced competitive balance in the UK Premier League, and that it may have improved it; the latter point is, however, as the authors recognize, based on a mere two seasons of reductions in the Herfindahl concentration index, and therefore rather inconclusive.[50]

While beyond the scope of this chapter, the FFP's troubles with EU law are a lingering question that should not be forgotten. A reference to the CJEU asking whether the system is compatible with EU competition law was declared inadmissible.[51] Several authors have argued that the FFP is, in fact, an unjustifiable restriction of competition, or have criticized the EU institutions for failing to act.[52] Some have argued that hard salary caps may be less anti-competitive and thus more palatable from an EU law perspective.[53] On a political level, representatives of the European Commission have expressed tentative support for the FFP,[54] while always bracketed by the need to ensure compatibility with EU law. In other words, the message from the EU has so far been inconclusive.

5. Concluding Reflections: Should the EU Look More Like the US?

In this chapter, we have presented two different sports regulation models, one heavily targeted towards achieving competitive balance, and the other that, despite paying plenty of lip service, is in practice quite dismissive of those concerns. They cannot both be right, unless of course the underlying differences justify a different approach. Thus, it is necessary to ask if there are such differences and what they may be.

To begin with, the US model is that of a closed league, whereas the European model is open. This difference does not say much per se. It is rather what this

[49] Plumley, Ramchandani, and Wilson (n 41) 130.

[50] Christopher John Freestone and Argyro Elisavet Manoli, 'Financial Fair Play and Competitive Balance in the Premier League' (2017) 7 Sport, Business and Management 188.

[51] Case C-299/15 *Striani v UEFA and URBSFA* [2015] ECLI:EU:C:2015:519.

[52] Oliver Budzinski, 'The Competition Economics of Financial Fair Play' (2014) Ilmenau Economics Discussion Papers vol 19, no 85, available at SSRN <https://ssrn.com/abstract=2409632>; Serby (n 34); Jesse Kalashyan, 'The Game Behind the Game: UEFA's Financial Fair Play Regulations and the Need to Field a Substitute' (2021) 18 European Competition Journal 1.

[53] Serby (n 34) 45–46.

[54] European Commission and UEFA, 'Joint Statement by Vice-President Joaquin Almunia and President Michel Platini' (21 March 2012) <www.uefa.com/MultimediaFiles/Download/uefaorg/EuropeanUnion/01/77/21/58/1772158_DOWNLOAD.pdf>. See also speech of former Commissioner Androulla Vassiliou, '"Financial Fair Play" Helping to Preserve the Real Values of Football, says Commissioner' (Informal meeting of EU Sport Ministers Rome, 21 October 2014) <https://ec.europa.eu/commission/presscorner/detail/en/SPEECH_14_706>. The FFP, as well as—more vaguely—competitive balance initiatives, is also expressly supported in the *2018 Arrangement for Cooperation between the European Commission and UEFA*, C (2018) 876 final, 19 February 2018 <https://editorial.uefa.com/resources/0242-0f842d5d2fe8-0bc0116a4b42-1000/arrangement_for_cooperation_uefa_ec_-_2018.pdf>.

difference entails that matters most. United States teams are playing for the championship ring. A typical European football team, on the other hand, is playing for the title in the national competition; participation in an UEFA competition; and to avoid relegation (because of the ensuing loss of income, which could be quite dramatic, especially in some leagues). Does the fact that the European clubs participating in open leagues compete for multiple achievements and not just league titles mean that there is no need to discuss competitive balance in Europe? Or does it only mean that the discussion should be refocused? Should stakeholders, for example, privilege the introduction of specific elements of competitive balance regulation only, say pool sharing (which could operate through compulsory centralized TV rights) to reduce the gap between high and low earners?[55]

Another complexity, as compared to the United States, is the existence of several national leagues. The clubs in those leagues compete only partially, but in significant ways: first, in European competitions (if they qualify); secondly, in the market for talent. At the same time, as explained above, UEFA's rules such as the FFP are in many cases limited to European competitions, while national leagues may or may not be covered by such rules. This creates regulatory divergence, which may have spillover effects. For example, one league may try to obtain an advantage in the player transfer market by not introducing a national regulation of competitive balance. It was widely reported, for example, that Spanish rules on financial fair play led to the transfer of Lionel Messi, one of the biggest stars in world football, to Paris Saint-Germain (PSG).[56]

We will entertain these questions in what follows. But first, we would like to highlight that some European sports do know of legal institutions *à l'americaine*. English rugby did introduce a salary cap, and, in a recent award, an arbitral tribunal (*Premier League Ltd v Saracens Ltd*[57]) was asked to decide whether the salary cap violated EU competition law. The arbitral tribunal (comprising the Rt Hon Lord Dyson, Aidan Robertson QC, and Jeremy Summers) found that the Rugby League salary cap was consistent with EU antitrust law as it did not constitute either an object infringement or an effect infringement. It found no infringement of UK law either.

5.1 The Substantive Issue

Let us start with the second question we asked above: in order to ensure competitive balance, is it sufficient or even advantageous if the most relevant sub-competitions

55 For one proposal, see Gayant and Le Pape (n 46).

56 Reuters, 'Keeping Messi Would Have Been a Financial "Risk" for FC Barcelona, Club Says' (*France 24*, 6 August 2021)<www.france24.com/en/sport/20210806-keeping-messi-would-have-been-a-financial-risk-for-fc-barcelona-club-says>.

57 Decision of the Disciplinary Panel, *In the matter of Premiership Rugby Salary Regulations, Premier League Ltd v Saracens Ltd* (SR/Adhocsport/201/2019).

(like the race for the championship or the fight against relegation) are 'balanced' among a narrow oligopoly of contenders?[58] Does the market take care of itself, or, at least, are we so unsure about the merits of intervention that we might prefer to leave the status quo undisturbed?

There are circumstances where even oligopolies are destabilized. What if, for example, a club—any club—complained that the financing of Manchester City or PSG, the two teams owned by governments, amounted to a form of state aid, perhaps violating EU rules on foreign subsidies?

Even if justified, condemning one or both of those teams would not necessarily mean that the road is wide open for introducing competitive balance in European sports. Indeed, the rationale for intervention against overspending is not necessarily one of competitive balance, as we have argued. Even from a competitive balance point of view, the argument against intervening would be that it is impractical to intervene and discipline the clubs in a situation where they do not all fight for the same trophies. It is not an argument of principle, which has value across all sports and across all territories. At what level, for example, should the salary cap be fixed? Does it make sense to introduce revenue sharing among teams that are as far apart (both financially and in terms of sporting success) as Arsenal FC and Hull FC? It is one thing for the Oklahoma City Thunder to share revenues with the New York City Knicks, since they make comparable income anyway and the burden is not disproportionate. It is a different thing to contemplate the same mechanism for the two aforementioned football clubs.

Recall, however, that the salary cap is just that: a cap. There is no obligation to exhaust it. The obligation is to avoid overspending, not underspending it. Why not set it at a level that will satisfy the leaders (Arsenal FC) and not the followers (Hull FC)? Revenue sharing, similarly, can be set as a mechanism of partial redistribution, and not total equivalence of monetary resources. After all, this is not the case, not even in the United States.

5.2 The Institutional Issue

The absence of regulation is, in a sense, a blessing in the current framework: no questions are asked as to who will do it. Moving to a regulation of competitive balance would, however, raise complicated questions, for example about consistency with EU or national antitrust rules, or about the competence of particular regulators to intervene. In order for UEFA to feel confident that it has the authority to strongly regulate competitive balance, it would have to secure *ex-ante* positive feedback from the EU authorities. Beyond general exhortations of a political

[58] Compare the thoughts, on this score, of Ross (2021).

nature, this would be difficult to obtain. While there is some track record of mutual support, the history between the EU and UEFA has not always been harmonious. And, of course, UEFA itself is not known for its efforts in ensuring compliance with EU competition law, never mind the many noticeable deficiencies plaguing its regulatory machinery. With these difficulties, it could be argued that the EU authorities themselves are better placed to regulate for competitive balance, or at least to take the first steps. However, even if they were so disposed (which is far from obvious), there would be numerous obstacles.

First, how to get around Article 165 TFEU? Recall that, according to that provision, the EU has only a support competence in the field. One possible avenue to explore would be for the interested Member States to utilize the 'enhanced cooperation' framework and coordinate their sports policies at the EU level. The risk is again a two-speed sports integration model. This mechanism would also be tricky to put in place, given the legal limitations on enhanced cooperation, which must 'comply with the Treaties and Union law' (and thus with the limits on EU competences set out in Article 165 TFEU), and which may not 'undermine the internal market', which could very well occur if European football markets were segmented.[59] If these obstacles could be overcome, this would be an (imperfect) improvement on the current situation, where there is no coordination at all.

Secondly, how to ensure that the many UEFA members who are not EU Member States will observe the EU Regulation on competitive balance? We could end up once again with a two-speed model, albeit a different one this time. Assume that all EU members agree on how to move forward, and certain UEFA members who are not members of the EU (the United Kingdom and its powerful football league comes to mind) do not. Thus, the regulation is binding only on clubs located in EU states. Non-EU UEFA members would be allowed to freeride and behave opportunistically.

But of course, the safer way forward would be for the EU and the UEFA to work together on these issues, assuming of course that the EU division of competences has been solved. The first steps could take place through dialogue between UEFA and the EU institutions, which should not, however, create an impression that the EU is merely rubberstamping the rules proposed by UEFA. European Union competition law would still have to be complied with in any new initiative. The UEFA has to live with Europe, and EU authorities need to develop their expertise in sports regulation.

[59] Art 326 TFEU.

13
No One is Bigger than the Game

*Okeoghene Odudu**

1. Introduction

A 2019 article in *The Christian Science Monitor* asked 'Do athletes make too much money?'[1] The fact that (some) athletes are (very) highly paid had prompted a debate as to whether 'the fact that athletes tend to be paid so much more handsomely than school teachers, nurses, firefighters, and others whose work is arguably of far greater benefit [is] a sign of an economic system with its values out of whack?'[2] The question is part of a broader debate about the stark disparities of income and wealth that prevail in the economy and whether we should be troubled by the situation.[3]

Athletes' remuneration is determined, of course, by the market—and competition law has played, and continues to play, a significant role in the functioning of the market for athletic services.[4] Does the fact that athletes tend to be rewarded much more handsomely than other roles we claim to value more highly, and the role of competition law in bringing about this situation, indicate a competition law

* The assistance of Stephen Ross and Barak Orbach in improving this contribution is gratefully acknowledged. The views however are mine alone, as is the responsibility for all errors and omissions.

[1] Phil Taylor, 'Age of the Megadeal: Do Athletes Make Too Much Money?' *The Christian Science Monitor* (13 May 2019).

[2] Lora Wuerdeman writes: 'When the highest paid public employee in nearly every state is either a basketball or football coach, the message being sent to public employees around the nation is sports are more important than anything else. Regardless of whether you are a chancellor of a university or the governor, winning in sports is more important.' ('Sidelining Big Business in Intercollegiate Athletics' (2017) 39 North Carolina Central Law Review 85, 90). See also Wanjiru Njoya, 'The Problem of Income Inequality: Lord Wedderburn on Fat Cats, Corporate Governance and Workers' (2015) 44 Industrial Law Journal 394.

[3] David B Grusky and Jasmine Hill, *Inequality in the 21st Century: A Reader* (Westview Press 2018); David B Grusky and Szonja Szelényi, *The Inequality Reader: Contemporary and Foundational Readings in Race, Class, and Gender* (2nd edn, Westview Press 2011); Harry Frankfurt, 'Equality as a Moral Ideal' (1987) 98 Ethics 21; Harry Frankfurt, 'Equality and Respect' (1997) 64 Social Research 3; Harry Frankfurt, 'The Moral Irrelevance of Equality' (2000) 14 Public Affairs Quarterly 87–103; Paula Casal, 'Why Sufficiency Is Not Enough' (2007) 117 Ethics 296; and, generally, Matthew Clayton and Andrew Williams (eds), *The Ideal of Equality* (Macmillan 2000).

[4] Sarah S Vance, 'Competition on and off the Field: An Analysis of the Role of Antitrust Law in the Continuing Evolution of Professional Sports and Intercollegiate Athletics' (2012) 86 Tulane Law Review 823; and Paul C Weiler, 'What Antitrust Did for Players' in Paul C Weiler, *Leveling the Playing Field: How the Law Can Make Sports Better for Fans* (Harvard University Press 2000).

Okeoghene Odudu, *No One is Bigger than the Game* In: *The Internal Market Ideal*. Edited by: Jeremias Adams-Prassl, Sanja Bogojević, Ariel Ezrachi, and Dorota Leczykiewicz, Oxford University Press.
DOI: 10.1093/oso/9780192867063.003.0014

regime with its values out of whack? Or do these observations indicate a role for competition law in increasing the rewards for labour in other markets?[5]

Section 2 of this chapter sets out the role competition law has played in determining the distribution of revenue between the 'game'—leagues, tournaments, and clubs—and 'athletes'. Leagues and clubs are the exclusive purchasers of athletes' services and thus have monopsony power. Leagues and clubs also fall within the scope of competition law, and the effective application of competition law has curtailed the monopsony power of the leagues and clubs, allowing athletes to extract a greater share of the revenue generated by sport than would otherwise be the case. There are limited and specific circumstances in which antitrust is suspended and the ability of athletes to extract their market value dampened. Though examples from the United Kingdom and the EU are provided in this chapter, given the global nature of sport, and though I write with no particular sport and no particular jurisdiction in mind, I would hope that the ideas and claims have relevance for most sports in most jurisdictions.

Section 3 considers whether it is harmful for athletes to extract their market value. Three arguments are considered: the first is that market salaries upset the competitive balance necessary for a sporting contest to be interesting; the second is that market salaries trigger an arms race affecting the financial viability of sport; and the third is that market salaries increase the cost of being a spectator or grassroots participant in a way that makes sport inaccessible.

The three arguments amount to a single claim that it is desirable to reduce cost in the game and Section 4 considers whether competition law might be used as a tool to reduce such cost. To do so involves reframing the discussion and moving away from issues of monopsony—of the 'game' wielding power over 'athletes'—to issues of monopoly: of either athletes or the game wielding power over sports fans. This is new territory, but the door has been opened by emerging work that seeks to explain why 'excessive' salaries are objectionable.

2. The Athletes' Market Value

It is often said that '[i]n the market for players, clubs must pay the going rate to attract stars … sellers can demand what they are worth'.[6] Athletes sell labour to employers in return for payment. A league, team, or club will hire an athlete if the wage, remuneration, or compensation that it must pay is exceeded by the value the athlete generates for the league, team, or club—a value known as the marginal

[5] See generally Organisation for Economic Co-operation and Development (OECD), *Competition in Labour Markets* <www.oecd.org/daf/competition/competition-concerns-in-labour-markets.htm> (accessed 19 October 2023).

[6] Thomas Hoehn and Stefan Szymanski, 'The Americanization of European Football' (1999) 14 Economic Policy 205, 216.

revenue product (MRP).[7] An athlete's MRP is usually thought of as the number of wins they are able to generate for the team multiplied by the value of each win. Although it is a team, rather than an individual, that wins, attempts to quantify the contribution to the win are made and generally accepted.[8] More elusive than the contribution to the number of wins is the contribution to the value of a win. Particular athletes may be the key to a team's success, both on the field of play and in the commercial arena.[9] These athletes have what Rosen calls 'the elusive quality of box office appeal, the ability to attract an audience and generate a large volume of transactions'.[10] It is also known that '[s]ome star athletes develop personal followings that go well beyond their contribution to the quality of specific competitions. "Star quality" is often elusive ... but fans apparently recognise it when they see it.'[11]

It may be that the audience is around 30 per cent bigger when certain athletes are involved.[12] Given that athletes in general—and superstars in particular—are so crucial to sporting and commercial success, it is natural that there is a vibrant market for athletes who can help teams and tournaments attract the talent that may bring them success; there is competition among employers to attract athletes' services.[13]

While there is necessarily competition for athletes, it has not always been the case that athletes have been able to obtain their market value. The Organisation for Economic Co-operation and Development (OECD) reports that:

> Until the 1960s it was possible to argue that professional athletes were underpaid. Salary levels in the team sports were maybe higher than those of many workingmen, but compared to many professions they were low. Moreover, although one can argue that it is the performances of the stars that people go to watch, the

[7] Marginal Product is a measure of how productive a worker is in terms of output. Marginal Revenue is a measure of the additional revenue generated by each new unit of output. MRP is the product of marginal product and marginal revenue (MRP = MP × MR).

[8] Michael Wallace, 'Labor Market Structure and Salary Determination among Professional Basketball Players' (1988) 15 Work and Occupations 294; Robert W Brown, 'An Estimate of the Rent Generated by a Premium College Football Player' (1993) 31 Economic Inquiry 671; Robert W Brown, 'Measuring Cartel Rents in the College Basketball Player Recruitment Market' (1994) 26 Applied Economics 27; and Robert W Brown, 'Research Note: Estimates of College Football Player Rents' (2011) 12 Journal of Sports Economics 200.

[9] Jerry A Hausman and Gregory K Leonard, 'Superstars in the National Basketball Association: Economic Value and Policy' (1997) 15 Journal of Labor Economics 586.

[10] Sherwin Rosen, 'The Economics of Superstars' (1983) 52 The American Scholar 449, 456; see also OECD, 'Competition and Sports' (2018) DAF/COMP(2010)38, 18 <www.oecd.org/daf/competition/competition-and-sports-2010.pdf>.(accessed 17 October 2023)

[11] Sherwin Rosen and Allen Sanderson, 'Labour Markets in Professional Sports' (2002) 111 The Economic Journal F47, F49; see also F55.

[12] Hausman and Leonard (n 9) 598.

[13] Pedro Garcia-del-Barrio and Francesc Pujol, 'Hidden Monopsony Rents in Winner-Take-All Markets: Sport and Economic Contribution of Spanish Soccer Players' (2007) 28 Managerial and Decision Economics 57.

players' share of the revenue generated was relatively low. Movie stars or pop stars in this period tended to be much wealthier.[14]

The first significant development since the 1960s is that there is simply much more money in sport. Fuelled by broadcast rights holders, advertisers, and commercial sponsors, annual revenues now reach some $13 billion in the National Football League (NFL), $10 billion in Major League Baseball (MLB), $7.4 billion in the National Basketball Association (NBA), and $6.3 billion in the Indian Premier League (Cricket).[15] Not only is there now considerably more money in the 'game', but athletes are also taking a greater share of the revenue.[16] In 2021, Forbes reported Conor McGregor as having combined on- and off-field earnings of $180 million over a twelve-month period, surpassing Lionel Messi's $130 million and Cristiano Ronaldo's $120 million.[17] What has enabled athletes to increase their share of this greater revenue is the ability to use competition law to remove or limit rules imposed by the game that hitherto prevented them from obtaining their market value. To substantiate this second development as a matter of EU and UK competition law it is necessary to show that the 'game' is within the scope of competition law and that measures limiting earning potential or forcing a non-market distribution can be seen as restrictive of competition.

2.1 The Scope of Competition Law

Athletes are able to use UK and EU competition law to challenge measures that would otherwise prevent earnings from being determined by market forces when the measure to be challenged is promulgated by entities that constitute undertakings, since Articles 101 and 102 of the Treaty on the Formation of the European Union (TFEU) apply only to the conduct of *undertakings* and *associations of undertakings*. The Court of Justice in *Höfner* considers entities to be undertakings when

[14] OECD, 'Competition and Sports' (n 10) 37, noting also that in baseball, the share of wages was around 35–40 per cent in the 1950s, while by 1990, it had risen to about 60 per cent. See also Gerald W Scully, 'Pay and Performance in Major League Baseball' (1974) 64 American Economic Review 915 (finding that over the length of their career, average players receive salaries equal to about 11 per cent of their gross and about 20 per cent of their net marginal revenue products) and Hausman and Leonard (n 9) 589.

[15] Dusan Randjelovic, '11 Most Profitable Sports Leagues: Their Value Will Surprise You' (*Athletic Panda*, 3 June 2020) <https://apsportseditors.org/others/most-profitable-sports-leagues/ (accessed 17 October 2023)>; Hoehn and Szymanski (n 6) 207–10.

[16] Gerald W Scully, 'Player Salary Share and the Distribution of Player Earnings' (2004) 25 Managerial and Decision Economics 77.

[17] Brett Knight and Justin Birnbaum (eds), 'Highest-Paid Athletes: The Top 50 Sports Stars Combined To Make Nearly $2.8 Billion In A Year Of Records' (*Forbes.com* 12 May 2021) <www.forbes.com/athletes/> accessed 8 April 2022.

'engaged in an economic activity'.[18] As explained by Advocate General Jacobs, it is necessary to 'focus […] on the type of activity performed rather than on the characteristics of the actors which perform it'.[19] Economic activity consists of offering goods or services on a market.[20] Those selling tickets for sport events, selling advertising at sporting events, selling media rights for sporting events, and transferring athletes in return for transfer fees are seen to be engaged in economic activity.[21] For this reason, in *Meca-Medina*, the General Court confirmed that 'high level sport has become, to a great extent, an economic activity'.[22]

While courts have naturally considered activities that bring money into the game to be economic activity, a different question is whether measures either affecting the distribution of revenue or limiting how revenue may be spent within the game are also activities of an undertaking and thus subject to scrutiny on that basis.[23] The prime example of a measure affecting expenditure of revenue within the game is the imposition of a salary cap. A salary cap functions as 'a limit on the amount of money a team can spend on player salaries, expressed as a per-player limit, as a total limit for the entire team, as a percentage of the team's total income, or some combination of these options'.[24] Craig and De Marco are of the view that when setting financial regulations in sport that limit the amount of money a club is allowed to spend, '[t]here is no doubt that the regulation of spending in sport by sports' governing bodies is subject to the principles of competition law'.[25]

In *Premier Rugby Limited v Saracens Limited*, it was accepted that for this purpose the clubs were undertakings, and that the league was an association of undertakings (so it was unnecessary to determine which of the two entities actually set

[18] Case C-41/90 *Klaus Höfner and Fritz Elser v Macrotron GmbH* [1991] ECLI:EU:C:1991:161, para 21; C-724/17 *Vantaan kaupunki v Skanska Industrial Solutions Oy* [2019] ECLI:EU:C:2019:204, para 36; C-280/06 *ETI* [2007] ECLI:EU:C:2007:775, para 48.

[19] Joined Cases C-264/01, 306/01, 354/01, and 355/01 *AOK Bundesverband* [2004] ECLI:EU:C:2004:150, Opinion of AG Jacobs, para 26.

[20] Case 118/85 *Commission v Italian Republic* [1987] ECR 2599, para 7. See also Case C-343/95 *Diego Cali* [1997] ECR I-1547, para 16; Joined Cases C-180/98–184/98 *Pavlov* [2000] ECR I-6451, para 75; and Case T-319/99 *FENIN* [2003] ECR II-357, para 36.

[21] Case T-193/02 *Piau* [2005] ECR II-00209, paras 69–70, 72, 75, 112, and 116; Commission Decision of 25 June 2002 in Case 37/806, *ENIC/UEFA*, paras 25–26 <https://ec.europa.eu/competition/antitrust/cases/dec_docs/37806/37806_7_3.pdf>; Commission Decision of 27 October 1992, *Distribution of package tours during the 1990 World Cup* [1992] OJ L326/31, paras 47, 52, and 53; Commission Decision of 23 July 2003, *Joint selling of the commercial rights of the UEFA Champions League* [2003] OJ L291/25, para 106.

[22] Case T-313/02 *David Meca-Medina and Igor Majcen v Commission* [2004] ECR II-3291, para 44.

[23] Examples of measures affecting the distribution of revenue are collective selling of broadcast rights and revenue sharing between teams.

[24] Michael J Beloff and others, *Sports Law* (2nd edn, Hart Publishing 2012) 4.62. A more granular account is provided by Nick Craig and Nick De Marco, 'Financial Regulation in Sport' in Adam Lewis and Jonathan Taylor (eds), *Sport: Law and Practice* (3rd edn, Bloomsbury Professional 2014) 284–355, B3.100. See also 'Commission Staff Working Document—The EU and Sport: Background and Context; Accompanying document to the White Paper on Sport, SEC (2007) 935, sec 2.3 fn 210.

[25] Craig and De Marco (n 24) 284–355, B3.166.

the challenged rules).[26] It seems clear that *the process* of setting a salary cap, the salary cap itself, and other measures affecting the distribution of revenue are subject to scrutiny under competition law. Rugby Union, rugby league, county cricket, and basketball are team sports in the United Kingdom that impose 'salary caps' on professional athletes.[27] In Sections 2.2 and 2.3, it is explained how competition law has been applied to such measures.

2.2 Restrictive Measures

Given that the express aim of a salary cap is to reduce the upward pressure that competition places on salaries, an agreement among competing employers to limit salaries is treated as being akin to price-fixing in all jurisdictions in which they have been examined.[28] Studies on athletes' salaries in the United States indicate that athletes are able to obtain around 15–20 per cent of revenue generated by the game when competition between employers is restricted, but between 50 and 60 per cent of revenue generated when restrictions are removed.[29] Bitel considers that '[t]here is absolutely no doubt that prima facie a salary cap is unlawful. It is an agreement (however you frame the limitation) between competitors to limit the amount that they spend on a key element of the production of that industry.'[30]

A cap on the salary payable to an individual athlete playing in a team was considered under the restraint of trade doctrine in *Johnston v Cliftonville Football and Athletic Club*. The Northern Irish Football League set out certain regulations applying to participating clubs, including provisions which prevented a club from paying any player (i) more than £120 as a 'signing-on-bonus'; (ii) more than £12

[26] *In the matter of the Premiership Rugby Salary Regulations: Premier Rugby Limited v Saracens Limited: Decision of the Disciplinary Panel* (2019) para 17 <https://media-cdn.incrowdsports.com/fa097ce0-fc01-4b01-bbb0-e147ffa67de6.pdf>.

[27] Beloff and others (n 24) 4.62; Craig and De Marco (n 24).

[28] See Nick De Marco, *Football and the Law* (Bloomsbury Professional 2018) 4.95 and Stephen F Ross, 'Player Restraints and Competition Law Throughout the World' (2004) 15 Marquette Sports Law Review 49.

[29] Scully, 'Player Salary Share and the Distribution of Player Earnings' (n 16) 78; John Twomey and James Monks, 'Monopsony and Salary Suppression: The Case of Major League Soccer in the United States' (2011) 56 The American Economist 20, 23 (reporting on US Major League Soccer's ability to keep athletes' salaries at around 25 per cent of revenue).

[30] Nick Bitel, 'Salary Caps: Lawful, Workable and Imminent' (2004) 12 Sport and the Law Journal 132, 132. See also Beloff and others (n 24) 4.43 ('The existence of a salary cap would, in our view and whether viewed in terms of free movement, competition or restraint of trade, constitute a restriction'). In 'Commission Staff Working Document—The EU and Sport', it was explained that:

> [t]here are currently a number of important outstanding legal issues relating to the application of Articles [101] and [102 TFEU] to sport, in particular football. The three subjects which have attracted considerable attention recently concern … the idea of introducing salary caps in professional football. No formal decisions have been taken on these issues so far by the Community courts or the Commission. Therefore, this document cannot at this stage, provide a definite or exhaustive legal analysis of the problems involved or establish whether these rules would violate Articles [101] or [102 TFEU]. (n 24) [2.3]

per week as wages; and (iii) more than £12 as a match bonus for a win or £6 for a draw.[31] Brian Johnston, a part-time professional footballer playing in goal for Cliftonville Football and Athletic Club, challenged these maxima as unreasonable restraints of trade.[32] Johnston argued that £12 per week did not reflect his skill—he had not missed a game for five years on the senior side, had played for the Northern Ireland under-21s and had been called up as stand-by goalkeeper for the Northern Ireland international squad—and he asked to be paid £15 per week. Murray J, comparing wages in comparable leagues in which no salary maxima had been set, found that in the League of Ireland, the average wage would be about £50 per week, and that one club, which employed full-time professionals, paid about £150 per week.[33] By way of contrast, in England, where no salary cap was in operation, players employed on a full-time basis could expect between £900 and £1,750 per week in Division One, £500–900 per week in Division Two, £300–500 per week in Division Three, and £100–300 per week in Division Four. It was also noted that for 'certain "big stars" the weekly wage can be as high as £2,000/£3,000 per week'.[34] Murray J ruled that:

> The maximum wage regulation does not in any way restrict the plaintiff's freedom to sign on and play football for any of the 14 clubs, but what it does undoubtedly do is to restrict his freedom to negotiate the financial terms on which he is to play. Is this a restraint of trade within the scope of the doctrine? ... In my judgment ... The maximum wage regulation undoubtedly interferes with the plaintiff's liberty of action in trading viz. with his liberty to negotiate the basic matter of the payment he is to receive for his service to his employer.[35]

Johnston can be compared with the more recent *Premier Rugby Limited v Saracens Limited*, a decision in which the disciplinary panel found that the Rugby Football Union (RFU) Salary Capping Regulations,[36] introduced in 1999 to limit the total amount that may be paid in salaries by clubs participating in the RFU premier league, were not shown to be restrictive.[37] In the case of *Premier Rugby*, unlike in *Johnston*, no limit is placed on how much an *individual* athlete can earn, though of course the global limit will have an impact on individual salaries. A further important distinction is that the restrictive effect examined in *Premier Rugby*

[31] *Johnston v Cliftonville Football and Athletic Club Limited* [1984] NI 9, 14–15; it was accepted that some of the maxima were habitually breached, but the maximum wage regulation was observed.

[32] ibid 9.

[33] ibid 15.

[34] ibid.

[35] ibid 19–20.

[36] Reg 1.1 and s 1(a)–(w) of Sch 1 define 'salary' to include salary, wages, fees, bonuses, insurance premiums, and accommodation costs. See further, Craig and De Marco (n 24) 284–355, B2.114–B3.120.

[37] *Premier Rugby Limited* (n 26) para 33.

concerns the inability of teams to attract talent within the cap.[38] *Premier Rugby* does not consider the impact of the cap on athletes' share of revenues vis-à-vis the 'game'.[39] In this regard, the position set out in *Johnston* remains uncontested.

2.3 External Limits on the Market Rate

Measures preventing athletes from obtaining their market value may be challenged under competition law, preventing the 'game' from unilaterally *imposing* such measures on 'athletes'. It has, however, been possible to limit athletes' power to bargain in the market by recourse to a mechanism known as the *non*-statutory-labour exemption. This operates as follows: the *process* of collective bargaining is exempt from antitrust scrutiny (on a statutory basis in some jurisdictions, eg the United States, and recognized by judicial authority in other jurisdictions, eg the EU).[40] The terms of any agreement reached under the collective bargaining process (ie the agreement negotiated and the agreement to negotiate) may then benefit from a *non*-statutory (ie implicit) exemption.[41] Under English law, James states the

[38] ibid para 85. Whether a league is open—allowing the possibility of promotion and relegation—and whether teams within a league are also able to participate in other competitions will affect the ability to attract talent within the cap. For example, a salary cap may restrict the ability of a club or team in its aspiration to compete in a higher league or division, or to compete in international competitions.

[39] It should also be noted that athletes' bargaining position may be affected by restrictions other than a salary cap. For example, the athlete may be subject to large contract termination fees if they wish to seek a new employer within the sport. Under art 17 of the FIFA transfer rules, a player may terminate their contract 'without just cause' and become a free agent, subject to payment of compensation. One idea is that the compensation equates to the cost of buying a player of similar quality in the transfer market; another is that wages outstanding on the old contract provide the appropriate measure; a third is that the compensation should be set out in the player's contact. The higher the compensation measure, the more significant the fact that the player is under contract. See Rosen and Sanderson (n 11) F54 (in-contract players have reduced bargaining power as compared to out-of-contract players) and Marko Tervio, 'Transfer Fee Regulations and Player Development' (2006) 4 Journal of the European Economic Association 957.

[40] In the United States, s 6 of the Clayton Act exempts the formation and operation of a labour union; s 20 of the Clayton Act and s 4 of the Norris-LaGuardia Act allow strike action by limiting the availability of injunctive relief. In the EU, the leading authority is Case C-67/96 *Albany* [1999] ECLI:EU:C:1999:430. See further, Gabe Feldman, 'Collective Bargaining in Professional Sports: The Duel between Players and Owners and Labor Law and Antitrust Law' in Michael A McCann (ed), *The Oxford Handbook of American Sports Law* (Oxford University Press 2018) 215–17; Stephen F Ross, 'The NHL Labour Dispute and the Common Law, the Competition Act, and Public Policy' (2004) 37 University of British Columbia Law Review 343, 378–84.

[41] See *Brown v Pro Football, Inc*, 518 US 231, 250, and 255 (1996), following *Mackey v National Football League*, 543 F2d 606 (8th Cir 1976) and *Powell v National Football League*, 930 F2d 1293 (8th Cir 1989). See also *Brown v National Football League*, 518 US 231, 255 (1996); *Wood v National Basketball Association*, 809 F2d 954 (2d Cir 1987); *Mackey v National Football League*, 543 F2d 606, 615 (8th Cir 1976); Kieran M Corcoran, 'When Does the Buzzer Sound?: The Nonstatutory Labor Exemption in Professional Sports' (1994) 94 Columbia Law Review 1045; Harvard Law Review Association, 'Note: Releasing Superstars from Peonage: Union Consent and the Nonstatutory Labor Exemption' (1991) 104 Harvard Law Review 874–95; and Michael S Jacobs and Ralph K Winter, 'Antitrust Principles and Collective Bargaining by Athletes: Of Superstars in Peonage' (1971) 81 Yale Law Journal 1, 21–28.

position as being that the legality of the restraints will depend not so much on their restrictive nature, but on the process by which the restriction comes into being, writing that '[t]he legality of modern salary caps will be dependent upon the engagement of the players, usually through their union, in negotiations of the earnings limits. If these are unilaterally imposed, they are less likely to be found lawful restraints.'[42]

That the exemption is dependent on the process by which the restrictive measure is established is well illustrated by the English Football League's failed attempt, as a response to the financial strain member clubs had suffered as a result of the Covid-19 pandemic, to limit the amount each club could spend on salaries to £2.5 million in League 1 and £1.5 million in League 2 for the 2020–21 season.[43] Although, as in *Premier Rugby*, no limit on how much an individual player could be paid had been set, it was argued that capping the amount of money a club could dedicate to salaries was a major change to the terms and conditions of employment between players and clubs. It was accepted that if a cap were to be agreed, the correct forum for doing so was the Professional Football Negotiating and Consultative Committee (PFNCC).[44]

One of the problems with assessing the process by which a restriction comes about, rather than the restriction itself, is that the process of collective bargaining may favour or disfavour certain groups.[45] For example, when a strike will last for a significant proportion of an athlete's playing career, and athletes lack alternative employment options using the same skillset, the prospect of using strike action can be remote.[46] The low prospect of striking puts athletes in a weak negotiating position. This is evident in the way negotiated settlements come before the courts. In ordinary labour markets, the collectively bargained measures are typically challenged by an employer, and it is the employees' representative (the union) invoking the non-statutory labour exemption in defence. In sport we see the reverse, with athletes (represented by the union) challenging the measure and employers invoking the exemption in defence.

A second problem is that the bargaining process is skewed towards the interests of current athletes.[47] The interests of future athletes, former athletes, and spectators

42 Mark James, *Sports Law* (2nd edn, Palgrave Macmillan 2013) 246.

43 Nick De Marco, 'The Cap That Doesn't Fit: Why Salary Caps Cannot Work in Football' (*Sports Law Bulletin, Blackstone Chambers*, 3 August 2021) <www.blackstonechambers.com/documents/PERSPECTIVES_-_Nick_De_Marco.pdf>.

44 EFL, 'EFL Statement: PFA Arbitration' (*EFL.com*, 9 February 2021) <www.efl.com/news/2021/february/efl-statement-pfa-arbitration/>. The Trade Union and Labour Relations (Consolidation) Act 1992 covers this collective bargaining agreement. The PFNCC agrees to the terms of the mandatory standard playing contract between the clubs and players.

45 See Stephen F Ross and Robert B Lucke, 'Why Highly Paid Athletes Deserve More Antitrust Protection Than Ordinary Unionized Workers' (1997) 42 The Antitrust Bulletin 641.

46 Feldman (n 40) 214. Player strikes or owner lockouts caused the cancellation or postponement of games in Major League Baseball in 1972, 1981, 1985, and 1994, as well as of spring training in 1990.

47 Jason A Winfree, 'No Seat at the Table: Representation in Collective Bargaining in Professional Sports' (2017) 38 Managerial and Decision Economics 697.

of the game are not represented. It is not clear, therefore, why third parties to a collectively bargained agreement should lose the protections that antitrust would otherwise confer (or why third parties should be forced to pay for the collectively bargained resolution).[48] At some point the question as to whether spectators or consumers are required to pay for industrial peace between athletes will have to be addressed. Some questioning as to how long the exemption can be maintained, or the basis on which it is justified, is surely warranted.

3. The Harm in Extracting Market Value

The commercial exploitation of sport now means that there is more money in the game. Competition law has played, and continues to play, a significant role in enabling athletes to obtain a greater share of the revenue generated by the game than had previously been the case. A question then is whether the ability of athletes to extract an increased share of the increased revenue generated by the game is somehow harmful. The most frequently cited harm is that such salaries have an adverse impact on 'competitive balance'. A further claim is that competition for athletes' services will destabilize the sport. And a final claim is that athletes' high earnings are a symptom of and indicator that sport is simply too expensive, whether for spectators or as participants in the amateur game or at the low level of the professional pyramid.

3.1 Competitive Balance

Competitive balance is the idea that there needs to be a degree of win-uncertainty for sport to be interesting.[49] The risk is that richer teams buy all the most able athletes and, in so doing, are able to buy success.[50] A contest in which the richer team always wins would be uninteresting and fans would turn away from the game. Limiting what athletes can be paid is thought to enable poorer teams to compete more effectively against richer teams—maintaining competitive balance.[51] Though

[48] It would seem, in the United States at least, that standing to challenge the collectively bargained agreement is available only to competing employers and only if they can show harm in a product market, rather than a labour market. See *Philadelphia World Hockey Club, Inc v Philadelphia Hockey Club, Inc*, 351 F Supp 462 (1972).

[49] David Forrest and Robert Simmons, 'Outcome Uncertainty and Attendance Demand in Sport: The Case of English Soccer' (2002) 51 Journal of the Royal Statistical Society Series D (The Statistician) 229; Peter J Sloane, 'Restriction of Competition in Professional Team Sports' (1976) 28 Bulletin of Economic Research 3; Simon Rottenberg, 'The Baseball Players' Labor Market' (1956) 64 Journal of Political Economy 242.

[50] On competitive balance, see Ross, 'The NHL Labour Dispute (n 40) 355–58.

[51] Stephen F Ross, 'The Misunderstood Alliance between Sports Fans, Players, and the Antitrust Laws' (1997) University of Illinois Law Review 519, 560–67.

preventing players from obtaining their market value, such a restriction of competition might therefore be justified on the basis that it improves the consumer appeal of the sporting competition.[52]

In *Johnston*, one justification offered for the salary cap was that it would prevent the wealthiest and strongest clubs from capturing all the best players by offering them higher wages (competitive balance).[53] Whether a salary cap is indeed effective at achieving competitive balance has been called into question.[54] It has also been demonstrated that not only is 'competitive balance' not universally accepted as a desirable quality, but also that less well-financed teams are able to achieve success.[55] The link between player restraints and the 'quality' of the product fans pay to see is therefore not clear. Further, a number of ways to achieve competitive balance without imposing player restraints, such as waiver rules and revenue sharing, are available.[56] An issue requiring explication is the claim that athletes (as distinct from their employers) should be the ones that pay to achieve 'competitive balance', if competitive balance is required and a restriction of competition is effective at achieving it.

3.2 Financial Instability

The rewards for success in team sport are considerable. However, only a few teams can end up in the prize-winning positions. Investments to increase the likelihood of success, ie finishing in a position that pays out, are rational and athletes are the key input in this regard. Investment, however, is cancelled out as other teams invest, meaning that further investment is required. And the cycle continues, creating a considerable risk of 'player costs spiralling out of control as clubs outbid each other to secure the best players'.[57] Athlete cost will consume all of (if not more than) a team's resources if the team is unsuccessful and fails to finish in a position that pays

[52] See ibid 537–40; Ross, 'Player Restraints and Competition Law Throughout the World' (n 28); Stefan Kesenne, 'The Impact of Salary Caps in Professional Team Sports' (2000) 47 Scottish Journal of Political Economy 422; Stefan Szymanski, 'Income Inequality, Competitive Balance and the Attractiveness of Team Sports: Some Evidence and a Natural Experiment from English Soccer' (2001) 111 Economic Journal F69–F84; Helmut M Dietl and others, 'Salary Cap Regulation in Professional Team Sports' (2012) 30 Contemporary Economic Policy 307.

[53] *Johnston v Cliftonville* (n 31) 21.

[54] Ross, 'The Misunderstood Alliance' (n 51) 567–77; Ross, 'The NHL Labour Dispute (n 40) 356–58; Bitel (n 30) 134–35 set out the position that percentage or 'soft' salary caps operate in a manner that is detrimental to competitive balance. On competitive balance, see Stefan Szymanski, 'The Assessment: The Economics of Sport' (2003) 19 Oxford Review of Economic Policy 467, 470–72.

[55] Ross, 'The NHL Labour Dispute (n 40) 386–91 shows that win uncertainty is not always desired by consumers.

[56] Ross, 'The Misunderstood Alliance' (n 51) 558–60, 577–80.

[57] *Premier Rugby Limited* (n 26) para 99. Rosen and Sanderson describe this as a variant of cutthroat competition in an arms race. It may also be described as a 'winner takes all' or 'positional race' ('Labour Markets in Professional Sports' (n 11) F65). See Michael Sabin, 'Antitrust and Positional Arms Races' (2007) 30 Harvard Journal of Law and Public Policy 1023.

out.[58] For example, the majority of football clubs within Europe have been found to operate at a loss, and the collapse of clubs due, in part, to player wages that are 'out of whack' with a club's revenues is not unheard of.[59]

In *Johnston*, a second justification offered for preventing athletes from obtaining their market value was to prevent a free-for-all on wages putting clubs into financial difficulty: ruinous competition.[60] In evidence, it was admitted that the desire to protect clubs and teams 'from their own financial folly' was the primary motivation for a salary cap, ie the main 'worry was that the financially weaker clubs would overreach themselves in an effort to keep up'.[61] As Bitel writes, 'the salary cap is not there to ensure the integrity of the competition. It is there to maintain the balance sheet, not the competitive balance.'[62] How has the 'cost certainty' justification fared?[63] The key barrier faced by this argument is to explain why the risk of insolvency in sports markets should have a different regime from other industries.[64] This is a particularly high barrier given that what is being claimed is that the 'game' is badly managed, but that athletes should immunize or indemnify owners/managers from the consequences of their folly.[65]

3.3 Participation Cost

Disputes between the game and athletes have been described as 'a food fight over their respective shares of the revenue pie, resulting in no dessert for the rest'.[66] The focus has been on the division of revenue between the 'game' and the 'athlete'.[67]

58 Wuerdeman (n 2) 85–96.

59 Josh Halliday, 'Bury FC: Despair As Club is Expelled from Football League after 125 Years' *The Guardian* (28 August 2019) <www.theguardian.com/football/2019/aug/27/bury-and-bolton-two-of-englands-oldest-clubs-face-tuesday-expulsion>. And see more generally the 2015 complaint from Football Players Worldwide, claiming 'hundreds of millions of football fans [have] been betrayed by the irresponsible administration of the transfer market'; 'FIFPRO Legal Action against FIFA Transfer System' <www.fifpro.org/news/fifpro-takes-legal-action-against-fifa-transfer-system/en/>; Charlie Gordon, 'Portsmouth FC: A Spirited Comeback from An Ownership Catastrophe' *Sports Gazette* (30 December 2020) <https://sportsgazette.co.uk/portsmouth-fc-a-spirited-comeback-from-an-ownership-catastrophe/>; and Darrell King, '140 Years of Rangers Liquidated ... After Just 8 Minutes of Meeting' *The Glasgow Times* (8 January 2015) <www.glasgowtimes.co.uk/news/13234824.140-years-of-rangers-liquidated-after-just-8-minutes-of-meeting/>. The perilous nature of football financing is not a new phenomenon. See Sloane (n 49) 4; Andrew Wenger, 'UEFA Financial Fair Play' (*Soccer Politics*, 27 December 2012) <http://sites.duke.edu/wcwp/2012/12/27/uefa-financial-fair-play/>. See also Craig and De Marco (n 24) 284–355, B3.85–B3.96 on the need for cost control.

60 *Johnston v Cliftonville* (n 31) 21. See also *Premier Rugby Limited* (n 26) paras 97–104; Bitel (n 30) 132–135; and Twomey and Monks (n 29) 20–28.

61 *Johnston v Cliftonville* (n 31) 21. Murray J considered that a limit on the number of players a club could sign was a natural solution to the first issue so that 'the point about the two wealthy clubs capturing all the good players does not bear examination and is a bad one'.

62 Bitel (n 30) 135.

63 Ross, 'The NHL Labour Dispute (n 40) 361–65.

64 ibid 394–98.

65 ibid 402–04.

66 ibid 344. Also Ross, 'The Misunderstood Alliance' (n 51) 521–22.

67 Hausman and Leonard (n 9) 586–624.

Relatively little attention has been given to the cost of being a sports fan, either as a spectator or as a grassroots participant.[68] The high salaries of athletes coincide with participation—either at the grassroots level or as spectators—moving beyond the reach of many.[69] As the cost of engaging in sport increases, participation in sport is shown to decline.[70] One idea is that athletes' earnings are in part responsible for the cost of being a fan, and restricting athletes' salaries will enable funds to be diverted to the grassroots level of the game or make the game more accessible in terms of lower gate prices.[71] Of course, the rewards reaped by others in the game should not be overlooked, but it is the high salaries of athletes that tend to attract outrage: 'owners insist that player salary demands are unrealistically high. Fans, caught in the middle, seem persuaded that the players are overpaid. Somehow, a $150,000 a year ball player claiming exploitation is anti-heroic.'[72]

4. Reducing the Cost of Sport

This final section picks up the points that relatively little attention has been given to the cost of being a sports fan, and that competition law limits the ability of the game to reduce athletes' salaries. We note that fans 'seem persuaded that the players are overpaid'.[73] And it is a very short leap to link athletes' high salaries with the increasing cost of being a sports fan. What is not tested, but what is tentatively

[68] There are a number of cases regarding the cost of merchandise (eg Joined Cases 1021/1/1/03 and 1022/1/1/03 *Jjb Sports plc v Office of Fair Trading; Allsports Limited v Office of Fair Trading* [2004] CAT 17) and availability of tickets for sporting events (eg *Distribution of package tours during the 1990 World Cup* (n 21).

[69] Kieran Devlin, 'Ever-Rising Ticket and TV Costs Risk Pricing Out Scottish Football Fans Battling the Cost of Living Crisis' *The Atlantic* (6 June 2022) <https://theathletic.com/3332466/2022/06/06/cost-scotland-fans-television/>. The pricing of tickets is generally thought to be inelastic: Dennis Coates and Brad R Humphreys, 'Ticket Prices, Concessions and Attendance at Professional Sporting Events' (2007) 2 International Journal of Sport Finance 161. But see Erik Thibaut and others, 'Financial Barriers for Sports Consumption: The Dynamics of the Income-Expenditure Relation' (2020) 10 Sport, Business and Management 245.

[70] Mark Hyman, *The Most Expensive Game in Town: The Rising Cost of Youth Sports and the Toll on Today's Families* (Beacon Press 2012); Michelle Cull and Keith Parry, 'Pay to Play: Is Participating in Sport Becoming Too Expensive for Everyday Australians?' (*The Conversation*, 6 September 2018) <https://theconversation.com/pay-to-play-is-participating-in-sport-becoming-too-expensive-for-everyday-australians-101826>; Nana Kwame Anokye, Subhash Pokhrel, and Julia Fox-Rushby, 'Economic Analysis of Participation in Physical Activity in England: Implications for Health Policy' (2014) 11 The International Journal of Behavioral Nutrition and Physical Activity 117; and Gwenno Edwards and others, 'Moving the Goalposts: Poverty and Access to Sport for Young People' (Centre for Analysis of Social Exclusion, Report 95) <http://sticerd.lse.ac.uk/dps/case/cr/casereport95.pdf>.

[71] *Johnston v Cliftonville* (n 31) 22 implicitly accepts that reducing athletes' salaries might lead to a reduction in the cost of being a sports fan or leave more money to filter down to the grassroots level.

[72] Scully, 'Pay and Performance in Major League Baseball' (n 14) 915. Note the suggestion in Ariel Ezrachi, Amit Zac, and Christopher Decker, 'The Effects of Competition Law on Inequality: An Incidental By-Product or a Path for Societal Change?' (2022) 11 Journal of Antitrust Enforcement 51–77, at 57 that '[u]nder certain assumptions, competition can limit excessive remunerations to executives and shareholders and curtail the growth of those in the very highest income groups'.

[73] Scully, 'Pay and Performance in Major League Baseball' (n 14) 915.

explored here, is whether competition law provides a useful framework for considering the possibility that athletes are taking 'too much' and leaving 'too little' for the game to sustain itself. To do so requires us to move away from ideas of coordinated behaviour and think of the unilateral conduct of each athlete. We must consider whether (i) athletes qualify as dominant undertakings, and (ii) make unfair demands that constitute an abuse.

4.1 Athletes as Dominant Undertakings?

Athletes participating in individual sports are within the scope of competition law when they participate in various tournaments but are not employed. It is recognized that the athlete may negotiate appearance fees, compete for prize money, and enter into sponsoring agreements.[74] In a team sport, because the athlete is employed, there has been some doubt as to whether athletes come within the scope of competition law. In *Bosman*, Advocate General Lenz considered that football players, as employees, were not themselves subject to EU competition law.[75] Advocate General Lenz goes on to say: '[t]here is in my opinion no rule to the effect that agreements which concern employment relationships are in general and completely outside the scope of the provisions on competition in the EC Treaty.'[76] In

[74] OECD, 'Competition and Sports' (n 10) 19 and Joined Cases C–51/96 and 191/97 *Deliège* [2000] ECLI:EU:C:2000:199, paras 46, 56, and 57.

[75] Case C–415/93 *Bosman* [1995] ECLI:EU:C:1995:463, Opinion of AG Lenz, para 263. Following this logic, see eg Kieron Beal and Emily Neill, 'Competition Law' in Paul Goulding (ed), *Employee Competition: Covenants, Confidentiality, and Garden Leave* (Oxford University Press 2016) A3.08, who write:

> As a general proposition, competition law does not apply to relations between an employer and an employee, since an employee is not treated as an economic undertaking distinct from the company or firm for which he or she works ... Generally, therefore, while employees are categorized as workers for the purposes of Article 45 TFEU ... their arrangements with employers fall outside the scope of Article 101 TFEU.

Alexandra Kamerling and Christopher Osman, *Restrictive Covenants under Common and Competition Law* (4th edn, Sweet & Maxwell 2004) 283 write: '[t]here appears to be no authority to say that an employee per se is an undertaking; *we do not think he is*; and see Sugar (40/73).' In their sixth edition, they write more assertively that 'Article 101 [TFEU] will not apply *as an individual employee is not "undertaking"* ... Article 102 TFEU by its very terms is of doubtful application.' Alexandra Kamerling and Christopher Osman, *Restrictive Covenants under Common and Competition Law* (6th edn, Sweet & Maxwell 2010) 204. Other commentators have given a more equivocal answer as to competition law in the employment relationship. For example, Guy Tritton writes: 'it will be *a rare case* where Art. 101 ... is potentially applicable to restrictive covenants in employment contracts', 'Employees, Trade Secrets and Restrictive Covenants in the United Kingdom' in Christopher Heath and Anselm Kamperman Sanders (eds), *Employees, Trade Secrets and Restrictive Covenants* (Wolters Kluwer 2017) 83.

[76] Case C–415/93 *Bosman* [1995] ECLI:EU:C:1995:293, Opinion of AG Lenz, para 273. See also the view of the Irish Competition Authority in Decision of the Competition Authority No E/04/002 *Agreements between Irish Actors' Equity SIPTU and the Institute of Advertising Practitioners in Ireland concerning the terms and conditions under which advertising agencies will hire actors* (Case COM/14/03, 31 August 2004) para 2.12, that, '[i]f one were to take a wooden approach and find that all [types of worker] were [not undertakings], the protections afforded Irish consumers by the Oireachtas in enacting the Competition Act, 2002 could easily be rendered illusory'.

Albany, Advocate General Jacobs acknowledges that there may be situations (such as in relation to an employer) in which an employee is an undertaking, writing: '[t]he future will probably show whether that principle [ie that employees are not to be treated as undertakings] applies also in certain borderline areas such as for example professional sport.'[77]

In 2018, when the OECD considered the status of athletes under competition law, it was felt that 'players can be considered as an undertaking due to the economic value they attract'.[78] As the existence of a 'transfer market' aptly demonstrates, there is clearly demand for athletes' services from clubs, teams, and tournaments; players (even as employees) are undertakings when they offer services on that market. The real question, then, is not whether athletes can be described as undertakings, but rather whether there is a sense in which an individual athlete can be said to be dominant or to monopolize the game? In *Replica Kit*, the market definition assumes that, in team sports, the relevant market is an individual club or team. The merchandise of one team or club is not substitutable with the merchandise of rival teams.[79] Can it be said that the market is narrower than a team or club, so that a single player constitutes the relevant market? This is a particular challenge to the idea that individual athletes make excessive demands. A sport may continue to thrive in the absence of a particular athlete or team—no one is bigger than the game.

4.2 Abusive Salary Demands

Competition law has hitherto had little to say about both absolute and relative salary levels both within and outwith sport. Indeed, though 'excessive pricing' is an established abuse of dominance, how to establish that excessive prices are being demanded is a highly contentious issue.[80] Beyond competition law, recent work by Collins has begun to set out how there may be a right to fair pay, and how to determine the fairness of pay.[81] Collins acknowledges that 'if current wage disparities

[77] Case C–67/96 *Albany* ECLI:EU:C:1999:28, Opinion of AG Jacobs, para 217.
[78] OECD, 'Competition and Sports' (n 10) 13. See also the view of the Danish delegate at 254.
[79] Decision of the Office of Fair Trading No CA98/06/2003 *Price-fixing of Replica Football Kit* (1 August 2003) (Case CP/0871/01).
[80] See *Competition and Markets Authority v Flynn Pharma Limited and Pfizer Inc* [2020] EWCA Civ 617; OECD, 'Policy Roundtables: Excessive Prices' DAF/COMP(2011) 18; Case 27/76 *United Brands Co v Commission* [1978] ECLI:EU:C:1978:22; *Napp Pharmaceutical Holdings Ltd v Director General of Fair Trading* [2002] EWCA Civ 796; Case C–95/04 P *British Airways plc v Commission* [2007] ECLI:EU:C:2007:166; and Case C–177/16 *Biedrība 'Autortiesību un komunicēšanās konsultāciju aģentūra—Latvijas Autoru apvienība' Konkurences padome* (*Latvian Copyright Case*) [2017] ECLI:EU:C:2017:689.
[81] Hugh Collins, 'Fat Cats, Production Networks, and the Right to Fair Pay' (2022) 85 Modern Law Review 1.

are largely the product of market forces, any law is likely to encounter considerable resistance to regulation that alters those outcomes'.[82]

If the services of an individual athlete are indispensable to a team, such that the athlete may command a stratospheric salary, can it be said that such a salary is anything other than a fair reward for what the athlete brings to the game?[83] An important point made by Collins is that '[t]he value of the job cannot be determined by reference to its prevailing market rate, for it is usually that market rate that is being challenged by the claimant'.[84]

Collins' focus is on fairness within a particular organization (what he calls interpersonal justice) rather than society as a whole (distributive justice).[85] The fair salary is one that is agreed to, is deserved (according to their valued contribution to the productive organization), and gives due recognition to the fact that productivity of the organization is a collective effort.[86] Separately, the case has been made that the customer has an interest in knowing the earnings of those in the institutions they patronize.[87] What we might add here is an element of accessibility. That is, we should think about the impact player salaries have on access to sport. Access is of course an under-explored concept, as a link between player salaries and the prices charged to play or observe sport is unclear. Further, taking as an example season tickets (providing access to all of a team's home games in a Premier League Football season, which might be had for anything between £750 and £2,000), sport seems reasonably affordable. Tickets are often sold out, with fans queuing for a chance to obtain one. How are teams or clubs to allocate such a scarce resource other than to search for market clearing prices? By the same token, how is sport to remain or become accessible to those unable to pay such a price?

Collins' account of a fair salary is focused on ratios between the highest and lowest earners within an organization. His approach would need to be modified and extended to consider the ratio between players' salaries and the cost of access to the game, either as a spectator or as a grassroots participant. Even then, as Collins concedes, it is 'probably impossible both practically and politically to impose a single formula on all employers or even on particular sectors of the economy. Instead, what must be required by a regulatory framework is for each organization to set its own standards with respect to ratios of pay'.[88]

Even if the salary exceeds an acceptable ratio, the challenges of (a) fitting the deviation within the concept of abuse, and (b) establishing standing on behalf of fans, as indirect purchasers of athletes' services, rather than the employing team or club,

[82] ibid 3.
[83] Rosen and Sanderson (n 11) F51–F52.
[84] Collins (n 81) 15–16.
[85] ibid 5–10.
[86] ibid 10–16.
[87] Colin Perkin, 'Directors' Remuneration: Enter the Customer' (2001) Journal of Business Law 166–78.
[88] Collins (n 81) 22.

remain to be overcome. On the first challenge, under EU law, the relevant abuse would be unfair pricing. This abuse has experienced something of a revival and has most recently been reviewed in the United Kingdom by the Court of Appeal.[89] What the court emphasized is that the basic test for abuse, which is set out in the Chapter II prohibition and in Article 102 of the TFEU, is whether the price is 'unfair'. There are a number of ways to show that a price is unfair and, depending upon the facts and circumstances of the case, a competition authority might use one or more of the alternative tests available. It therefore seems open for a comparator between athletes' salaries and the accessibility of sport to be developed. On the second challenge, competition law has been used in the battle between owners and athletes to influence the share of revenue each of the groups will obtain. There is, however, nothing in the jurisprudence that prevents fans or grassroots participants from mounting a challenge (either against the game or athletes) if they can establish a link between measures taken and a barrier to accessibility they experience. It is therefore possible to give thought to how competition law might be used to make sport better for fans.[90]

5. Conclusion

Though the high salaries of athletes can attract a certain degree of outrage, they are explained by there being more money in the game. The use of competition law has enabled athletes to negotiate a share of revenue that reflects the contribution they make towards generating the increased revenue. Though competition law has been very much present in the battle between athletes and the game, it has been largely absent in the relationships between fans and athletes and fans and the teams they support. If we assume a link between increased salaries and increased costs, either to spectators or to grassroots participants, a question arising is whether competition law can be used by fans and spectators. The key hurdle is to establish that an athlete is dominant or otherwise indispensable; no one is bigger than the game. If this barrier can be surmounted, it seems possible to build on emerging work that explains why excessive boardroom pay is objectionable to challenge athletes' salaries as abusive. Where this chapter differs from others in the genre is that it raises questions of affordability or accessibility for fans of the game, either as grassroots participants or spectators, rather than merely the distribution of revenue between owners and athletes. This raises questions as to who uses antitrust, how it is used, and who benefits from its use. Antitrust has long been used in sport and its use has contributed to athletes' increased share of revenue generated by the game. As further uses of antitrust are developed, we should pay attention to whether this is ultimately to the benefit of fans.

89 *Competition and Markets Authority v Flynn Pharma Ltd* (n 80). See also *United Brands v Commission* (n 80) paras 248–53 and *Latvian Copyright Case* (n 80).

90 See Weiler, *Leveling the Playing Field* (n 4).

PART IV

EU VALUES AND THE MOBILIZATION OF EU LAW

14

Public Interest Litigation, Legal Professionalism, and the ECJ: Deciding a Case or Managing Politics?

*Hans-Wolfgang Micklitz and Thomas Roethe**

1. In Friendship from Hans to Steve

Dear Steve,

The EU project on 'Emergency Management of Product Safety in the EU' brought us together in 1989 for a journey that has lasted more than thirty years now. It took us four years to transform the project into one of my favourite books to this day.[1] I remember you sitting in my office at the Berlin School of Business and writing your contribution on our research question: whether and to what extent one of the ECJ decisions under Article 30 EEC could be understood as establishing a responsibility of the EU for the health and safety of the EU citizens. When I pushed you hard in generalizing the possible findings, I heard you say 'Hans, it is just a case'. I learned my lessons in both projects: on the crucial but nevertheless limited relevance of a decision in a single case, and on the importance of the distinction between the law in the books and the law in action. I owe you what I learnt about the common law and the role and function of case law in a common law system, not least during my time as a visiting fellow at Somerville College, your intellectual home. We had a wonderful time. The contribution Thomas and I dedicate to you is an attempt to link the old days to the current days in focusing on the role of the Court of Justice of the European Union (ECJ), which is in the centre of your scholarly legacy.

In the best German *Festschrift* tradition, we tend to be provocative in our consideration of the impact of Public Interest Litigation on the 'European lawyer': on Judges, Advocates General, Attorneys, on those who bring the cases to the ECJ. In

* We would like to thank Emilia Korkea-aho, Dorota Leczykiewicz, Päivi Leino-Sandberg, and Urska Sadl for their insightful and demanding comments, without which the contribution would look very different, and Ariel Ezrachi for the language corrections. The usual disclaimer applies.

[1] Hans-W Micklitz, Thomas Roethe, and Steven Weatherill (eds), *Federalism and Responsibility: A Study on Product Safety Law and Practice in the European Community* (Graham & Trotmann 1994).

Hans-Wolfgang Micklitz and Thomas Roethe, *Public Interest Litigation, Legal Professionalism, and the ECJ: Deciding a Case or Managing Politics?* In: *The Internal Market Ideal*. Edited by: Jeremias Adams-Prassl, Sanja Bogojević, Ariel Ezrachi, and Dorota Leczykiewicz, Oxford University Press.
DOI: 10.1093/oso/9780192867063.003.0015

short, we want to examine if and how this particular form of litigation affects the *legal professions* and, through that, *EU law*. However, it is not our intention to discuss the legitimacy of juristocracy and the question of who is better equipped to carry out social regulation, the legislature or the judiciary, or who is accountable to whom.[2] This chapter is a kind of meta-reflection on what Public Interest Litigation is doing to the law and to the legal profession; it is not meant to blame the ECJ for producing 'bad law', let alone to reflect on the legal arguments presented. The wider context of our research results from the growing preparedness in legal scholarship to discuss the role of law and lawyers in the European integration process in a more distant critical perspective.[3] A note is needed—both of us have been heavily involved in the Brussels machinery on behalf of the European Commission, the Member States, and civil society organizations, as well as in providing consultancy to new Member States prior to their becoming members of the EU.

2. Public Interest Litigation, the ECJ, and Legal Professionalism

Our argument is that Public Interest Litigation transforms the role of the court and the judge and affects the legal profession and, thereby, the law. If this turns out to be correct, the question arises whether Public Interest Litigation should be kept separate from individual litigation and what the consequence of such a separation would be for the European judiciary. While we accept that there are difficult definitional issues,[4] we understand Public Interest Litigation as a form of strategic legislation in the name, and to the benefit, of the public interest, such as the promotion of environmental and consumer protection and the elimination of social discrimination. Particular individuals might draw benefits from Public Interest Litigation. However, in standard litigation, an individual party who is going to court would defend only their own interests, whereas Public Interest Litigation is characterized by its strategic purpose having a broader reach. Groups in society or, even

[2] Silje Synnøve Lyder Hermansen and Daniel Naurin, 'Holding Judges To Account: Policy, Performance and Impartiality' (European Consortium for Political Research (ECPR) Joint Sessions, 2 August 2022) <siljehermansen.github.io/project/court-of-justice-of-the-european-union/HoldingJudgesToAccount_HermansenNaurin.pdf> and many further references in the text.

[3] Antoine Vauchez, *Brokering Europe: Euro-Lawyers and the Making of a Transnational Polity* (Cambridge University Press 2015); Päivi Leino-Sandberg, *The Politics of Legal Expertise in EU Policy-Making* (Cambridge University Press 2021); Tommaso Pavone, *The Ghostwriters, Lawyers and the Politics behind the Judicial Construction of Europe* (Cambridge University Press 2022); Mikael Rask Madsen, Fernanda Nicola, and Antoine Vauchez (eds), *Researching the European Court of Justice, Methodological Shifts and Law's Embeddedness* (Cambridge University Press 2022).

[4] For discussion of public interests versus collective interests, and of the advocacy of civil society groups, state-sponsored NGOs, and public agencies, see, for a start, Hans-Wolfgang Micklitz and Andrea Wechsler, 'What is Collective in the Collective Interests?' in Stefaan Voet and others (eds), *Delivering Justice: A Holistic and Multidisciplinary Approach. Liber Amicorum in Honour of Christopher Hodges* (Hart Publishing 2022) 72–94.

more broadly, the society as a whole might benefit from the outcome achieved. The drivers of Public Interest Litigation are state-sponsored non-governmental organizations and public agencies, while the forum we are focusing on in this chapter is the European judiciary.[5]

The material we rely on comes from the European Research Council (ERC) project on European Regulatory Private Law.[6] We have carefully selected three highly controversial cases, each standing as paradigmatic for their respective policy fields, and have interviewed, as far as possible, all key actors: the national and the European judges, the Advocates General, the plaintiffs and the defendants, as well as their attorneys.[7] The analysis is qualitative, built around three cases and their potential impact on the EU legal order and society, therefore necessarily cursory and in need of counterchecking. The growing judicial activism in the climate change debate highlights the urgent need to take a more distant stand on the judicialization of political conflicts.[8] What might be 'good' for society might not be good for the law and for legal profession.

Defining legal professionalization is a demanding task. There is a whole field in sociology that discusses what constitutes a profession, what might be understood by professionalization, and what these developments mean for the legal profession.[9] Elsewhere, we have concretized our understanding of the legal profession,[10] inspired by Ulrich Oevermann.[11] Oevermann's critique of the sociological theories of professions is to argue not from the historical development of professions but from the problems arising in individual as well as collective life practice. Life practice has to cope with crises and requires decisions even when it does not have sufficient justifications for solutions at its disposal. The need to make decisions in

[5] R Daniel Kelemen, *Eurolegalism: The Transformation of Law and Regulation in the European Union* (Harvard University Press 2011).

[6] The project was conducted at the European University Institute between 2011 and 2016. The Principal Investigator was Hans-Wolfgang Micklitz. The quotes in this chapter are taken from the interviews and their transcripts are on file with the authors.

[7] See, for a full reconstruction of the cases and the methodology used, Betül Kas, '"Hybrid" Collective Remedies in the EU Social Legal Order' (PhD thesis, European University Institute 2017); with regard to interviews, see Emilia Korkea-aho and Päivi Leino, 'Interviewing Lawyers: A Critical Self-Reflection on Expert Interviews as a Method of EU Legal Research' (2019) 11 European Journal of Legal Studies 17.

[8] Laura Burgers, 'Justitia, the People's Power and Mother Earth: Democratic Legitimacy of Judicial Law-making in European Private Law Cases on Climate Change' (PhD thesis, University of Amsterdam 2020).

[9] For an overview of the sociology of professions, stressing the usefulness of Max Weber against taxonomic approaches, see Mike Saks, 'Defining a Profession: The Role of Knowledge and Expertise' (2012) 2 Professions and Professionalism 1.

[10] Hans-Wolfgang Micklitz, 'Legal Professionalism and Legal Expertise in EU Law Making' in Emilia Korkea-aho and Päivi Leino-Sandberg (eds), *Law, Legal Expertise and EU Policy-Making: Changing Roles for the Legal Profession* (Cambridge University Press 2022).

[11] More generally, Ulrich Oevermann, *Strukturprobleme supervisorischer Praxis. Eine objektiv hermeneutische Sequenzanalyse zur Überprüfung der Professionalisierungstheorie* (Humanities Online 2010). The paragraph is the result of a discussion we had on how to define and to explain the particularities of the legal profession.

the absence of justifications is the *topos* that has given rise to the evolution of 'professionalized' professions—priests, lawyers, and physicians—in manifest crises of personal and social autonomy. Professionalized action is the social place of the mediation of theory and practice under conditions of scientific rationality; ie under conditions of scientifically justified problem solving in practice. In essence, it is about severe losses of personal autonomy of clients—thus an expression of a societal problem—that render them helpless and in the same breath demand professionalized action.

We may have to formulate a clarification here for better understanding, thanks to which professions and professionalized activities can be distinguished. The farmer, the car mechanic, the carpenter, the bricklayer, the salesperson all provide indispensable services in their special skills of how this or that problem can be solved to the best standard. In other words, all the professions that have held society together for hundreds of years can rely on the knowledge they have acquired through practice and education. A car can be repaired in a standardized way, houses can be built following routine and knowledge secured over time. Another category consists of the professionalized professions that cannot deal with assured instrumental standard solutions, but that have to develop an understanding of the case. Routine and knowledge would—at least sometimes—fail because answers are not available in the canonized knowledge of the rules.

We experience this dramatically—to give just one example—as patients in relation to medical doctors when symptoms are puzzling in the face of available medical knowledge and thus there is no standardized answer to the question of how to treat the patient. Medical science must conduct research and gather empirical experience on the case in an unpredictable terrain. In these circumstances, the patient has lost their personal autonomy. The professionalized agent must act in a space located between the demands of an individual case and rule-based knowledge. This is also true whenever the subjects, ie individuals, partially or fully lose their personal autonomy in a legal conflict arising from business relationships or private conflicts which can no longer be resolved between the parties through communication, and which can now be dealt with only with the help of a lawyer and through their 'vicarious interpretation' (in German: *stellvertretende Deutung*) of the case. However, such crises also provide the opportunity to aggregate experience, which enriches the consolidated and archived knowledge laid down in books.

On the other hand, we can observe the phenomenon of de-professionalization. Actual cases of personal loss of autonomy of plaintiffs and defendants, in threatening crises and conflicts, can no longer be recognized by lawyers when they are acting merely professionally (similarly to car mechanics), rather than in a professionalized manner and, as a result, can no longer be dealt with appropriately. In such circumstances, case reconstruction is no longer possible; practising lawyers following routine knowledge, which ends in the stagnation of experience, expose themselves to the accusation of merely acting like a subsumption machine.

What we want to discuss in our contribution is whether Steve's observation that 'a case is just a case', a wonderful formulation reminiscent of Gertrude Stein's 'A rose is a rose', coiled around a tree and therefore also may be read as 'Rose is a rose', corresponds to what Steve had in mind. We doubt that this hopefully ever-relevant statement is always accurate and look at cases which can be characterized by the absence of a client (and thus also by no situational loss of personal autonomy), but rather involve litigants who no longer seek the legally capable consensus, the pacifying therapy in terms of scientific and theoretical law in the books. However, this also means that client-related judicial proceedings—ie the case- and rule-based actions of practice-oriented lawyers—may evaporate. Instead, we observe plaintiffs who are used as 'straw men' in the name of (N)GOs, and organizational plaintiffs who perceive themselves as societal institutions, committed to a goal. Now the question arises about the significance of such initiatives. What does this development mean for the legal profession and for the law? Is it justified to speak of the de-professionalization of the legal profession?

The sociology of European Public Interest Litigation, as developed by Thomas Roethe, constitutes the first section of the chapter. It offers a critical eye on the legal profession and its importance for the rule of law. Roethe argues in Section 3 that the three cases we examine lack the 'life practice' of professionalized lawyers, a practical, real-life context, as cases of conflict are 'politically constructed'. In a nutshell, the argument is that in the search for a legal solution to a 'non-case', courts are experiencing de-professionalization. The three cases in the distinct policy fields serve as evidence. In Section 4, Hans-Wolfgang Micklitz argues that most of what Roethe observes is structurally inbuilt in the preliminary reference procedure and is therefore the direct result of EU politics and programmatic EU lawmaking, which has turned the ECJ into an institutional hybrid—located somewhere between the judiciary, the executive, and the legislature. The changing role of judges brings to the fore the question of whether judges, at both the national and EU levels, are properly trained to handle European Public Interest Litigation. In the conclusion, we speculate about the consequences for EU adjudication of maintaining the distinction between individual cases and Public Interest Litigation, inspired by Rob van Gestel's 'Supreme Court Public Interest Chamber'.[12]

3. Legal Professionalization or De-professionalization in *Janecek*, *Feryn*, and *Invitel*

The three cases we have selected are paradigmatic for the three policy fields they represent—*Janecek* for environmental protection, *Feryn* for non-discrimination,

[12] Rob van Gestel, 'The Supreme Court's Public Interest Chamber' in Rpb van Gestel and Jan Vranken (eds), *Recht en rechtspraak vanaf 2040: Fred Hammerstein-bundel* (Boom juridisch 2021) 87–102..

and *Invitel* (Thomas Goethe) for consumer protection. One of the authors, Thomas Roethe, participated in interviews organized, conducted, and managed by Betül Kas and analysed them. The first two are typical Western European cases from Germany and Belgium. The third, *Invitel*, comes from Hungary. All three cases have risen to prominence: *Janecek* as a precedent for Public Interest Litigation in other Member States about the same or similar issues;[13] *Invitel* as a precedent for follow-on references to the ECJ, in particular in the aftermath of the Lehman Brothers collapse; and *Feryn* through strengthening the awareness about different forms of discrimination. In all three cases, the ECJ decided in favour of the plaintiffs—the non-governmental organizations (NGOs) and the public agency—leaving it to the Member States, their courts, and their authorities to transpose the judgments into the national legal systems. The analysis highlights the tension between well-meant judicial policies and the potentially erosive effects on the law. The sociological lens reveals a perspective in which the concrete legal arguments are shown to be much less important than the overall understanding, purpose, and function of Public Interest Litigation in a democratic society.

3.1 Public Interest Litigation and the Environment

Janecek[14] involved a resident who sued the Freistaat Bayern (Land of Bavaria) for not respecting the EU rules on emission standards for cars in the centre of the city. The litigation turned upon the question of how the politically agreed and European-wide set emission standards could and should be implemented, and what kind of remedies the citizens affected by their non-respect might need in order to put pressure on the public authorities to take the European benchmark seriously. The interview with the lawyer who brought the claim sheds light on how the case is built and on the strategic use of EU law:

> *Attorney*: How did it all begin? It started in 2004 approximately. But you have to say about my CV that I, as a lawyer, I've been a lawyer since '99 and started with environmental law and in the law firm of XXX, who had already decades previously operated in environmental law in a way that lawyers do not often do. It was often always the trial to continually find new ways to break new ground with which one can enforce the goals that you have. And since to look what developments can be seen, where will developments go to and then maybe also create cases with which you can apply these means and methods development—because

[13] 'Umweltklage gegen die EU: Die Emissionen müssen auf Null gefahren werden', interview with Gerd Winter (*Cicero Online*, 31 May 2018) <www.cicero.de/aussenpolitik/umweltklage-eu-schadensersatz-klimaschutz-erderwaermung-klimawandel>.

[14] Case C-237/07 *Janecek* [2008] ECLI:EU:C:2008:447.

> we experience so much what professors write beautifully in essays, only this is not interesting as long as it does not take place somewhere in the real application of law, namely in the judgments. For me it is the idea to find the ploy, the knack and to make the law fruitful in the development of law.[15]

Environmental problems should not be thought about only through the lens of their natural, chemical, physical, and social origins; instead, legal norms also have to shape reality:

> *Attorney*: We have, we have from January 1, namely 2005, for the first time fixed limits for particles that is 10 pm in the air. I do a lot in pollution control laws. And the limits are exceeded in almost all major cities and the municipalities they also will exceed. Let us simply turn the tables. Let us build suits/create suits with whom we can complain against the local authorities and complain against the states by saying: 'Listen! The limit is exceeded, you have to do something even blocking the streets temporarily to comply with the limits.' And then the German car manufacturers will pretty quickly seek for strict limits for their possible filters because otherwise they do not longer exist, then the technique is set very, very quickly. That was the background ... Then they were relatively fast also thrilled to turn the idea in this way. And then there was the question of how to build such a suit. Who is the one to claim and on what you can complain about?

So, it is not a matter of remedying a genuinely felt grievance, but of inventing a grievance in the first place:

> *Attorney*: There we actually are looking for the two/three best claimants who are possibly the most affected and these are often not those who are most active, like a pensioner or a person who finds it sympathetic, but is not involved but still is the most concerned person. That is not always a person involved in the organization of the resistance. That's usually not, it's usually someone else. We are looking for this person only to sign the legitimation to us. And we really only need the mandate. And I'll tell you, no client has to bother anymore ... Then we said, we need the places where the [monitoring] stations are. We need to know where they are and we need residents who practically live on this station. They quasi must sleep on the station. I do not want to meet the problem, in which the opponent raises the objection: Yes, but there the limit is not at all exceeded [because the claimant is not living directly there].

[15] The quotes in this section are from interviews conducted as a part of the ERC project (n 6).

The lawyer's intention is not to represent aggrieved individuals as clients, but to find people who are willing merely to slip into the role of a plaintiff without needing to fear the risk of litigation. It is not about personal concern; it is about initiating a court case in which national authorities have to face the accusation of disregarding EU directives. This, however, takes the form of a deliberate theatrical disguise in which a plaintiff-actor is sought who does not necessarily have to understand the meaning of the litigation in which they will be involved. The pitch would look approximately like the following text, which can be expanded if necessary:

> *Attorney*: I do a lot in pollution control laws. And the limits are exceeded in almost all major cities and the municipalities they also will exceed. Let us simply turn the tables. Let us build suits/create suits with whom we can complain against the local authorities and complain against the states by saying: 'Listen! The limit is exceeded, you have to do something even blocking the streets temporarily to comply with the limits.' And then the German car manufacturers will pretty quickly seek for strict limits for their possible filters because otherwise they do not longer exist, then the technique is set very, very quickly.

So the lawyer is not talking about the universal issue of air pollution in Munich or, say, Rome, but about restrictions on civic life in daily commutes or transport of supplies. He wants to talk about the German car industry, which risks being wiped out (*no longer exist)* if it is not able to present sufficient technical progress fast enough to obey EU directives. There are about 830,000 employees in the German automotive industry, not to mention suppliers worldwide. Who among them will have invented the 'possible filters' by the deadline and thus secure a job, a family, and an established social life? And of course we can guess how a non-professional lawyer imagines the evolutionary history of mankind, how such a lawyer understands the industrial history of the last 200 years—obviously it was legislation that built electrodynamics and steelworks.

Alas, the internal focus of the legal profession is to fortify and interpret the law. But still, the neglect exhibited towards natural persons—the clients—is astounding: they are regarded as mere pawns. Is the lawyer talking about real people who have been insulted by being deprived of their civil rights? Is he talking about common sense? No, not at all—he is talking about the reduction of complexity of world climate issues as he finds them represented in Munich, where the politically defined limits are exceeded. He concentrates on the particularistic formalistic essence (finding '*the best claimants*'); this is law pretending to solve universal problems. There is, of course, an element of trained and rabulistic 'professional'—or, better, 'expert'—knowledge of the discourse that enables the straining of the logic of legal thinking of court proceedings to the utmost limit:

Interviewer: And how then runs the financing?
Attorney: The funding runs in the background on the associations; no client/claimant has to take care about it.

The claimant is Deutsche Umwelthilfe ev (DUH), an environmental organization with a broad scope of political activities and the legal standing to sue all those infringing environmental protection rules. In 2019, DUH had a budget of eleven million euros, which came (to a considerable degree) from the German government and publicly financed projects.[16] DUH sees itself as an NGO—although it is also publicly funded—that specializes in taking legal action against producers, traders, and public bodies that may be accused of violating the law and regulations. In fact, one might wonder whether DUH would much better qualify as a 'quango', but this question is outside the bounds of the chapter.

There seems to be a structural conflict between the ardent desire to address air pollution and the unwieldy status of European regions which may inadvertently fail, or obstinately refuse, to follow the clean air standards, many of which may seem high-minded.[17] We find a disjunction caused by the benevolent mainstream political issues that have been transformed into EU law on the one hand, and real life, which does not comply with wishful political thinking, on the other. The ECJ is asked to fill this structural gap. If the ECJ responds, it is running into a dialectical trap of deciding how political Europe, in all its structures and articulated apparatuses, will apply legal norms in relation to the real social configuration of cases within twenty-seven nations having very different cultural histories behind them, all of which have to be harmonized and managed. This increases the danger of de-professionalization because European laws have to be applied in these often awkward realities. But there is another challenge. Given the varying historical context and the non-simultaneity of social development across the twenty-seven Member States and their different legal traditions and cultural certainties, there is also varying access to the scarce resource of 'law'. To this day, we have not heard of a state-funded NGO taking up similar litigation in Athens, Lisbon, or Helsinki. Should a German peculiarity pacify the entire EU?

European Union norms pave the way for environmental organizations to pressurize judicial personnel to take a decision which can hardly be made within the structures of professionalized deliberation and action. The following quote

[16] DeutscheUmwelthilfe, 'Transparenz' (Transparency) <www.duh.de/ueberuns/transparenz/>.

[17] Hans Rosling, Anna Rosling Rönnlund, and Ola Rosling, *Factfulness: Ten Reasons We're Wrong About the World—And Why Things Are Better Than You Think* (Flatiron Books 2018), dealing with the questions of how and why—transferred to our context—NGOs are turning a policy issue into an acute problem; in other words, why NGOs are so prone to misrepresentation of social reality.

documents how the German judge is at pains to apply the law to a case which does not fit into the standard procedural setting.

> *Judge*: The cry has to go to Brussels, where these arrangements were made. If it turns out what I understand from the different positions, to summarize it, it is not foreseeable in the near future or only could be done with measures that are considered as disproportionate from our point of view, then there is one possibility, by saying, so then we just change the directive. And then we do not have a value of 40 but 80-whatever, or 75. It may be—one could do that but as long as the laws are there, they must be followed in any way . . .
>
> Whether there are those measures, which are proportional it is something we do not have to decide. This is then the responsibility of the Ministry, which has to do this under certain circumstances, and the plaintiff to say, that's enough or not enough. We have not to decide this. And I think, as I said, the problem lies elsewhere, namely on the level where these laws were created, and I believe you [to the representatives of the Ministry] it's implementation for an official in the Ministry at *Rosenkavalierplatz* [residence of the Ministry] is simply inconceivable, to say, like Karl Valentin[18] did—all of Munich is open for cyclists on Mondays, and for pedestrians on Tuesdays—those days are gone. This will not actually be enforceable.
>
> That we know—we're not entirely stupid. And we know very well. However, it is not about whether we realize it or not, as long as the legal situation is such that a claim exists, that actions, appropriate actions have to be taken, we will probably have to require that those responsible take such appropriate measures.
>
> So the whole thing is, we can see quite clearly will fall on our feet again [a German saying: *auf die Füße fallen*, which means all efforts are in vain] and what we do here is a showcase. I know all that. And we are actually in the concrete form that we, PM10 and NO2 to reach next year, the year after next, we will not reach. You know that [to party Bavaria] and you know it [to DUH] and we know it. I know that the whole we are doing here just has just an appellative character. As long as I'm on duty here, we will not achieve that Munich can apply these values. That is very clear.

The judge comprehends the forced de-professionalization, that the Supreme Administrative Court is being 'abused' for a 'showcase', that nothing is actually being achieved in this artificially constructed case. Is the legal system eroded deliberately? Certainly not. But it is not an isolated phenomenon. Instead, our argument is, de-professionalization is systemically inbuilt in the interaction between the national courts and the ECJ in this type of strategic litigation.

[18] Karl Valentin, 1882–1948. A Bavarian humorist and logician of speech and meaning.

3.2 Public Interest Litigation and Non-discrimination

The *Feryn* case[19] concerned a company that specialized in the sale and installation of up-and-over and sectional doors. To this end, *Feryn* placed a large 'vacancies' sign on its premises alongside the main road between Brussels and Antwerp. On 28 April 2005, the newspaper *De Standaard* published an interview with Pascal Feryn, one of the firm's directors, under the headline 'Customers do not want Moroccans'. Feryn was reported to have said that his firm would not recruit persons of Moroccan origin, although, we should add, in his office two Moroccans are already working constantly:

> *Feryn*: Apart from these Moroccans, no one else has responded to our notice in two weeks ... but we aren't looking for Moroccans. Our customers don't want them. They have to install up-and-over doors in private homes, often villas, and those customers don't want them coming into their homes.

The plaintiff in the case was the Centre for Equal Opportunities and Opposition to Racism.[20] They accused Feryn of discriminating against migrants:

> *The head of the Centre*: Now, immediately, we reacted and we said that, given the anti-discrimination legislation in Belgium and in the EU, by the way, this what (was) not acceptable ... It was an idiot example of how prejudice tended towards results that nobody wanted. Not finding workforce and people staying unemployed because no match ... [T]he ambition, in a certain way, [was, THR] to educate the Belgian public so to say, things can go wrong, people can make mistakes, but they can correct it. And we offer the possibility to correct it.

There is a formally independent Centre, financed by taxpayer's money, and two angry ministers who put pressure on the Centre to act. The case was initially dismissed at first instance, but later transferred to the ECJ. The ECJ found that there was discrimination even though, if my understanding is correct, there was no aggrieved party, no person whose job application had actually been turned down. What can that mean? Law and litigation shall '*educate the Belgian public*'?[21] However, one has to recall that the ECJ does not have the capacity to make such findings. The only legal option was to treat the case as inadmissible because of its

[19] Case C-54/07 *Feryn* [2008] ECLI:EU:C:2008:397, para 5.

[20] The Centrum voor Gelijkheid van Kansen en voor Racismebestrijding (Centre for Equal Opportunities and Opposition to Racism or CGKR) is a body for the promotion of equal treatment and was established by a Law of 15 February 1993. That Law was amended by a Law of 25 February 2003 (the Law Against Discrimination), which transposed Directive 2000/43 into Belgian law. The CGKR has since been renamed 'Unia' <www.unia.be/en/about-unia>.

[21] The educational mandate of the law seems somewhat unusual to me and reminds me, from afar, of Mao Tse Tung's famous words: 'punish one and educate thousands'.

hypothetical nature. The attitude of the ECJ leads to de-professionalization of the EU judiciary by conforming to the official Belgian ideological views and accepting the Centre's premise from the outset.

In two different interviews with the Advocate General and another judge, the Advocate General argues:

> *Advocate General*: I find it very problematic, very problematic if we start saying, every company is entitled to discriminate because its clients want it to discriminate … it is precisely because of this sociological reality that it is important that the law imposes on any company, not to discriminate, otherwise how are you coming to overcome that? You never overcome it. So the fact is the law will impose on any company whatsoever that it cannot discriminate.

'Sociological reality' consists of theories and research findings. Sociological reality is certainly different from the social reality of general life practice, to which the Advocate General seems to refer. Life practice has to decide every day between possibilities for action (eg do I buy bread or cake, or more seriously—should I marry A or B or C?), a question that each individual has to answer for themselves. Choosing one option from several options means rejecting others; it means to 'discriminate'. We humans cannot escape such a decision-making situation. Over time, the term discrimination has changed its social meaning. It is understood as 'disparagement, disadvantage, denigration', which must be prevented and abolished. This judge of the ECJ dedicates his power to enforce European, value-based legal principles. Should we speak here of 'political judicial instead of sociological realities' or 'political thinking' when entering the court turns into a kind of 'jurisprudential wishful reality' rubbing up against social reality? This is very honourable conviction; however, it is refracted in the cultural conflicts that actually occur in inclusive Western societies. The Belgian population perceives what is happening in this small country in an unusual way.

To go a step further: in an interview led by Betül Kas with a second judge involved, this judge is full of doubts as to whether the right decision was taken after rereading the judgment. He is scrupulous ('it would have been better … *I would decide different[ly]* … ') ventilating all the arguments at stake. He brings us an irritating argument:

> *Judge*: There is one thing about judicial decision making, which in academia quite often is forgotten and this is the question of time … I had to work the whole weekend … you have much more time [pointed to the academic interviewer] than a judge himself … in there is always the interest to do justice in time …

De-professionalization occurs in this very moment. To produce justice can never be a function of time, and judges must defend their independence even in situations of stress. The *Feryn* case, with its intricate details, lasted for years, and an on-the-spot, de-professionalized judgment irritates the judge in charge years after it was passed. Additionally, we should not forget the costs that the litigation entailed for the defendant. After intervention of the interviewer ('… it cost them 5 hundred thousand (500,000)'), the judge replies:

> [T]hat is enormous … I know the tenor of the judgement can be published … interesting. I have never seen that… interesting [laughing] 500,000 Euros? That is enormous … [laughing]. The whole judgement? And that was the judgement? … The whole judgment? … [laughing] … Interesting.[22]

The judge, startled by the consequence of what the ECJ had evaluated and by the outcome of the national Belgian Court's decision, washes his hands of the matter. He has a strong feeling that the outcome of this lawsuit is overdone, exaggerated, and hard to accept. And in the end, he returns to the phenomenon that the ECJ is overloaded with cases and under greater time pressure than the supreme courts in other countries, such as the United States, the United Kingdom, Sweden, and Germany. In his Homeric laughter, he admits that everything in this case was overdone and that he would have decided differently after having been better informed and if only there had been enough time.

3.3 Public Interest Litigation and Consumer Protection

In *Invitel*,[23] the Hungarian Consumer Protection Agency (CPA) challenged the practice of requiring, in fixed-term 'loyalty contracts' (and, subsequently, to the conclusion of those contracts), that the consumer pay fees which had not initially been agreed by them. Invitel introduced into its general business conditions (GBC) a term providing for 'money order fees'; that is to say, the fees applied in the event of payment of invoices by a money order. According to that term, 'if the subscriber pays the amount of the invoice by means of a money order, the supplier of services shall have the right to invoice the additional fees which result (such as postal fees)'. Furthermore, the GBC did not contain any term specifying the method of calculating those money order fees. The CPA received no less than fifty complaints from consumers in relation to that term. As Invitel refused to amend it, the CPA brought an action before the Pest Megyei Bíróság (Pest County Court) with a view to obtaining a declaration that the contested term was void for unfairness, and an

[22] The court of last instance in Belgium ruled that the defendant had to publish the entire judgment verbatim at his own expense in the four most important daily newspapers in Belgium.
[23] Case C–472/10 *Invitel* [2012] ECLI:EU:C:2012:242.

order of automatic and retroactive reimbursement to subscribers of the amounts wrongly invoiced and received as 'money order fees'.

The interviews conducted by our researchers in relation to this case were linguistically complex, as the interviewer did not speak Hungarian and the Hungarian lawyers and judges were sometimes communicating in broken English. What shines through the interviews seems nevertheless paradigmatic. Advocate General Nils Wahl's irritation is well documented in his Opinion in *Macinský*, where he claims that even after having had the matter returned, the referring Hungarian court was unable to clarify the relationship between the different national legal rules and their position vis-à-vis EU law. Therefore, Advocate General Wahl remained uncertain whether he had properly understood the specific national context in which the preliminary reference question had arisen:

> Moving swiftly on, I will begin by recalling that, although in proceedings under Article 267 TFEU the Court may not rule upon the compatibility of a provision of national law with EU law or interpret national legislation, it may nevertheless provide the national court with an interpretation of EU law on all such points as may enable that court to determine the issue of compatibility for the purposes of the case before it. (18) Providing such assistance invariably requires a modicum of understanding by the Court of the relevant applicable national rules, even though that understanding obviously remains entirely subject to verification by the national court. With this general caveat in mind, I will state the following.[24]

I would join Advocate General Wahl. As a legal sociologist, I could not determine exactly what was the subject matter of the action in Hungarian law. Additionally, the judicial personnel questioned had only vague ideas about what could have happened and what should happen. In a complicated legal-historical situation, the Hungarian court tried to come to a reasonable decision while grappling with the combination of legal remnants of the 'KuK empire',[25] communist law, and the rediscovered national sources of law after the breakdown of communism, all in confrontation with the overarching EU law. There was an ECJ judgment urging the parties before the lower courts to agree to find a solution for the fifty plaintiffs trying to deal with the new terms and conditions of an IT company capitalized under EU law. In a nutshell, *Invitel* demonstrates the characteristics and the limits of litigation before the ECJ. The Court has neither the power nor the means to fully

[24] Case C-482/12 *Macinský and Macinská* [2013] ECLI:EU:C:2013:765, Opinion of AG Wahl, para 34.

[25] The adjective *kaiserlich-königlich* (usually abbreviated to k k), German for imperial-royal, was applied to the authorities and state institutions of the Austrian Empire until the Austro-Hungarian Compromise of 1867, which established the Austro-Hungarian Empire <https://en.wikipedia.org/wiki/Imperial-royal>.

reconstruct the case; it has to rely on the facts as they are presented to it by the referring national court. The ECJ is not aware that, as a consequence of its judgment, the service provider, Invitel, will in future collectivize the transaction costs arising from consumers paying via money order or 'yellow cheque'. The provider can live with this compromise.

An interview with a Hungarian judge and their colleague contained the following argument:

INTERVIEWER: So I heard today that it was not only one case right but two cases.
JUDGE: Yes two similar cases.
INTERVIEWER: And one went to the Constitutional Court and one went to the European Court of Justice.
JUDGE: Yes.

We have to keep in mind: the question here is whether Invitel is allowed to charge customers for the costs they incur because of the way the customers make their payments. The 'constitutional' aspect of this issue remains very unclear to me, as does as the European dimension:

INTERVIEWER: ... And with the European Court of Justice I was wondering why this question was put about the actio popularis and the erga omnes effect.
JUDGE: The Constitutional Court ... refused the question, it's some procedural problems. There is a new Constitutional Act in Hungary and the question it isn't good for the new Constitutional Act.
INTERVIEWER: And to the Court of Justice why was it not asked about the refund to the consumers at all?
JUDGE 2: Could you repeat the question?
JUDGE: My decision was cannot refuse the cost. It's the decision of the [to Judge 2: how do you say legal basis?]
JUDGE 2: Causal...
JUDGE: And other litigation came the customers to claim the money.
INTERVIEWER: But in this case not?
JUDGE: Not. And the opinion of AG Trstenjak is in my opinion too. It is impossible in one case and there isn't any legal national act possibility to refuse the money (he means there is no legal basis). In one case, because in the Hungarian Procedure Act [to Judge 2: how do you say stipulates? In Hungarian: a compensation can only be granted to a plaintiff that is a party to the case]. Third party, isn't in the process...
INTERVIEWER: Because it's a private relationship and a third party is not... OK.
JUDGE: Yes, there [isn't?] any rules in Hungary procedures [like] actio popularis and other system. [To Judge 2: what is a joinder of claims in English?]
JUDGE 2: Lot of parties in the claimer on the other parties...

JUDGE: If it's possible but . . .
JUDGE 2: A society of claimers. [he means a joinder of claims] [inaudible]

This conversation, which is a vital part of the whole interview, exceeds my possibilities of pure semantic and linguistic understanding, as I am not acquainted with Hungarian law; but still the question is whether Invitel was right when charging the customers for using the 'yellow cheques':

INTERVIEWER: And this yellow cheque? When you go to the post office? Is this a general problem in Hungary?
JUDGE: No.
INTERVIEWER: Because I know in Italy it's the same . . .
JUDGE: [In Hungarian to Judge 2: when the companies charged the postal fee onto the customers]. It isn't a big problem, low problem. I think that it's a very small problem but there is a general system in Hungary [to Man 2: what is provider in English?]
JUDGE 2: Provider.
JUDGE: The provider changed the services. It's one time, one moment, one fact. The yellow cheque, lots of another same problem in Hungary. Newer costs try to [?] to the customers.

After being reassured that the 'yellow cheques' are neither a general nor an individual problem for customers, and perhaps only a small problem for the society, we remain confused by the cryptic discussion. What follows is this statement:

INTERVIEWER: I see, and the answer from the court of justice, was it useful for the case?
JUDGE: Absolutely, very good indeed. In the first case, the provider said ok, it's right, I'll pay for the customers the money and [to Judge 2: how do you say terminate?].

The Hungarian judge is very satisfied with the ECJ's decision and, like the head CPA participating in the interview, he believes that Invitel will pay the yellow cheque fees out of the enterprise's piggy bank and is not aware that, in reality, the corresponding costs are now passed on to the entire clientele. 'In the real world there is no cup of coffee for free', said national economist Hayek at the time.

The Hungarian judge had to decide whether the CPA's claim was justified, and whether Invitel should return to the 'old' practice that customers using the yellow cheques should not pay fees. That would be the old socialist model of camouflaging the costs of service, and thereby now assisting the state-owned Hungarian Post, which sticks to the old model. The other option was to deny this claim because of the unfair treatment of different consumer groups in developing capitalism. He chose a third way: he took the opportunity to address the ECJ with questions regarding the national law. The ECJ ruled that this was possible.

A concluding remark on this case, which tells us something about the *conditio humana* whenever knowledge and exploratory case understanding suggest giving up in view of the dark complexity of the information received. The reader is likely to be perplexed, just as Advocate General Wahl was, by this almost Babylonian confusion of languages and multiple case descriptions, and the location in a historical transformation phase of the Hungarian legal system, suspended between EU law and traditional national law. A phase which—at least according to the sensitive Hungarian court—reveals incompatibilities and small-scale grey areas. The Hungarian court obviously is overwhelmed by EU laws, regulations, directives, rules, and side-rules, and seeks help. The ECJ is not equipped to understand the different and frequently alien national laws. Powerless to understand what is going on, the ECJ finds a wise Solomonic judgment, which delivers a decision against the background of blurred circumstances: it avoids dealing with the interests of the entrepreneurs and the fifty claimants. Its self-understanding in this specific situation is one of referee in an unknown playground. No matter what the question is, the ECJ is paving the way for Paul Feyerabend's reflections on 'Anything Goes', which, as a thought construct, means that science must repeatedly violate its own rules of knowledge aggregation in order to be successful—we remember Galileo and Copernicus, Einstein and Heisenberg. At the same time, we have to ask ourselves whether it is jurisprudence that really gives birth to new insights into the social and physical world, or whether it does not perhaps subsequently try to judge what is fact, or even adapt to the desired goals of the respective social organizations and institutions created from the political sphere.[26]

4. Legal Professionalization and Public Interest Litigation

When putting sociological analysis into the legal context, three particularities of the EU legal order spring to mind, all three operating at a different level: at the level of the institutional architecture of the preliminary reference procedure,[27] which enables Public Interest Litigation; at the level of the nature of EU law, which is often programmatic and complements Dworkin's[28] distinction between rules and principles, thereby increasing the role of the judiciary; and finally, at the level of legal education or, better, via the lack of a genuinely European legal education,[29] which

26 Paul Feyerabend, *Against Method* (Verso 1975); *Science in a Free Society* (Verso 1982).

27 In sociological language: to the structures of case processing within the legal disciplines that have developed architecturally in the context of meaning.

28 Ronald M Dworkin, 'The Model of Rules' (1935) 35 The University of Chicago Law Review 14.

29 See, in particular, the following publications by Bruno de Witte: 'The Scope of Community Powers in Education and Culture in the Light of Subsequent Practice' in Roland Bieber and Georg Ress (eds),

tackles the particularities of the EU legal order and the preliminary reference procedure (Hans-W Micklitz). Each of the three deserves a deeper presentation and analysis. For the purpose of this chapter, however, I will paint with a broad brush so as to be able to reconnect the three particularities to the impact of Public Interest Litigation on legal professionalization.

The preliminary reference procedure pursues a twofold purpose: the ECJ shall provide a useful answer to the referring court, and the ECJ shall give a valid interpretation for EU law as such.[30] The ECJ has no adjudicative power to decide the case. Therefore, the role of the individual case before the ECJ is neither institutionally nor structurally comparable to the adjudicative power of national courts. The diverse amendments of the Treaty of Rome are claimed to have transformed the rule-based 1957 Treaty into a programmatic Lisbon Treaty in 2007.[31] Secondary EU law, particularly in social regulation, is said to be ever more often read like an action plan, which the ECJ then has to transform into some sort of hard law.[32] The programmatic language tends to obscure the political dissent among the EU institutions and between the EU and the Member States, hidden in extensive, sometimes contradictory, recitals. Jürgen Habermas characterizes EU law as techno-law, an assessment which triggered a theoretical debate but has not yet made its way into legal doctrine.[33] The EU is the driving force in the ongoing transformation of the appearance—the external form—of the law, a phenomenon which can equally be observed in national law. Legal education has remained entirely in the hands of the Member States. With the exception of the University of Maastricht, there is no single institution where young lawyers are educated in EU law straight away. European law is an add-on in legal education, whose importance depends on the priorities of the Member States and the place they are ready to grant to EU law in the education of young lawyers. These crude facts determine the European legal expertise of national judges as well as the ECJ judges. Strictly speaking, there are twenty-seven versions of European legal expertise, which must be merged within

Die Dynamik des europäischen Gemeinschaftsrechts (Nomos 1987); *European Community Law of Education* (Nomos 1989); 'The European Dimension of Legal Education' in Peter Birks (ed), *Reviewing Legal Education* (Oxford University Press 1994).

[30] Lucía López Zurita, 'The Survival of the Fitted? Individual Protection in the European Court of Justice's Preliminary Ruling Procedure' (PhD thesis, European University Institute 2021).

[31] Ernst-Joachim Mestmäcker, 'Auf dem Wege zu einer Ordnungspolitik für Europa' in Ernst-Joachim Mestmäcker, H Möller, and HP Schwartz (eds), *Eine Ordnungspolitik für Europa. Festschrift für Hans von der Groeben* (Nomos 1987); Joseph HH Weiler, 'Deciphering the Political and Legal DNA of European Integration: An Exploratory Essay' in Julie Dickson and Paulos Eleftheriadis (eds), *Philosophical Foundations of European Union Law* (Oxford University Press 2012).

[32] Hugh Collins, 'The Revolutionary Trajectory of EU Contract Law towards Post-national Law' in Sarah Worthington, Andrew Robertson, and Graham Virgo (eds), *Revolution and Evolution in Private Law* (Hart Publishing 2017); Marten Scheffer and others, 'The Rise and Fall of Rationality in Language' (2021) 118(51) Proceedings of the National Academy of Sciences of the United States of America (PNAS) e2107848118 <doi.org/10.1073/pnas.2107848118>.

[33] Jürgen Habermas, *The Lure of Technocracy* (Polity Press 2015).

the European institutions' understanding of EU law and transformed into an 'autonomous' EU legal tradition.

4.1 *Janecek*, *Feryn*, and *Invitel* in the Institutional Context

How does the political commitment to a policy field affect the professionalization of the lawyers involved as 'professionalized professions', in whatever roles they are acting—as judges or attorneys for civil society organizations or public agencies fighting for the 'good cause'?[34] If we follow the sociological analysis, all three of the selected cases lack a client affected by a real-life problem, a client who has lost their autonomy. Public Interest Litigation looks like a tool to fine-tune the programmatic lawmaking and to instrumentalize the judiciary for policy purposes. The result is juristocracy.[35] The plaintiff acts as an instigator in setting the judicial machinery in motion. The claimants, the NGOs or the public agencies, are preparing the legal ammunition needed for identifying or 'creating' the 'appropriate' case. All key institutional actors are involved: the EU legislature provides vague laws, the ECJ integrates Public Interest Litigation into the preliminary reference procedure, and the Member States implement the ECJ decisions via their courts and/or via their laws.[36] The question is not really new. It suffices to remember Karl Llewellyn's[37] point that one should litigate disputes that make litigation respectable, or Frederick Schauer's[38] work on cases and bad law. The three cases are certainly more than 'just a case', as they are not really cases in the first place. Whether they produce bad law is not our primary concern. Instead, we are interested in a more general issue: the impact of European Public Interest Litigation on legal professionalization.

One might not share Thomas Roethe's analysis on the role of the courts, nor agree with the societal relevance of *Janecek*, *Feryn*, or *Invitel*. This is not a chapter on the legitimacy of social regulation. The question is whether judges are still acting as professionalized lawyers or whether they have turned themselves into social engineers; whether there are differences between national and European judges and, if so, what this means for EU law. In *Janecek*, the German administrative judge is

[34] In Germany, the DUH came under heavy attack from business circles, in particular from the car industry; see Remo Klinger, *Banal statt Skandal: Das Umwelthilfe-Urteil des BGH Verbraucher und Recht* (2019) Editorial Heft 10, 361.

[35] Ran Hirschl, *Towards Juristocracy* (Harvard University Press 2004).

[36] I am relying on previous research in *The Politics of Judicial Co-operation, Part II* (Cambridge University Press 2018) 112.

[37] See William C Heffernan, 'The Dual Problems of Legal Justification: A Key to the Unity of Karl Llewellyn's Jurisprudence' (1978) 45 The University of Chicago Law Review 654, 654–69; as to the problem of relying on disputes decided in courts, see George L Priest and Benjamin Klein, 'The Selection of Disputes for Litigation,' (1984) 13 Journal of Legal Studies 1.

[38] Frederick Schauer, 'Do Cases Make Bad Law?' (2006) 73 University of Chicago Law Review 883 and Frederick Schauer and Richard J Zeckhauser, 'The Trouble with Cases' (2009) Harvard Kennedy School Working Paper No RWP09-025 <ssrn.com/abstract=1523310>.

outraged ('showcase') and may be inclined to reject the 'invented' remedy, but ultimately remains loyal to EU law and decides 'the case' as he feels he has to. The ECJ expects the national court to force the authorities of the Freistaat Bayern to find ways and means to implement the European emission standards. Both courts break up the classical separation between powers. The courts are no longer just reviewing administrative action; they are pushing national authorities into action, thereby opening an endless back and forth between the plaintiff and the national authorities on whether the different steps in the action plan suffice to meet the EU emission standards.

In *Feryn* and *Janecek* the ECJ—'We the Court'[39]—accepts responsibility for surveying and monitoring the implementation of the environmental and equal treatment regulations. There is, however, a mismatch between the legally presupposed reality and the social reality. *Janecek*, even after the final judgment of the German administrative court, did not automatically lead to compliance with EU emission standards, nor did *Feryn* abolish discrimination against Moroccan immigrants in the installation of garage doors. The rulings ignore the social reality, the persistence of the executive, and the circumvention strategies of companies faced with the—in our case imputed—discriminatory wishes of their clientele. One might conceive the judgments as 'empty precedents' which could be later filled with social reality.[40] Much more than legal measures are needed. The judgments can only become social reality when they are accepted by the civil society. The ECJ attributes to the judiciary an educative function, imagining a civil society which does not (yet) exist. The sad alternative to societal integration would be that the judgments are leading nowhere, an assessment which would require a separate empirical study.

Public Interest Litigation requires a managerial judge, well-known from class action and group action,[41] whether based on opt-in or opt-out.[42] The vast majority of group/class actions are settled, often after many years of litigation. The judge has two tasks: to decide whether the law has been infringed and to manage how the compensation shall be distributed between the group or class. The managing judge cannot easily be reconciled with a more traditional understanding of the role of the judge. Public Interest Litigation can hardly be compared with collective redress. There are true victims in collective redress actions, and it is for the national judge to approve or reject compensation. The ECJ judges, on the other hand, are charged

[39] Miguel Poiares Maduro, *We the Court: The European Court of Justice and the European Economic Constitution* (Hart Publishing 1998).

[40] I would like to thank Urska Sadl for pointing me to the possibility of 'empty precedents'.

[41] Joel F Handler, *Social Movements and the Legal System: A Theory of Law Reform and Social Change* (Academic Press 1978).

[42] Hans-Wolfgang Micklitz and Astrid Stadler, 'Gruppenklagen in den Mitgliedstaaten der Europäischen Gemeinschaft & den Vereinigten Staaten von Amerika' in T Gabriel and B Pirker-Hörmann (eds), *Massen-verfahren Reformbedarf für die ZPO?* (Verlag Österreich 2005); critical but with emphasis on efficiency, Christopher Hodges, *The Reform of Class and Representative Actions in European Legal Systems: A New Framework for Collective Redress in Europe* (Hart Publishing 2008).

with resolving a conflict between the Member States' legal orders and the EU legal order. They must balance out market rationality with social rationality. Betül Kas' reconstruction demonstrates the limits of the ECJ and national courts in 'solving' conflicts with a strong societal dimension. At the very best, the ECJ may initiate a political debate in the national and EU fora and in the national and European society(ies). Therefore, the ECJ can be understood as a hybrid institution, combining judiciary with administrative and legislative powers.[43]

My reading of *Invitel* is deeply marked by my involvement in the Eastern enlargement and the experience I gained in the collaboration with lawyers.[44] I had two types of interlocutors, those who had received their legal education during communist times and those who had studied law in the West and had returned to their home countries after the fall of the Berlin wall. The communist legacy which I experienced prior to accession seems to be still alive, to which the national legal education might have contributed.[45] That is why I have some sympathy for the Hungarian judges who are struggling with EU law and the ECJ. The extract from the interview demonstrates that the Hungarian judges expected first and foremost a 'useful' answer from the ECJ, one which would help them to understand the distinction between individual and collective enforcement, the 'third parties' effect of the action for an injunction, and some guidance on where to place a European *actio popularis* in the national constitutional order. *Invitel*, decided in 2012, documents a miscommunication between the two courts. Neither the Advocate General nor the ECJ made an effort, similar to that of Advocate General Wahl in *Machinský*, to understand the intricacies of the Hungarian law. The ECJ's reasoning is extremely formal and, in a way, superficial. The judicial interaction is miles away from the dense exchange that has arisen in the context of a question about the legality of Swiss franc loans in the new Member States.[46] The series of references tells a story of the awakening of the Central and Eastern European civil society and the discovery of the preliminary reference procedure as a means of changing the national law.[47]

[43] Hans-Wolfgang Micklitz, 'The Transformation of Enforcement in EU Private Law: Preliminary Considerations' (2015) 23 European Review of Private Law 491.

[44] Michal Bobek, 'Prologue: Westernisation of the East and Easternisation of the West' in Michal Bobek (ed), *Central European Judges under the European Influence: The Transformative Power of the EU Revisited* (Hart Publishing 2015).

[45] Cosmin Cercel, 'The Destruction of Legal Reason: Lessons from the Past' (2019) 89 Acta Universitatis Lodziensis Folia Iuridica 15.

[46] Mónika Józon, 'Unfair Contract Terms Law in Europe in Times of Crisis: Substantive Justice Lost in the Paradise of Proceduralisation of Contract Fairness' (2017) 6 Journal of European Consumer and Market Law 157, 163; Emilia Mišćenić, 'Currency Clauses in CHF Credit Agreements: A "Small Wheel" in the Swiss Loans Mechanism' (2020) 6 Journal of European Consumer and Market Law 226, with reference to Opinion of the European Central Bank of 18 July 2019 on the conversion of Swiss franc loans (CON/2019/27).

[47] More generally, Bobek, *Central European Judges Under the European Influence* (n 46); Federica Casarosa (ed), *The Practice of Judicial Interaction in the Field of Fundamental Rights* (Elgar 2022).

4.2 *Janecek*, *Feryn*, and *Invitel* in the Programmatic Context

The cases also wonderfully document the programmatic language of EU environmental, consumer, and non-discrimination law, and the attempt of the ECJ to transform rather broad statements of intent into hard law. The common denominator of our analysis is the question of whether Public Interest Litigation implies a risk for the legal profession of 'going beyond the law', albeit for very valid, politically legitimate reasons. Who can be against social regulation? Again, the question is *not* whether the ECJ's legal reasoning is flawed. The perspective is more 'outside in' than 'inside out' on what Public Interest Litigation is doing to the law and to the legal profession.

Let us recall the key sequences of the respective secondary EU law, the questions of the referring courts and the answers by the ECJ. The underlying law, the question and the answer of the three judgments are reduced to the absolute minimum, so as to focus on their potential effect on legal professionalization.[48]

Janecek:

Article 7 of Directive 96/62, headed 'Improvement of ambient air quality—General requirements', provides: '1. Member States shall take the necessary measures to ensure compliance with the limit values ... 3. Member States shall draw up action plans indicating the measures to be taken in the short term where there is a risk of the limit values and/or alert thresholds being exceeded, in order to reduce that risk and to limit the duration of such an occurrence.'

Question of the referring Court: 'Is Article 7(3) of Council Directive 96/62 ... to be interpreted as meaning that a third party whose health is impaired is entitled to the preparation of an action plan even if, irrespective of any action plan, he is in a position to enforce his right to avoid any detriment to his health as a result of the emission limit value for particulate matter PM10 being exceeded, by bringing an action for intervention by the public authority?'

Answer of the ECJ: '(42) The answer to the first question must therefore be that Article 7(3) of Directive 96/62 must be interpreted as meaning that ... those persons may have other courses of action available to them for requiring those authorities to take measures to combat atmospheric pollution.'

[48] The two summary sections of *Janecek* and *Feryn* are created by merging different passages taken from the ECJ judgment, without changing the wording.

Feryn:

Article 15 of Directive 2000/43/EC: 'Member States shall lay down the rules on sanctions … which may comprise the payment of compensation to the victim, must be effective, proportionate and dissuasive.'

The sixth question (as reformulated by the ECJ) '(35) The sixth question asks, essentially, what sanctions may be considered to be appropriate for employment discrimination established on the basis of the employer's public statements.'

Answer of the ECJ: 'The answer to the sixth question must therefore be that Article 15 of Directive 2000/43 requires that rules on sanctions applicable to breaches of national provisions adopted in order to transpose that directive must be effective, proportionate and dissuasive, even where there is no identifiable victim.'

In *Janecek* and *Feryn,* the claimants—the German NGO and the Belgian Centre—faced a strategic challenge; at first glance, the two directives do not grant standing to either individual citizens or non-governmental organizations. The overall spirit behind the cases is the reliance on individual rights, also apparent in secondary EU law.[49] The addressees of those rights, if granted, are the Member States, which shall develop an action plan (*Janecek*) or provide for appropriate sanctions (*Feryn*). In both cases, the ECJ is 'inventing' a new remedy. In *Janecek*, it is the right for an affected 'strawman' (to use Roethe's language) to force the Member State to set up an action plan to ensure compliance with European emissions standards. In *Feryn*, the ECJ 'deduces' an action for an injunction to protect the potentially affected victims. How do these judgments fit into the overall picture of EU social regulation? The EU has no *Kompetenz-Kompetenz* and is dependent on the willingness of the Member States to delegate to it certain limited powers. The overly broad language of secondary EU law adopted on the basis of these delegated powers guarantees leeway to the Member States. However, it also opens up space for the European judiciary. In *Janecek* and *Feryn*, the ECJ is slipping into the role of the legislature or the executive, combining politics with policies. To repeat, the issue here is not the legitimacy of juristocracy, but staying true to legal professionalization. The ECJ is no longer just deciding a case but designing a particular element out of the social regulation mosaic, counteracting reluctance in the Member States, and setting aside conflicts within the national and European society(ies).[50]

[49] Eric Stein, 'Lawyers, Judges and the Making of a Transnational Constitution' (1981) 75 American Journal of International Law 1.

[50] Mikael Rask Madsen and others, 'Sovereignty, Substance, and Public Support for European Courts' Human Rights Rulings' (2021) 116 American Political Science Review 419.

The structural difference between an all-encompassing market order and a piecemeal social regulation is mirrored here. The ECJ judgments remain boxed in the respective policy fields. *Janecek* could be instrumentalized and tested for all sorts of claims against the Member States whenever they are not setting up action plans, for instance in financial services.[51] *Feryn* provides opportunities for reading in an action of injunction not only to other non-discrimination directives, but also, for instance, into product safety regulation. Silo-bound secondary EU law establishes a community of lawyers from all relevant actors in the field, who are strongly intertwined but are disconnected from other silos and from general law. This is not only true for substantive standards—emission standards or commercial practices—but also for 'rights, remedies and procedure'.[52] Public Interest Litigation enhances fragmentation within the legal profession, be they professionalized lawyers or technocratized ones, which means de-professionalized lawyers with legal experience.

In *Invitel*, we find the following:[53]

Article 3 of Directive 93/13/EC: 'A contractual term which has not been individually negotiated shall be regarded as unfair if, contrary to the requirement of good faith, it causes a significant imbalance in the parties' rights and obligations arising under the contract, to the detriment of the consumer.'

Article 6 of Directive 93/13/EC: 'Member States shall lay down that unfair terms used in a contract concluded with a consumer by a seller or supplier shall, as provided for under their national law, not be binding on the consumer.'

Question of the referring court: '(First question) May Article 6 be interpreted as meaning that an unfair contract term is not binding on any consumer where a (competent) body . . . seeks a declaration of the invalidity of that unfair term which has become part of a consumer contract on behalf of consumers in an action in the public interest (actio popularis)? May Article 6(1) . . . be interpreted, where an order which benefits consumers who are not party to the proceedings is made . . . in an action in the public interest, as meaning that an unfair term . . . is not binding on all consumers also as regards the future, so that the court has to apply the consequences in law thereof of its own motion? (Second question) May . . . that directive be interpreted as meaning that . . . a unilateral amendment . . . without explicitly describing the method by which prices vary or giving valid reasons in the contract . . . is unfair ipso jure?'

Second question reformulated by the ECJ: '(21) the referring court asks, in essence, whether, [respective articles] should be interpreted as meaning

[51] With regard to such a transfer, see Kai Purnhagen and Paul Verbruggen, 'Europäische Gemeinschaft' in Jürgen Keßler, Hans-W Micklitz, and Norbert Reich (eds), *Institutionelle Finanzmarktaufsicht und Verbraucherschutz. Eine rechtsvergleichende Untersuchung der Regelungssysteme in Deutschland, Italien, Schweden, dem Vereinigten Königreich und der Europäischen Gemeinschaft* (Nomos 2010).

[52] Walter van Gerven, 'Of Rights, Remedies and Procedures' (2000) 37 Common Market Law Review 501.

[53] Again, this is a merger of various passages of the judgment.

that ... a unilateral amendment of the fees connected with the service to be provided, without setting out clearly the method of fixing those fees or specifying a valid reason for this amendment, that term is unfair.'

Answer by the ECJ: '(31) ... to the second question is that the national court [has] ... to assess ... the unfair nature of ... [a term providing for] a unilateral amendment of fees ... the national court must determine, inter alia, whether ... the reasons for, or the method of, the amendment of the fees connected with the service to be provided are set out in plain, intelligible language and, as the case may be, whether consumers have a right to terminate the contract... [T]he answer to the first question is that ... the Directive ... must be interpreted as meaning that: —it does not preclude the declaration of invalidity of an unfair term ... [which] effects ... those consumers who were not party to the injunction proceedings.'

The difficulties in communication between the Hungarian and European judges, and the way in which the ECJ has reacted, result from the 'forced' character of the implementation of EU consumer law into the post-communist national legal orders. The political decision to apply for membership set a huge legislative machinery into motion. Progress in the candidate states was equalized with the transposition of the *aquis communautaire*. The one-size-fits-all approach left no room for seriously taking into account the communist legacy and its impact on the role of law in a political system. The result is a tripartite legal order:[54] the reinvigorated pre-communist private law rules, if there were any; the remainder of the civil law rules, ie those adopted during communist times and incrementally dealing with consumer protection; and, finally, the newly implemented secondary EU law. The three sets of rules are standing side by side, sometimes with overlapping scope of application and unclear legal boundaries.

What sounds complicated even at the surface level—the correct choice of the law—becomes truly difficult if we look into the differences between the legal cultures. During communist times, law had a programmatic political character. It was quite often implemented by public authorities even in private law relationships, with the communist party having the last word. Private law could survive only in an extremely formalistic understanding. Seen through the lenses of the new Member States, EU consumer law must look like another variant of what these societies had perceived in communist times, like just another political programme—merely the centre of power shifting from Moscow to Brussels, so to speak.[55] Those legal systems needed the Swiss franc loans references and the case law surrounding

[54] See the contributions in Paulina Bieś-Srokosz, Jacek Srokosz, and Ewelina Żelasko-Makowska (eds), *Mutual Interaction between Contemporary Systems and Branches of Law in European Countries* (S Podobiński Publishing House 2017); Fabrizio Cafaggi and others, 'Europeanization of Private Law in Central and Eastern Europe Countries (CEECS): Preliminary Findings and Research Agenda' (2010) European University Institute Working Papers Law 2010/15.

[55] These were, more or less, the words of a Serbian law professor whom the authors interviewed in the context of the adaptation process of Serbian law to EU consumer law, see Thomas Roethe, *Der Verbraucher. Rechtssoziologische Betrachtungen* (Nomos 2014).

them to build a connection between EU consumer law and the economic and social reality of the people. Seen in this way, *Invitel* came too early; there was not only 'no case', there was also no social issue which would have allowed the ECJ to delve deeper into the much broader problem behind the case. The takeaway from *Invitel* reaches beyond the particularities of the new Member States. It raises the question of whether the referring court and the ECJ really 'understand' each other when references are made. Or does the double-pronged function of the preliminary reference procedure—providing useful guidance vertically to the national court and horizontally interpreting EU law—render 'understanding' hard, if not impossible, due to the different functions the two courts have to fulfil? This is the pertinent query that needs to be constantly reiterated.

4.3 *Janecek*, *Feryn*, and *Invitel* in the Educational Professional Context

The institutional framework of the preliminary reference procedure and the institutional pressure on courts to decide political issues demonstrate the challenges to lawyers as a professionalized profession. Are the EU lawyers involved in European Public Interest Litigation prepared for the tasks they are supposed to meet? What do they know about EU law, and in what way are they trained to handle the preliminary ruling procedure on both sides, at the national and at the EU level, let alone the emerging features of European Public Interest Litigation? Legal professionalization in Oevermann's understanding builds on legal education, which is implicitly supposed to exist in the national context. But what does this mean for the European legal context?

The simple fact that even today there is no genuinely European legal education does not mean that the EU did not try to train the new 'European' lawyer. Attorneys in law triggered the Europeanization debate through their attempts to test the reach of the market freedoms in order to extend the reach of their professional activities beyond their home countries.[56] Implicit in such attempts is the idea that legal professionalism is universal and apt to deal with national differences in doctrine, tradition, and culture. In *Gebhard*, the ECJ cautiously paved

[56] Case 2/74 *Reyners* [1974] ECLI:EU:C:1974:68; Case 33/74 *van Binsbergen* [1974] ECLI:EU:C:1974:131; Case 107/83 *Klopp* [1984] ECLI:EU:C:1984:270; Case 71/76 *Thieffry* [1977] ECLI:EU:C:1977:65; Case C-340/89 *Vlassopoulou* [1991] ECLI:EU:C:1991:193; Case C-55/94 *Gebhard* [1995] ECLI:EU:C:1995:411; Case C-168/98 *Luxembourg v European Parliament and Council* [2000] ECLI:EU:C:2000:598; Case C-145/99 *Commission v Italy* [2000] ECR I-2235; Case C-35/99 *Arduino* [200] ECLI:EU:C:2002:97; Case C-309/99 *Wouters* [2002] ECLI:EU:C:2001:390; Case C-313/01 *Morgenbesser* [2003] ECLI:EU:C:2003:612; Case C-289/02 *AMOK* [2003] ECLI:EU:C:2003:669; Joined Cases C-94/04 and 202/04 *Cipolla* [2006] ECLI:EU:C:2006:758; Case C-305/05 *Ordre des barreaux francophones et germanophone* [2007] ECLI:EU:C:2007:383; Joined Cases T-125/03 and 253/03 *Akzo Nobel Chemicals* [2007] ECLI:EU:T:2007:287.

the way for such an understanding, which immediately triggered a legislative action:

> [I]n applying their national provisions, Member States may not ignore the knowledge and qualifications already acquired by the person concerned in another Member State. Consequently, they must take account of the equivalence of diplomas and if necessary, proceed to a comparison of knowledge and qualifications required by their national rules and those of the person concerned.[57]

The three Directives (77/249/EEC on Freedom to provide services (Lawyer's Services Directive), 2005/36/EC (Professional Qualifications Directive) concerning the recognition of diplomas, and 98/5/EC on the right of establishment (Lawyer's Establishment Directive)) open up three different pathways for migrant lawyers: (1) under Article 10(1) and (3) of Directive 97/5/EC through *three years of consecutive professional practice* without the need to take an aptitude test (in case of less than three years in the host state, the competent authority enjoys discretion);[58] (2) under Article 6 of Directive 97/5/EC through establishment as a qualified lawyer in the host state as a home state lawyer; and (3) under Article 10(2) of Directive 97/5/EC in connection with Directive 2005/36/EC through the application for recognition of the home state diploma in the host state. The EU has succeeded in opening up the market for temporary cross-border legal services for roughly 10,000 lawyers.[59] There is no empirical evidence that these lawyers are better equipped to initiate Public Interest Litigation. As the ECJ has de facto barred direct access of NGOs and public agencies to the ECJ through Article 263 of the Treaty on the Functioning of the European Union (TFEU), the plaintiff's lawyer has to construe the 'EU legal' argument through national legal lenses so as to overcome potential national barriers of access to court.

Recent years demonstrate a growing interest in the Europeanization of national judiciaries, including the question of why they are ready to cooperate with the ECJ, why they trust the ECJ, why they are willing to mobilize EU law against national legal constraints, and why there is a geo-spatial spread in the references to the ECJ.[60] However, there is amazingly little knowledge on what exactly national

[57] *Gebhard* (n 58).

[58] For an overview of the way in which the Member States have implemented the law, see Council of Bars and Law Societies of Europe, 'Guidelines for Bars and Law Societies on Free Movement of Lawyers within the European Union' (2016) 35 <www.ccbe.eu/fileadmin/speciality_distribution/public/documents/EU_LAWYERS/EUL_Guides___recommendations/EN_FML_2016_Guide.pdf>.

[59] Sjoerd Claessens and others, *Evaluation of the Legal Framework for the Free Movement of Lawyers* (Panteia/Maastricht University/European Commission (DG MARKT) 2012).

[60] Juan A Mayoral, 'Judicial Empowerment Expanded: Political Determinants of National Courts' Cooperation with the CJEU' (2019) 25 European Law Journal 374; Juan A Mayoral, 'In the CJEU Judges Trust: A New Approach in the Judicial Construction of Europe' (2016) 55 Journal of Common Market Studies 1; Juan A Mayoral and Aida Torres Pérez (2018) 'On Judicial Mobilization: Entrepreneuring for Policy Change at Times of Crisis' (2018) 40 Journal of European Integration 719; Virginia

judges know about EU law, and what exactly is undertaken and by whom in terms of training the national judges to act as 'European judges'.[61] Their knowledge depends on the education they receive in their home country and the degree to which they are entitled and prepared to participate in training courses, either at the national level through judicial training centres or at the Academy of European Law (ERA);[62] ERA has been set up on the initiative of the European Parliament. Since 2000, the EU Member States have financed ERA. Out of the 800,000 'EU justice professionals' (EU language for judges, prosecutors, court staff, lawyers, notaries, and bailiffs), 50 per cent had attended some training.[63] These figures, however, do not provide information on what the participants have learnt, taken home, and applied in legal practice.

To my knowledge, there is no systematic research on what exactly national judges know about EU law.[64] It seems fair to assume that everything depends on the competent judge. This explains why experienced Public Interest Litigation lawyers need to assume that the judges will have the relevant competence or perhaps better performance.[65] This was obviously not the case in *Invitel*, where the judge in charge was struggling with the EU legal jargon and with EU law and its impact on the national law, despite the extensive training judges in the candidate states had received prior to formal membership.[66] The reason might be an institutional flaw. The training offered consisted mainly of lecturing on EU law. The participants found it difficult to recognize the relevance of EU consumer law to their societies. A real transfer of knowledge presupposes that a concrete national consumer problem can be connected to the European legal environment. This is easy to write, but difficult to implement. The funded legal training programmes in the candidate states

Passalacqua, 'Legal Mobilization via Preliminary Reference: Insights from the Case of Migrant Rights' (2021) 58 Common Market Law Review 751; Tommaso Pavone, 'Putting European Constitutionalism in its Place: The Spatial Foundations of the Judicial Construction of Europe' (2020) 16 European Constitutional Law Review 669.

[61] Urszula Jaremba and Juan A Mayoral, 'The Europeanization of National Judiciaries: Definitions, Indicators and Mechanisms' (2019) 26 Journal of European Public Policy 386; Juan A Mayoral, Urszula Jaremba, and Tobias Nowak, 'Creating EU Law Judges: The Role of Generational Differences, Legal Education and Judicial Career Paths in National Judges' Assessment Regarding EU Law Knowledge' (2014) 21 Journal of European Public Policy 1120.

[62] Academy of European Law <www.era.int/cgi-bin/cms?_SID=c326b4518203df27da8c2564a02a1a28c77f430d00849254535564&_bereich=ansicht&_aktion=detail&schluessel=era&_sprache=en>.

[63] See the latest report of the European Commission: Commission, 'European Judicial Training 2020' (European Union 2020) <ec.europa.eu/info/sites/default/files/judicial-training-2020-web.pdf>.

[64] This does not exclude knowledge on particular issues such as soft law, where national judges look well informed; see Mariolina Eliantonio, Emilia Korkea-aho, and Oana Stefan (eds), *EU Soft Law in the Member States: Theoretical Findings and Empirical Evidence* (Hart Publishing 2021).

[65] Case C-392/92 *Christel Schmidt v Spar* [1994] ECLI:EU:C:1994:61; the president of the referring court was Ninon Colneric, later judge at the ECJ.

[66] Within the PHARE programme managed by the Centre de Droit de la Consommation, the TRACE programme run by the European Consumer Organisation BEUC, or within the activities of the German Gesellschaft für Zusammenarbeit (GIZ) in the Western Balkans and Georgia.

did not presuppose a serious stock-taking of what is called in Western language, a 'consumer problem'. The different legal education on either side of the iron curtain hampered communication, not forgetting that many participants were economists trained in crude Marxism-Leninism. What about today, and what about an East–West comparison of legal training strategies and their practical impact?

The knowledge base of EU judges (ie judges appointed to the ECJ) is slightly better. The Lisbon Treaty established a committee composed of former EU judges, supreme court judges of national courts, and lawyers with recognized competencies in charge of giving an opinion on the suitability of the candidates proposed by the Member States, under Article 255 TFEU.[67] The procedure is divided into three parts: first, the candidate needs the necessary support in their home country, the reasons for their selection having been made available to the committee; secondly, the candidate has to provide a CV, a letter of motivation, and a list of publications; and thirdly, the candidate has to pass an oral hearing. The committee regularly reports on the criteria and how they are applied in the selection procedure. The opinions, though non-binding, have been fully respected so far. Of candidates for a first-term office at the General Court 28 per cent were rejected; however, none were rejected for the ECJ.[68] The committee puts emphasis on the candidates' knowledge in 'general EU law' and their capacity to apply EU law in concrete cases. Lack of these skills constituted the major reason for rejection and explains the relatively high rejection percentage. However, the committee does not distinguish between the special knowledge required by the General Court and the 'constitutional' knowledge required for the ECJ.[69]

The 'entry exam' is the first step. The transformation of a national EU lawyer into a European EU lawyer occurs through learning by doing in the daily practice of preparing and discussing cases with the *référendaires* each judge is entitled to appoint, and with their colleagues in their respective chambers. The President of the Court may steer Public Interest Litigation through the appointment of particular Advocates General or the involvement of particular chambers.[70] The deliberations within the Court are confidential and not open to any kind of research. Judge Konrad Schiemann is one of the very few who provided a view into the engine room

[67] Michal Bobek, *Selecting Europe's Judges: A Critical Review of the Appointment Procedures to the European Courts* (Oxford University Press 2015); Mitchel de S-O-l'E Lasser, *Judicial Dis-Appointments: Judicial Appointments Reform and the Rise of European Judicial Independence* (Oxford University Press 2020), reviewed by Francis Jacobs (2021) 58 Common Market Law Review 1613.

[68] *Sixth Activity Report of the Panel Provided for by Article 255 of the Treaty on the Functioning of the European Union* (2019) <comite255.europa.eu/documents/5642886/5678369/6eme+Rapport+d%27activit%C3%A9+du+D255+-+EN.pdf/>.

[69] Tomáš Dumbrosky, Bilyana Petkova, and Marijn van der Sluis, 'Judicial Appointments: The Article 255 TFEU Advisory Panel and Selection Procedures in the Member States' (2014) 51 Common Market Law Review 455.

[70] Silje Synnøve Lyder Hermansen, 'Building Legitimacy: Strategic Case Allocations in the Court of Justice of the European Union' (2020) 27 Journal of European Public Policy 1215.

of European judicial lawmaking.[71] Potential conclusions on the self-understanding of EU judges may indirectly be drawn from the publication guidelines of the ECJ, as well as from the publications of the judges in leading journals on EU law.[72] The findings indicate a strong esprit de corps to support and to promote European integration. This might explain why ECJ judges are, overall, inclined to accept Public Interest Litigation claims, instead of declaring them inadmissible.

5. Coda: Afterthoughts

The analysis of these three cases has led us on a journey across the legal universe. Where do we land and how do we land? Public Interest Litigation fulfils an important function in the EU legal order. It bridges the gap between vague political statements in secondary EU law and enforceable hard law. The consequence might be that *le gouvernement des juges* takes the place of democratic legislation. There is a lot to say, not only on legitimacy, but also on whether judges can formulate the right questions necessary to construct the deeper architecture of the existing and developing EU law, or whether the questions they are raising are biased in all sorts of directions: because some national judiciaries are over- and others under-represented in the preliminary reference procedure; because judges at both levels have their own agenda; because NGOs are pursuing their view on the 'factfulness' of the case; because the legal order which is built through a biased Public Interest Litigation is not rooted in the societies it emerges from.[73] A wonderful place for research!

At the same time, European Public Interest Litigation runs the risk of disconnecting judgments from concrete facts, focusing on 'showcases' and not real disputes, thereby discrediting legal professionalization, or, to put it in a more forward-looking perspective, in establishing a new imagining of the role and function of judges and of courts. Karl Llewellyn, who along with Jerome Frank was at the forefront of the Realist movement, famously denounced the 'emptiness of rules without facts' and urged law schools to give consideration to the 'problem of turning legal or human knowledge into action'. Can this gap be closed through a new doctrine of empty precedents to be filled not only by the courts but, in particular, by the citizens, assisted by NGOs? Do we need more legal realism at the

[71] Konrad Schiemann, 'Europe—Our Common Legal Principles' (1999) 19 Yearbook of European Law 205.

[72] Päivi Leino-Sandberg, 'Enchantment and Critical Distance in EU Legal Scholarship: What Role for Institutional Lawyers?' (2022) 1 European Law Open 231.

[73] Carolyn Abbot and Maria Lee, *Environmental Groups and Legal Expertise: Shaping the Brexit Process* (University College London Press 2020); Emilia Korkea-aho, 'NGOs as Lobbyists: A Casualty of Environmental Law's Tunnel Vision?' (2022) 34 Journal of Environmental Law 1, who is praising the authors for engaging with civil society legal activism outside courts; Shai Dothan, 'A Virtual Wall of Shame: The New Way of Imposing Reputational Sanctions on Defiant States' (2017) 27 Duke Journal of Comparative & International Law 141.

ECJ, or perhaps a new legal realism which takes the particularities of European Public Interest Litigation into account? Damjan Kukovec[74] argues that in competition, state aid, and trade mark law, the ECJ vigorously engages with social facts, identifying this as a new move towards legal realism. However, his examples all come from the other side of EU law—from market integration, and not from social regulation. If our analysis of Public Interest Litigation is correct, there are only two possible options: either to tackle the challenges of European Public Interest Litigation comprehensively and prospectively, or to return to the role of courts as deciders of a single case, based on concrete social facts, which would mean the end of Public Interest Litigation in the current format.

Janecek was about strangely configurated and hardly controllable emission standards of air pollution. *Feryn* was about the toll of no longer being allowed to distinguish in an ever-more heterogenous ethnic society. *Invitel* was about the distribution of costs to be charged individually or collectively. Are *Janecek* and *Feryn* exemplary of the EU's renewed commitment to the well-being of the rest of the (European) world? Does *Invitel* demonstrate the difficulty of communicating between different courts at different levels in a transnational environment, one where East and West are coming together?[75] We find it difficult to interpret the significance of these cases because of the missing social facts.

It is highly unlikely that 'better and more facts' can overcome these difficulties, however. If that is true, the question is how to organize Public Interest Litigation before the ECJ. Where exactly is the difference between Public Interest Litigation before the ECJ and a 'normal' case where there is no NGO, no public agency, no social regulation behind it? After all, in a 'normal' case concerning primary EU law, market freedoms, and competition law, the rights of the parties invoked may very well affect the business community. Thus, the strategic dimension of the litigation may still be there, even if less obviously.

Taking seriously the hybrid function of the ECJ in Public Interest Litigation would require the consideration of setting up an equally hybrid institution, one where the different powers at the EU level and at the national level, as well as the civil society(ies), are represented. Such an institution would have to fill the gap in the programmatic decisions lawmaking produces. Unrealistic? Nonsense? The alternative is juristocracy and judgments which are hard if not impossible to implant into society. We concur with Rob van Gestel with one difference: we cannot wait until 2040. It is time to open a broad debate on Public Interest Litigation and the role and function of the ECJ in social regulation—and maybe not only in social regulation.

Dear Steve, are the three judgments 'just cases'? We have our doubts.

[74] Damjan Kukovec, 'The Realist Trend of the Court of Justice of the European Union' (2021) EUI Law Working Papers 2021/11.
[75] Ivan Krastev, *After Europe* (University of Pennsylvania Press 2017).

15
The Darker Side of the Internal Market Ideal: EU Migrant Workers Living in a Coastal Town

Catherine Barnard and Fiona Costello

1. Introduction

For many, the EU rules on free movement of persons have been seen as a positive, not just economically but also socially and culturally. Writing before the 2016 UK referendum on EU membership, Floris de Witte said that, for many younger European citizens, '[a]ll elements of their daily lives are infused with the results of free movement, whether it is their Polish classmate, their Belgian lecturer at university, their favourite Italian dish, a Czech football player on their favourite team, or Portuguese boss in the local restaurant'.[1] He noted '[Free movement] allows Europeans to pursue a way and quality of life that simply may not be possible in the state where they were born.'[2] This account largely reflects the experience of those EU migrants described by Adrian Favell in his book *Eurostars and Eurocities*.[3] He considers EU free movement of (mostly) skilled, mobile, multilingual (West) Europeans moving to EU capital cities—Amsterdam, London, Brussels. For this group, EU free movement law represents opportunity, benefits, excitement: 'Eurostars in Eurocities enjoy[ing] all these possibilities. The distinctive freedoms of European modernity.'[4]

However, both de Witte and Favell would probably recognize that this is not always the case, for either the movers or the stayers. Take the experience of EU migrants to, and the local residents of, the coastal town of Great Yarmouth, in the largely rural county of Norfolk, England. Since the accession to the EU of, first, Portugal in 1986, and then the EU8 countries in 2004, and the EU2 in 2007, Great

[1] Floris de Witte, 'Freedom of Movement is Not Simply an Economic Good, But a Bulwark Against Oppression' (*LSEBlogs*, 3 February 2016) <https://blogs.lse.ac.uk/brexit/2016/02/03/freedom-of-movement-is-not-simply-an-economic-good-but-a-bulwark-against-oppression/> accessed 10 March 2023.

[2] ibid.

[3] Adrian Favell, *Eurostars and Eurocities: Free Movement and Mobility in an Integrating Europe* (Blackwell Publishing 2008).

[4] ibid 11.

Catherine Barnard and Fiona Costello, *The Darker Side of the Internal Market Ideal: EU Migrant Workers Living in a Coastal Town* In: *The Internal Market Ideal*. Edited by: Jeremias Adams-Prassl, Sanja Bogojević, Ariel Ezrachi, and Dorota Leczykiewicz, Oxford University Press. © Catherine Barnard and Fiona Costello 2024.
DOI: 10.1093/oso/9780192867063.003.0016

Yarmouth has seen significant migration of EU nationals. They came mostly to do low-paid, low-skilled work in agriculture and food processing, work seen as undesirable by locals.[5] Local employers and recruitment agencies took advantage of this (cheap and willing) EU labour to meet worker shortages in these labour-intensive sectors.[6] The numbers are significant. Under the EU Settlement Scheme (EUSS) (introduced as part of the UK's commitments under the UK-EU Withdrawal Agreement 2020), all EU nationals and their family members had to register for Settled or Pre-Settled Status by 30 June 2021. Data on the EUSS shows there are now just over 14,000 applications by EU nationals and their family members in the Great Yarmouth local authority area (as of June 2023).[7] This compares to the local population of 100,000.[8] The 14,000 figure is substantially higher than the Office of National Statistics (ONS) 2019 population estimate for the town, which had put the entire non-UK population at approximately 5,000.[9] These EU populations are more pronounced in the town centre and neighbouring streets where the proportion of EU migrants may be as high as one in four. These central 'wards' (areas) in Great Yarmouth are among the most deprived in the country.[10] For example, in the Central and Nelson Wards, almost 50 per cent of the population is in receipt of at least one out-of-work benefit.[11]

In respect of the non-migrant local population, most were of course EU citizens prior to Brexit, but many were 'immobile'[12] or 'stayers'.[13] 'Immobile' is a broad category which includes those who could not afford to leave and those with caring responsibilities who were not able to leave, as well as those who actively chose not to exercise their rights of free movement. Nevertheless, this group has traditionally been left out of discussions of EU free movement. Many immobile EU citizens view(ed) free movement in negative terms, seeing EU migration both as putting

[5] Catherine Barnard and Fiona Costello, 'When (EU) Migration came to Great Yarmouth' (2023) 18 Contemporary Social Science 150. Maria Abranches and others, 'Cultural Violence in the Aftermath of the Brexit Referendum: Manifestations of Post-racial Xenoracism' (2021) 44 Ethnic and Racial Studies 2876; Jose Carlos Pina Almeida, 'Citizens of the World: Migration and Citizenship of the Portuguese in the UK' (2007) 23 Portuguese Studies 208.

[6] Samantha Currie, 'Scapegoats and Guinea Pigs: Free Movement as a Pathway to Confined Labour Market Citizenship for European Union Accession Migrants in the UK' (2022) 51 Industrial Law Journal 277.

[7] See UK Home Office, 'EU Settlement Scheme Statistics' <www.gov.uk/government/collections/eu-settlement-scheme-statistics>. Accessed 14 October 2023.

[8] See Great Yarmouth population change, Census 2021—ONS Accessed 14 October 2023.

[9] See Census 2021, 'How Life has Changed in Great Yarmouth' < https://www.ons.gov.uk/visualisations/censusareachanges/E07000145/> Accessed 14 October 2023. >.

[10] See Ministry of Housing, Communities & Local Government, 'English Indices of Deprivation' <www.gov.uk/government/statistics/english-indices-of-deprivation-2019> accessed 2 February 2022.

[11] Norfolk Insight <www.norfolkinsight.org.uk/> accessed 2 February 2022.

[12] Sarah Fine, 'Whose Freedom of Movement is Worth Defending?' in Floris de Witte, Ranier Baubock, and Jo Shaw (eds), 'Freedom of Movement Under Attack: Is It Worth Defending as the Core of EU Citizenship?' (December 2016) Robert Schuman Centre for Advanced Studies Research Paper 2016/69, 19 <http://dx.doi.org/10.2139/ssrn.2888363>.

[13] Favell (n 3) 11.

pressure on already hard-pressed public services and changing the face and identity of their town.

We shall argue that the arrival of so many migrants to Great Yarmouth has not generally been a happy experience for either migrants or local residents. Many EU migrants do low paid, physically demanding work in often poor working conditions,[14] while living in low-quality housing. Many locals resent the sudden influx of people who are seen as different and who do not integrate. There is a deep divide between the two communities, and both residents and migrants lack a sense of belonging to the town.[15] The most obvious manifestation of this unhappiness on the part of the local community was the overwhelming Leave vote in the 2016 referendum, the fifth highest Leave vote in the country. Although Brexit was about more than EU free movement,[16] the dominant view is that Leave voters tended to be particularly swayed by concerns about immigration, specifically the need to 'take back control' of UK borders.[17] It is perhaps no surprise, then, that the *Financial Times*[18] showed a positive percentage correlation between people without passports in 2014 ('stayers') and the share of the Brexit vote.[19]

So why has the experience of free movement been perceived as so negative for EU migrants in Great Yarmouth (and to the stayers)? In part it is about their working conditions which we have discussed elsewhere;[20] in part it is about housing which we want to focus on in this chapter. For the last three years we have been working with a charity, GYROS, which advises EU migrant workers. One of the main issues brought to GYROS by its clients concerns housing (see Figure 15.1). Housing has always been a sensitive issue for receiving states, as will be discussed in Section 3. Yet remarkably little attention has been paid to issues concerning housing in the studies and analysis of free movement. Using housing as a case study, we argue that the requirement of equal treatment—the key principle of EU free movement law and now carried over via the Withdrawal Agreement to those with EUSS—means little in practice for many EU migrant workers. This is because many live with other migrant workers in poor private sector accommodation (caravans when they first arrive, then moving to a house of multiple occupation (HMO), but not to local authority accommodation/social housing). Yet there is a perception among the local community that EU migrants are getting privileges, including in respect

[14] Catherine Barnard, Fiona Costello, and Sarah Fraser Butlin, '(Legal) Assistance in Employment Matters to Low-paid EU Migrant Workers in the East of England' (2022) 31 Legal Studies 1.

[15] Interview with community project worker (anonymous) (online, 3 March 2022).

[16] For more, see Aija Lulle, Laura Moroşanu, and Russell King, 'And Then Came Brexit: Experiences and Future Plans of Young EU Migrants in the London Region' (2018) 24 Population, Space and Place 1, 8–9; Alina Rzepnikowska, 'Racism and Xenophobia Experienced by Polish Migrants in the UK Before and After Brexit Vote' (2019) 45 Journal of Ethnic and Migration Studies 61.

[17] Fine, 'Whose Freedom of Movement is Worth Defending?' (n 12) 21.

[18] John Burn-Murdoch, 'Brexit: the Demographic Divide' *Financial Times* (London, 24 June 2016) (based on data from 382 voting areas in the UK).

[19] de Witte, Baubock, and Shaw, 'Freedom of Movement Under Attack' (n 12) 19.

[20] Barnard, Costello, and Butlin (n 14).

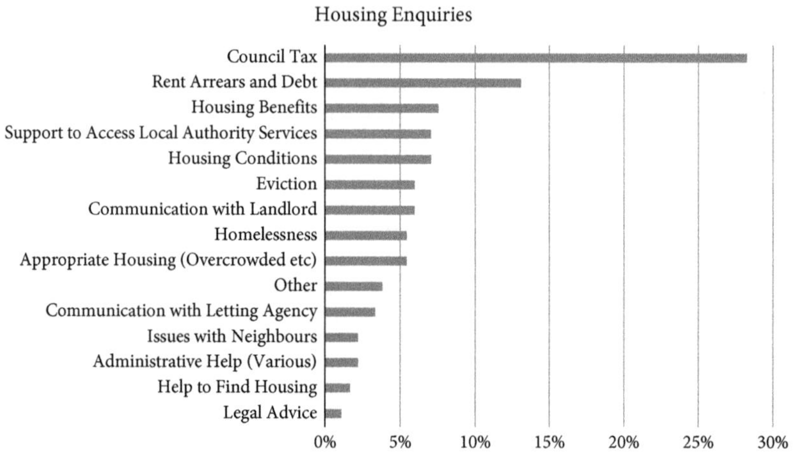

Figure 15.1 Housing enquiries brought to GYROS between 2015 and 2020, based on qualitative assessment of the queries undertaken by researchers*
*GYROS Database.

of housing, which mean that locals are put at a disadvantage. This has created tensions within the local community.

We therefore use housing as a lens through which to help us understand 'what it means [and now meant] to live in the EU and what it means to live under EU law'[21] in order to understand the realities of European integration—and resistance to it—'in a way that traditional accounts of EU law struggle with'.[22] In this way we wish to complement Steve Weatherill's own work on the internal market. He is, of course, one of the outstanding scholars in the field, helping to shape and deepen our understanding of not only the technical operation of the single market but also its values[23] through his excellent textbooks and other academic writing. But he has also always been interested in the human face of the single market: consumers,[24] workers,[25] footballers,[26] and even those caught on the wrong side of internal market laws.[27]

[21] Floris de Witte, 'Here Be Dragons: Legal Geography and EU Law' (2022) 1 European Law Open 113.
[22] ibid.
[23] Stephen Weatherill, *Law and Values in the European Union* (Oxford University Press 2016).
[24] See eg Stephen Weatherill, *EU Consumer Law and Policy* (Edward Elgar Publishing 2014).
[25] See eg Stephen Weatherill, 'Viking and Laval: The EU Internal Market Perspective' in Mark Freedland and Jeremias Prassl (eds), *EU Law in the Member States: Viking, Laval and Beyond* (Hart Publishing 2014); Stephen Weatherill, 'Use and Abuse of the EU's Charter of Fundamental Rights: On the Improper Veneration of "Freedom of Contract": Comment on Case C–426/11 *Mark Alemo-Herron v Parkwood Leisure*' (2014) 10 European Review of Contract Law 167.
[26] Stephen Weatherill, 'Case Note: Case C–415/93 (*Bosman*)' (1996) 33 Common Market Law Review 993.
[27] Stephen Weatherill and Paul Beaumont, *EU Law* (3rd edn, Penguin UK 1999) 529.

Building on Steve's interest in the human face of the internal market, we should like to look at EU migrant workers in the very deprived town of Great Yarmouth and specifically the question of their housing. We wish to argue that is a darker side of free movement, foreseen by those delegations involved in negotiating the texts of the original legislation facilitating free movement of migrant workers, with EU migrant workers living in poor standard private accommodation in certain wards (distracts) but who are considered by locals to be putting pressure on limited social (public) housing. This creates a picture of a geographically divided town and suspicion between the communities in the town.

The chapter is structured as follows: Section 2 provides a brief explanation of our methodology. Section 3 looks at EU rules on free movement, with a particular focus on housing. Section 4 considers the problems with housing in Great Yarmouth. Section 5 looks at some of the experiences of those EU nationals living in Great Yarmouth both pre- and post-Brexit. Section 6 looks at how the local community has responded to this migration. Section 7 concludes.

2. Methodology

As noted above, we have been working with a charity, GYROS, which offers multilingual information, advice, and guidance to migrant communities through a weekly 'drop-in' service in the town centre. We had access to a GYROS' dataset, which contained details of all the problems presented by its clients since 2015. This has given us a good insight into the range of issues facing this group of migrants. We have also used empirical data from over fifty semi-structured interviews and ten focus groups (n = 53) held with EU nationals living and working in the town (data collection 2019–22) and other professionals working in the town whose words we use in Section 4 to tell of their experiences. In addition, we have undertaken ethnographical research in the town itself, living in an HMO with eight EU national workers for two months and interviewing each of the residents and the landlord of the HMO. This has helped us to gain a thicker, more individualized understanding of what it means to be an EU migrant worker living in Great Yarmouth. The chapter therefore builds on the growing body of scholarship that 'stresses the relevance of spatial and geographical concepts' in the study of contemporary European free movement,[28] both pre- and post-Brexit.[29]

[28] Andrea Iossa and Maria Persdotter, 'Cross-Border Social Dumping as a "Game of Jurisdiction"—Towards a Legal Geography of Labour Relations in the EU Internal Market' (2021) 59 Journal of Common Market Studies 1086, 1086.

[29] Dora Kostakopoulou, '*Scala Civium*: Citizenship Templates Post-Brexit and the European Union's Duty to Protect EU Citizens' (2018) 56 Journal of Common Market Studies 854; Kate Botterill, David McCollum, and Naomi Tyrrell, 'Negotiating Brexit: Migrant Spatialities and Identities in a Changing Europe' (2019) 25 Population, Space and Place e2216.

3. Free Movement, Equal Treatment, and Housing

The right for people to move freely from one Member State to another is a central feature of the internal market.[30] As Chenchen Zhang puts it, '[h]aving emerged as an initiative to facilitate the circulation of goods, capital and workers in building the common market, free movement has now evolved into a defining character of, and an essential right associated with EU citizenship.'[31] The right to free movement of workers is found in Article 45 of the Treaty on the Functioning of the European Union (TFEU), with detail fleshed out in both Regulation 492/11 (replacing Regulation 1612/68) and the Citizens' Rights Directive (CRD) 2004/38/EC. The CRD gives every EU citizen the right to reside in another Member State for an initial period of three months, with no conditions on their stay (apart from possessing a passport/ID card). The right to reside for more than three months remains subject to certain conditions such as exercising Treaty rights as a worker, a jobseeker, or a self-employed person. European Union or third-country-national family members can also reside with the EU migrant. Those who have resided lawfully for five years have the right to permanent residence. These rights have been broadly protected under the EU Settlement Scheme (EUSS) for those migrating before 31 December 2020.

In the original Regulation 1612/68, there was an express provision on housing for migrant workers (Article 9). There was also a specific provision on housing for the family members of migrant workers in Article 10(3):

> [T]he worker must have available for his family housing considered as normal for national workers in the region where he is employed; this provision, however must not give rise to discrimination between national workers and workers from the other Member States.

As we have argued elsewhere,[32] agreement on this requirement was a major stumbling block in the negotiations of the draft Regulation. For example, in February 1968, the German and Belgian delegations proposed requiring migrant workers to have housing 'considered [to be of a] normal' standard before being permitted to have their family join them. The Commission considered that this was

[30] Catherine Barnard, *The Substantive Law of the EU* (Oxford University Press 2022) ch 9; Sandra Seubert 'Shifting Boundaries of Membership: The Politicisation of Free Movement as a Challenge for EU Citizenship' (2020) 26 European Law Journal 48.

[31] Chenchen Zhang, 'Free Movement and Social Citizenship: Towards a Politically Constructed Conception of Solidarity Across Borders' in Helle Krunke, Hanne Petersen, and Ian Manners (eds), *Transnational Solidarity: Concept, Challenges and Opportunities* (Cambridge University Press 2020) 331.

[32] Catherine Barnard and Sarah Fraser Butlin, 'Free Movement: A Case Study in State Autonomy and EU Control' in Mark Dawson and Markus Jachtenfuchs (eds), *Autonomy without Collapse* (Oxford University Press 2022).

discriminatory.[33] The German and Belgian delegations disagreed and argued that without a requirement for proper housing, families would join the worker and end up living in slums with precarious hygiene and sanitation.[34]

The Dutch delegation agreed and noted that, despite various efforts, an imbalance persisted between supply and demand of housing. They had introduced a system of waiting lists for housing allocation, depending on the length of wait, number of family members, and situation of the family, with priority given to those in most need and urgency. The waiting lists were open to all who were resident in the Netherlands, not just nationals. The Dutch delegation was concerned that if families of migrant workers were allowed to come to the Netherlands without having normal housing in place, and if they found themselves in a precarious position after arrival, they could use their situation to be given priority for housing and overtake Dutch families who had been living for a long time in unsatisfactory housing.

In July 1968, the Council met in Brussels to consider the draft regulations.[35] There was a lengthy discussion about the severe housing shortage in the Netherlands, a concern shared by the Belgian delegation. The Belgians raised concerns about overcrowding and the lack of proper housing at reasonable rents relative to workers' earnings. They were also worried about exploitation. However, the President of the European Parliamentary Assembly, Robert Schuman, said that 'the time had come to consider migrants from the Member States of the Community not as a complementary labour force, but as a settled population, and that it would not therefore be proper to introduce into the text of the Regulation a clause prohibiting such an establishment'.[36] He proposed the addition of the final clause of Regulation 10(3) that 'this provision [requiring the worker to have available for his family housing considered as normal for national workers in the region] ... must not give rise to discrimination between national workers and workers from other Member States'. It was in this form that the Regulation was passed and came into force on 15 October 1968.

Article 10(3) was repealed in Regulation 492/11, but Article 9 remains. Article 9(1) provides that a worker who is a national of a Member State and who is employed in the territory of another Member State must enjoy all the rights and benefits accorded to national workers in matters of housing, including being able to buy a home. Article 9(2) provides that a worker 'may, with the same right as nationals, put his name down on the housing lists in the region in which he is employed, where such lists exist, and shall enjoy the resultant benefits and priorities'.

[33] Historical Archives of the European Union, Council of the European Communities, CM2/1968–1005 <https://archives.eui.eu/en/fonds/93194?item=CM2%2F1968-1005>.

[34] ibid.

[35] Historical Archives of the European Union, Council of the European Communities, CM2/1968–1011.1297 f/68 (PV/CONS 21).

[36] ibid. The original reads as follows: 'le temps est venu de considérer les migrants en provenance des États membres de la Communauté non comme une main-d'œuvre d'appoint, mais comme une population d'établissement, et qu'il ne conviendrait pas par conséquent d'introduire dans le texte du règlement une clause interdisant cet établissement.'

So, what do these provisions mean in a town like Great Yarmouth where the housing stock is notoriously poor?

4. Great Yarmouth and its Housing Provision

4.1 The Socio-economic Profile of the Town

As we have seen, Great Yarmouth has a population of just under 100,000 residents. While life outcomes and well-being statistics for the borough as a whole are low compared with the wider county of Norfolk, the East of England, and England overall, there are also significant differences for individuals in the borough itself, with the innermost wards facing the highest levels of deprivation. For example, life expectancy is 10.7 years lower for men and 4.5 years lower for women in the most deprived areas of Great Yarmouth than in the least deprived areas.[37] More generally, Great Yarmouth is one of the most deprived local authorities in England. Of Great Yarmouth's sixty-one neighbourhoods, nine are ranked within the 3 per cent most deprived, four within the 2 per cent most deprived, and three within the 1 per cent most deprived neighbourhoods in England (including the central wards where our research takes place).[38] Some 20 per cent of children in Great Yarmouth live in low-income families and 13 per cent of its residents live in significant fuel poverty (a trend which has not improved over the past eight years).[39] The average weekly earnings are £354, significantly less than the East of England average (£462.70 a week).[40] The borough as a whole ranks poorly for income deprivation, where 43 per cent of households have an income under £20,000. This correlates with a higher-than-average number in receipt of welfare benefits and being incapable of work.[41]

4.2 Housing Stock

Great Yarmouth has had a long history of migration, not least because of its once successful herring industry,[42] and then the growth of tourism with the arrival of the

[37] Public Health England, Public Health Outcomes Framework <https://fingertips.phe.org.uk/profile/public-health-outcomes-framework/data#page/1/ati/101/are/E07000147>.

[38] Great Yarmouth Borough Council, 'Locality Strategy (March 2021–2026)' 50. Available at: Great Yarmouth Borough Council Locality Strategy (<great-yarmouth.gov.uk>).

[39] ibid 52.

[40] ibid 52.

[41] 'Housing Strategy—Evidence Appendix 2018' 1 <www.great-yarmouth.gov.uk/media/2712/Great-Yarmouth-Borough-Council-Housing-Strategy-Evidence/pdf/Housing_Strategy_-_Evidence_Appendix_2018.pdf?m=637025933557470000>.

[42] Frank Meeres, A *History of Great Yarmouth* (Phillimore 2007).

steam train.[43] However, a lot of this migration was temporary. The town suffered with the decline of both industries, a problem exacerbated by decades of under-investment and austerity.[44] Housing is both a symptom and a symbol of the decline of the town. Great Yarmouth was also heavily bombed in both wars, leading to the destruction of many of its famous 'Rows', 145 streets with houses packed closely together.[45] After the Second World War, prefabs or their equivalent were rapidly built to provide accommodation; this housing is still in use today, despite the problems it suffers with mould and damp. There is considerable Victorian housing stock, too, but serious flooding in 1953 damaged a lot of this housing and it continues to suffer from damp today.

Great Yarmouth also has some fine large Victorian and Edwardian houses which once served as accommodation for holidaymakers. As the tourism industry declined, these houses often fell into disrepair. In the late 1990s, they were used by London local authorities as cheap accommodation for asylum seekers (Kosovans, Afghans, and Iraqis). These asylum seekers, far from home and away from their own communities usually based in cities, struggled. GYROS was set up to support them. This housing has largely been converted into HMOs by private landlords and is now lived in by EU nationals. We return to this below.

The poverty of the accommodation makes life difficult for residents. Those who can move out do so—either to Gorleston, a somewhat more upmarket seaside resort on the other side of the river a couple of miles away, or to Norwich, a livelier university city about twenty miles away. This means that it is the most disadvantaged who are left behind living in these central wards in poor housing.

The Great Yarmouth Borough Council Housing Strategy (CHS) says that there are 45,318 dwellings in Great Yarmouth, of which 62 per cent are owner occupied, 20 per cent privately rented, and 18 per cent socially rented.[46] The Council notes that there has been significant growth in the private rented sector in Great Yarmouth in recent years, from 8 per cent of the total stock in 2001, to 18 per cent in 2011, to 20 per cent in 2017, the period which broadly spans the arrival of EU nationals. This is compared to the 9 per cent increase seen in England as a whole.[47] One council worker on the housing team said that the town has a high number of 'absent' landlords, individuals who buy up '5 or 6 properties' with no real link to Great Yarmouth or understanding of the communities and economic realities

[43] Frank Meeres, *Yarmouth & Gorleston through Time* (Amberley Publishing 2009).

[44] Norfolk Insight (n 11).

[45] Alfred Hedges, *Great Yarmouth as It Was* (Hendon Publishing 1973); Meeres, *Yarmouth & Gorleston through Time* (n 43) 17.

[46] 'Housing Strategy—Evidence Appendix 2018' fn 42 at 2.

[47] Great Yarmouth Borough Council, 'Great Yarmouth Borough Council Housing Strategy, 2018–2023' <www.great-yarmouth.gov.uk/media/2711/Great-Yarmouth-Borough-Council-Housing-Strategy-2018-2023/pdf/Great_Yarmouth_Borough_Council_Housing_Strategy_2018-2023.pdf?m=637025923792630000>.

of the town, as well as 'dodgy landlords', described as 'those who take anyone and everyone'.[48] This housing is often in very poor condition.[49] Some residents in the Nelson Ward speak of exploitative landlords who rent rooms to women and establish transactional-sexual relationships with their female tenants in lieu of rent.[50] The police say that the availability of cheap accommodation causes issues in the town. There is a consensus locally that cheap accommodation drives three things: vulnerability, criminality, and poor health and social issues.

The significant growth in the private rented sector in the town has not been matched by an improvement in the standard of the accommodation. One previous community development worker in the town said:

> They're paying the price now because the damp and mould issues and again, I guess it's the council not getting to grips with a place like Nelson ward. There's no plan for … the quality of housing stock across Nelson ward… [W]hat some councils have done is a big compulsory purchase of several streets as a major programme to improve. There's never been an intention to do that in Great Yarmouth. And it's … that issue with substandard housing across that ward.

The CHS (2018–23)[51] identifies four strategic objectives to meet current and future housing requirements in Great Yarmouth:

- New homes: ensuring there are enough good-quality new homes
- Our homes: improving the quality and use of the council's housing stock
- Decent homes: providing a good mix of decent homes across all tenures
- Healthy homes: meeting the needs of vulnerable households.

Under the 'decent homes' strand, the local government recognizes that 'the borough has a high number of Houses in Multiple Occupation (HMOs)'. While they do 'provide low-cost accessible accommodation, we would like to see the overall number of HMOs reduce over a managed period or become better managed'.[52] To this end, the Council has introduced a Selective Licensing Scheme for the most challenged parts of the Nelson Ward. The scheme came into effect on 7 January 2019 and runs for five years. Its aim is to improve housing and social conditions for

[48] Interview with Council housing team worker (anonymous) (Great Yarmouth, 26 November 2021)).

[49] cfDepartment for Levelling Up, Housing & Communities, *A Fairer Private Rented Sector* (White Paper CP 693, 2022).

[50] Right to Succeed Project (Great Yarmouth). 'Emerging Themes Working Document— Interviews with Nelson Ward Residents', shared with researchers (23 May 2022). For more on the Right to Succeed Project: <https://righttosucceed.org.uk/working-collectively/central-great-yarmouth/>.

[51] Great Yarmouth Borough Council, 'Great Yarmouth Borough Council Housing Strategy, 2018–2023' (n 47) 2.

[52] Ibid, 8

private sector tenants in this area, specifically targeting unethical landlords: 'the scheme has required landlords of most private rented housing … to be licensed and meet conditions around health and safety and standards.'[53] However, properties already subject to mandatory HMO licensing are exempt from the scheme (such as the HMO of our research).

What is striking about this description of housing in Great Yarmouth is just how reminiscent it is of the situation described by the Dutch and Belgian delegations in 1968 in their own countries: a shortage of good quality housing. It is against this background that more than ten thousand or so EU nationals arrived. What was their experience with housing?

5. EU Citizens and Housing in Great Yarmouth

5.1 Private Rented Sector

Of the clients in the GYROS database, over 55 per cent live in the private rented sector (PRS). For many, especially when they first arrived, accommodation was tied to their employment. They paid (usually private) individuals to help them travel to the UK, and then find work and accommodation. This initial cost was either paid up front, or the debt was 'worked off'. The accommodation usually consisted of shared rooms in houses or caravans. For example, Rasa[54] (sixties, Latvian) remembers her first night in England. She was brought to a caravan with six other people (men and women), and they all slept in the caravan's living room overnight in the same clothes they had travelled in. They were woken at 4 am and brought to the factory to work a full shift before they were then brought to their more permanent accommodation. This accommodation was cramped and had no washing facilities.

> We came to Great Yarmouth, and they put us in a little hotel. A double room. Very little room. We washed our jeans in a toilet sink. The basin … We washed our jeans there. And it was horrible.[55]

Edita (thirties, Latvian) was placed in a shared room with another woman:

> I still think it was wrong on so many levels that you don't even get asked if you want to be in a room or do you want to share or anything, you have no, you felt

[53] Great Yarmouth Borough Council, 'What Does Selective Licensing Mean?' <www.great-yarmouth.gov.uk/article/5263/What-does-Selective-Licensing-mean#_content>.
[54] All names used in this research have been changed.
[55] Interview with Rasa (name changed) (Great Yarmouth, 20 September 2021).

> you had no say. You could go and rent elsewhere but that meant you would need to pay, and you get deducted for it.[56]

She told us:

> [I shared with] a Polish woman and then another Lithuanian woman, and another Lithuanian woman. I mean there was one of them [who] was a proper hoarder, car boot [sales] was a big one, it was all about car boots and [she] just kept buying stuff and she was just bringing so much … And she had so much stuff, it was everywhere. It's like, she had two mattresses, and she was … yeah stuff everywhere. Wasn't a lot of room. And then after that there was another Lithuanian woman who, who was like, she was a compulsive cleaner and organiser, and … it got to the extent that she would reorganise my personal belongings and I couldn't find like, for example, my shoes.

Edita was physically assaulted by a male resident in this house and moved out. She had to pay £10 per week in order *not* to live in the house.

For the longer-established Polish, Lithuanian, and Latvian participants of our research, most were able to move on to 'better' accommodation. So, for example, Rasa (and, previously, Edita) moved into the same HMO in Great Yarmouth. Edita lived there for ten years before returning to Latvia (post-Brexit); Rasa still lives there. This HMO, where our ethnographic research was conducted, is a Grade II listed, three-storey sprawling building with eight residents in total (all Latvian and Lithuanian). The house itself has no central heating, suffers from significant damp and mould, has no Wi-Fi, only limited cooking facilities, and no communal areas. Residents each have self-contained bedrooms but share bathroom facilities. Everyone has a small, portable, plug-in heater. Rasa told us that her arthritis is particularly bad in the winter, and so she places the heater under the table next to her legs to ease the ache of the cold in the house.

Despite these privations, the residents suggest that the standard and experience of living in the HMO of our research is much better than previous experiences, not least because they are treated better by this landlord than by previous landlords. Vida (thirties, Lithuanian), on the third floor, says she has a leak in her ceiling and when it rains her belongings get wet. However, the landlord is 'too nice and too old' for her to bother him with this inconvenience (he has since died). Another resident (Camilla, fifties, Lithuanian) tells us her previous landlord took money from her for council tax, but never paid it. She ended up (years later) with a court fine and an attachment of earnings:

> First time when I come in England, I have a problem. I live in first my house two years and after I move and after about four years I have paper from council tax,

[56] Interview with Edita (name changed) (Great Yarmouth, 20 September 2021).

> but I no pay council tax. Because this landlord he says I no need to pay this. Just pay rent and everything is covered. It's included. And after two years. I have paper [bill] for £2000.

As Figure 15.1 shows, problems with council tax are the biggest issue facing GYROS clients under the housing label. But there are other issues, too. Take the case of Katia (sixties, Latvian):

> Client told me that she has a tenancy agreement in her name only, even though she is only renting a room and there are other tenants living in the other rooms. Client is registered for council tax as the only tenant in the property. Client is worried that water is not being paid for the property as she has seen a reminder letter to pay ... Client is worried she could be liable for utility debts for the whole of the property. Client wanted to know if she could apply for a council house as she is over 60. [57]

As Figure 15.1 also shows, issues about rent and debt arrears are the second largest issue facing GYROS clients.

Camilla (above) feels safer in the HMO of our research as she is confident that the bills are being paid (all utilities are included in the monthly rent). However, none of the residents has a tenancy agreement. All residents pay their rent in cash and receive no rent receipts, although they can ask for a receipt if they want or need one. These informal housing situations, where individuals have no tenancy agreement or proof that they are paying their rent, can cause problems for them when seeking to prove their status for the purpose of other claims (see Section 5.3).

Migrant workers often improve the standard of their accommodation, doing repairs and redecorating. For example, the tenants in the HMO of our research repainted, re-carpeted, and re-salvaged sections of the HMO, reclaiming and turning a 'junk' room on the ground floor into a spare bedroom for visitors (and lived in by our researcher).

5.2 Home and Work Combined

For some EU migrant workers, accommodation comes with the job. If they are working in the fields, it may be in a caravan. In factories, it might be a room in (now long-vacant) tourist accommodation. Those working in the tourist industry might get a caravan in a caravan park. This was the case with Jorge, a sixty-seven-year-old Portuguese national with no English language skills.[58] When he moved to the UK

[57] GYROS Database (Client ID 400).

[58] GYROS Database (Client ID 383).

in 2004, he lived in one of the holiday parks near Great Yarmouth, where he stayed for eleven years. When the park closed, he moved into the town, finding another job with associated accommodation. The case notes say: 'client started working in [a local chicken factory] for a while when he became ill and was dismissed due to long absence which also meant he lost his accommodation too, making him homeless.' Jorge approached GYROS for help to make a claim for universal credit (UC) .

In order to claim UC as an EU migrant worker in the UK, Jorge had to prove he had been 'habitually resident' in the UK by satisfying a 'right to reside' test.[59] In order to pass the 'right to reside' test, Jorge had to prove that he had been 'exercising his treaty rights' in the UK by working (proven by producing details of his work history, payslips, employment contracts, bank statements, etc.). As he was (involuntarily) unemployed, he also needed to prove his 'retained his worker status': that he was not working but this was only temporary. Satisfying this eligibility requires proof of his employment (payslips) and his accommodation (tenancy agreement) for the housing element of UC. This is where the informal employment/tenancy arrangements, described previously in this chapter, become a real issue for establishing entitlement.

After his initial application for UC, Jorge received an advance payment which he used to pay for two weeks' temporary accommodation. A fortnight later, he returned to GYROS for help with housing. His case notes show that he visited three different services: Housing Options at Great Yarmouth Borough Council (GYBC), which referred him to the local charity supporting homeless people (which had no availability), which referred him to the Job Centre, which referred him back to GYROS. GYROS called GYBC to understand what their housing team had advised; Jorge had not understood his conversation with them due to language difficulties. These difficulties also meant that he struggled to interact with other services, such as the Job Centre. Ultimately, GYROS helped Jorge to find private rented accommodation in the town (a room in a house share).

As Figure 15.1 shows, support in accessing local authority services is the fourth largest issue facing GYROS clients. Clients like Jorge need help from GYROS due to English language barriers. This is a common feature in all of GYROS' work: over 86 per cent of GYROS' clients rate their English language skills as 'limited' or 'very limited', and all the staff are multilingual.[60] For housing issues, staff are frequently called upon to bridge communication with landlords, housing agencies, and the local council (see Figure 15.1). Jorge's case also highlights the legal barriers facing an EU migrant worker. While EU nationals can live and work in another Member

[59] Citizens Advice, 'Check if You Have the Right to Reside for Benefits' <www.citizensadvice.org.uk/benefits/claiming-benefits-if-youre-from-the-EU/before-you-apply/check-if-you-have-the-right-to-reside-for-benefits/>.

[60] Catherine Barnard, Sarah Fraser Butlin, and Fiona Costello, 'The Changing Status of European Union Nationals in the United Kingdom Following Brexit: The Lived Experience of the European Union Settlement Scheme' (2022) 31 Social & Legal Studies 365, 381.

State as equal EU citizens, that equality (in the context of social rights) is conditional: EU citizens face additional eligibility tests to access social welfare benefits and housing support in their host Member States.[61] Those who cannot meet these additional eligibility requirements are considered to have 'no recourse to public funds (NRPF)' and are ineligible for state support. This lack of a safety net means that for those in low-paid, precarious work, problems can spiral quickly if that work stops.[62] This problem is considered in respect of access to social housing to which we now turn.

5.3 Housing Support: Social Housing and Homelessness Support

5.3.1 Social housing

As outlined in Section 3, there were initial concerns among some Member States that EU nationals and their joining family members might overwhelm social housing support in their host Member States. In the UK, many years later, this argument was echoed by the (then) Labour cabinet minister Margaret Hodge, writing in *The Observer* in 2007 that migrant workers from accession states (at the time) were benefiting from social housing in the UK at the expense of British citizens.[63] Her article caused considerable fallout in the UK, with some calling for her resignation, while others, such as the British National Party (BNP), supported her position.[64] However, '[e]vidence soon emerged revealing that relatively small numbers of foreign nationals, and virtually no migrant workers, were gaining access to and living within the social rented sector.'[65] This is because, historically, access to local authority housing support (social housing and homelessness support) is dependent on EU migrants satisfying the same tests described above, as applied to Jorge .

Post-Brexit, those granted Settled Status (more than five years' residency) under the EUSS will 'have the same access to social housing and homelessness assistance as comparable British citizens'.[66] Those who have only Pre-Settled Status (less than

[61] Charlotte O'Brien, *Unity in Adversity: EU Citizenship, Social Justice and the Cautionary Tale of the UK* (Hart Publishing 2017).

[62] Charlotte O'Brien, 'The Pillory, the Precipice and the Slippery Slope: The Profound Effects of the UK's Legal Reform Programme Targeting EU Migrants' (2015) 37 Journal of Social Welfare & Family Law 111, 111.

[63] For more see Philip Johnston, 'Hodge: "Give Natives Priority for Social Housing"' *The Telegraph* (21 May 2007) <www.telegraph.co.uk/news/uknews/1552180/Hodge-Give-natives-priority-for-social-housing.html>.

[64] For more, see Jo Revill and Jamie Doward, 'BNP Backs Hodge in Housing Row' *The Guardian* (26 May 2007) <www.theguardian.com/politics/2007/may/27/thefarright.communities>.

[65] David Robinson, 'New Immigrants and Migrants in Social Housing in Britain: Discursive Themes and Lived Realities' (2010) 38 Policy & Politics 57, 57 <https://bristoluniversitypressdigital.com/view/journals/pp/38/1/article-p57.xml> accessed 23 May 2022.

[66] EEA citizen's eligibility for social housing or homelessness assistance <https://assets.publishing.service.gov.uk/media/606349dbd3bf7f0c854ce227/LA_workshops_FAQ.pdf>. 1.

five years' residency) need a qualifying right[67] to access housing support (social housing, homelessness support), such as being in work. About 15 per cent of EU nationals in the UK are in social housing, a lower figure than that of UK nationals (16 per cent) and of non-EU nationals (19 per cent).[68] The GYROS database shows that about 10 percent of their clients report living in council accommodation (social housing), significantly lower than the national figure.

5.3.2 Homelessness

When it comes to those experiencing homelessness, like all applicants for statutory homelessness assistance, EU citizens must also meet four further tests (alongside the Pre-Settled Status 'qualifying right' requirement). Applicants must be legally homeless, have a local connection to the local authority to which they are applying, not be 'intentionally homeless', and demonstrate priority need.[69] European Union nationals represent 22 per cent of the homeless total in England, although in some boroughs in London the figure is closer to 50 per cent.[70] Just under 10 per cent of the GYROS dataset report being homeless, of no fixed abode (NFA), or in temporary accommodation at the point they accessed GYROS' services (homelessness was the eighth most common query for GYROS clients (see Figure 15.1).

The recent introduction of EU Settled Status and EU Pre-Settled Status, and their differential rights in access to housing support means understanding of EU citizens' rights on the frontline can vary. A 2021 report by the Public Law Interest Centre says:

> Lack of knowledge of EU citizens' rights and entitlements remains a serious problem across statutory and commissioned services, as well as in non-commissioned charities, day centres and soup kitchens. The (incorrect) blanket assumption that EU citizens 'have NRPF' is widespread among homelessness workers. As in other parts of the statutory sector (e.g. NHS, JobCentre Plus, DWP), culturally and linguistically appropriate provision is the exception rather than the rule.[71]

[67] Shelter England, 'People with EU Pre-Settled Status Eligibility for Homeless Assistance' <https://england.shelter.org.uk/professional_resources/legal/homelessness_applications/eligibility_for_homeless_assistance/people_with_eu_pre-settled_status_eligibility_for_homeless_assistance>.

[68] For more, see The Migration Observatory, 'Migrants and Housing in the UK' <https://migrationobservatory.ox.ac.uk/resources/briefings/migrants-and-housing-in-the-uk/>.

[69] Public Interest Law Centre (PILC), 'Still Here: Defending the Rights of Homeless EU Citizens after Brexit and COVID-19' (July 2021) <www.pilc.org.uk/wp-content/uploads/2021/07/PILC_EEA_A4_ONLINE.pdf>.

[70] Public Health England, 'Health Matters: Rough Sleeping' (Guidance, 11 February 2020) <www.gov.uk/government/publications/health-matters-rough-sleeping/health-matters-rough-sleeping>.

[71] PILC (n 69) 9.

Many EU nationals have been helped by the local authority in 'reconnecting' to their country of origin when they are facing homelessness in the UK, especially those who are considered 'NRPF' and therefore are not eligible for any other assistance locally. 'Reconnection' is a process whereby EU/European Economic Area (EEA) nationals who approach their local authority for support around issues with homelessness or destitution are offered help to return to their country of origin, as the only help available to them. This is paid for by the local authority. Based on previous research, the average amount being spent on reconnections is approximately £365.17 per person, but the figures range from £80 to just under £2,000 per person. Our research on this issue with English local authorities showed that (of the local authorities who provided data) as many as 1,350 EU nationals have been reconnected since 2016.[72] Norfolk—the county where our research is based—reported spending £200,000 on support for destitute EEA nationals between 2017 and 2020, including reconnecting 130 individuals and in some cases their families to their country of origin.[73]

5.3.3 Joining family members

It is quite a common pattern that one member of the family comes to the UK first and then their partner and children join afterwards, or that children are subsequently born in the UK. It is not unusual for grandparents to join to help with childcare. Some working mothers in one focus group (May 2022) told us that without their mothers joining them in Great Yarmouth, they would have been unable to work, as the twelve-hour shifts in the factories are not compatible with school hours. Hence, 10 per cent of the GYROS dataset live with their extended families (at point of enquiry). In the UK ONS data for multigenerational families in shared households, the figure is closer to just 1.1 per cent.[74]

Over 55 per cent of clients in the GYROS are dataset living with a family member at the point they access the service: a partner (19 percent), children (29 per cent) or extended family members (10 per cent). As mentioned previously, accommodation for joining family members was one of the original concerns of Member States, as extended family and children might put additional pressure on housing lists as well as other neighbourhood-level services such as schools and hospitals. Only 10 per cent of GYROS' clients report living in council housing at the point they accessed GYROS' service; the majority are in private rented accommodation.

[72] Catherine Barnard and Fiona Costello, 'Deportation and "Reconnection" of Homeless EU Nationals in the UK' (*UK and a Changing Europe*, 27 October 2020) <https://ukandeu.ac.uk/deportation-and-reconnection-of-homeless-eu-nationals-in-the-uk/>.

[73] ibid.

[74] For more, see Office of National Statistics, 'Families and Households in the UK: 2019' (Census 2021, 15 November 2019) <www.ons.gov.uk/peoplepopulationandcommunity/birthsdeathsandmarriages/families/bulletins/familiesandhouseholds/2019>.

The GYROS database shows instances of EU nationals struggling to find appropriate accommodation for their family.

> Client complained about her landlord as he does not give her a tenancy agreement and now he is complaining about the children, that she needs to keep them quiet and she feels he will ask her to leave. So, client is looking for another property. Clients pays £230 per week for 2 rooms in the house. One is for the children and the other is the living room which is now a bedroom for client and husband. (Client ID 439)[75]

In another example, the client moved to the UK to join her partner who had been in the UK for seven years.

> The client has been in the UK since December last year, her partner has been in the UK for 7 years always working for the same employer. They rent a room in a house and client is pregnant and the health visitor told them that they need to find another place as the room is too small and the house is not adequate for a baby. The client said that they do not have money for a deposit. I told them that we could make a claim for UC to help with housing costs, but they need to have a tenancy agreement or a letter from the landlord proving that they rent and rent receipts etc.[76] (Client ID 988)

As highlighted in this quote, the poor standard of accommodation available is often not appropriate for children, sometimes putting their health and well-being at risk.

> Client said her flat was not in good condition, part of the ceiling fell on top of her and her son and that she has already asked the landlord to fix this problem and he did not. (Client ID 1167)[77]

6. Preliminary Conclusions

Our case study shows how some of the initial concerns raised by Member States in the 1960s about pressure on scarce housing caused by migration (Section 2) have come to pass in Great Yarmouth. The EU migrant workers in our cohort are often in precarious and substandard housing, paying rents they struggle to afford. Ownership levels are low; the majority live in private rented accommodation, including those with family and extended family members. Some of the problems

75 GYROS Database (Client ID 439).
76 GYROS Database (Client ID 988).
77 GYROS Database (Client ID 1167).

experienced by EU migrant workers are common to any vulnerable group, migrant and non-migrant alike. However, we would argue that the EU migrant workers in our study are more vulnerable, given their lack of social networks, poor English language skills, and the additional statutory requirements imposed on EU nationals connected with obtaining benefits. The rights of equal treatment, while in theory observed, mean very little in the private sector where migrants are housed. As the manager of GYROS tells us:

> EU migrants live here. I mean, that's probably the downside, is that they're in desperate situations, and they rent whatever is available. So, they actually pay the price for accommodation that's not worth that price. So that's, I guess, the Council's job to make sure that the standard of the quality of accommodation, of property in Great Yarmouth goes up, not down.[78]

The experiences of EU migrant workers in the UK are more aligned with what the literature tells us of the experiences of (some) international migrant workers. Zhang talks of the 'trade off' international migrant workers accept when they move for work: their mobility to access the host country's labour market comes at the price of the rights available to them.[79] This, Zhang compares unfavourably to what she describes as the situation enjoyed by EU nationals: EU free movement allows not only unfettered mobility to another (EU) country, but also involves 'the enjoyment of a legal status that confers on the mobile citizen the right to be treated equally without discrimination'.[80] However, in the case of our research participants, the 'right to be treated equally without discrimination' has not been fully realized; their experiences appear more aligned with the precarious international workers who must accept a trade-off of rights for access to housing.

Further, due to strict eligibility requirements, migrants have not overwhelmed any social housing allocations—a concern also raised by the Member States in the original discussions in the 1960s—although the perception of this endures. That said, EU migrants have put additional pressure on local authorities, most evident around the allocation of homelessness support and assistance to families.

One final point: for many exercising their free movement rights to live and work in the UK, accommodation in Great Yarmouth has been chosen because it is cheap. But the factories where they work are up to forty-five to ninety minutes away. These factories often lay on buses which leave from the town centre at 3 or 4 am, or 5 or 6 pm, depending on the shift. Given that the migrants travel up to three hours a day and work for long hours in a physically tiring job in a chicken factory or food processing factory, they are often exhausted. After a long day, many just go back

[78] Interview with GYROS senior staff member (anonymous) (Great Yarmouth, 15 September 2021).
[79] Zhang (n 31) 332.
[80] ibid 331.

to their accommodation, eat, and then sleep. Camilla tells us: 'You need to work, work, work. No holiday, no weekend, no nothing, just pay money for rent and for water, for everything.' This means that these communities largely keep themselves to themselves. They live together in one part of town, mainly the streets in Nelson Ward. This 'ghettoization' creates further issues in the town, as we shall see in Section 7.

7. Local Residents' Response to Migration to the Town

It is clear that for local and migrant communities alike, the standard of rented accommodation available in the town is low. This is confirmed by interviews with members of the local housing team.[81] Local residents mention '[p]oorly maintained housing, majority of people are renting, generational households, exploitative private landlords' as key issues.[82] When asked about their experiences of living in the town's central Nelson Ward, local people identified four common themes: deprivation, housing, divided communities, and crime.[83]

Residents noted, in particular, that the East European communities (broadly defined) were not very well integrated within the wider community. The Portuguese community were considered somewhat more established because they had lived in the town for longer and had started opening local businesses (primarily local cafes and restaurants). However, even this was not always seen in a positive light. One of our interviewees noted that there are local residents living in Nelson Ward who have never worked in their lives, with families who had not worked either. He continued:

> I guess because migrant workers have come with a desire to improve lives and livelihoods … I guess that's where it rubs sometimes in the local community where they're like, how have they [migrant communities] opened up a cafe and how have they opened up this they must be getting grants from the council to do that … whereas you've got a local settled population that has become very sedentary in terms of 'my parents are on benefits, I'm on benefits'.[84]

The perception endures that Portuguese nationals were receiving grants and benefits from the council that local people were not eligible for, creating cross-community tensions.

[81] Interviews with GYBC Housing Team Members (n2 (anonymous)) (Great Yarmouth, 26 November 2021/19 November 2021).

[82] Right to Succeed, *Nelson Ward Interviews—Key Themes* (2022).

[83] ibid.

[84] Interview with ex-Council and community development worker (anonymous) (online, 3 March 2022).

One reason these myths are sustained is because, generally, cross-cultural interaction was considered limited by local residents. There are parts of the town, such as Nelson Ward, which, due to free movement, local people feel are now no-go areas for them. Local people mention that groups of (particularly) migrant men socializing on the street can feel intimidating. Maria Abranches et al, in their work in Great Yarmouth, have noted the same. They describe local residents being 'scared' of migrant (men) smoking on the street outside cafes, fearing they may become violent after drinking.[85]

The arrival of large numbers of migrant workers to disused tourist accommodation has also caused other difficulties with the local community. The police told us of tensions between newly arrived Romanian nationals working in a local poultry factory (recruited in Romania, housed in central Yarmouth) and local residents. This tension, the police say, was 'driven by xenophobic views':[86]

> So, speaking to the management agency [who] brought the people over, … They were basically saying because of Brexit looming, they couldn't recruit from Lithuania, Portugal, and actually, this is where they would normally go. So, they went to Romania, and engaged with a community that they hadn't before, which was Romanian gypsies. That's how they identified themselves. And so, they brought them over and they are a very identifiable community. And their education level was below the workers we normally have, their grasp of English just below, their social skills were below because of how Romanian gypsies are treated within their own country. They don't access education … And what this gave us was a very identifiable new community within Great Yarmouth, who have their own cultural … identity.

The police tell us that suspicions and rumours about the Romanian community caused significant difficulties in the town, compounded by perceptions that the new community was (very visibly) spending time together in the street or in the town centre. In reality, this was driven by the accommodation they had been given in the town, which did not have social space:

> And it just drew a massive wedge between that community when actually the big story around that was actually, they were put in probably very poor substandard accommodation. And because of that they were spending more time out in the community than normal.[87]

[85] Abranches and others (n 5) 2887.
[86] Interview with Great Yarmouth police officer (anonymous) (Great Yarmouth, 17 November 2022).
[87] ibid.

The 'Right to Succeed' project[88] is looking at community cohesion and experiences in the town. It says that local people feel that the 'transient' nature and increasingly diverse population in the town centre, a population which does not mix, has resulted in '[p]eople feeling there is a loss of ownership of the area, especially young people'.[89] Residents report that migrant communities have large families and that 'the parents can be difficult to engage'. However, it is striking that in interviews with local residents in the Nelson Ward, while housing is highlighted as a central issue for all, migrant communities living in local housing is not expressly mentioned. Instead, locals talk about a loss of ownership of the town, the broader lack of integration by EU migrants, and a lack of communication between communities, marking some areas as out of bounds in the town itself.

8. Conclusions

Brexit has prompted us to take a long, hard look at the lived experience of free movement and the reality of the internal market ideal, for both mobile and immobile European nationals, especially those who are poor, moving to and living in already deprived areas. For EU migrants/those with EUSS, there is a significant difference between the rights in the CRD, Regulation 492/11, and the Withdrawal Agreement on paper, and the lived reality thereof. As this case study on housing shows, EU migrants are not living the dream of free movement. Life as an EU migrant in Great Yarmouth is hard, expensive, and often precarious. And for immobile citizens, especially residents of deprived towns such as Great Yarmouth, free movement was something that happened to them, to their town, to their home, to their community identity. It was something other people did, and it has driven a sense of loss of ownership, and this continues to be the case post-Brexit. The equal treatment principle is also seen as eroding residents' own security and access to services, with what was already a small cake being shared among many more mouths.

In this scenario, neither group (mobile or immobile EU citizens) benefits, and the associated rights and opportunities of free movement and the internal market ideal were left for the 'Eurostars' (those benefiting from outward migration and the full realization of their rights) and local employers, landlords, and others benefiting from the inward migration of workers who suffer/accept a 'trade-off' of their rights and substandard accommodation. For those EU migrants who moved to

[88] Right to Succeed <https://righttosucceed.org.uk/>; see also James Weeds, 'Up to £1m to Improve Futures of Great Yarmouth Young People' *Great Yarmouth Mercury* (17 February 2022) <www.greatyarmouthmercury.co.uk/news/local-council/great-yarmouth-nelson-ward-1m-youth-endowment-fund-8696764>.

[89] Right to Succeed Project (Great Yarmouth). 'Emerging Themes Working Document—Interviews with Nelson Ward Residents' (23 May 2022).

Great Yarmouth and now hold EUSS or EUPS, it is not clear whether this new legal immigration status improves their everyday lives or, instead, entrenches the status quo. Yet EU migrants do add to the community, not only by opening new businesses but also in other ways—not least by spending their money locally. As the manager of GYROS noted: '[EU migrants] shop locally, you know? Very few migrants go somewhere else to shop. Yeah, they shop in Great Yarmouth.' And they improve the places they live:

> How many of our clients actually do the renovations in the properties they rent... They go in and they do all the painting, they change the flooring. They ask the landlord, and the landlord says, of course, do whatever you want. That's good for the landlord, obviously, and people do it.[90]

This chapter has shown the darker side of free movement, a side not often discussed in the textbooks, but one foreseen by those negotiating the texts of the original legislation facilitating free movement. However, the picture is not entirely negative. The local police officer told us:

> I think locally there is a real drive to enhance standard of living, our accommodation... I think there's real opportunity on the back of COVID to springboard this town. Which sits outside the police's realm, but we have a part to play. The amount of money, which is coming into the new marketplace, the harbour, the third river crossing. And there's a real scope you know what I mean for the selective licencing to just bring up a standard of the accommodation. It is not about having this glorious expensive accommodation. It's about actually having a standard which is fit for purpose, safe, and wholesome.[91]

This more positive message shows the opportunities that the levelling-up agenda can bring to a town—but, as the Right to Succeed consultation has shown, it will take more than some shiny new buildings to improve living and working conditions for EU migrants and locals alike and to heal the divisions in the town.

Free movement to the UK has stopped, but those EU migrants already in the UK continue to access the rights associated with the status. Some will return to their countries of origin, but many will stay and grow old in the UK. This will add further pressure on public services which, when facing the impacts of a government squeeze on finance and significant inflation, may struggle to cope. Deprived areas inevitably suffer.

[90] Interview with GYROS senior staff member (anonymous)(Great Yarmouth, 15 September 2021).
[91] Interview with Great Yarmouth police officer (anonymous) (Great Yarmouth, 17 November 2022).

16
The Paradigm Shift from EU Law to International Law of the Trade and Cooperation Agreement: A Swansong

*Katja S Ziegler**

1. Introduction

Steve Weatherill's retirement from the Jacques Delors Chair in European Union law following a career dedicated to research and teaching of the subject painfully coincided with the United Kingdom leaving the European Union. Although not a consolation, Brexit did not, however, herald an end to the application and relevance of EU law, even for the UK. This is true for EU internal market law so long as the UK has dealings with the EU (and because of the rules of the Northern Ireland Protocol), and, self-evidently, also for EU external relations law. The UK's exit also serves as a wake-up call for the EU to deal with the issues that contributed to the UK leaving, which are not uniquely British and range from the EU's continuing struggle to connect with the people of Europe to the internal responsibilities of a Member State flowing from the duty of sincere cooperation and EU values. The truly tragic geopolitical events of 2022, which saw Russia unleashing a war of aggression against Ukraine, not only demonstrated the need, benefits, and value of European integration, but at the same time both cast Brexit as a phenomenon of a much bigger challenge, and put it into perspective.

While EU law will continue to be relevant in the UK from the outside, the Withdrawal Agreement of 17 October 2019 (WA)[1] and the Trade and Cooperation Agreement of 24 December 2020 (TCA)[2] added a new field of EU–UK relations law, based on international law. The new relations reflect many aspects which are common in the EU's deep and comprehensive trade agreements, and, in that sense, they are still characterized and influenced by EU (external relations) law. But the

* The chapter was completed in July 2022. In some instances it was updated subsequently.

[1] Agreement on the Withdrawal of the United Kingdom of Great Britain and Northern Ireland from the European Union and the European Atomic Energy Community [2019] OJ C384/1.

[2] Trade and Cooperation Agreement between the European Union and the European Atomic Energy Community, of the one part, and the United Kingdom of Great Britain and Northern Ireland, of the other part [2021] OJ L149/10.

Katja S Ziegler, *The Paradigm Shift from EU Law to International Law of the Trade and Cooperation Agreement: A Swansong*
In: *The Internal Market Ideal*. Edited by: Jeremias Adams-Prassl, Sanja Bogojević, Ariel Ezrachi, and Dorota Leczykiewicz,
Oxford University Press. © Katja S Ziegler 2024. DOI: 10.1093/oso/9780192867063.003.0017

paradigm shift to international law also means moving to a less formalized framework of relations and less foreseeable relations, with a greater influence of political considerations..

This has already become apparent in the first year of the TCA's application, which was overshadowed by a wide range of conflicts. These conflicts hindered progress on discretionary, but intended, deepening of relations between the parties to mitigate the impact of the TCA. These included flashpoints right from the start after the provisional and then full entry into force of the TCA on 1 January 2021 and 1 May 2021, respectively: the debate about granting ambassador status to the EU representative in London; the short-lived but, nonetheless, impactful threat of the EU to take safeguard measures under Article 16 of the Northern Ireland Protocol (the Protocol) to prevent the export of Covid-19 vaccines through Northern Ireland and the possible requirement for export licences for Covid-19 vaccines leaving the EU; the UK's unequal treatment of different EU nationalities with regard to the cost of visas to work in the UK;[3] and disputes concerning the implementation of citizens' rights under the Withdrawal Agreement. Furthermore, conflicts over the granting of fishing licences, particularly around the Channel Islands, saw French fishermen blockade the port of Jersey in protest and a British military frigate make a show of force,[4] which demonstrated the potential for escalation (and the possible role of individual Member States as a potential for EU–UK conflict) in a sinister way.

Most of all, the fundamental conflict over the Northern Ireland Protocol hangs like the sword of Damocles over the new relations. The UK sought to renegotiate it immediately after its became effective, in regard to both trading and competition rules and the institutional architecture (the jurisdiction of the Court of Justice of the European Union, CJEU).[5] The UK unilaterally postponed the application of certain rules several times while trying to renegotiate the Protocol. The EU initiated, then paused and then resumed, infringement proceedings against the UK to force it to implement the Protocol, following the introduction of a bill in Parliament that would confer powers on the UK government to override it.[6] The disagreement goes beyond technical issues related to the rules of the Protocol and their practical application in the new relationship, but rather raises fundamental

[3] George Parker, Peter Foster, and Sam Fleming, 'After Brexit: The UK and EU Risk a State of "Permanent Alert"' *Financial Times* (London, 19 February 2021) 21.

[4] Daniel Boffey and Lisa O'Carroll, 'UK Sends Navy Vessels to Jersey amid post-Brexit Fishing Row with France' *The Guardian* (5 May 2021).

[5] *Northern Ireland Protocol: The Way Forward* (Cm 502, 2021). For analysis of the Protocol see Stephen Weatherill, 'The Protocol on Ireland/Northern Ireland: Protecting the EU's Internal Market at the Expense of the UK's' (2020) 45 European Law Review 222.

[6] Northern Ireland Protocol HC Bill (the bill was adopted by the House of Commons and reached Committee stage in House of Lords in October 2022). The UK Government declared that it intends to let the bill lapse with the end of the Parliamentary session, see Windsor Political Declaration by the European Commission and the Government of the United Kingdom of 27 February 2023.

questions of good faith and the binding nature of international law, and, therefore, trust between the parties.

Future relations will largely depend on whether these issues can be put to rest permanently—and how. For now, the Windsor Framework of February 2023 resolved the more technical questions. In particular, the formalities and procedures at point of re-entry relating to goods moving into Northern Ireland from Great Britain were eased and the application of state aid rules clarified.[7] Arguably, the most significant effect of the Windsor Framework was a reset in tone and approach in the EU-UK relations. The challenges to the Protocol have demonstrated the increased potential of disagreements in one area to 'infect' other areas of further envisaged cooperation, such as the UK's accession to the Lugano Convention,[8] which would, for example, allow the cross-border enforcement of judgments between its parties; further adequacy decisions for financial services; and the affiliation to the Union's Programmes, for example, the Horizon research programme[9] or electricity trading arrangements. In the future, the political relationship will be relevant for the extension of Sanitary and Phytosanitary (SPS) listing decisions, visa facilitation for short business activities in the EU, adequacy decisions regarding data protection, and agreements facilitating trade in services (such as the decision on the recognition of professional qualifications, the extension of the title on energy, the agreement on fisheries quotas, and cooperation on asylum and illegal immigration, to name but a few).

This chapter will outline and contextualize the paradigm shift of the TCA from supranational EU law to international law in selected areas, which—in spite of the long debate since the Brexit referendum in 2016—still seems to have surprised some. The paradigm shift is visible in all dimensions of the TCA: its substantive rules (which follow the paradigm of free trade agreements under international law, rather than the elaborate integration through the internal market and customs union); its institutional framework (with a much more limited potential for further development of cooperation through the TCA's Partnership Council, committees, and working groups, which replaces supranational legislative powers of the EU); and its dispute settlement mechanisms (which follow the paradigm of international arbitration between states, rather than the judicial dispute settlement, centralized enforcement, and enforcement mechanisms accessible to individuals in the EU).

[7] See e.g., Windsor Political Declaration (n 6) and subsequent Decision 1/2023 of the Joint Committee established under the Withdrawal Agreement of 24 March 2023, laying down arrangements relating to the Windsor Framework and Declaration of the EU and UK in the Joint Committee of 24 March 2023 on the application of Article 10(1) of the Windsor Framework.

[8] Convention on Jurisdiction and the Recognition and Enforcement of Judgments in Civil and Commercial Matters [2007] OJ L339/3.

[9] UK association was delayed by the disputes over the Protocol, but the UK rejoined Horizon in September 2023.

The most significant difference between the TCA and EU law lies, however, not in each of the substantive rules or its institutional architecture, and not even in its dispute settlement mechanism, but in its horizontal character of laying down obligations only between states, disempowering the individual, which was key to implementing EU law so effectively. First, individuals (natural persons and companies) do not have rights under the TCA (and hence the problem of the lack of access of individuals to an international enforcement mechanism under the TCA does not even arise). Furthermore, the TCA also tries to limit the extent to which individuals can directly invoke its provisions in the domestic legal orders of the parties (ie in the UK, the EU and, by extension, its Member States). Defining the relationship with individuals in the way the TCA has done is, however, not an automatic consequence of placing the EU–UK relations on an international law footing. It is a separate choice. Linked to the role of the individual, but also going beyond individual rights, is the weight of the values underpinning the EU on the one hand, and the values constituting the 'basis for cooperation' under the TCA on the other hand. It will be argued that the most fundamental paradigm shifts in the relationship between the UK and the EU lie in the lack of rights of individuals under the new treaty and the diminished role of values in the TCA.

The chapter will discuss first the paradigm shift with regard to the substantive rules laying down the structure of the new economic relations. The new arrangements for trade in goods will illustrate the new free trade agreement (FTA) paradigm to set the scene (Section 2). It will then consider the roles of the individual (Section 3) and of values (Section 4) in the TCA. In doing so, it will sketch out the paradigm shift from integration within the EU, based on EU law, and cooperation with the EU from the outside, based on international law.

2. Substantive Rules of the Economic Relations

The paradigm shift to an FTA and its effects can be sketched out by considering the mechanism of the new substantive rules on trade in goods. While considering the substantive rules, it also must be borne in mind that, in contrast to EU law, the trading rules of the TCA do not confer rights on individuals.[10]

2.1 Paradigm Shift

The TCA reflects the structure and content of a typical free trade agreement under international law, enriched by some elements specific to the EU–UK situation and

[10] The role of the individual will be discussed in more detail in Section 3.

the evolution of EU FTAs over time. Among the variety of possible models of integration, a free trade agreement is characterized by a lower intensity of cooperation, similar to—but above the level of—the World Trade Organization (WTO) rules. The choice of an FTA under international law means a paradigm shift: the new relationship between the EU and the UK is not only less intensive but is structurally fundamentally different from that of an EU Member State.[11] This has direct impact on its content and regulatory scope. This is due to two characteristics of EU law—the combination of the internal market and the customs union—which are both absent in an FTA. First, the starting point and the rule under EU membership are the internal market freedoms, with the goal of opening markets, facilitated by the mutual recognition of regulatory standards between Member States—the focus of much of Steve Weatherill's influential writing throughout his career.[12] As a rule, the country-of-origin principle determines the regulatory regime, which ensures only one regulatory regime must be followed. Almost every exception—that is, any restriction of internal market freedoms—requires a justification. In addition, European Union legislative harmonization measuresprotect legitimate regulatory interests, such as workers' rights and consumer or data protection, while avoiding the situation in which protection of such interests by different standards in the Member States becomes an obstacle to trade.[13] 'Level playing field' rules, such as competition and state aid law, provide a basis for the internal market to operate. Secondly, the customs union[14] ensures free circulation of goods once in the EU, without further formalities between EU Member States.

It follows directly from the fact that the TCA establishes neither a customs union nor an internal market between the UK and the EU (including its Member States) that non-tariff barriers to trade arise. To a large extent, the TCA's (future) role is to mitigate the effect of non-tariff barriers that the paradigm shift entails. However, an FTA takes a piecemeal approach to individual areas of trade rather than using liberalization as the starting point. An FTA, thus, reverses the rule-exception paradigm of EU membership. The conceptual starting point of an FTA is one of market

[11] See eg Catherine Barnard and Emilija Leinarte, 'Movement of Goods under the TCA' (2022) 13 Global Policy 106; Adam Lazowski, 'Mind the Fog, Stand Clear of the Cliff! From the Political Declaration to the Post-Brexit EU–UK Legal Framework: Part I' (2021) 5 European Papers 1105. For the different options under discussion, see Simon Hix, 'Brexit: Where is the EU–UK Relationship Heading?' (2018) 56 Journal of Common Market Studies 11, 12 and House of Lords European Union Committee, *Brexit: The Options for Trade* (HL 72, 2016). For comparison with WTO membership, see Freya Baetens, '"No Deal is Better than a Bad Deal"? The Fallacy of the WTO Fall-back Option as a Post-Brexit Safety Net' (2018) 55 Common Market Law Review 133.

[12] eg Stephen Weatherill, *Law and Integration in the European Union* (Clarendon Press 1995); Stephen Weatherill, *The Internal Market as a Legal Concept* (Oxford University Press 2017); Stephen Weatherill, 'Why There Is No 'Principle of Mutual Recognition' in EU Law (and Why that Matters to Consumer Lawyers)' in Purnhagen K and Rott P (eds), *Varieties of European Economic Law and Regulation* (Springer 2014) 401. See also references in nn 43, 44, and 79.

[13] See eg Consolidated Version of the Treaty on the Functioning of the European Union (TFEU) [2008] OJ C115/1, art 114.

[14] TFEU, arts 28 and 29.

closure unless specific rules are agreed to open access. As a rule, market access is granted on the basis of non-discrimination (equal treatment of nationals). That means that rules and regulations of the country of destination apply without discrimination as to the origin of the economic product or activity. But this leads, inevitably, to the application of two regulatory regimes, those of the country of origin and those of the country of destination, creating a 'dual burden', the very existence of which amounts to a non-tariff barrier to trade. An FTA can contain further rules that mitigate such barriers, for example through mutual recognition of product rules (in the context of trade in goods), professional qualifications (in the context of trade in services), and regulatory surveillance and enforcement regimes of the other party—on a case-by-case basis. Trade relations between the EU and the UK depend significantly on the extent to which non-tariff barriers to trade, such as additional regulations, approval procedures, controls, and formalities are or can be reduced in future. This is true for trade in goods and even more so for the provision of services. Because of the close connection of services with other dimensions of the internal market, which are not part of the TCA (especially the free movement of persons[15] and regulatory issues), the paradigm shift is even more visible for services than for goods. However, abolishing the free movement of persons and its 'right to regulate' were prominent aims of the UK's withdrawal from the EU.

In addition to creating a dual regulatory burden for trade between the parties, further obstacles arise if an FTA is not linked to a customs union. Even if an FTA eliminates all tariff barriers internally (ie tariffs and quotas are set at zero), it needs to be established that goods in fact originate in the territory of one of the parties and are not imported from the rest of the world. This necessitates rules of origin in an FTA, which require further formalities and controls and, thus, create barriers to trade.

The outcome of the TCA for UK–EU trade should be seen in the light of this paradigm shift in close alignment with WTO law. The TCA eliminates tariffs and quotas. Therein lies its added value as compared to WTO-level trade relations, which in some cases allow substantial tariffs.[16] Although both the UK and EU have praised the TCA as an ambitious agreement, it is not too different from other free trade agreements, such as that with Canada, which eliminates 99 per cent of tariffs.[17] However, obstacles to trade arise above all from non-tariff barriers. The TCA seeks to reduce these by facilitating customs and trade, for example through mutual recognition of the parties' so-called Authorised Economic Operators

[15] See, in more detail, Catherine Barnard and Emilija Leinarte, 'Mobility of Persons' in Federico Fabbrini (ed), *The Law & Politics of Brexit, Volume III: The Framework of New EU UK Relationships* (Oxford University Press 2021) 134ff.

[16] eg 50 per cent or more for meat and milk, up to 25 per cent for fish, 10 per cent for automobiles, and up to 12 per cent and 17 per cent for textiles and footwear, respectively.

[17] European Commission, *The EU—Canada Agreement Explained* <https://policy.trade.ec.europa.eu/eu-trade-relationships-country-and-region/countries-and-regions/canada/eu-canada-agreement/agreement-explained_en> (accessed 29 October 2023).

schemes, intended to avoid controls at the border.[18] Yet this only simplifies formalities, without abolishing them; the threshold and complexity to access the schemes are high and, therefore, the schemes are inaccessible for small- and medium-sized businesses. Further trade facilitation depends on future agreements.[19]

2.2 Example: Trade in Goods under the TCA

The paradigm shift can be demonstrated by reference to the TCA rules on trade in goods.[20] The TCA abolishes customs duties and quotas on imports and exports.[21] This corresponds to Articles 30 and 34 of the Treaty on the Functioning of the European Union (TFEU) but differs in one important aspect. Article 30 TFEU relates to all goods, including those imported from third countries which are in free circulation in the Member States as a result of the customs union, whereas the TCA is limited to goods 'originating' in the other party.[22]

Because there is no customs union, the TCA (like other FTAs) contains detailed rules of origin in its annexes. They define the criteria of when goods are deemed to originate in the UK or the EU and the extensive formalities of how to prove this.[23] Broadly, the rules of origin provide that goods which contain a significant number of third-country components and which have been processed only marginally in a contracting party (ie no value was added) do not qualify for preferential ('zero') tariff treatment. But the rules of origin are a complex maze of general and sector- or product-specific rules—for example for machinery or electric cars—and of many exceptions.[24] A much publicized but simple example of the effect of rules of origin (and of a gap in the TCA) were Marks & Spencer's Percy Pig sweets: the sweets were manufactured in Germany from ingredients (sugars) originating largely in third countries. Because the product was sufficiently modified through manufacturing, it qualified as an EU product and could then be imported without import duty to the UK (to a distribution hub warehouse). However, the product fell afoul of the TCA's rules of origin when exported back into the EU (Ireland): because there were only insignificant changes made in the UK, the product did not qualify as 'originating' in the UK when exported (eg to Ireland).[25] This shows that despite the TCA abolishing tariffs and quotas, obstacles to trade were created. Rules of origin

[18] cf TCA, art 110 and annex 18.
[19] House of Lords European Union Committee, *Beyond Brexit: Trade in Goods* (HL 249, 2021) paras 133–35.
[20] See, in more detail, Barnard and Leinarte, 'Movement of Goods under the TCA' (n 11).
[21] TCA, arts 21, 22, and 26.
[22] TCA, art 21.
[23] TCA, arts 37–68, in particular arts 39 and 43, and annexes 2–9.
[24] See eg TCA, art 60 for small consignments between private individuals and personal luggage.
[25] See eg Anthony Reuben, 'Rules of Origin: Why are Percy Pigs a Headache for M&S?' (*BBC*, 15 January 2021) <www.bbc.co.uk/news/55648201> (accessed 29 October 2023).

required (or set incentives for) the switching of supply chains and business models that had been established across the EU, including the UK while a member. The impact of rules of origin is is particularly pronounced where supply chains were highly integrated and where business models relied on single European distribution centres serving the entire territory of the two parties combined. In the interim, depending on the level of customs duties, paying the tariff may even be the more cost-effective choice for companies to avoid having to deal with complex formalities to prove origin. Data about the preference utilization rate will reveal in due course to what extent traders benefit from the TCA.[26]

In addition to obstacles to trade resulting from rules of origin (as a result of the lack of a customs union), there are a wide range of further (non-tariff) barriers to trade. In the EU, Article 34 TFEU prohibits not just tariffs and quotas but also any measures 'having equivalent effect'. The TCA does not abolish these other barriers to trade. Non-tariff, technical barriers to trade (TBT) and, in particular, the SPS with regard to agricultural and meat products remain in place, unless the parties agree further facilitations. These barriers flow from the general principle of national treatment in free trade agreements laid down by Article III of the General Agreement on Tariffs and Trade (GATT), to which the TCA also refers.[27] Non-discriminatory national regulatory standards are permissible in principle, for example, for health and consumer protection. This means that importers from the UK may have to comply with potentially different standards in each of the twenty-seven Member States (as importers in the EU will need to comply with UK standards, potentially diverging from those of the EU), which create barriers to trade. The TCA aims to facilitate trade and reduce non-tariff barriers in the three chapters dealing with such national measures.[28] They are based on – and refer to – the corresponding WTO agreements on:[29] Sanitary and Phytosanitary Standards (SPS Agreement),[30] Technical Barriers to Trade (TBT Agreement),[31] and Trade Facilitation (TF Agreement).[32] They include the general obligation not to create unjustified barriers to trade.[33] However, in contrast to the principle of mutual

[26] cf TCA, art 31 on statistical monitoring of preferential use, which will be informative for the actual benefit of the TCA in the future.

[27] TCA, art 19.

[28] TCA, pt 2, heading 1, title I, chs 3–5.

[29] TCA, arts 72 and 90.

[30] TCA, arts 69–87; see also WTO Agreement on the Application of Sanitary and Phytosanitary Measures (SPS Agreement).

[31] TCA, arts 88–100 and seven sector-specific annexes (including annexes 11–15: motor vehicles, pharmaceuticals, chemicals, organic products, trade in wine), which further define the TBT rules, but focus on cooperation and the development of international standards. See also WTO Agreement on Technical Barriers to Trade (TBT Agreement).

[32] TCA, arts 101–22. One example is the creation of the so-called Authorised Economic Operator schemes, which grant practical facilitations in trade between the partners; see TCA, art 110 and annex 18. See also WTO Trade Facilitation Agreement (TF Agreement).

[33] TCA, art 73(2).

recognition in EU law (no 'dual burden'), non-discriminatory regulatory standards are, as a rule, permitted, reversing the rule-exception paradigm.

For SPS, as a specific instance of a TBT, the TCA provides that the parties are free to determine the level of protection which they consider necessary for agricultural products of plant and animal origin, provided that restrictions do not go beyond what is necessary to achieve their objective.[34] This can lead to additional formalities, such as export declarations, additional checks such as veterinary checks on fresh/chilled meat, or even a complete prohibition of import. The SPS measures adopted by the parties must be based on scientifically identified risks and international standards,[35] but can be based on the precautionary principle, which is explicitly mentioned in the TCA.[36] This is relevant for the level of protection in the Member States, for example, in regard to the use of antibiotics, hormones, and genetically modified products, should the UK wish to diverge from its current regulatory standards (eg in order to implement a trade agreement with another country, such as the US).

The burden imposed by SPS rules has been highlighted by the example of UK fishermen who could no longer export some live shellfish to the EU because they did not meet the EU hygiene rules applicable to third countries once the transition period ended with the entry into force of the TCA (certain catch areas did not have the required water quality—something that did not matter under the previous mutual recognition regime).[37] The burdens imposed by SPS also featured prominently in the complaints of Northern Ireland unionists and the UK's challenge to the implementation of the Northern Ireland Protocol until the Windsor Framework was agreed in February 2023.[38] The Protocol requires that the EU's SPS rules need to be complied with when goods enter the island of Ireland (that is, even regarding the intra-UK trade routes between Great Britain and Northern Ireland) to allow free circulation in the EU (the Republic of Ireland).

The TCA refers to the WTO SPS Agreement, which provides for trade facilitation via bilateral agreements on the equivalence of regulatory standards and controls.[39] But the EU has not agreed to any such equivalence arrangements so far. Further cooperation measures may, in future, result from the Special Trade Committee on Sanitary and Phytosanitary Measures, established as part of the TCA institutional

[34] TCA, art 73(3)(d); WTO SPS Agreement, art 2(1).

[35] See also WTO SPS Agreement, art 3(1).

[36] TCA, arts 340, 356, 393, and 494.

[37] Rajeev Syal, 'Yorkshire Lobster Exporter Says Brexit Costs Have Forced it to Close' *The Guardian* (8 February 2021) <https://www.theguardian.com/politics/2021/feb/08/yorkshire-lobster-exporter-baron-shellfish-brexit-costs-forced-close> (accessed 29 October 2023).

[38] See above (n 7).

[39] The bilateral veterinary agreement between the EU and New Zealand can be cited as an example of a possible reduction in import controls: Agreement between the European Community and New Zealand on sanitary measures applicable to trade in live animals and animal products [1997] OJ L57/5.

architecture. It has the task of monitoring SPS measures and controls (and thus the impact of existing and new SPS as barriers to trade).[40]

The chapter on TBT aims to prevent, identify, and eliminate 'unnecessary technical barriers to trade'.[41] But TBT covers such a wide range of measures and controls[42] that its applicability to specific measures can be controversial. There is an inherent tension as divergence of regulatory measures (which could cause barriers to trade) result from the parties' 'right to regulate'. In the WTO context, the classification of measures as TBT that are not directly product-related, such as those aimed at compliance with environmental, social, or labour standards in the production process, is particularly controversial, recalling the debates, contestations, and choices regarding the scope of Article 34 TFEU in the context of the EU's internal market[43]—and now also the UK's internal market.[44]

In addition to the general prohibition of discrimination, the parties are obliged under WTO law to assess the impact of such standards and to be transparent about planned technical regulations, for example through notification.[45] Technical barriers to trade extend beyond the substantive regulatory requirements to the control mechanisms confirming conformity with the other party's standards. But in contrast to the Comprehensive Economic and Trade Agreement between the EU and Canada (CETA)[46] and the UK's negotiating objectives, the TCA provides for neither mutual recognition of standards, nor conformity assessment procedures. Such solutions would have enabled the parties to determine conformity with standards of the other party already in the country of origin, prior to export. Without this, for example, UK authorities can no longer determine that certain products meet the requirements of the EU's CE mark.[47] However, if conformity assessment procedures are required, they must be proportionate to the risk.[48] Product-specific rules allow manufacturers of certain low- or medium-risk products to self-certify the

[40] TCA, art 87 lit (d).

[41] TCA, art 88.

[42] TCA, art 90; TBT Agreement, annexes 1–3.

[43] See eg Stephen Weatherill, *The Internal Market as a Legal Concept* (Oxford University Press 2017) 2, ch 6, (esp 68–73, 76), 92, 99f, 223, 225–27; Stephen Weatherill, 'Free Movement of Goods' (2012) 61 International and Comparative Law Quarterly 541–43; Stephen Weatherill, 'After "Keck": Some Thoughts on How to Clarify the Clarification' (1996) 33 Common Market Law Review 885.

[44] Stephen Weatherill 'Comparative Internal Market Law: The UK and the EU' (2021) 40 Yearbook of European Law 431.

[45] TCA, arts 91 and 94.

[46] Comprehensive Economic and Trade Agreement between Canada, of the one part, and the European Union and its Member States, of the other part (CETA) [2017] OJ L11/23; CETA Protocol on the Mutual Acceptance of the Results of Conformity Assessment (Protocol on Conformity Assessment).

[47] The UK announced and then postponed plans to introduce its own safety mark: UKCA. The mandatory use, initially planned for 1 January 2021, then postponed twice (to 1 January 2023 and 31 December 2024, respectively). In August 2023, the government announced the indefinite recognition of the EU's CE mark. The introduction of the separate UKCA has been strongly criticized in business circles; see eg Peter Foster, 'UK Businesses "Not Persuaded" by New Safety and Quality Mark' *Financial Times* (19 December 2021).

[48] TCA, art 93.

conformity of their products.[49] The Special Trade Committee on Technical Barriers to Trade established under the TCA, is tasked with the further development of co-operation, particularly by creating future common or international standards and conformity assessment procedures, measures for market surveillance, and information exchange on, for example, hazards posed by products.[50]

In summary, the increased complexity and the lowering of the level of cooperation for trade in goods stems necessarily from the paradigm shift from the internal market and a customs union to a free trade agreement, and the fact that mitigating measures are oriented at the low level of WTO rules. However, the TCA offers opportunities for deeper cooperation, which are inherent in its specific rules and the institutional architecture and could further reduce non-tariff barriers to trade on a case-by-case basis.

3. The Role of the Individual

The previous section outlined the paradigm shift in the substantive rules from market integration to an FTA, with an overview of the structure of the new rules for trade in goods. This section will focus on the status and role of the individual (natural persons as well as companies).

The fact that the individual has direct (subjective) enforceable rights is a key feature of EU law and of its effective enforcement.[51] The TCA unravels what has widely been considered an advance in international law: by giving individuals immediate rights and status under (a type of) international law ('new legal order of international law'),[52] EU law has transcended the traditional state-centric nature of international law and its actors. In contrast, the individual has no direct role under the TCA which contains almost exclusively[53] inter-party obligations of the EU (including its Member States) and the UK. Individuals have no rights to start with and, therefore, no possibility under international law to enforce the rules that are aimed at benefitting them themselves and independently. Any benefits to individuals are mediated by the contracting parties to the TCA (the EU and the UK).

[49] TCA, arts 9(2) lit (b) and (5).

[50] TCA, art 100.

[51] For an overview of the widely discussed implications of individual rights and their enforcement in the EU and the Member States throughout the evolution of EU law, see eg Bruno De Witte, 'Direct Effect, Primacy, and the Nature of the Legal Order' in Paul Craig and Gráinne de Búrca (eds), *The Evolution of EU Law* (3rd edn, Oxford University Press 2021) 187ff, esp 223ff; Francesca Episcopo, 'The Vicissitudes of Life at the Coalface: Remedies and Procedures for Enforcing Union Law Before National Courts' in Craig and de Búrca, *The Evolution of EU Law*, 275ff.

[52] Case 26/62 *van Gend & Loos v Netherlands Inland Revenue Administration* [1963] ECLI:EU:C:1963:1; Case 6/64 *Flaminio Costa v ENEL* [1964] ECLI:EU:C:1964:66.

[53] With the exception of the individual rights contained in the Protocol on Social Security Coordination, art SSC.67 and, for the EU, TCA, pt 3 on law enforcement and judicial cooperation in respect of criminal matters.

The TCA rules, additionally, go out of their way to ensure that individual enforcement does not evolve dynamically, as it did in EU law. The TCA is unusually explicit about the application and interpretation of the TCA in the domestic sphere of the parties, even though it is mostly restating standard principles of international law, and even though the TCA does not provide for a central judicial dispute settlement body like the CJEU. The absence of a central judicial dispute settlement body already makes a dynamic and evolutionary interpretation of the TCA comparable to that of EU law by the CJEU unlikely, if not completely impossible. Despite these 'structural' safeguards, the TCA stipulates explicitly that it has to be interpreted in light of public international law (Article 4(1) TCA), and not in light of the internal law of the parties (Article 4(2) TCA). Article 5(2) TCA provides that the parties should not provide for actions against the other party under their domestic law, something that would follow from immunity from domestic jurisdiction of states for governmental acts. This seems to be, in part, driven by the desire to create a clear break with EU law (where Member States are subject to infringement actions before the CJEU) and, in part, to clarify beyond doubt that the EU, too, enjoys immunity under international law. This is assumed to be a customary rule of international law,[54] but an explicit rule disperses any residual doubts resulting from a general lack of practice around the customary rule.[55] These may be seen as largely unnecessary clarifications to contain indirect effects of EU law pre-emptively. The most far-reaching exclusions concern the status of the individual.

The TCA, naturally, places the relationship between the EU and the UK on the foundation of international law. This in itself does not rule out individual rights, which could be conferred by treaty. Excluding individual rights, instead, is a consequence of the concrete choices made when agreeing the TCA. In line with the objectives of Brexit, the TCA limits the new relations to inter-party relations (analogous to traditional inter-state relations). This has consequences for the (subjective) rights of individuals (both natural and legal persons) under the TCA and for the nature of the dispute resolution mechanism. It will have implications for the extent of the effect of the TCA within the domestic legal order of the parties and its enforcement overall.

3.1 Individual Rights

Under EU law, individuals have rights—including from the free movement provisions—which they can enforce by virtue of EU law before the CJEU and before national courts of the Member States (and against them). This was made

[54] Ramses A Wessel, 'Immunities of the European Union' (2014) 10 International Organizations Law Review 395, 414ff.

[55] ibid 415.

possible by the CJEU, which established in *van Gend* and *Costa v ENEL* that EU law is a 'new legal order of international law'.[56] The existence of subjective rights *by virtue of* EU law and their direct applicability in the Member States enabled a combination of extensive centralized and decentralized enforcement of EU law, before both the EU institutions and the Member States' courts. This dual mode of enforcement is, so far, unique in international law, at least to the extent that it is stipulated by an international treaty.

The TCA's approach stands in contrast to this. Article 5(1) TCA, like some other FTAs of the EU,[57] explicitly excludes an interpretation that the TCA provides individual rights *qua* international treaty; in other words, direct effect cannot be derived from the provisions of the TCA and applied to—or over—domestic law.[58] Article 5(1) TCA provides that:

> nothing in this Agreement . . . shall be construed as conferring rights or imposing obligations on persons other than those created between the parties under public international law.

Article 754(2) TCA reinforces this point by stating that decisions of the arbitral tribunal are also not creating individual rights, only rights and obligations between the parties.

The dispute settlement mechanism of the TCA is a direct reflection of the absence of individual rights. It is modelled on inter-state arbitration. Disputes, as a rule, are to be settled primarily politically/diplomatically in the Partnership Council or its committees. Failing that, the TCA provides for a general dispute settlement mechanism,[59] similar to recent EU and WTO FTAs (albeit without a second instance). It has three stages; first, formally initiated political or diplomatic consultations in the Partnership Council;[60] secondly, binding arbitration before an independent arbitral tribunal which is constituted for each dispute from a list of previously agreed potential arbitrators;[61] and thirdly, a compliance stage: if a party has not implemented the ruling of the arbitral tribunal in a reasonable time, the other party can enforce the ruling through temporary remedies.[62] This can be either temporary compensation (which needs to be agreed between the parties)

[56] *van Gend* (n 52); *Costa v ENEL* (n 52).

[57] See eg Agreement between the European Union and Japan for an Economic Partnership [2018] OJ L330/3, art 23.5; CETA, art 30.6; Aliki Semertzi, 'The Preclusion of Direct Effect in the Recently Concluded EU Free Trade Agreements' (2014) 51 Common Market Law Review 1125. This may strengthen the inter-institutional position of the European Parliament, but this may also be simply due to EU FTAs modelling the approach to WTO law.

[58] For the two exceptions, see n 53.

[59] TCA, pt 6, Title 1, art 734ff.

[60] TCA, art 738.

[61] TCA, arts 739ff, 754(2).

[62] TCA, art 749.

or a unilateral suspension of obligations under the TCA and/or Withdrawal Agreement,[63] for example, imposing duties or import restrictions.[64]

Because the TCA does not confer individual rights, individuals do not have direct access to the TCA's dispute settlement mechanism, in contrast to the situations under EU law, but also in contrast to CETA, which establishes 'investor-to-state' arbitration.[65] In cases of violations of the TCA, individuals are dependent on the EU or the UK taking up their grievance diplomatically in the Partnership Council or its committees and, if necessary, in the arbitration procedures foreseen by the TCA. This means that, to enforce the TCA rules vis-à-vis the other party, a party to the TCA must raise any concerns of its nationals as an inter-party complaint, exercising diplomatic protection on behalf of its own nationals.[66]

As is the case with arbitration under international law, the mechanism is characterized by greater control of the parties over the proceedings and weaker enforcement, compared to judicial dispute settlement.[67] Whether individuals have enforceable rights for diplomatic protection to be exercised on their behalf depends on the respective domestic law. In most circumstances, this will be subject, to a large degree, to the discretion of the party. The lack of direct access to enforcement mechanisms for individuals stands in sharp contrast to the direct and indirect actions under EU law (actions for annulment, preliminary rulings procedures) which have facilitated the centralized and decentralized enforcement of EU law. The absence of individual rights and individual enforcement mechanisms is likely to affect the effectiveness of the implementation of the TCA.

3.2 No Requirement of Direct Applicability in the Domestic Legal Orders

Article 5(1) TCA goes even further: it excludes not only a teleological interpretation in favour of individual rights, but also the direct applicability of the TCA in

[63] TCA, art 749(4) and Withdrawal Agreement, art 178(2). This is already provided for under the general international law of treaties, cf Vienna Convention on the Law of Treaties, art 60, in so far as there is a material breach of an obligation (see text near n 98 in Section 4).

[64] The suspension of obligations shall, as a rule, take place under the same heading of the TCA if the breach occurs in Heading One (trade) or Heading Three (road transport) of pt 2. However, this can be escalated to potentially suspending any obligation within the scope of the general dispute settlement mechanism, eg a breach under the fisheries Heading Five could lead to a suspension of obligations from the trade Heading One, subject to the proportionality of such a response.

[65] CETA, ch 8.

[66] For an overview, see John Dugard, 'Diplomatic Protection' in Rüdiger Wolfrum (ed), *Max Planck Encyclopaedia of Public International Law* (Oxford University Press 2021).

[67] TCA, arts 740, 741, and 752. Centralized enforcement of CJEU rulings through penalty or lump sum payments in TFEU, art 260(3) is replaced by the unilateral suspension of obligations under TCA, art 749.

the legal orders of the parties.[68] It stipulates that nothing in the TCA should be interpreted 'as permitting [the TCA] ... to be directly invoked in the domestic legal systems of the Parties'. This goes beyond the question of individual rights. It relates to the wider issue of the relationship between international and domestic law (and, by extension, EU law); in other words, the effect and status of international law in the domestic law of the parties. Such a provision would normally be unnecessary in an international treaty because the effect of international law is, in principle, already governed and controlled by each domestic legal order according to its own constitutional principles. For the EU, international treaties are generally an 'integral part' of the EU legal order (Article 216(2) TFEU) and are capable of direct effect,[69] subject to conditions the CJEU has developed in its case law. In the EU, an international treaty provision is directly applicable if it contains a sufficiently clear and precise obligation which does not require further implementation and direct application must not precluded by the 'nature and structure' or 'broad logic' of a treaty.[70] In the UK, international treaties are not directly applicable unless they are incorporated into domestic law by an act of 'transformation', a parliamentary statute that ensures that domestic law is not changed automatically by treaties in themselves. This is because the executive concludes treaties on the international plane. , Allowing them to be directly applicable automatically would bypass Parliament and contravene the UK constitutional principle of parliamentary sovereignty.[71] The EU's approach to treaties may, thus, be characterized as predominantly monist, whereas the UK takes a dualist approach.

Two reasons may explain why the TCA excludes direct applicability in the domestic sphere. On the one hand, an explicit exclusion of direct applicability of the TCA in the domestic legal orders of the parties fits the Brexit context. It ensures a categorical break with the *status quo ante* in EU law and seeks to rule out any eventuality of far-reaching teleological interpretations of the TCA à la *van Gend*[72] and its progeny. On the other hand, excluding the direct applicability of the TCA also avoids automatic asymmetries in the domestic application of the TCA between the EU and the UK, which would result from each party taking its 'usual'

[68] See also similarly CETA, art 30.6.1. cf Jens Brauneck, 'EU-VK-Handelsabkommen TCA: Streitbeilegung EU-rechtskonform?' (2021) 32 Europäische Zeitschrift für Wirtschaftsrecht 291, 296ff with concerns that art 5 of the TCA may be incompatible with the autonomy of the EU legal order.

[69] Case 181/73 *Haegeman v Belgium* [1974] ECLI:EU:C:1974:41, para 5; Case 104/81 *Kupferberg v Hauptzollamt Mainz* [1982] ECLI:EU:C:1982:362, para 13; Case C–162/96 *Racke v Hauptzollamt Mainz* [1998] ECLI:EU:C:1998:293, para 46; Case C–308/06 *Intertanko v Secretary of State for Transport* [2008] ECLI:EU:C:2008:312, para 38 (*Intertanko*); Case C–366/10 *Air Transport Association of America v Secretary of State for Energy and Climate Change* [2011] ECLI:EU:C:2011:864, paras 73 and 101 (*ATAA*).

[70] *Intertanko* (n 69) para 45; Joined Cases C–120/06 P and 121/06 P *FIAMM and Fedon v Council and Commission* [2008] ECLI:EU:C:2008:476 (GC) and *FIAMM* ECLI:EU:C:2008:98, Opinion of Advocate General Maduro, paras 27ff; Joined Cases 21–24/72 *International Fruit Co NV v Produktschap Voor Groenten en Fruit* [1972] ECLI:EU:C:1972:115, para 25ff; Case C–192/89 *Sevince v Staatssecretaris van Justitie* [1990] ECLI:EU:C:1990:322; *ATAA* (n 69) paras 53ff.

[71] *JH Rayner v Department of Trade and Industry* [1988] 3 All ER 257.

[72] *van Gend* (n 52).

constitutional approach—which differs between the parties. This is a rationale for such clauses in other EU FTAs.[73] However, if a treaty does not confer any individual rights under international law, its application within the domestic legal order is limited already. A further exclusion of direct applicability, then, seems to be unwarranted, if not superfluous. Asymmetries which would usually arise primarily with regard to the enforceability of individual rights in domestic courts do not, on the whole, arise if there are no individual rights under international law in the first place.

What, then, is the extent of the exclusion of direct applicability in Article 5(1) TCA? Is it *precluding* a party (or its courts), as a matter of international obligation, from considering the TCA to be directly applicable (even if that is the jurisdiction's standard approach)? In other words, is it a far-reaching exclusion of the TCA, excluded altogether from domestic application, even if a party's legal order allows for the direct application of an international treaty? Or is it simply clarifying that, as a matter of international law, the TCA itself is not *requiring* a direct application *qua* treaty of the institutional actors within the parties, eg courts (so: excluding a supranational effect), but still *allowing* the parties to apply it or make it applicable? The latter, narrower reading would be in line with the ordinary approach of international treaties. But the wording of Article 5(1) TCA is also amenable to a reading that supports the first, more far-reaching exclusion. Considering the wording, the English and French language versions[74] ('not ... permitting to be directly invoked' and 'ni ... permettant d'invoquer directement') are ambivalent in that they might be read to suggest a wider exclusion (if 'not permitting' is read as 'prohibiting') or a narrower exclusion (if 'permitting' is referring to the treaty, rather than to the parties to the treaty).[75] The German language version seems to be narrower in suggesting that there is simply *no obligation* under the TCA to allow it to be directly applicable and, therefore, also *no prohibition* against allowing it to be applied directly.[76] This reading is also in line with the ordinary approach to international treaties, which presupposes that the domestic effects of a treaty are to be decided by each party.

[73] De Witte (n 41) 200.

[74] The French language version is comparable to the English version: 'aucune disposition du présent accord ... ne peut être interprétée comme conférant des droits ou imposant des obligations aux personnes d'une autre nature que ceux créés entre les Parties en vertu du droit international public, ni comme permettant d'invoquer directement le présent accord ou tout accord complémentaire dans les systèmes juridiques internes des Parties.'

[75] The choice of the word 'permitting' in the English language version probably refers to other domestic actors (courts, individuals) rather than to the contracting parties themselves. The use of the word 'requiring' would be clearer in this respect.

[76] According to the German text of art 5, the provisions of the TCA 'sind ... weder dahin gehend auszulegen, dass sie andere Rechte oder Pflichten für Personen begründen als die zwischen den Vertragsparteien nach dem Völkerrecht geschaffenen Rechte oder Pflichten, *noch dahin gehend*, dass sie in den internen Rechtsordnungen der Vertragsparteien *unmittelbar geltend gemacht werden können*' (emphasis added).

The problem with this, however, is that it would run counter a rationale of the clause to create symmetry for the domestic effects in the legal orders of the parties, reflected in other EU trade agreements. Yet, while international law does not preclude that the parties agree a specific internal effect (as it is the case with the EU), this would require an explicit agreement, which does not appear to have been reached in the ambiguous wording of Article 5 TCA. First, such a wide interpretation of Article 5 TCA would reduce the effectiveness of the treaty. Because this is so, the wide interpretation could itself be considered to run counter to the objectives of the treaty, and so would need an even clearer indication of the parties' intent. In addition, for the EU, the direct applicability of international agreements ensures that Member States do not breach the EU's international treaty obligations (Article 216(2) TFEU). Secondly, excluding the internal effect of an international treaty *by* a treaty might also be questionable for reasons of EU constitutional law, eg the right to judicial protection.[77] Thirdly, the TCA itself requires the parties to make remedies against domestic decisions available under domestic law, eg Article 157 (trade in services) and Article 338 (transparency of regulation). This presumes some form of effect is given to TCA rules conferring a benefit to individuals, whether by specific implementing legislation or automatically and directly via the TCA. Specific incorporation is not required by the TCA. Fourthly, UK practice further supports a narrow interpretation. Section 29 of the European Union (Future Relationship) Act 2020 gives the TCA an unusually far-reaching scope to ensure the correct implementation of the UK's international obligations, namely direct law-amending effect in the UK,[78] by virtue of a statutory application order, in so far as this is necessary for compliance with obligations under international law arising from the TCA. Although this effect is mediated by a national statute (and not the result of direct applicability *qua* international treaty), it would be at odds with a wider reading that Article 5(1) TCA prohibits the parties from creating direct applicability of the TCA by virtue of a domestic implementing act. As the European Union (Future Relationship) Act 2020 was passed within days of concluding the TCA, section 29 casts a light on the understanding of the effect of the TCA at the time by one of the parties.

[77] Ernst-Ulrich Petersmann, 'CETA, TTIP, and TiSA: New Trends in International Economic Law' in Stefan Griller, Walter Obwexer, and Erich Vranes (eds), *Mega-Regional Trade Agreements: CETA, TTIP, and TiSA: New Orientations for EU External Economic Relations* (Oxford University Press 2017) 1838ff (pointing to the 'disempowerment' of EU citizens and fundamental rights concerns—effective legal protection); Lazowski (n 11) 1124ff (discussing unequal treatment of individuals in EU FTAs); cf also Brauneck (n 68) 296 (raising concerns about the autonomy of the EU legal order).

[78] European Union (Future Relationship) Act 2020, s 29(1) states:

> Existing domestic law has effect on and after the relevant day with such modifications as are required for the purposes of implementing in that law the [TCA] … so far as the agreement concerned is not otherwise so implemented and so far as such implementation is necessary for the purposes of complying with the international obligations of the United Kingdom under the agreement.

In addition, the Future Relationship Act gives the Executive wide powers to make regulations.

Article 5 TCA thus must be considered as solely concerned with the exclusion of individual rights under international law and clarifying that the domestic effect of the TCA is not regulated at the level of the international treaty, as a matter of international law, but left to the domestic law of the parties. Article 5(1) TCA *does not require* a specific domestic approach to implementing the TCA. This is in line with the context and interests involved, and the fact that in certain scenarios direct applicability might indeed arise under domestic law. It is unlikely that the parties would have wanted to exclude such a possibility.

In any case, Article 5 TCA cannot exclude the *indirect* application of the TCA through the interpretation of domestic law by the CJEU, Member States' and UK courts, or other domestic actors. Although interpretation in conformity with the TCA is not the same as directly applying it, the boundaries are fluid. Whether this is seen to support the narrower interpretation of Article 5 TCA or whether, to the contrary, this makes it less pressing, may be debatable. However, the intra-EU relations between the EU and its Member States call for a reading that favours direct applicability. As a result, there may be more scope for 'dialogue' between the domestic actors of both parties, including courts, than first meets the eye.

4. The Role of Values

The EU is also a union of values. Values are part of its identity, in both an aspirational and a constitutional sense.[79] Values already underpinned its creation, as the original communities were founded on the value of peace. Over the decades, the EU's values have become more defined, more nuanced, and more enforceable. Internally, values have been strengthened as fundamental rights of individuals and as constitutional values, or principles, which are also enforceable against the EU's own Member States.[80] On both counts, the TCA cannot be compared with the EU's increased protection of values.

European Union values have been strengthened most prominently through enforceable fundamental rights, both as general principles of EU law (referred to in Article 6 of the Treaty on European Union (TEU), alongside the European Convention on Human Rights (ECHR)) and their codification in the EU Charter of Fundamental Rights (the Charter). Whereas economic freedoms of individuals, discussed earlier in this chapter, have acted as an engine of integration, fundamental rights, conceptually, have the opposite effect: they function as limits to supranational integration—even though, in practice, they have also furthered it

[79] Stephen Weatherill, *Law and Values in the European Union* (Oxford University Press 2016) 393ff.

[80] Case C-156/21 *Hungary v European Parliament and Council of the European Union* [2022] ECLI:EU:C:2022:97, para 127; C-157/21 *Poland v European Parliament and Council of the European Union* [2022] ECLI:EU:C:2022:98, para 145.

by extending the EU's competences into the non-economic sphere. But the two types of rights are not hermetically sealed off from one another but can also mutually reinforce each other. The prohibition of gender discrimination in regard to pay[81] was originally driven by competitive concerns in the internal market law but gained a wider significance as a value. EU citizenship rights also evolved beyond their market origin in the fundamental (economic) freedoms. Conversely, the Charter protects the rights of market participants also *qua* fundamental rights, eg the freedom to conduct a business (Article 16 of the Charter).

Beyond fundamental rights of individuals, EU values have been codified in Article 2 TEU as its 'constitutional principles'. These are enforceable against the Member States through the special procedure of Article 7 TEU, activated against Poland and Hungary in 2017 and 2018 to address 'democratic and rule of law backsliding', which could ultimately lead to the suspension of membership rights. Article 2 TEU also gained independent force. The CJEU applied Article 2 TEU first in combination with Article 19 TEU[82] because of the direct relevance of judicial independence of national courts for the implementation of EU law. Then, the Court developed a prohibition of regression on rule of law standards applicable to accession states.[83] Most recently, when upholding the legality of the Budget Conditionality Regulation,[84] it developed what may be called a constitutional notion of 'defensive' (or 'militant') democracy in EU law. The CJEU held that there was a duty (and competence) of the EU to defend the EU's constitutional identity because a Member State's compliance 'with the values contained in Article 2 TEU is a condition for the enjoyment of all the rights' of that Member State under the EU Treaties. The values are 'shared by the Member States [and] define the very identity of the European Union as a common legal order'. This gives the EU the competence to 'defend those values'[85] also against the Member States, including by withholding funds from them, if the conditions of the Budget Conditionality Regulation are not met.[86]

The TCA also contains references to a number of shared values as the 'basis for cooperation' between the parties in Title II of Part 6.[87] But the substantive values are, on the whole, much more limited. To start with, the TCA does not contain any fundamental rights, which could act as limits to the TCA that could be enforced by individuals. The objective dimension of values agreed between the parties is

[81] TFEU, art 157.
[82] Case C-64/16 *Associação Sindical dos Juízes Portugueses v Tribunal de Contas* [2018] ECLI:EU:C:2018:117.
[83] Case C-896/19 *Repubblika v Il-Prim Ministru* [2021] ECLI:EU:C:2021:311, para 64.
[84] *Hungary v Parliament and Council* (n 80); *Poland v Parliament and Council* (n 80).
[85] *Hungary v Parliament and Council* (n 80) para 126ff; *Poland v Parliament and Council* (n 80) para 144ff.
[86] Regulation 2020/2092 on a general regime of conditionality for the protection of the Union budget of 16 December 2022 [2020] OJ L433 I/1. The Commission initiated the procedure against Hungary in April 2022.
[87] TCA, arts 763–71.

limited, too, if compared to the EU Treaties. The dispute settlement and enforcement mechanisms of the TCA are either completely excluded or weak in regard to TCA values. They are largely confined to a threat to cease cooperation under the TCA completely.

As to the substantive values underpinning the new UK–EU relations, Article 763 TCA identifies the principles of democracy, the rule of law, and human rights as common values and bases for cooperation. But the commitment to specific standards is much watered down, not least as a result of the UK's objection to horizontal values clauses during the TCA negotiations. The UK considered values clauses as, given the extent of alignment of values between the parties, and as going beyond the intended economic cooperation.[88] The Commission's proposal to include an explicit commitment to the ECHR[89] could not be agreed. Article 763 TCA mentions only the Universal Declaration of Human Rights and the 'international human rights treaties' which the contracting parties have ratified, all of which have weaker enforcement mechanisms.[90] Only Part 3, on police and judicial cooperation in criminal matters, contains more specific human rights obligations, in particular references to the ECHR, including a requirement to give them domestic effect.[91] The TCA also contains further and novel values, first and foremost the fight against climate change in Article 764 TCA,[92] to which it refers in strong terms[93] as an 'existential threat to humanity'. The TCA incorporates and requires parties to respect the obligations to reduce emissions under the Paris Agreement of 2015 and the process set up by the UN Framework Convention on Climate Change of 1992. This comprises the obligation to 'refrain from acts or omissions that would materially defeat the object and purpose of the Paris Agreement'. Other values which are not mentioned in the EU Treaties, but which are contained in recent EU FTAs, have been included. This is to ensure consistency among EU FTAs, reinforce the EU FTA 'template', and, hence, influence future EU FTAs.[94] In this vein, the TCA also includes as the basis for cooperation the following values: countering weapons of

[88] *The Future Relationship with the EU: The UK's Approach to Negotiations* (CP211, February 2020) <https://assets.publishing.service.gov.uk/government/uploads/system/uploads/attachment_data/file/868874/The_Future_Relationship_with_the_EU.pdf> (accessed 29 October 2023).

[89] European Commission, Task Force for Relations with the United Kingdom, Draft Text of the Agreement on the New Partnership with the United Kingdom (18 March 2020, UKTF 14), protocols 1, 6, and 13 and art COMPROV.4 <https://ec.europa.eu/info/publications/draft-text-agreement-new-partnership-united-kingdom_en> (accessed 29 October 2023).

[90] It is also ambivalent and possibly ambiguous, given the EU's lack of accession to human rights treaties so far, especially the ECHR.

[91] TCA, art 524.

[92] See also TFEU, art 191, in regard to the EU's external policy goal to fight climate change.

[93] See Markus Gehring, 'Analysis 5 of the Brexit Deal: Environment and Climate Provisions' (*EU Law Analysis*, 22 January 2021) <http://eulawanalysis.blogspot.com/2021/01/analysis-5-of-brexit-deal-environment.html> (accessed 29 October 2023).

[94] Strategic Partnership Agreement between the European Union and its Member States, of the one part, and Canada, of the other part [2016] OJ L329/45, art 2; Strategic Partnership Agreement between the European Union and its Member States, of the one part, and Japan, of the other part [2018] OJ L216/4, art 2.

mass destruction; countering illicit manufacturing, sale and distribution of small arms, light weapons, and other conventional weapons; prosecution and punishment of the most serious crimes against the international community as a whole; the fight against terrorism; protection of personal data; and a commitment to the promotion of multilateral solutions to common problems of 'shared economic, environmental and social interest'.[95]

However, enforcement of these values is weak. As a rule, the entirety of Title II on the 'basis for cooperation' is excluded from the general dispute settlement mechanism of the TCA,[96] so there is no recourse to inter-party arbitration in case of a dispute about values. Dispute settlement about values is essentially limited to diplomatic negotiations in the Partnership Council. However, a breach of certain values identified as 'essential elements' of the TCA gives rise to an accelerated right to suspend or terminate the TCA (Article 772 TCA). Essential elements of the TCA are democracy, the rule of law, human rights, combating climate change, and countering the proliferation of weapons of mass destruction (Article 771 TCA).[97] However, if one party breaches 'essential elements', there are no automatic consequences, but the other party may suspend or terminate the TCA in whole or in part after a thirty-day consultation period. This is quicker than termination under the general notice period of twelve months under Article 779 TCA, but the 'extraordinary' suspension or termination under Article 772 TCA is subject to the additional condition that the breach is 'serious and substantial'. Arguably, this means that the special suspension/termination rights under Article 772 TCA do not appear to go beyond the rights of the parties under general international law to suspend or terminate a treaty in case of 'material' breach.[98] As the general notice period to terminate the TCA is short anyway, the effect of an extraordinary suspension or termination for breach of 'essential elements' would largely lie in the swift and symbolic response. But in contrast to EU law, there is no mechanism to enforce these values while maintaining cooperation under the TCA. The effectiveness of an all-or-nothing solution lies in its threat and preventative disincentive to breach the essential elements of the TCA, not its activation.

Separately, Part 3, on law enforcement and judicial cooperation in respect of criminal matters, which are particularly sensitive areas for individual rights, can be terminated more quickly if the UK or a Member State denounces the ECHR or its Protocols 1, 6, or 13. Such termination is to coincide with the denunciation of the other party, but can be almost immediate (on the fifteenth day of giving notice

[95] TCA, arts 765–70.
[96] TCA, art 735(2) lit (h).
[97] TCA, arts 763(1), 764(1), and 765(1).
[98] cf Vienna Convention on the Law of Treaties 1969, art 60(1) and (3) and the equivalent provision in the Vienna Convention on the Law of Treaties between States and International Organizations or between International Organizations 1986 (not yet in force), art 60, which is considered to be customary international law.

to terminate Part 3); this is in contrast to the regular termination clause of Part 3, which requires nine months' notice.[99] In addition, Article 693 TCA allows for the suspension of Part 3 or its individual titles in case of 'serious and systemic deficiencies' in the protection of fundamental rights, the rule of law, and data protection, with three months' notice. These rights to terminate or suspend are important because of the human rights-sensitive nature of cooperation on law enforcement and criminal matters. But they are also important for the EU's relations with its Member States. If implementing the TCA (as EU law, cf Article 216(2) TFEU) could expose Member States to responsibility for breaches of the ECHR, it would affect their ability to fulfil their obligations under EU law to implement the international treaties concluded by the EU.[100]

Values also come into play indirectly through level playing field obligations of the TCA,[101] which contain provisions on labour and social,[102] as well as environmental and climate, standards.[103] The TCA also refers to instruments for trade and sustainable development (TSD).[104] While obligations regarding labour and social law and environmental and climate protection take the form of binding obligations not to regress on achieved standards, the obligations are not clearly defined. This is because the prohibition of regression is only violated if changes in the regulatory environment also affect trade or investment between the parties, with all the uncertainty around interpreting and evidencing this requirement.[105] In contrast, the TSD chapter has more precisely formulated obligations incorporating international standards. Article 399 TCA, for example, refers to multilateral labour standards of the International Labour Organization (ILO), such as freedom of association, prohibitions of forced labour and child labour, and the implementation of the European Social Charter.[106] Both the non-regression obligations and the TSD chapter are binding. While the ordinary dispute settlement procedure is excluded in these areas,[107] they can be subject to a special dispute settlement procedure before a panel of experts.[108] In contrast to the decisions of arbitral tribunals which are

[99] TCA, arts 692(1) and (2).

[100] See eg *Matthews v United Kingdom* (1999) 28 EHRR 361 (ECHR); *Bosphorus v Ireland* (2006) 42 EHRR 1 (ECHR).

[101] TCA, pt 2, title XI, heading 1 (Trade).

[102] TCA, arts 386ff; 387(2): 'A Party shall not weaken or reduce, in a manner affecting trade or investment between the Parties, its labour and social levels of protection below the levels in place at the end of the transition period, including by failing to effectively enforce its law and standards.'

[103] TCA, arts 390ff, 391(2).

[104] TCA, art 397ff.

[105] On the interpretation in the Dominican Republic–Central America United States Free Trade Agreement (CAFTA-DR), see *In the Matter of Guatemala: Issues Relating to the Obligations Under Article 16.2.1(a) of the CAFTA-DR* (Final Report of the Panel, 14 June 2017), para 167ff.

[106] TCA, arts 399(1), (2), and (5).

[107] TCA, arts 389(2), 396(2), and 407(2).

[108] TCA, arts 408 and 409. For an example of the possible impact of a TSD chapter, see the decision of the Panel of Experts established under the Korea FTA [2011] OJ L127/6: Panel of Experts proceeding constituted under Article 13.15 of the EU-Korea Free Trade Agreement: Report of the Panel of Experts, 20.1.2021, para 123ff. The EU–Korea FTA, art 13.4.3, corresponds to TCA, art 399.

considered to be binding, Article 409(9) TCA casts doubts on the binding nature of decisions of expert panels: '[f]or greater certainty the Parties share the understanding that if the Panel makes recommendations in its report, the respondent Party does not need to follow these recommendations in ensuring conformity with this Agreement.' However, this 'clarification' conflicts with the design of the expert panel procedure,[109] which suggests that panel decisions are binding. The procedure is intended to ensure compliance in all its facets. For the non-regression obligations (but not the TSD obligations),[110] this includes the right to take unilateral temporary remedies;[111] that is, to suspend obligations under the TCA in case of non-compliance with a panel ruling.[112] A violation of the non-regression obligations has a high substantive threshold but is linked to a comparatively stronger enforcement mechanism in the form of temporary remedies under Article 749 TCA (compensation, suspension).[113] In contrast, the TSD chapter has more stringent obligations, but a weaker enforcement mechanism, ending with the ruling of the panel of experts.

In sum, the TCA's focus on values contrasts strongly with the stance on values within the EU. In line with other EU FTAs, values have a much weaker, if not merely symbolic, weight in the TCA. In so far as values are enforceable, they are subject to a high political threshold of suspending or even terminating the TCA. This is likely to result in TCA values being compromised in order to maintain cooperation. Even the stronger, principled intra-EU enforcement of values does not seem free from compromise. A recent example is the need to maintain cooperation and EU unity in the response to the Russian aggression against Ukraine, while also enforcing the rule of law in its Member States. The 'milestones' agreed between the Commission and Poland in May 2022, which make the release of funds under the Recovery and Resilience Facility to Poland conditional on addressing aspects of its rule of law backsliding,[114] may be considered as such a compromise. They have been watered down to an extent that they would not lead to implementation of the rule of law as required by the CJEU and European Court of Human Rights, even if achieved.[115] The TCA's approach to values

[109] Likewise, Stefano Fella, *The UK–EU Trade and Cooperation Agreement: Governance and Dispute Settlement* (HC Library Briefing Paper 9139, 2021) 49ff.

[110] TCA, art 407(2) only refers to arts 408 and 409, but not to art 410.

[111] TCA, arts 410(2) and 749.

[112] TCA, arts 410(16) and (18). If the panel of experts rules that there has been a breach of obligations, the parties must agree on measures. If the parties cannot agree, they can again refer the matter to the panel of experts, which will then decide on the measures to be taken.

[113] See TCA, arts 410 and 749.

[114] European Commission, 'NextGenerationEU: European Commission endorses Poland's €35.4 billion recovery and resilience plan' (Press Release, Brussels, 1 June 2022) <https://ec.europa.eu/commission/presscorner/detail/en/IP_22_3375> (accessed 29 October 2023).

[115] See Roger Daniel Kelemen, 'Appeasement ad Infinitum' (2022) 29 Maastricht Journal of European and Comparative Law 177; Laurent Pech, 'Covering Up and Rewarding the Destruction of the Rule of Law One Milestone at a Time' (*Verfassungsblog*, 21 June 2022).

could make such compromise even more likely in the external relations of the EU.[116]

5. Conclusion

The paradigm shift from EU law to an FTA as a less intensive form of cooperation based on international law manifests itself in all areas of the TCA, including in its substantive rules and dispute settlement mechanisms. It is most prominently expressed in the status of the individual in relation to an international treaty. European Union law has given rights and status to individuals as actors and subjects under international law. In doing so, EU law is part of a wider trend, reflected as well in other areas of international law; for example, with regards to the ECHR and human rights law more broadly, or in international criminal law. The TCA goes against this trend.

Replacing EU law with a different type of international law in the EU–UK relationship is, therefore, more than just a paradigm shift from EU to international law. It is a distancing from, and attempt to reverse, that wider trend in international law, making individuals both subjects and actors, and not just objects (or beneficiaries) of international law. It reflects thus a return to the more traditional approach with regard to subjects of international law. This influences how the wider international legal environment may evolve.

Potential consequences for the wider international law environment also arise because of the reversal of two characteristics of EU law which affect the legitimacy of action on the international plane. Both accountability and democratic legitimation contribute to the legitimacy of international action. The TCA has disempowered individuals legally by not conferring rights under international law and, thus, access to international judicial enforcement, thereby deactivating previously existing accountability mechanisms. Moreover, there is generally no individual right in the domestic laws of the UK or EU that the UK (or EU) must enforce international law rules which create benefits for individuals at the international level. Whether one party holds the other party (the UK and EU and vice versa) to account (and exercises diplomatic protection) will be subject to a large degree of discretion as to whether and how to enforce international norms.[117] The TCA, therefore, has removed the legitimating effect that flows from accountability to individuals, at both the international and domestic levels, if compared with EU law.

[116] But see also the contrasting perspective of a 'bifurcation' between internal and external values policies of the EU: Andrew Williams, *EU Human Rights Policies: A Study in Irony* (Oxford University Press 2004).

[117] See eg *R (on the application of Abbasi) v Secretary of State for Foreign and Commonwealth Affairs and Secretary of State for the Home Department* [2002] EWCA Civ 1598. See also Dugard (n 66) paras 14ff.

The mediation of the individual by the state (and by extension, by the EU as a constitutional actor) also has consequences for the democratic legitimacy of the new relations as they evolve. One aim of Brexit was to increase democratic legitimacy by anchoring decisions more strongly at the national level. But this will not be an automatic consequence of the new relations under the TCA. It will depend on the national legal framework and its existing or new mechanisms for democratic accountability, eg through domestic parliaments. So far, British nationals' participation in the democratic legitimation of international decisions (through elections to the European Parliament) has been removed, but has not been compensated for by a comparable scrutiny of international treaties in the UK Parliament,[118] even though several parliamentary committees have inquired into the matter and called for more treaty scrutiny.[119] If one considers accountability (through individual rights at the international level) and democratic legitimation (through parliamentary scrutiny) as capable of complementing one another to some degree, this has so far not materialized. The loss of individual rights has, so far, not been compensated for by an increase in parliamentary scrutiny. At least for the time being, both accountability and democratic legitimation of international action have been diminished.

[118] Emily Jones and Anna Sands, 'Ripe for Reform: UK Scrutiny of International Trade Agreements' (2020) University of Oxford, Global Economic Governance Working Paper 144 <www.geg.ox.ac.uk/publication/ripe-reform-uk-scrutiny-international-trade-agreements> (accessed 29 October 2023).

[119] See eg House of Lords European Union Committee, *Treaty Scrutiny: Working Practices* (HL Paper 97, 2020) and *Scrutiny of International Agreements: Lessons Learned* (HL Paper 287, 2019); House of Lords Constitution Committee, *Parliamentary Scrutiny of Treaties* (HL Paper 345, 2019); House of Commons International Trade Committee, *UK Trade Policy Transparency and Scrutiny* (HC Paper 1043, 2018); and the ongoing inquiry of the House of Commons Parliamentary and Constitutional Affairs Committee on the scrutiny of international treaties and other international agreements in the twenty-first century.

17

The Single Market, the Rule of Law, and Access to EU Courts: Vigilance of Individuals before the EU Courts

Tamara Perišin and Nathan Cambien***

1. Introduction

Stephen Weatherill's academic writing and teaching have always placed internal market cases in their relevant social and historical context. He was well known at Oxford for quickly capturing the attention of his students with vivid examples. These ranged from a bottle of Cassis de Dijon labelled in German, which was evidence that the principle of mutual recognition established in a famous case has indeed enabled that French fruit liqueur to be sold in Germany,[1] to a football stadium sticker album, which set the scene for explaining the famous *Fratelli Costanzo* case on public procurement.[2] However, these legendary, colourful illustrations are just a small part of a broader approach to teaching, writing, and thinking about EU law in a way which takes account of the background, policy choices, and consequences of each case.

Stephen Weatherill's scholarship has sought to reveal legal norms in their full context so that his readers can grasp not only the importance of internal market rules and jurisprudence, but also their spillover effects on society and its values. His narrative demonstrates how free movement rules have profound effects on consumer protection, environmental standards, public health, personal names, morals, immigration, student standards, sports, fundamental rights, and possibly any other area of law and life. It also illustrates how intertwined the vigilance of

* All opinions expressed in this chapter are personal. I would like to thank Daniel Halberstam and Catherine Barnard for the invitation to present earlier versions of this contribution at the University of Michigan and University of Cambridge, respectively, as well as to the participants of those events for their questions and comments. Special thanks to Ilektra Antonaki, Alessandro Angelico, and Helena Kumpar Zidanič for their research assistance.

** All opinions expressed in this chapter are personal. I would like to thank the participants of the 19th Dubrovnik Jean Monnet Seminar on Advanced Issues of European Law for their questions and comments.

[1] Case 120/78 *Rewe-Zentrale AG v Bundesmonopolverwaltung fur Branntwein* ECLI:EU:C:1979:42 (*Cassis de Dijon*).

[2] Case 103/88 *Fratelli Costanzo SpA v Comune di Milano* ECLI:EU:C:1989:256.

Tamara Perišin and Nathan Cambien, *The Single Market, the Rule of Law, and Access to EU Courts: Vigilance of Individuals before the EU Courts* In: *The Internal Market Ideal*. Edited by: Jeremias Adams-Prassl, Sanja Bogojević, Ariel Ezrachi, and Dorota Leczykiewicz, Oxford University Press. © Tamara Perišin and Nathan Cambien 2024.
DOI: 10.1093/oso/9780192867063.003.0018

individuals is with the constitutionalization of the EU legal order and poses questions on how far constitutionalization should go.

In the same vein, this chapter seeks to put the narrative of the building of the single market in the broader framework of the rule of law and the role of individuals in guarding it. Section 2 deals with Court of Justice of the European Union (CJEU) cases dealing with the rule of law and highlights that such questions arise in different types of judicial proceedings including preliminary reference procedures, infringement actions against Member States, and direct actions against EU institutions or bodies, where each of these procedures can be initiated by more than one type of actor. While there is already abundant scholarship and even daily blogging covering some of the high-profile cases, the present chapter seeks to reveal a relatively less well-known part of the rule of law jurisprudence which arises from actions brought by individual applicants to the General Court. It explains the relevance of individual actions in ensuring effective judicial review of possible rule of law violations within one Member State, in a third country, or even at the level of the EU itself, and which—without the vigilance of individuals—might not be brought to the attention of EU Courts. This section suggests that the access of individuals to EU Courts might be particularly relevant in situations of a rule of law failure potentially affecting other courts.

Section 3 elaborates on how building a single market and ensuring the rule of law requires individual access to the EU Courts through direct actions. Indeed, while many academic contributions focus on the cases brought by individuals in the context of the preliminary ruling procedure, individuals can also play an important role by bringing direct actions before the EU Courts highlighting potential rule of law violations.[3] It is clear that the potential of such actions is highly dependent on individuals having access to the EU Courts, a possibility that centres on standing requirements and how they are interpreted. Against this background, this section examines some of the most recent cases on standing in fields related to the internal market, namely state aid law, public procurement, and the environment.

The chapter argues that the vigilance of individuals before EU Courts might now be as relevant for the rule of law as once the vigilance of individuals before national courts was for the building of the single market. In both cases, this vigilance points to possible violations of the most fundamental rules of the EU legal order which might otherwise pass under the radar. The novel contribution of this chapter lies in juxtaposing underexplored cases on the rule of law brought by individuals to EU Courts with the rules on the standing of individuals before EU Courts.

[3] This point is perfectly illustrated by Case T-791/19 *Sped-Pro S.A. v Commission* ECLI:EU:T:2022:67. In that case, the applicant brought an action for annulment against an EU Commission decision, arguing, inter alia, that it failed to respect the requirements relating to the rule of law.

2. The Rule of Law as the Backbone of the Internal Market and the EU

The rule of law is essential for the functioning of the EU legal order, and in particular for internal market law. It is well known that EU internal market law has developed through a series of cases that arose before national courts. On the one hand, some of these cases, such as *Van Gend en Loos*,[4] *Dassonville*,[5] *Bosman*,[6] and *Gebhard*,[7] became famous due to ground-breaking preliminary references to the European Court of Justice (ECJ) where the Court interpreted the relevant Treaty rules. On the other hand, there are also a large number of cases where national courts have directly applied EU rules without needing to refer a question to the ECJ. These latter cases might not have become well known at the EU level, but they have significantly contributed to the proper application of EU law. Therefore, while we cannot know the total number of cases in which national courts have applied internal market rules, it is certainly not an overstatement to say that the internal market could not function properly if there were no well-functioning courts charged with giving effect to EU rules. The rule of law is a prerequisite of the internal market.

Until several years ago, the rule of law in the EU was mostly mentioned in the context of EU enlargement as one of the Copenhagen criteria for accession. It was often the case that accession negotiations were most difficult in that field. While accession negotiations entail thirty-five negotiating chapters, the European Commission (Commission) has been known to insist most fiercely on the chapter covering the quality of the judiciary. Thus, for example, in the case of the last accession negotiations, namely those on the Croatian accession, the chapter on the judiciary was the last one closed, and much later than those related to the internal market.[8] One possible explanation for such an approach on the part of the Commission could be the following. On the one hand, for core EU policies such as free movement, it was not imperative to ensure the perfect application of EU law before accession, as any remaining problems could be 'fixed' later on. After accession, the Commission could have asked the Member State to improve its application of EU law, and possibly start infringement proceedings. Further, any individual could have invoked their free movement rights before a national court, asking it to set aside national rules that were in breach of EU law. On the other

[4] Case 26/62 *NV Algemene Transport v Netherlands Inland Revenue Administration* ECLI:EU:C:1963:1.

[5] Case 8/74 *Procureur du Roi v Dassonville* ECLI:EU:C:1974:82.

[6] Case C-415/93 *Union royale belge des sociétés de football association ASBL v Jean-Marc Bosman* ECLI:EU:C:1995:463.

[7] Case C-55/94 *Gebhard v Consiglio dell'Ordine degli Avvocati e Procuratori di Milano* ECLI:EU:C:1995:411.

[8] Ch 1, 'Free Movement of Goods', was closed on 19 April 2010, while ch 23, 'Judiciary and Fundamental Rights', was closed on 30 June 2011.

hand, it was common wisdom at the time that the Commission could not do much to affect the national judiciary after accession. Despite the fact that the rule of law was a fundamental value of the EU legal order, it was often thought that the EU had very limited powers in that field and in controlling national judicial systems of Member States, except in extreme situations such as those leading to proceedings under Article 7 of the Treaty on European Union (TEU). This no longer applies. This chapter will not examine the tools at the disposal of the EU's non-judicial institutions for overseeing and enforcing rule of law compliance in the Member States, such as Article 7 TEU, which makes it possible to suspend membership rights in the case of a serious and persistent breach, the Rule of Law Framework,[9] or budget conditionality.[10] Instead, the chapter focuses on judicial control over the rule of law.

The CJEU has special jurisdiction to review the procedural aspects of decisions of the Council or the European Council based on Article 7 TEU.[11] However, jurisprudence in the field of the rule of law is being developed through virtually all possible types of judicial procedures.

The door for judicial control over rule of law issues was opened in the landmark case *Associação Sindical*.[12] In 2016, Portugal's Supreme Administrative Court referred a question to the Court of Justice concerning a temporary reduction of judges' salaries introduced within the framework of the country's austerity measures seeking to cut public expenditure.[13] The national court inquired whether the lowering of judicial salaries which was 'imposed unilaterally and on an ongoing basis by other constitutional authorities and bodies' was contrary to the 'principle of judicial independence, enshrined in the second subparagraph of Article 19(1) TEU, in Article 47 of the [Charter] and in the case-law of the Court of Justice'.[14] While, at the time, it might not have been clear whether national rules on judicial salaries were within the scope of EU law, the Court took the opportunity to clarify that EU law was indeed applicable. It relied on Article 2 TEU listing the rule of law as a fundamental value of the EU legal order, in conjunction with Article 19 TEU on effective legal protection in the fields covered by EU law, as well as with Article 47 of the Charter guaranteeing the fundamental right to an effective remedy. It held that these provisions give the Court the jurisdiction to review the functioning of the judicial systems in the Member States, as such control was considered essential

[9] Communication from the Commission to the European Parliament and the Council: A New EU Framework to Strengthen the Rule of Law, COM (2014)0158 final.

[10] Regulation 2020/2092 of the European Parliament and of the Council of 16 December 2020 on a general regime of conditionality for the protection of the Union budget [2020] OJ L433I/1.

[11] Consolidated version of the Treaty on the Functioning of the European Union (TFEU) [2008] C115/47, art 269.

[12] Case C-64/16 *Associação Sindical dos Juízes Portugueses v Tribunal de Contas* [2018] ECLI:EU:C:2018:117.

[13] ibid para 2.

[14] ibid para 18.

for the proper functioning of judicial cooperation in the EU.[15] The Court emphasized that it would be contrary to EU law if courts were under any hierarchical constraints or subordinated to other bodies.[16] While the Court did not find that there was any violation, since reducing salaries was a general measure applying to a large proportion of the public sector as part of the austerity measures and was of temporary duration,[17] the case became a landmark one for rule of law adjudication.

Ever since, there has been a steady increase in the number of rule of law cases reaching the CJEU. The following sections present CJEU jurisprudence by systematizing it based on three different types of procedures through which they reached the Court. Each of the parts is further subdivided into two subparts depending on who initiated the type of procedure. The section thus covers, first, infringement procedures—initiated by the Commission or by a Member State (section 2.1); secondly, preliminary references—from the Member State concerned and from another Member State (section 2.2); and, thirdly, actions for annulment—brought by privileged or unprivileged applicants (section 2.3). An explanation will be provided on how this last type of procedure, namely those brought by unprivileged applicants, has a significant potential in drawing the attention of EU Courts to possible violations of the rule of law either at the national or at the EU level. Similarly, as in the development of the internal market, the vigilance of individuals complements the activities of EU institutions in safeguarding EU law.

2.1 Infringement Procedures Concerning the Rule of Law

Rule of law violations can be the object of infringement procedures initiated on the basis of Articles 258 and 259 TFEU. On the one hand, infringement procedures are one of the main tools that the Commission has at its disposal as the guardian of the Treaties when it considers that a Member State has failed to fulfil its Treaty obligations. Under Article 258 TFEU, if the violation of the obligations arising under EU law has not been remedied through an extra-judicial procedure, the Commission is authorized to bring a case against the Member State concerned before the Court of Justice. On the other hand, the right to seek the fulfilment of obligations under the Treaties was also given to Member States. Article 259 TFEU can be used by a Member State to start a procedure against another Member State if it alleges a violation of EU law. Each of these types of infringement procedure has also been used in the field of the rule of law.

As regards actions brought by the Commission, in recent years there have been a significant number of actions challenging the new Polish rules relating to

[15] ibid para 43.
[16] ibid para 44.
[17] ibid paras 46–51.

the functioning of national courts. For example, in Case C–619/18 *Commission v Poland*, the Commission successfully challenged Polish legislation lowering the retirement age of judges, including those of the Supreme Court, and giving the country's president the discretionary power to extend certain judges' period of service.[18] In Case C–791/19 *Commission v Poland*, the Commission successfully pleaded against several Polish rules relating to disciplinary proceedings against judges.[19] In a pending case, C–204/21, the Commission is challenging certain Polish rules concerning the functioning of ordinary courts, which has already led to two orders imposing interim measures.[20] These cases have been discussed in detail in numerous academic publications and will thus not be analysed here.[21]

In addition to these cases brought by the Commission, the rule of law is also beginning to be invoked in infringement proceedings initiated by an individual Member State against another. For example, Case C–457/18 *Slovenia v Croatia* concerned a border dispute between these two Member States.[22] Ever since the two countries became independent, they have disputed some parts of the joint border. Thus, prior to Croatia's EU accession, they committed to entrusting an arbitral tribunal with the resolution of the dispute. Later, when the arbitration process was compromised due to unpermitted collusion and instruction between the Slovenian arbiter and the Slovenian government, Croatia withdrew from the arbitration process. In contrast, Slovenia merely replaced its arbiter, so the arbitral tribunal continued its procedure and delivered a decision, the arbitral award. Croatia considered that it was not bound by this decision and that there was no obligation to implement it. In reaction, Slovenia initiated infringement action before the Court of Justice against Croatia, which, in the meantime, had acceded to the EU. Among other things, Slovenia argued that by not implementing the decision of an arbitral tribunal, Croatia had violated the rule of law.[23] This case shows that it is theoretically possible to interpret the rule of law very broadly. However, the Court of Justice found that it had no jurisdiction for deciding border disputes between two Member States or conflicts arising from an arbitration agreement, as these were regulated by international and not EU law.[24] In contrast, for disputes between Member States

[18] Case C–619/18 *Commission v Poland* ECLI:EU:C:2019:615.

[19] Case C–791/19 *Commission v Poland* ECLI:EU:C:2021:596.

[20] Case C–204/21 R *Commission v Poland* ECLI:EU:C:2021:593; Case C–204/21 R *Commission v Poland* ECLI:EU:C:2021:878.

[21] See eg Marco Antonio Simonelli, 'Thickening Up Judicial Independence: The ECJ Ruling in Commission v Poland (C-619/18)' (*European Law Blog*, 8 July 2019) <https://europeanlawblog.eu/2019/07/08/thickening-up-judicial-independence-the-ecj-ruling-in-commission-v-poland-c-619-18/>; Laurent Pech, 'Protecting Polish Judges from Political Control' (*Verfassungsblog*, 20 July 2021) <https://verfassungsblog.de/protecting-polish-judges-from-political-control/> accessed 19 October 2023; Renáta Uitz, 'The Price of Thrashing the Rule of Law: EC Requests CJEU to Impose Financial Sanctions on Poland' (*Bridgenetwork*, 10 September 2021) <https://bridgenetwork.eu/2021/09/10/cjeu-financial-sanctions-poland/> accessed 19 October 2023.

[22] Case C–457/18 *Slovenia v Croatia* ECLI:EU:C:2020:65.

[23] ibid para 1.

[24] ibid paras 103–08.

relating to EU law, the Court's jurisdiction would have been mandatory; had the dispute between Slovenia and Croatia concerned EU law, they would not even have been permitted to entrust settlement to an arbitral tribunal.[25] Thus, while one sees from this case that the concept of violation of EU standards of rule of law cannot be stretched so far as to cover disagreements on areas not covered by EU law, the case nevertheless remains relevant for this chapter in showing that Member States have the opportunity to challenge another Member State's rule of law violations related to EU law before the Court of Justice.

2.2 Preliminary References Concerning the Rule of Law

National courts have always played an important role in the development of EU law. Under Article 267 TFEU, any court or tribunal of a Member State may request the Court of Justice to give a ruling on the interpretation or validity of EU law, if that ruling is necessary for deciding a case pending before that national court. This system allows each national judge, regardless of the national hierarchy of courts, to directly communicate with the Court of Justice. This mechanism has been crucial in the development, interpretation, and application of EU law, and the same is true today in the rule of law domain.

First, a number of preliminary references have been initiated by national courts inquiring whether certain measures adopted by their own Member State were in accordance with EU law. Most prominently, several preliminary references came from Poland, and in several of these the Court found incompatibility with EU law. For example, in *AK*, the Court elaborated on which factors raised doubts as to the independence of the Disciplinary Chamber of the Polish Supreme Court entrusted with deciding cases concerning the retirement of Supreme Court judges.[26] In *AB*, the Court clarified which circumstances render problematic a new Polish rule preventing appeals on decisions on judicial appointments.[27] In *WB*, the Court stated that it was not compatible with EU law to permit a minister of justice to second judges to higher criminal courts where those secondments could be terminated by the minister at any time and without stating reasons, since such a system entailed the risk of political control.[28] Furthermore, examples exist of references from the other Member States inquiring about the compatibility of their national rules with EU law. For instance, in a case from Malta, a national court

[25] Case C–284/16 *Slowakische Republik (Slovak Republic) v Achmea BV* ECLI:EU:C:2018:158; Case C–459/03 *Commission v Ireland* ECLI:EU:C:2006:345 (*MOX Plant*).

[26] Case C–585/18 *AK (Independence of the Disciplinary Chamber of the Supreme Court)* ECLI:EU:C:2019:982.

[27] Case C–824/18 *AB v Krajowa Rada Sądownictwa (Nomination of Judges to the Supreme Court—Appeal)* ECLI:EU:C:2021:153.

[28] Joined Cases C–748/19–754/19 *Criminal Proceedings against WB* ECLI:EU:C:2021:931.

sought an interpretation under EU law regarding the prime minister's involvement in the appointment of judges, but the Court held that this was not contrary to EU law when the procedure also involved 'an independent body responsible for, inter alia, assessing candidates for judicial office and giving an opinion to that Prime Minister'.[29] In a case from Romania, a national court inquired about the compatibility with EU law of a rule preventing national courts from examining whether national legislation held constitutional by a national constitutional court was in accordance with EU law.[30]

Secondly, due to the fact that there is significant trans-European judicial cooperation and mutual interconnectedness between courts in different EU Member States, national courts started expressing concern about possible rule of law violations in other Member States. There were several such references in relation to the European Arrest Warrant (EAW).[31] While Member States have rules about the non-extradition of their own citizens, they can surrender their nationals to another Member State on the basis of an EAW, which is a legal mechanism made possible thanks to the mutual trust between the Member States and their respective judiciaries. However, when this trust eroded as a consequence of measures taken by the executive or legislative branch in some Member States which affected the functioning of courts in those states, national judges of other Member States started doubting whether they should indeed issue EAWs. In the *LM* case, the Irish court enquired whether it was obliged to surrender a defendant to Poland if it had doubts about the rule of law in that country.[32] The Court held that in cases where a national court called upon to execute an EAW 'has material … indicating that there is a real risk of breach of the fundamental right to a fair trial … on account of systemic or generalised deficiencies so far as concerns the independence of the issuing Member State's judiciary' there is no immediate obligation to execute an EAW.[33] Instead, that judicial

> authority must determine, specifically and precisely, whether, having regard to [the sought person's] personal situation, … the nature of the offence … and the factual context … , and in the light of the information provided by the issuing Member State … , there are substantial grounds for believing that that person will run such a risk if he is surrendered to that State.[34]

[29] Case C-896/19 *Repubblika v Il-Prim Ministru* ECLI:EU:C:2021:311, para 73.

[30] Joined Cases C-357/19, 379/19, 547/19, 811/19, and 840/19 *Euro Box Promotion* ECLI:EU:C:2021:1034. Other preliminary references from Romania were at issue in Joined Cases C-83/19, 127/19, 195/19, 291/19, 355/19, and 397/19 *Asociația 'Forumul Judecătorilor Din România'* ECLI:EU:C:2021:393.

[31] Council Framework Decision of 13 June 2002 on the European arrest warrant and the surrender procedures between Member States—Statements made by certain Member States on the adoption of the Framework Decision [2002] OJ L190/1.

[32] Case C-216/18 PPU *LM* ECLI:EU:C:2018:586.

[33] ibid para 79.

[34] ibid.

It thus follows from *LM*, as well as from *Openbaar Ministerie*, that a national court can refuse to issue an EAW under two cumulative conditions: first, if there is objective evidence of the risk of a breach of the right to a fair trial due to systemic or generalized deficiencies concerning the independence of the judiciary, and, secondly, if such deficiencies are liable to have an actual impact on the situation of the person concerned if she is surrendered to the judicial authorities.[35] The Court's case law is consistent in that there is no *carte blanche* for judicial authorities not to surrender a person sought by an EAW,[36] but exceptions exist in limited situations related to rule of law violations.

2.3 Actions for Annulment and the Rule of Law

Direct actions provided for by Article 263 TFEU give the CJEU jurisdiction to review the legality of legal acts adopted by EU institutions and bodies at the initiative of either privileged applicants, such as the EU institutions themselves or Member States, or on the basis of challenges brought by non-privileged applicants, namely natural or legal persons. In the field of the rule of law, both these groups have brought relevant cases, so this subsection will briefly examine both types. However, greater attention will be paid to the relatively unnoticed role that individuals can have in indicating to the CJEU possible rule of law violations.

As regards cases brought by privileged applicants, there have been several prominent decisions regarding the rule of law and, thus far, these have concerned challenges against EU acts in this area. For example, in Case C–650/18 *Hungary v Parliament*, Hungary brought an action for annulment based on Article 263 TFEU against the European Parliament's Resolution inviting the Council to determine whether there was a clear risk of breach by Hungary of EU values under Article 7(1) TEU. Hungary argued, inter alia, that there was not a sufficient majority for the adoption of the contested Resolution since abstentions were not considered in determining whether a two-thirds majority voted in favour. The Court disagreed with this argument and upheld the Resolution. In two other cases brought by privileged applicants, the so-called *Budget Conditionality* cases, Hungary and Poland challenged Regulation 2020/2092 introducing budget conditionality, ie making use of EU funds subject to compliance with rule of law principles.[37] The applicants argued that the Regulation lacked an appropriate legal basis and circumvented the procedure laid down in Article 7 TEU, and thus that the institutions exceeded their powers and violated the principle of legal certainty. The Court dismissed

[35] Joined Cases C–354/20 PPU and 412/20 PPU *Openbaar Ministerie* ECLI:EU:C:2020:1033.
[36] See also eg Case C–268/17 *AY* ECLI:EU:C:2018:602.
[37] Case C–156/21 *Hungary v Parliament and Council* ECLI:EU:C:2022:97; Case C–157/21 *Poland v Parliament and Council* ECLI:EU:C:2022:98.

the actions by finding that the Regulation's conditionality mechanism was within the power conferred by the Treaties on the European Union to establish 'financial rules' relating to the implementation of the Union budget.[38] Further, it held that the procedure based on Article 7 TEU and the one provided for by the Regulation pursued different aims and had distinct subject matter, since the Regulation served only the protection of the budget.[39]

In addition to direct actions brought by privileged applicants seeking annulment of acts of general application, rule of law issues are also increasingly arising in direct actions initiated by individuals challenging acts of individual application. In these cases, individuals often seek to draw the attention of the CJEU to rule of law violations which might otherwise escape judicial review at the EU level. In the first instance, the EU General Court, having jurisdiction for actions brought by natural and legal persons, is asked to conduct indirect control of rule of law compliance in three different types of situation—in a Member State, in a third country, or at the EU level.

The first subtype of this rule of law review in individual actions concerns alleged non-compliance with the rule of law by a Member State. For example, in *Trajektna luka Split*, the applicant brought an action against the Commission's decision rejecting his complaint that alleged certain breaches of competition law. In the case before the General Court, the applicant sought the annulment of the Commission's decision, arguing, inter alia, that 'the Commission ... erred in its finding that the national courts "appear[ed] to be well placed to handle the matters raised"'.[40] Further, the applicant claimed that:

> [A]s the Commission did not yet have any experience of the ability of the Croatian national courts to deal with such a case, the Republic of Croatia being a relatively new member of the European Union, [the Commission] ... was required to examine their ability in greater depth, since no national court had yet applied EU competition law.[41]

The General Court rejected these arguments by finding that Croatia had met the Copenhagen Criteria for EU membership which 'require the candidate State, inter alia, to have ... the ability to implement effectively the rules, standards and policies forming the EU legal framework'.[42] In the General Court's view, this meant that 'the ability of the Croatian courts to apply EU law cannot be called into question as a matter of principle'[43] and that 'the applicant has not produced

[38] Case C-156/21 *Hungary v Parliament and Council* ECLI:EU:C:2022:97,paras 133, 139, and 153.
[39] ibid paras 173 and 177–79.
[40] Case T-70/15 *Trajektna luka Split v Commission* ECLI:EU:T:2016:592, para 44.
[41] ibid para 52.
[42] ibid para 53.
[43] ibid para 54.

any specific evidence to demonstrate the inability of the Croatian courts to assess the situation at issue'.[44] This case is relevant because it shows that there is prima facie trust in the national courts of Member States. However, in situations where there is evidence that a court cannot be trusted, EU institutions would be obliged to react.

More recently, in *Homoki*, the applicant invoked a rule of law violation in Hungary. This access to documents case concerned a European Anti-Fraud Office (OLAF) investigation into possible corruption in the installing of public lights in Hungary. OLAF conducted an investigation, and the final report was distributed to the Member State concerned. Mrs Homoki, a representative of civil society, asked for access to this report, but OLAF rejected it based on several reasons, including protection of the investigation, commercial interests, and personal data. The applicant challenged this refusal before the General Court. She argued, inter alia, that the aims invoked by OLAF needed to be balanced with the superior public interest. In her view, access should have been granted because 'there [was] ... an overriding interest ... which justifie[d] ... disclosure of the document requested, given that the Hungarian national authorities did not carry out any substantive investigation into the public lighting projects, despite the fact that OLAF, in the course of its investigation, had revealed significant instances of maladministration'.[45] In the applicant's view, the overriding public interest in disclosure existed because 'it cannot be expected that the Hungarian authorities will conduct an examination on the substance as regards the serious abuses found by OLAF'.[46] Thus, in essence, the applicant was invoking the failure of the Hungarian authorities to comply with the rule of law.[47] This argument was amplified by the applicant's stance that it was particularly important to disclose the report to a non-governmental organization (NGO), bearing in mind the important role civil society has in guarding EU values, and this position was also bolstered with reasons connected to tackling corruption.[48] The General Court did not engage in a balancing exercise and in assessing superior public interest, but instead decided the case on the basis of another plea in law. It found that since all the procedures which followed the OLAF report were already closed, it was no longer possible for OLAF to rely on the general presumption that the objectives of the investigative activities could be undermined. It thus annulled the refusal decision on that basis. The case nonetheless remains interesting from a rule of law perspective because it shows how EU Courts can be asked to rule on the legality of an EU act on the basis of whether that act has taken account of rule of law compliance in a Member State. As a consequence, the vigilance

[44] ibid para 55.
[45] Case T-517/19 *Andrea Homoki v Commission* ECLI:EU:T:2021:529, para 35, translated into English by the authors.
[46] Action brought on 19 July 2019–*Homoki v Commission*, T-517/19, in relation to the 8th plea.
[47] Case T-517/19 *Andrea Homoki v Commission* (n 45), para 35.
[48] ibid para 38.

of individuals brings to the EU Courts cases which indirectly require assessment of the rule of law observance in the Member States.

The second subtype of rule of law review in actions brought by individuals concerns alleged non-compliance with the rule of law by a third country. In a number of cases on restrictive measures, the EU Courts have been asked to check whether the Council has considered various aspects connected to the rule of law, including the functioning of courts in a third country.

For example, the General Court was recently asked in *Ben Ali* to annul Council decisions imposing restrictive measures on the applicant.[49] Namely, in the aftermath of political events that unfolded in Tunisia in 2010 and 2011, the Council adopted Decision 2011/72/CFSP concerning restrictive measures directed against certain persons and entities.[50] This decision was intended to reaffirm 'full solidarity and support with Tunisia and its people in their efforts to establish a stable democracy, the rule of law, democratic pluralism and full respect for human rights and fundamental freedom'[51] and 'to adopt restrictive measures against persons responsible for misappropriation of Tunisian State funds and who are thus depriving the Tunisian people of the benefits of the sustainable development of their economy and society and undermining the development of democracy in the country'.[52] The Council was charged with establishing and amending the annex to the Decision listing persons whose assets were to be frozen, and it periodically renewed the Decision. In the case at issue, Ben Ali challenged the parts of the Council renewal Decisions 2018/141 and 2019/135 concerning his listing. He argued, inter alia, that the Tunisian authorities had not taken any procedural steps concerning him since 2011 and it was indeed confirmed before the General Court 'that none of the documents relating to the state of the proceedings in Tunisia which were communicated to the Council before it adopted [the contested] Decisions ... shows that there was any procedural activity relating specifically to the applicant'.[53] It was thus necessary for the Council to verify whether '[t]he absence of such activity over a period of seven or eight consecutive years' can 'be justified by particular circumstances specific to the case ... or ... specific to the applicant himself'.[54] However, the General Court found that the Council had failed to verify 'whether, as the applicant asserts, he has never been heard, or invited to a hearing, and has never been the subject of any investigative measures, and if that were the case, why he has not been the subject of such measures until now'.[55] The General Court confirmed that the 'Council cannot merely contend ... that it is required only to verify that there is an ongoing

[49] Case T-151/18 *Ben Ali v Council* ECLI:EU:T:2020:514.

[50] Council Decision 2011/72/CFSP of 31 January 2011 concerning restrictive measures directed against certain persons and entities in view of the situation in Tunisia [2011] OJ L28/62.

[51] ibid recital 1.

[52] ibid recital 2.

[53] Case T-151/18 *Ben Ali v Council* ECLI:EU:T:2020:514, paras 138 and 139.

[54] ibid para 139.

[55] ibid.

judicial investigation' so that the 'Council committed an error of assessment in considering that it was not required to carry out additional verifications' into the state and progress of the judicial proceedings which were ongoing for such a long time.[56] Thus, the case is relevant as it shows how individual actions can oblige EU Courts to examine whether an EU institution has sufficiently verified the proper application of the rule of law standards in a third country.

Finally, the third subtype of rule of law review in individual actions relates to alleged non-compliance with the rule of law at the EU level. Unlike in the previous two groups of cases, where the applicant argues that an EU institution breached EU law for not taking account of certain rule of law deficiencies in a Member State or in a third country, in these cases the issue is whether the EU itself has violated its own rule of law standards. A number of such cases concern judicial control over the rule of law standards in the appointment or termination of a mandate of the highest offices in the EU judicial structure. For example, a number of academics posed the question of whether the rule of law was endangered at the Union level when Advocate General Eleanor Sharpston's mandate ceased before the end of the six-year period to which she had been appointed as a consequence of acts adopted in relation to Brexit. However, the Court found that the acts in question were not acts of EU institutions, but rather were adopted by the representatives of the governments of the Member States exercising the powers of those states which were not subject to the review of the CJEU.[57]

Cases concerning the appointment of European prosecutors were also discussed in academic discourse and in the media as relevant for the EU's adherence to its own rule of law standards.[58] In *Mendes de Almeida*[59] and *Verelst*,[60] the applicants challenged the Council Implementing Decision on the appointment of European Prosecutors.[61] According to Council Regulation 2017/1939, European prosecutors are appointed by the Council following a reasoned opinion of a selection panel.[62] Both of the applicants in these cases had been shortlisted for the position of European prosecutor, and the selection panel had ranked each of them first among the three candidates from their respective Member State. While for most European prosecutors, the Council appoints the candidates with the highest

[56] ibid paras 156 and 158.

[57] Case C–684/20 P *Sharpston v Council and Representatives of the Governments of the Member States* ECLI:EU:C:2021:486, Order of 16 June 2021; Case C–685/20 P *Sharpston v Council and Representatives of the Governments of the Member States* ECLI:EU:C:2021:485, Order of 16 June 2021.

[58] See eg Miguel Poiares Maduro, 'Open Letter to the European Parliament: Call Out the EU Council on Its Rule of Law Hypocrisy' (*Euronews*, 4 October 2020) <www.euronews.com/my-europe/2020/10/03/open-letter-to-the-european-parliament-call-out-the-eu-council-on-its-rule-of-law-hypocris>.

[59] Case T–75/21 *Mendes de Almeida v Council* ECLI:EU:T:2021:424.

[60] Case T–647/20 *Jean-Michel Verelst v Council* ECLI:EU:T:2022:5.

[61] Council Implementing Decision (EU) 2020/1117 of 27 July 2020 appointing the European Prosecutors of the European Public Prosecutor's Office [2020] OJ L244/18.

[62] Council Regulation (EU) 2017/1939 of 12 October 2017 implementing enhanced cooperation on the establishment of the European Public Prosecutor's Office ('the EPPO') [2017] OJ L283/1, art 16.

ranking, in relation to three Member States, including those of the applicants, it departed from the ranking by selecting other persons from the shortlist. The applicants asked for a judicial review of the Council Decision, and in particular for a review of the statement of reasons. While the General Court found that the action in *Mendes de Almeida* was inadmissible as being time barred, and that the one in *Verelst* was unfounded, the cases remain relevant as they show that EU Courts have the task of checking that the EU itself adheres to its rule of law standards.

To conclude, this section has shown that rule of law issues can arise in three different types of proceedings, where each can be initiated by two types of applicants. While there is already abundant academic literature on most of these sorts of disputes, there has not been any writing on the potential of direct actions for bringing to the EU Courts possible rule of law violations, not just at the EU level, but also in Member States and third countries. The task of this section was to show that such actions are increasingly gaining importance for verifying rule of law standards in the Member States, in third countries, and at the EU level. Thus, ensuring that the vigilance of individuals is accompanied by the proper application of the standing criteria is relevant for the rule of law. The following section will examine the most recent EU Court cases with relevance to standing.

3. Standing of Individual Applicants before the EU Courts

Individuals can bring direct actions before the EU Courts provided that certain 'standing' requirements are satisfied. In this section, we analyse how the EU Courts have interpreted these standing requirements in recent case law in a number of important fields related to the internal market: state aid, public procurement,[63] and the environment. We also analyse the situation of a particular type of private applicant which has played an important role in bringing claims before the EU Courts in recent times: subnational entities. It will become clear that, while the EU Courts have shown signs of willingness to interpret standing requirements more flexibly in some fields, this has not happened in others.

3.1 State Aid

In the field of state aid, it is clear that EU Commission decisions declaring an aid measure incompatible with the internal market can be challenged, particularly by the aid beneficiary and by the Member State concerned.[64] However,

[63] On public procurement law as a subdiscipline of EU internal market law, see Stephen Weatherill, 'EU Law on Public Procurement: Internal Market Law Made Better' in Sanja Bogojević, Xavier Groussot, and Jörgen Hettne (eds), *Discretion in EU Public Procurement Law* (Hart Publishing 2018).

[64] See eg Joined Cases T–778/16 and 892/16 *Ireland v Commission* ECLI:EU:T:2020:338.

what happens if the Commission decides not to open a formal investigation procedure after an aid measure has been notified to it, meaning that the state aid measure is approved? According to settled case law, such decisions can be challenged by any 'interested party' within the meaning of Article 1(h) of Regulation 2015/1589,[65] ie any Member State and any person, undertaking, or association of undertakings whose interests might be affected by the granting of aid, in particular the beneficiary of the aid, competing undertakings, and trade associations.

This open-ended definition has been given broad interpretation by the EU Courts. The case law has recognized that not only direct but also indirect competitors of the state aid beneficiary can challenge the Commission's decision not to open a formal procedure. To that purpose, the indirect competitor must demonstrate that its interests could be adversely affected by the grant of the aid.[66] For instance, in *Deutsche Lufthansa*,[67] the Commission had approved, without opening a formal investigation procedure, the operating aid granted by the German authorities to Frankfurt-Hahn Airport. Lufthansa challenged this aid because it made it possible for Frankfurt-Hahn Airport to remain operational, and, consequently, for Ryanair, the main airline operating from that airport, to compete with Lufthansa in the Frankfurt region. The General Court ruled that even though Lufthansa was not a direct competitor to the state aid beneficiary, its competitive position was affected by the aid which would indirectly assist one of its main competitors in the region.[68] The General Court concluded, therefore, that Lufthansa had standing to challenge the aid measure.[69]

The EU Courts have even recognized the status of interested parties where the applicant was not an indirect competitor of the aid beneficiary, but where its interests were affected in another way. For instance, the Court has recognized that trade unions could be interested parties where their interests or those of their members might be affected by the granting of aid,[70] and the same was true for holders of subordinated debt in a bank that received state aid from the Italian government.[71] Similarly, the Court ruled that an association defending the interests of German motor sport was an interested party in relation to the sale of the Nürburg ring complex—which includes a world-famous race track—a transaction alleged to involve state aid.[72]

[65] Council Regulation (EU) 2015/1589 of 13 July 2015 laying down detailed rules for the application of Article 108 TFEU [2015] OJ L248/9.

[66] See, to that effect, Case C-83/09 P *Commission v Kronoply and Kronotex* ECLI:EU:C:2011:341, paras 63–65.

[67] Case T-218/18 *Deutsche Lufthansa v Commission* ECLI:EU:T:2021:282, unpublished.

[68] ibid paras 39–55.

[69] ibid para 56.

[70] See, to that effect, Case C-319/07 P *3F v Commission* ECLI:EU:C:2009:435, para 33.

[71] Case T-161/18 *Braesch v Commission* ECLI:EU:T:2021:102.

[72] Case C-647/19 P *Ja zum Nürburgring v Commission* ECLI:EU:C:2021:666, para 66.

In contrast to these cases where the EU Courts accepted the applicant's arguments that it constituted an 'interested party', there is also case law showing that this concept has its limitations. The recent *CAPA* judgment may serve to illustrate the point.[73] The case concerns a challenge brought by a French association of fishermen against a Commission decision not to raise objections against a French measure subsidizing wind farms. The fishermen had argued that the aid measure had a negative impact on their activities since they could no longer fish in the areas where the farms were constructed. The General Court ruled that the fishermen and the operators of the wind farms were not indirect competitors since they did not use the same resources. The mere fact that these activities took place in the same geographic zones was not sufficient to make the fishermen's association an interested party.

3.2 Public Procurement

An evolution in the interpretation of the standing criteria is also apparent in the field of public procurement, as illustrated by the *Leonardo/Frontex*[74] judgment. Frontex, the European Border and Coast Guard Agency, had issued a tender for surveillance services by drones. The tender documents stipulated that the drones were to satisfy a number of criteria, in terms of, inter alia, payload. According to the applicant in the case (a manufacturer of drones), these criteria were discriminatory because they excluded smaller drones, such as the one manufactured by the applicant, which allegedly would be able to carry out the surveillance services requested without satisfying all the mandatory requirements. Since it was clear that the applicant did not have any chance of winning the tender, it decided not to participate.

The interesting question was whether the applicant had standing to challenge the tender criteria before the General Court. Typically, such actions are brought by a company that participated in the tender against the decision rejecting its tender and awarding the contract to a competitor. In such circumstances, the applicant has a legal interest in bringing the annulment action, because the annulment would give rise to a new tender procedure—in which it could potentially win the tender—or, alternatively, to pecuniary damages.[75]

In *Leonardo/Frontex*, by contrast, the applicant did not participate, so it was not immediately apparent whether it had a legal interest in challenging the allegedly discriminatory criteria contained in the tender documents. The ECJ had already decided, in *Amt Azienda*, that, in the context of national public procurement procedures, it would be too much to require an undertaking allegedly harmed by

[73] Case T-777/19 *CAPA v Commission* ECLI:EU:T:2021:588.
[74] Case T-849/19 *Leonardo v Frontex* ECLI:EU:T:2022:28.
[75] See Case T-126/13 *Direct Way and DW Worldwide v Parliament* ECLI:EU:T:2015:819, para 44.

discriminatory tender specifications to submit a tender before being able to challenge such specifications.[76] The General Court ruled that this case law could also be applied, *mutatis mutandis*, in the context of European public procurement proceedings. However, its conditions were not satisfied *in casu* because the applicant had not proven that the tender conditions were discriminatory and had made it impossible for it to submit a tender.

The General Court's ruling that the reasoning used in the *Amt Azienda* case judgment is also applicable in the context of European public procurement procedures is an important step forward in terms of judicial protection. Indeed, where an undertaking has no chance of being awarded the contract precisely because of the presence of allegedly discriminatory specifications, it would be unreasonable to require it to participate in the tender—investing considerable time and resources—before it could challenge these specifications. Such a requirement would be tantamount to denying the right to effective judicial protection. Moreover, in order to obtain a speedy and effective judicial remedy, it is of the utmost importance that the undertaking be allowed to bring the action as soon as possible and already before the contract is awarded.

3.3 Subnational Entities

An evolution in the interpretation of the standing requirements is also clear when it comes to actions brought by subnational entities, such as regions or cities. In recent cases, such entities have played a leading role in challenging EU rules in, for instance, the field of environmental norms.[77] However, unlike Member States, subnational entities are not considered to be 'privileged applicants', which means that actions brought by them must satisfy the same criteria as those brought by private applicants, in particular those relating to direct and individual concern. The interesting question here is to what extent subnational entities can challenge EU measures that have an impact on the exercise of their competences.

In order to determine whether that is the case, the EU Courts have laid down a specific test. Indeed, according to settled case law, subnational entities are concerned by an EU act when they are entrusted with autonomous powers and the EU act prevents those entities from exercising those powers as they see fit.[78] While

[76] Case C-328/17 *Amt Azienda Trasporti e Mobilità* ECLI:EU:C:2018:958, para 47 and the case law cited.

[77] See eg the action for annulment brought by the Brussels Capital region against the Commission's renewal of the approval of 'glyphosate'. Case T-178/18 *Région de Bruxelles-Capitale v Commission* ECLI:EU:T:2019:130, unpublished; Case C-352/19 P *Région de Bruxelles-Capitale v Commission* ECLI:EU:C:2020:978.

[78] While this test was mostly developed by the General Court, it has recently also been accepted by the ECJ. A similar test has been applied in other situations (see eg Case C-872/19 P *Venezuela v Council (Whether a third state is affected)* ECLI:EU:C:2021:507, para 69).

in some judgments this test is used to establish individual concern, in others it is used for the purposes of establishing direct concern or even direct and individual concern.[79] Arguably, the test is relevant for determining both direct and indirect concern.[80]

Applying the test is straightforward where the EU measure is an individual decision notified to the subnational entity concerned, such as (in particular) a negative Commission decision following the notification of a local or regional aid measure.[81] In such circumstances, the Commission decision has the consequence that the region concerned cannot grant the aid it had envisaged and, therefore, cannot exercise its competences as it sees fit. The same is true where the Commission refuses a regional deviation from common EU rules under the procedure set out in Article 114(6) TFEU.[82]

By contrast, it is much less clear how to apply the test in the case of EU measures of general scope. Importantly, recent case law does not exclude the possibility of subnational entities challenging such acts.[83] That being said, the fact remains that, so far, all such actions have failed to pass the admissibility threshold. A case in point is the well-known *Ville de Paris* case, which concerns an action brought by the cities of Paris, Brussels, and Madrid against the new emissions standards introduced by Regulation 2016/646.[84] While the General Court found the action to be admissible, the ECJ disagreed, judging that the applicants did not satisfy the direct concern criterion.[85] More particularly, the ECJ found that the contested provision in the Regulation did not limit the exercise of the powers of the applicant cities in relation to the protection of air quality.

The relevance of this case stems from the fact that it recognizes the right of subnational entities to challenge EU measures of general scope.[86] Recognizing that subnational entities can be directly and individually concerned by general EU measures in fields in which they have autonomous competences is, arguably, in line with Article 4(2) TEU, which states: 'The Union shall respect the equality

[79] See eg for direct concern: Joined Cases C–177/19 P–179/19 P *Germany and Hungary v Commission and Commission v Ville de Paris* ECLI:EU:C:2022:10, para 72; for individual concern: Case T–167/13 *Comune di Milano v Commission* ECLI:EU:T:2018:940, para 34; for direct and individual concern: Case T–214/95 *Vlaams Gewest v Commission* ECLI:EU:T:1998:77, para 29.

[80] See in this sense Case C–352/19 P *Région de Bruxelles-Capitale v Commission* ECLI:EU:C:2020:588, Opinion of AG Bobek, para 61.

[81] See eg Case T–167/13 *Comune di Milano v Commission* ECLI:EU:T:2018:940.

[82] Joined Cases T–366/03 and 235/04 *Land Oberösterreich v Commission* ECLI:EU:T:2005:347.

[83] In contrast to earlier case law. See eg Case T–66/19 *Vlaamse Gemeenschap and Vlaams Gewest v Parliament and Council* ECLI:EU:T:2019:848, para 40.

[84] Commission Regulation (EU) 2016/646 of 20 April 2016 amending Regulation (EC) No 692/2008 as regards emissions from light passenger and commercial vehicles (Euro 6) [2016] OJ L109/1.

[85] See, respectively, Joined Cases T–339/16, 352/16, and 391/16 *Ville de Paris, Ville de Bruxelles and Ayuntamiento de Madrid v Commission* ECLI:EU:T:2018:927 and Joined Cases C–177/19 P–179/19 P *Germany and Hungary v Commission and Commission v Ville de Paris* ECLI:EU:C:2022:10.

[86] See Koen Lenaerts and Nathan Cambien, '*Regions* and the European Courts: Giving Shape to the *Regional* Dimension of Member States' (2010) 35 European Law Review 609.

of Member States before the Treaties as well as their national identities, inherent in their fundamental structures, political and constitutional, inclusive of regional and local self-government.' Indeed, in a number of Member States, competences in certain important fields of shared EU competences now pertain to subnational entities such as regions and communities in Belgium.

Crucially, in order to have standing, a subnational entity must demonstrate that the EU measure prevents it from exercising its autonomous powers as it sees fit. The extent to which this will allow such entities to challenge general EU measures will hinge on the precise interpretation of the expression 'as they see fit', which will need to be clarified in future case law. Obviously, not just any impact on the region's field of competences will be sufficient to demonstrate individual concern. Accordingly, the EU Courts have rightly held in a number of cases that the condition of individual concern was not satisfied because the region in question was merely relying on the general interest it may have in obtaining a result that is favourable to the economic prosperity of the region.[87] If, however, it is required that the EU measure make it *impossible* for entities to exercise their powers—as the *Ville de Paris* judgment suggests—they could challenge only those EU measures that either require them to entirely abstain from using their powers, or oblige them to use those powers in a very specific manner. A less strict interpretation has been put forward by Advocate General Michal Bobek, who has argued that it may be sufficient that the EU measure significantly alters the manner in which the subnational entity can lawfully make use of those powers.[88]

3.4 Environmental Cases

Environmental issues are one of the most pressing issues of our time. At the EU level, their importance is illustrated by the adoption of the ambitious Green Deal, which gives the impetus for EU action in different fields with a view to making the EU's economy climate-neutral by 2050.[89] It is clear from precedents in a number of Member States that national courts have an important role to play in environmental matters. A well-known example is the judgment of the Dutch Supreme Court in which it confirmed the order issued by a lower court according to which the Dutch state was obliged to reduce greenhouse gas emissions by 25 per cent by

[87] See, eg, order of 16 June 1998, Case T-238/97 *Comunidad Autónoma de Cantabria v Council* ECLI:EU:T:1998:126, para 49; Case C–142/00 P *Commission v Nederlandse Antillen* ECLI:EU:C:2003:217, para 69.

[88] Joined Cases C–177/19 P–179/19 P *Germany and Hungary v Commission* and *Commission v Ville de Paris* ECLI:EU:C:2021:476, Opinion of AG Bobek, para 86.

[89] See 'Communication from the Commission to the European Parliament, the European Council, the Council, the European Economic and Social Committee and the Committee of the Regions—The European Green Deal' COM (2019) 640 final.

the end of 2020.[90] Similar judgments ordering national governments to take more ambitious measures were rendered by courts in other Member States, including in France, Belgium, and Germany.[91]

The question arises whether individual applicants can also enforce environmental rights before courts at the EU level. A number of recent actions shed light on this question.[92] A noted example is the so-called *People's Climate Case*, brought by a number of families from various Member States and third countries active in the agricultural or tourism sectors, as well as a Swedish association representing young indigenous Samis.[93] The applicants argued that the EU's legislative package regarding greenhouse gas emissions was not sufficiently ambitious and, therefore, infringed their fundamental rights. The General Court ruled that the applicants did not have standing, since they were not individually concerned by the contested provisions. It held that, while it is true that the effects of climate change may be different for one person than for another, this was not sufficient to distinguish the applicants from other individuals who are affected by climate change.[94] The ECJ confirmed the judgment of the General Court, thereby rejecting the applicants' request to give a more lenient interpretation of the individual concern requirement.[95] The ECJ had adopted a similarly strict interpretation of the individual concern condition in another environmental case decided a few months earlier.[96]

One may question whether the current case law in the field of environmental matters succeeds in guaranteeing the right to effective judicial protection in a field of such capital importance. Under the current interpretation, it is difficult to see how an individual applicant could successfully bring an admissible action before the General Court against EU legislative measures concerning environmental matters.

While it is true that the conditions for admissibility of annulment actions are laid down in the Treaties, and that the EU Courts do not have jurisdiction to alter

[90] For an English summary of the judgment, see 'Dutch State to reduce greenhouse gas emissions by 25% by the end of 2020' (20 December 2019) <www.hogeraad.nl/actueel/nieuwsoverzicht/2019/december/dutch-state-case-reduce-greenhouse-gas-emissions/>.

[91] For an overview, see 'Climate Claims against Governments in Europe' (16 July 2021) <www.clearygottlieb.com/-/media/files/alert-memos-2021/climate-change-litigation-in-europe-increasing-judicial-scrutiny-over-state-climate-policies.pdf>.

[92] See also the discussion in Marc Willers, 'Climate Change Litigation in European Regional Courts: Jumping Procedural Hurdles to Hold States to Account?' in Ivano Alogna, Christine Bakker, and Jean-Pierre Gauci (eds), *Climate Change Litigation: Global Perspectives* (Brill 2021).

[93] Case T–330/18 *Carvalho v Parliament and Council* ECLI:EU:T:2019:324, unpublished.

[94] ibid; see also Case C–565/19 P *Carvalho v Parliament and Council* ECLI:EU:C:2021:252, unpublished.

[95] ibid. For a discussion, see Lena Hornkohl, 'The CJEU Dismissed the People's Climate Case As Inadmissible: The Limit of Plaumann is Plaumann' (*European Law Blog*, 6 April 2021) <https://europeanlawblog.eu/2021/04/06/the-cjeu-dismissed-the-peoples-climate-case-as-inadmissible-the-limit-of-plaumann-is-plaumann/>.

[96] Case C–297/20 P *Sabo v Parliament and Council* ECLI:EU:C:2021:24, unpublished.

them, their interpretation can evolve. Consequently, it might be possible for the EU Courts to modify their interpretation of these conditions, particularly by departing from the strict *Plaumann* case law,[97] without necessarily rendering these conditions meaningless. Would it not make sense to recognize that, while climate change will affect all of us, some individuals are more severely affected by reason of their particular circumstances? Should it not be possible for private applicants to bring actions against the EU if the latter were to fail to adopt the necessary measures to achieve its ambitious climate goals? A less restrictive interpretation of the standing requirements might allow the EU Courts to play a more important role in direct actions challenging measures involving the environment and climate change, similar to the roles played by courts in the Member States.[98] That said, one must not overlook the fact that the ECJ has issued important judgments on environmental standards in the context of the preliminary ruling procedure[99] or in infringement actions brought by the EU Commission.[100]

4. Conclusion

Individual applicants have always had a pivotal role in building and safeguarding the EU legal order. This has been true both for individuals pleading before national courts, and also for those seeking access to EU Courts. Stephen Weatherill's academic work in the field of the EU internal market has been essential for developing and understanding the narrative about the vigilance of individuals and the EU legal order.

This chapter has sought to stress that, similarly to other fields of EU law which have previously been developed through case law, individual applicants have a crucial role in safeguarding the rule of law in the European Union. Indeed, individual applicants have different procedures at their disposal to bring before the EU Courts

[97] Case 25/62 *Plaumann v Commission* ECLI:EU:C:1963:17; according to the classic interpretation of the individual concern condition first given in this judgment, persons other than those to whom a decision is addressed are individually concerned if that decision affects them by reason of certain attributes which are peculiar to them or by reason of circumstances in which they are differentiated from all other persons and by virtue of these factors distinguishing them individually just as in the case of the person addressed.

[98] It is worth noting in this context that the recent revision of the Aarhus Regulation (Regulation (EC) 1367/2006 of the European Parliament and of the Council of 6 September 2006 on the application of the provisions of the Aarhus Convention on Access to Information, Public Participation in Decision-making and Access to Justice in Environmental Matters to Community institutions and bodies (OJ L264/13)) failed to address the issue of standing before the EU Courts. For a discussion, see Ioanna Hadjiyianni, 'Access to Justice in Environmental Matters in the EU Legal Order—Too Little Too Late?' (*European Law Blog*, 4 November 2020) <https://europeanlawblog.eu/2020/11/04/access-to-justice-in-environmental-matters-in-the-eu-legal-order-too-little-too-late/>.

[99] See eg Case C-900/19 *One Voice and Ligue pour la protection des oiseaux* ECLI:EU:C:2021:211.

[100] See eg Case C-559/19 *Commission v Spain (Deterioration of the Doñana natural area)* ECLI:EU:C:2021:512.

possible rule of law violations in the Member States, in third countries, or at the EU level itself—violations which would otherwise escape judicial review.

The possibilities for individual applicants to bring direct actions before the EU Courts—possibilities which we believe are sometimes overlooked in academic literature on the rule of law—are heavily dependent on the standing criteria and the way these are interpreted. Traditionally, these criteria have been interpreted rather restrictively, but an evolution can be discerned in recent case law towards wider interpretation.[101] One factor contributing to this change may be the recent enlargement of the EU General Court—almost doubling its number of judges—which should provide it with an increased capacity to scrutinize a wider range of EU measures in different fields.[102]

While it is true that the same tendency is not apparent to the same extent in all fields discussed, this should not necessarily be viewed as problematic. Perhaps a 'functional' interpretation of the standing criteria is required, depending on the area of law concerned. In some fields, the General Court is better placed to develop the law which would justify a broader interpretation of the standing criteria. By contrast, in other fields, the ECJ may be better placed, meaning that a more restrictive interpretation of the standing criteria may be justified, given the ECJ's jurisdiction to issue judgments in the context of the preliminary ruling procedure or in infringement actions.

[101] It must be emphasized that a number of the General Court judgments discussed in this chapter are appealed before the ECJ, so it remains to be seen whether the ECJ will follow the reasoning of the General Court.

[102] While the General Court historically had one judge per Member State, the Statute of the Court of Justice of the European Union—since its amendment by Regulation (EU, Euratom) 2015/2422 of the European Parliament and of the Council of 16 December 2015 amending Protocol No 3 on the Statute of the Court of Justice of the European Union (OJ L341/14)—provides in its art 48 for a gradual increase in the number of judges: art 48(c) states that '[t]he General Court shall consist of two Judges per Member State as from 1 September 2019'. As a consequence of Brexit, the current total number of General Court judges is slightly lower than twice the number of judges before its enlargement.

PART V
TEACHING EU INTERNAL MARKET LAW

18

(Teaching) The Integrity of the EU's Internal Market

Niamh Nic Shuibhne, Dayana Baleva, Jovan Dimitrijewitsch, Rhian Jukes, Antonín Kotrba, and Lukas Schaupp

1. Introduction

Stephen Weatherill does not know this—but for the second semester of the 2019–20 and 2020–21 academic years, he was present every week in an Edinburgh classroom.

As first author for this chapter, I have taught courses on EU free movement, citizenship, and internal market law at Edinburgh Law School in some form or other for over two decades. On returning from research leave in 2019, I redesigned the LLM course in this field, partly because of the natural process of reflecting on the curriculum that a period of not teaching induces, but also because of what happened during that particular period of research leave: Brexit. In that context, questions about the extent to which the EU's internal market was 'divisible' (or not) provoked the lemonade out of lemons idea of using the concept of integrity to explore the internal market's nature, coherence, and future.

The first iteration of 'The Integrity of the EU's Internal Market' ran from January to March 2020, with a wonderful group of students who, individually and collectively, faced the starkest of challenges in completing their studies as a global pandemic intensified around them. In the final weeks of the course, Steve was one of a number of academic friends who sent us some thoughts on internal market integrity by email. These contributions enriched the students' overall understanding and appraisal of the defining course theme and are returned to in later sections of this chapter. Even more importantly, the willingness of Steve and other colleagues to engage with our mission at such a difficult time illustrated for the students the extraordinary generosity of the EU law academic community.

However, Steve's research provided the starting point for the course more fundamentally through his *tour de force* 2017 *Yearbook of European Law* essay on 'The Several Internal Markets'.[1] Paying tribute to that work was therefore an obvious

[1] Stephen Weatherill, 'The Several Internal Markets' (2017) 36 Yearbook of European Law 125.

Niamh Nic Shuibhne, Dayana Baleva, Jovan Dimitrijewitsch, Rhian Jukes, Antonín Kotrba, and Lukas Schaupp, *(Teaching) The Integrity of the EU's Internal Market* In: *The Internal Market Ideal.* Edited by: Jeremias Adams-Prassl, Sanja Bogojević, Ariel Ezrachi, and Dorota Leczykiewicz, Oxford University Press.

DOI: 10.1093/oso/9780192867063.003.0019

way to contribute to this volume (all the more so, given that—as Jo Shaw also writes about—Steve is himself an Edinburgh MSc alumnus). The chapter thus offers a research-led teaching assessment of the EU internal market's claims to integrity. It also provided an opportunity to involve Anthony, Dayana, Jovan, Lukas, and Rhian as co-authors; they were co-creators of the concept of integrity that emerged over the Integrity course's second iteration in 2020–21. Still in an intense phase of the pandemic, teaching was delivered entirely online, and we all know the disadvantages of trying to build a sense of community in those circumstances. For this group, though, somehow our intensive online discussions catalysed something special—not only evolving the concept of integrity in the context of the internal market through each individual part of the course, but producing, by the end of it, something genuinely more than the sum of those parts. As a result, what we constructed—and thus also this chapter—reflects the contributions and reflections of all six of us.

The structure of the chapter maps how the course was delivered. First, we outline in Section 2 how we developed a starting idea of the integrity of the EU's internal market (Weeks 1 and 2), showing how we drew heavily on Steve's *Yearbook* paper to establish foundations against which we evaluated internal market law's twists and turns in subsequent weeks. In Section 3, we demonstrate the fragility of the market's integrity by exploring different dimensions of free movement law, first addressing questions 'within' (Week 3) and 'across' (Week 4) the Treaty freedoms, and then examining free movement issues beyond the internal market (ostensibly at least) through developments in EU citizenship law (Weeks 5 and 6). We turn to the intersection of internal market law and non-market objectives in Section 4 (Week 7). In Section 5, we ask how the EU's internal market relates to markets outside the Union (Weeks 8 and 9), which by then included the post-membership relationship between the EU and the UK (Week 10). Across all sections of the chapter, we provide an account of how we taught and learned, unspooling in parallel our understanding of the internal market's integrity and the questions that trying to understand it provoked. Section 6 then presents post-course reflections from Anthony, Dayana, Jovan, Lukas, and Rhian, responding to the question: what was it like to learn about EU internal market law through this thematic approach? Finally, I conclude with a note on (the future of) teaching the internal market.

2. Constructing the Framework of Integrity

The internal market is a central policy goal of the EU and there is, at one level, remarkable continuity from the foundational legal framework developed principally through case law in the 1970s to the legal framework within which the internal market functions today. In Week 1 of the course, we examined key primary sources to introduce the foundations of internal market law (Section 2.1). In Week 2, we focused more specifically on agreeing a working understanding of the 'integrity' of the internal market (Section 2.2).

2.1 The Legal Foundations of the EU's Internal Market

Students will hopefully remember two key messages from this and other courses on which the first author has taught them: 'always start with the Treaties'; and 'it's not you, it's the case law'. We therefore first read Article 3 of the Treaty on European Union (TEU) and Articles 26, 28–36, 45–66, and 114–15 of the Treaty on the Functioning of the European Union (TFEU), alongside a powerful internal market case law quartet: *Dassonville*, *van Binsbergen*, *Cassis de Dijon*, and *Bosman*.[2]

We first compared how Article 2 of the European Economic Community Treaty (EEC) prescribed that:

> It shall be *the aim* of the Community, by establishing a Common Market and progressively approximating the economic policies of Member States, to promote throughout the Community a harmonious development of economic activities, a continuous and balanced expansion, an increased stability, an accelerated raising of the standard of living and closer relations between its Member States. (emphasis added)

with the more extensive list of Union goals now included in Article 3(3) TEU.[3] This comparison raised our first integrity problem: how can all the objectives that Article 3(3) stipulates be achieved in some kind of balance or harmony? This question is addressed in Section 4 below.

From the foundational case law, we extracted the restriction, derogation/justification, and proportionality method applied in free movement law; and the forms of discrimination (direct and indirect) that constitute free movement restrictions, as well as the challenges for market access that can still arise from non-discriminatory

[2] Case 8/74 *Dassonville* ECLI:EU:C:1974:82 (goods); Case 33/74 *van Binsbergen* ECLI:EU:C:1974 (services); Case 120/78 *Cassis de Dijon* ECLI:EU:C:1979:42 (goods); and Case C-415/93 *Bosman* ECLI:EU:C:1995:463 (workers).

[3] Art 3(3) TEU provides:

> [t]he Union shall establish an internal market. It shall work for the sustainable development of Europe based on balanced economic growth and price stability, a highly competitive social market economy, aiming at full employment and social progress, and a high level of protection and improvement of the quality of the environment. It shall promote scientific and technological advance. It shall combat social exclusion and discrimination, and shall promote social justice and protection, equality between women and men, solidarity between generations and protection of the rights of the child. It shall promote economic, social and territorial cohesion, and solidarity among Member States. It shall respect its rich cultural and linguistic diversity, and shall ensure that Europe's cultural heritage is safeguarded and enhanced.

restrictions.[4] We looked at the ruling in *Keck and Mithouard*, raising questions about 'types' of measures having equivalent effect to quantitative restrictions on the free movement of goods (Section 3.1 below).[5] We also considered the principle of mutual recognition, which facilitates 'negative' integration of the internal market, and the Treaty provisions on 'positive' integration; ie those enabling legislative harmonization.

Across that discussion, we developed a very basic sense of what integrity might mean, and we observed some obvious challenges to it within the case law and also within relevant Treaty provisions. But it is probably fair to say that in this opening seminar, we were alert to, yet not overwhelmed by, the prospect of digging more deeply into the integrity of the EU's internal market. Our impression of the concept was still diffuse—we used the term but had not yet examined what we meant to convey by using it. Nevertheless, we sketched a first attempt at 'defining and refining integrity as a legal concept', which entailed:

- Fragility/vulnerability of the internal market/of the EU as a system.
- Foundations: of the internal market and of the EU more generally.
- 'Who' can participate in it (third countries?)
- How the achievement of the internal market relates to other EU competences.
- How it relates to the concept of 'indivisibility'.
- How concepts migrate across different parts of EU law.

This became our rolling template, to which we added in each subsequent week, as unfolds below.

2.2 Conceptual Understandings of Integrity

In contrast, Week 2 required a conceptual deep dive into the meaning(s) of integrity, including how we might distinguish it from close yet different ideas such as coherence and convergence. This is when Steve 'joined' the class. Purposely provocative,

[4] eg Case C-110/05 *Commission v Italy* ECLI:EU:C:2009:66, para 34: 'Article [34 TFEU] reflects the obligation to respect the principles of non-discrimination and of mutual recognition of products lawfully manufactured and marketed in other Member States, as well as the principle of ensuring free access of Community products to national markets.' See generally, Jukka Snell, 'The Notion of Market Access: A Concept or a Slogan?' (2010) 47 Common Market Law Review 437.

[5] Joined Cases C-267/91 and 268/91 *Keck and Mithouard* ECLI:EU:C:1993:905, and esp para 16:

> [C]ontrary to what has previously been decided, the application to products from other Member States of national provisions restricting or prohibiting *certain selling arrangements* is not such as to hinder directly or indirectly, actually or potentially, trade between Member States within the meaning of the *Dassonville* judgment … so long as those provisions apply to all relevant traders operating within the national territory and so long as they affect in the same manner, in law and in fact, the marketing of domestic products and of those from other Member States. (emphasis added)

the first PowerPoint slide for Week 2 included, alongside images of the two protagonists to which he referred, the following extract from 'The Several Internal Markets':

> Michel Barnier wants to defend the four freedoms as indivisible, while Boris Johnson wants to shatter their unity. Michel Barnier adopts an elegantly thoughtful tone while Boris Johnson prefers oafish truculence. But in the background, both are working on a common understanding: that the EU's internal market is a political construct, and that its nature is open to contestation. They are right. It is not only a political construct—internal market lawyers are not out of a job. But there is a remarkable range of ambiguities in the legal definition of the EU's internal market (and related phenomena such as the EEA) and within those vacant spaces political choices are required to determine its shape and direction.[6]

I then distilled five key points from Steve's paper that indicate the (legal) nature of the internal market:

1. *(Almost) everything comes within the scope of the EU's internal market*: 'the handful of cases in which the Court places matters beyond the reach of EU law because they lack the necessary "marketizing" element reveal only unusual factual twists rather than any area that is in principle immune from the law of the internal market.'[7]
2. *It is significantly driven by negative integration*: 'free movement law bites where national measures diverge and ... it does not wait for the legislative process to catch up.'[8]
3. *There are limits, but they are rarely 'joined up' across internal market law*: '[t]he Court's case law resists distillation to a single test or explanation. It is, frankly, very hard work.'[9]
4. *Harmonization competence is not limitless*: 'Article 114 does not equip the EU with competence to harmonize diverse national rules per se. Instead it requires that that diversity shall exert a damaging effect on the internal market: that is the constitutionally proper target of harmonization.'[10]
5. *The EU's internal market has external dimensions*: 'it is not wrong as a matter of generalization to treat the EEA as a geographically extended version of the EU's internal market, even if at the level of detail that is to skate over the points of departure between the two systems ... large parts of the deal involve the extended application of EU orthodoxy.'[11]

6 Weatherill, 'The Several Internal Markets' (n 1) 125.
7 ibid 130, referring to eg Case C–268/99 *Jany* ECLI:EU:C:2001:616, para 49.
8 ibid 134.
9 ibid 137–38 and 141.
10 ibid 146.
11 ibid 170.

We then introduced different understandings of the internal market's integrity against that background. In the case law of the Court of Justice, there are threads that point, first, to the *interconnectedness* of different elements of the market, sometimes underpinned by references to Union citizenship. For example, in *Commission v Portugal*, the Court observed that '[t]he provisions of the [TFEU] on freedom of movement for persons are intended to facilitate the pursuit by [Union] citizens of occupational activities of all kinds throughout the [Union], and preclude measures which might place [Union] citizens at a disadvantage when they wish to pursue an economic activity in the territory of another Member State'.[12] Similarly, Advocate General Poiares Maduro argued that Treaty freedoms 'represent the cross-border dimension of the economic and social status conferred on European citizens' and that:

> [iI would be desirable for the same system to be applied to all the citizens of the Union wishing to use their freedom of movement or freedom to move services, goods or capital as well as their freedom to reside or to set up the seat of their activities in the Community.[13]

Secondly, integrity can relate to *interchangeability*—of both the Treaty freedoms,[14] and of the principles applied to interpreting them.[15] Thirdly, we debated the extent to which internal market integrity is in fact *required by* the Treaty. Here, we distinguished expectations of *uniformity* from the more integrity-leaning idea of *unity*.[16] In particular, we enthusiastically adopted Steve's compelling idea of '[Treaty]-sanctioned variation'[17] to determine ways to tolerate difference yet sustain integrity.

[12] Case C–345/05 *Commission v Portugal* ECLI:EU:C:2006:685, para 15.

[13] Joined Cases C–158/04 and 159/04 *Alfa Vita Vassilopoulos* ECLI:EU:C:2006:212, Opinion of AG Poiares Maduro, paras 40 and 51.

[14] eg Case C–390/99 *Canal Satélite Digital* ECLI:EU:C:2002:34, para 31:

> Where a national measure restricts both the free movement of goods and the freedom to provide services, the Court will in principle examine it in relation to one only of those two fundamental freedoms where it is shown that, in the circumstances of the case, one of them is entirely secondary in relation to the other *and may be considered together with it.* (emphasis added)

[15] eg Case C–55/94 *Gebhard* ECLI:EU:C:1995:411, para 37:

> National measures liable to hinder or make less attractive *the exercise of fundamental freedoms guaranteed by the Treaty* must fulfil four conditions: they must be applied in a non-discriminatory manner; they must be justified by imperative requirements in the general interest; they must be suitable for securing the attainment of the objective which they pursue; and they must not go beyond what is necessary in order to attain it. (emphasis added)

[16] eg Pedro Caro de Sousa, *The European Fundamental Freedoms: A Contextual Approach* (Oxford University Press 2015) 58–59; Peter Oliver, 'Of Trailers and Jet Skis: Is the Case Law on Article 34 TFEU Hurtling in a New Direction?' (2009) 33 Fordham International Law Journal 1423, 1426–27. See also Hans D Jarass, 'A Unified Approach to the Fundamental Freedoms' in Mads Tønneson Andenæs and Wulf-Henning Roth (eds), *Services and Free Movement in EU Law* (Oxford University Press 2002); and, in the same volume, Miguel Poiares Maduro, 'Harmony and Dissonance in Free Movement'.

[17] Weatherill, 'The Several Internal Markets' (n 1) 176.

Fourthly, we engaged in detail with the work of Alina Tryfonidou on the *convergence* of free movement law,[18] which is based on the idea, in my understanding, that 'the Court is consciously steering free movement law towards conceptual and definitional consistency irrespective of the Treaty provisions or free movement rights engaged'.[19] Guided by Tryfonidou's analysis, we first discussed the convergent evolution of the market access principle in case law on Articles 34 and 56 TFEU in particular.[20] We also queried whether convergence had deeper roots than judicial preference; whether it was, in other words, necessary to achieve the internal market—and in part, because of the increasingly complex nature of the internal market and greater (Treaty-compelled) consideration of non-market objectives.[21] We deduced that Steve was probably not convinced about this, noting his argument that:

> Reforms introduced by the Treaty of Lisbon such as the grant of binding force to the Charter and the embedding of the social market economy in Article 3(3) TEU are inapt to generate concrete changes in the existing law of the internal market, but they constitute recognition of the EU's vocation beyond trade liberalization.[22]

We return to this question in Section 4. Another possible catalyst of convergence is Union citizenship: for Tryfonidou, 'all market freedoms now form part of a general right for Union citizens to pursue an economic activity in a cross-border context'.[23] We also considered the significance of fundamental rights, discussing free movement rights *as* fundamental rights[24] and compliance with EU fundamental rights

[18] Alina Tryfonidou, 'Further Steps on the Road to Convergence among the Market Freedoms' (2010) 35 European Law Review 36.

[19] Niamh Nic Shuibhne, *The Coherence of EU Free Movement Law: Constitutional Responsibility and the Court of Justice* (Oxford University Press 2013) 32.

[20] Noting the cautions of AG Tesauro in Case C-292/92 *Hünermund v Landesapothekerkammer Baden-Württemberg* ECLI:EU:C:1993:863, para 1 of the Opinion ('[i]s Article [34 TFEU] a provision intended to liberalize intra-[Union] trade or is it intended more generally to encourage the unhindered pursuit of commerce in individual Member States?') and AG Tizzano in Case C-442/02 *CaixaBank France* ECLI:EU:C:2004:187, para 63 of the Opinion ('tantamount to bending the Treaty to a purpose for which it was not intended: that is to say, not in order to create an internal market in which conditions are similar to those of a single market and where operators can move freely, but in order to establish a market without rules').

[21] See, in particular, Tryfonidou (n 18) 39: 'The internal market policy is no longer the "lone and spoiled child" that monopolises the [Union]'s attention, but has to make room for other, now equally, important objectives that the [Union] has set for itself.'

[22] Weatherill, 'The Several Internal Markets' (n 1) 178.

[23] Tryfonidou (n 18). See further, Catherine Barnard, 'Fitting the Remaining Pieces into the Goods and Persons Jigsaw?' (2001) 26 European Law Review 35; Jukka Snell, 'And Then There Were Two: Products and Citizens in Community Law' in Takis Tridimas and Paolisa Nebbia (eds), *European Union Law for the Twenty-First Century: Rethinking the New Legal Order. Volume II: Internal Market and Free Movement Community Policies* (Hart Publishing 2004); Eleanor Spaventa, 'From *Gebhard* to *Carpenter*: Towards a (non-)Economic European Constitution' (2004) 41 Common Market Law Review 743; and Robin CA White, 'Free Movement, Equal Treatment, and Citizenship of the Union' (2005) 54 International and Comparative Law Quarterly 885.

[24] See further, Caro de Sousa (n 16) 70.

when justifying restrictions on free movement, reflecting on internal market law as 'porous to such non-economic interests' through the Charter of Fundamental Rights and 'the transversally applicable Treaty provisions such as Articles 11 and 12 TFEU [which] mandate the integration of concerns such as consumer protection, the protection of human dignity, and environmental protection into the elaboration of all the EU's policies and activities'.[25]

Our preliminary conclusion was that there was much 'integrity' to be found in internal market law when we loosened our understanding of it away from uniformity: when, instead, Steve's *sanctioned* variation benchmark could be satisfied. Certain concepts and principles of internal market law do seem closely aligned with convergence—for example, effectiveness of rights, equal treatment, and uniform application of EU law, all of which find expression in the 'autonomous concept' reasoning of the Court of Justice.[26] At the same time, other concepts and principles fit better with 'sanctioned variation'—for example, thinking about justification, mutual recognition, and minimum harmonization as examples of *permitted divergence*. Ultimately, we agreed that the internal market exhibits but does not require convergence in order to make claims to integrity—agreeing again with Steve, 'the internal market is an area within which the free movement of goods, persons, services, and capital is ensured, but they are not ensured in exactly the same way, and nor is their relationship with other EU policies fixed or clear'.[27] In that light, convergence and integrity are related but different frames of analysis—a thought shared by Tryfonidou, as she generously suggested to the previous year's students by email: in her view, steps that the Court might take to advance convergence do not 'question the integrity of the internal market but, rather, [demonstrate] that the latter is a "living organism" that needs to adapt to the EU's changing priorities in a manner that will, also, be acceptable to the Member States'.[28]

Disrupting this provisional mood of consensus and clarity, we then considered Brexit. Article 50(2) TEU requires that 'the Union shall negotiate and conclude an agreement with [the withdrawing] State, setting out the arrangements for its withdrawal, taking account of the framework for its future relationship with the Union'. Expanding on that mandate, the European Council's April 2017 guidelines for Brexit negotiations asserted that '[a]ny free trade agreement should be

[25] Weatherill, 'The Several Internal Markets' (n 1) 144.

[26] For example, classically, the definition of work/worker for the purposes of art 45 TFEU in Case 53/81 *Levin v Staatsecretaris van Justitie*, ECLI:EU:C:1982:105, esp para 12: 'enjoyment of the rights conferred by the principle of freedom of movement for workers could be made subject to the criterion of what the legislation of the host State declares to be a minimum wage, so that the field of application *ratione personae* of the [Union] rules … might vary from one Member State to another.' See also Case C-135/15 *Nikiforidis* ECLI:EU:C:2016:774, para 28: 'it follows from the need for uniform application of EU law and from the principle of equality that the terms of a provision of EU law which makes no express reference to the law of the Member States for the purpose of determining its meaning and scope must normally be given an autonomous and uniform interpretation throughout the European Union.'

[27] Weatherill, 'The Several Internal Markets' (n 1) 127.

[28] Email from Alina Tryfonidou to first author, 16 March 2020.

balanced, ambitious and wide-ranging. It cannot, however, amount to participation in the Single Market or parts thereof, *as this would undermine its integrity and proper functioning*.'[29] Moreover, '[p]reserving the integrity of the Single Market excludes participation based on a sector-by-sector approach … *the four freedoms of the Single Market are indivisible* and that there can be no "cherry picking" '.[30] These statements provoked debate about the extent to which they capture legal or political principles. For Steve,

> [t]here is in law no obstacle to dividing the freedoms in the way that some in the UK would wish, most obviously by privileging the free movement of goods and services over that of people. The indivisibility of the freedoms is a political construct: the legal reality is already messier and more heterogenous. But the political commitment to the indivisibility of the freedoms within the internal market is profound, and it is existential.[31]

His subsequent work then highlighted the carving up of the internal market through the Ireland/Northern Ireland Protocol.[32] In his view, '[t]he four freedoms are locked together by Article 26 TFEU … But those freedoms are divisible. More than that: they are divided.'[33]

The political dimensions of the market's indivisibility are clear; and '[w]e might … speculate about whether a commitment to indivisibility both so immediate and so sustained would have materialized had a Member State with a smaller economy than that of the UK been the first user of the Article 50 TEU withdrawal process'.[34] Indivisibility as a legal principle arguably rests on whether it applies only in a binary way—the single market is either indivisible or it is not—or whether it can, like other principles of EU law, be derogated from in proportionate ways for defensible public interest reasons (the situation of Ireland/Northern Ireland surely qualifying). Also relevant here is the European Commission's idea that 'Union policies and actions, including the Internal market with its four freedoms, form *a unique ecosystem* underpinned by instruments and structures that cannot be separated from each other'[35] so that cherry-picking engenders a 'risk for integrity and

29 European Council (Art 50) Guidelines for Brexit Negotiations, 29 April 2017, para 20 (emphasis added).

30 ibid para 1 (emphasis added).

31 Weatherill, 'The Several Internal Markets' (n 1) 178.

32 Stephen Weatherill, 'The Protocol on Ireland/Northern Ireland: Protecting the EU's Internal Market at the Expense of the UK's' (2020) 45 European Law Review 222. In March 2020, Steve kindly shared a preview of this work with that year's course students.

33 Weatherill, 'The Several Internal Markets' (n 1) 176; he also discusses arts 112–14 of the EEA Agreement (171–72).

34 Editorial Comments, 'Is the "Indivisibility" of the Four Freedoms a Principle of EU Law?' (2019) 56 Common Market Law Review 1189, 1190.

35 'Internal EU27 preparatory discussions on the framework for the future relationship: "Regulatory issues"', TF50 (2018) 32—Commission to EU 27, 21 February 2018 <https://ec.europa.eu/info/sites/info/files/slides_regulatory_issues.pdf> accessed 3 May 2021, emphasis added.

distortions to proper functioning of internal market, aggravated by [the] absence of [the] full EU "ecosystem" (including regulatory, supervisory, enforcement tools, with [the Court of Justice] on top'.[36]

With the group quite divided by the end of the seminar about whether, first, indivisibility is a legal principle and, secondly, integrity requires indivisibility, a final provocation was offered by the perspective that '[l]ooking in the case law for clear or consistent guidance about the conceptual foundations of economic integration is, as internal market lawyers know, a hopeless cause'.[37] Before leaving a perplexed—yes, even onscreen this was evident!—group, we agreed at least that integrity as a legal concept must connect to: (1) the nature of the internal market itself, which was acknowledged to be far from clear or settled; (2) an appropriate legal test/benchmark, which we admitted we did not yet have; and (3) legal certainty. But only two weeks into our excavation of integrity as a legal concept, we adopted our course image for the semester: *The Scream* by Edvard Munch.

3. Dimensions of Free Movement Law

We retreated to 'the law' with relief (misplaced, as it turned out) for Weeks 3–7, while continuing our quest to define and refine internal market integrity as a legal concept. We addressed questions *within* Treaty freedoms (Section 3.1); questions cutting *across two or more* Treaty freedoms (Section 3.2); and questions connected to Union citizenship (Section 3.3). We had detailed discussions on many legal (and wider) points in these classes, reflecting in some detail, for example, on what Union citizenship does, or should, mean. However, for this chapter, we focus here on specific integrity debates.

3.1 Questions within Freedoms

In Week 3, we explored questions on three Treaty freedoms. First, is the selling arrangement concept displaced by the ruling in *Scotch Whisky* and, if so, did that case render the Article 34 TFEU framework more unified?[38] Secondly, for Article 56 TFEU, does a consistent or inconsistent approach to the regulation of services emerge from *Uber Spain*, *Airbnb Ireland*, and *Visser*?[39] Thirdly, for Article 45 TFEU

[36] Editorial Comments (n 34) 1198.

[37] Gareth Davies, 'The Court's Jurisprudence on Free Movement of Goods: Pragmatic Presumptions, Not Philosophical Principles' (2012) 2 European Journal of Consumer Law 25, 27.

[38] Case C-333/14 *The Scotch Whisky Association* ECLI:EU:C:2015:845.

[39] Case C-434/15 *Asociación Profesional Elite Taxi (Uber Spain)* ECLI:EU:C:2017:981; Case C- 390/18 *Airbnb Ireland*, ECLI:EU:C:2019:1112; Joined Cases C-360/15 and 31/16 *Visser* ECLI:EU:C:2018:44.

but building on issues raised by *Visser*, does the ruling in *Saint Prix* offer a clear account of when (and why) primary law rights can change the boundaries of rights conferred by secondary law?[40]

On Article 34 TFEU and *Scotch Whisky*, we agreed with Niamh Dunne that 'price regulation no longer benefits from the presumptive safety of the selling arrangements category'.[41] What troubled us from the integrity angle was that we were not really sure *why* that was the case—is *Keck* still with us or not? Sitting in a (virtual) classroom in Scotland, we also had much sympathy with Dunne's criticism of the Court's approach to proportionality, advocating increases in excise—since 'it is clear that tax legislation constitutes an important and effective tool to discourage the consumption of alcoholic drinks and, therefore, to protect public health'[42]—yet completely ignoring 'the inexorable reality that the Scottish Parliament lacks competence in the area of excise duty'.[43] Dunne acknowledged that 'the logic of this decision is defensible to the extent that different Member States have different internal governance structures, and the ambit of the fundamental freedoms should not differ depending upon any national-level decision about internal division of competences' but also points out that 'it is impossible to conduct any meaningful proportionality assessment on the premise of a legal fiction'.[44] That provoked us to consider *territorial integrity*, which is more complex than Article 26(2) TFEU's airy idea of an area 'without internal frontiers in which the free movement of goods, persons, services and capital is ensured'.

For Article 45 TFEU, the Court's ruling in *Saint Prix* raised similar themes—here, displacement not of a concept of the Court's own making like in *Keck*, but instead, of an apparently finite legislative list of situations (in Article 7(3) of Directive 2004/38) in which the status of 'worker' can be retained after work itself has ceased.[45] By finding protection in Article 45 TFEU, so that worker status is also retained in 'the late stages of pregnancy and the immediate aftermath of childbirth, which require a woman to give up work temporarily',[46] the Court as creative artist on the canvas of free movement law was affirmed—we did not ignore the challenge that this presents for the integrity of free movement law, but it was a predictable challenge by this stage.

[40] Case C-507/12 *Saint Prix* ECLI:EU:C:2014:2007.

[41] Niamh Dunne 'Minimum Alcohol Pricing: Balancing the "Essentially Incomparable" in *Scotch Whisky*' (2018) 81 Modern Law Review 890, 896.

[42] *The Scotch Whisky Association* (n 38) para 44.

[43] Dunne (n 41) 901.

[44] ibid 903.

[45] Directive 2004/38/EC on the right of citizens of the Union and their family members to move and reside freely within the territory of the Member States [2004] OJ L158/77.

[46] *Saint Prix* (n 40) para 46. For further analysis, see Nicole Busby, 'Crumbs of Comfort: Pregnancy and the Status of "Worker" under EU Law's Free Movement Provisions' (2015) 44 Industrial Law Journal 134; and Samantha Currie, 'Pregnancy-related Employment Breaks, the Gender Dynamics of Free Movement Law and Curtailed Citizenship: *Jessy Saint-Prix*' (2016) 53 Common Market Law Review 543.

It was in our discussion on services, though, that controversies simmered and then boiled. We understood the Court's criteria on intermediation services as developed in *Uber Spain* and *Airbnb Ireland* and we benefited from insights from our Professor Emeritus and former Judge at the Court of Justice, Sir David Edward, on why transport services were detached from other services in the Treaty of Rome. The cases provoked ideas about *functional integrity* as both trade and society necessarily change over time. However, still in the domain of the platform economy, we disagreed about the extent to which 'the special characteristics of the collaborative economy' require 'new categories, principles, methods and (possibly) rules, in order to make sure that the promise of the fourth industrial revolution, made possible by technology, is not brought to its knees by inadequate and/or inappropriate regulatory framework'.[47] This was not so much a debate about regulatory innovation per se—rather, when we pushed the question through the integrity filter, further questions emerged about *relational* regulatory innovation vis-à-vis not only other Treaty freedoms but other aspects of services too. We found it easier to make claims about bespoke modes of platform economy regulation through some of the concepts discussed in Week 2: these *would* affect convergence, indivisibility, and uniformity. Would they also disrupt *integrity*? We were not sure.

However, it was in trying to make sense of *Visser* that the integrity storm properly exploded. We based our discussion on Jukka Snell's annotation, proceeding from his statement that 'Visser was a Dutch company seeking to lease premises to another Dutch company in violation of rules adopted by a Dutch authority'.[48] However, for restrictions on retail trade in goods that otherwise amounted to a 'selling arrangement' and thus fell outside the scope of Article 34 TFEU, the Court detached the requirement of the cross-border requirement in Articles 49 and 56 TFEU from Article 4(1) of the Services Directive.[49] It invoked the idea of a '*genuine* internal market in services', which 'requires, above all, the elimination of obstacles which are encountered by providers in becoming established in the Member States, *whether in their own Member State or in another Member State*, and which are liable to affect adversely their ability to supply services to recipients located throughout the European Union'.[50] Thus the Services Directive 'is capable of *extending, in certain cases, beyond what is strictly laid down in the provisions of the FEU Treaty*

[47] Vassilis Hatzopoulos, 'After *Uber Spain*: The EU's Approach on the Sharing Economy in Need of Review?' (2019) 44 European Law Review 88, 94. See further, Michèle Finck 'Distinguishing Internet Platforms from Transport Services: *Elite Taxi v Uber Spain*' (2018) 55 Common Market Law Review 1619; and Pieter Van Cleynenbreugel 'Accommodating the Freedom of Online Platforms to Provide services through the Incidental Direct Effect Back Door: *Airbnb Ireland*' (2020) 57 Common Market Law Review 1201.

[48] Jukka Snell, 'Independence Day for the Services Directive: *Visser*' (2019) 56 Common Market Law Review 1119, 1122.

[49] *Visser* (n 39) paras 99–103. Directive 2006/123/EC on services in the internal market [2006] OJ L376/36.

[50] *Visser* (n 39) paras 106 and 105 respectively (emphasis added).

relating to freedom of establishment and the free movement of services'.[51] The implications of this are surely seismic, yet the judgment received little academic attention.[52] For Snell, 'the Court opted for an autonomous and expansive reading of the Directive that does not tie it to the case law on Treaty freedoms but allows the Directive an independent and important role in internal market law'.[53] And we very much agreed with his view that '[t]he potential importance of the move to decouple the definition of service in the Directive from that in the Treaty should not be underestimated. It offers a way to activate the Directive in circumstances where the Treaty would not be of help.'[54]

Our debate on *Visser* and Snell's analysis of it mainly triggered questions about *different institutional responsibilities* for ensuring integrity, evident in this point made by Snell:

> A national rule establishing where a product may be sold is lawful under free movement of goods in the absence of discrimination, but now requires justification under the Services Directive. This undoubtedly represents a narrowing of Member State regulatory autonomy. However, the important difference with *Keck* is that the source of the rule is not 'just' the Treaty as interpreted by the Court. Instead, it is the Union legislature that has decided to go above and beyond the requirements of the Treaty freedoms.[55]

We disagreed about the extent to which this made a material difference in assessing *Visser* but agreed that responsibility for internal market integrity goes well beyond the Court. We therefore spent some time on what seemed, to us, a surprising set of concluding remarks—surprising in the sense that Snell had forensically critiqued the reasoning of the Court throughout his annotation yet offered an unexpectedly sympathetic final judgement. With what we might term forgiveness for the Court's approach, Snell suggested that *Visser* should be 'welcomed from the broader perspective of the dynamic development of the internal market' since the 'key priority for the Union is no longer just the opening of trade channels between countries, but the creation of a genuine economic union that can support the single currency'—something that 'represents a step-change from the single market' and 'calls for EU legislative action that is not limited just to cross-border situations but penetrates far deeper into their business environments'.[56] For Snell, these aims permit the hierarchy of norms inversion, suggesting that '[t]he Treaty freedoms should

[51] ibid para 107 (emphasis added).

[52] See, as an exception, Sara Iglesias Sanchez, 'Purely Internal Situations and the Limits of EU Law: A Consolidated Case Law or a Notion to be Abandoned? (Case Comment)' (2018) 14 European Constitutional Law Review 7.

[53] Snell, 'Independence Day for the Services Directive' (n 48) 1123.

[54] ibid 1125.

[55] ibid 1129.

[56] ibid 1134.

not be seen as the upper limit of EU's ambitions. Rather, *they are the starting point*, the bare minimum that the EU judiciary protects and enforces. *The Union legislature can go further*. It has a democratic mandate that the judges lack.'[57]

Bringing this together, we reached three conclusions. First, integrity as a legal concept has multiple layers—functional, institutional, territorial—and is substantive as much as conceptual. Secondly, observing Snell's change of tone when comparing his substantive analysis and final conclusions, we distinguished the market *and* law from the market *versus* law—we see *Visser* in the latter sense, since the pivotal cross-border requirement in free movement law had to bend for the purpose of achieving desired market results. Finally, building on Week 2, if legal certainty is critical to a legal understanding of market integrity, what *aspects* of legal certainty are critical?

3.2 Questions across Freedoms

In one sense, we had already looked across the freedoms in Weeks 1 and 3 when considering the market access test for defining restrictions of any of the Treaty freedoms, as well as in Week 2, when we discussed conceptual questions about unity or indivisibility necessarily relevant across freedoms. As brought out more clearly in Week 3, these examples also raise the integrity of the EU institutional system and the roles of different institutions in EU free movement law. Aiming to connect to but also progress that work in Week 4, we first revisited a question briefly introduced in Week 2: *interchangeability* of the freedoms. More specifically, we asked if it matters whether the relevant Treaty freedom is clearly identified in all circumstances. We considered here the extent to which legal protection for workers and self-employed persons overlaps or differs.[58] We also traced the concept of worker from free movement law to social policy, considering the *King* case on entitlement to paid annual leave and the role of the Charter in *Bauer*.[59] From the integrity perspective, though less dramatically than for *Visser* in Week 3, we again saw some erosion of the expected hierarchy of sources of EU law.

Secondly, using economically grounded justification as a case study, we considered the value but also the risks of *cross-fertilization of concepts*: where something starts life in the context of one freedom and is then transposed to the others. We unpacked ambiguities built into the Court's statement that while 'grounds of *a*

[57] ibid 1135.

[58] Case C-442/16 *Gusa* ECLI:EU:C:2017:1004, esp paras 42–44; and Case C-544/18 *Dakneviciute* ECLI:EU:C:2019:761, esp paras 31 and 35–36.

[59] Case C-214/16 *King* ECLI:EU:C:2017:914; Case C-316/13 *Fenol* ECLI:EU:C:2015:200; and Case C-569/16 *Bauer* ECLI:EU:C:2018:871. Directive 2003/88/EC concerning certain aspects of the organisation of working time [2003] OJ L299/9. See further, Denis Edwards, 'Chopping and Changing: The Self-Employed and Workers in EU Law' (2018) 134 Law Quarterly Review 374.

purely economic nature cannot constitute overriding reasons in the public interest justifying a restriction of a fundamental freedom guaranteed by the Treaties', it is nevertheless accepted that 'national legislation may constitute a justified restriction on a fundamental freedom when it is dictated by reasons *of an economic nature* in the pursuit of an objective in the public interest'.[60] Our core objective was to distinguish *protectionism* from (legitimate) *protection*, and we discussed in some detail the proposals in the 2016 Decision agreed between the UK and the other twenty-seven Member States before the Brexit referendum, which proposed discriminatory restrictions on workers in two key respects: eligibility for in-work benefits and indexation of exported family benefits.[61] We examined how the defence of 'economic but not purely economic' was drawn over to workers from case law on other Treaty freedoms in the justification arguments outlined in the Decision.[62] We thus observed the irony of the Commission's infringement proceedings against Austria, post-Brexit, for introducing benefit indexation in national law—a case pending before the Court at the time of writing, but with a clear signal of illegality from Advocate General Richard de la Tour.[63]

Fundamentally in this seminar, we interrogated the extent to which integrity can accommodate difference, testing the limits of Weatherill's 'sanctioned variation' against the benchmark of integrity. In some ways, we expected the anomalies that do arise across the freedoms because of the volatility already observed within freedoms in Week 3. That expectation freed us from surprise and pushed us more quickly to refine our understanding of integrity as a legal concept. Thus, in Week 4, we suggested that different Member States 'feel' the internal market (and/or the EU) very differently, which has implications for how justification, in particular, has evolved in free movement law. The Court is an obvious first point of institutional interest in that respect. However, borrowing from categorizations studied in the previous semester's course on 'The EU's Changing Constitution', we wondered too about the 'selfish v fearful' Commission; and leaned towards the latter.[64]

[60] Joined Cases C–105/12–107/12 *Essent* ECLI:EU:C:2016:732, paras 51–52 (emphasis added). See further, Sue Arrowsmith, 'Rethinking the Approach to Economic Justifications under the EU's Free Movement Rules' (2015) 68 Current Legal Problems 307 and Jukka Snell, 'Economic Justifications and the Role of the State' in Panos Koutrakos, Niamh Nic Shuibhne, and Phil Syrpis (eds), *Exceptions from EU Free Movement Law: Derogation, Justification and Proportionality* (Hart Publishing 2016) 12.

[61] Decision of the Heads of State or Government, meeting within the European Council, concerning a new settlement for the United Kingdom within the European Union, OJ 2016 C691/1; proposing amendments to, respectively, Regulation 492/2011 on freedom of movement for workers within the Union, OJ 2011 L141/1 and Regulation 883/2004/EC on the coordination of social security systems, OJ 2004 L166/1.

[62] eg Case C–542/09 *Commission v Netherlands* ECLI:EU:C:2012:346, paras 57–58, 68, and 81–82. See further, Niamh Nic Shuibhne, 'Reconnecting the Free Movement of Workers and Equal Treatment in an Unequal Europe' (2018) 43 European Law Review 477.

[63] Case C–328/20 *Commission v Austria* ECLI:EU:C:2022:468; Opinion of AG Richard de la Tour, ECLI:EU:C:2022:45. On the justification ground of 'establishment or restoration of the supportive function and the fairness of the social system', see esp paras 141–46 of the Opinion.

[64] Eleanor Spaventa 'A Very Fearful Court? The Protection of Fundamental Rights in the EU after Opinion 2/13' (2015) 22 Maastricht Journal of European and Comparative Law 35; Bruno de Witte, 'A Selfish Court? The Court of Justice and the Design of International Dispute Settlement beyond the

3.3 Free Movement Law beyond Internal Market Law: Union Citizenship

In Weeks 5–6, building on the public finance defence discussion in Week 4, we asked: does the imprint of internal market law still run (too?) deeply in EU citizenship law? We first addressed the controversial rulings on eligibility for social assistance in host states.[65] There is rich academic commentary in this field, but we did not read any of it before the seminar, aiming to make sense of the case law based on primary sources alone with further reading assigned as follow-up.[66] It seems fairly straightforward to state that we identified several points of confusion. We first raised the question of *selectivity* in legal reasoning as an integrity challenge.[67] Secondly, we used the language of *preserving* integrity almost by presumption in previous seminars; we now asked, more intensively: but *how* is it 'preserved'? Relatedly, thirdly, what is the appropriate balance between efforts to preserve integrity and an idea of *living integrity*? Finally, building on our interest in who, institutionally, is responsible for the integrity of EU internal market law, who is responsible for *breaches* of it?

We then contrasted the market concerns of the social assistance case law with the rights drawn from Article 20 TFEU in *Rottmann* and *Ruiz Zambrano*, which

European Union' in Marise Cremona and Anne Thies (eds), *The European Court of Justice and External Relations Law: Constitutional Challenges* (Hart Publishing 2014).

[65] At that time, we compared Case C-184/99 *Grzelczyk* ECLI:EU:C:2001:458; Case C-413/99 *Baumbast* ECLI:EU:C:2002:493; Case C-456/02 *Trojani* ECLI:EU:C:2004:488; Joined Cases C-22/08 and 23/08 *Vatsouras and Koupatantze* ECLI:EU:C:2009:344; and Case C-140/12 *Brey* ECLI:EU:C:2013:565, on the one hand; with the judgments in Case C-333/13 *Dano* ECLI:EU:C:2014:2358; Case C-67/14 *Alimanovic* ECLI:EU:C:2015:597; and Case C-181/19 *Jobcenter Krefeld* ECLI:EU:C:2020:794, on the other. Dayana examined this case law for her LLM dissertation in summer 2021.

[66] eg Michael Dougan 'The Constitutional Dimension to the Case Law on Union Citizenship' (2006) 31 European Law Review 613 and 'The Bubble that Burst: Exploring the Legitimacy of the Case Law on the Free Movement of Union Citizens' in Maurice Adams and others (eds), *Judging Europe's Judges: The Legitimacy of the Case Law of the European Court of Justice* (Hart Publishing 2013); Kay Hailbronner, 'Union Citizenship and Access to Social Benefits' (2005) 42 Common Market Law Review 1245; Dion Kramer, 'Earning Social Citizenship in the European Union: Free Movement and Access to Social Assistance Benefits Reconstructed' (2016) 18 Cambridge Yearbook of European Legal Studies 270; Niamh Nic Shuibhne, 'Limits Rising, Duties Ascending: The Changing Legal Shape of Union Citizenship' (2015) 52 Common Market Law Review 889; Charlotte O'Brien, 'I Trade, Therefore I Am: Legal Personhood in the European Union' (2013) 50 Common Market Law Review 1643 and 'Civis Capitalist Sum: Class as the New Guiding Principle of EU Free Movement Rights' (2016) 53 Common Market Law Review 937; Daniel Thym, 'The Elusive Limits of Solidarity: Residence Rights of and Social Benefits for Economically Inactive Union Citizens' (2015) 52 Common Market Law Review 17; and Herwig Verschueren, 'Preventing "Benefit Tourism" in the EU: A Narrow or Broad Interpretation of the Possibilities Offered by the ECJ in *Dano*?' (2015) 52 Common Market Law Review 363.

[67] A question investigated by undergraduate student Mateusz Pelka for his LLB thesis in 2021–22, by examining as many documents pertinent to the social assistance case files (including at national level) as he could access, questioning whether—and if so, how— *legal* research can derive evidence about 'selectivity' given the collegiate nature of the Court's judgments.

protect Union citizens in their home states,[68] using Advocate General Sharpston's Opinion in *Ruiz Zambrano* to bridge between the market roots of free movement law and a deeper understanding of Union citizenship beyond free movement.[69] In its ruling, the Court created a new pathway to citizenship rights under Article 20 TFEU, apparently removing the need for any free movement or cross-border element at all. In other words, Union citizenship gained significant legal substance beyond free movement law in some (exceptional) situations, which concern either the loss of Member State nationality or forced departure of a Union citizen from the Union territory—or it initially seemed that way, at least, considering the Court's later explanation that, in fact, protection in the home state has 'an intrinsic connection with the freedom of movement and residence of a Union citizen' into the future.[70]

Bridging back to Week 3, we asked if the loosening of the cross-border requirement was more justifiable in the context of Union citizenship than in the market-based context in *Visser* on the purely internal effect of the Services Directive (with no consensus). We noted how powerful the Charter had become in the Article 20 TFEU case law, compared to its exclusion in *Dano* from the social assistance context, when the Union citizen could not establish lawful residence on the basis of Directive 2004/38.[71] We considered the Court's less severe take on economic justifications in the context of restricting Article 20 rights, noting that 'a purely economic objective is *fundamentally different* from that of maintaining public order and safeguarding public security and does not justify such serious interference with the effective enjoyment of the substance of the rights deriving from Union citizenship'.[72] And we also addressed, again in contrast to *Dano* and *Alimanovic*, the continuing significance in the Article 20 case law of examining a citizen's individual circumstances to evaluate the proportionality of national restrictions.[73] Finally, bringing us back to *Dassonville* and early discussions on the scope of free movement law, we noted the discussion on the blurred boundary between potential and hypothetical

[68] Case C-34/09 *Ruiz Zambrano* ECLI:EU:C:2011:124; Case C-135/08 *Rottmann* ECLI:EU:C:2010:104. See further, Stephen Coutts, 'The Shifting Geometry of Union Citizenship: A Supranational Status from Transnational Rights' (2019) 21 Cambridge Yearbook of European Legal Studies 318.

[69] Case C-34/09 *Ruiz Zambrano*, ECLI:EU:C:2010:560, Opinion of AG Sharpston.

[70] eg Case C-165/14 *Rendón Marín*, ECLI:EU:C:2016:675, paras 73–75. See further, Stephanie Reynolds, 'Exploring the "Intrinsic Connection" between Free Movement and the Genuine Enjoyment Test: Reflections on EU Citizenship after *Iida*' (2013) 38 European Law Review 376.

[71] See art 7(1) of Directive 2004/38 (n 45); *Dano* (n 65) paras 85–91; and eg on art 20 TFEU and the Charter, Case C-133/15 *Chavez-Vilchez* ECLI:EU:C:2017:354. See further, Hester Kroeze, 'The Substance of Rights: New Pieces of the *Ruiz Zambrano* Puzzle' (2019) 44 European Law Review 238, and compare now Case C-709/20 *The Department for Communities In Northern Ireland (CG)* ECLI:EU:C:2021:602 (which LLB student Nadia Murray was exploring in her thesis at the time of writing).

[72] Case C-836/18 *Subdelegación del Gobierno en Ciudad Real (Spouse of a Union Citizen)* ECLI:EU:C:2020:119, para 48 (emphasis added).

[73] eg Case C-221/17 *Tjebbes* ECLI:EU:C:2019:189, paras 41–47.

deterrent effects in Advocate General Bobek's Opinion in *Banger*, underscoring the feeling that we seem doomed to have the same conversations in EU internal market (and also now in EU citizenship) law again, and again, and again.[74]

Three further integrity conclusions emerged by the end of Week 6. First, the importance of unpicking institutional differences was affirmed: the Court is confronted more directly with the (rights of the) individual than the legislator; yet we increasingly began to question the silence as much as the voice of the legislator as the course progressed. Secondly, the changing priorities of the Union, both in relation to but also independently in some respects from the Member States, became even more apparent, tracking the evolution of the Union as a polity with economic or market purpose to something much more complex. Finally, we asked ourselves directly: is the concept of integrity more elusive the more that we think about it, or had we, instead, changed our understanding—and expectations—of integrity and of what it could realistically deliver?

4. The Internal Market and Other Objectives

Weeks 8 and 9 addressed two questions: first, are 'other' objectives appropriately accommodated in EU internal market law; secondly, are they accommodated (or not) in ways that support or undermine integrity? In Week 8, we considered relevant case law and academic responses to it. In Week 9, we 'went' to Bruges—reflecting on contributions to a conference organized by Sacha Garben and Inge Govaere. That workshop (which Steve attended, and which took place 'in real life' in February 2018 at the College of Europe) interrogated *The Internal Market 2.0* and, fortunately for us, the proceedings were published in spring 2020.[75]

The starting point in Week 8 was the case law on posted workers, juxtaposing the Court's recognition of the fundamental right to strike with its approach to proportionality and business-privileging objectives, especially in *Laval*.[76] Promoting the freedom to trade of economic operators over the social interest in collective bargaining has been criticized in several respects, though from the integrity perspective, we focused on the intersection of justification and protection of fundamental rights in the *structure* of free movement law.[77] We considered the argument that 'nothing in the Treaty suggests that the [Union]'s social policy objectives must always take precedence over the objective of having a properly functioning

[74] Case C-89/17 *Banger* ECLI:EU:C:2018:225, Opinion of AG Bobek, paras 37–42.

[75] Sacha Garben and Inge Govaere (eds), *The Internal Market 2.0* (Hart Publishing 2020).

[76] Case C-341/05 *Laval un Partneri* ECLI:EU:C:2007:809.

[77] Catherine Barnard, 'Social Dumping or Dumping Socialism?' (2008) 67 Cambridge Law Journal 262, 264: 'The moment collective action is found to be a "restriction" and thus in breach of Community law, the "social" interests are on the back-foot, having to defend themselves from the economic.' See further, Dagmar Schiek, 'Towards More Resilience for a Social EU—The Constitutionally Conditioned Internal Market' (2017) 13 European Constitutional Law Review 611.

common market. On the contrary, the inclusion of both policy objectives in the Treaty signifies the aim of the [Union] to bring these policies together.'[78] We also addressed post-Lisbon shifts, not only in the Court's case law[79] but also in legislative and policy developments.[80] On the latter, we asked whether these shifts had done 'enough' to meet the criticism of *Laval*; whether the 'social' and the 'market' are now better balanced. After all, the Lisbon Treaty inserted the idea of the 'social market economy' into Article 3(3) TEU and we wondered whether that concept has more legal weight since *AGET Iraklis*.[81] Finally, we looked at *Josemans* to explore space for national difference within the internal market in a very different context.[82]

Across the seminar, alert to the unevenness of EU competence in different fields,[83] we discussed methods and strategies for realizing in better harmony the three elements of the *social market economy*. The 'fair balance' method applied in much of the case law was agreed to capture a worthy objective, yet it remains difficult to pin down.[84] We also examined the importance of the Charter of Fundamental Rights. As the Court affirmed in *Pfleger*:

> [W]here a Member State relies on overriding requirements in the public interest in order to justify rules which are liable to obstruct the exercise of the freedom to provide services, such justification, provided for by EU law, must be interpreted in the light of the general principles of EU law, in particular the fundamental rights henceforth guaranteed by the Charter.[85]

[78] Case C-438/05 *The International Transport Workers' Federation and the Finnish Seamen's Union (Viking Line)* ECLI:EU:C:2007:292, Opinion of AG Poiares Maduro, para 23.

[79] For an argument about the implications of Lisbon reforms for justification arguments, see Case C-515/08 *Dos Santos Palhota*, ECLI:EU:C:2010:245, Opinion of AG Cruz Villalón, para 53; cf Weatherill, 'The Several Internal Markets' (n 1) 178, noted in Section 2.

[80] See esp Directive 2018/957 amending Directive 96/71/EC concerning the posting of workers in the framework of the provision of services [2018] OJ L173/16, and the European Pillar of Social Rights <https://op.europa.eu/en/publication-detail/-/publication/ce37482a-d0ca-11e7-a7df-01aa75ed71a1/language-en/format-PDF/source-62666461>. See further, European Parliament, Resolution of 19 January 2017 on a European Pillar of Social Rights, 2016/2095(INI).

[81] Case C-201/15 *AGET Iraklis* ECLI:EU:C:2016:972. Compare AG Wahl's characterization of the EU as a 'free market economy' in para 1 of his Opinion (ECLI:EU:C:2016:429).

[82] Case C-137/09 *Josemans*, ECLI:EU:C:2010:774.

[83] See eg recital 17 of the Preamble to the European Pillar of Social Rights (n 80):

> Delivering on the European Pillar of Social Rights is a shared political commitment and responsibility. The European Pillar of Social Rights should be implemented at both Union level and Member State level within their respective competences, taking due account of different socio-economic environments and the diversity of national systems, including the role of social partners, and in accordance with the principles of subsidiarity and proportionality.

[84] eg Case C-283/11 *Sky Österreich* ECLI:EU:C:2013:28, para 60: 'Where several rights and fundamental freedoms protected by the European Union legal order are at issue, the assessment of the possible disproportionate nature of a provision of European Union law must be carried out with a view to reconciling the requirements of the protection of those different rights and freedoms and a fair balance between them.'

[85] Case C-390/12 *Pfleger* ECLI:EU:C:2014:281, para 35.

Dagmar Schiek's idea of the Charter-enriched 'constitutionally conditioned Internal Market' was important here,[86] and we also considered Floris de Witte's 'framework of procedural proportionality, which focuses on the coherence and consistency of national moral or ethical policies, and ensures a general regulatory equivalence between domestic and foreign situations' yet 'can as such ensure that the Union enhances, rather than decreases, the capacity of individual citizens to be in control of the moral and ethical environment in which they live'.[87]

After these reflections, we grafted six further thoughts onto our mutating conception of integrity. First, can internal market law ever *transcend or overcome* (the structure of) free movement law? In other words, is a *Ruiz Zambrano* moment—where the trajectory escapes expected constraints—also possible for social protection? Conversely, do expectations of integrity argue against these developments? Secondly, can an integrity-based market be achieved if *(national) political choices* are minimized in the Court's reasoning? Is avoiding confrontation best in the end—or not? Thirdly, can a truly integrity-based market ever be achieved without *harmonization*? Fourthly, based on our emerging consensus that integrity is *dynamic*, when/do/can we reach *enough* integrity? Fifthly, does integrity connect to what is *integral* to the market? Is social protection 'integral' to the EU internal market, as well as, for example, sustainability? Finally, sixthly, what does *exclusion* beyond the boundaries of the market—of, for example, moral or political choices, but also of citizens—tell us about the market's integrity? All class members particularly enjoyed pursuing these questions through reading the Bruges conference chapters in Week 9,[88] and we welcomed Edinburgh Law School colleague Raphaële Xenidis to the virtual classroom that week from her temporary home at iCourts in Copenhagen.

We agreed with Govaere's assertion that '[p]aradoxically, the internal market is one of the most prominent features of the European integration process but its specific internal and external dynamics are probably also among the least well understood',[89] and we structured our post-conference discussion agenda around five themes identified through pre-seminar submissions from the class members. First, we looked at the role of the Court, with Rhian highlighting Govaere's question about whether the Court has a responsibility to change (or not) with the times; Lukas asking whether the Court should adapt (or not) to changing politics, provoked by Gareth Davies' chapter; both Anthony and Rhian arguing that Davies

[86] Schiek (n 77) 639.

[87] Floris de Witte, 'Sex, Drugs and EU Law: The Recognition of Moral and Ethical Diversity in EU Law' (2013) 50 Common Market Law Review 1545, 1578.

[88] In Garben and Govaere (n 75): Inge Govaere, 'Internal Market Dynamics: On Moving Targets, Shifting Contextual Factors and the Untapped Potential of Article 3(3) TEU'; Bruno de Witte, 'The Freedom to Provide Services: The Controversial Freedom?'; Vassilis Hatzopolous, 'The Internal Market and the Online Platform Economy'; Stephen Weatherill, 'The Fundamental Question of Minimum or Maximum Harmonisation'; Gareth Davies, 'Originalism at the Court of Justice'; and Sacha Garben, 'The "Fundamental Freedoms" and (Other) Fundamental Rights: Towards an Integrated Democratic Interpretation Framework'.

[89] Govaere, 'Internal Market Dynamics' (n 88) 75.

had minimized the scale of the legal change brought about by *Keck*, *Dano*, and *Alimanovic*; and Dayana picking up on Steve's point about the Court as both driver of Union (social) change and respecter of diverse national contexts. Secondly, class members again emphasized the relationship between the Court and the legislator. For example, Lukas asked how Treaty change could be better reflected in case law, reading across Davies and Govaere. Rhian raised the idea of flexibility within integrity, through her reading of Steve's ideas on minimum harmonization; and Jovan, also inspired by Steve's chapter and our class discussion on market asymmetries, advocated minimum harmonization as a mechanism to balance the symmetrical design of free movement-based internal market law.

Perhaps unsurprisingly, given the intensity of our discussion on the platform economy and *Visser* in Week 3, a third theme connected to the Court/legislator relationship but more specifically in the domain of services. Jovan, Lukas, and Rhian again questioned the extent to which digital services spark—and should (or should not) spark—regulatory and thus market fragmentation, drawing from Govaere, Steve, Vassilis Hatzopoulos, and Bruno de Witte; Dayana stressed the considerable legal uncertainty that this debate produces; and Rhian challenged us to locate the line between problematic uncertainty and valuable flexibility. Anthony unpacked the extent to which slow-paced regulation of digital and technological markets stems from restraint in terms of not over-regulating in a dynamic area, or from legislative intimidation because of the sheer complexity and fast-paced nature of the field: either way, he argued, we find ourselves in a familiar place in EU internal market law—the legislature waiting and watching while the Court interprets 'old law' for new developments through the lens of an antiquated system. In that spirit, Jovan questioned the very idea of services as a distinct Treaty freedom in the contemporary world: is it still reasonable to retain that distinctiveness or could services be 'digested' by the other freedoms?

We grouped our questions under the fourth theme as *structural concerns*—notably, why, as Rhian expressed it via Davies and Govaere, is there still such a problem with the dominance of fundamental freedoms, since Article 3(3) TEU has provided a primary law impetus to pursue other objectives? For Dayana, considering Garben's chapter, the absence of clear hierarchical relationships is problematic since the Treaty does not help us to understand the ordering of economic and social economic objectives. Finally, fifthly, class members identified a series of *systemic concerns*. Jovan and Rhian asked what integrity ultimately means and *requires* in terms of guiding the internal market onwards into the twenty-first century and the necessarily changing contexts and objectives that entails. Rhian also wondered if cleaving too closely to the wording of the Treaty fulfilled or actually caused more problems for market integrity. Honorary class member Raphaële asked: is there something distinctly 'European' in the normative substance of the internal market or does Europeanization instead equate to procedural convergence in a normative vacuum, or at least in an under-determinate space in normative terms? She cautioned against *binary oppositions*, even linguistically—for example, between assuming the *positive* value of uniformity, coherence, and integrity on the one hand, compared to the *risks* of fragmentation and complexity on the other; between the *dangers* of centralization and power-grabbing, compared to the need to *safeguard* regulatory decentralization and national diversity. She also challenged us by asking: does a willingness to preserve the integrity of the internal market transform it into or reify it as a self-referential legal construct? In response, we articulated a new question: does internal market integrity as a legal concept takes us any closer to resolving the optimal balance of *proactive/reactive* institutional approach(es) to EU lawmaking (broadly understood): how might we better navigate the *complexity and (often) horizontality of the sources* of EU internal market law, or indeed uncover the *normative content* of the EU's internal market?

5. Relating the Internal Market to Other Markets

Taking seriously Raphaële's caution about self-referential market construction, our final discussions in Weeks 9 and 10 turned to markets *outside* the EU. We asked: can the internal market, or parts of it, be shared beyond the Union? How do these questions connect to the Commission's 'ecosystem' concept, introduced in Section 2, or to the indivisibility insisted on by the European Council throughout the Brexit process? These debates—more generally in Week 9 and focused on Brexit specifically in Week 10—were framed by further email contributions from academic friends. First, with strong resonance for Raphaële's perspective in Week 9, Marise Cremona had suggested to the previous year's class:

> In the external policies of the 70s and 80s, the Community saw the integrity of its common market primarily in terms of the need to protect its internal functioning and competitive structures (common conditions of entry from outside). In the 90s, as the EU model of market integration is exported to third countries, we can see a concern to protect the integrity of Community decision-making and institutional structures (only Member States have seats at the table). The current focus on autonomy as necessary to the integrity of the Union's 'eco-system' can trace its roots back to these concerns, while also reflecting an increased awareness of normative integrity (Union principles and values). But do we have to see integrity in terms of 'protection' from the external? Can we find a way to think of autonomy as a legal principle that helps to maintain the functional, institutional and normative integrity of the Union project while being open to external engagement and global commitments?

And from Christophe Hillion, leaning to the ecosystem:

> I do not think that the EU claims to have found the perfect system in terms of organisation/regulation of the market. But this system—the *acquis*—is based on

> treaties signed by the Member States and has been elaborated by common institutions, including a parliament. The least [that] one can expect from the Member States and the EU institutions is that they defend the integrity of these agreed rules when negotiating and concluding international treaties i.e. that they do not give out benefits associated with those rules (and the market) at a lower price. This would ultimately undermine membership. This does not mean that the EU imposes those rules on third states—the latter remain free to subscribe or not, based on their own interests, to what the EU proposes in terms of benefits and obligations, and to have a less ambitious arrangement, in terms of reduced market access.

Responding to these contributions, we first attempted to disentangle the legal qualities of sharing the market with third states 'near' and 'far'. Reflecting on Opinion 2/15 and relations-far, we were struck by Panos Koutrakos' language in his description of different threads of EU external policy coming together as an 'integrated whole' post-Lisbon, and by his conception of sustainable development as an 'integral part' of EU trade policy.[90] His analysis of the external sphere of integrity aligned closely with the integrity discussions we had progressed for the internal sphere.

In light of the discussion on Brexit planned for Week 10, we then spent considerable time on relations-near, noting the criteria in Article 8 TEU and exploring the extension of the EU's internal market through the European Economic Area (EEA) Agreement in particular.[91] We saw clear reflection of the ecosystem in Adam Łazowski's concern about '*partial* legal integration between the European Union and some of its neighbours'.[92] In that light, we reflected on the deeply unifying language of the preamble to the EEA Agreement alongside the unsettling argument that EU/EEA legal integrity might depend more on diplomacy, openness, and mutual willingness than defined infrastructure.[93] Considering the challenges

[90] Panos Koutrakos, 'The EU's Competence to Conclude Trade Agreements: The EU–Singapore Opinion' in Fabian Amtenbrink and others (eds), *The Internal Market and the Future of European Integration: Essays in Honour of Laurence W. Gormley* (Cambridge University Press 2019) 656.

[91] See further, eg Communication from the Commission to the Council and the European Parliament, Wider Europe—Neighbourhood: A New Framework for Relations with our Eastern and Southern Neighbours, COM (2003) 104 final (esp s 3); Matthias Oesch, *Switzerland and the European Union: General Framework, Bilateral Agreements, Autonomous Adaptation* (Dike/Nomos 2018); and Peter Van Elsuwege and Roman Petrov, 'Article 8 TEU: Towards a New Generation of Agreements with the Neighbouring Countries of the European Union?' (2011) 36 European Law Review 688.

[92] Adam Lazowski, 'Enhanced Multilateralism and Enhanced Bilateralism: Integration without Membership in the European Union' (2008) 45 Common Market Law Review 1433, 1443 (emphasis added).

[93] See esp Halvard Haukeland Fredriksen and Christian NK Franklin, 'Of Pragmatism and Principles: The EEA Agreement 20 Years On' (2015) 52 Common Market Law Review 640. We also reflected on the much more fragmented relationship between the EU and Switzerland (and Jovan went on to write his LLM thesis on this topic). See eg Case C–355/16 *Picart* ECLI:EU:C:2018:184, para 29. See further, Peter Van Elsuwege, 'Exporting the Internal Market Beyond the EU's Borders: Between Political Ambition and Legal Reality' in Amtenbrink and others (n 90) 637.

to market indivisibility and/or market integrity that the EEA Agreement thus raises,[94] is indivisibility then more damaging to than facilitative of integrity, since the EEA entails 'exporting' free movement of persons, for example, without the legal guarantees provided by the Charter or Union citizenship? We also reflected on the balance between compromise and integrity and about when costs or prices paid are worth it.

Peter van Elsuwege provided the final thought for Week 9 to bridge to the Brexit discussion in Week 10: 'it is impossible to have your cake (ie, internal market treatment) and eat it (ie rejecting any role for the [Court of Justice] with respect to the interpretation of EU internal market legislation).'[95] In our final seminar, we first assessed the Trade and Cooperation Agreement (TCA)[96] in light of themes raised by the EEA Agreement. We also examined the Ireland/Northern Ireland Protocol, re-engaging with Steve's work on indivisibility in trying to locate how integrity differs. On the TCA, we contrasted the political declarations by Prime Minister Theresa May and Prime Minister Boris Johnson on the post-withdrawal relationship between the UK and the EU, agreeing with Michael Dougan's observation about the 'very different (almost philosophical) starting points' on both sides.[97] We also compared the TCA preamble with the preamble to the EEA Agreement, finding little in the TCA of the 'proximity, long-standing common values and European identity' that ensure 'the fullest possible realization of the free movement of goods, persons, services and capital within the whole European Economic Area'. We then debated, in that light, the Court of Justice's finding in *IN* that 'not only the fact that the person concerned has the status as a national of an EFTA State, which is a party to the EEA Agreement'—in this case, an Icelandic national—'but also the fact that that State implements and applies the Schengen *acquis*, renders the situation of that person objectively comparable with that of an EU citizen to whom, in accordance with Article 3(2) TEU, the Union offers an area of freedom, security and justice without internal frontiers, in which the free movement of persons is ensured'.[98]

All of this really made us think hard about what it means, in legal terms, to have 'a *special* relationship with the European Union, which goes beyond economic and commercial cooperation'.[99] We recognized, in principle, that while '[i]t may seem incongruent that the binding effects of EU law as well as the jurisdiction of EU

[94] Specifically on the EEA Agreement and divisibility of the EU's internal market, see Weatherill, 'The Several Internal Markets' (n 1) 171–72.

[95] Van Elsuwege (n 93) 650.

[96] But guided through it by Steve Peers (at the time, <http://eulawanalysis.blogspot.com/2020/12/analysis-2-of-brexit-deal-euuk-trade.html>; see now, Steve Peers, 'So Close, Yet So Far: The EU/UK Trade and Cooperation Agreement' (2022) 59 Common Market Law Review 49).

[97] Michael Dougan, 'So Long, Farewell, *auf Wiedersehen*, Goodbye: The UK's Withdrawal Package' (2020) 57 Common Market Law Review 631, 697. Compare the first (Theresa May) political declaration setting out the framework for the future relationship between the European Union and the United Kingdom [2019] OJ C66/I/02; and the revised (Boris Johnson) political declaration [2019] OJ C384 I/02.

[98] Case C–897/19 PPU *Ruska Federacija v IN* ECLI:EU:C:2020:262, para 58.

[99] ibid para 44 (emphasis added).

institutions could outlive a State's membership of the Union', it might be possible that 'binding legal legacy effects could be conceived as a particular manifestation of the very specialness of EU law, and the corollary specialness of having been, once, a committed part of the EU's distinctive legal structure'.[100] The problem was that we could find no signs of such intentions in the TCA. In that light, the integrity argument could go both ways: the integrity of the EU's internal market could be argued to have been *preserved* by excluding a relationship premised on divided market freedoms; but it could also be argued that integrity was *eroded* by erasing the depth of the market connection that preceded withdrawal. In contrast, the Ireland/Northern Ireland Protocol sustains an integrated relationship with the internal market, but one based on dividing the freedoms—undermining any claims to indivisibility for Steve; forcing us to consider again whether that matters from the perspective of integrity. We broadly agreed that the wider context of the Protocol entails sustained claims to market integrity, but we remained as divided in Week 10 as we were in Week 2 about the implications of the Protocol for *indivisibility* as a legal concept. However, we agreed that the integrity of the market cannot—should not—be reduced to indivisibility: the latter is an element of the former, but the former is a much broader and deeper idea.

In the closing moments of the course, we then asked: are we always careful (enough) to distinguish integrity of the market, integrity of EU law, and integrity of the Union in a wider sense? We considered the extent to which 'future-facing' integrity is needed in addition to past-facing integrity. We also conceived three further dimensions of integrity: *technical* or *formal* integrity, reflecting indivisibility and convergence debates; *ecosystem* integrity, which also embraces wider dimensions of Union law; and *moral/ethical* integrity, which does have legal content but is more connected to Article 2 TEU values and EU policies around or beyond the internal market. What, then, was on our very final course PowerPoint slide? 'To be continued'.

6. Conclusion: Learning and Teaching the Integrity of the EU's Internal Market

In this chapter, we have offered our collective understanding of the integrity of the EU's internal market as a legal, and legally meaningful, concept. We have presented our evolving ideas through an account of how we formed them in the classroom. Formally, the final task for class members was the course assessment: to identify their own research questions from any part of the course, sketch their arguments briefly in a written abstract, and develop them in more detail in a video presentation

[100] Editorial Comments, 'Polar Exploration: Brexit and the Emerging Frontiers of EU Law' (2018) 55 Common Market Law Review 1, 15.

(another sign of the times). In these assessments, the students applied integrity reasoning to EU citizenship law (Dayana), regulation of technology (Lukas,) social policy (Jovan and Rhian), and to different case studies in continuing to explore integrity in a thematic way (Anthony).

For the purposes of this chapter, class members were asked to complete one further task after graduation: to send reflections by email on their experience of learning about EU internal market law through the lens of integrity. First, there were comments on integrity as a *concept*. For Dayana, the course provoked the distinction yet also interrelation between coherence and 'wholeness'—'the former referring to the logical consistence of the parts that comprise the system and, thus, best studied from within; while wholeness is best perceived and evaluated from the outside'. Other ideas connected to the *functional* purpose of integrity, especially in institutional terms. Dayana returned to Steve's idea of 'sanctioned variation', which, she argues, 'provide[s] some explanation about the hard-balancing act of the Court in maintaining balance between the converging—or conflicting—objectives of the internal market'. For her, sanctioned variation offers a way to 'normalize' apparently conflicting rulings, especially since it positions case law in 'the broader perspective on integration that the Court must maintain. Variation is still sanctioned—it means that the Court acknowledges its role in balancing between the objectives and catering to the different objectives of integration in a reality where priority is not signposted through primary law.' Similarly, for Lukas, given that

> the underlying reality is just too complex to fit into the narrow corset of the four freedoms ... the flexibility and the sometimes-criticised unpredictability ... displayed by the Court's judgments ensures that EU law finds answers to new challenges of the internal market. The fact that the Court does not always 'get it right' is regrettable, but also natural due to the often not solely legal but also political questions that end up in Luxembourg. Therefore, it seems not only acceptable but also natural that there are contrasts between freedoms as the Internal Market changes, at least for as long as the fundamental basis remains intact, and the underlying values[101] are protected.

Jovan emphasized the pivotal role played by the Court of Justice:

> [T]he Court has touched on a few supposedly unshakeable pillars several times so that we must abandon an overly narrow interpretation of integrity. For instance, the disregarding of the cross-border element in *Ruiz Zambrano*, the prevalence of secondary law in *Visser*, the overexpansion of the 'worker' concept in *King* or the

[101] Which change: for Lukas, 'all the different objectives of the Internal Market are subject to a constant process of re-organization and re-balancing, in the light of the law, which in turn is evolving over time'.

indirect acceptance of economic grounds to justify restrictions on free movement rights. Upon a closer look, those judgments per se might seem incoherent or even bizarre. However, from a distance, the overall structure is still perfectly readable and intact. Separate daring or unorthodox cuts to a tree do not necessarily impair its overall appearance. The same applies in a way to the aforementioned judgments of the Court.

Complementing that focus, Anthony considered what integrity might mean for different actors:

A lawyer may criticise the increasingly expanding lack of legal certainty resulting from the Court's role as a reactive co-legislator. A politician could argue the Court is overstepping its jurisdiction and interpreting the Treaties in a direction contrary to what are perceived to be current policy objectives. A Commissioner likely welcomes the arguably expanding margin of appreciation bestowed upon the Commission by the Court in cases concerning FTAs and competition law, while a neoliberal economist angrily screams in the background next to an ordoliberal, who is enjoying the show.

For Rhian:

What struck me the most throughout the course was the isolated nature of the internal market within the legal landscape of the EU. Considering how the internal market fits within the wider Treaty framework, I found the fundamental rights status attributed to the fundamental freedoms problematic. Discussions on this focussed on the centrality of freedom of movement to the internal market and the structural problems that this has created for furthering EU citizenship and social rights. With these objectives side-lined for what are essentially economic rights, it appears that the internal market has become a victim of its own integrationist success and its purpose less clear. With these discussions on conflicting interests within the internal market, I began to think of integrity as a facilitative tool, one which could be useful in guiding the examination of the different interests at stake.

At the same time, *dimensions of integrity beyond law* were underlined. For Jovan, 'when speaking about the integrity of the EU's internal market, it is not only about a contextualisation within the wider EU legal order, but also within the political, economic, scientific, technological or social realities'. Commenting on discordant EU citizenship case law and the possible influence of political mood, Rhian writes:

Whilst never implemented as a result of Brexit, a clear intention on the part of the EU institutions and Member States to sacrifice not only the integrity of

> Article 45 TFEU but also the integrity of the fundamental freedoms operating as a whole is flagrantly obvious [in the 2016 Decision] where it runs contrary to the market-building ethos behind jurisprudence such as *Dassonville*, *Cassis de Dijon*, *Mickelsson and Roos*, *Scotch Whisky* and *Visser*. A question mark hangs over the ability of political pressure to compromise the integrity of the fundamental freedoms, in particular the freedom of movement of persons and workers.

On that point, Anthony observes:

> [I]t seems reasonable to gingerly assert that the Court is likely to maintain its moral integrity and would have likely declared incompatible the changes introduced in the United Kingdom's renegotiated membership accepted by the Commission during the 2015–2016 negotiations. Whether such an approach would diminish legal integrity is another matter, but the damage done to legal consistency in other case law would remain.

Finally, class members reflected directly on their experience of learning internal market law in a thematic way. Lukas writes that:

> As a student of EU law, for a long time, I thought understanding the functioning of the EU's Internal Market was the 'bread-and-butter' business of any academic in this field, remembering the numerous times cases like *Dassonville* or *Cassis de Dijon* had come up over the course of my undergraduate studies. The decision to study the Internal Market from an integrity perspective has challenged this assumption every week since.

To illustrate:

> Influenced by pithy statements from the European Council and the EU's remaining Member States about the indivisibility of the four freedoms in the context of Brexit, I felt confident that a coherent concept of those freedoms exists, whose convergence forms the EU's Internal Market. The study of more controversial Internal Market case law has—in addition to being an emotional rollercoaster—shown that it is not that simple.

Rhian writes:

> When I began to consider the concept of integrity in the context of the internal market, as a British student, my mind immediately went to Brexit and Michel Barnier's infamous 'no cherry-picking' comment during the course of the Brexit negotiations. Indeed, it seems the indivisibility of the fundamental freedoms, a notion that certainly informed my understanding of integrity, has miraculously

emerged from Brexit with renewed vigour. However, the course provided me with an opportunity to shed my pre-conceived notions and to examine integrity outside of the question of if and how the internal market could be divided.

Jovan recalls:

In the beginning, the course title suggested to me that the internal market is to be conceived as a standalone, coherent entity with consistent and strict rules that have been developed and refined over time. Simultaneously, 'integrity' implied that there is an inherent obligation to preserve the internal market according to those rules and any departure from them would make the structure fall. As a result, I expected to study the four freedoms as they are laid down in the Treaties and as they are construed by the Court's case law. In order to protect the integrity of the internal market, so I assumed, any situation or challenge of the ever-changing reality must be brought in line with the Treaty provisions on the four freedoms. However, these (admittedly naïve) initial ideas were soon to be dissolved on different levels.

He further explains:

[M]y initial idea of integrity relating to the internal market has definitely changed. It does not mean to preserve a status quo of the internal market and its basic rules without allowing any leeway for divergent solutions. Integrity should rather be conceptualised as an underpinning ideal which shall guide us when construing the internal market, but at the same time *requires* us to depart from a strict, dogmatic application of the law in certain cases. Although this might seem a bit of an unusual comparison, sometimes I could not help thinking of the discussion on the right exegesis of religious sources. The textual sources are recorded and authoritative, yet it is widely undisputed that they must be interpreted according to shifting contextual factors. In doing so, the integrity of the underlying religious doctrine is not undermined, but 'translated' to the needs of the present. Perhaps this applies in a similar way to the integrity of the EU's internal market.

Finally, Anthony comments that, '[p]ersonally, the hardest general realisation in examining the integrity of the internal market is that "integrity" is not necessarily a singular absolute concept and, especially in the context of the EU, has many aspects and instances'. He adds:

[E]ven after all these considerations and quasi-objective conclusions, and as discouraging it may be, integrity is—at least to a considerable extent—subjective. As a European citizen with low trust in their country's government, I find myself in strong support of maximum harmonisation and further overall centralisation of

> the Union acquis and competencies. I see that as fair, integral, and a necessity for the global age. That is integrity for me, and of course, I always do my best to read and assess the scenarios of harmonisation or convergence from a legal perspective. Still, it would be dishonest of me to claim there are no strong personal ideals eternally tempting me in a specific direction.

But he ends on a note of optimism:

> Despite what it may seem from the above, it's not all doom and gloom. In fact, I would argue none of it is. Throughout the semester, I have come to realise that the at first seemingly masochistic undertaking to examine the integrity of a Union that has been often described as 'a roof without walls' is not only intriguing but necessary. With each unprecedented development, the 'roof' becomes larger, and the absence of the proverbial walls becomes less convenient to ignore. The time for structural action is ever approaching, and it will need to be done properly, hopefully drawing on those concepts of integrity through harmonisation, responsible decrease in reactive judicial co-legislation, convergence through EU citizenship, and appropriate yet incentivising third-country agreements.

In conclusion, on teaching through the lens of integrity, the course probably raised more questions than answers for the first author of this chapter, but in the best sense. For me, there is something inherently positive—noble, even—about the very idea of integrity and so I find it deeply and intuitively appealing to think about integrity as an organizing concept for EU lawmakers: in other words, it seems to provoke a 'good' standard or objective, somehow, even by the mere act of invoking it. But I was consistently reminded that concepts, even if also legal principles, cannot provide us with absolutes: integrity, as we have discussed, allows for difference. What we need to think more about is how we manage differences appropriately. Therefore, trying to ensure that concepts and principles still have meaningful and tangible value even when they are (rightly) fluid is one of the main challenges that I keep thinking about since this course ended. More broadly, the internal market is not just about the market. More broadly still, the EU is not just about the EU, or what happens within its borders.

The course has also made me think about trends in teaching EU law more generally. As this chapter demonstrates, the interested core group was already small in size, and the course did not run at all in the following academic year. As the Union's activities both expand and become more specialized, it is natural that students are drawn to courses that drill into more defined areas, such as data protection, climate change, and the legal dimensions of new technology. It is perhaps also not surprising that as student interest in internal market law contracted, 'The EU's Changing Constitution' course grew significantly. There, we addressed day-by-day developments on issues such as the rule of law and crisis management.

Nevertheless, the sense that EU internal market seems 'done'[102] does concern me, for that is how cases like *Visser* can slip through without much attention: yet a judgment upending the primary/secondary law hierarchy should surely attract quite a lot more of it?

Finally, to Steve: thank you for joining us, not only through the characteristically brilliant work that we focused on for this course but also through the vast contribution to EU law that your piercing insights have made more widely. It continues to teach us.

[102] We noted with relief and appreciation Inge Govaere's comment that '[t]he internal market is one of the few EU concepts which is expressly defined in the Treaties. All is not, however, thereby said and done' ((n 88) 75). Lukas also expressed the hope that 'even though my initial belief of having understood the Internal Market has been shattered, by looking at it through the lens of integrity, there will be a demand of students of EU Internal Market law for the foreseeable future to accompany this time-honoured and ever-changing field of EU law'.

19

The Archaeology of an Examination Paper

*Jo Shaw**

1. Prologue

In July 2021, just as I started to go back into the office after the second lockdown, an A5 envelope appeared in my pigeonhole. Perhaps it had been there for a while. I hadn't been into the staffroom to collect my post for some time, mainly because there was rarely anything of interest, as I had redirected all book deliveries to my home address.

I recognized the writing on the envelope. Do you remember those times when you knew the handwriting of your academic colleagues and friends? The slim envelope contained some pieces of paper and a Post-it. On the Post-it was written, in the same recognizable handwriting: 'Amazing the stuff you come across when you're clearing out your office xx'. No signature or other sign off. I knew that style of communication well.

I unfolded the pieces of paper and at the top of one of them I read the words:

'LAW TRIPOS Part II'.

Further details were set out below:
Friday 28 May 1982
9 to 12
Paper 46
E.E.C. LAW
Answer four *questions.*
I will return to those questions later.

The other piece of paper states that it is '© PJ Allott' and shows a graph illustrating some key aspects of the Common Agricultural Policy as it applied to cereals. The axes of the graph are price and time, and thus the curve shows the evolution of the price of cereals over time. I think it was part of a lecture handout. It looks vaguely

* Many thanks to Niamh Nic Shuibhne for comments on an earlier draft of this chapter, and also for sharing with me her contribution to this volume. That encouraged me to write something a bit different by way of my own tribute to Professor Stephen Weatherill.

Jo Shaw, *The Archaeology of an Examination Paper* In: *The Internal Market Ideal.* Edited by: Jeremias Adams-Prassl, Sanja Bogojević, Ariel Ezrachi, and Dorota Leczykiewicz, Oxford University Press. © Jo Shaw 2024.
DOI: 10.1093/oso/9780192867063.003.0020

familiar, although it would take me some time to work out what everything on the piece of paper means.

2. Starting Off by Looking Back

Let us go back to that date in May 1982 at the University of Cambridge. It represents one of the early occasions when Steve Weatherill ('SRW') and I were definitely in the same room at the same time doing the same thing. Writing an examination. We had been obviously in the same room for lectures in EEC Law, including Philip Allott's speedy guide to the Common Agricultural Policy, but the lecture hall did not offer such an intense experience as the examination hall and so left relatively little mark on me.[1]

That Friday morning, forty years ago, was one of the last written, timed, and closed-book examinations I ever had to take, following what seemed like a lifetime of sitting in examination rooms experiencing that familiar dread and rush of adrenaline (although it self-evidently was not a lifetime, with the benefit of hindsight; it was just over a decade, essentially between the ages of ten and twenty). I didn't know many other people who took the EEC Law course as an optional choice during their law degree, and I didn't know SRW. We are talking about a time long before EU law became a compulsory part of the qualifying law degree in Scotland (first) and then England, as one of the foundations of legal knowledge for legal practice in the UK. Probably for many people, at that time, it did not seem terribly relevant to their prospective lives as solicitors in the City of London or at the Bar (also in London). They were clearly wrong about that, although not necessarily always in ways that we could have predicted at the time. There was no one to supervise EEC Law in Trinity College that year, so I had to trek to other colleges for supervisions, including the rather new Robinson College. My memory is so poor that for all I know, SRW was in those same supervisions. I can't speak for SRW's motivation in choosing this subject, but I think for me it was something to do with referencing back to my 'roots' as a student, who did Part I Modern Languages (French and German), before changing to do Part IB and Part II Law. [I wrote about how those choices related to family circumstances in the preface to *The Transformation of Citizenship in the European Union*;[2] taking EEC Law both as an

[1] I do keenly remember one incident from the lecture room, and that came first thing in the morning on 5 November 1980, the day after the US presidential election. Someone from my class (James Brown, if I remember correctly: I wonder what happened to him ...) stood up at the front of the lecture hall before the lecturer arrived to tell us that we should fear for the end of the world as we knew it with the election of Ronald Reagan. I was so out of touch with day-to-day politics that this was the first time I had ever heard of Reagan. Because Steve studied law for three years at the University of Cambridge, and I studied it only for two, he would not have been in that lecture hall to hear that outburst.

[2] Jo Shaw, *The Transformation of Citizenship in the European Union: Electoral Rights and the Restructuring of Political Space* (Cambridge University Press 2007).

undergraduate and as a postgraduate represented an excellent way of triangulating between these two points of focus which related to my family life.] In the end, it was also the course in which I scored my highest mark in Part II. My path was set.

Although I did not know SRW in 1982,[3] we had a number of things in common that marked us out at the University of Cambridge at that time, such as a northern English grammar school background. Neither of us pursued the course that most of our peers took in becoming solicitors or barristers. Although Steve has now 'emerited', the core of that pathway continues in parallel. We went to university in 1979 and did not really leave again. Meanwhile, most of those who went into the City of London after university made partner very early on during the massive expansion of the legal profession in the UK in the 1980s and early 1990s, burned out, and were doing pottery courses at the Camberwell School of Arts or making chutneys in Devon by the time I saw them again at our thirty-year college reunion in the late noughties. Ten years later, at our forty-year reunion, they were bored stiff once again, and now looking for a third 'career'. Meanwhile, I had just kept 're-inventing' myself using different versions of the academic life, including teaching, research, and management. Retirement, but writing—SRW's chosen vocation for his seventh decade—will come to me, I hope, in due course.

Our pathways after Cambridge both took us to places of renown in relation to the study of European Community law. SRW came to Edinburgh, where I now work, and studied in what was then the Centre for European Governmental Studies (CEGLS) but is now the Edinburgh Europa Institute. He took an MSc, because at the time there was no LLM degree in the Faculty of Law.[4] The CEGLS had been founded in 1968 and was the first 'centre of excellence' for the study of European law (in its widest sense) in the UK, but it was always strongly connected—as it still now is—to the Faculties of both Law and Social Sciences (as they were then termed; now, the School of Law and the School of Social and Political Sciences, specifically the subject area of Politics and International Relations). SRW was a student soon after the sudden death in 1980 of JWB Mitchell, the first holder of the Salvesen Chair of European Institutions. It was during an interregnum in which the university had one of its periodic freezes on new professorial appointments. One of Steve's principal teachers at Edinburgh would have been John Usher, then a lecturer and later himself the Salvesen Chair in the 1990s and 2000s. Studying European Community law in Edinburgh under the shadow of JWB Mitchell's dramatic but prescient interventions in relation to how we should now understand the Diceyan concept of

[3] Or indeed any others of the 'Class of '82 lawyers' whose names are now reasonably well known in legal circles such as Vivien Rose, Justice of the Supreme Court of the UK, or Richard Hart of the eponymous publishing company.

[4] I am grateful for this information, which comes via my colleague Professor Niamh Nic Shuibhne from Professor Sir David Edward, who took up the post of Salvesen Chair in the Law Faculty in 1985. During Sir David's time in the Faculty of Law, the LLM, including the LLM in European Law, was created. See also Nic Shuibhne's and others' contribution to this book.

parliamentary sovereignty in view of the UK's membership of the EEC (on which more later), and shortly after John Usher published his ground-breaking book *The Irreversible Transfer?*,[5] represents an unbeatable grounding in the topic going way beyond what we had experienced in our one optional course in Cambridge.

Meanwhile, I went to Brussels and studied, largely in French, at the Institut des Études Européennes, part of the Université libre de Bruxelles, which had been around even longer than CEGLS, having been founded in 1962. There I learned about the horror of oral examinations (although I proved to be quite good at them, much to my surprise). Sadly, too much of that programme (a *licence spéciale*) comprised rote learning and regurgitation of course books that we had to buy, which comprised the essence of the professors' lecture notes. Our paths 'crossed' again soon afterwards, because after I left Brussels, I went to work at University College London as a 'research assistant' for John Usher, who had just moved from Edinburgh to UCL, and for Bob Hepple. In practice, they required no 'assistance' and both left me to my own devices to get on with whatever pleased me. At that time, I wasn't very sure what it was, although it was mainly European Community law. As it happens, neither of us went on to do a doctorate, which was quite common amongst academic legal scholars of our generation, and we both gained open-ended lectureships at an age, and with a level of research and teaching experience, which most today would regard as astonishing.

Whereas I spent much of the 1980s wondering what sort of academic I really wanted to be, SRW found his niche early, in the sub-field of EEC law that I had learned in Brussels to call *le droit économique*. This is one of those French terms for which there is no good English language equivalent. 'Trade law' and 'economic law' just don't do it. 'Common market law' was sometimes reserved for the whole subject, in homage to the UK's purported membership of the Common Market after 1973, and that was what the course was still called when I joined Keele University Law Department in 1990. By the end of the 1980s, SRW was a well-established and prolific publisher across the fields of free movement of goods, consumer law (a then-emerging area of Community legislation which raised fascinating and difficult questions about the scope and nature of competence), the evolving single market project, and competition law, with a side hustle in relation to some institutional questions especially surrounding the preliminary reference procedure. Before the end of the 1980s, SRW had also helped to establish the sub-field for which he is best known these days, namely EU sports law. His contribution came in the form of a paper in the *Yearbook of European Law* on discrimination on grounds of nationality in the field of sports.[6] The paper addressed the question of

[5] John Usher, *European Community Law and National Law: The Irreversible Transfer?* (George Allen & Unwin 1981).

[6] Stephen Weatherill, 'Discrimination on Grounds of Nationality in Sport' (1989) 9 Yearbook of European Law 55.

the extent of responsibility of private employers for discriminatory practices that would breach Article 48 EEC, building on the conclusions of the Court of Justice in *Walrave and Koch*.[7] This was, of course, long before the ship of *Bosman* sailed forth to grab everyone's attention in 1995 by confirming the applicability of Community law to the (national) regulatory side of sports, thereby significantly opening up the market for cross-national transfers of sports stars.[8] SRW tells us:

> My interest in writing the article published in 1989 was largely driven by the appreciation that sport offers a testing ground for an oddity in the structure of EU trade law. That is to say, I was using sport to try and develop a better understanding of EU law, rather than taking sport as the main focus of inquiry.[9]

Aye, right, Steve. Nothing to do with your passion for Hull City and various other football teams. Anyway, what we know for sure is that an interest in sports law and the EU has been an enduring *leitmotiv* of SRW's career. In 2022, and happily ensconced in retirement, we find SRW delivering the Mackenzie Stuart lecture at the Centre for European Legal Studies at his *alma mater*, the University of Cambridge, on the topic of 'Saving Football from Itself: Why and How to Re-make EU Sports Law'.

I cannot remember when SRW and I first met, but I do know that we lived in the same city (Nottingham) between 1993 and 1995 and we had definitely met before then. I was also by then the happy recipient of regular deliveries through the post of paper offprints (remember those?) of SRW's excellent publications, complete with more of those Delphic messages. Sadly, I rarely had anything quite so substantial and discipline-shaping to send in return, as I only properly found my academic voice in the late 1990s.

The delivery of paper offprints ceased at a certain point, but the Delphic communications (by now arriving via email) have continued, often as a commentary upon something I had put on Twitter, which led me to the conclusion that SRW is or has been a lurker there. Such as knowing that my dad had died and telling me which mountain top in the Lake District a certain photograph from my childhood that I'd put in an obscure corner of the internet had been taken on. [Helvellyn, since you ask.] Our most recent round of email communications came in February 2021, as I learned of SRW's decision to retire as a result of getting the invitation to contribute to this *Festschrift*. I wrote to offer him my congratulations on making such a life-shaping change in his circumstances. To me, this came as a double surprise, as not only was I a bit shocked that SRW was stepping back from frontline academic

[7] Case 36/74 *Walrave and Koch v Association Union Cycliste Internationale* ECLI:EU:C:1974:140.

[8] Case C-415/93 *Union royale belge des sociétés de football association ASBL v Jean-Marc Bosman* ECLI:EU:C:1995:463.

[9] Stephen Weatherill, 'Introduction' in *European Sports Law: Collected Papers* (TMC Asser Press 2014) 6–7.

work at a relatively young age (he's six months older than me), but the news also came in the month when I was signing back up to some managerial responsibilities and indeed to what now seems likely to be another five to six years at the coalface. This was after several years enjoying the luxury of a fellowship allowing me to focus on my research. Amidst discussions of the horror of EU lawyers being asked to teach not what they had been teaching for decades—ie EU law per se—but rather EU law in the (post-Brexit) UK (including the Withdrawal Agreement, retained EU law, the TCA, dynamic alignment, and so on), came a typical sign off: 'Daffs on the way, mind. It's soft down south.' At heart, we are both still northerners.

3. Settling Down to Answer the Questions

Back to that examination paper. By giving it closer scrutiny, I can also use it to offer some reflections on how the study of EU law and the context in which it is set has changed over the years. The examination paper doubtless reflects the preoccupations of the person who set it, and it comprises a mixture of some tricky problem questions and some standard 'regurgitative' essay questions, which would barely look out of place today. It contains quite a lot of competition law, but no question on the Common Agricultural Policy, despite our having taken a *tour d'horizon* of that topic with Philip Allott. Question 10 opens with a quotation from *National Panasonic*[10] about fundamental rights forming 'an integral part of the general principles of law the observance of which the Court of Justice ensures'. The question line is this: 'Do you consider that the form of protection envisaged by the Court is sufficient?' I was still setting versions of that question in examinations well into the 1990s. Even in the age of the Charter of Fundamental Rights, the 'general principles of EU law' remain an important topic of research[11] and are widely taught on EU law courses.[12]

I recall a few fragments of that morning forty years ago. One was my surprise (and disappointment) at finding that there was no question focusing directly on the relatively recently decided and obviously ground-breaking *Cassis de Dijon* case.[13] In addition, my comprehensive study of the Articles 9–12 EEC cases on charges having equivalent effect and the distinction between a tax and a charge was rendered nugatory as soon as I realized it did not feature in the examination, although

[10] Case 136/79 *National Panasonic (UK) Ltd v Commission* ECLI:EU:C:1980:169.

[11] For a recent example, see Giuseppe Martinico, 'Exploring the Platonic Heaven of Law: General Principles of EU Law from a Comparative Perspective' (2022) 3 Nordic Journal of European Law 1–18 <https://ssrn.com/abstract=4009794> accessed 11 October 2023.

[12] In fact, the University of Edinburgh's EU Law (Ordinary) examination paper for 2020–21 contained just such a question: 'What is the role of general principles of EU law? Are they still relevant today?'

[13] Case 120/78 *Rewe-Zentral AG v Bundesmonopolverwaltung für Branntwein (Cassis de Dijon)* ECLI:EU:C:1979:42.

it came in handy the following year in Brussels when I was forced to go into the topic in even more depth. This in-depth knowledge eventually found a home in my textbook (and obviously in my lecture notes, back in the day).[14] The only question on the free movement of goods was a complex one that linked Articles 30–36 EEC into a free trade agreement with a third state which contains those same provisions (so the question would be *how* these provisions should be interpreted), and which also combined elements of copyright law and national enforcement practices. It would take me weeks to unravel the complexities of that question, especially nowadays. I do not recall whether I attempted it, but I suspect not.

There was another tricky problem question on the free movement of persons, involving a Greek professor retiring from his university in Greece and being offered a visiting professor contract in Paris at the National School of Administration, which concerned mainly issues about the scope of the public service exception in Article 48 EEC.[15] However, if I remember correctly, I spied an opportunity to shoehorn some of my thoughts on indistinctly applicable restrictive national measures (as regards a general policy of the Greek government to refuse all age limit derogations in respect of academic appointments) into the scope of that question, allowing me to raise the issue of 'what if' the principles in *Cassis de Dijon* were to be regarded as applicable in the sphere of the free movement of persons. Perhaps the prescience of those observations is what secured me a first-class mark in this paper. In those days, we were given only the vaguest idea as to our individual marks in each paper, and it was indicated to me that EEC Law was my best paper. How those marks fed into the eventual class of degree we achieved was even more mysterious. So, I'm working with pretty sparse material here, but I think I did well.

Thinking about some of the questions on the paper does reinforce how far EU law has travelled. Take the question (which, from the annotations that he made, I would say is one that SRW answered) about the extent to which membership of the Communities derogates from the external sovereignty of the Member States. It is interesting to see this reference to *external sovereignty*, which for the time seems quite far-sighted. Those were the days of *ERTA*.[16] This question perhaps comes closest to acknowledging what has since become a core dimension of studying EU law: the recognition that, along with its Member States, the EU itself is also a polity and not *just* a legal order. And this has consequences. However, I doubt that many of those Cambridge students will have answered this question by reference to constitutional tenets relating to the delimiting effects of occupying the field. SRW's

[14] Jo Shaw, *European Community Law* (Macmillan 1993).

[15] No account is taken in the question of the fact that, at that point in time (1982), Greece was still in the transitional period for the free movement of workers. Perhaps there were points to be gained by spotting this. I don't think it was something that impinged upon me at the time; transition periods became much more of a 'thing' only after the 2004 enlargement.

[16] Case 22/70 *Commission v Council (ERTA)* ECLI:EU:C:1971:32.

step into this field in the 1982 examination presages his ground-breaking work in the following decade on competence, integration, and pre-emption.[17]

There are two questions in the examination paper about the relationship between national law and Community law in the internal domain. Question 6, where SRW has crossed out the number and not written any notes, looks at the distinction between direct effect and direct applicability and raises the impact of this distinction upon the status of Community legal acts within the national legal orders. Perhaps I answered that question, as it seems to ring a bell, but then the distinction between a concept (direct applicability) which relates to how Community law penetrates into the national legal orders and a concept (direct effect) which relates to the duties of national courts to give effect to obligations under Community law is something that obsessed me for several decades to come.[18] One is a federal variant on the question of the reception of international law and the other is a fundamental constitutional and institutional challenge. However, I find that surprisingly few people seem to see it in those terms. Never mind.

The other question is written from the perspective of national law. Question 8 builds upon a classic quotation from *Simmenthal (No 2)*:[19]

> A national court which is called upon . . . to apply provisions of Community law is under a duty to give full effect to those provisions, if necessary refusing of its own motion to apply any conflicting provision of national legislation.

The question line then continues: 'How do you consider that the English courts should reconcile this principle with the principles of the British constitution?' This question carries extensive annotations from SRW, so I assume that he did answer it.[20] What is significant about the question is that it *does not* ask the student to go deep into the nature of the principle of primacy and what it means for a non-state polity to have such a principle. This is a disappointing omission. The question dates from the time of Derrick Wyatt's significant contribution to the nature of the Community legal order, which was published in the 1982 *European Law Review*. This article muses on the question whether the Community constitutes a 'new legal order or old', by reference to classic understandings of national and international law.[21] However,

[17] Stephen Weatherill, *Law and Integration in the European Union* (Clarendon Press 1995); Stephen Weatherill, 'Beyond Preemption? Shared Competence and Constitutional Change in the European Community' in David O'Keeffe and Patrick Twomey (eds), *Legal Issues of the Maastricht Treaty* (Chancery 1994).

[18] See most recently Jo Shaw, *Law of the European Union* (3rd edn, Macmillan 2000).

[19] Case 106/77 *Amministrazione delle Finanze dello Stato v Simmenthal* ECLI:EU:C:1978:49.

[20] For the record, the annotations seem to indicate that aside from Q8 (primacy) and Q3 (external sovereignty), SRW also answered Q5 (abuse of a dominant position) and Q9 (a question about *Plaumann*, art 173 EEC, and direct and individual concern).

[21] Derrick Wyatt, 'New Legal Order, or Old?' (1982) 7 European Law Review 147. I remember reading this article the following academic year (and of course several times again since then).

I do not see traces of Wyatt's broader reflections in the question in the examination paper, highlighting a narrower and nationally focused perspective on this matter.

The question as set is preoccupied with the issue of national reception. In the UK, this concerned discerning how the courts could bend and rework that generally pliable instrument, the UK constitution, in the interests of achieving an appropriate acknowledgement of Community law in the UK. But one thing in that constitutional set-up is not so pliable, at least not according to orthodox constitutional theory, and that is the doctrine of parliamentary sovereignty and the principle that no parliament may bind its successors. In that context, how on earth could we understand the European Communities Act 1972 to be anything other than an ordinary Act of Parliament, vulnerable even to the risk of implied repeal, and certainly liable to be changed should the expressed will of the Westminster Parliament become such that European Community law should no longer apply in the UK (as it did in 2020)? In those pre-*Factortame* years,[22] the accommodation of the potentially competing demands of the British constitution and the demands of EU law achieved by the UK courts for around twenty-five years seemed a long way off.

4. The UK in the EU: A Matter of Both Legal and Personal Experience

Whenever I write about the EU legal order, especially from an historical perspective, I emphasize that what we could regard as the elements of the 'old constitution' of the European Union, namely the doctrines of direct effect, primacy, pre-emption, implied powers, and general principles of EU law, were all in place by 1970, before the UK's belated accession to the European Communities.[23] This belies, of course, the mantra that we were 'only' signing up in 1973 to join a so-called 'Common Market'. These doctrines together build what EU lawyers have now been calling for decades 'the constitutionalization of the treaties', although that language does not seep into this 1982 examination paper. But JWB Mitchell makes precisely this point in his 1979 *International Affairs* paper, which is intended to explain clearly to readers without expertise in law why the UK's parliamentary sovereignty, framed primarily by reference to Victorian jurist Dicey,[24]

[22] *R v Secretary of State for Transport, ex p Factortame Ltd (No 2)* [1991] 1 AC 603.

[23] Jo Shaw, 'The European Union: Discipline Building Meets Polity Building' in Peter Cane and Mark Tushnet (eds), *The Oxford Handbook of Legal Studies* (Oxford University Press 2003) and Jo Shaw, 'The European Union and Global Constitutionalism' in Anthony Lang and Antje Wiener (eds), *The Handbook of Global Constitutionalism* (Edward Elgar 2017).

[24] Martin Loughlin and Stephen Tierney, 'The Shibboleth of Sovereignty' (2018) 81 Modern Law Review 989.

is not a stumbling block to judicial and wider legal acceptance of the *Simmenthal* doctrine:[25]

> For the moment, what matters is simply the point that, already by 1973, the Treaty of Rome had become a constitution having its effects within the internal law of the whole Community and having consequentially effects, even then sufficiently clear, on the constitutional situation and internal law of each of the original Member States.

Indeed, there is something strangely lopsided about Question 8. It talks of the impact on the constitution of the UK. Of course, one could also talk in an answer to this question about reception of Community law in other Member States, as a point of comparison (and from his annotations that is what I discern SRW chose to do, drawing on what, by then, was a longer experience in some of the founding Member States). But there is nothing about the question which acknowledges the constitutional nature of what were then, in legal terms, the European Communities. Instead, it references the nature of the Community legal order only in terms of bare legal doctrines and misses out one of the key referents which has become and remains central to the idea of a multi-level constitutional order, the idea of 'constitutionalism beyond the state'. Throughout the examination paper, the European Communities come across as legal order without polity. This is hardly surprising. This was, after all, the orthodox perspective that a large proportion of the British legal establishment preferred to take throughout most of the nearly fifty years of the UK's membership. However, as a scholar of EU law, my perceptions of that legal order and of the role of constitutionalism grew to be quite different. This was not only about scholarly preferences, but also found its roots in personal experience.

My earliest political memory, which was not mediated via the agency of my parents (eg their reaction to the 1974 General Election victory by Harold Wilson), concerns the UK's 1975 referendum on the 'Common Market'. I attended a husting in Bingley Little Theatre for the referendum, although I was too young to vote. This referendum concerned whether to reverse the earlier decision to accede to the European Communities as of 1 January 1973. That decision had been driven forward by the 1970–74 Conservative government of Prime Minister Edward Heath, and was taken by a combination of executive action (signature of the treaties) and legislative action (adoption of a resolution of the House of Commons to pursue negotiations and passing of the European Communities Act 1972 to give domestic effect to the Treaties). In the end, the 1975 referendum was won quite comfortably by

[25] JDB Mitchell, 'The Sovereignty of Parliament and Community Law: The Stumbling-Block That Isn't There' (1979) 55 International Affairs 33, 34.

the 'remain' brigade. This success probably added something to David Cameron's evident and misplaced complacency in 2016.

I was part of a Tory-voting northern family, long before the days of the so-called Red Wall. This was true on both sides of the family, even the working-class maternal side, who were Conservative-voting miners from South Yorkshire and later wool factory workers in the West Riding. My grandfather was a scion of the Conservative Club in the Shipley constituency that elected Marcus Fox as MP for decades. But it was also a European family. In the late 1940s, while still at school, my mother had been a beneficiary of cultural exchanges for young people between the West Riding of Yorkshire and Lille in Northern France (started up with energy and a sense of adventure in the wake of the Second World War). She later studied and taught modern languages in high schools. And we regularly took our family-sized tent and motor caravan on lengthy summer holidays motoring across Europe, often meeting up with families she had known for decades in northern France and attending their family celebrations. To me, it seemed obvious that being 'part of Europe', as opposed to adjacent to Europe, was the right thing. Somewhere along the line, something changed, as I gather my late father voted Leave in 2016. In fact, my brother tells me that he probably voted to leave in 1975. Somehow, I think my mother would have voted to remain, so they would have cancelled each other out. However, she was sadly no longer around to vote in 2016. I never confronted my father about how his voting choices affected my life and my work. I had, in any event, been jerked out of any complacency about the 2016 referendum not only by the self-evident hostility of my father (and others of his ilk) to what they had come to perceive as the meddling works of 'Brussels' but also by the shock of the relatively narrow result in the referendum on that other union that I'd previously assumed to be enduring, namely that between Scotland and England. This had been put under the microscope in the September 2014 referendum on Scottish independence.

Mitchell's singular contribution to studies of the reception of Community law in the UK emerged out of his understanding of the UK as a union state. He highlighted that, just as in 1707 with the union of the parliaments, and indeed in 1931 with the establishment of the dominions (although in the latter case no one really seemed to notice), we stood in (legal) revolutionary times in 1973. This was in the sense that the UK was 'joining' a new constitutional settlement and thus changing the *grundnorm* of its own constitution in just the same way as it did with the union of the parliaments.[26] Consequently, what for Mitchell really mattered was accession itself—a treaty signed on behalf of the state by the executive, and buttressed by a parliamentary vote in 1971[27]—not the European Communities Act 1972 which,

[26] JDB Mitchell, SA Kuipers, and B Gall, 'Constitutional Aspects of the Treaty and Legislation Relating to British Membership' (1972) 9 Common Market Law Review 134.

[27] HC Deb 28 October 1971, vol 823, cols 2076–217.

according to dualist orthodoxy, was necessary in order to give effect to Community law (as a species of international law) in the UK.[28] However, he definitely admired the smart drafting of the Act, which was designed to reflect the dynamic and evolving character of European Community law. Of course, in a reflection of how life and practice can intersect, one of the principal drafters of that Act was none other than Philip Allott, during his years at the Foreign Office, before he returned to Trinity College.[29]

After the 1975 referendum, the contortions around the Treaty of Maastricht and the ultimately toothless European Union Act 2011, it was only through the reassertion of popular sovereignty in the guise of the 2016 referendum that this constitutional fact could legitimately be changed. This was yet another (legal) revolution, played out between 2016 and the end of 2020. As is well known,[30] the dominant players in the convoluted process of change after the referendum became the executive, the legislature, and the courts, and—as subsidiary actors in this context—the figure of the Speaker of the House of Commons, the political parties which went through a variety of contortions, and the devolved institutions within the UK's own unsettled and asymmetric constitutional settlement. While the popular sovereign receded into the background during the elongated process of leaving the EU, its shadow continued to hang over the post-referendum political and legal engagements within the UK and between the UK and the EU. This, in Eoin Daly's view, is hardly surprising, since 'popular sovereignty remains an inexhaustible principle irreducible to any contingent institutional expression'. Furthermore, 'this not only allows the people to reject the formal limits imposed by such contingent arrangements, [but] it also offers a symbolic resource to be instrumentalized by the constituted organs of government.'[31]

5. The Conundrum of Democracy in a Multi-level Constitutional Settlement

Yet still there is something missing, both in Mitchell's analysis and in the examination paper itself. This concerns democracy. I agree with Mitchell's claim that the European Communities of which he wrote in the 1960s and 1970s already constituted a polity. In that sense, accession brought the UK within a multi-level

[28] eg Henry WR Wade, 'Sovereignty and the European Communities' (1972) 88 Law Quarterly Review 1.

[29] Lesley Dingle and Daniel Bates, 'Second Interview: The Foreign Office Years (1960–1973)' in *Conversations with Professor Philip James Allott*, available at <www.repository.cam.ac.uk/bitstream/handle/1810/321157/allott%20INTERVIEW%202.pdf?sequence=1> (and part of the Eminent Scholars Archive: <www.squire.law.cam.ac.uk/cambridge-law-eminent-scholars-archive>).

[30] Stephen Tierney, 'Parliament and the Brexit Process: The Battle for Constitutional Supremacy in the United Kingdom' (2022) 12 Notre Dame Journal of International & Comparative Law 1.

[31] Eoin Daly, 'Popular Sovereignty After Brexit' (2022) 23 German Law Journal 1, 11.

constitutional settlement that provokes profound democratic challenges.[32] Speaking of the UK as a polity, with an evolving constitutional settlement, Mitchell refers to the role of (representative) democracy when discussing the role of 'schemes for readjustment of life', which provided—in his view—the reason why Common lawyers conceded the primacy of statute, and thus of Parliament. This was a Parliament which was, as he noted, elected on much wider franchise, although not universal, after the Reform Acts. Common law cannot build such schemes for 'readjustment of life'—that is to say, the things that became in the twentieth century public goods, such as pensions, unemployment insurance, and the National Health Service. Of course, Mitchell's comments long predated the enactment of devolution in the UK after the 1997 election, although in his lifetime Scotland had already failed once to agree by referendum to the re-establishment of the Scottish Parliament (in 1979). Thus, from Mitchell's perspective, all of these were matters—at the time—for the Westminster Parliament.

Yet Mitchell does not mention the conundrum of democracy in the decision-making processes of the European Communities. This is perhaps strange. By the time Mitchell wrote his final works, and certainly by 1982 (the date of the examination paper with which I began these reflections), the European Parliament had already transformed into a directly elected chamber, with the first elections taking place in 1979. Even so, the position of that institution within the Community's scheme for the adoption of legislation remained subsidiary to those of the European Commission and (especially) the Council of Ministers and the decisive juncture of the Single European Act (and its introduction of the cooperation procedure which began the process of the European Parliament morphing into a co-legislature with the Council of Ministers) still lay some way in the future (1985). Furthermore, at the time there was no doubt that in political terms the European Communities were firmly in the grip of political 'eurosclerosis', with only the role of the Court of Justice and the European Commission as animators of integration offering what could be seen as hopeful signs of a European Communities that could aim to match the objectives of the so-called founding fathers. Yet already by the time the UK joined the European Communities, a smattering of references to the 'democratic deficit' could be found in the scholarly literature; there were certainly some who were aware of the looming problem, even though the issue plays no role in either Mitchell's principal works or in the examination paper.[33]

It has taken decades to work through the paradox that a more successful and more political European Union is a less democratic and legitimate one. Thus, in the third decade of the twenty-first century, democracy is very much on the agenda,

[32] Richard Bellamy, *A Republican Europe of States: Cosmopolitanism, Intergovernmentalism and Democracy in the EU* (Cambridge University Press 2019).

[33] Prodromos Dagtoglou, 'European Communities and Constitutional Law' (1973) 32 Cambridge Law Journal 256.

although the paradox is still not fully resolved. While it remains true that the EU does not deal directly with the 'readjustment of life' in the sense that it runs no schools or hospitals or welfare schemes, nonetheless its actions can and do have a direct impact on human well-being, especially via the medium of laws and policies underpinning monetary union but also in other areas (especially in the context of post-Covid recovery). To that extent, democratic deliberation over crucial choices is a key issue and cannot be exhausted by the traditional threefold reference points: the direct election of the European Parliament, the accountability of the European Commission to the Parliament, and the indirect representative character of the government ministers who sit in the Council of Ministers and whose legitimacy stems from national elections. In 2021, University of Edinburgh EU Law (Ordinary) students were asked the following question: 'Based on an analysis of primary EU law, critically discuss the democratic nature of the EU as a polity.'[34] Any student who gave a strong answer to that question will have concluded that while there is plenty of primary material on concepts and practices of democracy, especially since the Treaty of Lisbon, there is less evidence of how that actually carries through in terms of democratic processes that materially engage 'the people'. The issue continues to be a challenge, notwithstanding the novel attempts to activate deliberative democracy through a citizens' assembly of randomly chosen citizens in the recently launched Conference on the Future of Europe[35] and the continuing usage of the European Citizens' Initiative. Both real and perceived democratic failures in 'Europe' and 'Brussels' certainly played a role in the successful campaign for a Leave vote in 2016. Those who voted Leave would, however, be as unmoved by statements from the Court of Justice about democracy as a value on which the Union is founded,[36] as they would be by what might be seen by some as the charade of a citizens' assembly or the pointlessness of a citizens' initiative that effectively cannot change the law.

The UK's withdrawal from the European Union hit academic lawyers of our generation hard. Membership of the EU has been part of both our personal and professional adult lives, and moving forward from here has been difficult emotional and sometimes practical labour. As democrats, we accept that the expression of political opinion may not always concord with our preferences. As legal academics, we acknowledge both the strengths and the weaknesses of the arguments made during the referendum campaign, although many bore little relationship to what we have seen as the 'reality' of the EU as either legal order or political settlement. As students of the EU, finally, we must acknowledge that the key issue lies not in being pro- or anti-EU, but in maintaining a critical distance from this curious and curiously

[34] University of Edinburgh EU Law (Ordinary) examination for the session 2020–21.

[35] Alberto Alemanno, 'Unboxing the Conference on the Future of Europe and its Democratic Raison d'Être' (2020) 26 European Law Journal 484.

[36] Case C-418/18 P *Puppinck v Commission* ECLI:EU:C:2019:1113, para 64.

durable experiment in multi-level constitution building. In SRW's case, that has resulted in him publishing some important works on the complex and interlinked topics of the Northern Ireland Protocol and the UK's own internal market.[37] They are rigorous academic works, but he rightly does not mince his words on the political duplicity which has led to such problematic legal solutions. My own approach has been to double down on the study of citizenship, touching upon issues of Brexit but focusing more than ever on placing the study of EU citizenship into a wider framing of multiple intersecting citizenship regimes across many different levels of the regional, the national, the supranational, and the international.[38] In both cases, the conversation clearly includes the impact of Brexit on how we understand the study of EU law to be evolving, but also places it in a wider context.

6. Concluding Reflections

I acknowledge that this short chapter is more akin to a piece of life-writing than a classic academic paper. Yet a major aim of the enterprise has been to demonstrate the intertwining of personal and professional experiences. My formation, and that of Steve Weatherill, stand in parallel: we are academic lawyers, who started to come of age in the 1980s. At that time, and well into the 1990s and 2000s, studying and writing about the EU and its legal order seemed to offer endless fruitful lines of enquiry. At the time when we started, it was possible to keep in view more or less the full range of developments in European Community law, both in terms of primary materials and the secondary literature. The 'generalist' EU lawyer was still a common figure. Now, not so much. After a relatively slow start, scholarship emerging from UK universities came to play a very important role in the emergent field of EU law, and within its subdisciplines, such as internal market law, competition law, and anti-discrimination law. There was a great deal of productive longer- and shorter-term mobility across (into and out of) UK universities at the level of students, postdoctoral scholars, and experienced scholars in the field of EU law.

Times have changed dramatically, across so many dimensions. Not only has the scope of EU law and legal competences expanded enormously, but the practical impact of EU law at the national level has led to its adoption as a key element of legal curriculums across a much larger range of countries, including but extending beyond the twenty-seven Member States (eg in closely connected countries like

[37] Stephen Weatherill, 'The Protocol on Ireland/ Northern Ireland: Protecting the EU's Internal Market at the Expense of the UK's' (2020) 45 European Law Review 222; Stephen Weatherill, 'Interpreting the Protocol' in Christopher McCrudden (ed), *The Law and Practice of the Ireland–Northern Ireland Protocol* (Cambridge University Press 2022); Stephen Weatherill, 'Comparative Internal Market Law: The UK and the EU' (2021) 40 Yearbook of European Law 431.

[38] Jo Shaw, *The People in Question: Citizens and Constitutions in Uncertain Times* (Bristol University Press 2020).

Norway and Switzerland and in candidate states). This in turn has fed a lively intellectual sphere, which is highly internationalized and multilingual, despite the continuing dominance of the Anglosphere and its many publishing outlets in terms of journals and book series. It also deploys an ever-widening range of research methodologies. At the same time, there has been a narrowing of horizons in the UK, which has been driven by Brexit (which provides both intellectual and practical (eg work visas) problems) and compounded by Covid-19. There are worries amongst my peers and colleagues that in UK universities we risk becoming peripheral to the most important developments, and those fears are compounded by politicking around the UK's future inside, or, it seems more likely, outside the EU's main research funding programmes.

Now is not the time, however, to dwell upon these dark clouds, as the purpose here is celebratory. In this chapter, my main objective has been to pay tribute to Steve Weatherill's immense contribution to EU law, in the UK (where he has concentrated his teaching) and beyond, through his contributions to conferences and collective projects and through his publishing, which knows no borders. I have mentioned only a few highlights in this chapter, many of them sparked by the curiosity of having an old examination paper to peruse as part of our shared heritage. I could have gone on at much greater length as there is so much other material with which to work, but I am sure that Steve would much rather I concluded by expressing the hope, for his sake, of a speedy return to the Premiership for Hull City and (in 2022, at the time of writing) the evasion of the dreaded drop to League One.[39]

[39] Dear Reader, they did. Hull City ended the 2021–22 football season in nineteenth place in the Championship, only three places clear of the relegation zone, but a comfortable fourteen points above it.

Index

For the benefit of digital users, indexed terms that span two pages (e.g., 52–53) may, on occasion, appear on only one of those pages.

Tables and figures are indicated by *t* and *f* following the page number